STOLEN HERITAGE

THE STRANGE DEATH OF INDUSTRIAL ENGLAND

ANTHONY WARWICK-CHING

Matador
9 Priory Business Park,
Wistow Road, Kibworth Beauchamp,
Leicestershire. LE8 0RX
Tel: 0116 279 2299
Email: books@troubador.co.uk
Web: www.troubador.co.uk/matador
Twitter: @matadorbooks

ISBN 978 1838593 988

British Library Cataloguing in Publication Data.
A catalogue record for this book is available from the British Library.

Printed and bound in the UK by TJ International, Padstow, Cornwall
Typeset in 11pt Adobe Caslon Pro by Troubador Publishing Ltd, Leicester, UK

Matador is an imprint of Troubador Publishing Ltd

*For my children
and grandchildren*

Contents

Foreword

To mourn the passing of industrial England is, of course, to exaggerate. But we have company. It has long been customary for the *Strange Deaths*[1] that haunt our age to overstate their case. Yes, Britain still makes things. It even clings to the premier league in a couple of fields. But once you have listed aero engines and upmarket cars the rollcall gets thin. If not outright extinction, the heartlands of industrial Britain have suffered a thousand little deaths. And some very big ones.

England was the cradle of the Industrial Revolution. This was, for centuries, a matter of intense pride. Somehow, that got lost in a welter of baseless self-doubt, doctrinaire delusion and partisan assault in the 1980s. Bizarrely, industry became almost a dirty word. How on earth did this happen? Why was so much of our industrial heritage lost? Why is so much of what's left a shadow of what was? Just how did the closing decades of the twentieth century become such a fateful era for manufacturing?

For me, these have long been baffling and troubling questions. This book seeks answers. It follows two strands. One tracks the rise and fall of Britain's historic industries by documenting the organisations that served them and offering a ready reference to hundreds of companies great and small. The other strand sets their stories within the political and economic context of the times. The book salutes a few winners but laments many losers. It looks at where things went wrong. It finds much to prompt concern, dismay and anger. In what I have written the tone is certainly polemical, occasionally tendentious, but not, I hope, unduly partisan.

In my working life I was privileged to have many close encounters with factories, foundries and forges, mines, smelters and refineries, plants, works and workshops, shipyards, rail yards and scrapyards, laboratories, research centres and head offices in the UK and overseas. Almost invariably, and slightly puzzlingly, their hard-working staff were eager to go out of their way to pass on some of their knowledge – esoteric, practical and always of value. To all of them, my eternal thanks.

I am also profoundly grateful for the array of published material – from the reminiscences of the incomparable Fred Dibnah (*Foundries and Rolling Mills – Memories of Industrial Britain*) and Negley Farson (*The Way of the Transgressor*) to the magisterial *Official History of Privatisation* – that touches on or illuminates the stories of our once-great industries. And I particularly appreciate our leading newspapers, notably the *Financial Times*, *The Guardian* and the *Daily Telegraph*, for the wealth of information in their contemporary despatches from the front lines of British industry. Without them any serious attempt at recording the decline of industrial England would be impossible.

I am, of course, deeply grateful to my wife and family for putting up with my long absences from the domestic hearth, and to friends for encouraging me in my endeavour. Errors of fact, interpretation or opinion are, for the most part, my own.

A word of warning, perhaps apology. Thankfully and surprisingly we still live in a unique political union, one whose magnificent industrial history is closely intertwined between its four members. I have therefore freely included many stories from Scotland, Wales and Northern Ireland with that of the central player, England. And for better or worse I have sometimes used the latter's name almost synonymously with those of Great Britain and the United Kingdom.

CHAPTER 1

Introduction

The business model of this country is broken. The role of the City of London, the huge current account deficits, dependence on the kindness of strangers and a model that relies on low wages, little regulation, zero hours contracts and an ideology of cheapness is not a good future for Britain, Brexit or no Brexit.

Yanis Varoufakis, Question Time, BBC1, 28 March 2019[1]

How on earth did it come to this? How did the cradle of the Industrial Revolution end up importing most of its cars, trucks, buses, trains, ships, airliners, machine tools, medical equipment, chemicals, electrical machinery, electronic equipment, steel, non-ferrous metals, paper, clothes and countless other goods that keep its citizenry in the style to which they have become accustomed? How did the power of the City, and that abject dependence on the kindness of strangers, come to dominate our economic life?

Only yesterday, Britain was a major industrial power, its stature placing it squarely in the front rank of advanced countries. As the first industrial country, England's identity was bound up, to a greater extent than anywhere else, with industry. Its manufacturing prowess sustained a unique global standing in the nineteenth century, bore it to victory in the great wars of the twentieth, was a trusty servant of its domestic needs and imperial pretensions, and was an enduring source of pride.

This industrial eminence was not lightly achieved. It was hard won, over centuries of invention, endeavour and toil. Yet, all that mighty advance, that expansionary momentum, came to an abrupt halt in the final decades of the twentieth century.

The impact has been most obvious in the way we earn our keep. In the flourishing fifties almost half the working population was in manufacturing. In the sunny sixties and sober seventies it was still 30–40 per cent. Now it's barely one in 15. This is partly because each employee produces more. But it is mainly a story of industrial decay. Within living memory an industrial giant, the UK is sliding into the third division.

Just where did so many of our great industries, and the companies that served them, go? How did they vanish? Why is so much of what is left a shadow of what was? What happened to all those household names – ICI, GEC, Courtaulds, British Oxygen, EMI, Dunlop, Leyland, Lucas, Metal Box, Pilkington, Raleigh, Swan Hunter, Vickers and countless others?

This book searches for answers.

The Elephant

For centuries manufacturing in England was on a broad upward path. At first some saw it as an interloper, but, as the scale of industry expanded and the power of the new middle class grew, manufacturing became pre-eminent. During the nineteenth century government policy increasingly favoured industry at the expense of agriculture. And for much of the twentieth century industry was a defining feature of Britain's way of life, its presence marking every town in the country.

Yet, the central role of industry in national life has been oddly neglected. Bookshops are full of closely written accounts of Britain's countryside, landscapes and agriculture, of villages, towns and cities, of social life, arts and customs, of sports, pastimes and interests. There are vivid accounts of every age. There are respectful portraits of industrialists and ponderous records of corporations, companies and family firms.

But the broad theme of industry – the creative, essential and fascinating business of devising, designing and making – often gets little more than a few paragraphs in a tome that may run to hundreds of pages.

It is almost the elephant in the room.

An elephant that is shrinking. Industry's long upward curve has been lost. The term deindustrialisation – no less cumbersome for its familiarity – masks many puzzles. Historians claim the seeds were sown a long way back. For economist Jim Tomlinson, it was the 1950s.[2] Others trace its origins to the locust years before the First World War, or even to the closing decades of the nineteenth century.[3]

Some assert that deindustrialisation is not a negative phenomenon. It is presented as something normal, an inevitable stage in a Darwinian evolution of the economy,[4] one that is common to all developed countries, though it takes longer to work through the economic fabric of some than others. It is claimed to be a feature of successful economic development.[5] It has even been described, when carefully handled, as positive deindustrialisation.

Yet, for many of those directly involved, for employees, owners and customers, the reality has been very different. In Britain the changes have frequently looked alien, incomprehensible and far from natural. They have often been more sudden, more baffling and more brutal than the cool detachment of economic theory might predict.

One reason is that, far from being the gradual shift implied by an evolutionary process, the impact was extraordinarily sudden. The charts tell a compelling story. Once it had begun its recovery from the Depression in the 1930s, manufacturing advanced steadily, robustly and continuously. It went on growing right through the post-war decades and well into the 1970s. True, there was at that point a distinct faltering. But there was still little warning of the shattering events that lay just ahead.

The clear fracture point was the 1980s. That doomed decade brought, with remarkable abruptness, a transformed economic landscape. It was marked by the annihilation of hundreds of companies, thousands of factories and millions of jobs, and economic devastation in many communities. Sedulous suburbs in the South, industrious towns in the Midlands and proud cities in the North were robbed of livelihoods, solidarity and communal strengths.

In the years since, the trajectory that took Britain onward and upward for centuries has never been restored. The towns hit by deindustrialisation never really caught up. They simply stayed left behind, signalling their distress in social dysfunction and giving angry voice in the EU referendum.

Weak or Strong?

Economists like to distinguish between weak deindustrialisation, reflecting a fall in manufacturing's share in national income, and strong deindustrialisation, where there is an outright fall in manufacturing output. Many of Britain's European peers have seen the weak version, with industrial output continuing to expand and only its relative share slipping.

The UK has been much closer to strong deindustrialisation. At the end of 2018 manufacturing output was lower than it had been 20 years earlier, and little more than it had been in the 1970s. It was 50 per cent short of what it would have been if the long-term trend had been sustained.

Such output as there is has been produced by a shrunken workforce. There has been a collapse in the number of people working in manufacturing. So in its impact the outcome has been as pronounced as it would have been if Britain had experienced strong deindustrialisation.

Much has been made of the growth in manufacturing productivity this implies. In fact, labour productivity appears to have risen no faster in recent decades than it did in the past. It notched up growth of 4.4 per cent a year for 1951–73. And it rose at the same rate in supposedly reformed 1999–2007.[6] A crucial difference was that output was growing quite strongly in the earlier period but has flat-lined ever since.

There was a brief moment in the 1980s when productivity appeared to have jumped. But this proved fleeting and illusory. The historic gap between UK productivity and that of its European neighbours has simply returned to where it was before deindustrialisation set in.

The UK has not, of course, been alone in the retreat from manufacturing. But the trend has been far more extreme here than in comparable countries. The challenge is to explain why deindustrialisation has been so much more marked in Britain than elsewhere.

Deindustrialisation has prompted a tide of academic debate. Commentators divide into those who argue the inexorability of what has happened and rivals who see at least some as avoidable. Partisanship is seldom absent.

At the risk of running into some technical fog it is worth a quick look at the inevitability case. This was summarised in a paper from the coalition Government Office for Science in October 2013.[7] Skating across the decades since 1945, it invoked two main explanations for the fall of manufacturing.

4

The first is the low income elasticity of demand for manufactures. The idea is that as people become better off they spend more of their income on services rather than goods. The second technical aspect is the fall in the price of manufactured goods relative to services. This is because manufacturing is supposedly more amenable to gains in productivity.

These explanations shed little light on the British case. The flaw in the first is that what may be true for the international economy does not necessarily hold for individual countries. Demand trends in one country are not a predictor of its output trends. The consumption of goods may rise more slowly than that of services, but this is no guide to where those goods will actually be made. They can just as well be produced at home – as in Germany and Japan, which run huge trade surpluses in manufactures – or they can be imported, as in the UK.

So it leaves unanswered the key question. The British have long been as keen on manufactured goods as anyone else. They used to make them in abundance, often rather well. So why are so many of those goods no longer made here? What happened to all those industries that used to supply them?

Nor is the relative prices argument much help. Valued at current prices, the share of manufacturing has indeed collapsed, diving from over 30 per cent of GDP in the 1970s to below 10 per cent today. The inevitabilists argue that the share should be measured in constant prices, to allow for the cheapening of manufactured output (and underweighting of its contribution to GDP) resulting from industry's faster gains in productivity. Even so, though industry's fall is not as dramatic as when the trends are measured in current prices it is still huge, plunging to 18.7 per cent in 2007 and less than 15 per cent today.

The difficulty, about which the Government Office for Science was distinctly insouciant, is recognised in a rival paper of greater clarity and balance.[8] Put simply, the differential productivity thesis is "fraught with data problems and limitations". What happened between the 1940s and the 1970s, when, despite a lot of inflation, the difference between the two measures was very much smaller? Indeed, the indicators ran almost parallel in the 1970s, a very inflationary decade, and it was only after 1979 that they diverged markedly. Again, what happened to manufacturing from then on? And, anyway, why should the two periods – pre-1970s and post-1970s – be gauged differently?

Shallow Trawl

Even if the inevitability proponents have a case, they concede that their two technical factors could account for no more than half the overall decline in the share of manufacturing in GDP.

This leaves an awful lot of the deindustrialisation story still to explain. A ragbag of considerations rounded up by the Office for Science includes statistical reclassification,[9] wartime overstimulation of manufacturing and official interventionism thereafter, excessive trade union power, employee intransigence, financial and investment inadequacy, and poor training.

It's a wide and indiscriminate trawl. Some of these themes emerge over the course of this book, and they are briefly revisited in the final pages. But most of our attention goes to three critical influences that are often simply ignored. These are the management of the economy, particularly in the 1980s and 1990s, the impact of privatisations, and the role of the City.

It is often claimed that the decline in the importance of industry does not matter because it reflected an overdue shift in the country's comparative advantage away from industry and into services, and this should be welcomed. Well, many of Britain's peers, particularly on the Continent, manage to combine industrial pre-eminence with being no slouch at services. Any such welcome should surely be extremely guarded.

And is it not disingenuous for the Government Office for Science to have referred approvingly to "a growing acceptance [since 1979] that manufacturing should sink or swim *along with other sectors*" [my emphasis] when the authorities had only recently had to find truly staggering sums of money to rescue the most prominent and self-congratulatory of all those other sectors, high finance?

It hardly needs pointing out that the 2008 emergency package of £133bn for bankrupt banks and £1,000bn to underpin the finance sector as a whole[10] dwarfs all subventions to manufacturing since the dawn of history. Moreover, those one-off costs were not the end of the story, with the taxpayer having to fund vast subsequent losses at the nationalised banks and take on board a Bank of England quantitative easing programme whose ultimate costs remain unknown.

If anything, this bizarre record prompts an urgent need to discover exactly what happened to Britain's manufacturing industries and how what is left might be sustained.

The Good, the Bad and the Ugly

The focus of this book is on the fate of British manufacturing companies, some large, some small, all reasonably representative of their industries. There are successes, and they are saluted. But they are few, and vastly outweighed by the casualties.

The terrain is vast, the subject broad and time has narrowed. It has proved impossible to cover the whole territory. Regrettably, some of my favourites, such as ceramics, clocks, footwear, furniture, instrumentation and jewellery, have had to be passed over.

Also excluded is the coal industry, partly for the pedantic reason that mining is classed as primary industry and this book is about manufacturing. But also because the history of coal[11] – particularly the haunting tragedy of its end[12] – has been so vividly described elsewhere.[13]

However, the status of oil production as an extractive industry, and therefore in the primary sector, has not deterred me from visiting Britain's brush with oil. This is because oil is closely linked to manufacturing and its fate in the UK exemplifies so much that has gone dreadfully wrong.

Among the big names shipbuilding perhaps receives too much attention, if only because its stories are so enthralling, the island race so careless of its heritage and the end so shocking. Of the other major industries only food processing gets notably less consideration than its stature deserves. But in compensation there is a brief taster of what was once a peculiarly British success story: confectionery. Our industrial survey ends with the one activity whose decline we can, despite all the misgiving about the loss of domestic industry, surely welcome – armaments.

CHAPTER 2

Steel Rusts

> *Everywhere it's the same story: coal mines and tin mines, mills and factories that were full of lovely old engines; steel mills with great big rolling mills and tilt hammers – all of them suffered the same fate when they were closed down…and so we lost much of our industrial heritage…but it's as important a part of our history as our great houses, abbeys and castles.*
>
> Fred Dibnah, Memories of Industrial Britain[1]

Iron Revolution

A steel industry was once regarded as an essential feature of any modern economy. Along with flying a flag and a state airline, every newly independent country aspired to make steel. Those days are gone. Globalisation and cheap transport allow steel to be traded in large quantities and there are states which have achieved great prosperity without making steel.

Yet the perception persists that iron and steel are integral to modern industrialism. Advanced economies without steel industries are still a minority. Countries as highly developed – and as small – as Austria, Belgium, Finland, Luxembourg, the Netherlands, Norway, Sweden and Switzerland have active steel industries, some of international stature.

Britain led the way, though the roots here lay not in steel but in iron.[2] Ironmaking in England stretches back beyond the Middle Ages. But it was

8

the metallurgical discoveries of the eighteenth century that allowed the use of iron on a scale unprecedented in history, and led on to the emergence of a major steel industry.

The critical development was the coke-based smelting of iron ore. The process was discovered by Abraham Darby, who in 1709 established a foundry using the new technique at Coalbrookdale. So momentous were the implications that this quiet Shropshire village is regarded as the birthplace of the Industrial Revolution. A fitting monument to the work of the Coalbrookdale pioneers is the graceful bridge over the nearby Ironbridge Gorge on the River Severn, recently restored with German funding.[3] The world's first cast iron bridge, it is still in use more than two centuries after construction.

Major steps in the progress of iron as an industrial material are credited to Henry Cort and Jeremiah Homfray of Tredegar, who devised a coal-fired "puddling" furnace for the production of wrought iron.[4] This proved more versatile than cast iron and between the 1780s and the 1880s – the malleable iron era – iron rapidly gained ground in a wide range of industrial applications.

Between 1788 and 1870 the output of pig iron, which in turn fed cast and wrought metal, grew nearly a hundredfold to 6.5 million tonnes. For most of this period Britain was much the largest producer in the world.[5]

Bessemer Brilliance

By mid-century the supremacy of wrought iron was about to end. In 1856 Henry Bessemer, a gifted English engineer, demonstrated a process for making steel (an alloy of iron and carbon) far more cheaply than anything previously achieved. Steel had been in use for centuries, with inventors such as Benjamin Huntsman pioneering crucible steel as long ago as the 1740s. But its high cost restricted its applications.

Henry Bessemer's technique yielded steel of adequate quality at dramatic speed and made its bulk production a practical proposition.[6] As so often with England's innovations, the industrial community was slow to adopt Bessemer's brilliant invention, but its value was eventually recognised and applied to commercial production.

In the following decade Karl Wilhelm (later Charles William) Siemens, from that extraordinary family with roots in both Germany and England, pioneered another approach. His development was refined by French inventor Pierre-Emile Martin, and the Siemens-Martin "open-hearth" process quickly gained favour as an alternative to Bessemer.[7]

However, both processes were restricted to ores low in phosphorus. The challenge was met in the 1870s when a self-taught chemist, Sidney Gilchrist Thomas, devised a new approach for the Blaenavon Ironworks in South Wales. The result was the Gilchrist Thomas or Basic Bessemer process. This countered the problems posed by phosphorus and was enthusiastically received on the Continent, where high-quality phosphoric ores were abundant.

The age of steel had been born.

Thereafter, the main techniques for making steel remained pretty much unchanged for the best part of a century. The most important development outside the three leading processes was the electric arc furnace, used for recycling scrap and making special steels.

Ironically, the inventions which Britain had pioneered soon allowed rivals to race ahead. US steel output rose from par with the UK in 1880, at around four million tonnes, to twice the British level at the end of the century and four times by 1913. German output rose from below that of Britain in 1880 to double the UK total in 1913, its producers benefitting from plentiful domestic ores, modern equipment and tariff protection. Britain's steel industry never again attained full parity with Germany's.

By the end of the nineteenth century carbon steel was being supplemented by new formulations. British names were still prominent. In 1882 Robert Hadfield, an energetic metallurgist who published over 200 research papers, patented one of the first steel alloys, manganese steel. Four years later he formulated silicon steel. He also pioneered chromium steels, later to assume importance in the new field of stainless steel.

The commercial application of stainless steel did not emerge until well into the twentieth century. History gives credit for the first successes to Harry Brearley, a self-taught chemist who started work in Sheffield at the age of 12.

His employer was slow to recognise the commercial potential of "rustless steel", but it was taken up by a US investor and promoted by the Firth Brearley Stainless Steel Syndicate. Harry Brearley completed his career as managing director of Brown Bayley, one of the leading makers of special steels. This admirable man never forgot his humble origins and at one point his board had to decline his request for a significant cut in what he felt was an unduly generous salary.

His successor, Dr W.H. Hatfield, distinguished himself by establishing the standard grade for stainless steel, 18/8 (18 per cent chrome, 8 per cent nickel). Nickel-based stainless steels are known as austenitic alloys in honour of yet another outstanding British metallurgist of the late Victorian age, William Roberts-Austen.

Wars and Recoveries

The UK may have been overtaken in carbon steel by the US and Germany, but its output saw steady growth. The main changes before the First World War were a gradual switch from Bessemer to open hearth and a wider geographical spread of production. There was further growth during the war, when steel capacity rose 50 per cent.

Thereafter trends became more erratic. A post-war boom pushed output to a new high at just over nine million tonnes before recession prompted a severe setback and Britain was overtaken for the first time by France. It was not until the late 1920s that output fully recovered, only to be hit within a couple of years by the Depression.

The collapse of shipbuilding and severe downturn in engineering cut deep into steel demand. However, when it came the turnaround was pronounced. By the mid-1930s recovery was well under way, thanks partly to the introduction of a hefty import tariff in 1932 and import quotas in 1935.

The traumas of the 1920s and 1930s prompted more reflective official attitudes. It was noted that the British steel sector was more fragmented than those of the US or Germany, with smaller plant sizes and less integration between iron and steel. In a gesture to reorganisation the British Iron and Steel Federation (BISF) was set up to foster rationalisation.

By the late 1930s the industry was in expansionary mood. The massive works at Ebbw Vale in the Welsh Valleys was reopened and enlarged to make it one of the biggest mills in Europe. And a new plant opened at Corby in the East Midlands.

The Second World War was followed by a period of remarkable growth, when output nearly doubled in a little over a decade.[8] In the face of post-war steel rationing the BISF had come up with a plan which would entail substantial investment in new capacity together with the elimination of outdated facilities. Demand proved so strong, however, that the retirement of older plant was shelved. The BISF target was revised upward to a capacity of 20.5 million tonnes a year in 1957–58.

When that had already been exceeded by 1956 the target became 29 million tonnes by 1962/63. Some of the projects at last reflected the need for larger units, for modernisation in the casting of blooms, billets and slabs, and for automation in tinplate. They also recognised the importance of the new basic oxygen process that was sweeping away the traditional methods of steelmaking.

Son of Bessemer

Basic oxygen steelmaking has been described as the "son of Bessemer". It is based on similar principles but uses oxygen rather than air to refine the iron. The technique became known as the LD process after the Austrian towns of Linz and Donawitz, where it was developed after the Second World War.

After demonstrating dramatic cost advantages over existing methods, the process was rapidly adopted in Japan and in the more progressive companies in Europe. Elsewhere, particularly in Britain and the US, steelmakers were slower to embrace the new technology.

This was despite a growing awareness of the extent to which productivity in the British steel industry was being outpaced. One of the last acts of the 1945–51 Labour government was to nationalise the bulk of the industry. Ideological motives were the main driver but there was already concern over the need to promote modernisation, above all to counter a history of underinvestment.[9]

Public ownership was soon reversed by the succeeding Conservative administration, and by 1957 all the nationalised firms save the largest and least profitable, Richard Thomas & Baldwins (RTB), had been returned to the private sector. Limited powers of oversight were retained by a new Iron and Steel Board.

The authorities did exercise some influence. Most notable was the "Judgement of Solomon" in 1958, when the Macmillan government coaxed the industry into splitting a project for a fourth major strip mill between two sites in deprived areas. One line went to Ravenscraig, in the west of Scotland, and the other to Llanwern in South Wales.

By this stage modernisation was at last under way. A major ambition was the replacement of open-hearth and Bessemer converters with basic oxygen furnaces. The first of these was not commissioned until 1960. Interestingly, this was not in the private sector but at the RTB works at Ebbw Vale.[10]

By then Japan had 13 LD converters in operation, and by 1965 its total had risen to 45.[11] In Continental Europe the share of LD output towards the end of the decade reached 29 per cent in Italy, 37 per cent in Germany, Belgium and Luxembourg, and 63 per cent in the Netherlands. The figure for the UK was just 24 per cent.[12]

Though the pace had slowed the 1960s had seen continued growth in UK steel. Output rose from less than 25 million tonnes in 1960 to 28 million tonnes ten years later.[13] At this point the UK was producing less than Germany, at 45 million tonnes, but rather more than France (under 24 million tonnes), Italy (a little over 17 million tonnes) or Belgium (12.5 million tonnes). For the UK, however, this was the peak. The early 1970s saw some slippage before a more serious relapse took production below 20 million tonnes in the recession year of 1975. For the rest of the 1970s there was modest recovery to an average of 21–22 million tonnes a year.

Slow Modernisation

The diverse pattern that characterised integrated steelmaking in Britain remained remarkably stable well into modern times. Two events were, however, to precipitate profound change – the first constructive in intent, the second shattering in the long run. The first was nationalisation in 1967. The second was privatisation 21 years later.

Nationalisation by the Labour government crystallised many of the issues facing the industry. Though there was a strong ideological element, a preparatory White Paper advanced three practical arguments: the steel companies had failed to invest at an adequate level, they would not invest in the right places and they had been fixing prices.[14]

The White Paper expressed aspirations which the industry still hoped to realise through private initiatives. The Benson Report published by the BISF in 1966 spelt out the issues. A central proposal was the concentration of integrated steelmaking on five sites – Lackenby, Llanwern, Port Talbot, Ravenscraig and Scunthorpe. All were large, modern and near the seaboard. They would be updated with the latest technologies, allowing the retirement of older plant and a third of the workforce. The industry's fragmentation, small plant sizes and low productivity would at last be addressed.

The government was frank about rationalisation and investment as major goals of state ownership. As so often in British industry, there was a huge backlog to address. Except in 1961/62 UK investment during the 1960s was much the lowest of all the main Western world steel-producing nations.[15]

The UK lagged in the adoption of basic oxygen smelting and continuous casting. True, the world's first continuous casting machine was installed at Shelton Bar, in Stoke-on-Trent, in 1964. But this was an exception. British industry was once again slow to cash in on native inventiveness. It was actually not alone here, since continuous casting did not gain widespread use until the 1970s.[16]

Birth of British Steel

The creation of the British Steel Corporation (BSC)[17] in 1967 involved a state buyout of all steel producers with an output of more than 483,000 tonnes a year, and covered four-fifths of UK production. The threshold excluded the smaller operations, such as the specialists of Sheffield, the non-integrated ironmakers, and the independent re-rollers and finishers. The resulting BSC tally was still 14 firms, which accounted for 21 fully integrated works and 39 producers of crude steel.[18] If the manufacture of downstream products is included, the total for plants taken into public ownership rises to 58 – a daunting array of operations to manage in a single corporation.

There is a curious but persistent feature of nationalisations and privatisations. Both are heavy on the taxpayer's pocket. The state often hands too much money to grateful owners of what may be an industrial burden. And when the state decides to sell them back to the private sector it lets them go much too cheap. True to form, the terms on which the state acquired the bulk of British steel were generous. The government paid £1.165bn for assets later valued at £834m. With the exception of a few business leaders, such as Raymond Brooks of GKN,[19] industry spokesmen were understandably muted in their criticism.

After a short-lived recovery, investment fell back again when the 1970 election brought in a Conservative administration less sympathetic to the BSC. Nevertheless, the Heath government set up a joint strategy group (JSG) involving industry representatives and civil servants. But not the trade unions. This was foolish, since it was quite clear that a priority would be big manpower savings.

The Ten Year Development Programme proposed by the BSC looked for a rise in capacity from 27 million tonnes a year to 36–38 million tonnes. Output would come mainly from the five big centres. In the light of what lay ahead the BSC's capacity plans now look fantastical. But at the time the economy was expanding fast, steel demand was strong and output still close to its 1970 high of 28 million tonnes.

Unfortunately, this was the moment long-term growth died. Little did anyone dream that in less than ten years the industry would be struggling to sell half the tonnage envisaged under the plan, or that further down the road production would slump to even lower levels.

From now on the BSC would have to realise its goals without the help of an ever-expanding market.

Modernisation and Rationalisation

The 1974 general election brought another change of government. The new Labour administration commissioned the Beswick Review,[20] which had much the same broad goals as Benson. Plant closures would, however, be cut from 19 to seven, and manpower reduction would be slowed. But Beswick recognised the desperate need for investment and for the corporation's new projects. Since these added to the strain on its finances, the BSC sustained losses from 1975 on and by 1977/78 it was relying almost entirely on public funds for its capital spending.

Investment rose from less than £460 million in 1970 to £3 billion by the end of the decade. BSC was racing to catch up. For one commentator, "where Japan invested in the 1960s the UK only got around to it in the late 1970s".[21] Dozens of small blast furnaces were replaced. LD converters rose from just one (Ebbw Vale) in 1960 to 20 in 1975. Continuous casters rose from two in the mid-1960s to 28 in 1980, hot strip mills from three to six.

There was still a significant productivity gap between British Steel and its counterparts,[22] but rationalisation was not being shirked. Over the 1960s and 1970s the workforce in iron and steel as a whole was drastically reduced. Headcount fell from nearly 330,000 in 1960 to little more than half that in 1980, with much of the manpower savings occurring in the second half of the 1970s.[23]

There were significant plant shutdowns. One of the first to go was the relatively small Cargo Fleet. More prominent were the Ebbw Vale blast furnaces and converters in 1975. In 1978 the open-hearth furnaces were closed at Glengarnock, the former Lancashire Steel plant at Partington was shut and the old Clyde Iron Works[24] was retired. Steelmaking at Shelton Bar[25] and East Moors closed in the same year, and Bilston and the Redbourn iron complex at Scunthorpe shut in 1979.

Despite the cuts in steel Stoke was still a long way from the post-industrial wasteland. It mined coal, made tyres and turned out the miraculous mix of beautiful ceramics and practical pots for which the Five Towns were world famous. Almost all of this has gone, and Stoke has become a centre for low-cost services. Even here it's been a rocky road, with the 2014 collapse of controversial mobile phone retailer Phones4U costing 1,700 jobs. Dismally, Stoke's biggest commercial employer is now Bet365, a secretive outfit that has made a fortune out of the squalid business of online gambling.[26]

Crude Confrontation

The attitude of the unions to the steel cutbacks of the 1970s is revealing. BSC industrial relations from the 1967 nationalisation up until the end of the 1970s have been described as "co-operative on the basis of industrial democracy, namely the coexistence of labour and capital".[27] One factor was a growing number of employee directors.

From quite early on the union leaders accepted the Ten Year Development Programme in principle. They were criticised on the political left for playing "a role as apologists for Lord Melchett [the chairman of the BSC] and for the government" and Dai Davies of the British Iron, Steel and Kindred Trades Association (BISAKTA) was jeered for having "publicly thanked Melchett for the humane manner in which he is imposing mass sackings".

Union cooperation came to an abrupt halt in the 1980s. The advent of a Conservative government in 1979 brought a doctrinaire approach to the challenges facing British industry and crudely confrontational answers. In 1980, Ian MacGregor, a US mining industrialist, was appointed chairman. He replaced the patrician Charles Villiers, a decent consensus manager still recalled today in the occasional piece of dim tabloid humour.[28]

The new management used the atmosphere of crisis as ammunition in pay talks. At a time when the cost of living was soaring the BSC labour force was offered a wage increase of 2 per cent. The response from those moderate unions was to call the first industry-wide strike in half a century. Steel production shut down for three months and output fell to its lowest since 1935. The immediate impact of the strike on the corporation's finances was, of course, gravely damaging.

MacGregor frequently cited the productivity challenge facing BSC, inciting outside commentators to point a familiar finger of blame at the workforce. In reality, a far more immediate problem for the corporation was a crushing fall in demand. Between 1979 and 1980, UK consumption plunged by a third under the bizarre economic policies unleashed by the new government, and it continued to slide.

This was acknowledged even by fervent disciples of Thatcherism. Former Labour minister Dick (by now Lord) Marsh, chairman of the British Iron and Steel Consumers Council, complained that the output of the main steel-consuming industries – mechanical engineering, construction, motor vehicles and metal goods – had fallen "massively" since mid-1979.

His answer was to open the flood gates to steel imports and urge "substantial" cuts in British steel capacity.[29] Marsh went on to betray his union origins by opposing safeguards for Scotland's Ravenscraig plant ahead of BSC privatisation.[30]

Biggest Fire Sale in History

The economic background became increasingly ruinous. Capital-intensive industries like steel have high fixed costs, and without 75 per cent capacity utilisation losses rocket.[31] The collapse in domestic demand left BSC on the front line of the monetarist experiment with little alternative to chasing its market downward. In one of the most extraordinary demolition drives in Britain's history, what should have been an orderly reorganisation turned into an industrial massacre.

The madness raged on for years. The spring 1982 issue of a US trade journal reported that Gavlick Machinery Corporation of Bristol, Connecticut, had teamed up with the appropriately named Henry Butcher to sell surplus equipment from operations being dumped by British Steel. This was no ordinary deal. Richard E. Gavlick gleefully described the $500m contract as "Maybe the largest sale of surplus equipment in world history".[32] No fewer than 14 iron and steel complexes were involved. Their assets included coking and sinter plants, walking drag lines, blast furnaces (including a brand new 14 metre vessel), arc furnaces, degassing equipment, direct reduction plants, blooming mills, roughing mills, billet and slabbing mills, bar and section mills, structural beam mills and rod mills. Enough to build an entire industry.

The Old World's loss was the developing world's gain. Among the flood of plant exports were consignments for South Africa,[33] Pakistan,[34] China[35] and the Dominican Republic.[36] Dismally, these disposals often involved equipment paid for with public money. An arc furnace sold to South Africa for £4m in 1983 had cost £35m, of which £31m had come from the taxpayer.[37]

Following the end of steelmaking at Motherwell and Cleveland in the second half of 1979, 1980/81 saw the outright closure of the integrated works at Consett,[38] Corby, Normanby Park[39] and Shotton. The latter was the largest single plant closure in Europe in 35 years.[40] There were also major cutbacks at Hallside, Cleveland and Barrow. They were followed by shutdowns at Barrow, Ebbw Vale and Parkgate, and at important finishing mills such as Gartcosh in Scotland.

Job losses were terrifying, with numbers employed by the BSC plunging from 166,000 in 1979/80 to 65,000 in 1984/85.

Nor did the independent sector escape, with Laird Group's Patent Shaft works at Wednesbury, Duport's new plant at Llanelli in South Wales, Tube Investments/BSC Round Oak mill (recipient of a Queen's Award for Export) and others withering in the economic blizzard.[41]

Privatisation Priority

By the mid-1980s the BSC was marching to a different drum. The focus had shifted from benign modernisation to narrow privatisation. In the face of abysmal demand, the only road to profitability was further ruthless cost-cutting and asset disposals.

In 1984 the BSC sold off its 91 per cent stake in one of the few British-owned offshore fabrication yards. BGC went to Trafalgar House, which had close links to the Conservative Party, for just £15m. The same company acquired world-famous bridge-builders Redpath and Dorman Long for £10m.

Order did occasionally break out in this mayhem, with three planned restructurings between 1981 and 1983. Phoenix I consolidated BSC and GKN rod and wire interests into Allied Steel & Wire. Phoenix II focused on engineering steels with the closure of Duport and one of Hadfield's two mills (subsequently Lonrho, BSC and GKN combined to close the other Hadfield mill).

Phoenix III saw the BSC's River Don mill put into Sheffield Forgemasters, in a joint venture with Firth Brown. Four years later Forgemasters was cast adrift on a management buyout and went on to navigate a long and perilous journey through financial crises and recurrent changes of ownership.

There were other cooperative restructurings. In 1986 BSC and GKN formed United Engineering Steels. This involved GKN's steel mill at Brymbo, three BSC special steels operations in Sheffield (Aldwarke, Templeborough and Stocksbridge), various rolling mills and six plants owned by GKN Forgings. These operations were far from being lame ducks, with the BSC gaining £592m from such disposals.

Tailoring for the 1988 privatisation was steered by Robert (Bob) Haslam, who after his unsuccessful bid to lead ICI succeeded Ian MacGregor at BSC in 1983. Haslam had "no time for MacGregor or his methods", yet was highly regarded by the few open-minded members of the government. For one-time energy secretary Peter Walker he was "one of the most outstanding nationalised industry chairmen I have come across".[42]

Privatisation was pursued with fierce tenacity by his number two, Robert ("Black Bob") Scholey, who took over as chairman in 1986. By 1988 the corporation was claiming a profit of over £400 million. This was achieved with a strong dose of window dressing. The corporation's costs had been suppressed through low depreciation and interest charges, debt forgiveness, tax breaks and meagre investment spending. Costs were also helped by low labour rates in comparison with Continental counterparts.[43]

This allowed the government, in the words of the *Financial Times*, to push it "to the front of the privatisation queue".[44] And, although the *FT* also noted that "investors have a deep prejudice against the steel industry" and "[t]he City has had little cause to understand it",[45] the corporation was priced at a level so low that even fund managers could recognise a bargain.

By the time the BSC was privatised the Labour and Conservative governments had together committed £7.6bn in state funding between the mid-1970s and the mid-1980s.[46] Against this can be set the £2.4bn realised on the sale of the corporation, leaving around £4.5bn to be written off in two tranches in 1980/81 and 1988/89.[47]

It would be quite wrong to think that the BSC was exceptional in its call on state funds. A parallel process had been going on all over Europe, where much of the industry made losses from the mid-1970s until the mid-1980s. All major OECD steel producers faced problems of spare capacity,[48] few more than in Western Europe.

The oil shocks of the 1970s had ended the *Wirtschaftswunder* and the *Trente Glorieuses*, dramatically slowing the growth in steel demand. Energy costs had shot up. Japan had shown that basic oxygen smelting and continuous casting were the way of the future. The minimum economic size of integrated plants was racing up. And coastal locations were the new fashion. At the same time steel companies were trying to make big labour cutbacks.

Manifest Crisis

All this implied huge expenditure. With the partial exception of the Germans, few of Europe's steel companies could finance this and they turned to their governments. Under the Davignon Plan,[49] from which Britain was idiotically kept aloof by the Thatcher administration, the European Commission was able to invoke "manifest crisis" conditions to impose floor prices and production quotas. As a consequence, the necessary adjustments on the Continent were gradual, sensible and humane.

If there was a difference between the approaches followed in Britain and its EEC counterparts after 1980 it was in the contrasting speed and harshness with which retrenchment and job losses were pursued. Here Britain stood out. By 1983 it was being claimed by ministers that the UK had made more cutbacks in steel than any other European country. Despite the UK suffering the worst collapse in its domestic market,[50] ministers were far from generous in their support. In the mid-1980s a *Financial Times* survey was reporting huge restructuring investment by European governments, with France planning to spend $3bn in 1985–87, Italy nearly $2bn, Luxembourg $1bn, Spain $3bn, and even Germany's Salzgitter and Saarstahl looking to their Länder for finance.[51]

The longer-term picture also puts Britain in perspective. The German Steel Federation estimated state aid of around DM27bn in the UK between 1975 and 1991. Comparable figures were DM7bn for Germany, DM12.7bn for Belgium, DM23.8bn for France and no less than DM39.4bn for Italy.[52] Indeed the support for the latter was an underestimate. It was reported in 1993 that Ilva, Italy's largest steel works, may have received as much as £14bn from the taxpayer between 1981 and 1992.[53]

Interestingly, the UK total for 1975–79, when there was a Labour government, was little more than the figure under the Conservatives in the 1980s. Moreover, the latter was weighted towards debt write-off, to window-dress the privatisation prospectus, rather than to the investment in new plant and equipment prioritised in the 1970s.

The newly privatised BSC was launched into choppy seas. UK steel output had remained below that of any year in the 1970s and the average for the 1980s was one-third down on the previous decade.

With its newly privatised status BSC was even freer to make cutbacks, however, and so they continued; 1990 saw the closure of Brymbo and a couple of years after that came the most dramatic shutdown of all, at Ravenscraig.

Following the decimation of shipbuilding, the closure of vehicle plants and the gouging of its engineering industry, Scotland's steel demand had collapsed. By the late 1980s barely 4 per cent of BSC output was going north of the border.[54] Scholey warned: "One of our big problems in Scotland is the lack of a local market".[55] This left the 'Craig very exposed,

MacGregor had proposed its closure as long ago as 1982, but this was resisted by ministers with Scottish responsibilities such as Malcolm Rifkind. He warned, presciently, that the "closure of steel making in Scotland would be a recipe for the resurgence of nationalism". Few pursued the case for Ravenscraig and the associated works at Gartcosh as tenaciously and rationally as the local MP for Motherwell, Labour's Jeremy Bray.[56]

The Raven Croaks at Motherwell[57]

On the eve of BSC privatisation minister Ken Clarke had opposed any extension of guarantees, but other ministers had offered reassurance about the future of the 'Craig. This was not allowed to stand in the way when the BSC board could cite commercial imperative. First to go was the strip mill, whose closure was announced in 1990.

The management handling of this sensitive issue had been crass. An all-party campaign against the closure had proposed the election of Sir Kenneth Alexander, chancellor of Aberdeen University, to the BSC board. This was opposed by Robert Scholey, who blocked a shareholder vote. He then refused to meet union representatives, in a communication to Malcolm Rifkind described by local Tory MP Sir Hector Munro as "quite unacceptable".[58] Rifkind himself described the decision to keep him out of the loop as "arbitrary and unreasonable".[59]

Not long afterwards, the Clydesdale tube works, busy supplying pipe for a new North Sea oil boom, was closed, Clyde Alloy shut and the future of the Dalzell plate mill was in doubt. The cold rolling mill at Gartcosh had been shut in 1986,[60] and the loss of all this local finishing capacity put the main plant at the 'Craig even more in peril.

In early 1992 its shutdown was confirmed. The tragedy prompted particularly thoughtful coverage in the *Financial Times*.[61] Once again the attitude of senior management had been execrable, with the Tory party's Scottish president accusing Scholey of a "slap in the face" to the workforce.[62]

That workforce showed astonishing magnanimity. Union convenors attributed the disaster to head office rather than local management, with whom "relations inside the plant [had] always been good".[63] BSC had been in the private sector just long enough for a cunning government to deflect blame away from itself.

The Scottish finishing mills were by no means the only capacity still being shed by BSC. The following year brought the end of the great

Templeborough Mills in Sheffield/Rotherham and the demise of product processing at Shotton.

At its formation British Steel had taken a number of specialty operations on board. They did not escape unscathed. In 1992 stainless steel was put into a joint venture with Sweden's Avesta, the first step in an assassination of stainless steelmaking in its very birthplace.

In 1999 the Shepcote Lane plate mill was closed and the book transferred to Avesta in Sweden. In 2000 the BSC stake was taken over by Finland's Outokumpu, which was buying market share via Avesta. Four years later the coil products division closed and its business went to Finland. The melt shop was cut back heavily, a process repeated in 2009, leaving the long-term viability of the plant further in doubt. In the same year Corus Engineering Steels made big cutbacks at its Rotherham works.

Corus and Tata

Once privatised, British Steel was free to embark on foreign adventures. Most of them flopped. But 1999 brought its biggest deal, when the company merged with Koninklijke Hoogovens of the Netherlands to form Corus. Smaller than its British sister, Hoogovens was modern and highly efficient. Strains soon developed when the UK operations came under pressure from a strong pound. In March 2001 Corus announced a 15-month loss of £1.17bn, as big as any of the operating losses of the BSC when it had been state-owned. Dutch investors demanded action – on this side of the Channel.

Cue for another round of swingeing cutbacks.[64] These were presided over by chairman Brian Moffat, an accountant whose dismal motto was "I'm interested in making money, not steel".[65] He was described in the *Daily Telegraph* as "the gloomiest man in British industry" when at the time thousands of jobs were being axed his salary more than doubled.[66] For the *Telegraph* he was the man who "refused to be bullied by Blair" (not exactly famous, whatever his faults, for bullying industrialists) since he flouted protocol by refusing to alert the government to his highly sensitive cutback plans.[67] For *The Guardian* the villain was a Labour government acquiescing in an overvalued exchange rate which had accelerated the decline of Corus's customer base.[68]

Measures included the end of steelmaking at Llanwern, the closure of Ebbw Vale tinplate and drastic cutbacks at Corby, Hartlepool, Newport, Port Talbot, Rotherham, Scunthorpe, Shotton, Stocksbridge and Stockton, most of which were already a shadow of what they had once been.[69]

Philippe Varin took over as chief executive in 2003, thought about Corus's share price for a second and came up with the same old solution – ruthless retrenchment. Plant closures included Stocksbridge and the rail mill at Workington. The City marked its approval of £600 million in cost cuts by ramping the share price up from 40p to nearly £4.

There was even more satisfaction when in 2007 the Corus board accepted a £7bn bid from India's Tata combine, looking to raise the profile of the family-controlled group outside India.[70] Karl-Ulrich Köhler, head of Tata Steel in Europe, set about rectifying a history of chronic underinvestment.[71]

Unfortunately, conditions deteriorated dramatically after the 2008 credit crunch and there was renewed pressure for cutbacks. The result was one of the most shocking events in the history of British steel. This was the shutdown of Redcar, which had been expensively updated in the 1970s.[72] Redcar was a flagship coastal plant which could ship raw materials in, and products out, by sea. Corus had signed a contract with four overseas customers.[73]

But those customers pulled out. Redcar had a brief reprieve when it was bought by Thailand's Sahaviriya Steel Industries (SSI) for almost £300m and reopened in 2012.[74] As so often in the history of Britain's traditional industries, the new owner expressed high praise for its acquisition.[75] Unfortunately, the SSI initiative proved unsustainable. In 2015 Redcar closed again, this time for good.

In the meantime, problems were brewing with the operations that Tata had retained, and in 2013 Tata Steel reported a loss of £840m.[76] In addition to a legacy of inadequate investment, weak global steel demand, a strong pound, excessive local taxes, high energy costs and environmental charges were cited.[77]

There was also an issue with imports of low-cost Chinese steel. Acting with alacrity, Brussels proposed anti-dumping tariffs. These were opposed by a British government all too ready to listen to its property development friends enjoying cheap steel imports.

For Tata this was the last straw. There were yet more cutbacks. Among the casualties were the Dalzell rolling mill and the Clydebridge plate mill. These were the last vestiges of Scotland's once-formidable steel industry.

After-Shocks

In June 2016 Tata sold one of its two remaining integrated steelmaking centres, Scunthorpe, to a private equity concern, Greybull Capital. In return for a major industrial complex, a high-quality rail mill, and £300m in raw materials and order books,[78] Greybull paid £1. The new owners resurrected the name British Steel for their acquisition, imposed wage cuts and claimed they would invest £400m.

The company reported a profit of £47m for its first full year, 2016/17.[79] This proved a false dawn. After taking many millions in fees and interest out of the business and investing just £20m, Greybull sought government assistance. Eventually a deal was cobbled together in which the plant passed into the hands of a Turkish pension fund.

Meanwhile, there had been bankruptcies in the Caparo Industries group of fabricators.[80] Liberty House bought these facilities and then added some of Tata's more specialised operations, including the two Scottish plants closed in 2015.[81] The spate of deals by Liberty House reportedly involved as much as £1bn.[82]

The combination of asset sales, demand improvement, a weaker pound, energy cost mitigation and belated anti-dumping tariffs allowed Tata UK to report a profit in early 2017.[83] This strengthened the hand of the group in its search for a buyer. The result was a deal which put all Tata's remaining steel interests in Europe, including Port Talbot and its associated mills in South Wales, into a 50/50 joint venture with ThyssenKrupp of Germany.

Only two other operations of note remain from Britain's once-mighty steel industry. The first, Sheffield Forgemasters, is the sole significant survivor of the destruction of Sheffield's steel. The company remains a world leader in massive steel forgings. In a rare act of constructive intervention a modest £36m (in place of a previous arrangement worth over £100m) was loaned to Forgemasters by the coalition government in 2011. This helped the company to continue offering the services of "probably the oldest steel business in the world".

The other survivor is the Celsa operation in Cardiff. This is run by a privately owned Spanish company, which bought out Allied Steel and Wire in 2003.[84] The facility uses an electric arc furnace to process scrap, and makes long products for construction. Highly efficient, it has nevertheless faced problems due to the volatility and high level of UK energy prices.[85]

A Triumph for Thatcherism?

A generation and more has passed since the 1980s, yet what remains of the steel industry is, like so much of Britain's economy, shaped by those turbulent years. For one historian, "the rehabilitation of British Steel is widely regarded as a triumph for Thatcherism".[86]

Was this "rehabilitation" attributable to privatisation? In a thoughtful 1998 study comparing the British steel industry under public and private ownership, David Parker and Hsueh Liang Wu concluded: "The UK steel industry, of which British Steel is the largest part, does not seem to have achieved a lasting competitive advantage in the early to mid-1980s on the back of its massive restructuring. By 1991, the position of UK steel in terms of technical efficiency was once again weak in relative terms."[87]

Indeed, within three years of privatisation the BSC had fallen into the heavy losses which prompted the cutbacks described earlier. This reinforces the view of Parker and Wu: "The change in the capital market did not lead to obvious performance gains."

One possibility is that the mere prospect of privatisation was the deciding factor. There is, of course, no way of knowing what would have happened in other circumstances. Interestingly, however, a parallel restructuring occurred in France's antiquated steel industry long before its privatisation in the late 1990s.

So what kind of legacy did Thatcherism's "triumph" really bequeath?

The Official History of Privatisation is unequivocal: "Privatisation did not secure for Britain a successful and expanding steel industry. But there again, the privatisation of BSC was *more about getting a troublesome loss-making industry off the government's books than securing its long term future.*" [my emphasis].

It is difficult to think of a more damning indictment of this cynical abdication of responsibility.

A striking feature of the steel industry has been its remorseless contraction. What was once the second biggest industry in Europe is now puny, its output pathetically small. Since 2010 crude steel production has averaged less than 10 million tonnes a year, barely a third of its 1970s peak. National output in 2018 was just 7.7 million tonnes – about what it was on the eve of the First World War.

Comparisons with peers are particularly troubling. Output in recent years has been twice as high in France and Spain, three times as high in Italy, and five times as high in Germany – all of which have endured their own ordeals on the journey into the modern world.

Nor has this decline been compensated for by higher-value production. In the country credited with its invention the stainless steel sector is a wraith. And the picture is the same for tool steels, high-speed steels, heat-resisting steels, electrical steels and the other important alloys so often pioneered in Britain.

Poor demand is much of the story. The hollowed-out industrial base bequeathed by Thatcherism has left Britain with steel consumption per head barely two-thirds of the European average. And there is another disturbing dimension. This is the extraordinary extent to which UK steel consumers, such as cars and construction, buy from abroad.

The UK steel industry may have dressed up its profitability in the 1980s, but it was not good at retaining its market. Imports of mill products rose from a fifth of demand in the 1970s to over a third in the 1980s and went on climbing. In recent years imports have taken nearly two-thirds of the market.[88]

The sources of these imports are telling. Yes, China sent 826,000 tonnes of steel products into the UK in 2015, providing a scapegoat for the problems of Tata. But these shipments were mostly at the lower end of the quality spectrum, such as sections for construction. They were dwarfed by the five million tonnes of EU steel shipped into Britain from across the Channel. Of this total almost 1.2 million tonnes came from Germany alone, and over 700,000 tonnes were from Spain.

It is the competition from the rest of Europe rather than the rest of the world that poses one of the biggest challenges to the survival of an integrated steel industry in Britain.

As for the independent sector, the picture in Britain remains desolate. The absence of a significant group of mini-mills is highlighted by the vast exports of ferrous scrap. These have been running at seven million tonnes a year, the second highest figure in the entire world. The exports of what should, in an old industrialised country like Britain, be feed for a big domestic recycling industry speak volumes about the death of steelmaking in this country.

Paving Over the Cracks

If Thatcherism's steel "triumph" now looks hopelessly illusory, the social implications have been huge. For many of the districts which once made iron and steel the industry is a fading memory. Among them is Corby, butt of plodding tabloid jokes as it struggles with its bereavement.[89] Another is Scunthorpe, one of only two towns to have retained a modest vestige of integrated iron- and steelmaking.[90]

Though it has Britain's only remaining major fully integrated steelworks, Port Talbot in South Wales also shows high levels of social and economic deprivation. Meanwhile, the demise of Ravenscraig and the closure of most of the downstream works left the Scottish steel industry with just two finishing mills, Clydebridge and Dalzell, in the entire country.

Perhaps the most poignant story is that of Sheffield, birthplace of modern steel. The city's heritage was decimated by cutbacks in both bulk steel and special steels, with the closure of Park Gate, Templeborough Mills, Tinsley Park, East Hecla and others leaving a chasm in the industrial heart of the city.

The outcome was a cynical fix all too symbolic of the Thatcher/Major era. The void left by former steelworks was not filled with brave new industries but paved over by Meadowhall, a retail centre built by Bovis, the family firm of 1980s Cabinet Minister Keith Joseph. A leading promoter was Paul Sykes, fervent supporter of Thatcher and the Conservative Party and financier of Leave in the EU referendum. He pocketed £280m when Meadowhall was sold.[91]

Like so many of the out-of-town shopping centres conceived in the 1980s and 1990s, Meadowhall merely camouflaged the wasteland left by the demolition of real industry and crippled the existing retail estate in the centre of the city.

Similar criticisms have been made of the sister development at Merry Hill, which is located on the site of the former Round Oak steelworks at Brierley Hill in the West Midlands and has had ownership or development links with Meadowhall.

Foundations

Does the withering away of British steelmaking matter? It would be easier to say no if the alternatives looked brighter. But it is impossible to find any basic industry – whether in chemicals, oil processing, non-ferrous metals, papermaking or even food manufacturing – on a sustained growth path. Nor are trends in the output of consumer and other manufactured goods reassuring. And the financial crash plainly demonstrated the perils of excessive dependence on services.

The arguments for sustaining sectors like steelmaking were persuasively set out in a PricewaterhouseCoopers (PwC) paper in 2013,[92] and in a paper from the Institute for Public Policy Research (IPPR) in 2016.[93] For the IPPR foundation industries make valuable contributions to regional growth, form important components of regional clusters and have been closely linked with key strategic sectors such as vehicle manufacture, aerospace and pharmaceuticals. They tap into and foster a unique combination of skills, knowledge and industrial tradition.

How to sustain them? A first essential for steel would be the removal of tax, fiscal or energy costs which place UK production at a disadvantage to its counterparts on the Continent. Low-cost imports should be barred if there is a hint of subsidy. Institutional support to foundation industries should be strengthened. There should be lavish availability of investment finance. Above all, there should be sustained pressure on UK consumers to step up their purchases from domestic suppliers.

And there should be much stronger intervention to ensure that public purchasing is steered in the direction of UK producers. The precedents here have been dismal. In July 2017 a typically arrogant Ministry of Defence told a weak defence minister, Harriet Baldwin, that steel for a new (Type 26) destroyer fleet should not necessarily be UK-sourced. Incredibly, this means that two-thirds of the material may come from Sweden.[94]

If Brexit is to bring any benefit to British industry, it has to mean that governments will feel freer to intervene clearly, boldly and decisively to ensure the survival of foundation industries like steel. But will the champions of Brexit, many of whom were captured by the ruinous dogmas foisted on Britain in the 1980s, be content to see the return of meaningful government intervention in industry?

CHAPTER 3

Mechanical Engineering – Spanner in the Works

The streets inside the great glass-topped works were a fifth of a mile long. They were whirring with machinery…and through the whole great works, from spectacled engineer-inspector in his long white coat to clog-footed puddler in the foundry, was a feeling of self-respect and pride in workmanship. They were making the best chains in the world – and they knew it. They were British workmen.

Negley Farson, The Way of a Transgressor[1]

Mechanical Milestones

Mechanical engineering is the oldest and mightiest of the engineering callings. Hatched before the Industrial Revolution, it fledged and took flight on the materials, processes and machinery to which that transformation gave birth.

In his classic *British Industries and Their Organization* G.C. Allen[2] traces the long march of engineering past such mileposts as stationary steam engines in the eighteenth century, textile machinery in the early nineteenth century, railway equipment in the 1830s, and steamships and marine engines in mid-century. Next came the development of machine tools and metal-working equipment, the small-scale manufacturing that made Birmingham the city of a thousand trades in the nineteenth century and amazingly prosperous in the twentieth.[3] The story goes on to gas engines, bicycles, electrical engineering and motor manufacture in the closing years of the Victorian era. And then to aircraft and electronics in the early decades of the twentieth century.

Since then there has been a tremendous proliferation. In its 1959 edition of *Britain – An Official Handbook* the Central Office of Information (COI) cited many of the sectors typical of British mechanical engineering near its zenith. It included agricultural machinery, boilers and boilerhouse plant, fabricated steelwork, food processing equipment, industrial valves and pumps, instrumentation, machine tools, mechanical handling plant, mining machinery, nuclear power plant, office machinery, ordnance, petroleum equipment, refrigeration machinery, stationary engines, textile machinery, and many other products.[4]

Strictly, such industries as car, truck and bus assembly, aircraft manufacture, shipbuilding, and the production of railway vehicles and armaments fall within mechanical engineering. But they normally receive separate treatment in any statistical and historical analysis, and this book gives them their due in separate chapters.

Craft Skills and Mass Production

As the nineteenth century advanced, great engineering industries grew up on both sides of the Atlantic. Though Britain and Germany were the leaders in Europe, other significant centres were developing in Belgium, France, northern Italy, the Habsburg lands and Switzerland. Where US industry was moving towards mass production, operations in Britain and Germany were still heavily dependent on the traditional craft skills of their industrial labour.[5]

Much of the industrial growth in the decades before the First World War was driven by engineering, with overseas markets taking about half of Britain's output.[6] Exports of machinery rose threefold between the 1880s and the pre-war years. Competition was keen, however, with German and the US already ahead as machine tool exporters.

One characteristic of British manufacture, a stubborn insistence on the highest standard of workmanship, may actually have handicapped

UK companies. In an affectionate account of his time in a Manchester engineering works in the 1900s, the American writer Negley Farson recalls the fury of the proprietor on learning that his employee had ordered a sample for a US customer. The Old Man rages: "Every foot of my chain is as good as any other foot. We don't send out *samples* to get orders."[7]

Once the short-lived boom after the First World War had deflated, engineering stagnated. In the mid-1920s the output of the general engineering trades was no higher than it had been a decade earlier, with a slump in steam engines, locomotives and textile machinery barely offset by newer industries such as motors and electrical manufacture.

Activity took another knock with the Depression, but when recovery came it was rapid. Between 1934 and 1937 engineering output rose 40 per cent, at which point it was 60 per cent higher than it had been in the mid-1920s.[8] Nevertheless, Britain's international standing slipped. Where on the eve of the First World War it had been level first with Germany in engineering exports, and both countries were ahead of the US, by the late 1930s the latter had moved into first place and Germany had overtaken the UK. The problem was not technical backwardness but stagnation in international demand for the goods in which Britain remained pre-eminent.[9]

The Second World War brought a big expansion in engineering, and when peace returned there were new technologies to draw on and new demands for plant and machinery. For G.C. Allen, writing at the end of the 1950s, "[t]he post-war years were a time of continuous growth to which *it would be difficult to find a parallel in history*."[10] [my emphasis]

Rich Heritage

The result was the extraordinarily rich heritage outlined in the prosaic pages of 1959's *Britain – An Official Handbook*. What is striking is the sheer range of activities that characterised engineering in Britain. It is difficult to find a single industry not represented.

The COI could even celebrate notable resurrections. Britain was once a leading producer of clocks and watches, birthplace of the Harrison chronometers which revolutionised sea-travel[11] and maker of the elegant long-case clocks gracing homes in England and abroad. By the end of the nineteenth century, production of clocks and watches had nearly died out, but the years following the Second World War saw the rebirth of an industry that eventually employed 15,000 craftsmen.[12] Much of this activity was the result of state sponsorship and promotion of industry in the development areas.

Another striking feature is the sheer scale of activity. In agricultural machinery Britain had come from nowhere to be the world's second largest producer of tractors and the largest exporter. It was a world leader in stationary engines for industrial and marine uses. It was still a major producer of textile machinery, exporting two-thirds of its output. In office machinery the UK was second only to the US, in the production and export of industrial valves it was again second to the US, and the same was true of equipment for the petroleum industry. Nuclear power plant was being pioneered in the UK, and the first export orders were being booked.[13]

The importance of industry ran right through the everyday life of the country, and almost every town had its complement of engineering activities. These included backstreet metal-working shops filling jobbing orders for local customers. There were medium-sized light engineering operations, often on neat government-inspired trading estates. And there were the mighty engineering works of Midland and northern cities, many still characterised by high levels of vertical integration and employing armies of skilled folk dwelling in their hinterlands. Layer upon layer in a rich industrial culture.

This broad pattern remained wonderfully intact well into the 1970s: 1973's *Britain – An Official Handbook* was able to paint a remarkably similar picture to its 1950s counterparts. At 1.2m, employment in mechanical engineering was at comparable levels to the late 1950s. And although it was less dynamic than chemicals and electrical engineering the output of mechanical engineering had grown by a third between the mid-1960s and the early 1970s.

Moreover, engineering was more than paying its way in the world, with exports of non-electrical machinery accounting for half the total output of the sector.[14] Agricultural equipment, machine tools, textile machinery, industrial pumps and valves, construction and earth-moving equipment, mechanical handling equipment, boilerhouse plant and office machinery scored particularly well overseas.

The mid-1970s brought the oil shock to an economy already destabilised by the reckless Barber boom of 1970–73. Nevertheless, mechanical engineering showed resilience. By 1977 it was second only to food, drink and tobacco among industrial sectors, with 12.6 per cent of total manufacturing production.[15]

Nevertheless, the flat trend for the 1970s as a whole contrasted with the heady advance of preceding decades. The heritage from the sunny 1950s and the ambitious 1960s was looking a touch frail, particularly in textile machinery, machine tools and shipbuilding supplies. But there were also problems where it would be difficult to argue a structural case. Motorcycles, only recently a world champion, had suddenly become a hospital case.

Some of the casualties, such as Alfred Herbert in machine tools and BSA in motorcycles, were granted a stay of execution through modest government intervention. And the outright closure of significant engineering plants remained remarkably limited.

Collapse and Doubtful Recovery

If the 1970s saw tremors, the 1980s brought an earthquake. In proclaiming the salvation of the British economy, the new Conservative government forgot to pass the message on to industry. With the onset of the worst recession since the 1930s, mechanical engineering, so dependent on other industries, was first to be affected. And in contrast to the upsets of the 1970s the recessions of the 1980s were excruciating.

From its 1979 peak mechanical engineering output fell heavily in 1980 and it went on dropping for years. By 1983 it was down no less than 20 per cent. And subsequent recovery was torpid. At the peak of revival in 1989, output was well below the level of ten years earlier and quickly slumped when another recession struck.

Earlier in the decade even conservative commentators had little good to say about the engineering scene. Looking at the pathetic vanguards of the new economy – Slush Puppy and juice cartons – journalist Patience Wheatcroft wistfully conceded: "The companies which have prospered throughout the recession have only one thing in common – their distance from the heavy engineering which was once the industrial backbone of Britain. …Britain's major businesses now languish in the sick room, many of them simply wasting away."[16]

The finance director at a medium-sized engineering company acidly commented: "We wonder why some of the harsher facts of industrial life since 1979 are glossed over in the support which the CBI gives the government. …When the history of these times is written, the UK banking system will surely be seen as hindering rather than helping to keep industry alive. …Redundancy is a threat which should be used exceedingly sparingly."[17]

Even when recovery was alleged to have started the picture remained sombre. A sceptical *Financial Times* review in 1987 pointed to "a wealth of contradictions", with better profitability but a bigger percentage of British companies locked in niche markets and an increasing dominance in the UK of big vertically integrated foreign companies that tended to use the UK as a manufacturing satellite.[18]

By the close of the decade it was obvious that all the retrenchments and restructurings of the 1980s had left corporate British engineering not stronger but very much weaker. A *Financial Times* survey of European engineering groups in 1989 split its sample into three – eight National Giants in the first, seven Pan Europeans in the second and 27 Nationally Based Medium Sized in the third. There were no British independents in the first division, none in the second and just seven in the third.[19]

The 1990s proved another flat period, with a modest upturn in the middle offset by downturn towards the end. The broad thrusts of economic policy were little changed from those unleashed by Thatcherism in the 1980s. A central justification for the attrition of the 1980s and 1990s was that the loss of companies, plants and jobs would be compensated for by the growth in productivity forced upon what was left.

Yet, any benefit to UK engineering was slow to emerge. True, there was no shortage of activity at the corporate level, with the press pointing to "schizophrenia" in mechanical engineering as British companies sustained a frenzy of spending on overseas acquisitions but continued to cut back at home.[20] But even by the late 1990s there was nothing positive to show. Incredibly, the *Financial Times* had to report that in terms of labour productivity UK mechanical engineering industry had actually fallen further. It now ranked eleventh out of 14 European Union nations, surpassing only Greece, Ireland and Portugal. Where in the UK productivity had risen just 7.1 per cent since 1990, in Italy it had jumped 60 per cent.[21]

At the corporate level the trend was further contraction. In a 1991 *Financial Times* listing of the top 20 European engineering companies only one was British.[22] A 1998 study found that despite a high quotient of "knowledge-based industries" the UK came only thirteenth out of 17 industrial countries for spending on innovation.[23]

Since 2000 the picture has been very mixed. A downbeat phase early in the new century was offset by an upturn in the mid-2000s. This was shattered after the financial crisis hit in 2008. Recent years have seen modest recovery, but the industry remains hopelessly short of recapturing its 1970s heyday.

The breadth and diversity of mechanical engineering is vast. To make it less unwieldy, the histories of a sample of companies involved in the sector have been divided into three. This chapter covers the first group. It comprises stationary machinery, ranging from textile machinery to pumps, valves and compressors. The next chapter has a little more coherence. It looks at wheeled vehicles of various kinds, from bicycles to motorcycles and from earth movers to forklift trucks. And the third chapter covers the rest.

Raising Steam

Together with iron and textiles, stationary steam engines were one of the foundations of Britain's industrial greatness. Even if they have now been superseded as a source of motive power, they deserve at least a respectful visit.

The relevance of stationary steam engines actually ended not long ago, with examples still to be found in industrial and utility plants for much of the twentieth century. In times of emergency they were sometimes brought back out of retirement. Together with its elderly operators the ancient workhorse at Syke cotton mill in Lancashire was coaxed back into use during the three-day week in 1974 and powered two-thirds of the plant's 450 looms.[24]

At water supply depots, stationary engines have been in service much more recently. A prime example is the Waddon. Built by James Simpson of Newark,[25] a pair of these magnificent horizontal cross compound machines was installed at the Metropolitan Water Board's Waddon pumping station in Croydon in 1910, and only retired in 1983. Also popular with waterworks was the Triple, a triple expansion engine built by Hathorn Davey of Leeds.[26]

The machines are often embellished by the instrumentation that guided them. The gauges are mounted in handsome brass cases, the lettering and numerals finely traced by hand. Manufacturers include George Kent,[27] Dewrance & Co,[28] and Schäffer & Budenberg of Manchester, London and Magdeburg.[29]

Fortunately, some of these mighty constructs have been lovingly preserved at centres such as the admirable London Museum of Water and Steam.[30] Powerful, handsome and enduring, they stand as magnificent monuments to the industrial prowess of which Britain has been robbed.

Textile Machinery

Textile machinery was another field in which Britain led the way. Spurred by the competition from the handloom weavers of south Asia, mechanisation spread rapidly through the UK textile industry in the eighteenth and early nineteenth centuries.[31] Major breakthroughs in carding, spinning, weaving, knitting, tufting and bonding of fibres were later followed by advances in colouring, finishing and printing.[32]

At first the new machines were developed by the textile mills themselves, but by the end of the eighteenth century independent manufacturers were emerging. Their position was strengthened by the tremendous growth of British textiles in the nineteenth and early twentieth centuries.

It was not until the interwar period that Britain's standing in textile machinery was seriously threatened by competition from Germany, Switzerland and Japan. Even so, only after the Second World War did UK textile machinery really began to stagnate.

Yet, as in so many other sectors, the critical turning point was not until the 1980s. In the 1960s the UK was still an important contender and second only to Germany in world exports. Shipments rose in the first half of the 1970s, and though this was reversed by the end of the decade there was no dramatic collapse. That came in the following decade, when the UK was the only major producer to see an outright fall in machinery exports and huge setbacks at home.[33]

The story of Britain's industrial development resonates with the names of textile machinery manufacturers. The nineteenth century saw the birth of many hundreds of independent firms, often specialising in one particular area of textile production. Among the earlier concerns was Asa Lees, which made preparation and spinning machinery. Other significant names included John Hetherington[34] of Ancoats, an area of east Manchester dubbed "the world's first industrial suburb" but now an industrial desert, and Howard & Bullough, whose Globe Works dominated Accrington.[35] Both firms were absorbed by Platt in the 1970s, and the Globe Works finally closed in 1993. Among other famous names is Singer, maker of the humble domestic sewing machine at its Glasgow factory until it closed in the 1980s.

Ernest Scragg emerged later in the nineteenth century and specialised in machinery for silk, rayon and synthetic fibres.[36] The company was eventually taken over by Switzerland's Rieter group, founded by a textile manufacturer hit by the Continental blockade during the Napoleonic Wars.

Perhaps the most famous name in British textile machinery was that of Platt, which originated in the late eighteenth century but survived until modern times.[37] Located in Oldham, Platt grew into the world's largest manufacturer of textile machinery.

It was not until well after the Second World War that business became more challenging. After the formation of Stone-Platt Industries[38] in 1958 the group diversified. Among its products were air conditioning systems. I had cause to be profoundly grateful for these on my travels in the 1970s, when I took refuge from the heat of the Nile valley in the sturdy East German electric trains that plied the lines between Aswan and Cairo.

In 1970 the group took over a leading US textile machinery operation to form Platt Saco Lowell. But the recession of the early 1980s delivered a fatal blow, with the company forced into bankruptcy – a rare fate for a large British group. The Oldham plant closed. Predictably, pleas for government assistance through development area funding had gone unanswered.[39]

Platt was not the last of the great names in British textile machinery. A rival for the title of world's largest was James Mackie (Mackies) of Belfast.[40] Established in 1858,[41] the company became a major employer and for many decades made machinery for textile mills at home and abroad.[42]

In 1977 the shares in Mackies were transferred to the Mackie Foundation, a cooperative trust. But within a decade Mackies was facing acute difficulty and approached Westminster for help.

Northern Ireland Secretary Tom King proposed £20m of conditional loans and temporary state control. Nationalisation by another name was, however, dogmatically opposed by Prime Minister Thatcher. For the *Official History of Privatisation* "the Mackies episode provides a vivid example of the difficulties that arise when a government adopts an ideological antipathy even towards temporary state ownership".[43] When US-based Lummus Industries stepped forward it was a different story. The taxpayer found £13m to underwrite an obscure US opportunist simply to avoid any semblance of public ownership.

Mackies went into receivership in early 1999.[44]

The international market is now dominated by producers in Switzerland, Italy, Japan and, above all, Germany,[45] where manufacturers talk earnestly about life-cycle costs and justify high prices with the slogan "buy cheap, buy twice".[46] As for Britain, it no longer sells on price – if it ever did – and still has a few contenders in textile machinery. But the industry is now no more than a niche player.

Machine Tools

The makers of textile machinery were among the first users of machine tools, defined as "mechanical devices for working substantial pieces of metal or other rigid material, usually by cutting, boring, grinding, shearing, shaping or forming". Traditionally those rigid materials had been temperate hardwoods, but the development of cast and wrought iron offered cheaper and more durable materials to the burgeoning industries of the Industrial Revolution. Iron was challenging to work, however, and this prompted the development of appropriate machinery.

The first recognisable machine tools appeared by 1800 and by mid-century James Nasmyth, Robert Whitworth and others had developed more sophisticated devices. The second half of the century saw a significant machine tool industry emerge in Britain, and its products acquired a reputation for quality and reliability.

Even before the First World War, however, they were being outsold in export markets by US and German machines.[47] British products were not as advanced in areas which required US-style standardisation nor as refined in fields which required the skills content where Germany excelled.

During the interwar years the UK machine tool makers continued to be squeezed. Pressure at home was, however, alleviated by protection. The industry was now concentrated in Halifax, Coventry and Leicester, with lesser centres in London and the South East.

After the Second World War the machine tool industry enjoyed buoyant demand in the late 1940s and in the 1950s. By the 1960s, however, business was tougher. This trend continued in the 1970s, which was marked by several closures in the Midlands. Nevertheless, the overall stature of the industry remained recognisably the same.

The situation deteriorated abruptly in the 1980s, when savage recession left structural weakness cruelly exposed. By 1983 the *Financial Times* was reporting: "Britain's machine tool industry is fighting for its life at a time when it should be leading the country's manufacturing industry into the brave new world of factory automation."[48]

The industry faced a crippling fall in sales. Between 1978 and 1981 shipments of lathes, boring machines and milling machines fell from 65,000 a year to 37,000. Employment dropped from 52,000 in 1978 to 37,000 in 1982. Overseas sales were also struggling. Incredibly, by 1983 the UK had a smaller share of the international market than East Germany.

There was a swathe of cutbacks. The most spectacular involved Alfred Herbert in 1980. John Brown cut back from four sites to one and slashed its workforce from 2,200 to 600. TI Group (formerly Tube Investments) halved employment at its Matrix and Churchill subsidiaries to 800. Kearney & Trecker Marwin shed a third of its workforce. US-owned Cincinnati Milacron cut its labour force from 2,000 to 800, Jones and Shipman's workforce was reduced from 1,550 to 850, and B Elliott cut back from over 1,770 to less than 840. Most of the operations of Staveley Industries and Brooke Tool were sold or closed.[49] And although the market recovered in mid-decade it was from "ridiculously low levels".[50]

Cutbacks and closures lasted throughout the decade, with John Brown, Brooke Tool, B Elliott, WE Norton, WE Sykes (The 600 Group), TI Group and the remnants of Alfred Herbert among continuing casualties. The crater gouged in machine tool demand was looking increasingly enduring. For one executive, "[t]he market is only half what it was".[51]

The owner of the privately owned Beaver Engineering protested at the upbeat CBI survey of the UK economy in 1987: "I would not echo those [optimistic] statements. There's simply no depth left in manufacturing in Britain. It is getting shallower all the time."

When this admirable company fell victim to the next recession the director general of the Machine Tool Technologies Association voiced the obvious truth: "The single issue which should be the prime concern of every industrialist, financier and minister in the UK at present [is] the collapse of capital investment, *which is far worse than in any other major industrialised country.*"[52] [my emphasis]

The next problem was Japanese imports, particularly computer numerically controlled (CNC) machines. Ever the pragmatic believers in a consensual approach, the Japanese signed an agreement to limit shipments of machining centres.[53]

The quid pro quo was a new Yamazaki Mazak export-oriented factory in the UK. At a time when government attitudes to British industry tended to combine abysmal ignorance and withering contempt, the Yamazaki president opened the works with some moving words. Reminding his audience that England was the birthplace of the Industrial Revolution whose offspring was the machine tool industry, he said that it had long been his dream to open a production plant in the UK.[54]

Despite such brighter moments, a *Financial Times* round-up late in the decade struggled to find anything to cheer. The *FT* pointed to a "sad and long trail of closures and receiverships" in traditional centres of the machine tool industry such as Halifax.[55] There were "tired and tatty buildings... dreadfully dated equipment rarely seen in the German or Swiss industries". On top of this was a familiar story: "The recession and the speed at which demand disappeared at the turn of the decade...was...too much to bear."

The UK continued to slide down the international league table. By the 2000s the country that had been a world leader as recently as the 1960s cut a sorry figure, falling to sixth place in Europe – far behind Germany, Italy and Switzerland, and eclipsed even by Spain and France. There was no sign of revival.[56]

The most prominent casualty of the 1980s was Alfred Herbert,[57] founded in the 1880s to supply the booming Midlands cycle trade.[58] After the First World War the company confirmed its position as one of the few machine tool makers that could compete with America's best. Alfred Herbert also fostered progressive employment practices, reflecting the philanthropic beliefs of its founder.[59]

After a merger with Churchill Machine Tools in the 1960s there were strenuous attempts at modernisation.[60] By the end of the 1970s the National Enterprise Board was heavily involved, but the change of government in 1979 killed off this constructive approach. In 1982 Alfred Herbert went into receivership.

A pleasing loyalty to many of the great names from Britain's industrial past lives on in India, where Alfred Herbert (India) is today a manufacturer of high-quality equipment for the motor industry.[61]

Few Survivors

Other big names from the heyday of Britain's machine tools included Asquith Machine Tool,[62] Birmingham Small Arms (BSA), Churchill,[63] George Cohen, Coventry Gauge & Tool, B Elliott, Jones & Shipman, Staveley, Webster & Bennett and Wickman. There were also hundreds of small family-owned businesses and operations such as Wadkin,[64] world famous for high-quality wood-working machines.[65]

Most have shrunk, become import distributors or disappeared. Asquith eventually became part of Staveley[66] and BSA fell apart in the 1970s. Elliott, in common with many British companies, owed its origins to an energetic immigrant from the Continent and became a sizeable operation with over 1,000 employees before going into decline.[67]

Matrix Churchill earned heavy publicity for dealing with Iraq in the 1980s. Having been encouraged by duplicitous ministers in the Thatcher government to supply machine tools to Saddam Hussein, Matrix Churchill's directors then found themselves facing prosecution for sanctions-breaking.[68]

Today's machine tool sector is modest, its output putting Britain twelfth in terms of world production and exports.[69] The great bulk of UK output is now accounted for by foreign-owned companies.[70]

Mining Machinery

Mining machinery was always a strong contender in a coal-producing country like Britain. For much of its history the coal industry was heavily dependent on manual labour, its vast workforce toiling in arduous conditions to win hundreds of millions of tonnes of coal every year.[71] But machinery, with its promise of less brutal working lives and greater productivity, offered the potential for change.

In contrast to Germany, mechanisation came late to Britain. It was not until after the mines were nationalised in 1947 that the industry launched an ambitious programme of modernisation. By the 1970s it had been transformed into the most highly mechanised in Europe.[72] The investment generated a big demand for plant and equipment. Most of it was made in the UK. This was no accident. When it came to equipment purchases coal favoured the home side. This evolved into a conscious policy under Derek Ezra, National Coal Board (NCB) chairman from 1971. Highly regarded in the wider world, he proved too consensus-minded and thoughtful for the Thatcher government and was retired in 1982.[73]

Remembered as clever but kind,[74] Ezra took pride in fostering special relationships with his suppliers and applied a kind of micro industrial strategy of his own.[75] Far from encouraging monopolistic practices and complacent attitudes, this proved extremely fruitful. When the NCB opted for automated coalface shearing it was approached by German interests but instead went to British manufacturers, who developed equipment so effective it was exported all over the world.

The productive patronage of the NCB nurtured a highly regarded British mining machinery sector.[76] The industry was concentrated in areas close to the major coalfields, such as South Yorkshire, the north-east of England and the west of Scotland. There were also outliers in South Wales and the West Country.

At its 1970s peak the UK was host to well-known multinational groups such as Gardner Denver and Joy Manufacturing. But the mainstay of the industry was British-based. It included companies like Anderson Strathclyde, Broom & Wade, Butterley, Dosco Mining, Dobson Park and Dowty Engineering, Fenner Gullick, Hawker Siddeley (flameproof electrical gear), Holman Brothers, Huwood, Meco, Mining Supplies, and Oldham.

The destruction of the coal industry in the 1980s and 1990s dealt a savage blow to the machinery suppliers. This obvious knock-on rarely figured in the calculations of a government apparently indifferent to the death of coal. Even before the long coalfields strike began in 1984 the equipment industry had been hit by a slump in NCB orders, simply because the board's cash limits were slashed by the government to half the levels of the late 1970s.

In a 1987 appeal to the government to stand by domestic coal, the British Longwall Mining Association pointed out that the mining machinery industry employed 50,000 people, had a turnover of £400m and exported 36 per cent of its output. In the previous year it had, amazingly, won all ten major non-US export orders in the Western world.[77] It still desperately needed a decent home base to thrive.

Yet the attrition continued. In 1992 a backbencher in John Major's ruling party angrily demanded whether the mining equipment manufacturers would at last be taken into account in a pending government review of the coal industry.[78] And he reminded his minister that in overseas markets, where British companies had made heroic efforts to offset the loss of domestic business, the significant subsidies enjoyed by German coal producers sustained home demand for their equipment suppliers and assisted their penetration of export markets.

One of the first UK casualties was Huwood Mining Machinery. Based on Tyneside, the company had for many years supplied conveyors, drive machinery and supports to the NCB and employed 2,000 people. Within two decades it had virtually disappeared.

The same fate awaited Wigan-based Gullick, a major supplier of pumps since 1969. Dobson Park[79] supplied half the requirements for powered roof supports in the 1970s, so it was severely affected by the collapse of NCB investment. In 1993 Dobson Park combined with Meco International to form Longwall International. The company survived until 1995, when it was taken over by the Joy Manufacturing division of US-based Harnischfeger Industries and decimated.[80]

Cornwall has a long history of underground hard rock mining and open pit mining of china clay. Base metal mining, now ended, was in the past a ready market for the equipment makers. The leading locally based firm was Holman Brothers, which specialised in rock drills, compressors and other pneumatic tools. Holman became the principal industry of Camborne, where it had three factories and over 3,000 employees, and enjoyed a major export business.

The decline of the local tin industry prompted the 1968 merger of Holman with Cornish-based Broom & Wade[81] to form CompAir. Twenty years later the group was bought by Siebe Gorman. It changed hands again in 1999, when Siebe merged with rival engineering empire BTR to form Invensys. This proved fatal for what had been Holman. In 2003 its activities were moved to Simmern in Germany and Camborne closed. And in 2012 the meagre remnants of CompAir were bought by Gardner Denver of the US.

Anderson Strathclyde

Perhaps the most egregious story in mining machinery was that of Anderson Strathclyde.[82] The company had emerged in 1966 from the combination of long-established Anderson Boyes[83] and Mavor & Coulson.[84] Anderson Boyes was a pioneer in longwall mining, an intensive method evolved in Britain which could deliver huge improvements in productivity and safety.

Anderson Boyes had been closely involved in the development of the Anderton shearer loader on behalf of the NCB. Following the merger and limited rationalisation Anderson Strathclyde's main centre of operations was in Motherwell, in the heart of the Scottish engineering belt. The company was noted for good apprenticeships, excellent facilities and modern production techniques.[85]

By the end of the 1970s the derivations of the Anderton shearer loader were extracting most of the coal produced in Britain. Much of the machinery was supplied by Anderson Strathclyde, now the world's largest manufacturer of high-capacity coal-cutting machines.

This made it an intriguing takeover target for a company which had roots in mining but had lost its way. Charter Consolidated,[86] later renamed Charter, was a successor to the British South Africa Company, the vehicle for Cecil Rhodes' ruthless grab for the mineral wealth of Africa. By the late 1970s, Charter's main assets were some hopeless mining ventures and some dull – though more lucrative – shareholdings. Unsurprisingly, the plan was to dump the former, diversify the latter and create a dynamic new giant out of the slumbering hulk.

One of the first steps was to acquire 28.4 per cent of Anderson Strathclyde in 1980. This triggered a referral to the Monopolies and Mergers Commission (MMC), which came out against the takeover. At the end of 1982 the government ignored strong objections in Parliament[87] to overrule the MMC.[88] It instead applied simplistic criteria known as the "Tebbit Rules".[89] These required mergers and acquisitions policy to be based solely on crude competition grounds rather than employment, industrial relations, regional impact and other "public interest" criteria applied by the MMC. The decision was contentious,[90] partly because of a concealment of personal interest in Charter on the part of the secretary of state for industry, Lord Cockfield.

Ironically, government policies toward the coal industry were not exactly helpful to Charter. Within a few years there were severe cutbacks at Bridgeton and outright closures at East Kilbride, Glenrothes and Kirkintilloch.[91] The Motherwell labour force was reduced from 3,000 in its glory days to just 450.

Within a decade Charter had lost interest and sold what was now Anderson Group to the Chicago-based Long-Airdox. Two years later Motherwell closed and production was transferred to the US. What was left of Anderson was sold on to Deutsche Bergbau-Technik in 2001,[92] then to Bucyrus International in 2007. Finally, in 2010 it went to Caterpillar, which shut down the last remnant of the old company in 2011.

Yet another icon from Scotland's rich engineering heritage had passed into history.

Charter stumbled on down the restructuring road, buying ESAB, a Swedish welding technology concern, in 1994 and ventilation specialist Howden in 1997. In 2012 the group surrendered to Colfax Corporation, an obscure US conglomerate controlled by two brothers who had surfaced in the junkbond corporate raids of the 1980s.[93]

Today's mining machinery industry is a shadow of what once was. True, it has a voice in the Association of British Mining Equipment Companies (ABMEC). Some of its members are little more than representatives of foreign-owned groups, however, and most of the rest manufacture on a small scale. Though ABMEC claims its members export over $1 billion worth of equipment and services, the figure it quotes for employment in the industry – just 1,800 people – tells the real story.[94]

Industrial Engines

Among the great success stories for British engineering was industrial engines. These are widely employed in pumps, power generation and other static uses such as specialist road and off-highway vehicles and marine applications.

Established in the late nineteenth century, the industrial engine industry enjoyed rapid growth before the First World War and in domestic and empire markets between the wars. There was another boom following the Second World War, with shipments rising from 250,000 in 1948 to 430,000 in the mid-1950s.[95]

Thereafter they levelled off, but lower volumes were offset by higher values. Moreover, British manufacturers continued to score extremely well in export markets. In 1971 60 per cent of the industry's sales were overseas[96] and a strong export performance was sustained throughout the decade.

Diesel engines led the field. A *Financial Times* survey in 1979 paid tribute to one of the few sectors in which the UK could match Germany. Its share of world end-use markets ranged from 14 per cent in cars and commercial vehicles to 27 per cent for tractors.[97] Another area of strength was diesel generator sets, where the UK was in the top rank alongside Germany and Japan, and small marine engines, where UK manufacturers long had a worldwide reputation.

On the back of its success in diesel engines the UK had also built an outstanding position in components, with Lucas the world number two in fuel injection systems and Holset and Garrett the leaders in turbochargers.

Moreover, the UK diesel industry was remarkably diverse. At the end of the 1970s there were 17 significant players – a dozen if the big automotive companies were excluded. Though two of the mainstream vehicle-makers (Vauxhall and Ford), a specialist producer (Caterpillar) and one engine maker (Cummins) were US-owned and one, Perkins, was Canadian, all the rest were British. These included Amalgamated Power Engineering, British Leyland, Dorman, Doxford, Gardner, Kelvin, Lister, Mirrlees Blackstone, Paxman, Petters, Rolls-Royce and Ruston.

Apart from Doxford, a maker of big marine engines and part of British Shipbuilders, most of the UK manufacturers were neatly grouped into two major combines, GEC and Hawker Siddeley.

GEC Diesels

GEC inherited its diesel interests from the 1968 merger with English Electric. This brought the newborn giant a portfolio of engineering operations with wonderfully redolent names. They included Ruston, builder of mid-size ship and power generation engines, Paxman, renowned for rail traction motors, Kelvin, maker of boat engines, and Dorman, manufacturer of engines for a range of uses.

In contrast to companies like Perkins all of these were specialists, supplying craftsman-built high-quality products tailored to client needs. Output ranged from a few hundred a year in the case of Ruston to thousands for Dorman. GEC Diesels was highly competitive internationally, exporting more than half its production each year.

There was some reshuffling of interests under GEC but the biggest changes – and the demise of this heritage – followed from the disintegration of the parent company that began in the late 1980s. There were hefty cutbacks for Ruston, and its more important operations, such as gas turbines, became part of Siemens in 2003. Paxman, long associated with Ruston, was parcelled up with the latter and sliced up by France's Alstom in the 1990s.

Within a few years it had been sold on to Germany's MAN group, and the name and most of its operations died out. Kelvin Diesels was sold off in 1994. Dorman was sold by GEC in 1987 and then sold again in 1994. The last buyer was Perkins, which rationalised operations and dropped the venerable Dorman name.

Hawker Siddeley Diesels

By the end of the 1970s Hawker Siddeley had also built a nice balance of interests in diesels, ranging from the magnificent machines offered by Mirrlees (Stockport) and Blackstone (Stafford) to the fine tailor-made engines from Gardner and the mass-produced products from Lister and Petters. Ranked among the top ten manufacturers in the world, Lister and Petters exported more than half their output.

Wretchedly, most of this inheritance has vanished. After being sold to GEC Mirrlees Blackstone eventually ended up in Alstom. MAN bought what was left and closed it down. Gardner was sold to Perkins when Hawker Siddeley was taken over by BTR and came to a similar sorry end. And the story was much the same for Lister and Petters.

Gardner

L Gardner & Sons was founded in Manchester in the 1860s. The company offered a range of bespoke products for stationary uses and also for lorries, buses and marine applications. Its products were lightweight, fuel efficient and low revving, making them durable and cheap to run.

The 1980s brought very tough times, with a slump in commercial vehicle production exacerbated by ferocious recession. Between 1980 and 1985 Gardner's workforce halved. Much of its traditional business with bus-makers was hit by the government's chaotic approach to bus deregulation and privatisation. In 1986 Perkins Engines bought the company from Hawker Siddeley, bringing yet more sweeping redundancies.[98]

Since it was already a maker of high-quality engines, Perkins' takeover was in reality just buying market share. The traditional outlets for its new acquisition, both buses and commercial vehicle tractors, were in severe decline. Inevitably, within a few years Gardner was closed.

Lister

RA Lister was another renowned name in industrial engines.[99] Founded at Dursley in Gloucestershire in 1867, Lister initially served the agricultural sector. But eventually it became a prolific supplier of small petrol engines for use in pumps, power generation and small marine craft. Few owners of dinghies, fishing boats or yachts were without their trusty Listers.

Such was their durability that many continue in use today. Yet, after Lister was taken over by Hawker Siddeley in 1965, it never again looked forward. In 1986 it was merged with Petters, and when Hawker Siddeley was itself bought by BTR in 1992 the seas became still choppier. In 1996 what was now Lister-Petter was split between Germany's Deutz and Schroders Venture Capital and after further trimming the latter off-loaded its interest on to a management buyout. Yet another round of cutbacks proved terminal. In 2003 the company went into administration.

Naturally the pension fund was left empty.

Petters

The closest rival to Lister was Petters,[100] which began making stationary engines in Yeovil in the 1890s. In 1957 Petters was taken over by Hawker Siddeley and activities were reorganised, with production of small engines concentrated in Staines, near London. Eventually the rivalry with Lister was ended and the two companies combined into Lister-Petter. The Staines factory was closed in 1988 and all production was concentrated on the Lister site at Dursley – only for this eventually to close.

Perkins

A rare survivor in industrial engines is Perkins. Established in Peterborough in 1932 after founder Charles Chapman had developed the world's first high-speed diesel, Perkins Engines has long been a world leader. Though the company has produced a variety of successful vehicle engines, its main interests are in off-highway diesel and gas engines. Applications include industry, agriculture, construction, material handling, marine and power generation.

In 1959 Perkins was taken over by its largest customer, Massey Ferguson. Fortunately, it was managed at arm's length, and when Massey passed into the fumbling hands of Varity Corporation Perkins remained semi-independent. During the 1960s and 1970s Perkins extended its international operations and by 1979 it was the world's leading manufacturer of diesel engines, with plants in the UK, Brazil, the US and Germany.

In common with the rest of the UK engineering industry, Perkins was nearly wrecked by the recession unleashed in 1980. Output at Peterborough crashed from 245,000 engines in 1979 to 130,000 in 1983 as home demand froze and exports halved. The workforce was cut from 13,000 to 5,600.

However, huge improvements in productivity were secured through hefty investment and changes in working procedures. In the words of the managing director, "[t]he co-operation from the workforce has been outstanding". In a candid press interview he voiced concern that the (Thatcher) government was not more appreciative of manufacturing industry, dismissing the "sunset" label so readily applied.[101]

Perkins endured a spell under Varity. In contrast to Lucas, which had also been taken over by Varity, Perkins was not broken up but kept as a distinct entity. In 1988 it was sold to Caterpillar, creating the world's largest diesel engine maker.

In a rare exception to the pattern with many takeovers of British companies, the results have been positive. Perkins has sustained a well-defined brand and a strong research presence. Despite having associates in Brazil and elsewhere, it has kept a significant manufacturing base in the UK. Capacity at the two main factories, Peterborough and Stafford, runs at 500,000 units a year.

Cummins

Long the world's biggest independent diesel manufacturer, Indiana-based Cummins has been building engines in the UK for over 60 years. Its first European plant opened at Shotts, in Scotland, in 1956, and by the late 1970s there were plans to double capacity. Meanwhile, the company opened factories at Darlington in 1964 and Daventry in 1972 to make mid-sized engines for vehicle, industrial and marine uses.

The momentum built in the 1960s and 1970s came to a brutal halt in the hostile climate of the 1980s. The first half of the decade saw deep retrenchment. A strenuous anti-closure campaign saved Darlington, but not without a cut in the labour force from 3,000 to 1,100. Component manufacture was transferred to Shotts.[102]

Shotts itself was closed in 1998 and its activities transferred to Darlington and Daventry.[103] In 2016 a factory at Manston in Kent was closed and its work went overseas.[104] Nevertheless, with an output of around 40,000 units a year, Cummins continues to be one of the few players left in Britain's once-flourishing engine industry.[105]

Industrial and Mechanical Handling Equipment

Industrial handling equipment includes mechanical lifting and handling machinery of all kinds. One of the foremost makers of cranes, hoists and lifting devices was Herbert Morris.[106] Founded in 1884, the company began production in Loughborough in 1897.[107] By the 1970s the company had a labour force of 2,000.

Herbert Morris remained privately controlled, internationally respected but conservative, slow-growing and underinvested. This began to change after the retirement in 1969 of Frank Morris, who had run the company for four decades. Tall and courteous, Morris was a distinctive figure around the works, tipping his hat to staff, maintaining an open style of management and fostering good relations with his workforce.[108]

After his departure a programme of restructuring and expansion was initiated. But somehow a large shareholding slipped into the hands of Babcock & Wilcox. A referral to the Monopolies and Mergers Commission brought approval and in 1977 a takeover was completed.

Unfortunately, this launched yet another distinguished British company down the slipway to oblivion. Despite its intention to rebuild a presence in cranes Babcock sold Herbert Morris on to Davy, the Stockton-based plant builder. There were further changes of ownership and eventually a skeleton – Morris Material Handling, with just 300 UK employees – was sold to a management buyout in 2001.[109]

Far from reinvigorating struggling companies, management buyouts are often a stalking horse for a new owner, frequently foreign. Sure enough, the remnants of Herbert Morris were soon peddled on to the Finnish company Kone.

An overseas parent in pursuit of market share is no guarantee of survival and in October 2009 Loughborough was shut down. The *Leicester Mercury* was scathing: "The [manner of the] announcement yesterday of the closure of one of Leicestershire's oldest manufacturers by its Finnish owners certainly did nothing to belie the uncaring and distant stereotype often associated with overseas business owners."[110]

Coles Cranes

Another crane maker to suffer major setbacks in the 1980s was Coles Cranes. Originating in south London in the late nineteenth century, Coles moved to a large factory in Sunderland after the Second World War.[111] In 1972 it was bought by the Acrow engineering group and claimed to be Europe's (and the world's) largest manufacturer of mobile cranes.[112]

Coles was hit in the early 1980s by the economic collapse at home. Orders for standard cranes fell from 2,800 in 1979 to just 1,100 in 1984.[113] The year 1982 brought the closure of plants in Manchester and Grantham, and there were severe cutbacks in Sunderland.[114] When Acrow went bankrupt in 1984 Coles was acquired by US-based Grove Cranes, which shut its Oxford and Bicester operations. Sunderland finally closed in 1998.

As so often, the closure of a major factory was to evoke powerful emotions in the people who had served it, with a former employee mourning his time at Coles as "a way of life…just like one big happy family".[115]

Pumps, Valves and Compressors

Industrial pumps, valves and compressors are vital components in many industrial processes, and Britain was long an important producer. Established during the nineteenth century, the manufacture of pumps was often in shipbuilding districts, such as the west of Scotland and England's North West. Valves became associated with South Yorkshire, following the invention of the modern household tap by Richard Chrimes in the 1840s. Other manufacturers, notably Dewrance, Hattersley, Hopkinsons, IMI, Pegler and Serck, developed in a variety of locations.

In the 1950s the UK was second only to the US in the field of pumps, valves and compressors, and accounted for a fifth of world exports.[116] The sector remained buoyant in the 1960s and its international standing was still strong in the 1970s, when it employed over 80,000 people.[117] Even in the more challenging climate of the second half of the decade, over 50 per cent of the industry's production was exported.

The 1980s brought swift deterioration. The harsher climate was particularly evident in valves. Business had been remarkably strong in the 1970s, with sales rising from £100m a year early in the decade to over £400m by the end of it. But by 1985 the *Financial Times* was reporting that "[i]n real terms sales since 1981 have collapsed", with employment dropping from 25,000 to just 12,000.[118] Acute problems arose from constraints on municipal house-building, drastic cuts in water authority spending, the tailing off of the national power station programme and – incredibly, at the height of the North Sea oil boom – the lack of new oil refinery projects.

The nightmare conditions facing "honest engineering ventures" were vividly brought to life in a *Financial Times* interview of the manager of a medium-sized Manchester pump manufacturer in the mid-1980s.[119] This unassuming industrial hero had had to institute three rounds of sweeping redundancies, handle a one-month strike, supervise a wholesale reorganisation of production and somehow sustain an output of 20,000 industrial pumps a year. And all for a salary that an apprentice stockbroker would have scorned.

Hardly surprisingly, he no longer shared his directors' faith in the Conservatives. "I am pessimistic about manufacturing in Britain. All I see is the decline of manufacturing on such a large scale it's very worrying, and that's a hell of a price to pay."

Some of the pumps and valves industry has nevertheless survived. Successes include Spirax Sarco and Rotork, whose stories are told in Tom Brown's revealing *Tragedy and Challenge*.[120] Overall, however, the pumps and valves industry operates on a much smaller scale than in the past and increasingly under foreign ownership. And in an international context the UK is now mostly a bit player.

Weir Group

The most famous survivor is Weir Group, founded by George and James Weir in the 1870s to supply the booming Clydeside shipbuilding industry. Weir later became a key supplier to power plants and chemical works.

An engaging history of this impressive company – for long a rare British *Mittelstand* – has been written by a fourth-generation Weir.[121] Its

Middle East desalination business brought clients who could be wise as well as wealthy. The emir of Kuwait responded to a comment on the good fortune of discovering oil: "I was born in a tent in the desert and we had no money. One day a successor of mine will be born in a tent and he will have no money."[122] He founded the world's first sovereign wealth fund.

His admirable example was not followed by Britain.

In the 1960s and 1970s Weir moved into the oil industry. After a "perfect storm" in 1980 the workforce of 9,000 was halved.[123] Despite the involvement of financiers the engineers fortunately retained control.

By the late 1980s the balance sheet was sound enough for renewed acquisitions, such as a run-down Mather & Platt.[124] There was also ample potential across the Atlantic because, as William Weir put it, pumps and many other useful products were "rust-belt" to a stock market which had inverted its role to become a "driver of American industry" rather than "an innovative and effective means of raising capital for industry".[125]

The parallels on this side of the Atlantic are all too close.

More recently the company has focused on mining, oil and gas, and power. The first two proved testing after the commodity markets turned sour in 2015.[126] As profits lapsed[127] the downturn inevitably brought significant cost-cutting and job losses.[128]

With its strong position in specialist markets and renowned name, Weir has inevitably been a target for City-driven speculation about a potential takeover. Descendants of the founders have, however, demonstrated a commitment increasingly rare in family-controlled British companies. Long may it continue.

Howden Group

Among significant operators in parallel fields was the Howden group.[129] Founded in the 1850s, Howden was a counterpart of Weir's but handled gases rather than liquids. Like Weir, Howden was family-controlled.

Though never as large as Weir, Howden became a sizeable concern, with a workforce of 2,500 in the 1960s and 1970s. Operations were based at Renfrew, near Glasgow. Here, in a rare exception to the cascade of closures that typified her reign, Prime Minister Thatcher actually opened a large new plant in 1981.

The investment had been part of a drive to turn Howden from a narrow base in gas-handling into a bigger diversified international group. The new activities included construction and mining machinery, notably the giant tunnelling machines in which it became a world leader.

In less than a decade such ambitions were severely curbed. The year 1990 saw cutbacks at Renfrew due to the loss of business in Iraq, the shelving of three coal-fired power stations and the appalling blight hanging over the electricity supply industry in the run-up to privatisation.[130]

Eventually Charter made an offer for Howden,[131] and after Weir had declined to be a "white knight"[132] Charter took over in 1997. When Charter was itself taken over in 2012 Howden fell into the hands of US-based Colfax. To no one's surprise there have been big cutbacks and redundancies at Howden operations in Glasgow,[133] with many jobs moved to the Continent.[134] Howden was simply following the path to oblivion so familiar to Britain's historic companies and their industries. In most cases that path has proved impossible to reverse.

Is there one overriding theme in the decay of mechanical engineering since the 1970s? Privatisations had limited direct impact, because the sector saw few. City meddling, so often negative in its longer-term effects, was undoubtedly an issue.

But government action has most to answer for. The once-flourishing mining equipment business was wrecked by the assassination of coal at the hands of government. And the economic and commercial climate resulting from government policy was exceptionally adverse in the 1980s and early 1990s. With its dependence on other sectors at home, and on export markets in the wider world, mechanical engineering was inevitably susceptible to severe damage when both the domestic economy and the exchange rate were hopelessly mismanaged. The sector became littered with casualties, and simply never recovered its former status in the years since.

CHAPTER 4

Mechanical Engineering –
The Wheels Come Off

> *A motorcycle functions entirely in accordance with the laws of reason, and a study of the art of motorcycle maintenance is really a miniature study of the art of rationality itself.*
>
> Robert M. Pirsig, Zen and the Art of Motorcycle Maintenance[1]

Wheels Within Wheels

Many wheeled vehicles are unquestionably products of the mechanical engineering industry but for good reason fall outside the usual catchment of cars, trucks, buses and vans. They include motorbikes, off-highway trucks for construction and mining, tractors and other agricultural vehicles, and forklift trucks. Not all are motorised, of course, since they also include the bicycles in which Britain was once a world leader. This chapter looks at the stories of the industries that made these products, and revisits the companies which were the main players.

Motorcycles

An industry where Britain made a swift descent from international dominance to near-extinction is motorcycles. The first steam-powered two-wheelers were patented in France in the 1860s, but it was not until the 1880s that more practical petrol-fuelled machines appeared elsewhere. By the 1890s designers were particularly active in the UK, and within a decade some of the best-known names, such as Birmingham Small Arms (BSA), Norton, Royal Enfield and Triumph, were well established. Home to the bicycle boom of late Victorian times, Birmingham soon hosted many of the leading motorcycle makers.[2]

Over the course of the twentieth century well over 600 brands of British motorbikes were registered.[3] This offers a clue to the kind of industry it was to become: diverse enthusiasts supplying a diverse range of hand-built machines to diverse enthusiasts. There were, of course, notable exceptions. But they were few in number, and though one or two were quite large their size was in the end no guarantee of survival.

Motorcycles proved their value in the First World War, with British manufacturers supplying large numbers of competent machines to the armed forces. Though there was some rationalisation, the interwar period still saw the British market served by over 80 makes of motorbike, with none of the manufacturers comparing in size with the largest US and German concerns. The Second World War brought another surge in demand for motorcycles and during the conflict British and Commonwealth forces acquired more than 400,000 machines,[4] the bulk supplied by BSA and Norton.

The post-war years offered a wonderful opportunity for British motorbikes. Producers in Germany and Italy had yet to recover, Japanese competition was still in its infancy, and the US industry had shrunk to a couple of manufacturers. British exports – mainly to the Commonwealth and North America – boomed. Indeed, in the 1950s motorcycles were outpaced only by cars and whisky in export to the US, where "Britiron" enjoyed a legendary reputation in the one market prosperous enough for motorcycling as a popular leisure activity.[5] Triumph and Norton became iconic names on both sides of the Atlantic.

The renown of British motorbikes was worldwide. When a young Argentine doctor set off on a trip round South America in the early 1950s his steed was naturally British. Ernesto Che Guevara and his friend were mounted on a sturdy Norton 500, dubbed La Poderosa.

UK motorbike production rose from under 100,000 at the end of the war to over 170,000 in 1950 and remained at high levels for some years. By the end of the decade, however, strains were appearing.[6] Both domestic and export markets were under pressure. Inexpensive cars were vying with motorcycles for personal transport. There was competition from Italian scooters and Italian and German motorcycles. And the first phalanx of machines from giant new factories in Japan was on the starting grid to world domination. UK motorbike production fell to 127,000 in 1959 and within a few years it was below 100,000 and speeding down.

What had gone wrong? In its post-war heyday Britain was a major producer of carefully built hand-made motorcycles of many types and sizes. But they were typically assembled from bought-in components made in ageing factories on worn-out machinery. The designs were too often rooted in the 1930s and 1940s, aesthetically pleasing but lacking in modern technology. There was a heavy emphasis on performance or even race potential.

There was, in abundance, complacency. In response to worries about the reliability of BSA products a director famously commented: "Most motorcycle owners love to spend their Sunday mornings taking off the cylinder head and re-seating the valves".[7] There was little interest in fostering a market for cheap and reliable utility motorbikes for day-to-day personal transport.

Investment Failure

The industry's decline can be laid at the door of one overwhelming problem – the failure to invest.[8] Quite why the industry did not modernise when it had the chance remains baffling. Most manufacturers entered the 1950s with profits at a comfortable level, and even though returns dipped from 25–43 per cent in the first half of the decade to 14–19 per cent in the second half[9] there should have been ample funds for investment. The industry had a high international reputation. It had resourceful engineers and inventive designers. It had a loyal workforce and good industrial relations. No serious commentator has ever tried to lay its eventual demise at the door of the unions.

There is evidence that the industry, or at least its leading players such as BSA, had a lower skills base than its counterparts in Germany and

Japan. What it undoubtedly had was poor leadership. Indeed, the biggest manufacturer, BSA, was burdened by top management that was both complacent and erratic.

The group's management was too readily distracted by diversification and the complexities of coordinating new acquisitions. Few gave much thought to the way personal transport was evolving in the new-found prosperity of the consumer society. And like other British industry the motorcycle sector was fragmented just when economies of scale were becoming critical. At the end of the 1950s, when the Japanese industry was gearing up to make half a million machines a year, Britain's biggest brand, Triumph, was making barely 30,000.[10]

As so often with the decay of Britain's industries, government was far from blameless, displaying a "blind and often suicidal devotion to free trade".[11] This applied as much to motorcycles as to textiles. Politicians were slow to recognise the new competitive threats. Thus an Anglo Japanese Trade Agreement in 1962 left the industry astonishingly defenceless against incursion from the East. The story was different elsewhere. Italy, for example, imposed sensible protectionist measures to ensure the survival of its scooter and motorcycle makers.

Exposed to the blast of competition, the British manufacturers engaged in "segment retreat". They deserted the markets for mopeds, scooters and utility motorcycles in favour of more specialised heavier machines. This worked fine until, of course, the Germans and Japanese began offering bigger products. Worse, Japanese bikes got a good reception in the UK. Where BSA Bantams had ceded to Benleys and Dreams in the lightweight sector in the 1960s, in the 1970s the mighty Bonnevilles, Commanders, Dominators and Thunderbirds gave way to more sophisticated machines with agreeable names like Gold Wing.

By the time another famous biker set out on his grand tour in 1990 British brands had long ceased to be the machines of choice. On his global odysseys Jim Rogers, author of *Investment Biker*, was mounted all the way on trusty BMWs.

The decay of the British motorcycle industry had been evident more than two decades earlier, when sales were going into continuous decline. A succession of forced mergers and bankruptcies culminated in the failure of one of the two main groups, Associated Motor Cycles, in 1966. Its rival, BSA, was only saved from a similar fate by government intervention in the early 1970s. And the remnants of that group survived for only a few more years.

By 1968 motorcycle production was down to 84,000 and the end was in sight. Before long output had dwindled to less than 10,000 and in the mid-1980s it was close to zero. Only with the revival of Triumph in recent years has the tide turned. But even here there has been substantial offshoring of manufacture.

Brands Proliferate

Of the hundreds of British motorbike brands registered in a century of motorcycling, some never even graced the badge on a roadworthy machine. And many involved production on a scale risibly small by modern standards. Among the better known were AJS, Ariel, Associated Motorcycles, Brough, Birmingham Small Arms (BSA), Francis Barnett, Norton, Royal Enfield, Triumph, Velocette and Vincent.

Most of the smaller makers disappeared with little trace, but a few names were rescued by defensive consolidation of the industry. Notable among them was Norton, whose survival owed much to the enduring glamour of its image. The heroine in the 1968 film *Girl on a Motorcycle* naturally rides a Norton Commando en route to trysts with her lover.

Norton lived on for some years as part of Norton Villiers Triumph (NVT), the last bastion of the traditional British motorbike industry. Despite modest financial support from the Heath government in the early 1970s, NVT collapsed in the harsher climate ten years later.

Triumph

Triumph had its origins in a bicycle manufacturer in Coventry in 1888.[12] The founders were Siegfried Bettmann, an immigrant from Nuremberg, and his compatriot Moritz Schulte. The company sold its first motorcycle in 1902 and quickly built up operations, diversifying into cars after the First World War. Financial problems during the Depression prompted a change of ownership and the car division went to the Standard Motor Company.

Motorbike production was resumed after the Second World War, when Triumph moved to a new factory outside Birmingham and the Meriden plant became a shrine for motorbike enthusiasts. After Triumph was sold to BSA in 1951 it was the group's most prestigious marquee, with the Triumph 650 holding the land speed record almost continuously for 17 years.[13] The T60 model was the machine on which Steve McQueen made his bid for freedom in the 1963 film *The Great Escape*.

By the late 1960s, however, even the company's most successful models were beginning to look dated. Nevertheless, Triumph was the most promising component of a newly formed combination of Norton, Villiers and Triumph. The cooperative set up by the workforce at Meriden managed to maintain production as Triumph Motorcycles (Meriden) until the 1980s but went bankrupt in 1983.

This was still not the last of the world-famous brand. It was bought by John Bloor,[14] who brought the business back to life and re-established production at Hinckley, in Leicestershire. Triumph became the centrepiece of a modest revival in the British motorcycle industry, whose output lifted from less than 3,000 in 1990 to 30–40,000 a year in the mid-2000s. Since then production has drifted back again, falling from 38,000 in 2006 to less than 20,000 a year.[15] Though total company output has been running at 50–55,000 a year,[16] Triumph's British heritage has been heavily diluted by moving manufacture overseas.

The company concentrates on large machines such as the 2.3-litre Rocket III, the biggest bike on the market. There are, as yet, no other contenders to restore the momentum of UK motorbike manufacture.

Bicycles

The claims of England to be the birthplace of the modern bicycle are as good as any. The critical moment in the evolution of the two-wheeler came in 1876, when an English engineer, Harry John Lawson, registered his new "safety" model bicycle.

Harry Lawson's design was not, however, a commercial success. That achievement went to the Starleys. James Starley patented the all-metal

Ariel bicycle in 1870 and John Kemp Starley put his ideas into practice in the mid-1880s, calling his invention the Rover Safety Bicycle.[17]

It was an immediate hit, and quickly supplanted the contraptions that had preceded it. Starley established the world's first modern bicycle factory in Coventry,[18] naming his company the Rover Cycle Company – later the Rover Company.

The 1890s saw a boom in popular cycling. Within a decade Britain was the world's largest exporter of bicycles, sustaining its pre-eminence for much of the twentieth century. The main centres of production were Birmingham, Coventry, Nottingham and Oxford.

The West Midlands saw a number of firms enter the industry in the late nineteenth and early twentieth centuries. Among the more enduring names were Hercules, Humber, Phillips, Rover, Rudge, Sun and Whitworth. These were joined by Armstrong, Birmingham Small Arms (BSA)[19] and Norman in the interwar period.

One of the more distinctive early entrants to the industry was the Triumph Cycle Company. Run by Siegfried Bettman and Moritz Schulte of motorbike fame, the new concern began production in 1894. After moving into motorcycles and cars the bicycles operation eventually became a separate business. In 1951 it was bought by BSA and then sold on to Raleigh, which put the brand on a succession of stylish upmarket models.

Raleigh's Rise

Raleigh Bicycle Company was by far the most successful and long-standing of UK bicycle makers. Its origins go back to the 1880s, when Richard Woodhead and Paul Angois, a French immigrant, established a bicycle workshop on Raleigh Street in Nottingham.[20] In 1887 local businessman Frank Bowden bought a stake[21] and the company embarked on a long period of growth.[22] By the 1910s Raleigh was the world's biggest bicycle manufacturer.

Expansion continued during the interwar years, and there were acquisitions of rivals such as Humber. There was a prompt return to normal after the Second World War, and in the post-war years Raleigh and other British manufacturers accounted for nearly all the bicycles imported into the US.

Further Raleigh acquisitions included Triumph and Three Spires in 1954 and BSA's cycle interests (New Hudson and Sunbeam) in 1957, and for many years it remained the world's largest bicycle maker.[23] By now Raleigh's operations were on a vast scale, with the world-famous Nottingham factory covering 60 acres and employing over 6,000 people.[24]

Raleigh's main competitor was Tube Investments (TI Group),[25] which was building a substantial engineering conglomerate. TI's bicycle brands included Phillips, taken over in the 1920s, Armstrong,[26] acquired in the 1930s, and Hercules, Norman[27] and Sun,[28] bought in the 1940s and 1950s. In 1956 the parent combined its interests in the British Cycle Corporation and rationalised some of its operations.

The biggest acquisition by Tube Investments was Raleigh itself, which it bought in 1960 and put into a grouping called TI-Raleigh. Meanwhile, Raleigh had taken over Carlton Cycles, and shortly after there was an agreement with Moulton to make its revolutionary small-wheeled unisex model under licence.

In its traditional products Raleigh now had a huge market share, with 75 per cent of domestic bicycle sales and a major presence in the US and Commonwealth markets. At this point Raleigh still had a strong position in the global industry, making around two million machines a year.

By present-day standards it had a very high level of integration. This included lightweight steel tubes (Reynolds), gears (Sturmey-Archer) and saddles (Brooks), and the company made its own wheel rims, spokes, brakes, handlebar grips, washers and other components.

Conditions were, however, more challenging. The ready availability of motorbikes, scooters and mini-cars was sapping the domestic market for utility bicycles, and between 1950 and 1962 total sales halved. Overseas, there was competition from Asian producers. And imports from the Continent were growing.

Nevertheless, there were major successes,[29] such as the Chopper,[30] and large traditional markets in the Netherlands, Canada and Nigeria sustained the company through the 1970s. The traditional reputation for style, quality and durability was maintained throughout this period.[31]

Raleigh's Fall

In the 1980s the road got much bumpier. The pressures of domestic recession, an overvalued pound and government policies that were not –

despite the windy rhetoric – business-friendly conspired with a fashion for narrower corporate vision. Tube Investments downsized. First to go was the Carlton factory in Worksop, which closed in 1981. In 1982 Raleigh's hold over its US market slipped away when it inexplicably sold the local brand to Huffy Corporation. Within a couple of years almost all Raleigh bicycles sold in the US were being made in the Far East. Further erosion of the brand followed. In 1987 TI finally abdicated and sold the operation outright for just £13m.

The buyer was Derby Cycle Corporation, registered in Luxembourg. Further cutbacks followed and in 1999 what was left of Raleigh was sold on again, this time to two US venture capital groups, for $180m. The dead hand of financial opportunism was now at work.

Bits continued to fall off the machine, with Raleigh terminating frame production and auctioning off its high-tech equipment.[32] For the writer Alan Sillitoe this was a watershed: "Raleigh is a kind of soul of Nottingham. I'm very sad about it." Drawing on personal experience, Sillitoe's novel *Saturday Night and Sunday Morning* had brilliantly evoked the life of a shop-floor worker at Raleigh in the 1950s, his attitudes a blend of truculence and resentful pride in the skills he brought to the world's greatest bicycle maker.[33]

In 2000 the rest of the Raleigh site was sold.[34] The following year there was a management buyout and at the end of 2002 all manufacturing ceased,[35] with final assembly transferred to the Far East.[36] A modest design and marketing presence remained in the UK, but in 2012 even this was finally sold[37] to the Dutch company Accell[38] for $100m (£62m).[39]

The brilliant story of what had been a British flaghip had come to an end.

One of the ironies of Raleigh's fate is that the market for bicycles has seen a striking rebirth.[40] From little more than two million in 2000 annual sales jumped to nearly four million in the mid-2000s, and have remained in the low millions.[41] Yet UK production has fallen from 1.2m annually to less than 100,000.[42]

This comes from three specialists, Brompton, Pashley[43] and Moulton,[44] highly rated but operating on a relatively small scale.[45] There have also been moves to reshore Holdsworth bicycles.[46] The modest revival has brought better times for makers of components and parts. These include Brooks saddles, Reynolds steel tubing and Sturmey-Archer gears, now owned by Sunrace of Taiwan.[47]

So is mainstream bicycle production finished in Western Europe? Has it all followed Raleigh to the Far East? Far from it. Output is well over two million a year in Germany and Italy and nearly a million a year in France and the Netherlands.

With more commitment, investment and vision, it could all have been so different for Raleigh.

Farm Tractors

Agricultural equipment, particularly tractors, was an outstanding British success of the post-war years. It was also one of the more surprising. Historically, farm machinery was not one of the major industries of these islands.[48] Rural mechanisation was much slower to take hold in Europe, including the UK, than in North America.

As a result, the output of tractors and other mechanised equipment in Britain remained modest, even when agriculture started to recover in the years before the Second World War. All this quickly changed after the war, when agricultural machinery was among the engineering sectors which showed the strongest growth.[49]

Yet, barring just two rather small-scale manufacturers, the British tractor industry has almost vanished. With an annual output of barely 20,000 machines, and a modest local content, the industry is a shadow of what it once was. In the 1970s the industry was making nearly 200,000 tractors a year and was the world's third largest producer and its biggest exporter.[50] Since then there has been dramatic attrition, with three major shutdowns in the 1980s and another three in the 1990s and 2000s.

Ford and Fordson

The first modern producer of tractors in the British Isles was Ford, which launched its Fordson (Ford & Son) brand in 1916/17[51] and opened a factory at Cork in 1919. In 1933 production transferred to Ford's new plant at Dagenham.[52] During and after the Second World War the

Fordson Model N became the workhorse of the British countryside. Nearly 140,000, more than 80 per cent of total national output, were produced.

In 1964 the production of tractors was transferred to a purpose-built factory at Basildon.[53] By doing so Ford benefitted from the financial incentives offered for investment in the New Towns. In 1986, after Ford had bought the New Holland agricultural machinery interests of Sperry, it renamed its tractor division Ford New Holland. Five years later the division was sold to Fiat. Further opaque corporate deals resulted in a group called Case New Holland, or CNH International, the world's second largest manufacturer of agricultural equipment.[54]

Having built over 1.6m tractors since it opened, the Basildon plant is now the last major tractor manufacturer in Britain. However, its output of around 20,000 machines a year is well below capacity. Moreover, it is little more than a final assembly operation. With engines imported from Italy, transmissions from Belgium and cabs from France, only 30 per cent of the finished vehicle is locally sourced. Research and development are based elsewhere and CNH is expanding production in China and India.[55]

The hope is that Basildon will not go the way of Ford Langley and Seddon Atkinson, two fine operations taken over and closed by Fiat in the recent past. As an export-oriented operation with a high dependency on imported components, however, Basildon looks intensely vulnerable to almost any new trade arrangements applying after Brexit.

David Brown

Soon after Ford started tractor production at Dagenham a competitor emerged. This was David Brown Ltd,[56] a manufacturer of gears and associated machinery. In the 1930s it formed a short-lived partnership with a talented Irish engineer, Harry Ferguson, and David Brown was launched into the tractor market with an innovative model.

Assembled at a new plant at Meltham in Huddersfield, the tractor enjoyed considerable post-war success, particularly overseas. However, other interests, such as Aston Martin cars, strained the company's finances. In 1972 David Brown's tractor interests were sold to the US group Tenneco, which wanted a foothold in the UK for its JI Case tractor subsidiary.

In 1984 Tenneco bought part of International Harvester and combined its tractor interests in Case IH. Within two years the decision was taken to invest in the company's Doncaster plant and suspend product development at Meltham. Unusually for a Conservative government, the factory's case was strongly supported by the minister of state for industry, Peter Morrison. In a document circulated by the municipal council he pointed out: "Meltham has an excellent productivity and labour relations record which provides the basis for a secure manufacturing future."[57]

The plea was in vain, and when the factory closed in 1988 another illustrious name vanished from the countryside.[58] Case IH eventually became part of the Fiat offshoot CNH, Britain's last big tractor maker.

International Harvester

Though Ford led the way in Ireland the first of the multinationals to set up in England was International Harvester Company (IHC),[59] which opened an assembly plant in Liverpool in 1923.[60] Following the Depression business recovered enough to justify a large new factory in Doncaster (Wheatley Hall Road) in 1938.[61] In addition to balers, combines and other equipment the new operation produced the Farmall tractor.

In 1955 IHC bought the Bradford premises of the defunct Jowett car company. Bradford became a significant operation, shipping much of its output to developing countries and employing over 2,000. Meanwhile, another Doncaster factory was opened at Carr Hill in 1964. IHC was a big exporter and made an important contribution to the global sales of the parent company.

However, the 1980s sowed the seeds of sweeping change in both global and national economies, through a climate in which managements felt freer to treat their assets more as financial packages than historic manufacturing enterprises. Far from immune, the venerable agricultural engineering sector was soon enmeshed in a succession of complex asset exchanges. Already facing financial strains, the IH group was under pressure to restructure.

Bradford, Doncaster Doomed

The first step was the closure of IHC's Bradford operation in 1982.[62] The plant was only the latest in a plague of closures (eg Thorn Consumer Electronics, GEC Large Machines, Rank Wharfedale) "turning [Bradford] into an industrial desert".[63] Mothballing of Carr Hill soon followed. Then in 1984 International Harvester sold its entire agricultural division to Tenneco, which had just added David Brown to its JI Case stable to form Case IH.

The Doncaster Wheatley Road factory remained a highly regarded operation, and when Case rationalised its European capacity it switched production from Neuss, in Germany, to its UK plant. It did so because of the latter's lower costs and greater worker flexibility.[64]

However, Case IH subsequently came under the control of Fiat. When the latter took over the New Holland interests of Ford it hived off the former IH tractor operations into an obscure Italian organisation called Argo. At the same time the Doncaster factory now became the main asset of an entity called McCormick Tractors International.[65]

The end was not long in coming. First to go at Wheatley Hall Road were the smaller machines, which moved to Italy. Then came the announcement – nicely timed for Christmas – of outright closure, with all production transferring to Italy. In December 2007[66] the last tractor rolled off the line,[67] and after turning out 436,836 tractors over a lifetime of nearly 60 years Doncaster's Wheatley Road shut for good.[68]

Harry Ferguson

Ford, David Brown and International Harvester made major contributions to the British tractor industry, but the most famous name is that of Ferguson. Harry Ferguson was an engineer who played a unique role in the evolution of modern farming machinery.[69] After his brief involvement with David Brown Ferguson went on to a "handshake agreement" under which Ford was to produce a Ferguson tractor at Dagenham. The arrangement was rescinded by Ford in 1947. This did not stop Ford using Ferguson's ideas in its Ford 8N, which became North America's top-selling tractor of all time.

In the meantime Ferguson arranged for the Standard Motor Company to make the TE20 model at its Banner Lane factory in Coventry. Tractor production began in 1946. Noted for exceptional ease of use, reliability and durability, the Little Grey Fergie became a much-loved feature of farmyards throughout the British Isles and beyond, with over half a million produced in the ten years following its launch.

Massey Ferguson

In 1953 Harry Ferguson merged his tractor interests with those of Canada's Massey-Harris, to form Massey Ferguson.[70] By the time Harry Ferguson died in 1960 this name was one of the most celebrated in British engineering, and the magnificent operation at Banner Lane was well on the way to becoming the world's biggest tractor factory.[71] At its late 1970s peak the factory was making 90,000 tractors a year, exporting 90 per cent and employing 6,500 people on the best wages in Coventry's flourishing engineering industry.

In addition to Banner Lane Massey Ferguson also had a large factory at Kilmarnock, in Scotland, built for the company by the regional development agency Scottish Industrial Estates. Opened by Ferguson in 1949, the factory concentrated on combine harvesters. With 90 per cent of self-propelled combines sold in Britain coming from Kilmarnock, Massey Ferguson's handsome red machines dominated the countryside at harvest time.

At the start of the 1980s the company faced pressures and Kilmarnock came under threat. After a long debate in Parliament[72] closure was staved off. But the harsher economic climate ushered in by the Thatcher government encouraged a more simplistic approach to industrial issues. In 1980 the factory was closed, with production moving to Marquette in France.[73] Ironically, Marquette's industrial relations were worse than Kilmarnock's. But it had the benefit of a large protected domestic market and an unashamedly interventionist government. The new administration in Britain was not ready to save the Scottish factory.

With the domestic recession biting deeper, Massey Ferguson next announced the closure of its tractor-digger plant at Knowsley, near Liverpool, with the loss of 550 jobs. And by mid-decade Banner Lane itself was facing a crisis. The strength of sterling was hampering export sales and tractor output slumped to half the levels of the 1970s.[74] Meanwhile, even its domestic market had been hit by the government's withdrawal – for doctrinaire reasons – of capital allowances to farmers.

Though the workforce had been more than halved since the halcyon days of 1979, more cuts were demanded. And in November 1987 a proudly independent workforce granted sweeping concessions to the management. These included further redundancies, job flexibility, pay cuts and radical reductions in union representation. A union convenor warned: "They have made a hell of an inroad into the trade unions here [but] the multinationals… could close us down in the morning and transfer all the work to France".[75]

That prediction was wrong only in timing. Massey Ferguson's successes – and the contribution of its workforce – proved little protection in the long run. The 1970s and 1980s had been turbulent years for the Canadian interests of Massey Ferguson. Control passed through various hands, including those of newspaper proprietor Conrad Black. An enthusiast for the dogma of the Thatcher government, Black's appetite for lecturing the world on how it should conduct its business was eventually tempered by a conviction on felony charges – albeit unrelated to his involvement with Massey Ferguson.

In 1986 the remnants of the group re-emerged under the control of Varity Corporation, named after chief executive Victor A. Rice who ran an obscure Toronto-based farm equipment company but was not noted for modesty.

Prior to its re-emergence in Varity Corporation Massey Ferguson had acquired some high-quality interests in the UK. Notable among these was Perkins Engines in Peterborough, which had been bought in 1959 but fortunately kept a distinct identity. Perkins added the Rolls-Royce diesels division to its portfolio in 1984 and two years later it bought the Gardner engines operation. And finally Perkins bought Dorman Diesels from GEC in 1990.

Banner Lane Closes

Varity was run on an opportunistic basis. Within a few years its tractor interests were sold to a US farm machinery group and in 1994 Banner Lane became the largest tractor factory in the portfolio of AGCO Corporation of Duluth, Georgia. In another big retreat from the British industrial stage, Varity (by now LucasVarity) sold Perkins on to Caterpillar in 1998. Meanwhile, Massey Ferguson's new owner, AGCO, claimed to be "the world's largest manufacturer of machinery and equipment focused solely on the agricultural industry".[76] Its commitment, according to its website, is "as vast as the land of our machines cultivate [sic]…AGCO is committed to so much and so many".

Unfortunately, this vast commitment had its limits. One was the entire UK operation. After grumbling about the strong pound[77] and Britain's failure to join the euro, the company abruptly announced the closure of Banner Lane in June 2002.[78] By the year end the factory, which in over half a century had made more than three million tractors[79] and had an exemplary operating record,[80] was shut down and production transferred to France.[81] This extraordinary act of destruction evoked not a bleat from a Labour government hopelessly compromised by its pact with Thatcherism.

Perhaps the most fitting testimonials to Massey Ferguson are its 135 and 165 tractors. Still wonderfully reliable half a century after they were built, these legendary machines are favourites at second-hand tractor auctions and shipped off in their hundreds every year for service in the developing world.[82]

Nuffield and Leyland

Among newcomers drawn into tractor making by the post-war boom was the Nuffield Organization, whose Morris Motors Agricultural Division launched its tractor range under the Nuffield name in 1948.[83] Production was based at the Wolseley works in Birmingham, and there was little change when Nuffield combined with the Austin Motor Company to create the British Motor Corporation (BMC) in 1952.

The first significant upheaval came with the alliance of BMC and Leyland Motors in 1968, when the British Leyland Motor Corporation (BLMC, subsequently BL) was formed. Nuffield Tractors became Leyland Tractors and in 1969 production was moved to the former BMC factory at Bathgate, in Scotland.[84] Eventually the Conservative government that had come into office in 1979 pressured BL into divesting its tractor business and in 1982 it was sold to Marshall-Fowler.

Marshall-Fowler

Production of the Leyland tractor was moved to Gainsborough in Lincolnshire for sale under the Marshall name. Marshall, Sons & Co had its origins with the output of steam engines and agricultural machinery in the mid-nineteenth century.[85] The move into conventional tractors with the Leyland brand lasted ten years, before production ended in 1992.

Another independent producer of tractors was County Commercial Cars,[86] which began operations in the late 1920s. At its operation in Fleet, Hampshire, County concentrated on large four-wheel-drive vehicles, mainly based on Ford tractors. Competition in the four-wheel drive and tracked vehicle sectors from the major players increased the pressure on County, and it ceased production in 1965.

JC Bamford Tractors

Apart from Fiat's CNH, the only company now making tractors in the UK is JCB, based at Rocester in Staffordshire. Still privately owned, JCB was founded in 1945 and is now the world's third largest maker of construction equipment and has over 20 factories around the world. While JCB is famous for diggers and excavators, it makes a range of other products, including tractors.

When it was launched in the early 1990s the JCB Fastrac was the first tractor capable of high-speed travel on metalled roads. However, the JCB presence in the UK tractor market is small, with sales of only a few hundred a year. Most of the company's customers are overseas.

Other Farming Equipment

Manufacturers of other farming equipment have fared as badly as the tractor-makers. Again, the biggest damage occurred in the 1980s. After a buoyant 1970s, following Britain's admission to the EEC and Brussels' farm support, conditions deteriorated in the following decade. By 1987 the *Financial Times* was recording a 40 per cent decline in the total UK market for farm machinery since the 1970s.[87] There were extensive ownership changes and rationalisation for many smaller concerns. These included Bettinson, Bomford & Evershed, Javelin Irrigation, Wright-Rain and Stanhay-Webb, and liquidations for AC Bamlett, British & General Tube, Howard Machinery and Weeks.

Among the larger casualties was the well-known firm of Ransomes, Sims & Jefferies.[88] Based in Ipswich, on the edge of the wide farmlands of East Anglia, the company was long the second largest manufacturer of farming implements and equipment in the country. This made it an attractive target for Sweden's Electrolux, whose Overum and Tive subsidiary exported ploughs to the UK, and in 1987 Ransomes sold its agricultural business to the Swedish company. Within two years all production had been moved abroad.

Construction Equipment

Construction and earth-moving equipment was another of the success stories of the post-war era, with the UK developing a full range of crawler tractors, graders, scrapers, trenchers, dozers, dumpers, excavators, shovels and loaders in those busy years. The 1959 edition of *Britain – An Official Handbook* noted that production had risen from just £2m in the mid-1930s (when the pre-war house-building boom was under way) to £80m in 1957.[89]

By 1971 it had reached £250m, 65 per cent for export,[90] and the trend remained upward for the rest of the decade. Despite the destabilising impact of the Barber boom, whose intemperance was nowhere more evident than in property, business in construction equipment proved surprisingly resilient. Sales of hydraulic excavators, for example, rose from 1,300 in the mid-1970s to over 2,000 in 1979.

The 1980s brought unprecedented strains, and 1983 found the construction industry in Britain reeling from the double impact of a long slump in demand and the arrival on the UK market of Japanese producers.[91] Though it was fashionable to blame the Japanese, the real culprit was the recession, which had driven domestic demand down by a third since 1979. Exports were also collapsing. By mid-decade production had halved.

The casualties mounted. Caterpillar, Priestman, Ruston-Bucyrus and Terex had all taken measures by the end of 1983. The following year saw Ransomes & Rapier and its sister company Newton Chambers make heavy cutbacks, and Priestman go into receivership. Aveling-Barford laid off a fifth of its workforce in 1986 and the Ipswich factory of Ransomes & Rapier was closed by Robert Maxwell in 1987, when the company was sold for a knock-down price to Stothert and Pitt.

The few beneficiaries of the decimation of the British-owned construction equipment industry included Japanese companies such as Komatsu, which opened a "screwdriver" plant at Birtley, on Tyneside.[92]

Caterpillar

Caterpillar built a major UK presence after opening its first manufacturing venture outside the US in the 1950s. After decades of growth, the group was hit hard by the 1980s recession and had to cut back. One of the first facilities to go was Birtley Engineering, which made components for earth-moving equipment. After cutting employment from over 2,000 at the end of the 1970s, the factory closed in 1983, making nearly 1,000 employees redundant. Most lived on south Tyneside or Wearside, where unemployment was already 20 per cent.[93]

Another resounding blow was the closure of the company's crawler tractor plant at Uddingston, near Glasgow, in 1987.[94] As the Uddingston plant was profitable the decision was particularly puzzling. It looked very much like a panic measure to shrink the company's cost base – by moving production to China – in the wake of a modest loss in third quarter 1986.

With the government clearly taken by surprise, there was forthright condemnation by Scottish Secretary Malcolm Rifkind.[95] Angered by the lack of consultation the workforce reacted with a peaceful sit-in. Inured by now to the savage recessions launched by Reagan and Thatcher, the American managers were perplexed. One remarked to the union convenor: "Back home, they would just shoot us [them]."[96] The occupation failed and the plant closed, robbing Scotland's industrial heartland of yet another 1,200 engineering jobs and pushing local unemployment to 50 per cent.

Unlike other multinationals who have cut back in the UK, however, Caterpillar has not deserted the field. Indeed, it remains a successful player in what is left of British engineering. With a workforce of around 10,000 the company operates at 16 sites, and its products include diesel engines (Perkins, acquired in 1998), off-highway trucks at Peterlee, and construction products at Leicester and Stockton-on-Tees.[97]

Aveling-Barford

Between the 1950s and the 1970s the most prominent name among British-owned manufacturers of earth-moving equipment was Aveling-Barford, formed by the merging of Barford & Perkins and Aveling & Porter during the Depression.[98] With financial backing from diesel engine maker Ruston & Hornsby, Aveling-Barford opened the Invicta works at Grantham in 1934.[99]

"Father of the Traction Engine" Thomas Aveling had built the world's first practical steam roller in 1867 and the first internal combustion-engined roller in 1904. Such machines proved invaluable in applying those other great British inventions, macadam and tarmac.

By the late 1930s Aveling-Barford could claim three-quarters of the British roller market. In the post-war years the company extended its activities into dump trucks, graders, front-end loaders and other construction equipment, and built up a thriving export business, with overseas sales eventually reaching 75 per cent of its business.[100]

Notable deals included the supply of dump trucks for the Aswan Dam at the end of the 1950s and dump trucks and front-loaders for an open-cast coal mine in Zambia[101] a decade later. Both contracts were backed by government overseas aid funds, and the trucks performed well in testing conditions. Other significant export destinations were pyrites mines in Spain and hydroelectric developments in Norway. The company won several Queen's Awards for Exports.

At peak the labour force at the Grantham factory exceeded 2,000 and there were 1,000 employees at other sites. Just when the company was reaching its zenith, however, it was facing much tougher competition. The challenge was to match the big off-highway dump trucks under development by competitors such as Euclid and Caterpillar.

In 1967 Aveling-Barford became part of Leyland Motors, and eventually part of Leyland Special Products under BL. It was hoped that the new subsidiary would have an assured source of engines within the group, meanwhile giving the latter a secure outlet for its bigger motors.[102]

There were at last funds for modernising some of Aveling-Barford's antiquated plant. In 1977 Aveling-Barford International was launched and there was appreciable expansion, both at Grantham and at the recently acquired Marshall-Fowler works in Gainsborough, not far away.

The upgrading and restructuring were barely completed before the firm was hit by the 1980s recession, when sales withered. There were sweeping cutbacks and Aveling-Barford was earmarked for disposal as part of the demolition of British Leyland. By the time a buyer was found in 1983 the workforce was down to 800 and operations had shrunk drastically.

The new ownership – a US entrepreneur and a Singapore financier – was obscure, and the slide continued. By 1988 Aveling-Barford was bankrupt. Rescued from receivership, the Invicta works resumed production of some products. However, its glory days were long past, and after other corporate changes the last 30-tonne dump truck left the Grantham site in October 2005.[103]

Ransomes & Rapier

A nearly forgotten name is that of Ransomes & Rapier. Originally established as a general engineer at the end of the eighteenth century, the Ipswich company developed into a supplier of cranes and contractors' plant, and it also became the sole UK maker of giant walking draglines for open-cast mining.

By the early 1960s the Ipswich factory was a sizeable operation, with around 2,000 employees. After the firm was taken over by Newton Chambers Koehring in 1958 excavation products were sold under the NCK-Rapier brand. The graveyard decade of the 1980s brought the firm's downfall, and in 1987 it was wound down and the dragline activities were sold to US-based Bucyrus-Erie.

JC Bamford Excavators

A lone British success in the earth-moving equipment business is JC Bamford Excavators (JCB). A standing reproach to those who hold that the UK can no longer host major home-grown engineering companies, JCB is the world's third largest manufacturer of construction equipment and commands half the domestic market for excavators. The company makes numerous vehicles for use in earth-moving, agriculture and military applications, and a range of lighter equipment for construction and other activities.

Manufacturing sites include the long-standing base in Staffordshire, factories at other UK locations and operations in Continental Europe, the US, China and Brazil. Its biggest overseas facility is at Ballabgarh, in India, which has, ominously, been designated the company's principal manufacturing centre.

The ingredients of JCB's success are complex, but echo those of the *Mittelstand* that buttress Germany's economic prowess. They include a high level of R&D spending, evolutionary development of established products, resistance to lateral expansion through acquisition and refusal to court the financial markets through share offerings. Enlightened employment policies also play an important role. And the development of a strong corporate identity – JCB is now a global generic term for the mechanical digger – has made a valuable contribution.

Until the 2008–09 financial crisis JCB had enjoyed continuous growth since its foundation by Joseph Cyril Bamford in 1945.[104] In the subsequent recession the company shed 2,000 employees, but was then able to rebuild its workforce. By 2015 there were 12,000 employees, spread across 18 factories. That year brought another slowdown and several hundred job losses were announced.[105] Even for a company as successful as JCB, growth – at least at its home base – may not be eternal.

One aspect which exemplifies the trends in UK manufacture of vehicles of all kinds is the collapse of locally built content. In 1979, no less than 96 per cent of a JCB digger was made in Britain.[106] By 2010 that had dropped to 36 per cent, and it has since slid even further.

Forklift Trucks

For three decades Britain led Europe in forklift trucks. Picking up an idea originally conceived in the US, a couple of outstanding entrepreneurs took it forward and turned it into a series of highly successful products. Unfortunately, the companies they nurtured turned out to be all too dependent for their progress and independence on their founders. Once they had gone the industry quickly became prey to takeover, absorption and, ultimately, annihilation.

Lansing Bagnall

Established by an American salesman (W.G. Bagnall from Lansing, Michigan) in the 1930s, Lansing Bagnall was bought by Russian-born Emmanuel Kaye and his partner John Sharp in 1943[107] and developed into an international leader in mechanical handling equipment.[108]

The company became the foremost European manufacturer in the new forklift truck industry in the 1950s. For a German rival "they were the envy of the industry", commanding nearly half the UK market and shipping 60 per cent of output abroad.[109] There were Queen's Awards for Exports and for technological innovation in the 1960s and 1970s, and at peak the workforce at its Basingstoke factory reached 3,500.

The boom years came to a sudden halt with the 1980s. Indeed, the abrupt change could be timed, with remarkable accuracy, to the weeks following Conservative Chancellor Howe's budget of spring 1980. In the words of managing director John Allenby, "[t]he market for fork lift trucks collapsed with a bruising thump in the second quarter of 1980. We had read the signs early, but the fall-off in orders was very sudden."[110]

Within weeks the company was looking at its lowest order book in two decades. And added to fears for its own survival were those for its component makers. When an upturn came many of its subcontractors had vanished, forcing the company to look abroad for suppliers.

Partly by taking subcontracted work in-house, Lansing Bagnall survived. By 1989, however, the company's founder was in his 70s and looking to retire. Where in Germany the proprietor of a *Mittelstand* might strive to find a way to keep the business in private – preferably family – hands, with

Lansing Bagnall this was not to be. Kaye sold the company to Germany's Linde, which was building its interests in materials handling.

Things started well, with Lansing-Linde investing £50m in Basingstoke. But in another grim recession sales fell 20 per cent in 1990 and the more advanced products "died a death". The setback was not shared in other countries, since the recession was made at home.

Bob Bischof, shrewd UK head of Jungheinrich, pointed a critical finger at government policy. The government had raised interest rates to extraordinary levels, first to curb the Lawson boom and then to bolster membership of the European Exchange Rate Mechanism (ERM). Bischof again denounced industry's reluctance to invest for the longer term in sophisticated capital equipment.[111]

Once again there was recovery, but it was limited. In 2004 the production of internal combustion engine trucks was transferred from Leighton Buzzard to Germany. And in 2006 Linde gained control of BOC (British Oxygen), one of the giants of industrial gases and considerably bigger than its new owner. Linde hastily dumped its materials handling interests in the portentously named Kion (supposedly Masai for "take the leadership") for sale to a private equity consortium led by Kohlberg Kravis Roberts (KKR) and Goldman Sachs.

Private equity ownership usually brings a licence to pursue investor advantage, under the guise of shareholder value, of a peculiarly narrow and short-term nature. Barely two years on, Kion was announcing the closure of the Basingstoke factory and the transfer of all production to Germany and France.[112] Nor was this sweetened by a familiar sop to critics of offshoring – the retention of design and engineering facilities in the UK.[113] All too soon they moved to Germany. Despite a commitment to maintain production of heavy lift trucks at the company's Merthyr Tydfil factory, that also closed within three years.[114]

Lancer Boss

Another famous name in British forklifts was Lancer Boss, founded in the 1950s by the notoriously autocratic Neville Bowman-Shaw.[115] From its factory in Leighton Buzzard,[116] Lancer Boss became a significant player at home and overseas, exporting the bulk of its output in the 1960s and 1970s.

The company ran into severe problems in the recession of the early 1990s, but survived. There followed a revealing interview in the *Financial Times*. Along with many industrialists Bowman-Shaw had been looking to Michael Heseltine, one of the few senior ministers in the Thatcher or Major administrations with any knowledge of industry, for a better balance of economic priorities. Despite being a fan of Margaret Thatcher, Bowman-Shaw's view was: "By God she was wrong about manufacturing."[117]

His blistering criticism was matched by trenchant views on British managers: "I would say 45 is the oldest you would want to employ an Englishman, because they are poorly educated and, even worse, badly trained vocationally." This perhaps justified his own remuneration of £455,000 a year.[118]

After its German subsidiary went bankrupt the parent was itself forced into receivership in 1994[119] and was acquired for a nominal sum by Jungheinrich. The sale of Lancer Boss meant that Britain no longer had an indigenous player in an industry it had done so much to develop. And dependence on overseas manufactures rose to 50 per cent, with imports up fivefold since the 1970s. In 2003 Jungheinrich closed the Leighton Buzzard factory and transferred production to Germany.[120]

Neville Bowman-Shaw nevertheless went back into business. Sadly, he did so by importing lift trucks from China.

Coventry Climax

Better known as an independent manufacturer of high-performance car engines, Coventry Climax was also a sizeable producer of forklift trucks. The company made its inaugural forklift in 1946, when it claimed to be the first British producer of lift trucks with pneumatic tyres.

In 1963 Coventry Climax was bought by Jaguar Cars but continued its involvement in mechanical handling. Following the merger of Jaguar with the British Motor Corporation (BMC) in 1966 and the subsequent emergence of state-supported BL in 1975 there was considerable expansion, with new production sites in Batley, Yorkshire, and Warrington, Cheshire, and a workforce of over 2,000.

When recession struck in the early 1980s and the market for lift trucks shrank by more than half, the company ran into heavy losses. Soon the messy privatisations of state assets got under way and Coventry Climax was handed over – effectively free – to a consortium, the ownership structure of which had always, in the words of the *Financial Times*, been "murky".[121] Emmanuel Kaye, owner of Lansing Bagnall, somehow ended up with a 50 per cent stake in the new organisation.

This was not for long. Within four years Coventry Climax was close to bankruptcy and sold to Sweden's state-owned Kalmar. For one reporter Coventry Climax exemplified both the state some of Britain's engineering factories – dirty, dishevelled and in desperate need of investment – and a clash of industrial cultures between Britain and the rest of the world. Coventry Climax was no exception. In the words of its new Swedish managing director, "[w]e were shocked. It was a mess. It was awful."[122]

Kalmar-Climax continued in production for a few years, but manufacturing was run down and ownership eventually passed into the hands of a Finnish-based mechanical handling group.

The death of some of the industries considered in this chapter – notably motorcycles – is not so difficult to explain, with poor management and investment starvation the obvious culprits. For others government policies must be held to account. Privatisation affected a few, with Aveling-Barford perhaps the most prominent. And mismanagement of both the economy and the exchange rate clearly had a crippling impact on sectors such as construction equipment, heavily dependent on the domestic building industry and on exports.

This leaves at least two activities, farm tractors and forklift trucks, whose demise is less easy to account for. What it is now fashionable to call predatory capitalism undoubtedly played a major part in the downfall of agricultural vehicles. And together with ruinous economic policies in the early 1980s it played a role in undermining the forklift truck business.

CHAPTER 5

Mechanical Engineering –
Bearings to Chains

> *It was a hard life at Hoffmanns, but the closeness to colleagues and friends is something almost impossible to find today. …Management and the unions had worked together to create procedures over the years that made the place work as a well-oiled machine 24-seven 365 days of the year.*
>
> *Former employee, Hoffmann bearings factory, Chelmsford*

Foundries Founder

The foundry was often where it all began. No longer as central to mechanical engineering as they once were, foundries still have a role in supplying its basic metal requirements. Operations may be ferrous, making products from iron or steel, or non-ferrous, using aluminium, brass, copper, bronze, magnesium or zinc.

Foundries are essentially factories that produce metal castings. Liquid metal is poured into a mould and then allowed to cool and solidify. The resultant casting is broken out of the mould, trimmed and cleaned. Casting is most often used for complex shapes that would be difficult or uneconomic to make by other methods. Foundries became less prominent as new approaches to supplying the raw materials for mechanical engineering were adopted. Nevertheless, they remain of considerable significance and world production averages 100 million tonnes a year.[1]

The most important outlet for ferrous foundries in the UK was traditionally the motor industry. A cluster of operations developed to serve the vehicle-makers of Coventry, Birmingham and Oxford, and for much of the post-war period foundries in Smethwick, Tipton, Wednesfield, Wolverhampton and Halesowen enjoyed good business with a booming car industry. There was also a significant foundry industry in Yorkshire, with Halifax counting at least 50 operations in the 1970s.

Output ran at around three million tonnes a year in the 1960s, though iron castings were declining as aluminium became more popular for engine blocks, cylinder heads and other automotive components. The 1970s brought much slower trends because of stagnation in vehicle production and substitution. Despite this, even in the late 1970s the foundry industry was still in surprisingly good shape. It had invested an impressive £250–300m and cautiously restructured in response to government incentives.[2]

In 1979 the total UK output of castings was over 3.2 million tonnes, mainly iron and steel.[3] This put Britain at second place in Europe, well behind Germany (4.6 million tonnes) but on a par with France and ahead of Italy.

The 1980s marked the end of anything resembling buoyancy for the heartlands of British engineering. The onset of ferocious recession following the arrival of a radical Conservative administration brought setbacks on an appalling scale. As the *Financial Times* put it, "[n]owhere is the rapid decline of the UK manufacturing base more apparent than in the ferrous foundry sector".[4]

In just three years ferrous castings output fell by half and non-ferrous castings were down by two-thirds. More than 300 plants closed and the workforce was decimated. The Foundry Economic Development Committee reported an entire sector in deep and protracted crisis.[5]

Among the bigger players who cut back were GKN (Halesowen), Ley's Foundries & Engineering[6] and Triplex (the Tipton and Vowles foundries). A particularly controversial closure was Ford's Thames Foundry at Dagenham, which had been rebuilt in the 1950s.[7]

Repeatedly in the eye of the storm was the Birmid group, whose mighty Smethwick operations had pioneered the use of aluminium castings in the motor industry. Another significant closure was CB Smith in Wolverhampton, which made cylinder heads for diesel engines.[8] Even though retrenchment began early in the 1980s Birmid was still cutting back in mid-decade. With the 1986 shutdown of Sterling Metals in Nuneaton, the group had closed half a dozen big foundries since 1979.

The fate of Sterling Metals was particularly salutary. This was the only remaining UK foundry making cylinder blocks for high-speed diesels used in trucks, farm equipment and construction machinery. The group had faced a devastating slump in its markets, with the output of castings for the motor industry falling from a million tonnes a year at the end of the 1970s to less than 300,000 tonnes in the mid-1980s.[9] Also savagely affected was Qualcast in Derby. In just half a dozen years Birmid Qualcast slashed its workforce from 12,000 to 3,500.

Closures were not confined to iron and aluminium. There were sweeping cutbacks among the steel foundries supplying the makers of pumps, valves and other high-value products for railway equipment, turbines, nuclear power plant and specialist construction machinery. Business saw unprecedented declines in all of these sectors. Among the hardest hit was earth-moving equipment, where castings offtake slumped from over 34,000 tonnes in 1976 to barely 7,000 tonnes in 1983.[10]

In the face of this crisis merchant banker Lazard Brothers devised an emergency restructuring. The initial result was a 22 per cent fall in capacity, with the number of foundries cut from 70 to around 50.[11] As so often with such voluntary schemes, there was no guarantee that it would be the healthier operations that survived.[12]

Working conditions were often hot, dirty, dusty and dangerous.[13] Yet, each foundry closure was a local tragedy, particularly to the migrant communities who often provided much of their labour, and another savage blow to Britain's industrial heritage. The collapse of the industry naturally had a severe impact on one of Britain's oldest and most highly skilled crafts, patternmaking – the design and forming of moulds in the inverse shape to the desired casting.[14]

Foundry activity saw modest revival from the worst of the 1980s recession and then had to ride out the collapse of the Lawson boom. Even at the end of the 1990s output remained below two million tonnes, and it soon began to slide again. An important factor was the shrinking of the vehicle component industry. By 2007 UK foundry output had dropped well below a million tonnes and the financial crisis took it below half a million tonnes in 2009.

Casualties since the millennium have included Hydro Aluminium Motorcast of Leeds, one of the West Yorkshire Foundries, whose history and working life were movingly described in the *Yorkshire Evening Post* when they closed in November 2004.[15] Among other significant closures was the Ford plant at Leamington in 2007.

The years since the financial crisis have seen only the feeblest upturn, and Britain's foundry industry remains a shadow of what it once was. With a total output in 2015 of 518,000 tonnes, UK castings production is pitifully small in comparison with its European neighbours – less than a third the size of that in France (1.7 million tonnes), a quarter of that in Italy (2 million tonnes) and barely 10 per cent of Germany's 5.3 million tonnes.[16]

Forges Founder

Forging is a technique in which metal, usually iron or steel, is heated and then pressed or pounded into units known as forgings.[17] The process has been used since classical times, though the Industrial Revolution replaced hand-working with machine operations. Forgings are widely used when a high degree of strength and integrity is required. Modern applications are dominated by the vehicle industry but include mining, oil extraction and agricultural equipment.

For centuries Britain had a flourishing forging industry, with the main centres in the West Midlands and West Yorkshire and significant outliers in Scotland and South Wales. Historically the industry was fragmented, with over 100 separate operations in different parts of the country, but by the 1960s it had begun to consolidate.

Much the largest grouping was GKN Forgings, based mainly in the West Midlands. GKN had eight plants (Garringtons, Shardlow, Forgings and Presswork, Kirkstall, Smethwick Drop, Smith Clayton, Scottish Stampings, Birfield Extrusions) and accounted for nearly half of national production.[18] Other significant players included the West Yorkshire plants of Daniel Doncaster and Firth Brown, and South Wales-based Deritend and High Duty Alloys.

The growth of the motor industry kept the forgings makers buoyant up until the 1960s. From mid-decade on trends softened as substitution began to impact. From a high of over 650,000 tonnes in 1965 the output of forgings fell below 550,000 tonnes at the end of the decade and by 1979 it was down to around 450,000 tonnes. The fall in output was, however, gradual enough to allow for orderly rationalisation of the industry.

This was not the case with the next round of decline. This was so abrupt and so extreme that the industry was almost wrecked. In just four years output plunged by more than half to barely 220,000 tonnes as the recession unleashed in 1980 bit into the heartlands of UK engineering. Employment in drop forging fell 40 per cent, and press forging was not far behind.[19] Many of the smaller operations closed for good.

The forging industry never really recovered from the collapse of the 1980s. Except in specialist fields such as those served by Sheffield Forgemasters, it is dwarfed even in a European context. UK output of under 250,000 tonnes in 2015 was little more than half that of France (476,000 tonnes), a quarter that of Italy (1.1 million tonnes) and less than 10 per cent of Germany's 2.8 million tonnes.[20] Again, revival prospects look remote.

Industrial and Process Plant

British industry manufactures almost every type of industrial plant. Of particular importance are fabricated products such as pressure vessels, heat exchangers and storage tanks for chemical and oil refining process plant, steam-raising boilers, sinter plants, metallurgical furnaces, lime and cement kilns, nuclear reactors, water and sewage treatment plants, and fabricated steelwork for bridges, buildings and industrial installations. The industry has many large-scale enterprises, including nine with over 2,000 workers, and in all employs 196,400 people.

This was the cheerful story from the Central Office of Information (COI) in the mid-1970s.[21] Britain still had a broad industrial base offering a sophisticated market for plant suppliers. Even at the end of the decade, despite some rationalisation and restructuring, the COI was still able to paint an impressive picture.[22]

Today such confidence would be impossible. The withering of much of Britain's industrial heritage since the 1980s – in power engineering, nuclear engineering, oil refining, bulk chemicals, ferrous and non-ferrous metallurgy, and even food manufacturing – has made the COI's boast impossible to sustain.

The industrial plant business has traditionally comprised both the contractors responsible for the design of plants and the fabricators and builders. The contractors have included both British and foreign companies, with the latter led by US players such as Bechtel, Enserch, Fluor and Foster Wheeler, all of which had flourishing UK operations.

Prior to the 1980s British-owned contractors often had substantial manufacturing facilities. Familiar names in plant building included Davy Corporation, Head Wrightson, John Brown Engineering, Babcock & Wilcox, Clarke Chapman, Haden, Matthew Hall, Simon Engineering and Capper Neill. In food and drink processing plants the leaders were APV and Baker Perkins. Contractors such as Humphreys & Glasgow and Seltrust Engineering kept out of manufacturing.

Davy and Head Wrightson

Davy had its origins in Sheffield steel but by the 1960s it was a global name in non-ferrous metallurgy, oil refining and chemicals, as well as steel plants. Managing director John Buckley guided Davy out of financial crisis at the end of the 1960s and was a charismatic champion of the company – and of his country's engineering prowess – on the global stage.[23]

In 1977 Davy acquired Head Wrightson, the big iron and steel fabricator based on Teesside.[24] Part of the magnificent concentration of industry that had grown up in England's North East, Head Wrightson's output included marine and industrial boilers, distillation columns, pressure vessels and other major components for process plants.[25] By the 1960s the company employed 6,000 people at its Thornaby site.

Cruelly, within a few years of Davy's purchase, process plant was in crisis. The policies of the Conservative government that took office in 1979 triggered a ruinous collapse in investment. In just three years, work in progress for process plant contractors fell by a quarter. New orders plunged 80 per cent.

The industry went into huge retreat. Humphreys & Glasgow cut its workforce from 2,500 to 700 and was then sold at a knock-down price to Enserch. Incredibly, at the peak of the North Sea oil bonanza refinery specialist Capper Neil was allowed to collapse.

One factor in the dearth of UK business was the government's doctrinaire abolition of tax allowances on capital investment. Worse, export business slumped, with UK-made content on overseas contracts falling from over 70 per cent in 1980 to less than 30 per cent three years later.[26] The government had withdrawn the export credits vital to British firms competing with rivals from the US, Japan, Germany, France and Italy, all of whom benefitted from financial incentives.

Before long even Davy was struggling, and in 1987 Head Wrightson was closed and the works bulldozed. In a surreal incident soon after, the prime minister was photographed at the derelict Thornaby site. Standing alone in the industrial wasteland which owed so much to her economic policies, she made a thoughtful if unrepentant figure.

She had made a desert, and called it peace.

Babcock & Wilcox

A traditional area of strength for British plant contractors was industrial boilers. Demand was dramatically reinforced by Charles Parsons' invention of the steam turbine in the 1880s. By the 1950s the boiler makers employed 30–40,000 people and were big exporters.

The main contenders were Babcock & Wilcox and Clarke Chapman. The larger of the two, Babcock & Wilcox was founded as an offshoot of its US parent in the 1890s.[27] By the 1950s it was a global giant, employing thousands at its Renfrew works on Clydeside.

Thanks to sustained economic growth and high levels of investment the 1960s were a rewarding time for suppliers to the electricity industry. Business slowed in the oil shock years, but Babcock's return on capital remained buoyant and averaged around 15 per cent in the mid-1970s.[28]

In 1982 the core was floated on the Stock Exchange as Babcock International, and the company became vulnerable to predatory investors. In 1987 it was bought for £416m by the obscure FKI Electricals,[29] which set about the expected dismemberment. Within months the Inbucon consultancy was being paid £1m to oversee sweeping cutbacks. Four thousand highly skilled jobs were to go,[30] including many hundreds at Renfrew.

Babcock cited damaging delays in the flow of orders by the Central

Electricity Generating Board (CEGB).[31] Although preparations for privatising Britain's enviable state-owned power industry did not begin until 1989, the mere threat of sell-off was already casting a pall.[32]

The cull at Babcock included six out of seven group managing directors. The aggressive comment from the FKI boss was: "It's not that they're not capable of doing it [restructuring]. It's that they don't want to do it."[33] So sweeping were the dismissals that Inbucon had to rush in its own staff to fill the gaps.

Presiding over this fiasco was chairman Lord King, one of the prime minister's favourite businessmen. King was an ardent disciple of Margaret Thatcher, and in a fit of pique had withdrawn Babcock from the CBI when its director general, Terry Beckett, made a courageous public attack on her economic policies.[34]

Within two years Babcock was demerged again. In 1995 it sold a majority stake in boiler-making to Mitsui, which eventually passed it on to a Korean concern. The rest of the group has enjoyed taxpayer largesse as a supplier of services to the Ministry of Defence and a contractor for the Queen Elizabeth-class aircraft carrier programme.

Clarke Chapman

Clarke Chapman was yet another mainstay of the North East, having established itself at Gateshead in the 1870s. Much of its work involved bespoke equipment for shipbuilding, power generation and eventually nuclear engineering.

In 1969 Clarke Chapman bought Sir William Arrol, the bridge builder; in 1970 it acquired John Thompson, a Wolverhampton boiler maker; and in 1974 it took over the UK arm of International Combustion.

Government efforts to nudge British industry into stronger groupings prompted an unexpected merger of Clarke Chapman with Reyrolle Parsons three years later. The result was Northern Engineering Industries (NEI), intended as a rival to GEC.

In 1989 NEI was taken over by Rolls-Royce, keen to reduce its dependence on aero engines. However, the business climate remained challenging and in 2000 NEI was sold on to new owners. The most recent proprietor of what is left of Clarke Chapman is Langley Holdings. The original factories have, of course, closed and all that survives is a small producer of mechanical handling equipment.

Whessoe

Like its Teesside neighbour Head Wrightson, Whessoe developed as a supplier of heavy iron and steel fabrications for the booming engineering activities of the North East in the nineteenth century. The group went on to the assembly of industrial plant and installations and eventually became a specialist supplier to gas, oil, chemical and nuclear energy. The 1950s and 1960s were a particularly buoyant time and Whessoe employed over 3,000 people at its main works in Darlington.

The 1980s brought a dramatic fall in investment in heavy industry and Whessoe's attempts to build a significant stake in offshore oil were disappointing. In 1989 the main factory closed. The little that was left passed through the hands of Preussag, Kvaerner, Al-Rushaid and, in 2013, Samsung of Korea.

Bridge-Building

Until the eighteenth century, bridge-building in Britain was noted for the conservatism of its designs.[35] All this changed with iron and steel. Their low cost and matchless properties took Britain from a laggard in infrastructure to the front rank.

The first significant iron bridge was erected at Ironbridge Gorge, on the River Severn in Shropshire, in 1781. Produced by Abraham Darby's process developed early in the century, its cast iron components were fitted together on site. The structure is still in use, having survived a lunatic Shropshire County Council proposal to replace it in 1956.

Ironbridge was followed by hundreds of other iron bridges, and then by steel when that became readily available. In the early days iron bridges would often have been made locally, but gradually national specialist suppliers became the main producers. Often these were based at iron and steel works.

William Arrol

A leading example was Sir William Arrol & Co, founded at Dalmarnock Iron Works in Glasgow in the 1870s.[36] The company went on to build the famous bridges over the River Tay (replacing the first, which had collapsed) and the Forth in the 1880s, and London's Tower Bridge not long after. Important overseas projects included the Nile Bridge in Cairo and the Hawkesbury Bridge in Australia. In addition to bridges Arrol supplied giant cranes to shipyards and harbours.

By the time of his death in 1913 William Arrol had become a Scottish industrial hero.[37] The company remained a significant engineering contractor and was acquired by Clarke Chapman in 1969. As the new parent ran into increasing problems in the graveyard decade of the 1980s, however, operations were severely curtailed. In 1989 Dalmarnock closed.

Redpath Dorman Long

Like William Arrol, Redpath Dorman Long had roots in iron- and steelmaking.[38] The main bridge-building structures were normally cast and fabricated at the company's operations in Middlesbrough and shipped for assembly on site.

Remarkably, one of Redpath Dorman Long's first big contracts was the huge Sydney Harbour Bridge, commissioned in 1932. In the meantime the company had completed the Tyne Bridge in 1928. It also built the mighty Storstrøm Bridge in Denmark in 1937 and many significant projects in Africa and the Far East.[39]

Among them was the Omdurman Bridge, located where the two Niles – the Blue and the White – unite and the great river starts its journey across the driest desert on earth. When I backpacked through Africa in the 1970s the bridge was still serving Sudan half a century after it was built.

By the 1960s the constructional business of Dorman Long employed more than 4,000. After nationalisation it remained a division of British Steel until 1982. Redpath Dorman Long was then sold off as part of the Conservative government's privatisation programme. It was bought, for just £10m, by the Trafalgar House property conglomerate. Trafalgar House already owned its great rival, Cleveland Bridge & Engineering, and merged the two operations in 1990. The result was the largest structural steel fabricator in Europe, with 7,000 employees.[40]

The manufacturing side was gradually run down, however, and all that remains today is a consultancy specialising in structural projects.

Cleveland Bridge

Unlike its Middlesbrough rival, Cleveland Bridge was an independent structural engineer from the start.[41] The typical pattern for Cleveland Bridge was to fabricate the components at home and then ship them out for assembly on site.

In the years before the First World War, Cleveland Bridge built many bridges throughout the empire. Among celebrated early projects was the railway bridge connecting Northern and Southern Rhodesia at Victoria Falls on the Zambezi. A later venture was the first great bridge across the Bosphorus, the longest suspension bridge outside the US when it opened in 1973.

In the meantime the company was acquired in 1967 by the Cementation Company, a construction firm which was itself taken over by Trafalgar House in 1970.[42] In 1990 Cleveland Bridge was merged with Redpath Dorman Long but six years later it changed hands again when Trafalgar House was itself bought by Norway's Kvaerner group.

Trafalgar House had been an uneasy alliance of engineering and shipping with tabloids and property speculation. Contributions to Conservative Party funds lubricated rapid growth in the 1980s. A notorious episode when the company demolished the art deco Firestone building in west London in anticipation of a preservation order did nothing to damage its standing in government circles.

Towards the end of the decade the company reverted to type by piling on property assets in the later phases of the Lawson boom and was heavily exposed when the boom went bust. Stern warnings about its accounting practices forced the disclosure of one of the biggest losses in British corporate history.[43]

Somehow Hong Kong Land was not deterred from taking a large stake in Trafalgar House in 1992. The new owner then presided over even bigger losses. The mess was eventually cleared up when Kvaerner bought

Trafalgar House for its engineering subsidiaries. Most of the directors were dismissed.[44] They included deputy chairman Charles Powell, who had been private secretary to both Margaret Thatcher and John Major before taking lucrative sinecures in the private sector.

In 2000 there was a management buyout (MBO), which took Cleveland Bridge back to independence. As so often, the MBO was prelude to another sale and within two years a controlling stake had gone to a group based in the Middle East. Cleveland Bridge UK maintains a fabricating facility at its home base in the north-east of England, but its 300 headcount[45] points to a greatly shrunken manufacturing base.

Diversified Engineering Groups

The emergence of the vehicle industries at the start of the twentieth century prompted the birth of many suppliers of components and parts, and some of these were eventually to grow to immense size. Among the early beneficiaries of the new industries was a range of rubber components.

Dunlop Deflates

Much the most important was the pneumatic tyre, developed by Irishman John Boyd Dunlop in the 1880s. By the end of the First World War the Dunlop Rubber Company was a major international player, with a huge factory at Fort Dunlop, on the edge of Birmingham.

The years after the Second World War saw further development of Dunlop as a global brand, with sports goods added to its traditional products. Inventions such as the Denovo self-sealing tyre and the Maxaret anti-lock braking system were notable achievements, and by the 1970s it was a big multinational, with over 100,000 employees.

The subsequent demise of this well-regarded giant remains puzzling. Despite good business conditions in the 1960s, profitability was lacklustre and in 1971 Dunlop went into an ill-conceived alliance with Pirelli.

The Dunlop-Pirelli Union combined one financially weak giant with an even weaker one. Pirelli was an uneasy combination of dull cable-making and glamorous motor-related activities, and even less profitable than Dunlop. Neither partner was prepared to share technology or pursue economies of scale. Within ten years the Union had collapsed.

A debt-ridden Dunlop never reclaimed its former glory and there were hefty retrenchments.[46] These accelerated in the grim conditions of the 1980s, and in 1982 the company announced a loss of £26m. The deficit was actually quite modest in comparison with other tyre makers. In the same year Michelin, the market leader, lost £354m.

But it was Dunlop that deserted European tyre-making, selling its core brand to former subsidiary Sumitomo Rubber Industries. The development was welcomed in the City, where an analyst gleefully predicted that Sumitomo "would go through Fort Dunlop like an avenging fire"[47] – a comment which revealed a remarkable ignorance of the cautious, constructive, consensus-seeking Japanese approach to business.

Dunlop Holdings was subjected to sweeping financial reconstruction. Between 1979 and 1984 the company had axed 23,000 jobs before newly arrived executive chairman Michael Edwardes pronounced: "This is a case where more wholesale reductions [in jobs] is not the answer to the company's problems."[48]

What was left was bought by acquisitive conglomerate BTR.[49] The cost was offset by the gradual sell-off of Dunlop interests. The disposals reached a peak in the mid- to late 1990s, when BTR itself was shedding its conglomerate image.

In 1999 Sumitomo went into a joint venture with Goodyear, giving the US company control of its UK operations. The main interest was a plant at Washington, County Durham, which closed in 2006. A specialist motorsport operation continued to manufacture at the original Fort Dunlop site until 2014, until that too disappeared.

Michelin, Pirelli, Goodyear Go Flat

Since the demise of Dunlop, mainstream UK tyre production has been in the hands of three majors, Michelin, Pirelli and Goodyear. All have seen heavy retrenchment from the 1980s on. From 44,000 in the mid-1970s the workforce in tyre-making across the country fell to less than 20,000 in 1984.[50]

At the start of the 1980s Michelin had 15,000 UK employees at six separate sites – Aberdeen, Ballymena, Belfast, Burnley, Dundee and Stoke-on-Trent. Virtually all of these have been decimated or closed.

Meanwhile, in mid-2015 Goodyear announced its withdrawal from UK tyre-making with the closure of the Wolverhampton plant. And the Pirelli story is also dismal. Despite huge productivity improvements the company's operations at Burton and Carlisle[51] have both shut,[52] with production switched to Italy and Turkey.

BTR

BTR Industries, the main player in Dunlop's carve-up, started out as an offshoot of the US-based Goodrich tyre company.[53] Registered as the British Tyre & Rubber Company in 1934, the company changed its name to BTR when tyre production ended in the 1950s. It became a conglomerate in the 1980s, a transformation driven by managing director Owen Green, who built up a pliant City following.

Easy parallels have been drawn between BTR and Hanson, another high-profile conglomerate of the 1980s. Both chased short-term success by banging down costs, jacking up prices and chasing operational and financial efficiencies. Like Hanson, BTR had little compunction about shedding employees. A typical view was: "Companies...are for sale because the owners won't take the hard decisions, which mostly come down to people." In the case of Dunlop, "[t]hey had too many people, and couldn't afford the costs of getting rid of them".[54]

Yet, under both Owen Green and his successor John Cahill there were differences in the BTR approach. The *Financial Times* noted a genuine taste for manufacturing management as well as financial engineering, quoting John Cahill: "I'm a factory man. I don't like to go into a factory which is dirty and provides rubbishy service." Hanson and his henchman Gordon White boasted they never set foot in their factories. Moreover, BTR's culture was distinctly austere, with many executives receiving modest remuneration and John Cahill paid less than an eighth the salary of Hanson.

Apart from Dunlop, BTR's major targets included Pilkington, which resisted takeover in 1985, and Hawker Siddeley, which surrendered in 1992. This was the last milestone in the career of Owen Green, who retired the following year. With his departure the conglomerate fad was fading. In 1999 BTR merged with Siebe to form a new engineering giant with the clumsy name of Invensys.

Siebe Gorman

Siebe was founded in London by a young Prussian artillery officer, Augustus Siebe, after the Battle of Waterloo. His firm, Siebe Gorman, specialised in diving gear, underwater apparatus and breathing equipment.[55]

The 1970s brought a series of acquisitions, including CompAir in mining equipment and APV in food processing. There was also a move into industrial controls through the acquisition of Barber-Colman and Foxboro. Despite some successes, opportunistic investor pressure prompted the £9bn merger with BTR in 1999. The deal was billed as bringing together two of the most powerful UK engineers to compete with global giants such ABB, General Electric, Rockwell, Schneider and Siemens.

Invensys Fantasy

This was fantasy. On paper Invensys may have appeared formidable. In practice its management struggled with such a disparate group.[56] By 2002 Invensys found itself with debts of over £3bn and under pressure to divest.[57] A typical comment was: "While Siebe had a strong focus in controls and software…BTR had degenerated into a ragbag of interests, whose shares had fallen 75 per cent behind the market."[58] Dependably fickle, City sentiment had turned heavily against its former favourite, with one trader remarking: "If BTR were a horse, it would be taken out and shot."[59]

The reign of its first chief executive, Allen Yurko, saw 23,000 jobs go in three years. Yurko then followed, his departure sweetened by a £5m pension pot.[60] His successor, Rick Haythornthwaite, grumbled about excessive management time spent on restructuring. He might have mentioned the cost. In 2001 he blew £165m on retrenchment, mostly for redundancies.

The scene was now set for major divestment. As so often, good assets went first. Power storage went to EnerSys of the US for $505m. Siemens snapped up the best Invensys activities, railway signalling and traffic control. Much of what was left was bought by France's Schneider Electric to strengthen its presence in industrial software, automation and energy control systems.

The rueful comment from Robert Bischof, a friendly but frank German observer with many years' experience of British business ways, was: "Short term shareholder value rules and the Brits will sell anything and everything to please the City. I am aghast...In 2005 the board appointed Ulf Henrichsson as chief executive. ...Enter Nigel Rudd as chairman...he fired Henriksson, an engineer, because 'he could not see the big picture' and replaced him with the chief financial officer, Wayne Edmunds. The break-up of the company...the sale of the signalling business to Siemens...and the rest to a French company...*such deals are a sure way to UK manufacturing oblivion*".[61] [my italics]

The Nigel Rudd who presided over the carve-up had form. Previous career lows had included peddling off important British companies such as Pilkington and Boots to new owners abroad.

Ever Ready

Another venerable name which fell to the conglomerate fad was Ever Ready. The UK offshoot of American Eveready Battery became British Ever Ready on the eve of the First World War. By the 1970s the company enjoyed a major share of the UK market, its operations including a major plant opened with government assistance at Tanfield Lea, County Durham, in 1968.

Ever Ready also had big research and development laboratories in north London. Yet it was slow to recognise the potential for long-life alkaline batteries. This was despite a holding in Mallory, whose Duracell brand was to become market leader. Indeed, Ever Ready eventually sold its stake in Mallory.

In 1981 the company, by then pointlessly rebranded Berec (British Ever Ready Electrical Company), was taken over by Hanson Trust. Hanson followed its well-worn path to short-term profitability. There were sweeping cutbacks, research and development was slashed, a third of the workforce was sacked and capital spending frozen. Worse, valuable subsidiaries in Germany (Daimon) and Italy (Superpila) were sold. Of all possible contenders they were handed to rival group Mallory/Duracell.

In one of its few constructive decisions Hanson restored the name Ever Ready. This turned out to be window dressing ahead of an eventual sale to US-based Ralston Purina. Having started life in catfood, Ralston Purina was diversifying into batteries.

Within a few years most of Ever Ready's remaining UK facilities – hopelessly underinvested by Hanson – had closed. They included the now run-down factory at Tanfield Lea. Generous taxpayer funding when it opened in the 1960s had made this a flagship.

By the time the new owners took over it was a "shit pit".[62]

Lucas Leads

An even more famous household name was that of Lucas,[63] which straddled the worlds of electrical and mechanical engineering. Founded in King Street, Birmingham, in the 1860s, the company eventually became Britain's leading supplier of components to the motor industry.

A succession of mergers with other component makers included CAV, strong in diesel fuel injection, and Simms in a similar field. The interwar period also saw the takeover of Rotax, a specialist supplier of aircraft components, and Girling, a major producer of brake systems, clutches, shock absorbers and dampers. The post-war years saw Lucas well established as a multinational. A significant presence in Continental Europe was reinforced through a subsidiary in Germany and a joint venture with Ducellier in France.

By the 1970s Lucas was a giant of UK engineering, employing over 100,000 people at home and abroad and a backbone of the Birmingham economy. Despite robust unions, the company's illustrious name, technological expertise and product quality prompted great affection at many of its operations.[64]

While the 1970s proved challenging the 1980s were calamitous. In 1980/81 Lucas made its first ever loss, around £20m. The response was sweeping retrenchment, with 22,000 jobs lost by 1985. Half of these were in

Lucas Electrical. For one manager, "Electrical is 20 per cent of our turnover and 80 per cent of our problems".[65]

Given the appalling economic climate it would be quite wrong to accuse the Lucas management, headed by Godfrey Messervy and Tony Gill, of simply wielding the Hanson hatchet. Reacting to City criticism, a director commented: "It is easy to increase profits on paper by cutting everything back quickly. But that capacity and the skilled people are lost for ever. It is much more of a challenge for management to try to turn a business around. That is the real test in the long term."[66]

Attrition nevertheless continued. There were major cutbacks in the Midlands and at CAV and Simms in London. One of the biggest shocks was the closure of King Street in 1986. In one of Birmingham's biggest shutdowns of the 1980s, 1,200 employees lost their jobs.

Tony Gill still defended a gradualist approach: "We spend two per cent of annual turnover on training and six per cent on research and development…other companies have got their profits up higher than ours and sooner…but have abandoned some of the things without which they are going to be struggling in the longer-term."

The financial community continued to carp. "There seems to be a total inability on Lucas's part to understand why the City was so brassed off with it," bleated a fund manager after a rights issue to finance just the sort of activity the City relished – takeover bids.[67]

Varity Virus

Despite recovery in the mid-1990s, the company remained vulnerable to the corporate reshuffles that had taken such virulent hold in industry. The end came in 1996, when chief executive George Simpson, who had moved from Rover and would go on to lead GEC to disaster, acquiesced in a reverse takeover by Canada's Varity Corporation.

Varity had just 9,000 employees against the 46,000 still working for Lucas. The new organisation, LucasVarity, lasted less than three years before the company was sold to US-based TRW. Chief executive Victor Rice walked away from the wreckage with £17m in cash and options.

TRW promptly hacked chunks off its new acquisition. Prized diesel injection went to Delphi, the US-based automotive parts company.

Aerospace went to Goodrich, also of the US. The remaining automotive interests were bundled up with those of Varity and TRW and hawked to the Blackstone investor group.

The once-great name of Lucas flickers on in minor components made by an outfit called Elta Lighting Ltd.

GKN

With origins going back to the Industrial Revolution[68] GKN is one of Britain's oldest companies.[69] Its historic homeland was the Black Country, where GKN was a major employer in Bilston, Wolverhampton and other great manufacturing towns. For most of the twentieth century it remained synonymous with screws, nuts, bolts and other fastenings.

Most of GKN's steel interests were eventually nationalised, and GKN sought other interests.[70] One was GKN Birfield Industries, whose subsidiaries included Hardy Spicer, a pioneer of the constant velocity joints (CVJs) used in front-wheel-drive and four-wheel-drive cars.

By the 1970s GKN was still a dominant presence in steel fastenings but also a major supplier of forgings, bearings and other products for the car industry. There was a successful line in fighting vehicles for the military.

The dependence on the motor industry left the group heavily exposed when activity stagnated in the 1970s. It proved almost disastrous in the following decade. The first major shock was a plunge into loss after centuries of profitability. From a profit of over £100m in 1979, GKN slumped to a pre-tax loss of £1.2m in 1980, in what the *Financial Times* described as "one of the most gruesome horror stories in engineering".[71]

Leadership of GKN had just passed from the charismatic Barrie Heath, a "forceful but incredibly kind and generous" Second World War flying ace noted for consensus labour relations. His successor was Trevor Holdsworth,[72] who belied a mild demeanour by launching four years of savage cutbacks. His wild spending on retrenchment, cutting GKN's UK workforce from 69,000 to 33,500, cost £200m.

At the end of it all the company's return on net assets was no better than it had been in 1979.[73] Lamely, GKN explained this fiasco as a strategic necessity arising from "the diminution of the customer base in the United Kingdom" – in other words, the desperate hollowing-out of the industrial economy.[74]

Attrition continued. By 1988 GKN's UK workforce was down to 19,000. Yet, on taking up the presidency of the CBI, Trevor Holdsworth proved a diffident champion of manufacturing. Unlike more courageous contemporaries such as Terry Beckett and John Harvey-Jones, Holdsworth was forgiving of the Thatcher experiment. The extraordinary job losses and industrial devastation that scarred its record were brushed away with fashionable myths: "I remember one calculation – I don't know its source – that around 10m people in the UK were underemployed in 1980."[75] For Holdsworth the answer was self-flagellation: "We had a terrible reputation for old equipment. Not only that, we were proud of it."[76]

The second recession of the Thatcher era, at the end of the 1980s, brought more cutbacks, notably the closure of the Brymbo steelworks jointly owned with British Steel.[77] By 1991 GKN's global workforce had plunged from over 100,000 in 1980 to just 30,000.

From now on the company's emphasis was on aircraft, automotive and powder metallurgy. There was a short-lived foray into helicopter building when GKN took over Westland. More recently, GKN's business has demonstrated its long-standing skills in automotive[78] and aerospace.[79] This, and the scope for divesting, inevitably attracted a corporate vulture. Since March 2018 the new owner of GKN has been Melrose Industries, run by a quartet which had pocketed £170m in 2017.

One is a protégé of James Hanson. Inevitably, dismemberment has already begun. The auspices for what remains of GKN are not good.

IMI

Originating in the Nobel Explosives division of ICI, IMI was floated off as Imperial Metal Industries and concentrated on non-ferrous metallurgy, the manufacture of plumbing fittings and related areas.

These activities were increasingly seen as low growth underinvested commodity businesses. A *Financial Times* profile of IMI in the late 1990s painted a picture of the Yorkshire Fittings factory in Leeds as "a pre-war brick pile on an old industrial estate, which despite an impressive drive to raise performance offered a depressing contrast to the company's operations in Germany and the US".[80] Eventually it was sold, along with other traditional interests, to concentrate on flow control systems and other precision engineering products.

Other Component Suppliers

With the exception of Smiths Industries, other suppliers to the automotive sector have proved less resilient than GKN. Companies like Champion, Ferodo, Lodge, Rubery Owen, Quinton Hazell and Trico once formed a thriving group of what were almost household names. Many were based in the West Midlands, in easy reach of the volume car plants. Most survived the stagnation in car production in the 1970s only to hit dreadful conditions in the 1980s, when the setbacks in cars were exacerbated by a collapse in trucks, buses and vans.

Rubery Owen's main works at Darlaston in the West Midlands closed in 1981 and many of its peers were cut back, closed or, like Ferodo, sold to foreign buyers. Others survived the 1980s and 1990s only to face heavy retrenchment more recently. Quinton Hazell, once the largest independent supplier of auto parts in Europe, eventually sold its operations. Two of these, in Wales and Lancaster, were closed in 2013 after the bankruptcy of their parent, Klarius.

Their shrinking UK supply base has prompted warnings from carmakers that the component sector may have fallen below a minimum critical mass, and that the future is one of ever greater import dependence.[81] As Tom Brown spells out in his vivid account of the travails of engineering, *Tragedy and Challenge*,[82] the revival of car production in the UK is much less robustly based than often claimed.

Ransome Hoffman Pollard

Essential components of moving machinery, bearings were pioneered in the UK in the eighteenth and nineteenth centuries. There is now nothing left of a British-owned industry which had included three significant concerns, Hoffmann Manufacturing, Pollard Bearings and Ransome & Marles Bearing Company.[83]

Hoffmann was named after a Swiss-American businessman[84] who opened a factory in Chelmsford in the 1890s and was for many years the town's largest employer. Subsequently Hoffmann commissioned a factory at Stonehouse,[85] near Bristol, to supply bearings for aircraft and other specialist applications.[86]

In 1969 Hoffmann was steered by the Industrial Reorganisation Corporation (IRC) into a merger with Ransome & Marles and Pollard to form RHP.[87] The aim was a unified British bearings industry with a better chance of survival.

The largest partner was Ransome & Marles, which had for many years been the leading UK producer. It was not, however, a strong presence in an industry dominated by global players such as US-based Timken, Sweden's SKF and NSK of Japan. Even RHP had less than half the UK market, and the gruelling conditions of the 1980s proved lethal.

The main casualty was Hoffmann's Chelmsford works, which closed in 1989. A former employee voiced the moving epitaph quoted at the start of this chapter.[88] And the remnants? A small facility at Stonehouse went to SKF in 2002.[89]

In 1990 what was left of RHP went to NSK.[90] In addition to its own plant in Peterlee, opened in 1976 as NSK's first factory outside Japan, NSK has maintained production at the former Ransome works in Newark.

Steel Chains

Industrial steel chains are used in vehicles, construction machinery and materials handling. Britain's leading manufacturer is Renold,[91] founded by a Swiss engineer who bought a small business making textile chain in Salford in 1879.[92]

Renold became the leader in its field and its bush roller chain is still the bicycle industry standard. By the 1970s the company could claim to be the world's largest chain maker. A workforce of 12,000 was concentrated mainly at its Manchester operations in Wythenshaw and Burnage (where investment was described by a union spokesman as "terrible").[93]

The company was hit very hard by the recession of the 1980s, with demand for industrial transmission chains and gears falling by a third in the first half of the decade. Between 1981 and 1984 the workforce was cut from over 11,000 to 5,000. Further redundancies followed after cutbacks in hydraulic motors and robotics, and the company's workforce was soon down to just 2,500.[94]

Eventually the company revived, helped by acquisitions at home and abroad, and business in the 2000s proved more stable. More recently there has been some retrenchment and renewed job losses. The main casualty was the Bredbury factory in Stockport, whose closure was announced in 2013.[95]

Pilkington – Triumph to Tragedy

"Pilkington was once a national treasure. From its St Helens base in England's North-West, it was a pioneer of the world of glassmaking. Now, that same cradle of innovation is an operational outpost of a disparate Japanese empire. Britain's biggest glassmaker has all but slipped from public view."[96]

How did this national treasure come to earn this accolade from the *Daily Mail*? The story is one that starts promisingly, peaks brilliantly and then, as so often when the money men come calling, fades into twilight.

Founded as the St Helens Crown Glass Company in the 1820s, Pilkington Brothers[97] eventually entered the most challenging sector, plate glass. When new markets opened up in the auto and optical industries after the First World War, Pilkington quickly became a major player, taking a stake in Triplex to develop laminated and toughened glass for the motor manufacturers. There were also pioneering moves into fibre glass and related products.

Meanwhile, Pilkington became the epitome of the long-established, paternalistic family firm, providing a virtual welfare state for employees, pensioners and their families.

For most of the twentieth century Pilkington fostered an active research and development effort. This paid off spectacularly with the invention in 1952 of float glass. The new process involved floating liquid glass on a bath of molten tin, avoiding the casting, grinding and polishing that made plate glass much more expensive.

The invention transformed a major capital industry, revolutionising architecture and conceiving new energy-saving and safety glass products. Technical director Alastair Pilkington[98] (no relation) enjoyed well-deserved fame. In the early 1960s Pilkington began to license the float glass process to other manufacturers and develop a wider network of overseas interests.[99]

After nearly 150 years wholly in family hands, the company offered its first public shareholding in 1970 and eventually joined the Stock Exchange blue chips. Nevertheless, it remained under family control.

Meanwhile, the cash flowing from float glass royalties financed major expansion in the 1970s, and the St Helens labour force reached an unprecedented 16,500. Diversification included a stake in Rockware Glass, the leading maker of glass containers.[100]

In the early 1980s Pilkington bought major overseas rivals such as Germany's Flachglas and US-based Libby-Owens-Ford. This confirmed Pilkington's status in the top rank of glass manufacturers. Through Triplex the group supplied glass for 20 per cent of the world's auto production and enjoyed a similar standing in spectacle lenses.

The strength in international markets was fortunate, since the 1980s brought savage recession at home and the company's domestic operations went into loss. By mid-decade there were huge retrenchments, cutting the workforce by more than half at a cost of nearly £100m.[101]

Hard-won recovery attracted a hostile takeover bid from BTR in 1985. With the Pilkington board marshalling employee, shareholder, community and parliamentary support to back its long-termist philosophy, the approach was repelled.

At the end of the 1980s the second recession in a decade hit the company. More retrenchments and disposals followed, taking the St Helens workforce below 5,000. There was, however, renewed expansion overseas. By the time of Alastair Pilkington's death in 1995, float glass had been licensed to 42 manufacturers in 30 countries and there were 170 plants operating or planned around the world.

Two events in the 1990s proved critical to the fate of Pilkington. One was the acquisition by Nippon Sheet Glass (NSG), Japan's second biggest glass manufacturer, of a 20 per cent stake in Pilkington's Triplex Safety Glass. The other was the appointment of Nigel Rudd as the first non-Pilkington chairman. Over the next few years the balance of non-executives (NEDs) crept up from four out of 11 directors at the time of the BTR bid to five out of eight 20 years later.

This was to prove crucial when in October 2005 Pilkington received another takeover approach. The suitor was NSG, and the board eventually announced unanimous acceptance.[102] Shareholder support was far from unanimous. Approved by the few big institutions which held most of the Pilkington shares, the takeover was bitterly opposed by the smaller shareholders, many of them existing or retired employees. Under the takeover code's ludicrously undemocratic rules, their position was outvoted.

Chief executive Stuart Chambers declared himself "excited about Pilkington's future as part of the NSG group".[103] City opinion was mixed. "This…makes strategic sense from an NSG perspective," said Paul Rogers, dutiful analyst at Deutsche Bank.[104] But more thoughtful Japanese analysts were sceptical.[105]

NSG Not So Good

They were right. The synergy so often claimed for corporate mergers was, as usual, spurious.[106] NSG, which thought bigger meant better, was half the size of Pilkington. Moreover, it became heavily dependent on Pilkington management, giving them half its board seats and instating Stuart Chambers as president. Chambers had little loyalty to NSG, and left after a year. And the financial record has been dismal, with NSG in loss or wafer-thin profit for eight consecutive years.[107]

Why did this matter to Pilkington? Because the takeover was debt-financed. Unusually for a Japanese company, this left NSG highly leveraged. The resulting financial constraints have put severe limits on investment. And, despite clear assurances at the time of the takeover, there have been job losses and plant closures.[108] Total UK employment is just 2,500, of which perhaps half are in St Helens, and the organisational command has moved to Germany. In both size and status, the company is pathetically reduced.

So how did the deal come about? The answer lies with the changes in business philosophy and corporate governance that have become embedded since the 1980s. A thoughtful case study[109] highlighting the dubious role of NEDs in corporate mergers and acquisitions put it bluntly: "The firm has [since Thatcher] become a bundle of saleable assets on the assumption that this makes markets work better and improves competitiveness."

NEDs, who may have little technical skill and less long-term commitment to the companies whose remuneration they take, are "not only sympathetic to the notion of *everything for sale* [my italics] but also well-practised in running an auction".[110] So a financially robust and technical exemplar like Pilkington, facing an opportunistic bid from a smaller rival, could be surrendered for a few more pence on the bid.

It is now fashionable to disregard almost everything but the short-term valuation set by the share price. The *Financial Times* felt able to report, without apparent irony, "The Board and its chair had the confidence of City investors who agreed that 'Sir Nigel Rudd knows what he is doing'".

He and his fellow NEDs would certainly have known about the millions in share options that they were able to pocket on completion of the takeover. Whether they gave a moment's thought to the implications of handing over yet another of Britain's national flagships to an inappropriate suitor is not recorded.

Metal Box Rusts

Metal Box was for many years Britain's main manufacturer of packaging, supplying containers for storing and shipping foods, liquids and other materials.[111] Tinplate was its main raw material.

The First World War accelerated collaboration. In 1921, four can-makers combined to form Allied Tin Box Makers, eventually Metal Box.[112] Their cleverest coup was a series of market-sharing agreements with Continental Can of the US, which gave Metal Box insight into its rival's technology while restricting access to the British market. The 1930s saw Metal Box confirm a commanding presence at home and overseas.

Its position was reinforced in the decades after the Second World War. Much of the achievement was credited to Robert Barlow, the dominant figure in Metal Box until his retirement in 1961. At this point the firm was the leading packaging supplier to some of the world's largest companies.

The 1970s brought keener competition at home, but this was more than offset by expansion in the US and Europe. By the end of the decade annual revenues had reached $2.7bn.[113]

Then trouble struck. Metal Box was severely affected by the recession unleashed in 1980. Though the company's finances were far from weak the management resorted to the usual measures. In little more than five years 13 factories were closed and the labour force was slashed 43 per cent,[114] with heavy casualties at Carlisle, Liverpool, Manchester, Mansfield, Salford, Swindon and Reading.[115]

Meanwhile, a new chairman, Brian Smith, had taken up office. A *Financial Times* profile conveyed an aura of brisk no-nonsense, with ugly overtones of the hatchet man now in fashion. Smith proudly reported that in four years as head of ICI Fibres he had cut the headcount by 40 per cent, including a halving of the research department in a company whose very life owed everything to its research achievements.[116] "Research is too important to be left to the researchers" was Smith's breezy view.

He then set in train events that led to the end of Metal Box, turning it into a rudderless conglomerate and killing off its identity as leader in its field. He and his successors spent years in frantic and fruitless trading of the group's assets. There were moves into building products, plumbing fittings and cheque-printing. The year 1988 saw the packaging operations merged with those of Brussels-based Carnaud to form CMB, with control ceded to French managers.

Before long the cash from the deal was spent on Caradon, which brought more construction and plumbing brands on board. The result was dubbed MB-Caradon. Following exit from CMB and the acquisition of RTZ Pillar's industrial interests in 1993 the company called itself Caradon, and the last reference to one of Britain's great industrial names was finally buried.[117]

There were more ventures into building products, this time doors and windows in Germany and the US. By 2000 chief executive Jürgen Hintz had to admit to restless investors that the mess over which he presided had no real core business. The Caradon badge was dumped and yet another new name, Novar ("freshness and a new start"), adopted. And in 2005 the sorry residue of yet another British industrial flagship was sold to an overseas interest. This time it was the US group Honeywell, which promptly disposed of two out of the three divisions of its new acquisition.

Like so many fine British companies, Metal Box had now been well and truly buried.

Disparate though they are, the industries visited in this chapter have all, to a greater or lesser extent, been assaulted by one or other of the villains that have conspired to dig the graves of British manufacturing. Closely tied to the heartlands of heavy industry, foundries were an immediate casualty of grotesque economic mismanagement in the 1980s. Process plant was crippled by the investment collapse that accompanied that mismanagement, and also suffered from the dire handling of the exchange rate. And, having ridden out the recessions of the 1980s and 1990s, outstanding companies like Pilkington and Metal Box eventually succumbed to the fashionable management myths that took hold in an era when short-termism and malign City meddling reigned unchecked.

CHAPTER 6

Cars – Changing Gear

> *It was still possible to feel, but not to think, that farming England was the real England, and industry a mere brutal interloper to be fought or ignored. The motor car was still an instrument of pleasure. My Rover 8 was milk chocolate colour, a colour they haven't tried since, and it was squarish and had two enormous air-cooled cylinders which stuck out of vents on each side of the bonnet. After a long day they glowed cherry red in the twilight.*
>
> *René Cutforth, Order to View[1]*

Slow Start

Britain came late to carmaking. Having offered its unique contribution to the steam age, it was a slow starter in the internal combustion stakes. True, it has made valuable contributions to the development of the automobile. British inventions include pneumatic tyres, fuel injection, disc brakes and power steering. And the down-at-heel London suburb of Acton hosted the world's first factory devoted to six-cylinder engines.[2] But the key mileposts on the road to the motor car were elsewhere.

Germany has the distinction of being its birthplace but France was where its commercial potential was first realised. By the end of the nineteenth century France's annual output was over 10,000 vehicles. Britain and Germany produced barely 2,000 and even America made fewer than France.

As Europe's most affluent country, the UK led the way in private motoring[3] but remained dependent on imports. It was not until the eve of the First World War that a significant proportion of new sales at last came from domestic sources. The largest was Ford. Other British manufacturers included names later to dominate the industry, such as Morris, Austin and Wolseley.

Car sales and carmaking fell back during the war, partly due to a high level of import tariff. Imposed at 33⅓ per cent as a wartime deterrent to luxury consumption, the duty survived, with only brief interruption, for nearly five decades.[4]

After the war, the land fit for heroes presented carmakers with a boom. Companies such as Morris and Austin had greatly expanded their activities, and workplace controls exercised by craft unions in the interests of the war effort reverted to management. Dozens of new manufacturers started up and by the early 1920s there were almost 90 British makes of cars on the market.[5]

Few survived. Recessionary conditions were aggravated by government austerity, initiated to help Britain repay war debts and return to the gold standard. By the end of the 1920s the number of producers was down to around 30 and the industry was dominated by just three companies. All were British, Ford having slipped from its earlier pre-eminence.

Though it dropped in 1929–30, car production in the UK was not as severely affected by the Depression as it was on the Continent. Indeed, from 1931 on the British motor industry enjoyed a remarkable revival. By 1938 car production had raced up from 150,000 early in the decade to around 450,000 units a year, compared with fewer than 230,000 in France. Even German output was 25 per cent below British levels.

The UK boom was fuelled by managed trade and, after the 1931 exit from gold, economic stimulus. Tariff walls were high enough to deter imports. Imperial preference stimulated sales to the dominions and colonies, and Britain accounted for half of all the cars exported from Europe in the 1930s.

In contrast to the US, the British market favoured model diversity, product differentiation and limited standardisation. By the mid-1930s the UK car industry offered a wide range of products, often at attractive prices. My grandfather, a City underwriter, could afford a stately Armstrong Siddeley 20/25, and on a modest professional salary my mother ran an Austin Seven Ruby.

Modern and Efficient

A fast-growing UK market was served by some efficient modern operations. William Morris had built up production at his Cowley works on the edge of Oxford and by the late 1930s was making 90,000 vehicles a year. Herbert Austin was manufacturing on a comparable scale at Longbridge in Birmingham.[6] Ford opened a giant new plant at Dagenham integrated all the way from foundry to final assembly. And the industry was supported by a broad base of component suppliers such as AC, Bendix, Dunlop, Hardy Spicer, Lucas, Pressed Steel, Smiths and others whose names survived until the culls of the 1980s and 1990s.

The growth of the British industry in the 1930s was organically driven, and restructuring was limited. Morris had rescued Wolseley from bankruptcy in the 1920s and bought Riley in the late 1930s. General Motors bought Vauxhall in 1925. Hillman, Humber and Commer merged to form the Rootes Group. Nevertheless, the industry remained fragmented, with the big three accounting for less than two-thirds of output in the late 1930s. This compared with almost 70 per cent for the top three in Germany, 75 per cent in France and 85 per cent in the US.

Car output fell to low levels during the Second World War, but there was a bonus for the motor industry. The shadow factory scheme was expanded, with investment in new industrial sites, buildings and machinery. These stood the industry in good stead once civil production resumed.

There were, nevertheless, the first questions about the future. A 1945 official report described a sector with too many units and too many models. The lack of consolidation and standardisation would leave the UK industry more vulnerable in the longer term.

For a while, however, any such weakness was forgotten. Car output surged from a few thousand a year to over 200,000 in the first 12 months of peace and in 1948 total production exceeded the 1938 peak of nearly 450,000. By the end of the decade output had neared 800,000 a year.

A major preoccupation was exports to compensate for the depleted gold reserves and huge debts bequeathed by the war. Britain strove to meet strong car demand in the US and the Commonwealth. Raw materials were allocated to companies with a good export performance, and by the end of the decade the industry was shipping two-thirds of its output abroad. Among notable offspring of the export drive was the Land Rover, which proved an immediate hit at the 1948 Amsterdam motor show.

The late 1940s saw the first post-war models from leading manufacturers. Popular newcomers included the Devon and Hampshire from Austin, the Minor[7] and Oxford from Morris, the Standard Vanguard and the Vauxhall Wyvern. The new family saloons were conventional in design but there were exceptions. One dashing initiative was Austin's top-of-the-range offering, the Atlantic. A handsome sports coupe, with triple headlights, bench seats, a sleek radio and nice art deco touches, the Austin Atlantic failed to make an impact in its main market, the USA, and was pricey for Europe. This was no longer a deterrent when I bought a battered second-hand model, my first car, in the early 1960s.

The 1950s brought a golden age to British cars and output raced away, more than doubling over the decade. If not sharing in the Continental miracle, the economy was growing steadily. Under consensus Conservative governments, policy was Keynesian, constructive and internationally admired. Long-term unemployment was mostly eliminated and consumer demand taking off. Taxes on car ownership were cut. Private motoring was at last within sight, if not always the grasp, of lower income groups.

Never Had It so Good

Serving the new demand was a remarkable array of carmakers. Catering for the mass market were the big five. Austin and Morris merged in 1952 to form the British Motor Corporation (BMC), the largest car company outside the US. BMC commanded 40 per cent of its domestic market in the mid-1950s and had a big overseas presence. A reinvigorated Ford, with a fine new model range, had over a quarter of the British market, while the others – Rootes Group (Hillman, Humber, Sunbeam and, from 1955, Singer), Vauxhall and Standard-Triumph – shared around 30 per cent. Imports were an exotic rarity.

The balance went to a group of companies which was peculiarly British and often highly inventive. They came with names like AC, Allard, Alvis, Armstrong Siddeley, Aston Martin, Bentley, Bristol, Daimler, Gilbern,

Healey, Jaguar, Jensen, Jowett, Lagonda, Lanchester, Lea-Francis, Lotus, Morgan, Reliant, Rolls-Royce, Rover and TVR. Later entrants included McLaren, maker of racing cars, Caterham Cars and a clutch of tiny specialists. There was even a factory in Slough assembling a stylish saloon for France's Citroen.

The independents varied from substantial publicly quoted firms like Rover to privately owned workshops. Their output ranged from Reliant's humble three-wheelers to the magnificent limousines offered by Rolls-Royce. Some succumbed to competition from the big five. Some merged with one or other of the big five. But a surprising number survived into the modern era.

BMC remained the vanguard of Britain's car industry. While domestic demand boomed, the export imperative became less urgent. Nevertheless, Britain remained the world's leading car exporter until the mid-1950s, with a particularly strong position in the US. Increasingly, however, this rested on sports cars and high-performance saloons.

It was in those sunny years of "never had it so good" that cars took a lasting hold on the popular culture. Before the war British car ownership had been very restricted, and motor sport remained a minority taste. Apart from flashes of glory for Bentley and Lagonda at Le Mans, there was only limited British participation in the sporting events popular on the Continent.

All this changed in the 1950s, when Britain made a thrilling return to Le Mans. A single decade brought six outright victories – five for Jaguar, one for Aston Martin – and the 1957 result was astounding, with British cars taking 12 of the first 16 places. Drivers like Peter Walker, Mike Hawthorn and Roy Salvadori became popular heroes, a tradition sustained in following decades by charismatic characters such as Stirling Moss,[8] Graham Hill and James Hunt.

Nor were Britain's new celebrities confined to the wheels of high-performance models. Maurice Gatsonides, the father of modern rallying, specialised in extraordinary performances from ordinary cars.[9] He came second in the 1950 Monte Carlo Rally in a stately Humber Super Snipe, and in 1953 carried off first prize in a Ford Zephyr family saloon.

The global challenge for the British car industry was a mass market now much more competitive with the resurgence of Continental manufacturers. For any Briton, the Volkswagen story is a poignant one. While its post-war manager Heinrich Nordhoff fostered the legend of his role in the company's resurrection, the credit for its salvation belongs to an enlightened British trusteeship between 1945 and 1949.

Long after, the company historian generously recorded: "The success of Volkswagen had strong British roots."[10] As a result Volkswagen entered the 1950s in remarkably good shape and, under the control of the Lower Saxony government, quickly became the country's biggest producer. Its success helped to ensure that state ownership of industry would never be a serious issue in German politics in the way that has bedevilled the British scene.

Other Continental producers were also recovering. Renault had been nationalised after its owners' wartime collaboration with the widely popular Petain regime. With state funding Renault was growing rapidly. Its flagship was a key mass market product, the Dauphine, which eventually sold over two million.

Following the post-war eviction of its Agnelli family owners for their friendship with fascism, Fiat was also thriving under state direction and evolving into the sole major carmaker in Italy. Such concentration by the big Continental carmakers brought them greater focus and economies of scale than the UK producers, notably BMC, and offered a warning for the future.

Nevertheless, British car exports rose from 400,000 units in 1950 to 570,000 in 1960. But they were still heavily dependent on North America and the Commonwealth. Belatedly, BMC came up with the revolutionary new Mini, brainchild of Alex Issigonis,[11] who had designed the Morris Minor.

Born in 1959, the Mini became an immediate favourite[12] and remained in production for four decades. By the end of its run in 2000 it had won three Monte Carlo rallies, sold 5.4m and become the "second most influential car" (after the Model T Ford) of the twentieth century.

Four years after its launch the Mini was followed by the innovative 1100. For a while BMC had a pair of serious contenders for the Continent. Moreover, they at last brought the volumes enjoyed by the leading manufacturers in Germany, France and Italy. They did not, however, generate the profits they deserved. BMC's production techniques were seriously underinvested and antiquated, and the cars were underpriced.

Merger Moves

The industry had not yet run out of growth, with output rising from under 1.4m cars in 1960 to 1.8m in 1968, but there were mounting pressures for consolidation. Standard (now Standard-Triumph) merged with Leyland Motors, the country's leading heavy truck-maker, in 1961. The group then concentrated on a suite of handsome Triumph-badged cars, such as the TR and Spitfire sports cars and the Herald, Vitesse and 2000 saloons, all given styling panache by designer Giovanni Michelotti.

After premature launch of the Hillman Imp, dashing and innovative but handicapped by a paltry development budget, Rootes had to sell a minority stake to Chrysler Corporation in 1964. Chrysler wanted a European presence like those of Ford and General Motors, and gradually built its stake to 100 per cent.

One of the more puzzling developments of the 1960s was the end of independence for both Jaguar and Rover. For the former the usual story is that although it remained profitable its owner, William Lyons, was approaching the end of his career and was persuaded that consolidation was the future. In 1966 he sold Jaguar Cars to BMC to create British Motor Holdings (BMH). Jaguar continued to make original cars, though production bottlenecks after the launch of the popular XJ6 in 1969 highlighted a perennial problem of underinvestment.[13]

Buoyed by the enduring appeal of the Land Rover, Rover Cars had also been very successful. The company had launched two outstanding new models within five years – the P5 3 Litre in 1958 and the acclaimed P6 (Rover 2000) in 1963. Nevertheless Rover accepted a takeover offer from Leyland Motors in 1967. The result was a Leyland group that combined a lean approach to production, ample design talent and a portfolio of distinctive cars and highly regarded trucks and buses. The company was rewarded with the only gains in market share for any of the UK motor manufacturers.[14] The portents looked good.

Yet consolidation was still in the air. Official policy favoured concentration of industry to compete with the American multinationals and the Continental giants. This was not a command economy so government's instrument was the Industrial Reorganisation Corporation (IRC), which was encouraged by modest progress in industrial bearings, paper and aluminium.

Industrial conglomerates were the fashion on both sides of the Atlantic, with economists breezily extolling the virtues of central purchasing and cheaper capital. In this context the IRC's aims were laudable. Unfortunately, the results of consolidation were sometimes unwieldy far-flung empires rather than streamlined powerhouses of industrial progress.

British Leyland Challenge

Having helped save Rootes from bankruptcy, the IRC then nudged Leyland into an alliance with BMH in 1968. The new group was headed by Leyland's chief executive, Donald Stokes, a gifted salesman who cheerfully pocketed under-the-counter commissions on his deals.[15] The combine was christened the British Leyland Motor Corporation (BLMC), or BL for short. With 48 factories and 23 major plants, the new giant was a daunting managerial challenge.[16]

Its products included coach-built limousines, the handsome upmarket models of Jaguar, Rover and Triumph, an assortment of decent family saloons from the former BMC, a wonderful array of sports and performance cars, a worthy collection of vans and light commercial vehicles, high-quality heavier trucks and specialist behemoths from Leyland, buses and coaches, off-road trucks, construction equipment, agricultural tractors, and military equipment. And a dozen overseas subsidiaries making some of these products and some of their own.

What BL did not have was major long-term contenders, other than the Mini and 1100, for the mass market. And the need for standardisation, rationalisation, constructive labour relations, and effective managerial and accounting systems still cried out for attention.

These problems were masked by the Barber boom of the early 1970s, when car sales raced up under the reckless economic pump-priming of the Heath government. Unfortunately, imports surged, jumping from just 158,000 cars in 1970 to over half a million three years later – enough to kick-start an irreversible ratchet. Some of the demand did feed into domestic production, however, and in 1972 British car output reached an all-time high at over 1.9m.

The boom was abruptly stalled by the first oil shock and car demand slumped, with UK output plunging to 1.5m in 1974 and below 1.3m in

1975. Much of the brunt was borne by BL, which recorded a loss for 1975 of £76m – uncomfortable, but by motor industry standards far from terminal.

The main problem was that the group still needed major investment. With internally generated funds drying up the last resort was government. So the Labour government guaranteed the company's loans pending the release of a comprehensive review of its prospects.

The Ryder Report was published in 1975. It recommended that BL continue to compete in both the mass-market and the specialist car sectors to an extent no other European manufacturer was attempting. Among Ryder's more realistic aspects was an acknowledgement of the need for investment on a heroic scale. The big private shareholders were bought out and British Leyland became state-controlled.

Apart from ideological objections to this quasi-nationalisation, public comment ranged from the sceptical to the defeatist. Faint-hearted critics expressed doubts about the ability of British industry to supply the machine tools on the scale required. There were claims that UK workers were genetically unable to work in mass production environments. They were said to be better suited to craft activities of the kind required by the specialist carmakers.

The Front Line

Don Ryder[17] had managerial oversight of BL for a couple of years, then in 1977 he handed over to Michael Edwardes, a tough industry outsider. Edwardes was determined to secure three things: viable new models – particularly the Mini successor – rationalisation of capacity and labour relations peace. In new model development he made valuable progress by signing a far-reaching agreement with Honda in 1979. The first fruit was a version of the Honda Ballade, assembled in the UK and marketed as the Triumph Acclaim. Several good quality new models with a substantial Honda content followed over the next few years.

Edwardes also shed a lot of capacity. He closed the Triumph factory at Speke, on Merseyside, and imposed hefty cutbacks and closures elsewhere. This reinforced a confrontational approach to labour relations which produced mixed results.

Many commentators, notably in the popular press, obsessed about labour relations as the key to the future of the company. Typically, their analysis missed the point. A much fiercer challenge was the abrupt deterioration in external conditions. The 1979 oil shock was magnified by the savagely deflationary policies of the new Conservative government.

At the 1980 Confederation of British Industry (CBI) conference Michael Edwardes had the courage to spotlight the lunacy of a laissez faire approach to oil: "If the Cabinet does not have the wit and imagination to reconcile our industrial needs with the facts of North Sea oil, they would do better to leave the bloody stuff in the ground."[18]

He was on the front line. UK car sales were collapsing. Worse, an overvalued pound crippled exports, which fell from 410,000 units in 1979 to 219,000 in 1984 and a pitiful 200,000 in 1986. Car output dropped from 1.07m in 1979 to fewer than 890,000 in 1982, half the peak levels of ten years earlier and the lowest since the 1950s.

The political climate had, of course, changed profoundly. The government that took office in 1979 continued grudgingly to tolerate BL but was impatient to privatise. And so began the process of downsizing, dismembering and selling off state-owned assets wherever and whenever possible.

Many BL operations were terminated but among the more senseless tragedies was the closure in 1980 of the MG factory at Abingdon, birthplace of the lovely T-series before the war and the popular MGA, MGB and MGC in more recent times.[19]

The privatisation process for BL was set in train by a government that posed as canny and business-oriented but actually followed the same dismal template of struggling companies since time immemorial. Sell the tastier bits first and dump the rest at the first moment you can get away with it. Early departures included Alvis, sold to a private buyer in 1982, and Jaguar, peeled off from BL in a stock market float in 1984. Then followed a succession of disposals in trucks, buses and other sectors. And, finally, the big one, the deal with a British buyer who would take the whole of what was left of BL.

Rover Sell-Off

The government had held preliminary talks with Ford and General Motors, but these foundered on concerns that under one of the American multinationals the identity of the nation's greatest motor group would quickly disappear. This obstacle vanished when in 1988 a "British" solution suddenly presented itself.

British Aerospace (BAe) was showing interest. Seldom slow to a quick fix, the government struck an exclusive deal with BAe.[20] The group would run BL, by now called Rover Group, as a stand-alone subsidiary under the continued management of Graham Day.

Dedicated and austere, but less confrontational than Michael Edwardes, Day knew that the days of widespread labour unrest were history and was nothing if not loyal to the cause. At the meeting to confirm terms for Rover's residual small shareholders, who were to receive £1 per share compared with 2.7p for the government, there was predictable carping from the floor at the (vastly reduced) workforce. Day's admirable response was: "I am content to accept whatever criticism is levelled at me. That comes with the job. But I bitterly, bitterly resent the accusation that our people are slackers or incompetent."[21]

The motive driving the disposal of Rover to British Aerospace was not complicated. For the *Financial Times*, "[t]he story begins with the order from Margaret Thatcher…to Lord Young…to sell its loss-making Rover Group subsidiary at any cost".[22] BAe knew that a tempting deal was certain, simply because the government was so eager to offload its responsibilities on to any new parent politically acceptable to its backbench MPs.

Sweeteners Swing It

BAe got everything it wanted. In return for a business with net assets of £1.1bn and annual sales of £3bn (and by now in modest profit), BAe would pay the government just £150m. Moreover, this payment was deferred for 19 months and BAe received "sweeteners" over which Parliament was misled. BAe also received a capital injection of £547m for Rover and big historic tax losses. Gross state funding of £2.9bn for BL/Rover since 1975 was written off.[23]

The scheme was described as "a triumph…the deal of the decade" for the taxpayer by trade and industry secretary David (by now Lord) Young.[24] Knowing better, the City dubbed the shabby fix as the deal of the century for BAe. The Square Mile had spotted that Rover brought a vast endowment of property with development potential on sites where factories had closed – or were likely to close.

There was immediate scepticism in Parliament on the right (Jock Bruce-Gardyne) and left (Bryan Gould), and official criticism of the terms. Within months there were calls for a Public Accounts Committee (PAC) investigation of claims that BAe would make a £1bn "killing" from land owned by Royal Ordnance and Rover Group.[25]

Commentators had little to say about the all-important issue of the implications for Rover. Yet, it is difficult to think of a more unsuitable foster parent for the carmaker. There were none of the usual synergies conjured up by advisers and bankers when a takeover is in the wind. Yet, the new parent quickly covered most (£128m) of the direct cost of its acquisition through disposals.

A more profound problem was that though BAe had itself been privatised on generous terms in 1983 it was not in robust financial shape. So it was never in a position to provide the major new investment so desperately needed by Rover, and the latter had to get by with annual investment of barely £200m. Indeed, in the view of one observer BAe had "quite ruthlessly used Rover as a vehicle to generate the cash that other divisions are squandering".[26] Shockingly, while under BAe's stewardship Rover had little more to invest than its own depreciation flow.

BMW Rescue

It was stipulated that BAe should not sell Rover within five years. This did not stop BAe from looking for a buyer before the moratorium was over. It soon found one in the shape of BMW, which paid BAe £800m and took over Rover in March 1994. Honda had had a close technical relationship with Rover for 15 years, and each had held a 20 per cent stake in the other's UK operations. So the Japanese responded with justifiable bitterness to the abrupt sale of Rover to BMW and terminated the development agreements.

BMW soon realised that Rover was essentially a rump left by the domino collapse of seven brands and the sale of Jaguar.[27] Rover still had twice as many car platforms (common engineering and design patterns) as BMW, and huge excess capacity.

The new regime brought investment of over £3bn,[28] a streamlined labour force and radical working changes. Successes such as the Rover 75, Car of the Year in 1999,[29] highlighted the previous dearth of resources. Its project director explained, "[s]ince BMW took control we have had access to facilities we could only have dreamed about".[30]

Rover's quest for survival came at a price. UK sourcing of components was driven dramatically downwards. Up until 1999 domestically supplied components made up 90 per cent of Rover, Land Rover, Mini and MG production. This then fell to 70 per cent with the Rover 75 and 50 per cent or lower with Land Rover and Mini.[31]

Rover was still sinking. The huge Longbridge plant was the main problem. In the words of one observer, "[i]t was obsolete fifty years ago [and] its layout is a nightmare".[32] The exchange rate moved disastrously against Rover, its market share slipped again and losses mounted. In 2000 BMW quit. It retained the Mini factory and its engine plant, and got £1.8bn out of Ford for Land Rover. For a token £10 it handed the remainder, now MG Rover Group, to Phoenix Venture Holdings, known as the Phoenix Consortium.

Phoenix Flies and Flops

Phoenix's main asset was Longbridge. This included the Rover assembly lines and the Powertrain plant, which made transmissions and the well-regarded K-series engine. Phoenix was born with a dowry of £500m in cheap loans, £65m in cash and £450m in unsold stocks. Yet, within five years[33] it had crashed with debts of £1.4bn.[34]

It remains difficult to see Phoenix as ever a serious player. The launch of a new car model can cost £1bn. Yet, under Phoenix MG Rover's research and development outlays fell 80 per cent to just £15m, a fraction of what rivals were spending.[35]

By the end of their involvement the "Phoenix Four" who ran the operation, John Towers, Nick Stephenson, John Edwards and Peter Beale, had paid themselves and managing director Kevin Howe a total of £42m. The 6,000 redundant employees received next to nothing. The Phoenix Four's adviser, leading accountancy firm Deloitte, was severely reprimanded and fined £14m for its role by the Financial Reporting Council.

For Longbridge it was the end. The nation's largest factory was sold to a property developer. As so often, the gravedigger was St Modwen. The MG brand went to a Chinese company, Geely, which re-established design, marketing and manufacturing[36] on a modest scale only to back-pedal on production in 2016.[37]

The closure of Longbridge was a sombre moment. It meant that the enterprises which had made all those dashing MGs, Triumphs and Healeys, those sturdy Austin, Morris, Riley and Wolseley family cars, those sober Rovers for the government minister, the civil servant, the doctor, the solicitor and the accountant, those stately but unpretentious limousines with names like Sheerline and Van den Plas, became – outside the arcane world of classic cars – a melancholy memory.

Since the formation of BMC in 1952 the principal British carmaker had undergone no fewer than six major restructurings and radical changes of ownership. Each one left it tragically weaker. In the words of the German executive who had to organise the exit of its last effective owner, by the time it reached the hands of his company Rover was too small to be a contender in the mass market and too weak to be a premium brand.[38]

French Lessons

It is commonly claimed that the disaster which overtook the British-owned part of the motor industry can be laid at the door of both government, for prompting the creation of British Leyland, and management, for repeatedly taking the wrong decisions.

The challenge posed by the giant conglomerate formed by BL has been well documented, but it was not inevitable that its fate was doomed from the start. There have been plenty of precedents for successful motor industry mergers, from General Motors in the 1920s to the rationalisations in Germany (Auto Union/Audi, Volkswagen), France (Ford/Simca/Talbot/Peugeot, Renault/Berliet), Italy (Fiat/Lancia/Alfasud) and Japan (Nissan/Renault).

For British Leyland, two critical things were missing. One was time. The build-up to a major diversified group was much too fast, the trawl much too broad. Companies like Volkswagen have developed a vast portfolio but have had half a century to do so. The other element missing for BL was funding to take the new venture forward. Firms like Renault, Peugeot

Citroen and Fiat have also grown to huge size, but they have all secured immense investment by the state.

"By 1986 it was a company known for the low quality of its products. Losing $3.5bn between 1984 and 1986, inefficient and $9bn in debt, it survived only because of government support. In 1987 it stopped selling cars in the United States, where its name had become synonymous with shoddy products."[39] No, this was not BL/Rover, but Renault. The challenges faced by BL were no worse than those of other carmakers, none more than the state-owned French flagship.

After decades of borderline profitability the 1980s brought gigantic losses to Renault. In just three years the group lost more than FF25bn (£3bn).[40] All of it was underwritten by the state, prompting the comment on the street: "There go my taxes."[41] The losses took the company's debt to FF62bn (over £7bn).[42] As with BL/Rover, the crisis prompted plant closures, dismissal of intransigent employees and big job losses. Labour relations were at least as difficult in *le Petit Kremlin*[43] as they were at Longbridge. The chief executive who initiated the restructuring was assassinated for his pains.

Yet the state went on funding its flagship on a heroic scale.[44] Between 1983 and 1985 alone the group planned to invest FF28.5bn.[45] The largest subventions to Rover, the sweeteners attached to its sale to BAe, sailed through the European Commission because they were so small and Brussels had recently nodded through yet another £2bn for Renault.[46]

With investment sustained at three or four times the levels of its British counterpart, the policy paid off. But, far from then being precipitously dumped into the private sector like Rover, Renault was privatised only gradually and only partially. The government entrusted Renault's leadership to the distinguished public servant Louis Schweitzer,[47] and displayed the kind of pragmatism of which the British were once so proud. A state-guided Renault went from strength to strength, going on to sort out the managerial mess at Nissan and become a global giant.[48]

Other major carmakers have benefitted hugely from official intervention. PeugeotCitroen suffered losses of more than FF8bn (around £1bn) in the early 1980s and its debt reached FF33bn by mid-decade.[49] The company had to make even larger workforce cutbacks than Renault. The cost was borne partly by the early retirement (*préretraite*) system funded by the state. Similar assistance helped Fiat restructure at about the same time. In 1980

Chrysler was supported through a $1.5bn loan guarantee from – of all people – the Reagan government.

Such sensible interventions have continued. In 2009 the French government loaned more than £5bn to Renault and Peugeot to tide them over the recession.[50] The latter came back for another €6bn in 2014 and there was more assistance in 2016/17; 2008–09 saw governments in Italy, Spain and other countries offer special measures to their carmakers, and President Obama extended $82bn to General Motors and Chrysler.[51]

It all makes the total state funding of less than £3bn for BL/Rover – before asset sales – over the entire 1975–88 period look almost modest. Particularly compared with the gigantic bailout of the financial sector a couple of decades later.

Management and Labour

The ghost of British Leyland has often been attacked for poor management. It is far from clear that the charge really stands the test of time. True, like all managements the company's leaders made mistakes. But they were determined, conscientious and energetic. Their critics have always been short on detail, and most tend to fall back on complaints that not enough operations were shut down, factories closed and employees sacked. In the end, terrible retrenchment was forced on BL, with products terminated, subsidiaries sold, factories shuttered and workforces decimated. All to no avail.

Actually, not to no avail. Large chunks of BL went on to new life in other hands. These included Alvis, Hams Hall (BMW engines), Jaguar, Land Rover, Leyland Trucks, Mini and Unipart.

The failure of British Leyland/Rover raises puzzling questions over the fate of British car production in other – supposedly better – hands. Vauxhall has been in retreat for decades. Despite a dominant market position Ford has deserted UK car assembly, and even its position in automotive engines looks very vulnerable.

One area where there were big challenges was labour relations, butt of stale tabloid yarns. In contrast to the US and Germany, where single-union plants and fixed-term agreements were the norm, multi-union operations in Britain were characterised by shorter periods of strife-free working. The irregularity of employment and the lack of mutual loyalty it engendered damaged working relations. The episode in 1956 when BMC laid off one in eight employees without notice sowed deep destructive roots in the folklore of Longbridge.

Is it fair to lay the responsibility for poor labour relations at the door of management? This is one area where it is difficult to see mitigation. Strikes were rare before the war and infrequent for many years after. Only between the late 1960s and the 1980s did days lost to disputes reach high levels, particularly at Longbridge and Dagenham. And since the 1990s the incidence of strikes has been negligible, not just at the newer car plants but at the older survivors in the traditional industrial heartlands of the Midlands and the North West. Yet, all these plants are staffed and managed by employees every bit as British as their 1970s predecessors. What has profoundly changed is management ethos.

While handy to a press looking for easy headlines, the notion that poor labour relations were a uniquely British phenomenon is both insular and confounded by comparison with carmakers elsewhere. French factories saw scenes of ferocious confrontation in the 1970s. Fiat also saw major disturbances at its Turin headquarters during those difficult years. Moreover, other criteria – such as absenteeism, labour turnover and even vacation downtime – put British workforces in a less unfavourable light.

Poor labour relations may have had a subtle effect on the quality and consistency of output at some UK plants. But clear evidence that except in a couple of notable episodes, such as the BL strikes of 1977 and the 1988 Ford strike, car output was systematically and severely curtailed by strike action is absent.

And it cannot escape notice that despite the harmony that reigns in today's car plants the total output of the industry has remained far below the all-time peak of the strike-prone 1970s.

CHAPTER 7

Cars – Back on the Road?

| *The period between clocking on and clocking off was like a living death.*

Ford employee, Dagenham[1]

| *I've loved working at Ford. It's been like a big family.*

Ford employee, Dagenham[2]

Chrysler Crisis

The glory of British carmaking in the decades after the war was its sheer diversity. By the 1970s this had become a handicap. As in motorcycles, there was a rich heritage of makes, marques and models. But, as in motorcycles, this was less relevant to the mass market that had emerged in the 1960s. And the car manufacturers were under some of the same pressures as the motorcycle makers.

While the focus of public and press had been the challenges faced by BMC and its successors, other traditional players were in trouble. The first to run out of road was Chrysler UK, formed from the Rootes Group brands in the 1960s. Even after its rescue by Chrysler the group remained weak. Apart from Linwood, its operations were antiquated, with one observer describing the group's factories as "more like mediaeval blacksmith's shops".

Chrysler was soon in trouble. In April 1976 the company threatened to shut down all its UK operations unless it received major government support. Eric Varley, minister for industry, opposed the demand as blackmail.[3] But Chrysler employed 25,000 in Coventry and Linwood, near Glasgow. The administration came up with a £200m package which kept the company going for another two years.

By 1978 Chrysler Europe was again close to collapse, and sold up. Along with Chrysler in France (Simca) and Spain (Barreiros), the UK operations were dumped into the lap of Peugeot Citroen, for whom the acquisition was a cheap route into one of Europe's biggest markets. Peugeot wasted little time. To the huge distress of workers and townsfolk, Linwood closed in the bleak economic conditions of the early 1980s. Peugeot then focused all its activities on Ryton, near Coventry.

Although Ryton remained profitable, Peugeot sought investment finance from the government in 2002.[4] The operation received modest assistance but was increasingly treated by its owner as marginal and in 2006 Peugeot opted to invest in Slovakia rather than Ryton. Despite the original undertakings safeguarding its future, Ryton closed at the end of the year.[5]

French politicians criticised the British prime minister, Tony Blair, for failing to intervene.[6] The demise of Ryton would have been almost unthinkable in France. Since the ruthless closures of Linwood and Ryton, Peugeot has supplied the UK simply by shipping its products in from factories on the Continent.

The takeover of General Motors' European operations by Peugeot in 2017 points to a similar fate for Vauxhall.

Ford's Dagenham Dream

More puzzling has been the fate of Ford UK. Rootes was always weak, but Ford of Britain was not. In most years Ford returned a decent profit to its owner. Yet in 2002 Ford of Britain built its last car in the UK.

For most of the post-war period Ford had adequate plant, popular products and good marketing. And outstanding management in chief executives like Pat Hennessy,[7] Walter Hayes, Ian Gibson, Sam Toy[8] and Terry Beckett.

Terry Beckett is affectionately remembered for an approachable style and his courageous attack ("a bare knuckle fight") on the Thatcher administration after he had left Ford for the CBI.[9] Describing the Conservative government, all too accurately, as a narrow alliance in which few had ever run a business, he was fiercely critical of its destructive economic policies.[10] He had earned his spurs: to his eternal credit he could claim to be father of the Cortina.

When it opened in 1931 Ford's Dagenham works was the largest car plant in Europe and quickly restored the company to a leading place in Britain. After the war Ford re-established its status with the Consul, Zephyr and Zodiac, drawing on American styling themes. These were followed by more original designs, such as the Anglia, and the brilliant Cortina, of which 4.3 million were made between 1962 and 1982.[11] Then came the Escort, whose prowess as one of the greatest rally cars was beautifully evoked in the 2010 BBC documentary *Ford's Dagenham Dream*.[12] And finally the dashing Capri and another bestseller, the practical little Fiesta.

By the late 1980s such successes had driven Ford to first place in the UK market, with a share of about a third. Under the surface, however, more ominous trends were emerging. They went back to the steps taken by Ford in 1967 to coordinate its European subsidiaries.

One result was that Ford of Britain began to source its products from the Continent – a sister operation at Cologne and a big new plant opened at Valencia, in Spain, in 1976. By the 1970s the Franco regime was fostering new industries for a new Spain. Car manufacturing was one of them. The programme epitomised the managed trade policies that had served so well elsewhere. Key features were investment incentives, protection and ambitious thresholds for local content and exports.

Valencia was launched with a big domestic content (over 90 per cent) and a high export ratio (two-thirds of sales). The project became an important new supplier to the international market. By the time it was in full production a new Conservative government in Britain was displaying scepticism over the merits of domestic industry and indifference to its fate.

Ford's tied imports into the UK jumped from less than 30,000 cars in 1976 to 240,000 in 1979. Despite the collapse in UK car demand in the first half of the 1980s, shipments from overseas remained high. This applied to components as much as finished products.

Historically, Ford in the UK had had a high level of local sourcing for components, and until the 1980s had been a net supplier of parts to other vehicle-makers. The position was enhanced by a new engine factory at Bridgend in South Wales at the end of the 1970s. Built with government assistance of more than £100m,[13] Bridgend was to ship a million "leanburn" petrol engines a year to Ford, Volvo, Jaguar and elsewhere. In recent years, however, there have been huge cutbacks and job losses at Bridgend and the prospects have darkened with the impact of Brexit.[14] Bridgend was Ford's last significant greenfield initiative in the UK.

As the turn of the century approached, Ford's UK manufacturing presence was sinking. In 2001 the company declared a loss of £892 million. Much of this was write-offs rather than operating losses. And part was attributable to activities outside the traditional Ford stable. The company had acquired several prestige brands during the preceding decade and failed to make any money out of them.

Brutally, this was taken as a cue to end car production at Dagenham in 2002.[15] All that Dagenham was to keep was diesel engine manufacture. Local reaction ranged from gloomy puzzlement to fatalistic acceptance.[16] Working life at Dagenham could be both hard and yet personally rewarding. But beneath the personal responses was a deeper despair. The anguish, born of crushing economic decline as a workforce that had once numbered 40,000 shrank to a couple of thousand, was movingly evoked by writer Ian Jack.[17]

The reaction of the Labour government to the end of car assembly at Dagenham was meek acceptance. Interestingly, despite the earlier criticism of its productivity Halewood did not close. Production of Ford cars had ended there in 2000, but transmission manufacturing continued. And the car plant was successfully converted to making Jaguars.

Ford still has an industrial presence in the UK, with petrol engines at Bridgend and diesels at Dagenham. And it has a research and development facility in Essex. But, shockingly, its status as a centrepiece of the British car industry has almost vanished.

Vauxhall Survival

Founded in the 1860s, Vauxhall Motors was acquired by General Motors in 1925 and its Luton factory became the first volume car plant in Britain.

During the Second World War Vauxhall and its Bedford subsidiary produced 5,600 Churchill tanks and a huge number of trucks. This cemented a long association with the armed forces.

Some years after the war Vauxhall made a stronger pitch to the UK market. The Luton cars followed Ford in adding American styling, with fins, wrap-around windows and wide radiator grills offering a modern alternative to the dowdier products of other manufacturers. The 1960s brought more capacity when a new factory opened at Ellesmere Port on Merseyside.

By the 1970s Vauxhall was shifting towards blander styles, and this left it without a well-defined positioning in the UK market. It was not seen as a manufacturer of luxury cars, its products had no sporty connotations and it had a lacklustre quality image.

Following the example of Ford, General Motors began coordinating its European operations. In 1979 commercial vehicles were centred on the UK, while Opel at Russelsheim in Germany became the headquarters for cars.

Vauxhall felt free to switch its product sourcing to Germany. This enhanced its brand in the UK, but not the viability of its manufacturing. Tied imports into the UK shot up from less than 50,000 in 1979 to over 100,000 three years later, and by mid-decade they were 170,000 a year. Meanwhile, exports, mainly to the Commonwealth, were abandoned.

Vauxhall's dependence on imports left its UK factories underutilised. Despite Luton's good record for productivity, efficiency and quality this was where the axe fell. In March 2002, nearly a century after the first car rolled off its lines, the plant closed. This was only a few weeks after the end of carmaking at Dagenham.[18] Unfortunately, Vauxhall was not finished with its UK cutbacks. The year 1994 saw the closure of its engine plant, a joint venture with Fiat at Ellesmere Port.[19]

The 2008 financial crisis brought the threat of closure to Ellesmere Port. Instead, however, General Motors closed Bochum, in Germany.[20] European output of the popular Astra was transferred to Ellesmere Port, and the company invested £125m in the plant. The decision was a tribute to the efforts of industry secretary Vince Cable, the Unite union and local Vauxhall management.[21]

The downside of Ellesmere Port's survival was that its output would have a UK content of just 25 per cent. This compared with 95 per cent for a typical Vauxhall in the 1970s. Former Vauxhall chairman Nick Reilly has pointed out that for long-term viability the British car plants need to have nearby clusters of suppliers rather than sourcing components from abroad.[22]

General Motors struggled to regain prosperity after the recession and in March 2017 announced the sale of its European operations.[23] The buyer was Peugeot.[24] Peugeot has declared that Vauxhall could have a future as a brand "warm to the hearts of UK consumers".[25] Yet sales fell to 164,000 in 2017, half the level of ten years before.

The last time Peugeot bought a British carmaker it took over the Rootes plants in the Midlands and Scotland. All were eventually closed and their markets given to imported Peugeot and Citroen vehicles.

Even without Brexit the prospects for Vauxhall could only be described as very uncertain.

Jaguar Sensation

One of stars of the British motor industry has long been Jaguar Cars. It raced into the headlines with its first modern production model, the XK120, in 1948 and its successors the XK140 and XK150 remained uniquely popular throughout the 1950s. They were bought by comfortably off young men, film stars and celebrity authors. The 18-year-old Françoise Sagan spent the royalties from her 1954 bestseller *Bonjour Tristesse* on an XK140.[26] (And, such was the appeal of those lovely English sports cars, she followed it with an Aston Martin and a Lotus.) The replacement for the XKs, the E-Type, earned from Enzo Ferrari the accolade of the most beautiful car ever made.

All these cars used the XK engine, the legacy of chief engineer Bill Heynes, Jaguar's resident genius from 1935 till 1969. The unique styling and design for the Jaguar roadsters were the work of proprietor William Lyons, one of that noble but vanished breed of English craftsmen who could not even draw.

Lyons was nothing if not frugal. Once when visiting the West End Jaguar showroom he was asked to replace the threadbare carpet surrounding the display area. Lyons baulked at the cost, and the next time he entered the showroom he was shocked to see what looked like a new carpet. On demanding an explanation, he was relieved to hear that the old one had simply been turned round so as to show the unworn edge.

After surrendering its independence in 1966, Jaguar spent nearly two decades under the wing of BMC/BMH/BL, until it was floated off at the instigation of the Thatcher administration in 1984. The sale realised £294m, which was retained by BL.[27] Returned to the private sector, Jaguar faced the challenges of a relatively small and specialised carmaker. But initially, hefty price rises, severe cost-cutting and a buoyant US market gave the company a spell of prosperity.

It was also helped by a new top-of-the-range model, a late offspring of the BL years. The BL board had managed to find £100m to seed development of a new flagship for Jaguar, together with an engine to replace the legendary XK. The result was the XJ40, launched to acclaim for its style and engineering in 1986.

Towards the end of the decade problems were surfacing. Production and sales had lifted from under 40,000 in 1985 to over 50,000 three years later. But there was an urgent need for investment. Fortunately, Jaguar found a saviour with deep pockets – Ford.

Unsuccessful in attempts to develop its own upmarket brands, the Ford Motor Company of the US had taken the acquisition route. It bought a majority stake in Aston Martin in 1988 and added Land Rover and Volvo to its portfolio. Meanwhile, the Thatcher government, eager to shrug off any vestige of stewardship, lifted a veto on foreign ownership of Jaguar and in 1989 Ford bought the company for £1.6bn.[28]

Ford had serious ambitions for Jaguar.[29] The aim was to build the company into a serious player in the executive cars. The company put in a request for government development aid of £100m.[30] There were objections from other carmakers but strong support from Michael Heseltine, and some state encouragement trickled through.

The first task was to modernise the main works at Browns Lane, Coventry. This epitomised so many British engineering plants – exemplary craftsmen working with antiquated machinery in premises that were "dark, dirty and behind the times".[31] As frugal with equipment as he was with showroom carpets, Sir William Lyons had run his lines on installations bought from the Standard Motor Company back in 1953.[32]

The first generation of new models did not, however, make the required impact. Technically flawless, the S-Type, launched in 1999, lacked traditional flair. The X-Type, unveiled in 2001, used Ford components and compromised on exclusivity.[33] And, although completely re-engineered, the top-of-the-range XJ models were criticised for lacklustre styling.

Nevertheless, annual output rose from 50,000 cars in the year before the takeover to 130,000 at their 2003 peak. Much of the increase was attributable to the X-Type, made at Ford's Halewood factory.

By the mid-2000s, however, demand for the X-Type was flagging and Jaguar sales were falling. When the US parent faced global losses of $15bn in 2006–07 it began selling assets, among them Jaguar. It also divested itself of Land Rover, which it had bought from BMW in 2000.

Ford never made money from Jaguar and at one appalling moment considered closing it down. But it had been a generous patron. It revitalised Jaguar's research effort, invested heavily and initiated a major programme of model development. By the time it passed Jaguar and Land Rover on to a new owner in 2008, its investment in the two operations had reportedly been $10bn.[34] This was at last bearing fruit, and a succession of superb new models has rolled out over the last few years.

The beneficiary was Tata Motors,[35] which bought Jaguar and Land Rover as a single package for $2.3bn (£1.15bn).[36] Tata was now Britain's biggest manufacturing employer, with a workforce of 47,000.[37]

At first the purchase looked spectacularly ill-timed. Within months vehicle demand ran into the credit crunch, Jaguar Land Rover (JLR) sales crashed and in its first year Tata lost £300m. JLR made cutbacks and approached Whitehall and Brussels for assistance. The aid was not forthcoming, but Tata's JLR deal was soon looking like the turnaround of the century. Costs had been cut, the market had revived and by 2012 Tata had made enough profit to recoup its entire outlay.[38]

Despite grumbles about the poor work ethic of British managers[39] (but not the shopfloor), the company geared up for major expansion and a new engine plant.

Land Rover Successes

It has to be said that Land Rover was the main element in the financial success of JLR. Inventor of both the four-wheel-drive off-roader and the luxury four-by-four, Land Rover's viability has never been in doubt. When its original parent Rover Cars went down with the wreck of British Leyland, Land Rover continued to survive and, mostly, to thrive.

True, it ran into a lean phase in the 1990s, but Ford's massive investment and the move to Halewood for the new Evoque model proved rewarding. JLR sales were particularly strong in China and other new markets.[40] There were even gains at home. This defies a fickle public which, improbably, gives imports from Mercedes-Benz, BMW and Audi their third biggest Western world markets.

There has been substantial outsourcing of components by JLR, but its products still have the highest domestic content of all British carmakers. About half its parts come from the UK, many of them from the West Midlands, and the proportion has risen with the new £500m engine plant in Wolverhampton.[41]

Within six years of the recession JLR doubled the output of Jaguars and quadrupled the production of Land Rovers and Range Rovers, becoming Britain's biggest carmaker.[42] Since its design, engineering and management are all based in the UK, JLR is the most "British" of the volume carmakers.

More recently, however, the company has faced severe setbacks due to slower sales in China and diesel doubts at home. Nevertheless, with its strong British identity it may well be best equipped to withstand the strains of Brexit. The worry is that after Brexit the company will continue to expand production overseas rather than at home.

Mini Majors

Another post-BL success story is that of Mini, retained by BMW when it bailed out of Rover in 2000. While the brand has been kept on the road the cars have been radically restyled. BMW has made major investment in the Cowley factory and the engine plant at Hams Hall near Birmingham. Mini output in the UK has run at around 200,000 a year. However, the management has expressed concern over the implications of Brexit, and is hedging its bets by developing an alternative base for Mini production in the Netherlands.

Roller Coaster

First offered to the public in 1904, Rolls-Royce cars soon established an unrivalled name.[43] For nearly 70 years the carmaker was an important subsidiary of the Rolls-Royce group, and based for much of the time in Crewe. Two years after the parent had to be nationalised to save it from collapse, the car business was floated on the Stock Exchange as a separate entity.

The year 1980 saw a successful takeover bid for Rolls-Royce Motors by the Vickers engineering group. Rolls remained in the hands of Vickers for nearly two decades, during which it added the prestigious Cosworth Engineering operation to its automotive division. Despite the link with Cosworth, which specialised in engine technology, the period of Vickers ownership was marked by significant erosion of the UK content of Rolls-Royce cars.

The shift was accelerated by a financial crisis in the early 1990s. Mismanagement of the US and British economies had thrown both sides of the Atlantic into severe recession. Sales of Rolls-Royces and Bentleys withered. The carmaker plunged into a loss of over £100m, a shock in a business which had generated profits for two decades and averaged a 30–35 per cent return on capital.[44] A faint-hearted board was soon talking about "looking at the ways to obtain the best value for shareholders, including an outright sale".[45]

There was no firesale. But there was a pressing need for successors to the Silver Spirit and Silver Spur models. Lacking the courage to develop the updates on its own, Vickers went cap in hand to BMW. In 1994 the German company agreed to supply replacements for the existing Rolls-Royce engines.[46] When the RR Silver Seraph and Bentley Arnage were launched four years later, they were powered by BMW V12 and V8 engines.

Meanwhile, Rolls-Royce was on a much sounder footing. Belated modernisation of Crewe, coupled with wide-ranging contributions from the unions, had achieved a big jump in productivity. Decent profitability had been restored.

So why were there still strong come-on signals to would-be buyers? The answer was that Rolls-Royce was eminently saleable. And the group was now headed by a salesman. Colin Chandler,[47] knighted by Margaret Thatcher for clinching the Al Yamamah arms deal with Saudi Arabia, had become chairman of Vickers in 1997. He was only too delighted to receive an offer from BMW the following year.

Ever since the link-up in 1994 an approach had obviously been possible. BMW now offered £340m for Rolls-Royce Motors. At this point

Volkswagen (VW) made an offer of £430m. VW also proposed £100m for the excellent operation that was Cosworth. The chilling response from BMW was that a sale to VW would end all cooperation with Rolls-Royce and, by implication, terminate its car production.

Competition from British interests soon faded. Mayflower, a Midlands-based components maker already closely involved with the car industry, was bullied out of the running by BMW.[48] A couple of other groups, lighter on their industrial connections than their patriotism, were ignored in favour of VW. And Britain's most famous brand slid, pathetically easily, into foreign hands.

Drolly, Rolls-Royce plc (the aero engine group) had granted its approval only to the BMW option. So VW found it had not secured the vital name. Thanks to a shabby £40m side deal, BMW got the marque and the logo (though not the mascot and radiator grille). VW ended up with the factory and the brand for Bentley cars, which had been hand-made alongside Rolls-Royces at the Crewe works.

Chided for being quite so eager to cede Rolls-Royce to a foreign rival, Chandler boasted: "We have saved the car marque [and] restored it to health".[49] More tellingly, he resorted to the usual excuse of short-term shareholder value, or something very like it: "We have been able to pay our investors an 80p special dividend, the equivalent of 11 years of dividend payments all at once. ...We got a very good price...as good as best City estimates."[50]

Once again, City-driven short-termism had triumphed.

The last Rolls-Royce came out of Crewe in 2002. The factory became the home of Bentley Cars and Rolls-Royce moved to Goodwood in Sussex. Since then both brands have followed a parallel course, importing their technology and most of their components.

The decay of local content epitomises so much of what has happened to the UK car industry. Prior to the Second World War it would have been difficult to find any foreign-made components in a Rolls-Royce. By the 1960s the use of Chrysler's superb TorqueFlite automatic transmission and imported technology in brakes and suspension would have brought UK content down to 75 per cent. But even at the start of the 1990s major items such as body panels, sub-frames, engine blocks, cylinder heads, pistons, crankshafts, propshafts, differentials, wiring, instrumentation, glass, wheels and tyres were all made in this country, and UK content would still approach 70 per cent.[51]

Today, according to one coy owner contacted by the author, the only identifiably British-made parts in the latest Rolls-Royce saloons are the leather hide and the wood trim.

Sales rose fairly steadily in the 2000s. Even so they took a long time to match the 3,347 cars sold back in 1978,[52] the heyday of the Callaghan government, whose policies were supposed to have been so punishing to the classes which could afford the world's best car. In recent years they have been averaging a little over 4,000 a year.

Meanwhile, VW was able to report sales of 11,023 Bentleys in 2016. The figures were boosted by the arrival of the Bentayga, an SUV capable of 300km an hour. Dismayingly, the Bentayga was to have been built in Slovakia. But ministers in the coalition – notably Vince Cable – took the trouble to make representations and the vehicle is being assembled in Crewe.

Bouncing Czech

The Germans have played a valuable part, and the Indians have had a very productive role. But it was mainly thanks to the Japanese that the story of car mass production in Britain was not remorselessly downhill. Since the mid-1980s the big three Japanese carmakers, Nissan, Toyota and Honda, have invested £10bn in the UK to make cars for the mainstream market. For over a decade they have accounted for around half of all British car production, and until Brexit threatened their stature continued to grow.

The arrival of Japanese cars predates these manufacturing operations by over a decade. A key role was played by Octav Botnar, a secretive émigré who cornered the distribution of Nissan products when he set up Datsun UK in 1971.[53] From fewer than 7,000 in its first year, Datsun sales rose rapidly as the Sunny became a favourite with mini-cab drivers and impecunious family motorists. Within a few years annual sales were in six figures.[54]

Datsun's appeal was partly its miserly pricing, underpinned by colossal tax evasion on the part of Botnar. Eventually accused of defrauding the Inland Revenue of £97m, Botnar fled to Switerland.[55] This does not seem to have damaged his standing with the Conservative Party, to which he was a large secret donor.[56] Indeed Lord McAlpine, Tory treasurer, described him as an "incredibly generous" philanthropist, who had saved the country a great deal of money by fleeing in order to avoid prosecution.[57] The logic of his comment was obscure, but the sentiment was all too clear.

Whether Botnar ever regretted damaging the viability of the UK car industry while failing to pay his dues to the country which had given him shelter is not recorded.

Nissan Novelty

Within three years of taking office in 1979 the Thatcher administration was implored by the Association of British Chambers of Commerce (ABCC) to stem the desperate slide in car production.[58] The ABCC urged import restraint on the Japanese and encouragement to set up factories in the UK.

With the collapse in manufacturing looking increasingly catastrophic, the government at last adopted a more positive attitude towards investment by the Japanese. Nissan, still looking for an EEC production base, chose a greenfield site near Sunderland in return for incentives of at least £100m. The company insisted on single-union employee representation, and was set an absurdly low hurdle for domestic content. Its factory opened in September 1986.

Prime Minister Margaret Thatcher attended the proceedings. Her presence was claimed by Octav Botnar to have been secured through his furtive collusion with the Conservative Party.

Sunderland went from strength to strength, becoming the world's most productive car plant outside Japan.[59] Its success ensured that it would remain unscathed when, after forming an alliance with Renault in the late 1990s, Nissan had to trim corporate debts of $22bn. By 2013 Nissan had invested £3.3bn in Sunderland, taking capacity to 550,000 cars a year. It has been the UK's largest car factory for over a decade.[60]

Two developments have, however, raised new concerns. In 2015 the French government lifted its stake in Renault to almost 20 per cent and its voting rights to 30 per cent.[61] Critics feared that through Renault's 43.4 per cent holding in Nissan the French government might one day use its influence to steer investment and production away from Sunderland to France.[62]

The more alarming threat to Nissan UK is Brexit. The loss of traditional trade relations with the EU, to which Sunderland has been shipping most of its output, could cause major problems.[63] One desperate resort, if free trade with the Continent were ruled out by a post-Brexit deal, would be for Sunderland to concentrate on the UK market. In other words, go for import substitution.

Toyota Threat

Six years after Nissan's start-up, Toyota opened an assembly plant at Burnaston in Derbyshire and an engine plant in Deeside, North Wales. Toyota "believes in localising its vehicles to meet the specific needs of Europe's varied customers and this means that the company's operations in Europe are generally located within the communities they serve".[64]

The company only recouped start-up costs after 17 years[65] – an impressive tribute to the long investment perspectives of corporate Japan. And it was not until 2005, after unfavourable productivity comparisons with the company's French factory,[66] that Toyota's UK operations matched Japanese efficiencies. By 2012 the company had invested over £2.1bn at Burnaston and Deeside, and in recent years output has been around 180,000 cars a year.

Despite the EU referendum Toyota has announced an investment of £240m to upgrade Burnaston, with the help of £21.3m from the government.[67] However, the company has warned that tariff-free access to and from the Continent is vital to the success of an operation which imports 60 per cent of its components and exports most of its output. Brexit poses a huge challenge.[68]

Honda Hopes

Honda has been involved in UK cars since it began collaboration with British Leyland in 1979. After the sale of Rover to BMW Honda went ahead alone with local production. An engine plant was opened at Swindon in 1989 and car assembly started in 1994. In all the company has invested over £2bn at the site and taken capacity up to 250,000 cars a year.

This potential has, however, never been fully realised. Output in 2018 was only 160,000 vehicles, of which 90 per cent were exported to the rest of

Europe. Nevertheless, as at Toyota UK profitability is thin. In February 2019 the company abruptly announced the closure of its Swindon operations in 2022, and the loss of 3,550 jobs. Brexit was not directly cited as a reason for closure, but since most of the factory's output goes to the EU it cannot have been helpful to the cause of Honda UK. The sensible suggestion that BMW might take over the factory to make its own brand cars have not, so far, been followed up.

A Hollow Recovery

Forty years have brought a complete transformation of British carmaking. There remains a handful of specialist producers, still showing characteristic flair and originality. But in mass production output is dominated by producers who were little more than fledglings a generation ago. After such profound changes, how does the balance sheet look today?

Clearly, a 2001 prediction by consultants AT Kearney that mass car assembly had no future in Britain has proved hopelessly wrong.[69] But the reality is a long way from the wildly misleading claims of the tabloids.[70]

At 1.52m, 2018 output was far below the all-time peak of nearly two million in the early 1970s, and it was close to the average for the 1990s and the 2000s. But it had made a decent recovery from the recessionary low of 2009, let alone the dark days of the 1980s when it slumped to less than 900,000. The UK now clings to fifth position as a European car manufacturer and fourteenth place for the world as a whole.

There are, however, serious distortions. The trade pattern for the British car industry is now very skewed. Eighty per cent of output goes to export, while over 80 per cent of demand is met by imports. The result is a consistent deficit in overseas trade in motor vehicles.

True, the shortfall – £4.6bn in 2017 – has narrowed in recent years.[71] But any improvement has been swamped by the slide in parts and accessories, where the deficit has rocketed from £2.4bn in 1998 to £8.7bn.[72] Combined, the trade deficit in finished vehicles and components has been over £13bn a year.

The KPMG consultancy has estimated that only 36 per cent of the content of British cars comes from domestic sources, compared with at least 60 per cent in Germany. The British figure has recently lifted a little, but it is not clear that this is a sustained trend since there has been further retreat in component manufacturing.[73] Employment in the sector fell 25 per cent in 2009–10.[74]

Because their initial domestic sourcing was set so low, the Japanese carmakers all import a high proportion of components for their UK factories. Vauxhall is in the same position. And there have been similar if less pronounced trends for Land Rover, Jaguar and other UK-based producers. Experts like Professor Karel Williams have long urged that the target for domestic sourcing should be set at much higher levels.[75] When content is allowed for, total value added by the UK car industry is barely two-thirds of the levels achieved in the 1970s.[76] Worse, the fragmented nature of today's industry makes it much harder for a large auto component supply sector to develop.[77]

Even in traditional areas of strength, such as engines, trends have faltered. The output of 2.5m engines in 2016 compares with more than 3.1m in 2007–08.[78] Moreover, there are obvious question marks over the future. How will Ford's Bridgend plant survive the loss of business from JLR[79] and the recent output cutbacks?[80] Will Ford Dagenham survive the slump in demand for diesels? Would the two remaining Japanese plants and Mini survive the uncertainties and costs imposed by Brexit?

Post-Mortems

The profound upheaval in the structure of the British automotive industry in the closing decades of the twentieth century prompted extensive comment at the time. Much of it is neatly summarised in Roy Church's *The Rise and Decline of the British Motor Industry*, published in 1994.[81] Are the explanations any different, or any clearer, now?

The biggest permanent change in the commercial environment came with the loss of import protection and the end of imperial preference. For nearly half a century the industry was shielded by the 33⅓ per cent McKenna Duties imposed on non-empire imports in 1915. The

GATT Kennedy Round cut the tariff to 25 per cent in 1963. It was then progressively reduced, falling to 17 per cent in 1969, 11 per cent in 1972 and 8.3 per cent on British accession to the EEC the following year. It finally disappeared in 1977, when the British market became fully open to all EEC manufacturers.

The British carmakers then faced a new challenge in imports from Japan. The response was the 1977 Voluntary Export Restraint (VER) agreement between the Society of Motor Manufacturers and Traders (SMMT) and its Japanese counterpart. Criticised by commentators, particularly on the right, VERs were far from uncommon in the traditional car manufacturing countries.[82] At 11 per cent of the market the UK agreement was similar to that in the US but looser than elsewhere. Initially, imports into France were limited to 3 per cent of the market[83] and in Italy the ceiling was 2,000 cars a year.

The Japanese were far from uncomfortable with the managed trade that had served them so well. While Japanese imports, particularly through Datsun UK, undoubtedly added to the pressure on Britain's domestic manufacturers, without the VER their position would have been far worse. The quid pro quo of the VER was that the Japanese car companies start manufacturing in Britain and build EEC market share from within. By the time the British VER ended in 1999 the transplants had all become well established.

Poor Productivity, Inadequate Investment

Until the Japanese operations were in full production, productivity at British car plants compared poorly with their counterparts elsewhere. It had not always been so. In the 1950s UK carmakers had higher levels of output per employee than German companies. By the mid-1960s, however, the position had been reversed and the gap widened further in the 1970s and 1980s. The productivity gap between British Leyland and Ford also widened.

Interestingly, European factories were generally far less productive than their counterparts in the US. The US manufacturers have generally served markets abroad from overseas subsidiaries, and limited their direct export efforts. Given their excellent productivity, however, it remains puzzling that the American carmakers were to find it so challenging to compete with imports, whether from Europe or Japan.

Productivity differences can reflect many things, such as scale, standardisation, the pattern of inputs and outputs of each particular factory, the character of the labour force, industrial relations, and, above all, the quality and age of the equipment. The latter was a particular critical problem for the British-owned carmakers. One survey showed that by the early 1970s British Leyland had the lowest level of fixed assets per employee in Europe.

This reflected grossly inadequate levels of capital spending. Between the mid-1960s and the mid-1970s, investment at BMC/BL was 30 per cent lower than at Renault and 60 per cent below that of Volkswagen. Far from improving when Rover came under the wing of British Aerospace, its investment shortage became a famine and its long-term demise more certain. When the company launched its award-winning Rover 75, its success reflected the contribution of BMW's lavish model development facilities.

Though less meagre than in the past, investment by the car industry has remained shabby by international standards. For the period 2000–16 total net investment for the sector was £29.5bn. This was an average of less than £2bn per year, or 3.4 per cent of turnover.[84] And since 2017 the figure has plunged alarmingly in response to the Brexit threats.

A key indicator of industrial health is spending on research and development. Here the historical record was pathetically weak. British Leyland spent far less than its counterparts in the US, Germany, France and Japan. At the same time Britain's US-owned operations, particularly Ford and Vauxhall, saw their research and development effort increasingly siphoned off to their associates on the Continent.

Total motor industry research and development spending of £2–3bn in recent years looks distinctly ungenerous in a sector where ceaseless innovation and product development are the lifeblood of progress.

Government Policies

Government policies towards industry have often been cited as burdensome to British carmakers. The Conservative governments of 1951–64 encouraged the location of new factories in areas with no history of vehicle manufacture, and this was said to have handicapped the industry.

Transport and management costs were claimed to be higher and labour productivity lower. It was said that former shipyard hands were unsuited to the production line at Linwood, that unemployed engineering workers made an uncomfortable transition to Bathgate, and that Merseysiders were constitutionally unfit for work at the Triumph factory opened at Speke, near Liverpool, in 1959.

Linwood's existence was problematic right from the outset, since it was making the hopelessly under-researched Hillman Imp. Bathgate closed during the decimation of British Leyland, itself damaged by crippling economic recession, in the mid-1980s. And Speke closed in 1978 after the introduction of a flawed product (the Triumph TR7), low productivity and bad labour relations undermined its viability. Those truculent Merseysiders were said to have struck themselves out of a job.[85]

This slander might have had a hint of credibility but for the success of Halewood, in the next parish to Speke, and Ellesmere Port, just across the river. Opened by Ford in 1963 to make the Anglia, Ford chose Halewood for the Jaguar X-Type because of its good labour relations and productivity. And when Vauxhall made its big retreat it closed Luton rather than Ellesmere Port.

Other initiatives away from the traditional carmaking centres have been just as constructive. Ford's Bridgend plant has made hundreds of thousands of engines each year for export. And thanks to investment incentives all the Japanese transplants have been located outside traditional carmaking centres.

Turning the Import Tide

Despite a downturn in recent years, British car demand has been at a reasonably high level by historical standards. Yet, more than 80 per cent of this market is supplied from overseas, giving the UK the highest import ratio of any major car producing country. Does this matter?

Not for *The Economist*: "Britain now exports most of the fancy cars it makes while importing most of the basic ones it drives."[86] Typically, this is only half the story. In addition to huge volumes of small cars Britain also imports an awful lot of fancy cars. All four of the upper tier registrations are headed by imports – BMW or Mercedes-Benz – with Volkswagen and Audi not far behind.[87] The picture is even more dispiriting when content is considered.

BMW at least assembles the Mini in this country and sources 40 per cent of the components here. For Audi, Mercedes-Benz and Volkswagen, however, UK content is abysmally low. Between them Germany's carmakers have been shipping 700–800,000 cars a year to Britain,[88] buying little in return. The same is true of the French and Italian car companies who enjoy such good business here.

Can anything be done to redress the imbalance? A meaningful start could be made in parts and components. Locally sourced content of UK-assembled cars can certainly be increased. A 2012 study identified £3bn worth of annual parts purchases where manufacture could be expanded in Britain. It should be explained to carmakers who benefit from rewarding business in Europe's second biggest car market that one of their corporate goals must be a meaningful rise in local content.

Finished vehicles are more of a challenge. But there has to be scope for more UK assembly by foreign manufacturers. Obvious candidates would be the Koreans. Their rise to global stature is an astonishing story. Korea had no history of vehicle manufacture, yet in 1974 the Hyundai group went into the motor business. Hyundai hired George Turnbull, distinguished former head of Austin Morris at British Leyland.[89] Using the Morris Marina as the template, they launched the company's first car, the Pony, just two years later. Today Hyundai is a global giant.

As for the big Continental producers, a more radical approach is long overdue. Given an appropriate post-Brexit trade deal for components, why not local assembly of finished German and French cars? The car industry represents a rare potential bonus for a post-Brexit UK, but it will need a purposeful interventionist government. A BMW purchase of the Honda plant would be a relatively easy start.

The consumer side needs to be tackled. More than half the car market comprises business purchases. The resulting expenditure is eligible for tax relief. Yes, the taxpayer is subsidising the import of cars from the competitors of hard-pressed British-based carmakers. This is mad. It is surely well within the competence of policy makers, post-Brexit, to structure the system so that it is less unfavourable to the home side.

147

The private car market is a tougher proposition. English nationalism is a light sleeper, yet Buy British seems to be a difficult flame to light. Even the founder of the Brexit party has displayed the shabby reality of his patriotism by driving a Volvo.

If this is too challenging another segment of the market can be more easily addressed. This is the public sector. A recent survey recorded that three-quarters of vehicles procured by police authorities were made overseas.[90] And the Highways Agency, the Environment Agency, the Ambulance Service, the Fire Service and local councils also buy improbable numbers of imported vehicles.

The contrast with Germany, France, Spain and Italy is striking.[91] When the Italian authorities announced a few years ago that the top brass of the armed forces would be issued with 19 locally made cars "because they are Italian",[92] nobody in Brussels batted an eyelid. It was the fact that they were Maseratis that caused a stir.

One place where the message went home was Downing Street. Shortly after pledging to "get Britain working" and before Chancellor Osborne's "March of the Makers", the coalition prime minister was seen getting into a Lexus saloon car. Members of the public were quick to point out that not a single Lexus is made in this country.[93]

Ever since, ministers have been more careful to use Range Rovers and Jaguars, which are made in England.

CHAPTER 8

Truck Stop

Scammell is a name people live for. We are like a big family. The management takes us fully into their confidence.

Union convenor, Scammell, 1988

When I started as an apprentice in 1954 there were 23 British truck manufacturers; now there are none.

Dai Davies, Director, ERF, 2009

Slow Road

It was evening on the motorway some years ago. The light was still good but the traffic was crawling. Before long it was clear why everyone had slowed. There was a military convoy on the road. Eventually I overtook. Being army, the vehicles were strictly within speed limits and immaculate. As I passed I noted the makes and models. There were a few Land Rovers, a handful of smallish Leylands, a fleet of sturdy Bedfords, some hefty Seddon Atkinsons, a couple of giant Scammells.

Apart from Land Rover, these names have all vanished from our highways. The only place you can be sure to find venerable British makes is fairgrounds and circuses. Resting behind the carousels and the marquees you may see handsome old workhorses with badges like AEC, Albion, Atkinson, ERF, Foden, Leyland, Scammell, Seddon and, on a good day, Dennis, Guy and Thornycroft. All giving faithful service many years after they were built.[1]

British carmaking may have revived but the same cannot be said of commercial vehicles, where the picture is desolate. Today's production of vans, trucks and buses is a fraction of what it once was. Buses are a particularly sorry story, with output just 5 per cent of what it was at peak and the last British manufacturer going out of business in 2019. Heavy commercial vehicles (HCVs), where production is down 90 per cent, are little better. And even in light commercial vehicles – mainly vans – output is barely a third of its all-time high.

Britain's lorry industry, once the world's second largest, dates back to the late nineteenth century. At that time steam was dominant, and it did not finally go out of fashion until the 1920s. The industry then motored confidently ahead, and except in the Depression years of the early 1930s production rose steadily. Though it fell back during the Second World War, some manufacturers were allowed to maintain operations.

After a hesitant post-war restart, HCV output rose strongly in the 1950s. The economy was expanding steadily, freight was migrating from rail to road and export demand was strong. Lorry production raced ahead, accelerating from less than 7,000 in 1950 to almost 100,000 at the end of the decade.[1]

At this point the industry had developed some peculiarly British features. The big integrated car companies all offered a range of commercial vehicles. But alongside them were a couple of dozen specialists, buying in their major components – engines from manufacturers like Cummins, Gardner, Perkins and Rolls-Royce – and tailoring their products to customer requirement.

Most of these concentrated on heavy trucks, some were active in buses and coaches, and others in utility or military vehicles. Articulated models eventually became more popular at the heavy end of the market and replaced rigid flatbed styles. For these the specialist builders often supplied a "tractor", with the customer choosing between the trailers offered by York Trailer, Crane Fruehauf and others.

The 1960s brought tremendous growth, with HCV output jumping from 127,000 in 1960 to almost 200,000 at the end of the decade. There were still 20 British truck-makers of varying size, a third of the total for the whole of Europe.[2] This was a measure of just how diverse the UK industry was relative to its counterparts on the Continent.

The early 1970s saw lorry production reach a peak, and the rest of the decade brought a significant decline. Oil shocks and a volatile economy were partly to blame. But so was the loss of protection at home and preferential markets overseas, following British accession to the European Economic Community. Another factor was the stubborn refusal by the UK authorities to raise legal weight and speed limits for commercial vehicles in line with the Continent. This meant that British manufacturers lagged behind in upgrading their products to higher-performance specifications.

All of this left the UK market increasingly open to outside pressures. Imports, notably from Volvo, began to make inroads.[3] By the end of the 1970s HCV production had slipped below 120,000 a year.

Far worse was to follow. From around 100,000 trucks in 1980, output crashed to fewer than 60,000 the following year. Demand had collapsed. An overvalued exchange rate was hampering exports and the domestic economy was being crushed by monetarist economics. And in a foretaste of what was to hit the railway industry a decade later, truck demand was stifled by the impending privatisation of state-owned British Road Services (BRS).[4] Ahead of the sale to management, the country's biggest haulage contractor kept a tight lid on investment to minimise the asset book for which they would have to pay.[5]

The truck market did not improve. The rest of the 1980s brought devastating cutbacks and plant closures, and the demise of some of the best-known names in the industry. By 1989 output was well below 50,000, and with the renewed recession in the early 1990s it slumped again. At the end of the 1990s it was well under 20,000 a year and except once it has never again reached even this level.

The closures which annihilated so many commercial vehicle builders got under way in the 1980s and intensified in the 1990s. True, there had been some amalgamations and mergers before this. But they were evolutionary and involved careful restructuring through rationalisation and the elimination of duplicate capacity. None of this had prepared the industry for the challenge of the 1980s, when the realities were a catastrophic decline in demand and emergency action to kill off capacity. The 1990s brought no relief.

The history of some of the better-known names is vivid testimony to the industry's decline.

Bedford

One of the most familiar names in British lorries was Bedford, established as General Motors' commercial vehicle arm after it bought Vauxhall in the 1920s.[6] After considerable success in the 1930s, Bedford turned out many thousands of vehicles for the military during the Second World War. Manufacturing capacity was increased in 1942 by the opening of a huge new plant at Dunstable, near the company headquarters in Luton.

From the 1950s to the 1970s Bedford enjoyed thriving markets at home and abroad, with 60 per cent of output exported to Commonwealth countries. The army remained a loyal customer, and the company extended its range into the largest weight classes then permitted.

The big challenge, however, was the 1980s recession and the appalling slump in the medium and heavy trucks market. Bedford was particularly hard hit. JT Battenberg III, its chief executive, put it bluntly: "The industry peaked in 1979–80 at 85,000 units and then the bottom fell out in 1981. That year was an absolute disaster, with [national] sales falling to 42,000. We could build enough trucks in our Dunstable plant alone to supply the whole UK market."[7] Only a decade earlier Britain's heavy commercial vehicle output had still been in sight of 200,000.

Bedford, which had been profitable until 1980, made continuous losses. Negotiations to buy the commercial vehicle interests of BL foundered on fears that a merger would prompt a swift rationalisation of the Leyland operations. That was the end for Bedford. In September 1986, General Motors announced that it would terminate all truck production in the UK. After making over two million vehicles since 1931, the largest volume of any British marque, Dunstable fell silent.[8]

In the political row that ensued the right-wing MP for Luton North, John Carlisle, flailed about wildly, first trying to blame the Leader of the Opposition for the "decimation of the truck industry of this country", and then turning his ire on Trade and Industry Secretary Paul Channon.[9] The seeds of the disaster lay, of course, not with a powerless Opposition or even the complacent incumbent at the head of the DTI, but in the ruinous policies pursued by the government that took office in 1979.

Bedford operations did not die at once. There were military contracts and modest export commitments to complete, but efforts by a new owner, AWD

Ltd, to sustain operations eventually failed. In 1992 the great Dunstable works closed for good.[10]

Ford

Ford was for many years a big producer of commercial vehicles, and the bestselling brand in the British van market since the 1960s. Truck production was established in the 1930s under the Fordson badge, and during the war tens of thousands of lorries were made at Dagenham.[11] Subsequently, Ford's commercial vehicle output was centred on Southampton for heavier trucks and Langley for mid-size lorries.

Naturally Ford suffered severely in the dreadful conditions of the 1980s. It held on until 1986, when it sold a majority stake in Langley. The buyer was Iveco, controlled by Fiat. Ever alert to the potential for rationalisation, Fiat closed Langley in 1997.[12] This left Ford's van production at Southampton as its only remaining UK involvement in commercial vehicles. Eventually this too closed when Transit production was transferred to Turkey.

Commer, Karrier and Dodge

The Rootes Group[13] made a range of lorries, light commercial vehicles and buses, its main brands being Commer, Karrier and Dodge. Commer had been founded in south London before the First World War, and was bought by Humber in the 1920s. In 1931 Humber was itself bought by Rootes, which acquired Karrier in 1934. Both names were retained for Rootes' light trucks, with output centred at a Dunstable factory in the 1960s.

Chrysler UK took over Rootes in the mid-1970s and sold the entire group to Peugeot Citroen in 1978. The new owner had little interest in commercial vehicles and ran the Dunstable factory in partnership with Renault. The latter phased out the former Rootes models in favour of its own, eventually ending all UK production in the 1990s.

Renault's involvement with Dunstable had rewarded its owner with the ultimate goal of so many multinational takeovers – additional market share for its imports.

Leyland Motors

For most of the twentieth century, Leyland, which took its name from the Lancashire town where it was founded, was the most celebrated marque in commercial vehicles.[14] Leyland was an early convert from steam to internal combustion and greatly expanded around the time of the First World War.

Between the wars the company became a leader in truck and bus design. Among other initiatives was the development of its own diesel engines and the launch of the Leyland Zoo series, with the company's vehicles given names like Lion, Tiger, Hippo and Beaver.

The Second World War saw large-scale production of tanks, trucks and munitions by the company's workforce, now grown to 11,000. Under the benign stewardship of the Spurrier family, which ran the company for three generations, the post-war years were a time of strong expansion. In 1946 Leyland set up a collaborative venture, British United Traction, with AEC. The year 1951 brought the acquisition of Albion Motors, 1953 a joint venture with Danish Automobile Building (DAB) and 1955 the establishment of Ashok Leyland in India.

Post-war success was reinforced by the introduction of the successful Comet and Royal Tiger models. Leyland also introduced its new Titan bus, which brought large sales to London Transport and big orders from Cuba. Meanwhile, the takeover trail continued, with Leyland buying Scammell Lorries in 1955 and ACV, best known for its AEC operation, in 1962. Three years later Leyland took minority stakes in Bristol Commercial Vehicles and Eastern Coach Works.

At this point the company could claim to be the world's biggest truck-maker.[15]

Meanwhile, Leyland had moved into cars. In 1961 there was a merger with Standard-Triumph. The lure was a volume car business to reinforce the company's motor industry standing. Such thinking may have prompted Leyland to acquire Rover and Alvis in 1967 and to merge with British Motor Holdings (BMH) to form British Leyland (BL) the following year.

In 1969 the Leyland arm of British Leyland formed a joint venture with the National Bus Company. At first successful, the venture eventually came to grief on the rocks of privatisation and market collapse in the 1980s.

Critics claim that the merger of Leyland with BMH allowed the management to raid the profits from trucks to shore up volume cars.[16] The truck side nevertheless produced a line of vehicles which won Truck of the Year at the end of the 1970s. Nationalisation of the BL group in 1975 had actually brought much-needed finance and in 1979 a fine assembly hall, technical centre and computerised warehouse were opened at Leyland.[17]

In 1981, Leyland Trucks became a separate division of BL, but this did nothing to shield it from the devastating recession, which was to drive outfits as big as Bedford out of the lorry business, set Ford and Chrysler on their downhill paths and close many smaller concerns. Profit remained elusive at Leyland, and as part of the dismemberment of BL it was privatised in 1987. Leyland and Freight Rover merged with DAF, the Dutch truck-maker with operations in the Netherlands and Belgium. The arrangement proved highly controversial, and is worth looking at more closely.

Downing Street ensured that most press comment was complacent, with frequent references to the success of Anglo-Dutch ventures such as Shell and Unilever. But the head of Unilever, Floris Maljers, wisely cautioned: "Make absolutely sure that the two partners are equals. If some are more equal than others it is lost."[18]

A fair deal for the home side was just what Downing Street typically failed to ensure. Although the UK would account for almost 60 per cent of sales,[19] DAF was given a controlling stake (60 per cent) in the new group. And all the sacrifices – in products, plants and jobs – were to be borne by Leyland/Freight Rover. DAF engines were to replace the Leyland series in heavy trucks, and Leyland models were replaced by DAF products. Leyland was to close the Scammell factory in Watford and the engine plant and foundry at its home base in Leyland, and impose hefty cutbacks at the Albion works in Glasgow and the Chorley warehouse.

There was fallout further afield. Engine builder Cummins in Scotland shipped a quarter of its output of diesels to Leyland. This was clearly in jeopardy following DAF insistence on sourcing its needs from the Netherlands.[20] Shotts eventually closed in 1998.

"The Deal Stinks"

In all, 2,200 job cuts were to be forced through at Leyland,[21] with no closures or job losses in the Netherlands or Belgium. And all this was to be financed by a £750m subvention from the UK taxpayer. In the words of the independent-minded Tory MP for Chorley, Den Dover, "[t]he whole deal stinks".[22]

Nevertheless, the new company secured a stock market flotation. But by the end of the 1980s the febrile upturn in the British economy was withering and UK truck demand once more collapsed. Between 1989 and 1991 the market was halved and Leyland DAF plunged into a fresh crisis. In 1993 the group went bankrupt.

In contrast to the Netherlands and Belgium, where there was support from patriotic customers, financiers and, above all, government, Leyland DAF received no backing from John Major's administration.[23] Indeed, the response from Downing Street was actually damaging. The Dutch economics minister had to point out that dreary clichés such as "it is not proper to use British taxpayers' money to support lame-duck industries" were not helpful.[24]

With hefty assistance from state and other sources, the Dutch and Belgian operations of Leyland DAF became DAF Trucks under a management buyout (MBO). But it was only after heroic efforts by the chief executive and his colleagues – and token intervention by industry minister Michael Heseltine – that Leyland (now the UK arm of Leyland DAF) survived the shabby official treatment this side of the Channel, and went into a management buyout in June 1993.[25]

The operation had come perilously close to shutdown – not least by a predatory takeover from a rival hungry for market share. The biggest threat was Volvo. The Swedish company's stalking horse may have been Ian McKinnon, who had publicly declared that he wanted to lead a takeover within days of the receivership. It was he who had led the buyout of Leyland Bus in the late 1980s, only to peddle it on with indecent haste to Volvo.[26]

Part of the deal involved hiving off the van-making side that had been Freight Rover. This emerged as a new entity, LDV (Leyland DAF Vans), based at Washwood Heath, in Birmingham. Unfortunately, the orphaned LDV was too fragile to survive and eventually closed.

At Leyland the new management implemented the usual formula of severe workforce cutbacks and cost savings, and there was a minor recovery in the market. It was just enough to restore viability, and in 1998, for a sum still not disclosed the Leyland MBO team got its sale. The buyer was PACCAR, which had bought DAF in 1996.[27] Two years later the output of Foden, already owned by PACCAR, was transferred to Leyland and Foden was killed off.

Leyland was assigned the production of light and medium trucks. Heavy trucks were reserved for the Netherlands, which also retained the group's technical centre and proving ground.[28] The UK end of the group has won a string of awards for operational efficiency and product quality.[29] As if in recompense for decades of government neglect, it was commended by business secretary Vince Cable in 2013.[30] Yet, its output remains a modest 14–15,000 units a year. And for reasons that are not obvious the Leyland brand has been suppressed, all its trucks being sold under a DAF badge.[31]

Yet, the legendary name of Leyland lives on, in a country with a saner approach to industrial dilemmas. The alliance with Ashok that Leyland built in the sunny years of the 1950s and 1960s has borne rich fruit. Ashok Leyland is today a giant, its annual output of 70,000 heavy trucks and 30,000 buses putting it among world leaders in commercial vehicles.

The company has paid generous tribute to its heritage: "Over the years, Ashok Leyland vehicles have built a reputation for reliability and ruggedness. This was mainly due to the product design legacy carried over from British Leyland." By a curious turn of fate, the link with Britain has been rejuvenated; Ashok Leyland's parent, the Hinduja Group, adopted UK residence in the 1990s.

Into the Leyland Fold

The British truck industry once had a wealth of smaller firms, often supplying the more specialised end of the market. They followed two routes to their fate. Many migrated into the British Leyland fold. And others remained independent until they were taken over or sunk in the economic blizzards of the 1980s or 1990s. None survived in British hands.

Those that ended up within British Leyland were taken aboard either when the British Motor Corporation (BMC) was formed in the 1950s or via takeovers by companies which eventually joined BL. A founding member was Austin, which had combined with Morris to form BMC in 1952.

Austin offered a range of small and mid-size lorries[32] with an excellent reputation for reliability and robustness, as I know from personal experience. When I travelled from Ethiopia to Sudan in the 1970s, many of the flatbed trucks doing duty as buses were sturdy little Austins which raced along dried-up riverbeds at bone-jarring speed.

Some years after the formation of BMC the company was persuaded to set up a factory at Bathgate, near Edinburgh. Production was based on Nuffield and Leyland agricultural tractors and light trucks. However, tractor output ended in 1982 and truck assembly ended in 1986, when the factory closed in one of Scotland's many devastating industrial shutdowns.

Even after becoming part of BMC, Morris Motors continued to sell light trucks.[33] Offering economical transport for short journeys, the Morris Commercials were grimly shorn of refinement. The little wagons I drove when delivering soft drinks for Corona in the 1960s offered appalling heat in the summer, numbing cold in the winter, oppressive noise and vibration at all seasons, and, thanks to a governor on the gearbox, sluggish journeys everywhere. It was a relief when the company invested in stylish Commer vans. With a walk-through cab, cab-over design and under-floor engine, they were the last word in sophistication.

AEC – Sure as the Sunrise

Another specialist manufacturer was AEC,[34] whose origins went back to the world's first great public transport system, that of London. AEC became famous for its Routemaster double-decker bus, and enjoyed export success in Latin America and Southern Europe. After a series of restructurings in the 1940s and 1950s, AEC was taken over by Leyland Motors in 1962 and made its last vehicle in 1979.

Founded in Glasgow in 1899,[35] Albion was famous for its striking art deco logo and slogan "Sure as the Sunrise". The firm was eventually taken over by Leyland and after the formation of BL its truck production moved to Bathgate in 1980. Long after Bathgate was closed the Albion tradition lives on in a modest component factory near the original site in Glasgow.

Guy Motors started life in Wolverhampton on the eve of the First World War.[36] In addition to trucks the company made luxury cars during the 1920s, including a model powered by the first British V8 engine. Subsequently Guy had considerable success with military vehicles and then buses and trolleybuses. In 1961 the company was bought out of bankruptcy by William Lyons, the owner of Jaguar, which passed it on to British Motor Holdings and then British Leyland. Despite Guy's modest profitability, government pressure obliged British Leyland to close it in 1982.

Scammell Giants

A specialised operation that ended up in the BL fold was Scammell. Established in Watford shortly after the First World War, it became "the greatest name in British commercial transport".[37] One of its founders was Lt Colonel Alfred George Scammell. "Officious but fair, he knew everyone."[38]

Following early successes with the Pioneer six-wheeler in oilfield and logging duties and the Hundred Tonner[39] in military uses, Scammell was associated with heavy haul trucks such as the Contractor and the Crusader. Taken over by Leyland in the 1950s, it eventually became a specialist division of British Leyland.

One of its spectacular products was the Commander, used to transport Challenger 2, one of the heaviest tanks ever built. Seventy of these magnificent behemoths served during Operation Desert Storm in 1990, travelling 200 miles a day in the deserts of Arabia.[40]

Scammell tendered for 1,500 heavy haul trucks for the army in 1986, but soon after the £120m contract was awarded Leyland was forced into association with DAF. One of the consequences was closure of Scammell, and production ended in 1988. Despite the formation of a successor, Alvis Unipower,[41] the Watford factory shut for good, with the loss of 600 jobs.

Scammell's demise prompted yet another bereavement in the passing of industrial England. Interviewed for the *Financial Times*, the works union convenor pointed with pride to a history of remarkable industrial harmony, with two and a half days lost to disputes in 66 years. "Scammell is a name people live for. We are like a big family. The management takes us fully into their confidence." And the chief shop steward said simply: "We take a pride in the job. The customer only has to tell us what he wants from his vehicle and we will do it."

Such tributes refute once again the absurd calumny that the death of industry can be laid at the door of an intransigent workforce. Leyland Trucks made this absolutely clear by commenting that the closure had nothing to do with labour relations, productivity or quality, but was simply due to excess capacity.[42] It had been trapped in the ruinous economic conditions of the 1980s. It was reported that the redundant employees, many with more than 25 years of loyal service, typically received compensation of just £2–3,000.[43]

When the time came to replace the Commander as its tank transporter, the Ministry of Defence had to order an overpriced monster, the Oshkosh 1070F,[44] from America.

An early rival to Scammell in heavy haul trucks was Basingstoke-based Thornycroft. Among its memorable products was the Mighty Antar,[45] named after an Arab warrior-poet of ancient times and used as a tank transporter in the 1950s. In its final version, the Antar, fully loaded with a Chieftain tank, was road-tested to over 120 tonnes. It was replaced by the Scammell Commander in the 1980s.

Thornycroft had been acquired by AEC parent Associated Commercial Vehicles in 1961 and then became part of Leyland when ACV was itself taken over the following year. There was so much overlap with the output of Scammell that it was inevitable Thornycroft would eventually be phased out, and Basingstoke closed in 1969.

Independent Oblivion

In a vivid history of ERF, founded at Sandbach in Cheshire in 1933,[46] former director Dai Davies poignantly commented: "There isn't a day in my life when I don't think about ERF. When I started [as an apprentice] in 1954 there were 23 British truck manufacturers. Now there are none."[47]

Badly hit by the market collapse of the 1980s, ERF was eventually bought by Canada's Western Star and then sold on to Germany's MAN. As so often, a Continental owner meant the end of the road for the British subsidiary. A large contract with the Ministry of Defence was redirected to MAN's operations at home without the smallest protest from the customer, the British government, and eventually all UK production ended.

Founded in Preston in 1907,[48] Atkinson was a well-regarded independent truck-maker for many years. It eventually built up a solid following among both independent operators and British Road Services, concentrating at the heavier end of the market. The company also went into buses and coaches. In 1970 it was taken over by Seddon to form Seddon Atkinson.

Dennis dates back to a bicycle business established in Guildford in the closing years of the nineteenth century.[49] After diversifying into car production and buses and coaches,[50] the company eventually specialised in public service vehicles such as dustcarts and fire appliances.

In modern times the firm has been subject to pass-the-parcel ownership so familiar in British industry. In 1972 the company was bought by Hestair, whose chairman commented: "It's a typical British industrial museum piece. ...Even in good years we knew it wasn't suitable."[51] Dennis bus operations went successively to Trinity Holdings, Mayflower Corporation, Transbus International and finally Alexander Dennis, now one of Britain's last makers of buses and coaches. Otherwise the name lives on in fire appliances and refuse carts.[52]

Foden started life in the 1880s and went into diesel-engined trucks in the 1930s.[53] Thereafter it remained an active independent supplier of tractors, dropsided and flatbed lorries for many years. After financial difficulties the company went into receivership in 1980 and was taken over by US-based PACCAR.

Events then followed a wretched and all too familiar pattern. Within two years of the 1998 takeover of Leyland Trucks by PACCAR,[54] Foden production ended, though the name was tacked on to some of the Leyland products. This contrivance ended in 2006, when the Foden name was finally killed off.

Seddon and SAMs

Robert Seddon set up his eponymous lorry manufacturing operation in Salford in the late 1930s.[55] A post-war move to a shadow factory in Oldham allowed a big expansion in output. The company added buses to its portfolio and enjoyed considerable success in the Commonwealth and Southern Europe. Meanwhile, Seddon developed a range of heavy trucks.

In 1970 Seddon took over Atkinson Lorries[56] to form Seddon Atkinson Vehicles. Four years later the company was sold to the US group International Harvester and repaid its new owners with considerable success, its new range voted European Truck of the Year in 1976.[57] However, the 1980s brought fierce recession and Seddon Atkinson was not exempt. In 1984 it was bought by Spain's Enasa to complement its Pegaso brand. In 1990 Enasa sold Pegaso to Fiat's Iveco subsidiary, and Seddon Atkinson followed the next year.

Iveco dropped the Pegaso name in the mid-1990s, but Seddon Atkinson was spared. The company had developed a popular line in municipal refuse vehicles and the logo of the smiling dustman SAM (Seddon Atkinson Municipals) became a familiar sight. In 1992, however, production was transferred to the Iveco factory in Madrid and UK operations ceased. In 2010 even the famous brand was finally dumped.[58] Half the UK municipal truck market now goes to costly imports from Germany.

Light Commercial Vehicles

Britain has a long history of making light commercial vehicles. Typically these comprise vans, pickups and flatbacks, but they include a wide variety of small utility vehicles.

UK output picked up rapidly after the Second World War. From 132,000 in 1946 production rose to 243,000 in 1950 and 312,000 a decade later, and peaked at 322,000 in 1961.[59] Although the industry never again matched this, the trend for the next couple of decades was reasonably resilient, with averages of 258,000 a year for the 1960s and 242,000 for the 1970s.

The 1980s saw a break with this pattern, with particularly poor out-turns for the middle of the decade when output fell below 180,000 a year. Though it had a couple of bad years the average for the 1990s held at a little above 200,000 a year. Since then, however, there have been some terrible years – only partly explained by recession – and the underlying pattern has been broadly downward.

Traditionally, most of the bigger car manufacturers made light commercial vehicles. Some models were simply car-derived vans and pickups but the major producers also had a portfolio of vehicles specifically designed for commercial uses, including short distance all-purpose delivery or special applications.

The post-war decades saw a wide variety of vehicles on the UK market, almost all supplied by domestic manufacturers. BMC's output ranged from derivatives of the Austin A40, Morris Minor and later the Mini to the larger J4 and J2 vans. Standard produced a van based on its small family saloon and then the more suitable Atlas, and among Ford products was the

Thames 400E, a small mid-engined forward control van. Rootes' contender was its Commer PB range.

Bedford was the market leader with the CA, which sold well on both domestic and export markets. Among its popular callings was the ice cream van, and it is possible to see the occasional veteran still in action after more than half a century of use.

Ford Transit

Even the prosaic world of British vans has had its moments of excitement. One of these was the arrival in 1965 of the Ford Transit.[60] With their wide track, large capacity, racy performance and American-inspired styling, Transits quickly became market leaders. Over the years more than seven million have been built.

At first the Transit was made at Ford's Langley factory, but in 1972 production was transferred to Southampton. And there it remained for 40 years. Then came a shock announcement that along with two other Ford Europe operations Southampton would close.[61] Transit production moved to Turkey.

Southampton's closure brought Ford UK plant shutdowns to 16 in just 15 years and ended a century of vehicle production in the British Isles. For a prominent union leader, it epitomised a situation in which the British workforce "remains among the easiest and cheapest to fire in Europe". He pointed bitterly to the readiness of the French government to provide €7bn in financial support to get Peugeot through its rough patch.[62]

Ford's "exit by stealth"[63] meant the company now had only three manufacturing operations left in the British Isles – petrol engines at Bridgend (now earmarked for closure), diesel engines at Dagenham and gearboxes at Halewood.[64] Britain is a very important market for Ford. Its abandonment of vehicle manufacture raises urgent questions about corporate responsibility and the reluctance of British governments to insist on a proper contribution to local manufacture by free-wheeling multinationals.

Leyland Sherpa

British Leyland's belated answer to the sharper competition in vans was the Sherpa, launched in 1974 and destined for a surprisingly good innings.

The 1981 reorganisation of BL made it the main product of Freight Rover. When Leyland Trucks was sold to DAF in 1987, Freight Rover went with it, though the Sherpa name was dropped. The year 1993 saw more upheaval when DAF went bankrupt and Leyland DAF Vans was formed by a management buyout.[65] The following year brought a change of name to LDV.[66]

After a couple of years the new company was hit by the inexplicable award of a major Ministry of Defence truck contract to a German competitor. LDV found its way into the hands of Russian interests, Oleg Deripaska's Gaz group, in 2006.

In the wake of the financial crisis a Labour government only too ready to hand countless billions to bankers dragged its feet over a £5m loan for LDV. The trade minister loftily declared: "The British taxpayer cannot be expected to pay for the company's losses." By the early months of 2009 LDV was in a terminal condition[67] and by mid-year it had entered administration. The chairman of Gaz paid handsome tribute to the "supportive and patient" employees at his factory and at dealers and suppliers. Manufacturing consultant Lord Battachariya pointed out the obvious: "In a competitive market you need critical mass."[68]

LDV was the last big private-sector concern in Washwood Heath, a deprived area of inner Birmingham. The *Financial Times* offered a grim portrait of a once-thriving cradle of the Industrial Revolution turning into one of its graveyards.[69]

The Survivors

Bedford followed its CA van with the CF. After its launch in 1969 it became the second most popular van in the UK. It was eventually superseded after the van factory in Luton was put into a joint venture with Isuzu, under the name IBC Vehicles, and the Bedford name was dropped.

Through Adam Opel, its German subsidiary, General Motors bought out Isuzu. Luton now mainly assembles light commercial vehicles under the Vauxhall marque. It is the sole remaining van plant in the UK. The year 2016 saw an upturn in demand for its products and production was lifted by around 20 per cent. Whether IBC survives the sale of Vauxhall to Peugeot, and the impact of Brexit, remains to be seen.

The only other UK manufacturer of light commercial vehicles of any note is Tata, which makes 5–10,000 Land Rover commercial vehicles each year.

Buses and Coaches

After a slow start in the nineteenth century public bus services became widely established before the First World War and saw further growth after the war. Meanwhile, coach travel also became more popular for long-distance journeys.

Most of the truck-makers also offered buses, but some bus-makers started life as production divisions of operators. Gradually such activities were run down in favour of purchases from the established manufacturers, or they became separate manufacturing entities. Some companies favoured a high degree of integration while others concentrated on making the bodies and buying in most of their components.

The period after the Second World War brought some rationalisation. But new owners were often content to keep their acquisition in production, often capitalising on popular names and long-established customer relationships. The 1940s saw extensive nationalisation of bus services, but many municipal bus services retained their distinct identity and fostered close relations with vehicle suppliers.

AEC – Red Routemaster

One of the best-known bus-makers was AEC, which had a large factory at Southall, in west London. Main line rail travellers to Paddington were able to relieve the vista of dull suburbia with the sight of rows of scarlet Routemasters waiting to join London Transport's magnificent double-decker fleet.

AEC took over two significant rivals, Crossley and Maudsley, in 1948, two coachbuilders, Park Royal Vehicles and Charles H Roe, in 1949 and part of Thornycroft in 1961. AEC was itself taken over by Leyland the following year, but continued to lead a separate existence until 1979. In that year Southall was at last closed and production for London Transport moved to the nearby suburb of Park Royal.

Leyland Buses

Leyland was a household name in both buses and coaches and had a strong presence in export markets. It was typical of the panache with which the company was run that in 1964 its managing director Donald Stokes cheerfully signed off an order for 620 buses for Cuba in the teeth of a US government boycott of the Castro regime.

Leyland built its market share by buying Albion in 1951 and taking on AEC's portfolio of established bus-makers when it acquired the parent company in 1962. It bought stakes in Bristol Commercial Vehicles and Eastern Coach Works and after the formation of British Leyland in 1968 found itself with still more bus-making capacity at Guy Motors. Rationalisation, however, remained limited.

For much of the post-war era business was booming. After a slower phase in the 1950s activity raced up in response to higher government subsidies and incentives for bus operators. Long-distance coach travel was becoming popular and there was strong export demand from Commonwealth countries. From a low of 7,200 buses in 1953 output accelerated to 17,000 at the end of the decade.

Royal Tiger

My memories of the 1950s include school excursions in smart coaches – all plush upholstery, wide windows and art deco trim – with stirring names like AEC Regal, Duple Vega and Leyland Royal Tiger. At its launch in 1950 the Royal Tiger was the first coach with an underfloor-engined chassis, and it was an immediate success at home and abroad.[70] I vividly recall a trip to the Pyrenees when we gazed in wonder at the old-fashioned French buses, tall, narrow and wheezing, with protruding bonnets and odd names like Berliet, Chausson and Saurer.

Despite the competition of private motoring, UK bus manufacture averaged more than 19,000 a year in the 1960s, and the 1970s were even better, with annual output running at a remarkable 29,000 vehicles.[71] At its 1975 peak of over 35,000, UK bus output was far ahead of any other European country and third in the world behind the US and the Soviet Union.

It all ended in the 1980s, which brought a devastating slump. Output fell below 22,000 in 1980, paused at 12–15,000 for a couple of years, then hurtled on down. It fell below 5,000 in 1984, below 4,000 in 1985 and averaged 2,400 a year for the rest of the decade. In the years since it has shown little sign of recovery.

Deregulation Devastation

What on earth triggered that extraordinary collapse? The jump in fuel prices following the 1979/80 oil shock was a factor. As was the gruelling recession unleashed by the new government. But it took an exceptional set of circumstances to bring a previously thriving industry so low, and to keep it down.

The critical events were deregulation and privatisation. The crippling effects of these doctrinaire and wretchedly planned policies were to have a disastrous replay in what happened to the railways a decade later and deserve to be revisited.

The Conservative government that took office in 1979 soon indicated that it wanted the publicly owned bus companies deregulated and sold off to the private sector. And there were strong signals that management/employee buyouts would be welcome. This raised an immediate problem for the bus builders. Why would any managers intending to bid for their public transport concern want to push the price against them by adding to the assets of the enterprise? Sure enough, once privatisation started to loom, orders for new buses froze.[72]

The first big legislative change was the Transport Act of 1980, which deregulated long-distance bus and coach travel. This was followed by the Transport Act of 1985, which deregulated all urban bus services outside London and Northern Ireland and accelerated privatisation.[73] (The reorganisation of London's buses had begun in 1984 and by the end of the decade the system had been split into smaller companies and mostly privatised – though under a more sensible regime than its provincial counterparts.)

While deregulation and privatisation were working their way across the bus and coach industry, operating conditions were being made more difficult by the ending of fuel subsidies. These were progressively phased out between 1980 and 1985. To add to the chaos there were fickle changes in the regulations relating to one-man operation.

At first these favoured single-decker buses at the expense of the double-deckers historically popular with transport authorities. And then there were policy reversals which brought back more traditional designs. Demand collapsed, with new bus registrations falling to just 300 in 1986. For the surviving bus-makers business conditions were becoming increasingly nightmarish.

Privatisation Pillage

Like most of those involved in privatisation, the architects of bus deregulation, such as Professor John Hibbs,[74] were remarkably insouciant about the wider impact of their pet wheezes. But even they could hardly have envisaged the chaos and squalid profiteering they were to unleash. A warning shot came in 1986, when the National Bus Company (NBC), operator of most buses outside the larger towns, declared a huge one-off loss. The intention was to dump all kinds of non-recurring costs (notably sweeping redundancies) onto its owner, the taxpayer, on the eve of sell-off. That way the owners would have a nice debt-free balance sheet to display to would-be buyers.

Within a few years the new owners – mostly former managers – had made fortunes from shabby ploys like selling off bus stations and garages for shopping developments.[75] Meanwhile, many were peddling their stakes to larger groups, thus concentrating rather than opening up the industry. Some of the business practices of the newcomers were appalling. Stagecoach, fast emerging as Britain's biggest bus operator, was heavily criticised by the Monopolies and Mergers Commission for anti-competitive behaviour.[76]

Some of the more scrupulous managers in the municipal bus companies had never been enthusiastic about privatisation. In 1984, the retiring NBC chief criticised Transport Secretary Nicholas Ridley for his "inexplicable" privatisation plans.[77] Later the same year Ridley faced angry jeers when he outlined government policies at the annual Bus and Coach Council conference. At the same event, the managing director of Hestair Dennis spoke for manufacturers when he pointed out that production had fallen by two-thirds since 1979 and was set to plunge further.[78] And, the following year, a leading transport executive voiced alarm that deregulation was threatening all that had been achieved.[79]

Nor were the post-mortems more favourable. Colin Curtis, who as vehicle engineering manager for London Transport had played a key role in the design and development of the much-loved Routemaster, was saddened by the casual discarding of so much industry expertise.[80] A letter from the editor of *Local Transport Today* to the *Financial Times* summed up the record: "In an industry whose business has shrunk by 25 per cent... since privatisation...what has been the purpose of the exercise? To make millionaires of several dozen lucky bus managers while they squeezed the wages of their staff, and to enable quick returns for shareholders while fares have risen ahead of inflation."[81]

The brunt of the order cutbacks fell on Leyland, which had once supplied 60 per cent of all the buses sold in the UK. By the mid-1980s British Leyland had had to close most of the bus-making ventures it had acquired over the years. The forced rationalisation involved consolidation into a single concern, Leyland Bus. This had been established in the late 1960s as a sensible collaboration between the state-owned National Bus Company and British Leyland. Its main assets were a new factory at Workington in Cumbria and subsidiary operations at Farington in Lancashire.

Workington Sell-Out

Workington was a flagship. It was a modern state-of-the-art plant which, as the local MP put it, "prospered throughout the 1970s on the back of [government] transport policy...a fine example of good planning, stemming import penetration and providing substantial employment for Workington". Among pioneering features were a rolling production line, multi-skilling and flexible working, and the adoption of radial tyres, air suspension, turbocharging and low floor construction in single-decker buses.[82]

Its main product was the Leyland National bus. Despite problems with the original engine, the bus was a considerable success. Even more popular was its successor, which sold well at home and overseas and was still in service decades later.

In its eagerness to shed all vestiges of industrial stewardship, the Thatcher government was looking for opportunities to dump BL/Rover. This, of course, included Leyland Bus. What followed was one of the shabbiest episodes in the dismal history of privatisation. At the end of 1986, with no meaningful due diligence, the government nodded through the sale of Leyland Bus to a management buyout (MBO).

It was yet another instance of insiders pocketing fortunes from the disposal of public assets. Headed by Ian McKinnon, a former BL executive, the MBO team comprised six middle managers who had been drafted in to the bus subsidiary from the truck side of Leyland during one of the company's reshuffles. The buyout terms were fantastically generous with taxpayers' money. For just £4m – mostly not even their own money but loaned by Bankers Trust and Bank of Scotland – the new owners acquired a company capitalised at £17.4m. They also gained £2.5m worth of stock contracted for British Rail, a debt write-off of £55m and no restrictions on resale.

The reaction of the few bus operators back in the market for new vehicles was mixed. Two big orders from British Rail helped to keep the new venture in business, and Ulsterbus promptly placed a large order. But Badgerline, no longer part of the National Bus Company and thereby apparently absolved from loyalty to the home side, took its chequebook to Volvo.

Within weeks of the buyout the new owners were slashing the workforce and closing Eastern Coachworks in Lowestoft, with most of the costs borne by former parent BL/Rover.[83] And before long the MBO was clearing the decks for a resale. It took little more than 12 months for the MBO to pass the company on to Volvo for £25m.[84] Since Volvo had already sounded out British Leyland and the government about a possible purchase in 1982 and again in 1984 it was always the obvious contender.[85] Indeed, there were rumours that the MBO team had made furtive overtures to Volvo even before the end of 1987.

The sale to Volvo prompted familiar platitudes about complementarity of products and activities. Volvo was strong in Scandinavia, Central Europe and South America. Leyland had a historic claim on the Commonwealth. Yet, their relative standings made the deal a coup for Volvo. Where there

170

were said to be 45,000 Volvo buses on the road there were 65,000 Leylands in use, implying a big potential for parts and replacements.[86]

The usual pieties about continuity, investment and a secure future were dusted off. There were promises that all jobs would be preserved at Farington and Workington.[87] But there were hints of less agreeable changes. Although production at Workington and Farington would rise, there would, for example, be a decline in UK content, historically over 90 per cent, as the buses moved over to Volvo engines and other components.[88]

In the event the changes would be far more profound, and ultimately disastrous for both Farington and Workington. There were job cuts, product rationalisation, and experiments with dock-building and team working.[89] In all this upheaval the management was given the full cooperation of its labour force and unions. Yet, there were threats to hand over responsibility for all bus production outside Sweden to Renault, now in an alliance with Volvo.[90]

False and Shabby

In the end a decision was made to close Workington, without consultation with local managers, in December 1991.[91] Meanwhile, Farington had shed three-quarters of its workforce and become a minor components supplier. It was the end for Leyland Bus. Even its name was changed to Volvo Bus.[92] Recalling that Volvo had promised a great future for the plants, junior minister Robert Atkins declared himself "misled and deceived [and] angry that a company with Volvo's reputation should behave in such a false and shabby manner".[93]

Production – by now little more than final assembly – was transferred to the Volvo factory at Irvine in Scotland. Even Irvine lasted only a few more years. Following the end of bus assembly in 1998 and the transfer of truck production to Belgium and Sweden in 1999, the last of Volvo's UK manufacturing operations closed.[94]

The Swedish takeover of Leyland Bus had been driven by four factors. Volvo had a short-term requirement for more capacity. It needed a bus factory within the European Community, of which Sweden was not yet a member.[95] It wanted a production facility in its largest market outside Scandinavia. Above all, it wanted to grab more market share by buying out its main UK competitor.[96] In all of these it succeeded. But for Leyland Bus it was a disaster, and for the UK it meant the death of its last major integrated bus manufacturer.

A former managing director had once said of Volvo: "There is a special Volvo culture. Everybody is so proud of what they are doing and it is like a huge big family."[97]

Whether he felt so warmly about his corporate family in later years is not recorded.

Survivors

Out of the wreckage just three British bus assemblers survived. The oldest was privately owned Wrightbus, founded in the 1940s in Ballymena, Northern Ireland. Wrightbus entered the midi-bus sector in the early 1990s and subsequently moved on to double-deckers.

Among its more distinctive products was a trial successor to the Routemaster, developed under a £7.8m contract with Transport for London when Boris Johnson was mayor of London.[98] While it was refreshing to see a British transport operator actually foster a stylish and innovative design from a UK manufacturer, the "Boris Bus" had technical issues and the project was abandoned by Johnson's successor. Sadly, Wrightbus has more recently been on life-support.

Another significant manufacturer, Alexander Dennis, combined Alexander of Falkirk, Dennis of Guildford and Plaxton of Scarborough in the early 2000s. After Transbus went into administration in 2004, Alexander Dennis was bought by investors, among them Brian Souter, who had made a fortune out of bus service privatisation in the 1980s and rail services in the 1990s and seemed at last ready to put something back into the country which had been so generous to him. Factories in Belfast and Wigan were nevertheless closed. However, Alexander Dennis bought Plaxton back into the fold in 2007.[99] In 2019 the UK operations, claimed now to be the world's largest makers of double-decker buses, were bought by Canada's NFI group.

The last of the survivors is Optare (Latin "to choose"), whose bizarre corporate history epitomises the demented times that such organisations have had to endure. Since it was formed, Optare has been through at least half a dozen changes of ownership.

After the closure of Leyland Bus subsidiary Charles H Roe in 1984, Optare was set up by a group of municipal bus companies to make buses in Leeds. In 1990 it merged with DAF Bus to form United Bus, but this initiative collapsed with the bankruptcy of DAF and Optare went to a management buyout. In 2000 it was bought by North American Bus Industries, but in 2005 Optare again went into an MBO. This ended in a takeover by Jamesstan Investments in March 2008 and a reverse takeover by Darwen Group later the same year.

At this point Optare had facilities in Blackburn and Rotherham, in addition to Leeds. All three eventually closed and a modern purpose-built facility opened at a new site in 2012. Meanwhile, Ashok Leyland had taken a 26 per cent interest in 2010, and the following year it increased its stake to 75 per cent.[100] Now that Optare is in the hands of owners who are in the business for the long haul, the company may at last have a future as secure as it or any of its peers have seen in a long time.

Whatever the fate of the survivors, however, the British bus industry will surely never return to its once-great stature.

Whatever the problems of underinvestment facing some individual companies (for example, Dennis), it is clear that Britain's commercial vehicle manufacturing was crippled by two familiar villains. These were the abysmal economic mismanagement which killed off major operators such as Bedford in the 1980s, and the doctrinaire, clumsy and irresponsible privatisations of the 1980s and 1990s. The sell-off in road haulage was carried out without a thought for the implications for domestic manufacturers, and in bus services this problem was exacerbated by the chaotic way the policy was actually implemented. The appalling destruction of Leyland in the bus field and the reduction of its truck-making side to a small foreign-owned residual stand as egregious examples of how not to run an industrial economy.

CHAPTER 9

Train Wreck

Enter the great hall of the National Railway Museum in York and you walk smack into Mallard, an iconic object of such outrageous beauty that genuflection seems the only proper response.

Maev Kennedy at the National Railway Museum, 2002[1]

Valhalla

Reverence is fitting, for this is a cathedral of the railway age. A few paces from *Mallard* the pilgrim would find *Deltic*, a mighty diesel surprisingly handsome in blue and silver. Or a great black steam locomotive shipped to China in the 1930s and returned home when put out to grass half a century later. Or *Princess of Hamilton*, a vision of art deco streamlining in carmine and gold. And more recently a graceful *Flying Scotsman*, which, after post-retirement alarms, was restored in the museum's workshops to the apple green livery in which it was born a century ago.

Apart from their style these exhibits have something unique in common. They are, to the core, British – conceived, designed and built by hand in Britain. This is true of nearly everything on display. Britain has been one of the great locomotive-building countries of the world. The US leads the field, with over 175,000 steam engines made between the mid-nineteenth century and 1970. Germany has a rich railway history. But Britain beats

174

it, with over 110,000 steam locomotives built since the first miraculous prototypes of the early 1800s, and thousands of diesel and electric engines assembled in the years since steam was retired.

Britain was the first country to have a locomotive-hauled public railway when Robert Stephenson's Locomotion No 1 inaugurated the Stockton–Darlington line in 1825. The network spread rapidly during the nineteenth century and this small island still has the world's eighteenth largest railway system and one of the most densely spread. It is one of the busiest in Europe, second only to Germany in the number of services, and is the fifth most heavily used in the world.

The growth of the network in the first half of the nineteenth century was based on a patchwork of local links developed by small companies. Most of these firms did their own maintenance and many built their own rolling stock. During the second half of the century railway amalgamation became more common and there was some rationalisation of locomotive-building, but overall capacity remained very substantial.

The in-house operations of the railway companies were passed on to British Railways when the system was nationalised in 1948. Alongside them was a group of independent operators who had survived into the second half of the twentieth century. These included names of international renown such as Vulcan Foundry, North British Locomotive, Metro Cammell and Brush. And they also included the locomotive-building interests of the great electrical engineering combines, AEI, English Electric and GEC.

A roll call of independent locomotive builders of the twentieth century lists almost 90 operations.[2] Today this heritage has almost vanished. The entire in-house capacity of the railways has gone. A couple of specialist outfits linger on. And just one broad-based independent plant has survived – perilously.

Vulcan Foundry

Among the many factories in Great Britain which for over a hundred years have specialised in engineering, those making locomotives are of outstanding importance. The engineers who work in the factories have spent a lifetime in the design and construction of railway engines for use in many lands, and their skill has accumulated from generation to generation. One such engineer is Ted Wilson, the Production Engineer of this factory. He has worked here for nearly thirty years...every day passing on his knowledge to others, no matter which country they are from, for the language of engineers is becoming universal.

The comment is from *Portrait of an Engineer*, one of many fine documentary films made by Merton Park Productions in the 1950s.[3] Set in the Vulcan Foundry ("the Foundry") in Newton-le-Willows, Manchester, this affectionate study offers a picture of calm and constructive industry, labour-intensive, painstaking and craft-based. Even in the 1950s the company was still highly integrated, with its own design and pattern departments, in-house foundry, forge, boiler fabrication and wheel-making facilities, and, of course, its own locomotive assembly hall.

It was axiomatic in those days that skills were passed on, and the film closes with a rather touching scene in which the pipe-smoking engineer is quietly instructing a student from India in the lore of locomotive-building. Financed by his parents to come to England to acquire his skills, that apprentice would go back to reinforce the railway tradition so vital to the life of his great country.

The Vulcan Foundry dated back to the early days of the railways. Opened in 1832 to serve the Liverpool and Manchester Railway, Vulcan Foundry was soon supplying customers in the US, France, Austria, Russia and later India,[4] Japan and China. Famous for their durability, some Vulcan machines clocked up two million miles on the plains of India.[5]

Vulcan Foundry was eventually taken over by English Electric as a route into diesel-electrics in the 1950s.[6] After English Electric was itself taken over by GEC in 1968, Vulcan Foundry concentrated on the manufacture of diesel motors. But it retained a strong link with the railway industry as a supplier of power units to British Railways workshops.

North British Locomotive

A prominent contender among the independent rolling stock makers was North British Locomotive, established in the Springburn district of Glasgow in 1903. Glasgow was then in its industrial prime, its dense network of marine, mechanical and precision engineering and textiles reinforcing its status as the second city of the empire.

On its three sites North British produced a remarkable 600 locomotives a year[7]– as many as the Vulcan Foundry delivered in six years. Many of these went out to serve the empire, South Africa alone receiving more than 2,000. Unfortunately, North British did not survive the transition to the modern world. When railway modernisation began in the 1950s and steam was replaced by diesel and electric, North British failed to adapt. It went bankrupt in 1962.

Associated Electrical Industries

Other rolling stock builders found a role on a smaller scale or in more specialist areas. British Thomson-Houston, one of the founders of Associated Electrical Industries (AEI) in 1922, built limited numbers of locomotives at its Birmingham works in the 1950s. Metropolitan Vickers (Metrovicks), the other great arm of AEI, made successful diesel locomotives for British and Irish railways at Trafford Park in the 1950s.

The AEI operations were rationalised when the company was taken over by GEC in 1967. This was also the fate of Robert Stephenson & Hawthorns (RSH), which had been formed in 1937 and included the world's first dedicated locomotive works in Darlington (closed in 1964), and Newcastle (closed in 1961).

English Electric

Even before it bought Vulcan Foundry, English Electric had made diesel and electric locomotives at Preston. However, its new acquisition greatly enhanced the group's standing in railway engineering, and English Electric workhorses were shipped from the Vulcan Foundry to export markets in Africa and elsewhere.

Vulcan Foundry was only one of a series of acquisitions by English Electric. In 1962 the company formed English Electric Traction to rationalise the resources of Vulcan Foundry with those of other acquisitions such as Robert Stephenson, Dorman & Co and W.G. Bagnall.[8] And in 1968, under the banner of English Electric Diesels, it united various long-established engine makers such as Ruston & Hornsby[9] and Davy, Paxman.

Among the celebrated products devised by English Electric were the mighty Deltic diesels. Fondly remembered by railway veterans, they were named for their ingenious coupling of twin Deltic motors originally designed for marine applications by the Napier subsidiary of English Electric. Assembled at Newton-le-Willows, these formidable machines were claimed to be "the fastest and most puissant diesel locomotives ever to run in Europe".[10]Averaging more than three million miles in 21 years, they proved unbeatable on one of British Railways' busiest routes, the East Coast Main Line.

They also found their way to punishing postings overseas. When I backpacked through Sudan in the mid-1970s, battered but magnificent workhorses from Newton-le-Willows were doing sterling service on the long desert haul from Khartoum to the shores of Lake Nasser.

Sadly, but typically for British engineering, where such illustrious names as English Electric live on they are ghosts of their former selves. But in the late 1960s English Electric was, like its rival AEI, still one of two formidable home-grown empires. And ripe, in the view of many, for rationalisation.

GEC

That came with the takeover of both groups by GEC in 1968. This took GEC straight into the railway market as a major manufacturer of rolling stock.[11] English Electric-AEI Traction was formed in 1969 and in 1972 the various operations were combined as GEC Traction. For 18 years the company was a leading supplier to British Railways. It also continued to make locomotives for its own account at Attercliffe Common in Sheffield, which closed in 1984.

Rationalisation had been initiated by the combination of English Electric, AEI and GEC, but the pattern had been sensible, necessary and gradual. The next major step in the history of the group heralded something very different. The catalyst came from across the Channel.

France's Compagnie Générale d'Electricité (CGE) had been looking for ways to extend its reach and had cast envious eyes at the standing of GEC at home and abroad. By the late 1980s GEC was itself coming under malign pressure from the City to divest. One of its defences was "poison pill" alliances which would be difficult for predators to disentangle. So in 1989

GEC management merged the company's power and transport divisions with those of CGE to form GEC-Alsthom.

This was the prelude to a disastrous deterioration in the fortunes of railway engineering in Britain. The causes were mainly home-grown. First was the severe recession that followed the reckless Lawson boom of the late 1980s. The second and more deadly was the dearth of rolling stock orders accompanying rail privatisation.

It was the start of a terminal decline in GEC's rolling stock business. By the late 1990s the Trafford Park site inherited from AEI had closed. Production was moved mainly to France. The next few years brought further retreat. In 1998 Alstom [*sic*] was listed on the Paris Stock Exchange. GEC-Alsthom became Alstom Traction Ltd and eventually simply the traction division of Alstom. UK operations were reduced to minor contractual repair and overhaul.

Metro Cammell

The collapse of the once-formidable rolling stock interests of English Electric, AEI and GEC did not entirely kill off GEC's involvement in locomotive manufacture, since soon after it was formed GEC-Alsthom had bought the Metro Cammell works in Birmingham. Metro Cammell originated in a railway works established at Saltley in the mid-nineteenth century,[12] and became a joint venture with Vickers in 1923. Manufacturing was eventually concentrated at Washwood Heath a few miles away.

Metro Cammell supplied main line railways and was also a leading rolling stock maker for the underground systems of London, Glasgow and other cities. Major assignments included the carriages and power cars for London Transport's Piccadilly Line, and for the highly regarded Hong Kong Mass Transit Railway (MTR) in the 1970s.

Among notable achievements was the supply of over 300 cars for the new Victoria line in the 1960s. The trains incorporated the world's first fully automatic train operating system (ATO), with the driver replaced by an operator who simply controlled the doors and restarted the train after each stop.[13] The cars were designed by the celebrated industrial designer Misha Black, and made in Birmingham. They were naturally powered by AEI or GEC motors.

In 1989 the company was sold to GEC-Alsthom. It survived renewed recession in the early 1990s and the threat of rail privatisation. But its new owner, Alstom (as it now was), had capacity to fill and was looking to supply customers from its French base. On completion of a final contract, the assembly of Pendolino tilting trains for the West Coast Main Line, Washwood Heath closed in 2005. To rub salt in the wounds, big orders for London Underground were transferred to Alstom's plant in Spain.[14]

The Brush

Little specialised rolling stock capacity has weathered the difficult conditions of recent decades. A venerable survivor is the Brush group, established at the Falcon Works in Loughborough since 1889. Like many of its contemporaries, "the Brush" produced railway locomotives to order for many years, supplying diesel-electrics for British Railways' modernisation and specialist locomotives to steel works, coal mines and other outlets at home and abroad.

In 1956 the locomotive activities were restyled Brush Traction.[15] Like so many historic British industrial concerns, the Brush has been passed like an orphan through a succession of corporate hands. In 1957 it was taken over by Hawker Siddeley, which was in turn acquired by BTR (1991) and later sold to FKI (1996). More recently, in February 2011, Brush Traction was bought by Wabtec, a US-based railway specialist.

Brush Traction faced its greatest challenge under Hawker Siddeley,[16] which made sweeping cutbacks in the grim conditions of the 1980s. The position of the Brush was not helped by a government refusal to provide export credits for an Iraqi order for 80 mainliners. An odd decision, given the subsequent eagerness of the Thatcher administration to underpin the military ambitions of Saddam Hussein.

Fortunately, the 1990s and the 2000s saw the Brush working on sizeable orders for the Channel Tunnel service. The project was cold-shouldered by the Thatcher government and, hardly surprisingly, the high-speed trains that were to ply between London and Paris or Brussels were all made by GEC-Alsthom/Alstom in France. Worse, most of the shuttle service equipment – car transporters, freight wagons, flat wagons, maintenance locomotives, service vehicles, scrubber units and other equipment – was supplied by Continental manufacturers.[17]

However, there was a requirement for high-performance vehicles to haul freight and passenger car wagons between the Folkestone and Calais terminals. Here the quality of Brush manufacture counted, and the company shared with ABB Zürich the supply of 42 electric locomotives, the new Class 92, to haul night and freight services through the Tunnel.[18]

Ominously, under Wabtec the focus for Brush Traction now appears to be less on new-build than on service, upgrade and maintenance.

Specialists

Another specialty rolling stock maker taken over by Wabtec in recent years is Hunslet. Founded in Leeds in 1864, Hunslet became a well-known supplier of shunting and short-haul industrial locomotives to customers at home and abroad. I have spotted the company's name on veteran machines still doing duty in copper mines in South America and steel works in Australia. Hunslet made the last industrial steam engine sold in the UK, but adapted to the modern world by serving niche markets, supplying rolling stock for the Channel Tunnel Shuttle and other customers.

In 2004 Hunslet was taken over by the LH Group, which transferred production to Barton, near Burton-on-Trent. It changed hands again with the Wabtec takeover in 2012,[19] and has since offered both small specialist locomotives and rolling stock overhaul and refurbishment.

Other small rolling stock makers have vanished. Powell Duffryn was for many years a dependable supplier of freight wagons to coal mines and industrial operations in South Wales and elsewhere. Excluded, bafflingly, as a supplier of rolling stock when the Channel Tunnel was being developed in the 1980s, the company closed down its wagon-making activities and left the railway business.

Privatisation Perils

For most of the twentieth century even the biggest of the independents was eclipsed by the facilities owned by the railways themselves. When Britain's railways were nationalised in 1948, long after Italy (1905), Germany (the 1920s) and France (1938),[20] British Railways found itself with an impressive heritage of workshops serving both maintenance and new-build requirements of the former company networks. Though they were concentrated in the North, there were major railway workshops in most regions, some meeting the needs of a particular area, others filling a national role.

Reorganisation in the 1960s brought both new-build and maintenance into a single organisation, British Railways Workshops.[21] Rationalisation, the shift to diesels and the network cutbacks prompted by the Beeching Report (2,000 stations and 5,000 miles of line) meant closures. Even so, when British Rail Engineering Ltd (BREL) was formed in 1970 there were still 14 major centres in the system.[22]

The 1970s were a reasonably buoyant time for British railway engineering. Though the opportunity for wholesale electrification had been missed, investment was recovering from low levels in the wake of Beeching, and the transition from steam to diesel-electric and electric had been completed. Despite meagre support from the public purse, BREL achieved notable technical successes such as the High Speed Train and the prototype Advanced Passenger Train.

This was, however, the final phase of that long constructive era that had begun with nationalisation – which itself drew on the advances of the big four railway companies before the war. The 1980s, in contrast, opened the way to fragmentation, bewildering changes of ownership and the senseless destruction of Britain's rolling stock industry.

The merits of railway privatisation were fiercely debated in the years following the Major government's 1996 sell-off. To be accurate, there was fierceness on one side. Faced by soaring subsidies, safety lapses and abysmal service, privatisation's proponents have always had difficulty countering the superb polemic of commentators like Christian Wolmar,[23] Ian Jack[24] and Andrew Martin.[25]

Naturally there was strong support from dogma-obsessed civil servants such as the Treasury's Steve Robson, who steered privatisation.[26] And the tracks were greased by compliant management insiders benefitting on a shocking scale from employee buyouts. But other supporters of privatisation – usually academics or politicians rather than railwaymen or businessmen – have shuffled responsibility for mistakes on to the defective model peddled to the government by the Adam Smith Institute.[27]

One aspect little analysed is the devastating impact of privatisation on the supply industries. At first, though they robbed British Rail of useful revenue the privatisations were not directly damaging to railway engineering. Mostly they involved hotels, property and ancillary services.

Under pressure from the Thatcher government, BR Hotels, one of the largest chains in the country, was sold off between 1981 and 1985, with magnificent establishments like Gleneagles going for a song.[28] BR Hovercraft was given to a management syndicate, which sold it on for £5m. Ferry operator Sealink, with a fleet of 37 seagoing ships and ten entire ports, was snapped up by Bermuda-based Sea Containers for just £66m.

By the late 1980s it was the turn of the some of the direct suppliers to BR. The focus was now on the workshops, where BREL was under pressure to tailor itself for privatisation. First to go was the Temple Mills wagon works and repair yard in East London. Reduced to a minor repair facility, it finally disappeared a few years ago.

Another early casualty was the Shildon Works in County Durham. Built for the Stockton & Darlington Railway in 1825, Shildon had maintained a distinctive role as an assembler of specialist wagons for British Rail and a major producer of components. Hit by the 1980s recession, Shildon's future was sabotaged by the sale of its forge – the only one in the railway system – at a quarter of its book value.[29]

After 150 years' service, the works which built the world's first locomotives and enjoyed excellent labour relations, union moderation and rising productivity closed in June 1984.[30] In a town already suffering from the effects of recession and the collapse of coal mining the impact was devastating. Worse, redundancy payments were set at "pitifully low" levels.[31]

For a government so keen to jettison public property the approach to whetting the appetite of potential buyers was odd. In 1985, Transport Secretary Nicholas Ridley insisted that in future British Rail would not necessarily buy British.[32] Just why he wanted British Rail to diverge from the sensible policy of its European counterparts who typically sourced their needs at home[33] he did not disclose. Even splenetic government supporters like Woodrow Wyatt found Ridley's approach baffling and argued strongly for a kind of practical patriotism.[34]

Added to the threat of foreign invasion was a squeeze on supplier business. The public service obligation (PSO) grant to British Rail fell by a third between 1983 and the end of the decade, taking investment in the system to its lowest since the 1940s. The government was able to push through drastic cuts with surprising ease partly because Robert Reid, BR chairman since 1983,[35] foolishly curried favour with ministers by acceding to reduced funding.[36] The shortcomings of appeasement had clearly passed him by. Indeed, on his watch British Rail was accused of connivance in its own rundown.[37]

It would be wrong to infer that the railways were friendless. Conservative MP Robert Adley, a veteran rail enthusiast, caustically compared taxpayer support to the railways with the generous funding for roads.[38] Adley accused some Tory MPs of being ready to privatise "even the armed forces".[39] As chairman of the Parliamentary Transport Committee, he had to point out the blindingly obvious connection between failing services and cuts in the PSO grant.[40] Given Margaret Thatcher's praise for "the great car economy" and derision for public transport,[41] his battle remained a lonely one.

Swindon Closes

The financial squeeze on BR was a critical element in the tragedy now unfolding. The next casualty was the Swindon Works. Opened by Brunel's Great Western Railway in 1844, it became the heart of the town, with 14,000 employees at its 1930s peak. Locomotive-building continued through the 1950s and in 1960 Swindon launched the last main line steam locomotive for British Railways. Named *Evening Star*, this handsome machine now resides in the museum at York.

Locomotive-building ended at Swindon in 1965 and activity focused on repairs and maintenance, making the works a prime candidate for closure. When the melancholy end came in 1986 it was movingly described by the writer Jeremy Seabrook.[42]

Doncaster Closes

Meanwhile, BREL had been split into two divisions – the Maintenance Group workshops in Doncaster, Eastleigh, Glasgow and Wolverton, and the New Build and Repair Group, based in Crewe, Derby, Horwich and York.

Doncaster Works ("the Plant") had been opened by the Great Northern Railway in 1858, and by the end of the century was building locomotives, carriages and goods wagons. Between the wars it produced some of the finest steam locomotives ever made. These were the Gresley Pacifics, famed for streamlining and speed. Prime examples were *Flying Scotsman*, the first steam engine to reach 100mph, in 1934, and *Mallard*, which set an unbroken steam speed record of 126mph in 1938.

With the end of steam locomotive production in 1957, activity focused on diesels and electrics. But by the mid-1980s activity had been scaled down to a shadow of what it had been. Some of the facilities at Doncaster were handed to a management buyout, RFS Industries, in 1987, and later sold on to Bombardier Prorail.

After sweeping rationalisation they closed in 2002, when ongoing work was transferred to Wakefield.[43] Other facilities went to Wabtec, but these also closed in 2007. A hundred and fifty years of distinguished history for the Plant ended in a humdrum residential and retail development.[44]

Next to be privatised was Horwich Foundry, near Bolton. One of the last major railway engineering facilities when it opened in 1886, Horwich catered for London Midland & Scottish Railway (LMS) before the war and British Railways after nationalisation. When locomotive production ended in 1964 the works concentrated on carriages and other rolling stock.

Following heavy cutbacks in the mid-1980s the remaining operation was sold off in 1988 as Horwich Castings, for just £2m. At this point it was the last manufacturer of railway brake blocks in the country and reputedly one of the biggest foundries in Europe. Although the firm won significant new business, including a large contract to supply base plates for the Jubilee Line extension, it was abruptly put into receivership in 2004 and closed.[45]

BREL Blitzed

In 1989 BREL itself was sold.[46] This brought privatisation into the heartlands of railway engineering. The maintenance yards at Eastleigh, Glasgow and Wolverton were retained by British Rail, so BREL's main assets were now the facilities at Crewe, Derby and York.

BREL's new owner was a consortium comprising employees (20 per cent), Asea Brown Boveri (ABB) (40 per cent) and Trafalgar House (40 per cent). ABB was a Swiss/Swedish engineering giant with strong credentials in railway engineering. Trafalgar House was a seedy property and services conglomerate. For just £13.6m the group was handed four major engineering works, with more than 8,000 employees, assets of over £150m and an order book of £330m.

The new enterprise was launched into the teeth of another economic blizzard. The recession that followed the Lawson boom of the late 1980s naturally hit railway business. Still worse was the impact of approaching privatisation on new rolling stock orders, which stopped dead in their tracks.

By now the ownership lottery was playing again. In 1992 ABB bought out its partners and became ABB Transportation Ltd. After soldiering on for four years its rolling stock interests were merged with those of Daimler Benz to form AdTranz. This in turn was sold in 2001 to Bombardier Transportation, which had become the world's largest rail equipment manufacturer.

Early in 1993 BREL chairman John Darby issued a blunt warning: "We now have very effective production units at Crewe, Derby and York. None are fully occupied as the proposals by HM Government to privatise British Rail, together with the government's economic policy, have precluded either British Rail or London Underground putting orders for new rolling stock out to tender."[47]

David Gillan, director of the Railway Industry Association, wearily explained: "There is a mistaken belief in the minds of ministers that a short gap in production is sustainable. But shareholders don't allow production capacity to be kept open against the *possibility* of getting business."[48]

Andrew Cook, chairman of component maker William Cook, was furious at the way even the crumbs of business still coming from British Rail – freightliner and Channel Tunnel wagons – had gone to a French supplier operating from a protected home base, forcing Cardiff-based Powell Duffryn to close. And he pointed out: "It is no use pleading EC rules: no one else obeys them and there are any number of legal loopholes… such as insistence on adherence to national quality standards."[49]

York Closes

So the toll of British railway engineering went on. Next to go were the historic operations at York. The city had been the focus of a complex of works over the years and there had been some carefully planned rationalisation under British Rail.

The most significant facility to survive into the privatised era was the Holgate Road Wagon Works. Opened in 1880 to make carriages for the North Eastern Railway, the works went on to build Nigel Gresley's celebrated Jubilee train in the 1930s and a variety of other locomotives.

Manufacturing continued until the mid-1990s, but by that point a workforce that had numbered 5,000 at nationalisation had shrunk to 750. Crippled by the dearth of orders from British Rail ahead of privatisation, the works closed in 1996.[50] Prime Minister John Major displayed his characteristic lack of insight and fondness for clumsy metaphor by commenting: "Privatisation is no more responsible for those job losses than it is for an outbreak of measles."[51]

Attempts by Thrall Car Manufacturing to reopen to supply 2,500 wagons to English Welsh & Scottish Railway (EWS), which had taken over most of British Rail's freight business,[52] proved short-lived.

Crewe Closes

A railway centre even more impressive than York was that of Crewe. Originally opened by the Grand Junction Railway in 1840, the works became the main engineering centre for its successor the London & North Western Railway, and the workforce eventually reached 20,000. The works shaped the town and nurtured a rich tapestry of mechanics' institutes, libraries, meeting halls, churches, homes and public parkland, laid out by the celebrated railway engineer Francis Webb.[53]

At a time when British Railways was the largest employer of apprentices in Britain, with 11,000 on its books, Crewe was chosen for a new training school. When it opened in the 1950s it was the largest establishment of its kind in the country. Ponderous and conservative British Railways may have been, but the stated aims of the school reflected a noble philosophy at its heart: "the whole of the training is designed to ensure efficiency and complete happiness in one's daily work".[54]

Crewe built more than 7,000 steam locomotives. Among the most celebrated was the Coronation Class. Built to rival the Pacifics of the LNER, these were routinely capable of over 100mph. Its expertise led Crewe to develop the power cars for the Intercity 125 High Speed Train in the 1970s and 1980s. However, by the end of the decade recession and impending privatisation were starving Crewe of orders. In 1991 locomotive production ended and that superb training school closed.

Derby Despair

The closure of Crewe left Derby as Britain's last major train-builder. Dating back to 1840, Derby became one of the two main engineering centres for LMS when the big four railway companies were formed in 1923. Retaining their separate identities, the Derby plants were closely associated with the LMS Scientific Research Laboratory. Among their notable designs was the Princess Coronation Class, brainchild of the chief mechanical engineer for LMS in the 1930s, William Stanier.

Derby sustained a significant level of production, completing nearly 3,000 steam locomotives by the 1940s. Meanwhile, diesel-electric development was gathering pace, and the first mainliner for the domestic network was completed at Derby in 1948. By the time the production of standard units ended in 1966, over 1,000 diesels had been built at Derby.

Derby came under the aegis of BREL in 1970 and maintained its role as a development centre. BREL worked successfully on the diesel multiple units (DMUs) and claimed three major achievements in a more advanced field. These were the development of the High Speed Train (HST), which became British Rail's Intercity 125 and Intercity 225, and the Advanced Passenger Train (APT).

The latter had been the original objective of engineers working on the fast train concept as long ago as the late 1950s. But management lack of vision slowed the work on the APT and development was suspended. Efforts were instead concentrated on the HST as a stopgap into the world of rapid rail. The HST was original, involving a rake of passenger coaches sandwiched between two power cars. All the main components were naturally from British manufacturers. They included Paxman (GEC group) Valenta diesels, Brush Traction motors and alternators, and GEC Traction motors.

For a design developed and built on a modest budget in just two years, the HST was extremely impressive.[55] The first prototype rolled out of Derby in August 1972 and nine months later clocked up a diesel speed record of 143mph. This made it the world's first high-speed train outside Japan, a year ahead of France's TGV. The first operational sets were delivered in 1975 and 40 years later most of the 197 units eventually built were still going strong. Designated the XPT, the HST made a successful export to Australia.[56]

Meanwhile, the APT reached prototype, established a new UK speed record of 162mph in 1979 and entered service at lower speeds on the Glasgow–Euston run. But under pressure from a hostile Thatcher government management killed the project.[57] Yet again, short-termism and a blinkered approach to research and development had aborted long-term promise.

Having survived the preludes to privatisation, the Derby locomotive works passed from BREL to the ABB-led consortium in 1989 before being earmarked for closure the following year. The final shutdown came in 2004. Salvaging something of worth from the wreckage, part of the site went to make a football ground.

Now only the Carriage and Wagon works at Derby was still operating. With a workforce of over 5,000 in the 1950s this made rolling stock for British Railways and London Underground. One of its celebrated products in the 1970s and 1980s was the Mark 3 passenger carriage, a high-quality vehicle which came to form the bulk of Britain's long-distance rolling stock.

By the end of the 1980s Derby was the only remaining integrated British rolling stock manufacturer. In this it offered a sharp contrast to its largest rivals, such as GEC-Alsthom, which was predominantly an assembly operation using parts from outside sources, often imported.[58]

Despite orders for electrical multiple units (EMUs), refurbishment contracts and some export work, business conditions remained erratic and difficult right through the 1990s and the climate did not improve in the 2000s. Derby survived the savage cutbacks to its UK operations by Bombardier in 2004, but by the end of the decade the outlook for Britain's last train-building plant was still looking bleak.

Causes of Collapse

How to explain the extraordinary collapse of what was once one of Britain's leading industries?

Go back a few decades and we can point to one obvious factor. The loss of export customers made life difficult for some of the independent workshops, but this was inevitable as traditional markets loosened their trading links with the UK.

Another challenge has been recurrent changes of ownership. This was a significant factor in the demise of at least one great name. When Arnold Weinstock, the canny, tight-fisted, patriotic autocrat who built the GEC empire, at last retired, it did not take long for his successors to unravel the group and drop train-making into the lap of the French, only too eager for their Continental plants to supply UK contracts.

Overshadowing the whole sector, however, has been government policy, which ranged from complacent in the 1970s to wildly destructive in the 1980s and 1990s and negligent in the 2000s. Only very recently, with the industry in desperate straits, has there been some effort to maintain a more constructive approach.

There has often been a problem at the top. Since nationalisation in 1948 there have been more than 50 government ministers with responsibility for the railways. Few could have been as unhelpful to their cause as Labour's Dick Marsh. On his appointment in 1968, Marsh's reaction was: "I could not see the slightest reason why I should be shifted into a ministry about which I knew nothing and cared even less."[59] His predecessor, the inspiring Barbara Castle, described him as cynical, superficial and lazy.[60] He lasted just long enough to close the 98-mile Edinburgh–Carlisle line, one of the last major victims of Beeching.

He went on to become chairman of the British Railways Board for five undistinguished years. His successor in that role could not have been more of a contrast. For an annual salary of just £23,000,[61] the brilliant Peter Parker took on a "bed of rails", challenging the anti-rail lobby, defeating the Serpell Committee proposals for drastic closures in 1982,[62] charming away union suspicions and battling for adequate funding.[63]

Right-wing pressure groups find the railways an irresistible target. Thirty years on from Serpell, the Institute of Directors (IoD) was recommending the axing of 3,000 miles of secondary and branch lines.[64] More recently, the

Institute for Economic Affairs (IEA) wheeled out a bizarre proposal that rail lines should be converted to busways. It fantasised that air pollution would be "questionable" and anyway "the quieter, constant hum of buses" would be preferable to the noise from trains.[65]

Peter Parker's efforts were to little avail. Railway investment fell to a post-nationalisation low in 1981–84.[66] By 1987 a critical report from the House of Commons Transport Select Committee was pointing out: "Compared with other European railways, British Rail receives a low level of support both per head of population and as a percentage of GNP."[67] The report noted the government intention to halve state grants by 1990. That was the year in which Prime Minister Margaret Thatcher spoke admiringly of "the great car economy" and reminded the public that she did not use public transport if she could help it.

Worse was to follow. After the 1992 general election the Major government stepped up its preparations for privatisation.[68] The next few years were a nightmare for any company dependent on a regular flow of orders from the railways.[69] Business virtually dried up.[70] The problem was a moratorium on purchases of rolling stock, and for almost three years there was a freeze on new orders – a famine of over 1,000 days.

This was an incredible situation for a system which required 300 new units a year merely to replace worn-out stock, let alone upgrade its equipment.[71]

TOCs, ROSCOs and Feeding Frenzy

When the train-builders' business came back it was a different world. In place of a single buyer charged with a clear public service mission, they faced a bizarre new structure in which the users of their products were an assortment of train operating companies (TOCs) to whom route franchises were dished out, on the basis of opaque criteria, by Department for Transport civil servants.

The TOCs did not own the trains. Shortly before privatisation the rolling stock pool had been parcelled out to three rolling stock companies (Roscos) – Angel Train Contracts, Eversholt Leasing and Porterbrook Leasing – who then leased the trains to the TOCs. Replenishment of the rolling stock, as it wore out or needed upgrading, was steered by the Department for Transport.

In other words, the industry had been privatised but, more than ever, the civil servants were still in charge.

The assets had been sold to the Roscos absurdly cheaply because the civil servants and their City advisers misunderstood the dynamics of the quasi-market they were cooking up and overestimated the risks. The businesses taken on by the Roscos were remarkably secure. Most rolling stock was route specific. The contracts under which it was leased varied, but the majority were for a minimum seven–eight years (or for a shorter period with renewal options).[72] The default risk (TOC vs Rosco) on these contracts was negligible.[73] And the Roscos were guaranteed 80 per cent of the initial lease rentals and a government contribution to the cost of mandatory safety modifications.

Yet the government was warned about the impending fiasco. In a back-of-the-envelope calculation based on the £150m cost of 160 new electric carriages put out to provisional tender, Professor Bill Bradshaw briskly pointed out that at the £1bn sales target set by the government the 11,260 BR locomotives and carriages intended for sale would be grotesquely undervalued.[74]

Being little more than nameplates leasing their assets to the operators and contracting out the maintenance, the three Roscos were fantastically profitable. In 1994/95 they made £332m on a turnover of £797m.[75] This meant huge windfalls for owners who promptly jumped ship. Sandy Anderson, managing director of Porterbrook, grabbed £40m in cash and shares when the company was sold to Stagecoach. Car-hire salesman Ray Cork took £17m, Tim Gilbert £11m and chairman Peter Watson £4.8m.[76]

The story was repeated with Eversholt, where managing director Andrew Jukes pocketed £16m for his paltry £110,000, and Angel Trains, where the chairman took £15m and two "railway consultancy" partners were given £3.4m each. And there was a lot more than 30 pieces of silver for middle-ranking railwaymen who had put up modest stakes in the Roscos they happened to be employed by.

The *Official History of Privatisation* drily comments: "The pecuniary gains made during the various sales by a number of British Rail managers would become highly contentious."[77]

Worse still was the feeding frenzy as the financial institutions swarmed over the scene. Nomura made £334m out of Angel Trains and Victor Blank's Charterhouse bank lifted £224m from Porterbrook.[78] It was plunder of the public purse on a scale that might have embarrassed the oligarchs who looted post-Communist Russia. The taxpayers' largesse could have been avoided simply by the insertion of profit clawbacks into the sales contracts.[79]

The whole process drew severe censure from both the National Audit Office and the House of Commons Public Accounts Committee (PAC). It was difficult to find a single aspect of privatisation that had not been handled badly. Even a more modest event, the sale of seven British Rail maintenance depots in 1995, was mishandled in a "quite appalling" way in the view of the PAC. Conservative MPs were particularly sharp in their criticisms, noting the Department of Transport's failure to monitor the sale process and its giving away of £17m in cash held by the depots.[80]

Among other grotesque scandals were the extraordinary fees handed out to packs of accountants, bankers, financial advisers, lawyers and surveyors ahead of the main sell-off. Most of these costs were dumped onto the railway administration. Railtrack spent £78m, the Office of the Rail Regulator handed out £97m and British Rail spent an astonishing £278m on the privilege of having itself carved up.[81] Not surprisingly, the government tried to keep the sell-off fees secret ahead of the deed.[82]

Poll Tax on Wheels

The Conservative-dominated Transport Select Committee of the House of Commons was very uncomfortable with the programme as a whole. Chairman Robert Adley described the policy as a "poll tax on wheels", a memorable phrase usually attributed to CBI director general John Banham.[83] If Adley had known that annual government funding for the system would jump from less than £1.2bn in 1996/97 to £5.4bn ten years later, his language would have been even less temperate.

Inexplicably, the execrable financial consequences of privatisation were never rectified by subsequent Conservative or Labour administrations. Indeed, the systemic abuses went on for years. Even a decade on, James Sherwood, head of operating company GNER, was protesting: "A huge amount of money is being thrown away to the rolling stock companies. It's grotesque and the government should step in immediately to put a stop to that."[84]

Unlike their unrepentant leading adviser, Steve Robson,[85] more thoughtful Tories later confessed to their errors. Nevertheless, when David Willetts, the party's policy chief, admitted in 2003 "we were wrong on rail" he was referring to the new structure of the industry rather than the way it had been plundered.[86]

It would be a mistake to think that the Roscos had cornered all the spoils. There was no shortage of takers for the operating franchises. Though a couple turned sour, for most of the operators they were very rewarding. After many years with the West Coast line in Virgin's pocket, one of Richard Branson's colleagues bragged that the franchise was "a licence to print money".[87]

The rolling stock owners were unrepentant about their ill-gotten gains. Profitability having been so easy, they were in no rush to spend. True, by a process of monitoring, evaluation and assessment the Department for Transport was supposed to indicate when new rolling stock was required. But the process was opaque and the order stream faltered even when it finally got going.

Invasion

By the end of the 1990s orders were at last recovering. This was when the final and deadliest blow hit the UK train-builders – the invasion from abroad. As David Gillan, long-suffering director general of the Railway Industry Association, put it, "I don't think the Europeans believed Britain would open up its market to overseas tendering as completely as it has". The result was a stream of orders flowing out from the Roscos, in collaboration with the TOCs, to Continental suppliers.

Buying specialist requirements from abroad was not new. In the 1980s quarry companies and electricity generators – post-privatisation, of course – had imported high-powered locomotives from General Motors. And, although Brush Traction had landed contracts for the Channel Tunnel Shuttle, most of the other equipment had come from the Continent. Moreover, most of the work on the Eurostar passenger trains was carried out in Alsthom/Alstom workshops in France and Belgium.

Although the threat of main line privatisation had crippled new rolling stock business for UK train-builders, London Underground (LU) was still placing large contracts. One of the biggest came up in 1994 in the form of a £750m contract for new Northern Line trains. The order went, however, to GEC-Alsthom/Alstom, by now rapidly assuming a French identity, with most of the work directed to the Continent.

These were emotional times, and a valiant ABB works manager broke down as he announced the news to assembled colleagues in the "U" shop at Derby, where "everyone had worked so hard as a team" on Central Line trains for LU.[88] Transport Secretary Brian Mawhinney could only come up with the callous comment that the project was "a perfect example of how the Government's deal-driven Private Finance Initiative [PFI – later hopelessly discredited] can deliver more and better quality investment in essential projects".[89]

In contrast to their predecessors in British Rail, loyalty to UK train-building was rarely in the lexicon of the new railway owners and operators. Porterbrook, whose founders had taken £73m off the taxpayer, cheerfully handed big orders for haulage locomotives to General Motors plants in Canada and Spain. And Angel Trains gave a succession of contracts for mainline multiple units to Siemens.

The headline deal was one involving South West Trains as the franchise holder. South West was controlled by Stagecoach, a company whose main shareholder, Brian Souter, carved his fortune out of undervalued bus services privatised in the 1980s. He then replayed this winning trick with Porterbrook in the 1990s. Somehow, the extraordinary generosity of the British taxpayer gave him no pause in handing a £750m contract to a foreign manufacturer.[90]

By this stage the supplier concerned, Siemens, was being given so much UK business that it had to spend £7m modifying – that is, downgrading – its Wildenrath test track to match the dilapidated conditions its trains would face in Britain.[91]

Even more controversial was a huge agreement announced in February 2009. This was the £7.5bn project to replace the magnificent 125s and 225s on the Intercity routes, dubbed the Intercity Express Programme (IEP). The decision was devastating for UK train-builders (by this stage, of course, only Bombardier at Derby) because the consortium involved was led by Hitachi, based in Japan. Hitachi has subsequently opened what is ostensibly a train-building plant but is in reality just a final assembly warehouse, or what used to be known as a "screwdriver" operation.

There was a lot of windowdressing in the announcement. In presenting the news, Labour minister Geoff Hoon made the absurd claim that 12,500 jobs would be created or saved by the decision.[92] He failed to mention that most of those jobs would not actually be in the UK. True, Hitachi has since opened a "global rail headquarters" in London[93] and a workshop at Newton Aycliffe in County Durham.[94] But its UK workforce will be engaged in the final assembly of components designed, developed and manufactured in Japan.[95] It is yet another wretched instance of the hollowing-out and deskilling of what remains of Britain's industrial economy.

Further blows to the future of UK train-building came with the announcement in 2011 of a £3bn contract with Siemens for 1,200 units for the Thameslink route. The decision was confirmed in December 2012, with a vapid comment from Conservative minister Teresa Villiers that the contract offered "the best value for the UK taxpayer". Before long Bombardier had to cut its Derby workforce by another 1,200 craftsmen.

March of the Makers?

By now the alarm bells were at last ringing with a government that had earlier announced a "March of the Makers". In late 2011, Vince Cable, one of the few senior ministers to have any working experience of industry, announced £80m financial support for a sizeable order for Bombardier to make multiple units for the Southern rail franchise. Almost uniquely, the chief executive of Southern had expressed mild interest in the fate of the UK rolling stock industry.

There was hope of a new approach to contracts involving public money (which is of course still the case with the "privatised" railways). There would in future be a more careful approach to the drafting of tender documents. Instead of confining themselves to narrow cost considerations (the cliché of "value for the taxpayer"), tendering would have to take account of wider industrial, economic and social issues. All of this has long been entirely legitimate within European Union public purchasing rules. The EU philosophy of an open and even-handed market for bidders was never intended to drive industries into annihilation.

However, 2015 brought a new Conservative government, and the new climate that had been tentatively emerging under the coalition government

Train Wreck

receded again. In 2016 a £490m contract for hundreds of carriages for Northern Rail was awarded to CAF of Spain. The deal was signed off by Arriva Rail North, which had just been handed the Northern Rail franchise.[96]

Fortunately, the impact on Bombardier was alleviated when later in the year the firm won a £1bn contract to make 660 carriages for East Anglia, where Abellio had retained the franchise.[97] However, though the Derby factory was saved from closure Bombardier said its survival still depended on winning more business. Its future seemed only a little more secure when a £1bn contract to supply and maintain the rolling stock for the new Crossrail service was awarded to the Derby factory in 2014.[98]

Behind any lasting change of heart on the part of the UK authorities has to be the realisation that a major reason for the plight of industries like train-building is the failure of governments, both Conservative and Labour, to formulate anything resembling industrial policy – even to the extent permitted by Brussels.[99] This means they have allowed manufacturing to be picked over by foreign firms in a way that would be inconceivable in France, Germany or Italy.

Rail expert and historian Christian Wolmar quotes a professor of European business law on the long tradition of British failure to understand the finer points of European legislation. "The British tend always to go for the lowest bid but actually they could take into account many other considerations."[100] The problem is: "The UK decided quite a while ago that it would have a competition policy, and no other considerations."[101]

If yet another British industry is not to fade into history, those forgotten considerations must be dusted off, polished up and put back on the rails. Brexit will at least remove an important alibi for future governments who fail to support UK manufacturing.

It would be difficult to find an industry more damaged by official policy than railway engineering and rolling stock. Not so much the vagaries and parsimony of funding when the railways were publicly owned, extremely debilitating though these were, but the near-lethal injury caused by the needless and badly handled privatisation of the 1990s. Added to this was the insult of looting – by private, professional and City interests – on a scale almost unmatched in the whole wretched history of state sell-offs. Restoring this industry will take a commitment and clarity of vision foreign to government since that appallingly destructive era.

CHAPTER 10

Shipbuilding Founders

> *In my early days I was afraid to come to John Brown's because the requirements were so high, and I felt as a tradesman that I might not meet up with what they wanted. So that when I did come in here eventually, I felt an immense pride.*
>
> Shipyard worker, *The British Seafarer, BBC Radio 4, 1980*[1]

Island Nation

Quizzed in a poll some years ago about the commercial activities they associated with Britain, a sample of Germans was none too sure. Aero engines? Racing cars? Pharmaceuticals? Strangely, none of these. Theatre? Design? Architecture? Yes, these scored points. But the biggest vote was for financial services. Fair enough, this was pre-crisis, pre-recession, and the City still had a half-decent name for its expertise.

The surprise was the second most popular choice. It was ships and shipbuilding. Which just goes to show that popular perception can run far behind the reality. Britain long ago ceased to be in the first division for shipping, and in shipbuilding its pre-eminence faded even further back. Nowadays Britain builds fewer ships than any other maritime country, and in world terms it is just a speck on the charts. Without naval shipbuilding it would not even be on those charts.

Which is extraordinary for an island nation, dependent on trade and with a long history at the forefront of developments in ships and shipbuilding. True, Britain's real ship design revolutions were not realised until the 1840s and 1850s, when vessels like *Great Britain*, the first screw-driven steamer, and Brunel's mighty *Great Eastern*, the first all-iron ship, were launched. But others soon followed, and by the 1860s iron was rapidly replacing timber in Britain's oceangoing ships. Having been on a par with the US until mid-century, when wood was still supreme, UK shipbuilding rapidly pulled ahead once the new technologies had been demonstrated.

The combination of an advanced iron industry, expertise in steam and a fast-growing merchant fleet proved invincible, a position reinforced by the rapid switch to steel once it became cheaper. Charles Parsons' development of the turbine for marine applications gave Britain's shipbuilders yet another advantage. By the 1890s the UK was producing three-quarters of the world's shipping.[2]

At the turn of the century other nations, such as the US, Germany and France, were emerging as builders of modern ships, and Britain's share of the market inevitably fell.[3] Nevertheless, it was still supplying over 60 per cent of the world's ships on the eve of the First World War. Though Britain supplied substantial tonnages for overseas buyers, however, only about a quarter of UK shipbuilding was for export. And to its ultimate detriment the industry was to remain heavily dependent on domestic custom for the rest of its life.

In total shipbuilding employed around 200,000 people, most with craft skills. Conditions were often gruelling. Well into the twentieth century a working week of 54 hours was common, with men toiling outdoors without breaks in the cold and wet of the northern winters. The bulk of the workforce was employed on a casual basis and subject to an hour's notice.[4] The resulting insecurity and group loyalty prompted militant political attitudes and a hostility to change in working practices that was profound and enduring.[5]

The geography of British shipbuilding was well defined. The most important centre was the Clyde. A stretch of this modest river, extending 20 miles downstream from the centre of Glasgow, offered the biggest concentration of shipyards and marine engineering in the world. Legendary names such as John Brown, Fairfields, Lithgows, Scotts and Yarrows were supported by engine builders, boiler makers, foundries, steel fabricators, chandlers, finishing trades and a host of other activities supplying the great yards.

Comparable with Clydeside in output was a trio of rivers in the north-east of England. The Tyne, Tees and Wear supported such companies as Austin & Pickersgill, Clelands, William Doxford, Smiths Dock and Swan Hunter. Again, these were a focus for regional clusters of steelworks, engine builders and engineers. The Mersey was home to another grouping of shipbuilders, of which the most prominent was Cammell Laird at Birkenhead. And, in addition to its base on the Tyne, Vickers had a major warship yard at Barrow-in-Furness, in Cumberland.

Other shipbuilding centres included Aberdeen (Hall Russell), Belfast (Harland & Wolff and Workman, Clark), Dundee (Caledon), Goole, Lowestoft, Portsmouth and the West Country, notably Appledore and Falmouth. On the lower Thames the bigger operations had, by the early twentieth century, moved elsewhere.[6] One of the few major seaboard cities without significant shipyards was Cardiff.

The Clyde and Belfast were noted for passenger liners, Tyneside and Barrow for warships, and the Tees and Wear for cargo ships, freighters and tankers. The smaller yards of the east and south coasts made tramp ships, coasters, trawlers and specialist vessels. And in addition to the commercial yards were the great royal dockyards such as Portsmouth, which had built warships for the navy since the reign of King Henry VIII.

The commercial yards often had close ties with the shipping lines, and shipbuilding activity tended to follow their needs. For most of the twentieth century the merchant marine assumed an astonishingly favoured position in British commercial life, with shipowners often at the core of the financial and industrial elite and enjoying a privileged role in the City.[7]

Supremacy Challenged

At the start of the twentieth century the UK accounted for at least half the global tonnage of merchant shipping. Though the fleet was now expanding more slowly, launchings rose from 1.2 million tonnes a year in the 1890s to 1.4 million tonnes a year in the 1900s and a peak 1.9 million tonnes on the eve of the First World War.

This was in spite of growing competition from the more export-oriented German yards. Leading the rivals was the legendary Blohm & Voss of Hamburg, whose founders had learnt their trade in Britain. Returning home, they opened what was to become one of the world's great shipyards, launching ocean liners and the mighty warships that challenged the Royal Navy at Jutland. In the words of a commentator, "[t]o Blohm and Voss goes some of the credit – or blame – for loosening Britain's nineteenth century stranglehold on world shipbuilding and for establishing Germany as…an envied and feared industrial and military giant".[8]

The loss of eight million tonnes of British shipping in the First World War, coupled with reviving world trade, fuelled a post-war boom. In 1920 British yards raised their output to an all-time peak of over two million tonnes, with tonnage under construction approaching four million tonnes. Production constraints in other countries pushed new orders on to British yards, and the proportion made for foreign owners reached an unprecedented 40 per cent.

The boom was brief. International trade was still lower than it had been in 1914. Shipping business slowed, new-build orders shrank, and there was a swift decline in warship commissioning. In a business that was becoming increasingly volatile, merchant shipbuilding plunged to 650,000 tonnes in 1923.

By the mid-1920s, however, activity was picking up again. One of the more aggressive British lines, Furness Withy, broke with precedent by ordering five vessels from a German yard. Nevertheless, the UK share of world shipbuilding actually rose from 49 per cent in 1922–25 to 53 per cent in 1927–30.

The upturn was not sustained. This time a cyclical fall in orders was aggravated by the Depression. Merchant shipbuilding collapsed, with completions plunging from 1.5 million tonnes in 1930 to 131,000 tonnes three years later. Many yards fell silent. Unemployment exceeded 60 per cent. The unprecedented situation prompted the first coordinated attempts at rationalisation.

National Shipbuilders Securities, established at government prompting, set about cutting capacity. In total over 30 yards were mothballed. The most dramatic case was on Tyneside, where the closure of Palmer's threw 80 per cent of the population of Jarrow out of work and into desperate poverty. Such terrible events go a long way to explain the difficult labour relations that dogged the industry even when better times returned.

When economic recovery appeared, British yards were for the first time looking slightly behind the times. The switch from riveting to welding caught on late. Shipowners were slow to adopt diesel-fuelling in place of steam. They were also late in exploiting the growth of the tanker trade and other specialist areas.

One aspect the industry could do little about was the rise of subsidy and protection elsewhere. By the late 1930s Germany had confirmed a much stronger position in export markets than the UK, and Japan was fast emerging as a significant player. Both were eager participants in a new naval arms race.

War and Peace

The Second World War encouraged fresh approaches to production, with the Anglo-US alliance allowing for specialisation of output. British skills combined with American mass production to make standardised cargo carriers such as the *Liberty*, with an all-welded hull and low-cost steam engine. In one of the great industrial achievements of the Arsenal of Democracy over 2,700 of these ships were commissioned.

Peacetime brought strong demand and the biggest labour force since 1914. Yet British shipbuilding never quite regained its former scale. At an average of over 1.2 million tonnes, annual output in the second half of the 1940s was well short of all-time highs. And it rarely approached full capacity of 1.7 million tonnes a year. Nevertheless, Britain still accounted for 45 per cent of the tonnage under construction in 1949.

From this point on, however, the UK share of the global market went into continuous decline, slipping to 38 per cent in 1950, 27 per cent in 1954 and 21 per cent in 1956. This was not for want of demand. The Korean War and European economic recovery stimulated a boom, but although UK output reached a new short-term peak at nearly 1.5 million tonnes in 1955 it was simply not keeping up with the growth in the world market.

One reason was competition. Despite only being allowed to re-enter the international market in 1949–50,[9] Germany and Japan were resurgent, and Scandinavia and the Netherlands were strong contenders. These rivals had newer facilities than British yards, used more modern techniques and concentrated on products with greater growth prospects. Where British yards were still launching general cargo ships and cargo/passenger liners, others were developing expertise in tankers,[10] bulk carriers and specialised vessels.

Britain's deep-seated reluctance to invest was glaringly obvious. Twenty years on a *Financial Times* profile of one of the leading yards was devastating: "There is not much doubt that Swan Hunter is the most versatile of British Shipbuilders' companies and has a reputation for building extremely sophisticated vessels with the minimum of fuss. …This reputation for good workmanship has, however, been achieved largely without investment in modern facilities. The tooling in some of the yards is pre-war."[11]

As in other cyclical businesses, British shipbuilders looked back to the harrowing experiences of the 1930s rather than the buoyant conditions of the post-war world. Only one new greenfield yard was opened in the decade after the war, there was little radical modernisation and limited restructuring. Even existing capacity was not fully realised, with production persistently falling short of potential by 300,000 tonnes a year.

Unfortunately, the British merchant marine was itself stagnating. The growth of fleets in other European countries, the drift to flags of convenience and the erosion of captive Commonwealth markets were partly to blame, as was the bias towards general cargo and passenger ships in the UK fleet when tankers were the fastest-growing sector of the business.

A recurrent complaint from the British was the persistence of protection and subsidy for their competitors. Cabotage rules effectively closed the US, Germany, France, Italy, Spain and Japan to British contenders, and shipbuilders in these and other countries benefitted from valuable financial incentives.

Though there had been limited government measures before the war, the British authorities in the 1950s were averse to intervention. Instead, they stressed the need for the industry to find its own ways to adapt. Yet, there was growing awareness that, although British skills, construction and build quality remained first class, low productivity, high costs and poor labour relations were hampering competitiveness.

The post-war boom faltered. Shipowners had rushed to order Cape Size tankers and bigger bulk carriers in the wake of the 1956 Suez crisis, but while the industry was absorbing this capacity the global economy slowed. The year 1956 had seen Japan launch more merchant tonnage than the UK for the first time, and Germany followed suit two years later. A growing problem was desertion by the British shipowners. In 1959 the UK became, for the first time in its history, a net importer of ships.[12]

Geddes and After

Just in time, the market once again came to the rescue. By the mid-1960s world order books were rebuilding and over the following decade they grew sixfold. The UK industry benefitted, with production reviving to a million tonnes in 1964 and an average 1.2–1.3 million tonnes a year for the next decade. At the worst point of the downturn in 1963 the government had at last introduced a Shipbuilding Credit Scheme, which yielded £75m and a sharp upturn in orders. Although activity levels were more respectable, however, the UK's standing was continuing to slide, its share of world launchings dropping from 10 per cent in 1964 to less than 4 per cent ten years later.

The underlying economics of the industry were raising concern. An early move on the part of the interventionist Labour government that took office in 1964 was to commission the Geddes Report of March 1966.[13]

The report pointed to a multiplicity of fiercely independent firms, short-term management philosophies, poor labour relations, high levels of absenteeism, inefficient deployment of resources, and weaknesses in research, planning and marketing. There was strong evidence of a link between low levels of investment and chronic labour problems. Worse, Geddes highlighted profits and cash flows that were wholly inadequate to sustain the yards.[14]

Sensibly, Geddes recommended concentration into four or five merchant groups, three naval yards and four engine builders. It urged reformation in employment conditions, labour relations and working procedures. And it proposed state funding for restructuring via a Shipbuilding Industry Board (SIB).

Crises in Scotland and Ulster

Before Geddes had even reported, the industry was hit by a crisis. This was the bankruptcy of Fairfields. Since 1958 there had been half a dozen yard closures on the Clyde, but apart from Harland & Wolff's Linthouse these had involved small operations and orderly rationalisations.[15] Fairfields was different. It was one of the oldest yards on the river and one of the biggest. But a ten-year modernisation programme had left it indebted, and although it had a two-year book its orders were loss-making. In February 1965 it filed for bankruptcy.

Rescue came under the leadership of Iain Stewart, a noted Scots industrialist. He engineered a new start with the Fairfield Experiment. An enthusiastic government acquired 50 per cent ownership, and funds were raised from private and union sources. Resenting the shoring up of struggling competition, however, an incorrigibly individualistic industry was less pleased.

Nevertheless, some of the leading shipbuilders were persuaded by SIB funding to participate. One of the bigger groups, Upper Clyde Shipbuilders (UCS), brought together Barclay Curle, John Brown, Connell, Fairfields, Stephen and Yarrow, though the last – still profitable – was a reluctant and semi-detached partner.

On the Lower Clyde, Scotts, Lithgow and Greenock Dockyard eventually formed a single group. In the north-east of England two combines emerged, one led by Swan Hunter on the Tyne and the other by Austin & Pickersgill on the Wear. There were also mergers involving smaller concerns such as Caledon and Robb on the east coast of Scotland and Thornycroft and Vosper on England's south coast.

This left four major operations – Cammell Laird on the Mersey, Doxford & Sunderland on the Wear, Harland & Wolff in Belfast and Vickers at Barrow-in-Furness – unaffected by reorganisation. And there was little restructuring of the struggling engine-building sector.

In the herculean task of pushing a venerable industry into the modernisation that would allow it to survive Geddes could claim a few successes, but no victories.

At the very moment Fairfields was facing bankruptcy, a tempest was brewing across the Irish Sea. Contract losses, modernisation costs and underperformance by its Scottish subsidiaries had culminated in losses for Belfast's giant Harland & Wolff. Its status as Ulster's largest employer secured financial assistance from the Northern Ireland government, and funding from the SIB was enough to stave off bankruptcy.

Meanwhile, the yards tacked together in Upper Clyde Shipbuilders had very different cultures and histories. Worse, the group was still hopelessly undercapitalised,[16] leaving it short of finance not just for investment but even for day-to-day business. Moreover, official encouragement was replaced by a much more restrictive attitude to SIB assistance after a Conservative government took office in 1970. Despite new management, a full order book and progress towards profitability, in June 1971 UCS went into liquidation.

The crisis was precipitated by a new government policy of not supporting "lame ducks".[17] Faced by the imminent closure of the UCS yards, shop stewards such as Jimmy Reid and Jimmy Airlie led a disciplined work-in, financed, among others, by John Lennon. Strong popular support prompted an official change of heart and fresh finance.

Three of the yards were reorganised into Govan Shipbuilders and one (John Brown) was sold to Houston-based Marathon Oil for rig production. This was despite the caustic observations of one of the American executives, struck by the contrast between the skill and pride of the workforce and the antiquated equipment they had to work with.[18] The lone profitable partner, Yarrows, withdrew from UCS.

One other group had turned to government for assistance shortly before UCS. This was Cammell Laird, which had incurred heavy losses through fixed price contracts and late completions. Mainly a warship builder, the company was ineligible for SIB funds but on the eve of the 1970 election it was offered a substantial loan through the Industrial Reorganisation Corporation. This commitment was sustained by the new Conservative government despite its hard line on industrial casualties. The funding of Cammell Laird brought total government assistance to the big three of UK shipbuilding to nearly £140m.

There were notable exceptions to the pattern of struggling shipyards. Austin & Pickersgill on the Wear made a profitable living with its standardised bulk carriers. Neighbouring Doxford & Sunderland had modernised in the early 1970s and only got into trouble because of losses outside shipbuilding. The Appledore shipyard in Devon remained viable, as did the smaller south coast operations of Vosper and Thornycroft.

Ironically, the crisis developing in British shipbuilding had coincided with a marked upturn in business conditions. This only emerged once the economy had been stabilised by the new Labour government after Chancellor Reginald Maudling's reckless "dash for growth" in the early 1960s. More to the point, a more generous flow of SIB funds helped yards to win orders. And, paradoxically, the tail-end of the long post-war economic upswing was marked by rocketing world shipbuilding orders, their ascent briefly accelerated by the Yom Kippur war in 1973.

False Recovery

Following the massive injection of finance into the industry from around 1966 on, British shipping was distinctly buoyant. By 1973 the investment in new tonnage had reached astonishing levels, equivalent to a quarter of all capital spending by British manufacturing industry.[19]

Shockingly, little of this money went to British shipbulding. The Heath government was remarkably careless about how the subsidies thrown at the shipowners were being spent. State subventions, investment allowances and other incentives were handed to the powerful shipping lines with no conditions on where their new vessels were built.[20] This was a scandalous contrast to other maritime countries such as France and Germany, where there were implicit or explicit requirements to buy domestic. In the UK, important firms such as European Ferries never bought British.[21]

Nevertheless, business did pick up at UK yards. Output of ships rose from a million tonnes in 1969[22] to over 1.3 million tonnes the following year, and it averaged around 1.2 million tonnes for the next three years. The year 1973 saw new orders approach 4.4 million tonnes and total work booked reached 7.5 million tonnes. Unfortunately, this only encouraged complacency. The shipping business was actually at a classic cyclical peak and when the world economy turned down it contracted fast.

The terms on which British shipbuilders were winning business often remained uneconomic, and the Heath government had to acquire all the equity in Govan Shipbuilders and controlling stakes in Cammell Laird and (indirectly) Harland & Wolff. So the tide was already flowing in the direction of state involvement when a new Labour government took office in 1974.

The previous year had seen a party/union report which recognised the industry's challenges and recommended state ownership. While preparations were made for nationalisation, a new £65m shipbuilding intervention fund was established to sustain some sort of order book.

British Shipbuilders

At vesting day in July 1977 the assets of British Shipbuilders (BS) included nearly 30 shipbuilding, engineering and training companies, and more new-build and repair yards were added soon after. Even without Harland & Wolff, which remained outside BS, the new corporation had a daunting portfolio. It included 32 shipyards, 19 ship repair yards and six marine engineering works. BS now controlled 97 per cent of mainland merchant shipbuilding, the whole of warship and slow speed diesel engine production, and half the ship repair capacity.

Though these assets generated sales of over £700m, their book value was less than £140m, profits were barely £9m and 15 companies were loss-making. Despite their plight, the Shipbuilders and Repairers National Association (SRNA) and its Conservative allies put up strenuous opposition to nationalisation.

They merely succeeded in delaying it by two crucial years, ensuring that the new corporation would be launched into the gale now blowing through shipbuilding. From its 1974 peak global output halved in less than four years and it remained depressed for another decade. British completions plunged from over a million tonnes in 1977 and 1978 to less than 700,000 tonnes in 1979 and only 427,000 tonnes in 1980 – the lowest total since 1933.

Though the downturn in shipbuilding was worldwide, at least one country stood against the tide. This was Korea. In a fascinating replay of history, when they had transferred their knowledge to nascent industries on the Continent, British naval architects and technicians were now taking their skills to Korea. There were 40 technology transfer contracts from the UK alone and, as one industry veteran put it, "[t]he major Korean shipyards were built by frustrated Brits who couldn't get things done at home".[23] The Koreans could not have wished for a better pedigree. Between 1980 and 1986 they doubled capacity.

Admirable Admirals

In its early days British Shipbuilders was blessed with impressive leaders. For the first three years the chairman was Admiral Anthony Griffin, former controller of the navy and a passionate advocate for Britain's maritime heritage.[24] Griffin had the daunting task of reconciling the rugged individualists who managed the yards and the doughty trade unionists who represented their employees.

He nevertheless negotiated a corporate plan that projected cuts of a third in capacity and employment. But the scope for planned rationalisation was once again overtaken by events. Orders for new-build were still sliding, the slump had pushed the repair yards into heavy losses, and engine-building had virtually stopped. In its first two years BS ran up a trading loss of nearly £160m.

For any administration this would be disquieting. For the Thatcher government, which had a distaste for heavy industry surpassed only by its abhorrence of public ownership, it was anathema. Griffin was replaced by Robert Atkinson, who had experience in shipbuilding as well as the navy. Able and fiercely patriotic,[25] Atkinson promptly reorganised the corporation, closed several operations, cut merchant yard employment by a third through voluntary redundancies and slashed the losses.

Unfortunately, the improvement then went into reverse, partly due to Atkinson's pursuit of offshore business. The development of the North Sea oilfields had been an extraordinary technical success but it was being marred by the loss of rig and platform orders to foreign yards. Atkinson was naturally determined that more of this business should stay at home.

The BS shipyards which took on this work were not really ready for it. Nor did the home side help. Even the state-owned British National Oil Corporation (BNOC), a natural ally for a Buy British policy, placed two big orders with Continental yards. It only awarded a third to BS after mild intervention by an otherwise indifferent Conservative government.

"Margaret Wants Rid of Shipbuilding"[26]

There was another problem. Atkinson stoutly opposed government plans for piecemeal privatisation of the warship yards, which were still profitable. He had a vision for Britain's magnificent shipbuilding heritage. The government did not. Indeed, the prime minister "wanted rid of shipbuilding". Norman Lamont, a struggling merchant banker who became a minister for industry in June 1983, was totally unsympathetic to Atkinson's view and "only seemed happy when I [Atkinson] had closed down a yard or laid off 500 men".[27]

Once he had retired, Atkinson's verdict was damning. In late 1984 he accused the government of doing all in its power to force the extinction of shipbuilding because of political dogma. He said that during his period at BS he was never once asked about research and development or the future of the industry. "But if I talked about closures or redundancy, their eyes shone."[28] Worse than that, Conservative dogma had actually made it even more difficult for shipbuilding to survive. Access to a huge Brussels fund which paid 20–25 per cent of the cost of a ship to compete with Japan and Korea was scandalously denied to British Shipbuilders. This was simply because the government wanted Brussels' approval for privatisation.[29]

Norman Tebbit, who took over as secretary of state for industry in October 1983, consigned Atkinson to that growing band of distinguished public servants in whom the government was "disappointed". Tebbit had form. As early as 1979, when a trade minister, he had made it clear that the fate of British shipping, as much as its shipbuilding, was a matter of complete indifference.[30] An indifference which could only be compared with the truculent apathy of Labour's Dick Marsh when he was put in charge of the railways a few years earlier.

In his attitudes Tebbit was, of course, in step with colleagues, above all the prime minister herself.[31] As one commentator was to put it, years later, what was so baffling and appalling about the attitude of Mrs Thatcher and her keenest cronies in handling sectors such as shipbuilding was not the desire to privatise but "the panting eagerness to get rid of entire industries".[32]

The indifference was not shared by some of the older backbenchers. In a 1986 Bow Group paper Edward du Cann MP belatedly called for the government to abandon its blind adherence to free market ideology in shipping to avert a "catastrophic" decline in the fleet. By then the UK-owned and -registered fleet had collapsed to less than a third of its 1970s peak.[33] Winston Churchill's vision of the British as "a seafaring race who understand the call of the sea"[34] was indeed being denied.

It would be wrong to assume that apathy bordering on hostility pervaded the entire government. Underlying ideological tension continued to flare up long after British Shipbuilders had been scuttled. August 1994 found Michael Portillo, chief secretary to the Treasury and fervid Thatcherite, upbraiding Michael Heseltine for failing to extol policies that might cut taxation by slashing funds for industry.[35]

An advocate for measured intervention, Heseltine was resisting Treasury demands for termination of any support for the relics of UK shipbuilding. An immediate consequence of Portillo's stance was the resignation of Noel Davis, chief executive of Vickers Shipbuilding and Engineering (VSEL) and president of the Engineering Employers Federation, from the Institute of Directors (IoD). The IoD had been making its usual nauseating obeisance to Conservative government policies.[36]

Sell-Off Day

A decade earlier the replacement for Robert Atkinson was stepping forward to head British Shipbuilders. This was Graham Day, later to lead Rover Group. His first priority might have been to persuade British shipowners to patronise British yards. Compared with 77 per cent in France and 82 per cent in Germany, only 44 per cent of their new vessels were built at home.[37] Instead his mission was to privatise the warship builders in short order. This did not stop him making the first disposal that of a merchant yard, Scott Lithgow. After 3,000 redundancies Trafalgar House acquired the yard for £20m in March 1984, in a deal that somehow cost BS over £71m.

Now it was the turn of the warship builders. First was Brooke Marine of Lowestoft, sold to a management buyout (MBO) in March 1985. The following month saw Yarrows go to GEC for £34m. Later in the year Vosper Thornycroft went to its management for £18.5m, and early in the new year Swan Hunter was handed to its own management for £1.5m. Hall Russell, a small warship builder in Aberdeen, was sold to a local consortium in March 1986, and at about the same time the Vickers Shipbuilding and Engineering (VSEL) grouping – which included Cammell Laird – was sold to a MEBO for £60m.

Day's job finished, he went off to Rover and the leadership of British Shipbuilders passed to Philip Hares. He and his successor John Lister presided over a sad shadow of what had been. By mid-1985 merchant yard employment had sunk to just 8,400 and, robbed of critical mass and valuable specialisms, BS was actually recording lower productivity and higher unit losses than ever before.

Yet another minister, Ken Clarke, was now responsible for shipbuilding. His contribution was furtive lobbying for the final extermination of BS. In public he hinted at further closures with a breezy reference to the reduction of France's industry to a single yard. This was both inaccurate, since French shipbuilding was now in two groupings, one naval and one merchant (both of which have since done rather well) and not pertinent, since France had traditionally had a much smaller industry than the UK.

Overriding John Lister, Clarke pressed for the sale of the remaining BS operations.[38] The modernised facilities at Govan were handed to Norway's Kvaerner for just £1.3m. And at the end of 1988 Appledore and Ferguson were given away at a cost to the corporation of over £7m. North East Shipbuilders, including the formerly successful Austin & Pickersgill, was closed.

By Easter the following year the rest had gone. This included the Clark-Kincaid engine builder, which went to its management for just £3. Naturally they soon passed a controlling stake on to Norway's Kvaerner – for a lot more money.

British Shipbuilders had finally sunk, without trace.

Refuge in Repair and Maintenance

Its appalling demise brought to a close a decade in which shipbuilding had suffered more in Britain than in any other country. There had been a fall of over 75 per cent in jobs in the UK compared with a decline of 19 per cent in Italy and a *rise* of 37 per cent in Germany. The tonnage of shipping built in Britain fell 81 per cent, but in Italy it actually *rose* more than 60 per cent.[39]

All but two of the British yards still open either took refuge in ship repair and maintenance (Ailsa, Appledore and Austin & Pickersgill) or eked out a living from small, specialised vessels (Ferguson) and rare government contracts (Cammell Laird). The exception was Govan, which, after its takeover by Kvaerner, worked on chemical and gas carriers, a field in which its new parent specialised. After heavy losses in other areas, however, Kvaerner sold Govan to GEC-Marconi in October 1989, and the new owner promptly converted the yard to naval work.

This was the end of significant merchant shipbuilding on the mainland.

But not quite the end of the industry in the British Isles. Harland & Wolff had remained in business through the long recession in shipbuilding. By the mid-1980s the yard had ventured into the market for more complex ships but was still making losses. The Westminster government put it up for sale. Potential buyers included tanker owner Ravi Tikoo, who, in the spirit of the magnificent *Canberra*, launched in Belfast in the 1960s, wanted to follow it with a great cruise liner. Predictably, inadequate government incentives scuppered the project and in 1989 the yard was sold to a management buyout.

This was led by chief executive John Parker and backed by Norwegian ship-owner Fred Olsen. Spells in tankers, bulk carriers and then in offshore vessels proved challenging and work in more conventional shipbuilding began to run out, particularly after the Cunard line showed its familiar lack of support by ordering a new liner from France rather than Belfast. Harland & Wolff opted for heavy engineering and in 2003 the yard launched its last vessel.

The long history of merchant shipbuilding in these islands was almost at an end.

Warship Builders Fight On

The warship sector lived to fight another day. Not all of it, since there was major restructuring in the wake of Graham Day's privatisations. Hall Russell went into liquidation in 1988 but subsequently re-emerged as part of a larger ship repair group. Brooke Marine downsized to yachts before liquidating in 1993. Swan Hunter eventually closed, its equipment hawked off to India in 2007. Yarrows was sold by GEC/Marconi to BAE Systems (BAES). Shorn of Cammell Laird, which closed most of its operations in 1992, Vickers went to BAES in 1995. Govan was bought by BAES in 1999. After protracted manoeuvrings, Vosper Thornycroft shipbuilding activities also went to BAES when the latter bought out the stake in their BVT joint venture in 2009.

The Ministry of Defence (MoD) was now dealing with one main contractor in the procurement of warships. This was a reversal of the muddled philosophy which had previously prevailed, when the MoD followed competition dogma by trying to keep a number of players in the field. The policy had led to some unfortunate decisions in the handling of orders in the years following privatisation. It also reflected contractual tensions between the MoD and BAES during the 1990s and 2000s.

The resentments were mutual. In 2004, when there were rumours that BAES might sell its shipbuilding side, defence minister Geoff Hoon warned that in the interests of sovereignty he would veto the sale of the warship interests. The latter were responsible for the work on the Trident and other submarine programmes, while the surface yards were preparing for the new Queen Elizabeth-class aircraft carriers.

The disposal by British Shipbuilders of its warship yards still left an issue for a government which held as an article of faith that when it came to management private would always be better than public. What to do with the royal dockyards? These were the great complexes that had for centuries built, serviced and repaired ships for the Royal Navy.

In July 1985 Michael Heseltine, for the moment secretary of state for industry, coined the unlovely word "contractorisation".[40] The management of the yards would be run through a four-year cycle of competitive bids. In the event both Rosyth and Portsmouth were eventually sold. Portsmouth went to BAES but closed in 2014. Rosyth was managed then eventually purchased by Babcock International and has a role in the construction of the Queen Elizabeth-class carriers and the new Type 31 frigates for the Royal Navy.

Where have the tumultuous upheavals of recent decades left shipbuilding in Britain? Apart from valiant efforts to keep Ferguson building small ferries on the lower river and the two warship yards (Govan and Scotstoun) upstream, the Clyde is silent. Auden's haunting "glade of cranes" is long gone. So deep has been the decay – of tradition, skills and aptitudes – that one of the challenges for BAES has been to change a Scottish mindset now less than thrilled by the idea of shipbuilding. Along with pits and forges, yards have been relegated to folk memory. As the writer Ian Jack movingly put it, there were so many years of grieving when heavy industry was in a kind of hospice. But the bereaved have at last let go.[41]

Elsewhere in Scotland, in Aberdeen, Dundee, Leith and Troon, silence reigns. All that remains beyond the Clyde is the warship activity at Rosyth. On the east coast of England, from the Tyne to Lowestoft, all is quiet save for ship repair and maintenance. In the south, from the Thames to Falmouth, the picture is the same, though Devonport and Portsmouth still service the navy. On the western seaboard, Cammell Laird has intermittently operated on a cottage industry scale in Birkenhead but only the submarine base at Barrow is still a major shipyard. And Belfast? Harland & Wolff has not launched a new ship in years.

Elsewhere in the marine industries the picture is not entirely bleak. The UK retains a useful ship repair capacity. This reflects Britain's location on the great sea-lanes of the world. It also reflects the heartening recovery of the British merchant fleet from its 1980s collapse. Most of the repair capacity is in yards which gave up on new-build. In scale the British ship repair industry is comparable with Spain, Italy and Poland, but far behind Germany and the Netherlands.

The UK also has a presence in marine equipment. Britain is a significant supplier of engines, mainly from Rolls-Royce, and also makes electronic and other specialised equipment.

Yacht-Building

The UK has a fine tradition in smaller boats, and ranks among the larger builders of yachts.[42] Though well behind the big three of Italy, Britain's two leading yacht-makers, Princess Yachts and Sunseeker, ranked fourth and fifth in Europe in recent years. As with so many distinctive UK companies, however, the ownership story has a familiar dismal ring. Both the leaders have sold out to foreign owners. Princess Yachts is now part of the ragbag of interests controlled by LVMH, the Paris-based "luxury goods" conglomerate, and Sunseeker is in Chinese hands.

The smaller yards often import hulls from the Far East and finish them in the UK, so the domestic value added is less impressive. However, bigger vessels have occasionally been made in the UK. The magnificent *Vava II*, at 4,000 tonnes the largest private yacht launched in Britain, was built for London-based entrepreneur Ernesto Bertarelli in 2012 in a combined operation at the Appledore and Devonport dockyards.[43] Appledore has since closed.

The French Way

Could the story of British shipbuilding have been different? A glance at its Continental rivals gives the answer. Though it has ceded ground to Asia, Europe's shipyards still dominate in cruise ships, where they have a near-monopoly, offshore supply vessels (over 40 per cent), luxury yachts (65 per cent) and military craft.

Among the great survivors is France. Like Britain it was hit by crises in the 1970s and 1980s. But there the parallels end. Drastic cutbacks and rationalisation were required. But in contrast to the Thatcher administration the Mitterrand government of the 1980s was determined to save as much as possible. Among its imaginative instruments was a Ministry of the Sea. It also committed huge funds for rationalisation, retraining and modernisation.[44] Eventually the industry was tailored into two groups, one specialising in warships and the other in merchant vessels.

Both have had to navigate stormy seas but have won France a rewarding place in world markets for naval vessels and specialised merchant ships. DCNS, France's naval shipbuilder, operates from ten sites and has developed an impressive foreign clientele. Among major contracts it has sold submarines to Brazil, Chile, India, Malaysia and Poland. And in 2016 it won an extraordinary deal, valued at €34bn, to build a new submarine fleet for Australia.

At least some of France's clients would once have been customers for British yards. But BAES, custodian of Britain's warship tradition, has been an also-ran. For the Scottish yards the last significant order was two frigates for the Malaysian Navy in 2001–02.[45] In 2012 BAES switched an order for three small ocean patrol ships from Trinidad to Brazil, where the vessels were to be built.[46]

Meanwhile, France's main merchant yard, Chantiers de l'Alantique at Saint-Nazaire on the Loire estuary, has made a success of cruise ships. It reinforced its position with an order for four vessels in early 2016, and shortly after launched the world's biggest cruise ship, the 227,000 tonne *Harmony of the Seas*.

Chantiers de l'Atlantique also retains a capacity for warship construction, building two much-admired Mistral-class advanced amphibious assault ships (a kind of compact aircraft carrier). Both were originally for Russia, but after the annexation of Crimea one of the contracts was diverted to Egypt.

Originally established with the help of John Scott of Greenock in the 1860s,[47] the yard has had a number of owners over the years. After severe crises in the 1980s and 1990s it reorganised and retrained a workforce so combative it had earned the town the nickname *la ville rouge*.[48] By the year 2000 the yard had won 40 per cent of world cruise ship orders, the balance going to other yards in Continental Europe.[49] One of France's former government ministers was adamant: "If the yards had not had subsidies [since phased out] they would have closed long ago."[50]

Eventually Saint-Nazaire came under the control of Korea's STX Corporation in 2008. Wisely, and with no ideological inhibitions, Sarkozy's conservative government took a one-third stake.[51] Similarly, after the bankruptcy of STX threatened to push Saint-Nazaire into the arms of Italy's state-owned Fincantieri in 2017, President Macron briskly renationalised this flagship of France's maritime tradition – to keep it in French hands.

The Spanish Way

Almost as impressive is the recent history of Spanish shipbuilding, particularly in the naval sector. The main player is Navantia, whose origins owe much to technical assistance and investment by Vickers and John Brown in the 1900s. Navantia is still state-owned, and a successful exporter to half a dozen countries.

Following major sales to Norway and Thailand, in 2007 the company won a spectacular coup with a clean sweep of the global competition to rebuild much of Australia's surface fleet. The $11bn deals included three air warfare destroyers and two amphibious assault ships.[52] Yet, like India, Australia was once a natural customer for British yards.[53] Indeed, the Royal Australian Navy picked up a second-hand *Largs Bay* (a smaller version of the ships being supplied by Spain) for just £50–60m in the wake of the 2010 UK defence review.[54]

Spain's success has naturally been built on major government investment. EU enquiries into state funding of well over €3bn in the 1990s and 2000s appear, moreover, to have been quietly shelved.

The German Way

This is also true, perhaps more surprisingly, of Germany, where state-owned Howaldtswerke Deutsche-Werft and Bremer Vulkan benefitted from large subsidies after the fall of communism. In those difficult years five yards in former East Germany received government funding of €3bn.[55] The industry had to endure traumatic closures, major restructuring and fierce industrial strife. But today Germany is still a significant player in cruise ships, where Mayer Werft is a leading contender, builds other sophisticated merchant vessels, and is a leading exporter of surface warships and submarines.

The Italian Way

Though it tut-tutted over the $400m state aid it had received the previous year, *The Economist* was full of praise for Fincantieri, Italy's state-owned shipbuilder.[56] This was the mid-1990s. After re-entering the merchant business following a 25-year absence Fincantieri had captured a big slice of the world order book for cruise ships. The group also made other merchant ships, military vessels, fast ferries and marine engines, and was a leader in new shipping technologies. Italy has had particularly strong support from British lines such as P&O, whose directors – fervent advocates of private industry at home – had no inhibitions in handing vast contracts to Italy's state shipyards.

Fincantieri's accounts are opaque, but there can be no doubt that there has been major financial support from the government over the years. Would Fincantieri still get accolades from *The Economist* today? The answer is surely yes. Very large state subventions necessary during reconstruction phases have helped to build a highly successful operation. Eight shipyards, together with ancillary facilities, make Fincantieri the biggest shipbuilder in Europe and the fourth largest in the world.

The British Way

What has been missing in UK shipbuilding? First, support from the British shipping industry. Historically the main customer for UK yards, once this custom was withdrawn the yards were plunged into an intensely competitive international market. Why did domestic demand sink? One reason was that the merchant fleet, equal first with that of Japan in the 1970s, collapsed when its traditional owners walked away in the 1980s.

The secretive Cayzer dynasty, for example, had sidled into the financial services that became so lucrative under the Thatcher government and only broke cover in a demeaning family squabble in the 2000s.[57] Ironically, the UK merchant marine was by then recovering after supportive policies had been introduced by the Labour government on the initiative of John Prescott.[58]

A profound historic problem lies at the door of British shipping interests. As an American historian has put it, in Britain the names of shipowners were at the core of the financial and industrial elite.[59] However, this favoured sector was not obliged to use its investment subventions to buy from domestic yards like its Continental counterparts. Thanks to one or two outstanding leaders such as Lindsay Alexander, British shipping lines were well to the fore in developments such as containerisation.[60] But domestic shipbuilders drew relatively little benefit when it came to orders for the new vessels.

Lack of loyalty to the home side became much more acceptable in the 1980s, when many collaborative and constructive ways of doing business were jettisoned. A legend in shipping for nearly two centuries, P&O stepped up its overseas orders for vessels once routinely built at home.

A prime example was a 31,000 tonnes luxury ferry for the Hull/Rotterdam route ordered from Japan in 1985.[61] Then followed a stream of orders to state-owned Fincantieri, culminating in two 60,600 tonnes "cruiseferries" in January 1999.[62] P&O's largesse was soon spread even wider, with $2bn worth of orders going to Japan, Italy and France later the same year,[63] and a 76,000 tonnes cruise ship delivered by Mayer Werft in 2000.[64] The new ships were to service a booming demand for cruises, where the market on P&O's own doorstep, the UK, was the largest in Europe. Struggling British yards received not a crumb of all this business.

Under recurrent pressure from short-termist City fund managers executive chairman Jeffrey Sterling, ennobled as "Mrs Thatcher's favourite business man" [yet another one] after long years of financing the Conservative Party, capped a long innings with P&O by selling it off in bits. The highly successful cruise line was handed to its leading US rival.

In a profile of Sterling in the *Financial Times* there was much talk of loyalty, trust and other good old-fashioned virtues.[65] The appalling behaviour of P&O in the wake of its *Herald of Free Enterprise* disaster, Britain's worst peacetime maritime calamity since 1919,[66] went unremarked.

The record at Cunard – US-owned but crewed and promoted as British to its gunwales – is also dispiriting. In 2000 the company ordered its gigantic new flagship, the *Queen Mary II*, from Chantiers de l'Atlantique,[67] and followed this by an order for the 90,000-tonne *Queen Victoria* from Fincantieri.[68]

Life on MARS

The greatest handicap faced by the British merchant shipbuilders was the lack of appropriate state guidance and support.[69] True, like its overseas counterparts, Britain's shipbuilding industry received substantial public subventions. Whether it is to bail out General Motors or revamp a corner shop, restructuring usually costs serious money. Between vesting day and privatisation, the government spent hundreds of millions of pounds on British Shipbuilders. But the finance was all too often directed towards working costs rather than investment in plant, equipment and labour force retraining.

Worse, the political environment in which shipbuilding faced its last desperate crises was characterised by dogma, hostility to traditional industries and ministerial incompetence. The industry should have been steered towards the activities that did so well in the rest of Europe: cruise ships, offshore services, modern ferries, naval craft and other specialities. Instead, British shipbuilding in the 1980s was treated like a tiresome basket case, a stark contrast to the incredible featherbedding that finance got 30 years later.

Subsequent developments have not been reassuring, even in the one area that survives on any sort of scale – military. In clear breach of the sovereign capability rule a £452m order for four MARS (Military Afloat Reach and Sustainability) tankers for the Admiralty in 2012 was given to a Korean company.[70] An offer by Fincantieri to build at least one of the ships in Britain if it won the order was ignored.[71]

This was a bizarre decision for a government whose under-secretary of state for defence (a Thatcherite banker) had only recently stated: "It is about time that the UK woke up to the fact that we have immense engineering skills in Britain, that the companies with these skills are world class and Britain's future prosperity will not be found on the back of financial services."[72] The minister, Gerald Howarth, had been impressed by a visit to Govan.

It is obviously too soon to point to the end of warship building in these islands. Indeed, the orders for five cut-price Type 31 frigates from the Rosyth yard run by Babcock in September 2019 offer a fresh lease of life. But the death of significant merchant shipbuilding is fact. In the words of writer Adam Nicholson, lamenting the neglect of England's historic ships from the more distant past, an entire tranche of national life has been erased from the world.[73]

As the French, the Germans, the Spanish and the Italians have demonstrated, for Britain it could all have been so different.

CHAPTER 11

Electric Shock

> *Between the Industrial Revolution of the 18th and 19th centuries and the Technological Revolution of the 20th century there was a period which has justifiably been called the Machine Age. This was a time when the mechanisms of industrialisation had become well understood and when, perhaps, the more exploitative aspects of the industrialised workplace had been tempered with a little humanity.*
>
> *Jim Lawton, Metropolitan Vickers Electrical Company, 1899–1949[1]*

Late Start

For a country so advanced in mechanical engineering – the harnessing of wind and water, coal and steam to the needs of industry and everyday life – Britain made a late start in the electrical field. Yet the intellectual soil could hardly have been more fertile. The astounding discoveries of William Gilbert, Robert Boyle and Stephen Gray in the early days of the Industrial Revolution were followed by those of Michael Faraday,[2] James Clark Maxwell and William Thomson in the nineteenth century. And the practical applications of electricity were pursued by Peter Watkins and Robert Davidson[3] with the electric motor, Joseph Swan with the incandescent lamp,[4] and Charles Parsons, who invented the steam turbine.

Yet as the nineteenth century drew to a close the leisurely response of industry was of growing concern. "A great many of us…have been alive to the fact…that England is in a deplorably backward state with regard to electrical development. It is extremely painful for anyone who has watched the progress…in America and Germany…to see the thoroughly backward position we are in, in England." This was the lament of Joseph Lawrence, director of the British Westinghouse Electric and Manufacturing Company at its first shareholder meeting in 1899.[5]

Britain's sluggish embrace of the Machine Age remains an enigma. Was the entrepreneurial spirit suffocating in the complacency of late Victorian England?[6] Steam was still king in industry and town gas the major source of lighting. Were vested interests getting in the way of the new technology?

Fortunately, a new generation of entrepreneurs, often American and German, was about to redress Britain's strange backwardness. The twentieth century was to see the emergence of three great British combines in electrical engineering. It was also to witness the annihilation of their legacy in one of the most appalling acts of corporate destruction in modern history.

When US inventor George Westinghouse opened a lavishly equipped factory at Trafford Park in Manchester in 1902, all this lay far ahead. Trafford Park was the world's first industrial estate and Westinghouse its most prestigious resident. For many years the plant remained one of the most important engineering centres in the country.

Metrovicks

But it remained financially overextended, and in 1919 the company merged with the electrical interests of Vickers to form Metropolitan Vickers Electrical (Metrovicks).[7] By the following year the labour force, now based on Tyneside as well as Trafford Park, exceeded 20,000.

The 1920s brought better times for Metrovicks. The First World War cost German electrical engineering its pre-eminence in world markets, where it had once held a 50 per cent share,[8] and British manufacturers were able to catch up.

Metrovicks' production was mainly at the heavy end of the electrical spectrum. Orders flooded in from the newly established Central Electricity

Board,[9] from railways, mines and factories at home, and from export markets in the empire, South America and Eastern Europe.

The company earned an almost legendary reputation for design, quality and durability. In the mid-1970s the Mulungushi hydroelectric dam in Zambia still depended on a turbo-generator which bore the legend *Metropolitan Vickers, Newcastle upon Tyne*. When I visited the little turbine hall, its beautiful machinery was still turning – quietly, dependably, economically – half a century on from its installation.

Nor were the monuments to Metrovicks confined to the Commonwealth. The immaculate turbine installed by the company at a hydroelectric station in far-off Tajikistan only finally stopped turning in 1991. It had run out of the spare parts supplied when the plant was built in the 1940s.[10]

The company had a highly regarded training scheme, and the board was at times composed entirely of former apprentices.[11] Metrovicks was also unusual for a strong emphasis on research. And it was noted for enlightened labour relations, drawing strength from the works committee established in 1917.

By the late 1920s, however, General Electric (GE), the industry leader in the US, was pushing significant restructuring though its UK associate, British Thomson-Houston (BTH). In 1929 Metrovicks was taken under the wing of a new financial holding company, Associated Electrical Industries (AEI).[12]

Having just acquired BTH, AEI promptly became the largest player in the industry. For the next 30 years successive managements struggled to consolidate the two great rival subsidiaries.[13]

British Thomson-Houston

BTH had been formed in 1896 by the US company Thomson-Houston, and the links with General Electric brought an enduring American influence. In comparison with the extravagance of Westinghouse, the birth of BTH was a model of prudence. The Rugby factory commissioned in 1902 was a third the size of Trafford Park. Its output covered a similar range to Westinghouse, with one crucial addition. This was incandescent lamps, a very profitable activity thanks to the international Lamp Ring cartel.

Rugby was to become a legend in electrical engineering, boasting the first electric street lamps, the devising of many domestic appliances, the invention of holography, the design and manufacture of the jet engine, and "the best dynamos and steam turbines ever made".[14] The effects on those who worked there, and their families, were powerful. As with many of Britain's older industrial towns, there was for generations a strong spirit of kinship.[15]

In contrast to the experience in the USA and Germany, the Depression left British electrical engineering remarkably unscathed. Output fell in only one year, 1931.[16] Thereafter, activity rose continuously, with growth rates outpacing even the 1920s and electricity enjoying faster expansion than any other major sector.

An important influence was the development of the National Grid, which allowed rapid advances in electricity consumption. With tariff protection at home and preferential markets in the empire, the 1930s saw British electrical engineering catch up with the best that Germany or the US could offer.

Associated Electrical Industries

Few benefitted more than AEI. But the buoyancy of business masked continuing departmental rivalry. Metrovicks and BTH both worked separately on the world's first jet engine in the 1930s and made competitive bids for a big Argentine contract in the 1950s.

AEI chairman Felix Pole was far too mild to tackle such anomalies and when he retired in 1945 they remained untouched. His distinguished successor, Oliver Lyttelton, was from a very different social mould. But his determination to improve matters had to wait. Post-war recovery dictated production as the priority, and by the time Lyttelton returned as Lord Chandos in 1954 business was reinforced by the long pent-up demand for consumer goods and a UK dependence on electricity twice that of comparable countries.[17]

Chandos was an unrepentant expansionist, and in those sunny years he endorsed a remarkable surge in investment, with capital commitments rising tenfold in the 1950s. Projects included a massive turbo-generator plant at Larne in Northern Ireland in 1957.[18] In 1958 the group could proudly point to 26 new factories and to joint ventures with Thorn Electrical and EMI in consumer products.

The late 1950s and early 1960s saw major new challenges. These included a drive to build much bigger steam generators for the Central Electricity Generating Board (CEGB) now that post-war restrictions had been lifted. This imposed technical strains on AEI.

Urbane, witty and well-connected, Chandos was handicapped by the serpent that so often lurks in the English Eden – class. He was snobbish, particularly towards the diligent engineers who had built the proud institutions that were Metrovicks and BTH.[19] So when conditions turned less favourable and he at last took action he found it as hard as ever to take his staff with him.

The 1960s were more financially testing. When Chandos departed in 1964 there was no tangible improvement and by 1967 the group was ripe for intervention. For the Ministry of Technology (Mintech) and the Industrial Reorganisation Corporation (IRC), set up to foster consolidation in British industry, electrical engineering was a prime target. When GEC made an offer for AEI in September 1967, it was swiftly approved.

AEI was now in the hands of GEC's extraordinary executive chairman, Arnold Weinstock, who promptly set about that long-overdue reorganisation.

English Electric

Weinstock's next target, English Electric (EE), was reputedly the best run of the big electrical combines. The company had its origins in a group of operations brought together just after the First World War. A major constituent, Dick, Kerr,[20] had bought the UK interests of Algemeine Elektrizitäts Gesellschaft (AEG) and Siemens Dynamo from the Custodian of Enemy Property during the conflict.

At the end of the 1920s the company received a big infusion of American finance and a new managing director. George Nelson was an exceptionally able engineer who had spent nearly a decade with Metrovicks. He remained at the head of English Electric for 32 years.

Profitability recovered but remained dependent on heavy electrical equipment. The situation was alleviated only late in the 1930s, when English Electric developed the aircraft interests that were to bring some spectacular achievements in years to come. By 1945 the company claimed to be the largest engineering organisation in the country, noted for its research and training facilities.

English Electric remained in the front rank of heavy electrical engineering in the 1950s, benefitting from big public investment programmes in the UK and Commonwealth. It enjoyed strong positions in aircraft and railway locomotives, and also in electronics through the post-war purchase of the Marconi Company. By 1962, when George Nelson died and his son ("young George") took over as chairman and chief executive, the company had 80,000 employees.

A move to acquire GEC in 1960 had failed, but more successful takeover forays included Elliott Automation in 1967. The following year brought the biggest deal of all, when the management of English Electric was persuaded into a merger with GEC. In reality it was a reverse takeover, since English Electric's turnover was twice that of GEC and it was nowhere near the kind of crisis that had hit AEI.[21] The catalyst was a bid from Plessey. To most observers the Plessey approach made little industrial sense. The government concurred.

GEC

So GEC was drawn into the picture. The authorities still looked favourably on a merger in which English Electric would come under the control of the man regarded as a potential saviour of Britain's industrial heartlands, Arnold Weinstock.

GEC had had modest beginnings. Like many British companies it owed much to the energy and enterprise of immigrants, once again from Germany. Gustav Binswanger (later Byng) and his brother Max moved from Munich to London in 1880 and within a few years they incorporated themselves as the General Electric Company, or GEC.[22]

By this point the dominant presence was Hugo Hirst, also German but more extrovert, ambitious and expansionary than the Byngs. His reign lasted from 1906, when he became managing director, to 1943, when he died in office as chairman.[23]

Hirst cleverly defused wartime hostility to the German origins of him and his able colleague Max Railing – by boasting that since it was not backed by US money GEC was the foremost British electrical enterprise.

He became a dedicated proponent of the protectionism that was to serve the industry well in years to come.

The takeover in 1918 of Fraser and Chalmers took GEC into turbines and soon after the company opened one of the country's first stand-alone industrial research laboratories.[24] Expansion during the interwar boom took the workforce from 19,000 in 1919 to 40,000 20 years later.

Following the Second World War there was major investment under Harry Railing, Max Railing's brother, but profitability stagnated. By the end of the 1950s GEC was actually seen as a takeover target.

In 1961 everything changed. GEC merged with Radio and Allied Industries, a fast-growing manufacturer of radios and TV sets. It was run by two men, Michael Sobell and his son-in-law, Arnold Weinstock.

The latter had proved outstanding at shaving input costs, controlling outgoings and driving up profitability. The merger stipulated that he should join GEC senior management and command one of its major divisions. Within two years he was managing director of the entire group. A key colleague was Kenneth Bond, who applied to GEC the financial controls he had introduced at Radio and Allied.[25]

Weinstock and Bond quickly made their mark. Though there was rationalisation, retrenchment was limited. So were corporate deals, though gas appliance manufacturer Cannon was bought in 1964 and GEC's turbo-generator business was sold to CA Parsons the following year. The main impact of the new regime was financial discipline. Weinstock and Bond slashed head office costs, imposed tight spending controls and squeezed stocks. Within three years profits had trebled and GEC's reputation was transformed.

This made GEC an obvious home for AEI and English Electric when concentration came into fashion. The formation of a single diversified group that could stand comparison with overseas competitors was the key aim of the IRC. Concern over the redundancies bound to accompany rationalisation was mitigated by the fact that it was a time of extremely low unemployment and ample job alternatives.

The New Giant

The decade following the merger of AEI and English Electric with GEC did see considerable rationalisation. The Witton works in Birmingham was cut back and other activities curbed. By the late 1970s the new group had shed 60,000 jobs from a workforce of 300,000. At the same time, Weinstock was keeping stocks under control and squeezing creditors. The result was the growing cash mountain for which GEC and Weinstock became famous.

By the end of the 1970s a distinct pattern had emerged. There were alliances and takeovers in telecommunications and office equipment, particularly in the US. And there was further emphasis on the military field – communications, avionics and even naval shipbuilding. An involvement with defence was to remain a long-running theme for GEC under Weinstock.

The verdict on the giant's first decade was distinctly favourable. Even two waspish observers of the economic scene, Michael Grylls MP and John Redwood MP, praised "the creation of one of the UK's most successful large corporations" in their 1980 report *National Enterprise Board, a Case for Euthanasia*.[26]

Alongside the cautious restructuring GEC was strengthening its standing in traditional areas. In turbine generators (inherited from AEI and English Electric) it retained an international status astonishing to many of its British peers. By the early 1980s GEC could boast that in the previous three–four years it had exported more steam generators than any other company in the world.[27] Between 1981 and 1986 it booked 12.5 per cent of all international export orders, putting it second only to Mitsubishi and well ahead of giants like Kraftwerk Union (Siemens), Brown Boveri, General Electric and Westinghouse. Indeed, its export sales topped those of the latter two combined.[28]

Though GEC's export books were full, domestic orders were insufficient to fill all four manufacturing centres. These were the plants at Trafford Park (Metrovicks), Rugby (BTH), Larne (AEI) and the crown jewel English Electric plant at Stafford. There were cutbacks at the first three, and GEC Gas Turbines at Whetstone was closed – an unfortunate move with the government's ludicrous "dash for gas" just round the corner.[29]

The background at home was becoming ever more unfavourable. Not only was there a dearth of new plant orders, but there were profound changes to the corporate environment. The new climate was one in which effortless fortunes could be made through slick deals, asset stripping and loading company balance sheets with debt. In came the quick-fix managers, the investment bankers and the accountants looking for an easy route to riches. Out went conservatism, caution and the long view, the slow, steady fostering, nurturing and building of businesses for the years to come.

Confronted with this new world, Weinstock snapped: "We don't deal in companies. I don't approve of raising money to plunder other companies."[30] Weinstock had not, of course, flinched from rationalisation when necessary. But such measures were never aimed at opportunistic gambling with companies, assets and people in pursuit of easy gain. In its way intensely conservative, the underlying theme was always to consolidate, squeeze costs and secure the company's position in its traditional sectors.

Initially a supporter of the 1979 Conservative government's pro-business pose, Weinstock soon became disenchanted. In 1985 he joined other industrialists in criticising the Thatcher regime's industrial policy, appalled that an indigenous manufacturing base was being destroyed in favour of services and foreign-owned assembly plants. He was strongly opposed to the privatisation of British Telecom and the electricity supply industry, on the grounds of both the enhancement of monopoly power and the threat to native equipment suppliers.

The City attitude to GEC gradually shifted from admiration to scepticism. The cash mountain irked. It was not being used for a dash into microchips or consumer electronics. Or a takeover spree that would fill the pockets of bankers and brokers. There was a stubborn refusal to load the balance sheet with debt. Instead, Weinstock stuck to solid stuff like defence, railways, power plant and telephones. And his famous cash mountain was invaluable in financing long gestations and tiding the company over the terrible recessions of the 1980s and 1990s.

Critics and Threats

The right was not alone in attacking GEC. For the *New Statesman* the company had "never developed into an integrated electrical and electronics company like Hitachi or Matsushita because, for the past 20 years, it has been in productive retreat".[31] Sales had stagnated and employment fallen. Research and investment levels were "pitiably low". The World Socialist Website claimed that, in contrast to ICI, GEC's "international ventures were not a success, leaving the company largely dependent on the domestic market, government procurement, and markets and governments in the former British Empire".[32]

The critics had half a point. But they had absolutely no answers. Rightly, they did not trust the City to come up with anything other than destructive short-term gambits. But even they could not foresee the utter disaster that lay ahead when a City-driven philosophy was finally applied.

There had been several plots to mount a takeover of GEC as the 1980s wore on. At least one was approved by a prime minister quick to bridle at criticism and slow to recognise manufacturing success. Her lofty declaration that she was "disappointed"[33] with Weinstock was taken as a cue by every investment banker, broker and deal-hunting chancer inside and outside the City.

Thatcher's view was, incidentally, not shared by Michael Heseltine, one of her few colleagues with any business experience. He was later to describe Weinstock as "one of the greatest industrialists of the second half of the twentieth century".[34]

Weinstock saw off some half-baked wheezes. But the clouds were gathering. The threat of an unwanted bid remained. As with ICI and other great industrial companies, management energies were increasingly eaten up in the effort to deflect and dodge the corporate raiders.

The main ploy in making GEC less vulnerable was a series of associations with other major companies. After an abortive counter-bid for Plessey in 1986 Weinstock settled for a cooperative approach to the development of the System X electronic telephone exchange through GPT (GEC Plessey Telecommunications). In 1989 he took over Plessey on a joint venture basis with Siemens. In the same year GEC combined its transport and power engineering interests with France's Compagnie Générale d'Electricité to form GEC-Alsthom.

Since they made GEC a much tougher prospect to unbundle, such arrangements were not popular with the City. But the formation of GEC-Alsthom got a breezy endorsement from *Management Today* as "a merger of power giants" that "created a Cross-Channel duo with global muscle".[35] Yet, it is quite clear that such alliances were the start of a deadly slide into oblivion for what was – now that ICI was increasingly crippled – Britain's industrial flagship.

Privatisation Tragi-Comedy

GEC-Alsthom was a particularly telling story. The new organisation absorbed about a quarter of GEC's assets. Yet French influence dominated from the outset. Seven of the company's nine divisions were based in France and high-level committees invariably had majority French membership.[36]

Barely had the ink dried on the agreement than it was in trouble – not of the company's own making but of the British government's. At the end of the 1980s the electricity supply industry was to be peddled off under the Thatcher government's privatisation programme. In the view of the *Financial Times*, the administration's mishandling of the sale of the generating sector was, however, almost comical.[37]

The process may have been risible but it had very grave consequences. Since it shared features with other privatisations, it is important to look at it in some detail.

Right from the start, the immediate expenses were grotesque. Over £100m of taxpayers' money was squandered on swarms of advisers, with hundreds of lawyers, accountants, tax professionals, surveyors and even estate agents piling in.[38] As the privatisation deadline approached, the legal profession enjoyed a feeding frenzy. Slaughter and May, a collaborator on electricity privatisation for two and a half years, deployed 55 lawyers. McKenna's had 38, Linklater and Freshfields 35 each, Herbert Smith 25, and Clifford Chance and others fielded significant teams. In one fatuous episode, countless documents were being rushed up and down between dozens of lawyers seated at makeshift tables in the corridors of a gloomy office block in the City.[39]

The only party to play an honourable hand, by relying on in-house advisers, was British Coal.

All this was before the investment bankers and investors had got to work. And before the emergence of the corporate predators to feed on the corpse of one of the world's finest publicly owned power supply systems. Within months Hanson was stalking PowerGen, one of the three generating companies carved out of the industry. Meanwhile, their directors were plotting to make thousands redundant, switch from British-mined to imported coal and double their salaries. In the words of one official, electricity privatisation was a "mess from beginning to end".[40]

Even more serious consequences followed. Many had been foreshadowed by Conservative critics of the sell-off. Lord Weir made a bitter attack on "a simplistic and almost ideological commitment to competition" which could cause "confusion and uncertainty…for the power station construction programme".[41] And the Tory-controlled House of Commons Select Committee on Energy criticised most aspects of energy secretary Cecil Parkinson's privatisation proposals.[42]

To facilitate the sale of power supply capital spending had been frozen, sowing the same blight that hit the manufacturers of railway rolling stock, trucks and buses ahead of the privatisations of their customers. In the case of power supply it meant a standstill in the entire power station building programme, with the sole exception of a politically inspired nuclear go-ahead at Sizewell.

Recession and the public spending squeeze had already stifled investment in new generating capacity, and by the end of 1989 there had been no new conventional station orders for a decade. Although GEC/ GEC-Alsthom had picked up some work at Sizewell, the wider freeze hit its British operations hard. The entire workload of the magnificent works at Larne vanished. Within two years it had closed[43] and Trafford Park[44] had been decimated.

Once power distribution (the electricity area boards) was included in the scramble to privatise, the coordinated long-range planning which had been one of the glories of public ownership collapsed.[45] A phony competitive market was cobbled together[46] and a plethora of opportunistic projects emerged from the new power supply entities.

This gave the foreign manufacturers their chance. Siemens, ABB (Asea Brown Boveri) and Mitsubishi plunged into the new free-for-all. They often secured their positions by taking a stake in a project and bidding low to lever their way into what had suddenly become the most open market in Europe.

One of the first beneficiaries was Siemens, which was awarded a £300m contract for a new power station by PowerGen in April 1990.[47] ABB took a leading stake in Lakeland Power to win a big long-term supply contract for the north-west of England, and Bechtel of the US signed up for a commercial station for British Coal.[48]

By mid-1990 a dozen projects had been proposed but only one, Corby Power,[49] went to (part) British interests in the form of GEC-Alsthom.

A crucial factor was the choice of technology suddenly favoured by the government – combined cycle stations using gas turbines, in which UK power engineering had limited experience. Even for Corby the gas turbines were to be made in France.

Egregious Enron

Among the newcomers to British power supply was US energy services company Enron, which was licenced to open a big (1,875MW) gas-burning power station on Teesside in 1991 and eventually a large (819MW) gas-fired plant at Sutton Bridge, in Lincolnshire.

Natural gas had hitherto been sensibly regarded as a premium fuel too precious to use as a bulk commodity in electricity generation. But the Thatcher and Major governments realised it offered a handy weapon for killing off Britain's use of domestically mined coal, and that as a "clean" fuel gas provided a lazy way for the UK to cut its carbon dioxide emissions.

John Wakeham, who signed off the Teesside project as energy secretary, was rewarded with a directorship of Enron in 1994. Despite his accountancy qualifications he brushed aside whistle-blower warnings about the financial scandal about to explode in the company.[50]

Enron exercised a mysterious hold on both sides of the Atlantic. It was later revealed that in 1997–98 the UK ambassador to Washington, Christopher Meyer, put "enormous pressure" on ministers in the new Labour government to ingratiate themselves with Enron head Kenneth Lay. One of Meyer's colleagues gushed: "Ken Lay would be on anyone's list of the most highly respected and influential businessmen in the US."[51] And as late as June 2001 *The Economist* was praising Enron for creating "the most successful internet venture of any company in any industry anywhere".[52]

Kenneth Lay was not quite so highly respected, even by sycophantic British diplomats and journalists, after Enron had filed the biggest bankruptcy in US history and he was convicted on ten counts of fraud. Among the more heinous activities of Enron's directors was swindling their own employees by selling them shares (often, indirectly, their own) that they knew were worthless. John Wakeham at last resigned from the company in February 2002,[53] but was never admonished or sanctioned in any way.

Astonishingly, even as this squalid fiasco was playing out vocal commentators were still floating up to defend the indefensible. A position as "director of regulatory studies" [*sic*] at the Hudson Institute did not deter Rupert Murdoch's crony Irwin Stelzer from enlarging on "Why Enron deserves our gratitude".[54]

The execrable story of Enron and its involvement with British ministers is of direct relevance here. The two gas-fired power stations built by the company cold-shouldered British suppliers of equipment such as GEC and Northern Engineering Industries (NEI). Teesside's eight big combustion turbines were from Mitsubishi. Its steam turbines and two generator sets were from Westinghouse.[55] And Sutton Bridge (819MW) used only General Electric turbines and generators.

Carve-Up

Weinstock was now over 70 and, following the tragic death of the son he had hoped would succeed him, he stepped down in 1996. The new managing director was George Simpson, veteran of Rover Group, who received a golden handshake of £10m when he took over.[56] He played to the City with breezy pledges to "open the window" and "jerk up earnings".[57] The following year a new chairman was appointed. This was Roger Hurn, "quietly astute" chief of Smiths Industries and supposedly the man to bring instant credibility to "lumbering" GEC.[58]

The third key player was John Mayo, former Warburg investment banker who had been intimately involved in the disembowelling of ICI a few years earlier. He was appointed GEC finance director in September 1997, and was later to make the bizarre claim that he had joined a "disastrous, dysfunctional, corrupt conglomerate".[59]

Simpson and Mayo then embarked on the most extraordinary corporate restructuring spree in memory. They were following the dim gospel of the business school – the unbundling of slow-growing complex organisations to concentrate on fast-growing specialisms, all in the pursuit of short-term shareholder value.

Hatched in corporate finance departments in the Square Mile, Project Superbowl[60] was a plot to ditch the bulk of GEC's activities in electrical engineering, defence, consumer goods, medical equipment and industrial controls in a bid to coat-tail the high-tech fad. In a rare understatement the press reported that the City had "warmed to the Simpson-Mayo double act".[61]

A wave of decent businesses, including AB Dick, Express Lifts, Marconi Instruments, GEC Plessey Semiconductors, Satchwell Controls and Wire & Cables, was sold off. Most fetched prices which reflected their long histories and first-class names. An even bigger departure was the 1998 flotation on the Paris Stock Exchange of GEC-Alsthom. GEC's new management jumped at the chance to surrender half its stake for £1bn.[62]

The new company promptly became a French citizen, dropping the first half of its name and calling itself Alstom. When there was a dearth of orders some years later it was the UK workforce that faced savage job cuts.[63] In fairness, Alstom put the blame where it actually belonged. Not on its 10,000 UK employees but on the government – for its failure to foster a sustainable market for trains and power plant instead of the "intelligent procurement process" about which "we have been talking to the government for the last two to three years".[64]

Among the crown jewels bequeathed by the old GEC regime to the new was its military electronics. Sure enough, Simpson and Mayo sold virtually the entire defence portfolio – warship production, rockets, satellites and radar – to GEC's old rival British Aerospace in the biggest deal in the whole saga. There was also some reshuffling of former Plessey activities, most of which handed the driving seat to Siemens.

The core of the new company was to be GEC Plessey Telecom (GPT), focusing on digital phone systems, electronic exchanges and other dot-com activities. The company now adopted the venerable name of Marconi.

To realise its new aims Marconi had to go on a spending spree, buying 15 companies around the world in the course of 1999–2000. These included two big US acquisitions, Reltec, for £1.3bn, and Fore Systems, for £2.8bn. Thanks to the high-tech fad, the prices paid were vastly inflated. Insanely, the new acquisitions were all bought with cash.

The whizz-kids were breaking rule number one in the City's grubby takeover manual. If you are going to overpay for an acquisition, use your own overpriced shares.[65] In less than four years of deal-making Marconi found it had gone through £14bn – the £3bn cash mountain inherited from Weinstock, £8bn from asset sales, and another £3bn from borrowings dumped on to a balance sheet debt-free for decades.

Rotten Plum

The Economist ran a gushing accolade to George Simpson for turning "stodgy old GEC" into "a high-tech plum" that could attract a friendly takeover.[66] In the real world, the plum was already rotting. The high-tech bubble had burst. Since many of its new acquisitions were not actually profitable, Marconi was hurtling into losses about which the management was rather too coy for rather too long. It finally dawned on the City that its grand wheeze had gone hopelessly wrong.

Having hyped the shares all the way up to £12.50, it then panic-sold them all the way down to £1. A company with a peak market capitalisation of £35bn was now worth under £100m – a destruction of shareholder value on a scale rare in history. City ghouls watched with repellent glee, Edmond Warner of Old Mutual Financial Services declaring: "There is something invigorating about the collapse of Marconi. Investors and bankers have received a rude reminder of the inherently precarious nature of their activities."[67] For a fickle financial press, its former heroes were now the "£11bn wreckers".[68]

What the *Daily Telegraph* dubbed the nightmare on Bruton Street (Marconi's shiny new headquarters) ended in the abrupt departure of the trio who had engineered the fiasco.[69] Less than four years after joining, GEC Mayo left, later resurfacing in private equity with a partner called Freke [*sic*].[70] Simpson resigned and was eventually rewarded with a Labour seat in the House of Lords. His exit package from Marconi ("disgusting and appalling", in the words of shareholders) was said to be £1m.[71] Hurn left with a mere £300,000, though this was thought to be rather more than the paltry pay-offs for the thousands of blue-collar staff axed in the disaster.

The new Marconi managers had to devote its energies to restructuring the debt they had inherited. There were still some valuable subsidiaries that could be sold off, among them Gilbarco, a world leader in petrol retailing equipment. But a deal with creditors had to be stitched together. In the final settlement the creditors waived £4bn in debt in return for control of the company, leaving just 0.5 per cent of the equity in the hands of the existing shareholders.

Chairman John Devaney cheerily told them they were lucky to get anything. "That's life. Shares can go up as well as down [He meant down as well as up] the company is now owned by its creditors, and them's the rules".[72] This did not stop chief operating officer Mike Donovan, a member of the Simpson-Mayo board who had overseen 20,000 job losses, leaving in 2004 with £8.5m in compensation, options and other sweeteners.[73] For the *Daily Telegraph* this was a pay-off that "sticks in the craw".[74]

Worse was to follow. Marconi's largest customer, accounting for more than a quarter of its revenues, was BT Group. After 20 comfortable years of privatised monopoly, the dozy giant was embarking on a £10bn "21st Century Network" project to upgrade its network with a unified internet-based system. Marconi and its predecessors had supplied most of the existing equipment – much of it a gift from a generous taxpayer, since BT had been shamefully underpriced at its privatisation – and its technology was competent. So there was widespread expectation that at least some of the business would go to the British bidder.

All the more shocking, then, that in April 2005 BT awarded not a single contract to Marconi, choosing instead contenders from China (yes, Huawei!), France, Germany, Japan, Sweden and the US.[75]

Telentless

BT did not bother to clarify a decision with devastating implications for British jobs, research and technological competence. Chairman Christopher Bland's vapid observation was that the new network would allow the company to offer services "which are both world-class and cost-effective".[76] Paul Reynolds, head of BT wholesale, denied that the failure to include a British-owned company would hurt the country's prospects in the high-tech economy and even made the baffling claim that "all these suppliers will be hiring new people and that will be good for UK plc".[77]

The contract winners took no notice of his advice – except, of course, in their own countries. Marconi announced hundreds of job losses, the closure of its century-old Liverpool factory and the transfer overseas of responsibility for many key products.[78] Apart from the pious hope that Marconi sustain its UK research and development, where it had been in the top ten spenders, the Labour government hid behind the "commercial" nature of the BT decision and offered no advice or assistance of any kind.[79]

It was left to the Amicus union to state the bleak truth: "As far as the UK's telecoms research and development capability goes, Marconi is it. There are no others left."[80]

Marconi's share price again collapsed and the company cast desperately around for a new owner.[81] After abortive contacts with Huawei[82] and with Alcatel and Siemens, Ericsson stepped in. In October 2005 the venerable Swedish telecoms company agreed a price of £1.2bn for the bulk of Marconi.[83]

All that was left was a rump given the forgettable name Telent. A service operation, its employees represented less than 1 per cent of what had once been the biggest private-sector workforce in Britain.

The corpse of GEC was still not quite cold. The last chief executive of Marconi, Mike Parton, had reportedly received £8m in options prior to the BT fiasco and took another slice in the low millions before quitting a year after the formation of Telent.[84] Another year on and Telent itself faded into private obscurity.

Could the slaughter of GEC have been avoided? Unquestionably yes. This was a company which had never made a loss, which had sustained its labour force as unemployment soared in the recessions of the 1980s, and had built a cash fortress to take it through those grim years.

True, it was conservatively run, risk-averse, and stinted on research and development. But most of what it did it did quite well. It had conserved some of the heartlands of Britain's industrial base in the 1980s, when great tracts were being laid waste. It had sustained a major international presence when many of its peers were in retreat. Only when a new management picked to bits the construct so tenaciously built by Arnold Weinstock did it crash. And then it could not elicit help from a Labour government fatally infected by the toxin of non-interventionism inherited from Thatcherism.

Alstom Alternative

The contrast with what happened to Alstom, France's equivalent to GEC, could not be more stark. Having built a corporate giant much like GEC over the two decades following its merger with Compagnie Générale d'Electricité (CGE), Alsthom/Alstom ran into severe financial difficulties in the early 2000s. By 2003 its share price had fallen 90 per cent and its debts reached $5bn.

Chairman Pierre Bilger was paid off, but in a remarkable contrast to the GEC/Marconi directors (and British executives in general) he made the startling announcement that he was returning his €4.1m departure package.[85] This honourable man had no wish to be "an object of scandal" for employees and shareholders.

Since Alstom had the good fortune to be French, its government stepped in with a huge rescue package. This was a potential challenge to EU competition policy, but the French knew perfectly well that no Brussels commissioner was going to risk the wrecking of one of France's crown jewels. If pushed, moreover, the French administration could cite the "manifest crisis" precedents in EU lore.

Defying doctrinaire carping in *The Economist* and the financial press, the rescue worked. Alstom emerged as a formidable giant, with global sales of £20bn. Many of these were in power engineering and rail – the very areas in which GEC had once been so strong. When the time came to swap assets with Siemens a dozen years later it was able to secure a huge price for its jewels.

Parsons

No other company in British electrical engineering has compared for size with GEC in its prime. But the roll call includes distinguished names. Among them is CA Parsons, founded by the inventor of the steam turbine.[86] Charles Algernon Parsons, an Irish landowner, patented his design for marine applications in 1884. His revolutionary development was scaled up by George Westinghouse for land-based power generation. Though there were other turbine designs, the reaction model conceived by Parsons was the most efficient.[87] That this device has been the source of 90 per cent of all the electrical power ever generated on earth is a measure of Parsons' towering achievement.

Following his discovery he established his own company[88] at Heaton, on Tyneside. By the early twentieth century Parsons was constructing up to 50 steam turbines a year.[89]

Overseas business was particularly buoyant, and by the late 1940s exports exceeded home sales. The 1950s brought a commitment to the nuclear industry, and during the 1960s Parsons supplied generators for half the nuclear plants at home and a major unit abroad. Following a ruling that there should be only two designs for new CEGB power stations, Parsons bought the turbine generator division of GEC in 1965.

The 1960s were the heyday of Heaton, with the workforce rising to a peak 8,000. In 1968 Parsons merged with the company with whom it had worked closely for many years to form Reyrolle Parsons.

Reyrolle Parsons

Established in 1886, Reyrolle had been founded by yet another enterprising immigrant, this time from France. Alphonse Reyrolle opened a factory to make heavy electrical equipment at Hebburn, on Tyneside, in 1901.[90] The main activity was switchgear, and this eventually developed into an even bigger business than Parsons, with a peak workforce of 12,000.[91]

Union with Reyrolle may have brought benefits to Parsons, but by the mid-1970s there were new pressures on the industry. Higher oil prices combined with economic stresses to slow investment in both conventional and nuclear power. The Labour government was keen to see further industrial restructuring to build on the successes of the AEI/English Electric/GEC merger in the 1960s.

Two new groupings were proposed. One would consolidate the generator builders within GEC. The other would combine Clarke Chapman,[92] a manufacturer of boilers and a specialist in nuclear power, with Babcock & Wilcox, its main competitor. Clarke Chapman had already absorbed the third player in its sector, International Combustion of Derby, in 1974.

Northern Powerhouse

The subjugation of Reyrolle Parsons to GEC and Babcock was, however, too much for the Tyneside engineers, and they opted for a union of Reyrolle Parsons with Clarke Chapman. The result was Northern Engineering Industries (NEI), a new industrial giant employing over 40,000 people and based at Gosforth, in Newcastle.[93] Four years later NEI acquired Amalgamated Power Engineering, a Midlands maker of industrial engines.

Arguably, Parsons had ceded the technical edge in turbine technology to GEC, and in a world of giant groupings it was too small. Where GEC had secured 12.5 per cent of the world steam generator market in 1981–86, NEI won just 2.7 per cent.[94]

Challenges at home had been exacerbated by a CEGB switch from nuclear advanced gas-cooled reactors (AGRs) to pressurised water reactors (PWRs). NEI had to close its dedicated AGR plant in Gateshead in 1983[95] and picked up little of the work from the Sizewell B PWR go-ahead in 1984.

Moreover, its international business was crippled by the dogma-driven withdrawal of government backing for British exporters. Within a few years the workforce had been halved. Implausibly, the *Financial Times* lent a brave face in 1984: "A slimmer and fitter NEI moves nearer a clean bill of health."[96] But NEI's profitability remained fragile, with restructurings and cutbacks continuing for most of the 1980s.[97]

The year 1989 brought a surprise approach from Rolls-Royce, a move later described as "folly".[98] Long recovered from the crisis of the early 1970s, Rolls was keen to reduce its dependence on traditional markets. The new acquisition's strong emphasis on international contracts had some success, despite unhelpful government attitudes. Following a breach of undertakings by Peter Lilley, trade secretary, to compensate for the loss of business in Iraq, NEI had to go after difficult contracts elsewhere.

Moreover, the pendulum of financial fashion had swung against diversification. So in 1996 Rolls-Royce put most of what it had acquired with NEI up for sale.[99] This time it went to Siemens.[100] The German company was buying a share in the world's fifth biggest market for electrical equipment.[101]

However, it took on only part of the Parsons business,[102] and before long it was cutting back on what it had picked up so inexpensively. In 2002 it terminated all manufacturing at Heaton in favour of Budapest, where labour was "cheaper". Today, the factory which was one of the cradles of modern material civilisation is a modest administrative base for Siemens Energy Service.

Siemens has the irony – perhaps unconscious – to call the building CA Parsons Works.

Siemens Brothers

Siemens also acquired the activities built up by Reyrolle. Hebburn was sold in 1998 to VA Technologie and was subsequently bought by Siemens, which now maintains only a modest operation where thousands once worked.

The acquisitions of recent times complete a full circle for Siemens. In the mid-nineteenth century the three Siemens brothers, Werner, Wilhelm and Carl, had formed Siemens and Halske to make telegraph and electrical cables in Hanover.[103] Wilhelm was sent to England to represent the firm[104] and in 1863 opened a cable factory at Woolwich, in London. Two years later the British operations were reconstituted as Siemens Brothers.

The company had many firsts. These included the inaugural undersea telegraph cable between England and France, the world's first commercial power station, the first electric street lighting and the first electric train, supplied to Bushmills whiskey distillery in Ireland. By now a distinguished British subject, Wilhelm Siemens was knighted for services to science in 1883.

Siemens Brothers eventually set up the Siemens Dynamo Works in Stafford (later sold to English Electric) and a lamp works in East London. During the First World War the company was taken over by the Custodian of Enemy Property. In the 1950s the company became part of AEI, and in 1967 it joined GEC.

Bruce Peebles

One of the few independents which did not end up in the great combine was Bruce Peebles, founded in Edinburgh in 1866. The company opened a large factory at East Pilton in the early 1900s, and specialised in traction motors and large transformers for the national grid. The heyday of the plant was the 1950s, when it had a workforce of over 3,000.

In 1969 Bruce Peebles became part of the newly formed Reyrolle Parsons. Subsequently it became the transformer division of Northern Engineering Industries (NEI) when that was established in 1977. Eventually this was sold to VA Technologie, before it became part of Siemens. Eventually transformer manufacture ended and the East Pilton works closed.

Crompton Parkinson

Crompton Parkinson, another early starter in the electrical field, goes back to the formation of Crompton & Co in 1878.[105] Founder R.E.B. Crompton was a distinguished engineer whose Chelmsford factory was one of the world's first large-scale manufacturers of electrical equipment. Initially it specialised in lamps, made under licence from Joseph Swan.

After a merger with FA Parkinson, a producer of electric motors,[106] Crompton Parkinson built a large factory at Guiseley, near Leeds, in the 1930s. The post-war years saw considerable expansion and in 1968 Hawker Siddeley Group, now a rising conglomerate, bought Crompton Parkinson. Hawker Siddeley was itself taken over by BTR in 1992.

Both before and after that event the various strands of Crompton Parkinson were broken up, demerged and downsized. The main factories at Chelmsford and Guiseley have long been closed.

The venerable name of Crompton is half-forgotten. But not everywhere. Crompton Greaves is still a significant producer of heavy electrical equipment in India, and a major supplier to that country's great railway system.

South Wales Switchgear

South Wales Switchgear was established at Treforest in South Wales in 1941[107] to bring industry to a depressed area.[108] The workforce eventually reached 2,000 in 1961, but like so many British industrial concerns South Wales Switchgear has gone through a succession of ownerships. Each change has seen it shrink in stature.

In its drive to build an engineering empire Hawker Siddeley took over South Wales Switchgear in 1973. Following the takeover of Hawker Siddeley by BTR, this was consolidated with Brush Switchgear to form Hawker Siddeley Switchgear in 1991.[109] In 1996 it was sold on again to FKI to become part of FKI Switchgear, based at a new factory in Blackwood. In yet another deal in 2008 the operations were taken over by Melrose plc, which renamed them Hawker Siddeley Switchgear. The Melrose takeover has been followed by predictable cutbacks, with 75 jobs lost out of a total 400.[110]

The Brush

The last of the significant survivors is the Brush group, which takes its name from yet another American inventor who brought his energies to Britain. Charles Francis Brush founded the Brush Electric Light Company in Chicago in 1879,[111] merging it with Thomson-Houston Electric in 1890 and with Edison Electric two years later. The result was General Electric, long the global giant of electrical engineering and still an icon of industrial management.

The Brush name lived on in Britain, where production was based at the Falcon Works in Loughborough. Brush was eventually taken over by Hawker Siddeley Group in 1957, and Brush Electrical Machines took on a new lease of life. By 1960 the workforce exceeded 4,000, with four-fifths involved in transformers, generators, electric motors and switchgear.[112] In the early 1970s 5,000 were employed in Loughborough.

The recession of the 1980s brought severe strains to Hawker Siddeley and to the Brush, which at one time faced a real possibility of closure. A *Financial Times* survey conveyed a picture of "a very big, old engineering site" characterised by the cramped and cluttered layout familiar to British engineering.[113] Despite this the Brush was getting some things right, and after hefty retrenchment it survived. It changed hands again in 1991, when Hawker Siddeley was subject to a hostile takeover by BTR.

Brush Electrical Machines was sold on yet again five years later, when Hawker Siddeley Electric Power Group was bought by FKI. FKI was sold to Melrose in 2008, and employment at Loughborough slipped again, to just 700.

There are rare success stories in today's electrical engineering, but the industry is a pitifully poor relation to what it once was. Such as they are the more significant operations are in the hands of foreign owners. The largest is Siemens, whose website describes a "proud history" of engineering in the UK. Fair enough, Siemens Brothers was an early offshoot of the original Siemens enterprise and a significant presence well before the First World War.

In recent years Siemens has reported a UK workforce of around 15,000, of whom over half were in the electrical sector. Over 1,500 were employed on industrial gas turbines at the former English Electric works at Lincoln, Alstom having sold the plant to Siemens in 2003. A couple of hundred were based at the Parsons site in Newcastle, and a handful in Hebburn.

In the website snapshot of its activities Alstom invoked for some years the legendary names of Robert Stephenson, Joseph Swan and other British pioneers in a "long and proud history of Alstom in the UK". It also took credit for building more than half the country's operational power stations. This startling take on history can of course only be based on the long rollcall of operations Alstom inherited through its joint venture (as Alsthom) with GEC in 1989.

Since then the record has been downhill most of the way. Notable among cutbacks were the events of 2003, when Alstom accused the Labour government of failure to foster industry and slashed 1,000 jobs in train-making and 4,000 jobs in power engineering. After subsequent deals with Siemens and General Electric, Alstom has further reduced its presence in recent years and reports employment of just 2,000 in the UK.

If not coming full circle, the UK has slid a long way back down that path which took it from a leisurely start in electrical engineering in the nineteenth century to the first division in the twentieth. Following catch-up with Germany between the wars, Britain's electrical engineering retained its pre-eminent position long after 1945. Approaching its pinnacle at the end of the 1950s, the UK was one of the world's top three manufacturers of electrical engineering products. From £155m in 1938, production rose to nearly £1.3bn two decades later, when Britain was the world's second largest exporter of electrical goods.[114]

The 1960s were good to British electrical engineering, with output rising by more than half between 1963 and 1971.[115] There were still the three great corporate groupings that were to combine in GEC and a full contingent of respected second-division players. British industry could offer the entire spectrum of electrical products. Thanks to the restructurings of the 1960s and 1970s, UK electrical engineering sustained its status right up until the 1980s.

That world has gone. There is now not a single British company that stands the remotest comparison with the global giants of Germany (Siemens, Bosch), France (the descendants of CGE), Italy (Ansaldo), Sweden/Switzerland (Asea Brown Boveri), the US (General Electric) and Japan, or the new giants of Korea and China.

The second division is equally bleak. And although some of the great historic centres of electrical engineering – Birmingham, Manchester, Rugby, Stafford and Tyneside – keep a flicker of their tradition alive, it is typically under foreign ownership. And the scale is a shadow of what once was.

The swift decline of electrical engineering from first division in the 1970s to third division today can fairly be laid at the door of government and the City of London. Dreadful mismanagement of the economy in the 1980s and 1990s was perhaps less crippling for electrical engineering than it was for other areas of industry. But privatisation was at least as badly handled in power supply as it was in other sectors and City meddling, so evident in the disastrous fate of GEC, was as malign in electrical engineering as anywhere.

Could Britain's once-great electrical engineering industry now begin to be restored? Except in marginal respects, it is difficult to see how.

CHAPTER 12

Electronic Short Circuit

Radio has no future. Heavier-than-air flying machines are impossible. X-rays will prove to be a hoax.

Lord Kelvin, 1899

I think there is a world market for maybe five computers.

Thomas Watson, IBM Chairman, 1943

Electrical or Electronic?

Electronics has a remarkably short ancestry. Though it was born with telegraphy in the nineteenth century and nurtured on radio and telephony in the twentieth, it was only recognised as a distinct academic subject in the 1960s.

Yet, Britain was far from backward in the research from which modern electronics sprang. At the end of the nineteenth century the Cambridge scientist J.J. Thomson had carried out experimental work that led to the cathode ray tube, an essential feature of television receivers for the next century. And the first thermionic valve, integral to radios, was demonstrated in the Electrical Engineering Department at University College London in 1904. Indeed, it was radio that led the way in the practical applications of electronics.

The years after the First World War saw rapid progress towards public broadcasting. In 1922 the British Broadcasting Company was established by American and British electrical companies eager to exploit this new field. And in 1926 it was replaced by the British Broadcasting Corporation (BBC). The scene was set for rapid expansion of the medium, and a vibrant industry to serve it.

Baird and Shoenberg

Within a decade the world of broadcasting was revolutionised by the arrival of television. Though scientists worked on television in the USA, Germany, Russia, France and Japan, Britain was in the lead. And with this triumph two names will always be associated – John Logie Baird and Isaac Shoenberg.

An inventive Scots engineer whose university career was interrupted by war, Baird persisted with experimental work, often in primitive conditions, to produce the world's first electromechanical television device and the first electronic colour television tube. As early as 1926, a year ahead of his US counterparts, Baird demonstrated the television system used for the BBC's first experimental broadcasts.

However, Baird's technology was inadequate and the BBC eventually adopted a superior rival.[1] This was the system developed in less than four years by Isaac Shoenberg,[2] a brilliant Russian-born engineer who had joined the Marconi Wireless and Telegraph Company in 1914 and later led research and development at Electrical and Musical Industries (EMI).

In November 1936 the BBC launched the world's first high-definition public television service, using the EMI "Emitron". Public uptake was slow, however, and when broadcasting closed down in September 1939 fewer than 20,000 TV sets were in operation.[3]

Other industries in which electronics would become all-important were still in the early stages of development. The Second World War naturally accelerated the advance of military radio, telephone communications, defensive radar and marine radar.[4] But in civilian telecommunications and consumer appliances modern electronics was in early infancy. And the semiconductors and microchips which would one day lie at its heart were scarcely thought of.

In the post-war world UK electronics advanced quickly. First to take off were computers, capitalising on the wartime achievements of mathematicians and scientists. Next came semiconductors, developed on the back of the transistor, which quickly became vital building blocks in electronics. Microcircuitry allowed rapid advances in consumer appliances in the 1960s.

By the middle of that decade Britain's successes in computers, consumer electronics and military applications were prompting widespread satisfaction. In his book *What's Wrong with British Industry?* Rex Malik described electronics as the wunderkind of the British industrial scene – diverse, resourceful and resilient.[5]

True, he qualified his accolade by designating British electronics a technical success but a commercial failure. But even he acknowledged a dynamism to the sector that was harder to match elsewhere. Was this the turning point in electronics, and if so what happened to that success story?

Computer Challenge

The first programmable computers appeared in Germany and the UK at about the same time.[6] Britain's pioneer was Colossus, built by a Post Office team in 1943 and deployed at Bletchley Park. It was the progenitor of the rich experimental environment that blossomed after the war. The first stored-programme computer, the Small Scale Experimental Machine (SSEM), was unveiled at Manchester University in 1948.[7] This was quickly followed by the more sophisticated Electronic Delay Storage Automatic Calculator (EDSAC) at Cambridge.[8]

Commercial computers came on to the market in both the UK and the US in 1951. Britain's pioneer was the Ferranti Mark I, which owed its genesis to the work done at Manchester.[9] In its early days a traditional electrical engineer, Ferranti had developed a major interest in radar and defence equipment during the Second World War and produced a succession of computers for military and commercial uses.

In the same year that the Mark I was launched the first electronic computer designed for data processing was unveiled. This was the legendary Lyons Electronic Office (LEO), devised to manage the stockholding and accounting routines of the J Lyons catering empire.[10]

The 1950s saw UK computer technology sustained at a high level, though in contrast with the vast official support for the US industry, UK funding via the National Research and Development Corporation (NRDC) and the military was paltry.[11] There was growing pressure to consolidate, and in 1959 British Tabulating Machines (BTM) and Powers-Samas merged to form International Computers and Tabulators (ICT). BTM had sold equipment designed by US-based Tabulating Machine Company (TMC), forerunner to the mighty International Business Machines (IBM).

ICT acquired EMI's computer activities in 1962 and Ferranti's interests in 1963. In the same year English Electric combined with Lyons to form English Electric LEO and, in 1964, English Electric LEO Marconi. The British computer industry was now dominated by just three players, ICT, English Electric and Elliott Automation.

ICL and After

In the meantime IBM was becoming a superpower. "No one ever got fired for buying IBM" was its triumphant slogan. And the other US players were far from small. When the Seven Dwarves became the Bunch – Burroughs, Univac, NCR, Control Data and Honeywell – each of them outclassed the British contenders in size.[12]

Anxious to preserve one of its flagship industries, the British government prompted further consolidation. Elliott Automation was taken over by English Electric, which in turn merged its computer interests with ICT to form International Computers Ltd (ICL) in 1968.

The government extended a modest £17m through the National Enterprise Board (NEB) and steered a succession of departmental orders to ICL, ensuring that the UK was the only major non-US market where IBM was not dominant. ICL was to hold on to this position until the mid-1980s, when a newly privatised British Telecom betrayed its traditional UK suppliers by handing a big batch of orders to IBM.

In little more than a decade the British computer industry had had to shoehorn half a dozen separate companies, systems and product ranges into a single group. It had an urgent need to develop a new generation of computers under one badge. But there was a shortage of money, "exacerbated", as an avowed critic of state support put it, "by the [Heath] government's less generous approach compared with that of many international governments for their indigenous computer industries".[13]

The Conservative government eventually renewed support in 1972, and the Labour government that took office in 1974 extended some assistance through the NEB. This paid off, and in one of its first privatisations the Thatcher government sold the NEB's 25 per cent holding in ICL at a good profit.

The 1980s brought a very different economic environment, however, and the diverse electronics sector shepherded through the 1970s soon unravelled. The competitive pressure from the American giants was huge. The domestic market was squeezed by severe recession. And the Thatcher administration was hostile to the promotion of manufacturing. With fresh NEB funding ruled out by the government and the financial markets less friendly, ICL adopted an "open systems" approach[14] and in 1981 formed a link with Fujitsu.

There was one last attempt at a British solution to ownership of the UK computer industry. In 1984 ICL was bought outright by Standard Telephones and Cables (STC). Traditionally one of the big equipment suppliers to the British telephone system, STC was pursuing newly fashionable convergence between telecoms and computing.

As the 1980s wore on STC itself faced recurrent financial pressure, due mainly to the loss of domestic custom in the telephone sector. Meanwhile, ICL slashed its labour force from 34,000 in 1979 to 22,000 in 1985.[15] Despite this, ICL was the mainstay of STC's profits as the decade went on.[16] Unfortunately, STC had insufficient funds to secure the development of ICL and satisfy the City, which had come to expect annual dividend growth in double figures.[17]

In 1990 ICL was accordingly sold to Fujitsu.[18] The surrender to the Japanese brought consequences. ICL was expelled from the European Information Round Table and from Europe's biggest semiconductor research programme, the Joint European Submicron Silicon venture (JESSI).[19]Not long after, Fujitsu redesignated ICL as Fujitsu Services, and UK production withered.[20] Ironically, the sale of ICL left STC no stronger, and the following year it was itself taken over by Canada's Northern Telecom (Nortel).

So ended half a century of brilliant theoretical work, pioneering development and successful manufacturing by a distinct British-owned computer industry, one in which the government had made a modest but rewarding financial intervention, abruptly terminated in the early 1980s. Thereafter the philosophy of non-intervention prevailed. It now became fashionable for politicians to deride the challenging business of "picking winners" in the industrial stakes. Essentially, they were playing safe. As one obituary put it, at least nobody could accuse them of blowing it.

Truth was, they didn't even try.[21]

French and German Ways

Europe's other big players, Germany's Siemens and France's Machines Bull, did not give up so easily. Nor were their stories the tales of hopeless disaster so often retailed in histories of the computer industry.

Machines Bull[22] developed into a significant competitor to IBM in the 1950s and 1960s. Its Gamma computers were a technical success but the company had to navigate a path between avowedly nationalistic French governments and the need to form commercial and technical alliances.

French administrations backed their protectionist instincts with serious money, however, and were loyal to their industrial champions. After it had been nationalised in 1983, Bull received $1bn to allow it to restructure, absorb the rest of the French computer industry and invest. After privatisation in the 1990s Bull found a sustainable role as a provider of IT systems to commercial and military clients. In 2014 the group was bought as a going concern by the Atos services group for no less than €620m.[23]

Siemens developed a presence in computers in the 1960s and benefitted from significant government support through the 1970s and 1980s. In 1989 it took over Nixdorf Computer, a specialist in small-scale systems. Although Siemens Nixdorf Information Systems was now the largest European computer group, it opted for a joint venture with Fujitsu in 1999. Siemens then soldiered on far longer than ICL ever did, and only abandoned the field in 2009 when Fujitsu bought out its German partner.

Micro Computers

An interesting footnote to the story of the UK computer industry – and an all-too-fleeting monument to the resourcefulness of British inventors

– is the emergence of micro computers in the 1980s. With remarkable rapidity Acorn, Amstrad, Sinclair and others became household names as consumers acquainted themselves with the world of small computers for personal entertainment and educational uses.[24] The spread of personal computers spelt the end of this sector, however, and 30 years on from their heyday they and their successors have disappeared.

McKinsey Mauling

How did the electronics industry look in the late 1980s, after nearly a decade of self-proclaimed business-friendly government under the Thatcher administration?

Unfortunately, not good. A gloomy study by McKinsey in 1988 pointed to average annual growth of 9.4 per cent in UK electronics demand in 1976–86, above the average for the leading industrial countries. Yet at just 2.6 per cent a year output had advanced much more slowly, allowing foreign companies to grab two-thirds of the UK market and turn the trade balance customary in the 1970s into an alarming deficit.[25]

UK companies had become too dependent on defence and telecommunications. They were slow to develop international business and, despite high profit margins, were tight-fisted with investment and training. Industry short-termism was attributable to the portfolio organisational structure of UK companies and the over-decentralisation accompanying the conglomerate structures of many groups.

The broader criticisms – over-decentralisation, inadequate investment, undue dependence on government business – applied particularly to GEC. But it was also relevant to STC, Thorn and Plessey. In their defence they pointed out that the UK market had opened up much more abruptly than others, in large part because of government privatisation programmes.

Integrated Circuits

After the US development of the transistor in 1947, the science of semiconductors spread quickly to Europe. Although British companies focused on more specialised products, they were well up with the vanguard. Thanks to the Royal Signals & Radar Establishment, the world's first integrated circuit (IC) was made by Plessey in 1957, a year before Texas Instruments launched its inaugural microchip.[26] And the 1960s saw government funding for promising development work by Elliott, Ferranti, Marconi and Plessey.

Unfortunately, the merger of AEI, English Electric and GEC in 1967/68 took Britain out of big areas of the microchip market. Arnold Weinstock, head of the new electrical giant, baulked at the volatility of microchips and the investment required. So he curtailed the group's interests. By the time he tried to get back into microchips the terms on offer were much less favourable.

Others were still active in specialist areas. Plessey was a world leader in emitter-coupled logic (ECL) devices and Ferranti led the way in semi-custom chips. By 1974, however, Ferranti was facing serious financial difficulties. Modest funding was obtained from the NEB, and Ferranti went on to make semiconductors for Sinclair, Acorn and other microcomputers, only dropping out when it sold its microchip interests to Plessey.

Inmos

The 1970s saw other government initiatives in semiconductors. Among the largest was a £50m NEB investment in 1978 in an ambitious IC start-up, Inmos. Founder Ian Barron wanted to commercialise the transputer – an ingenious "computer on a chip". A high-tech factory opened at Newport, South Wales, in 1982,[27] and a design centre was commissioned in Bristol. With a view to shaping it for privatisation, the Thatcher government merged the NEB and the NRDC to form the British Technology Group (BTG). In 1984 the BTG sold Inmos off to Thorn EMI at a knock-down £192m, and within a couple of years its new owner was selling it on again.

The BTG went on to a management buyout and stock market flotation. After a couple of decades specialising in medical innovations – some of the more brilliant ones developed at public expense – the BTG was sold to a US-based company in 2018. The BTG's chief executive pocketed £20m from the deal.[28]

Plessey, the microchip industry leader, should have offered a natural home for Inmos but its proposed purchase was allowed to fail and Thorn EMI eventually passed Inmos on to the state-controlled French/Italian SGS-Thomson.

Again, the outcome was not a happy one. The government was approached for £50m to upgrade the factory in Newport. The request was turned down by trade secretary Peter Lilley, so Inmos closed Newport and transferred production to Italy, France and the US.[29] Within a few years the Inmos name was buried and its Bristol design centre closed.[30]

Though direct intervention in industry was out of favour, state funding had somehow been found for the Alvey project, a response to the Japanese Fifth Generation computer programme. Alvey was an ambitious pre-competitive collaborative microchip programme initiated in 1983 by Kenneth Baker, who took his responsibilities unusually seriously and earned an improbable accolade from *The Guardian* as a "highly effective" minister for information technology.[31]

Baker had succeeded in creating an oasis of creative intervention in a laissez faire world, persuading two major private-sector participants, GEC and Plessey, to join the initiative. Unfortunately, GEC dropped out in 1987 and Alvey's death knell sounded when its leading sponsor, the Department of Industry, became infected with the "enterprise culture" of David Young, Margaret Thatcher's favourite minister. Starved of meaningful funding, Alvey was, in effect, killed by the very short-termism it had sought to mitigate.

GEC Plessey Semiconductors

There was a more positive development in 1987, when Ferranti's micro-electronics business was sold to Plessey. Only a couple of years after it had completed this deal, however, Plessey was carved up by GEC and Siemens.[32]

For semiconductors, the original plan was a joint venture between GEC and Siemens. Faced by objections from the Ministry of Defence, Siemens withdrew, and in April 1990 the entire heritage of the former microchip operations of GEC, Plessey, Marconi and Ferranti was amalgamated into GEC Plessey Semiconductors (GPS).

This proved a retrograde step. The University of Sussex Science Policy Research Unit[33] contrasted GEC's lack of enterprise with Plessey's innovative niche market strategy. It predicted that GEC would not invest in risky markets such as the semi-customised chips (ASICs) in which Plessey was a leader.

Plessey's renowned research team was cut back and dispersed.[34] Moreover, the deal had put what was left of UK semiconductors into a tidy saleable package. As the terminal dismemberment of GEC got under way in the late 1990s, GPS was sold to Canada's Mitel, which in turn parcelled it up for sale to others.

This marked the end of a British-owned mainstream semiconductor industry. Nor did foreign-owned operations compensate. A big microchip plant built by Fujitsu in the North East in 1991 closed in 1998,[35] and a major operation commissioned by Siemens on Tyneside in 1997 closed within two years.[36]

There were still a few surviving innovative ventures in semiconductors. In recent years Imagination Technologies has excelled as a designer of microchips for mobile devices. And ARM Holdings, spun off from Acorn Computers in 1990, has retained world leadership in processors for mobile phones and tablets. Naturally it offered a tempting takeover target, and when Japan's Softbank made a bid in 2016 Britain's last major specialist high-tech company was handed to foreign owners.

The government of the day merely voiced a mild regret.

GPO Tradition

Sophisticated electronics came late to telephony. Research into electronic switching got under way in the 1950s but not until the 1970s did the first viable product became available in Britain. Though this was a fully electronic telephone exchange, designed entirely in the UK, its progress had been hampered by the procurement protocols of the only major domestic customer, the General Post Office (GPO).

Prior to this, telecommunications had still been wedded to technology little changed since the turn of the century. Exchanges were big electromechanical constructions, labour-intensive and transmitting messages along copper cables whose design would have been familiar to Victorian engineers.

Although the GPO had a substantial research capacity radical advances encountered significant obstacles in their adoption and led the sleepy management of the Post Office down some blind alleys.

Historically, the Post Office had fostered a group of five telecom equipment manufacturers – Automatic Telephone and Electric (AT&E), Ericsson Telephone (ETL or "British Ericsson"), GEC, Siemens Brothers and Standard Telephones and Cables (STC). GEC and Siemens Brothers[37] were broad-based manufacturers of electrical equipment, while the others were more specialised. British Ericsson was founded in the early 1900s as a joint venture between Sweden's LM Ericsson and the National Telephone Company, an offshoot of the GPO. When LM Ericsson sold its holding in 1948, ETL became independent.

STC was established as a British concern in the 1880s but became a subsidiary of the American group ITT in 1925.[38] Although it was run at arm's length, it only resumed full independence in 1982. The company was a leader in international and subsea cables, and retained its status as the world's largest supplier of submarine telecommunications cables right up until the 1980s.

STC had pioneered major developments such as multi-channel communication, microwave transmission, coaxial cabling and pulse code modulation in the 1930s, and played an important role in the spread of television reception in the 1950s. Subsequently it took a lead in the new science of fibre optics and was active in the first commercial installations in the 1970s.

The five suppliers shared the major GPO orders through bulk supply agreements. Though not formally a member of the group, the Plessey Company also sold to the Post Office, and its position was greatly enhanced in 1961 when it merged with AT&E and Ericsson Telephones Ltd (ETL)[39] to become the country's largest manufacturer of telecommunications equipment.[40] Siemens Brothers had become a subsidiary of AEI in 1954 and then GEC when it took over AEI in 1968.

Thus, by the end of the 1960s the group supplying the Post Office had shrunk to three – GEC, Plessey and STC.

Until the 1970s the UK telephone system was wedded to traditional Strowger exchange technology, and with electronic systems on the way it was reluctant to invest in the more modern Crossbar system widespread in the US.

After some costly false starts it was clear by the mid-1970s that the main contender for electronic switching should be System X, developed through collaboration between the GPO, Plessey, GEC and STC. In 1977 the system was formally adopted by the Post Office. In the meantime semi-electronic systems named TXE2 and TXE4 were installed as a stopgap.

GPO Telephones

The GPO was soon to undergo the most profound changes in its long history. The Royal Mail traced its origins back to 1516, when King Henry VII created a Master of the Posts to supervise the transmission of written messages across his realm. The other main branch of the Post Office, telecommunications, dated back to the formation of the Electric Telegraph Company, the world's first nationwide communications network, in 1846.

This inevitably brought an accretion of archaic practices. Tony Benn's diaries are revealing. Eager to attend his inaugural meeting as newly appointed postmaster general in October 1964, the earnest young technocrat was greeted at GPO headquarters by a flunky in scarlet frock coat and top hat, and discovered a gigantic quasi-civil service, with 400,000 employees and many critical functions.[41] Keen to modernise after the years of neglect by Conservative predecessors, Benn had to tussle with entrenched interests, conservative prejudices and cautious management.

Yet it would be wrong to assume that GPO Telephones was hopelessly backward. It was a typical British combination of clever research and dusty tradition. It was a pioneer in subsea cable, particularly for the early transatlantic links. The world's first programmable electronic computer, Colossus, was designed and built by a Post Office team. The GPO commissioned the world's largest satellite earth station at Goonhilly Down in Cornwall in 1962. And it was a pioneer in fibre optics, installing the first public network optical cable link in 1978. The following year the Post Office played a key role in setting up Inmarsat, the global system that remains the leading player in maritime communications today.

However, a major setback was the failure to foster a successful electronic telephone switching system until late in the day. True, there had been some impressive development work. The world's first electronic exchange was opened at Highgate Wood in 1962.[42] But it proved unsuitable and the subsequent delays in commissioning a viable product left British suppliers at a serious disadvantage to overseas competitors.

In the 1960s Britain had a fairly high level of telephone usage, and demand was growing rapidly. To Tony Benn, the case for a complete separation of telecommunication and postal services was obvious. Ironically, the first step on the road which would eventually turn one of the biggest government departments into one of the biggest private companies in the land was initiated by a Labour government in 1969. But a full and formal split between post and telecommunications did not occur until the 1980s.[43]

Privatisation Pressures

The Post Office was fortunate to have two notable leaders during the 1970s. The first was Bill Ryland ("a very bright man" – Tony Benn), chairman between 1971 and 1977. He was succeeded by William Barlow, who served as chairman from 1977 to 1980 and oversaw the creation of British Telecom (BT) as a state corporation in 1980.

Barlow pressed for privatisation[44] and the government soon realised that BT was eminently saleable. The sell-off revenue would make a useful offset to the public sector borrowing requirement (PSBR), the modish preoccupation of the day. The privatisation of BT was to prove profoundly destructive to the British telecoms industry and needs to be looked at in some detail.

During the run-up to 51 per cent privatisation in 1984, two concerns were the potential for monopoly and the long-term threat to the traditional equipment suppliers. By mid-1984 BT had placed orders for over 400 System X exchanges but still had many hundreds of centres to upgrade. On the eve of privatisation BT shortlisted overseas manufacturers for a large order and hinted that a previous undertaking to limit foreign buying to 10 per cent of total purchases would be broken.

The privatisation itself drew fierce criticism for gross underpricing of public assets,[45] for the monstrous fees[46] handed to City institutions[47] and for the weak regulatory climate into which the new giant was launched.[48] Within months the unease over the buying policy of what was now the most potent single influence on the future of information technology in Britain, with nearly £2bn a year to spend,[49] was turning to concern.[50, 51, 52]

BT had begun to place big orders with foreign suppliers of digital equipment, booked £100m worth of computers from IBM rather than ICL[53] and acquired 51 per cent of Mitel, a Canadian supplier of private telephone exchanges.[54] This was rightly seen by the stock market as ominous for BT's traditional suppliers. Share prices fell 5 per cent in the case of Plessey and 7 per cent for STC.

The policy whereby a newly privatised BT was abandoning its traditional suppliers was chided in *The Times*: "The trouble is that, while Plessey and GEC had a captive customer in the old BT, they were also captive suppliers. ...System X was built to BT specifications and the companies geared up investment to sell it to BT. Export orders have failed to materialise so far, partly because the other big markets have similar cosy arrangements with domestic suppliers, partly because British export aid is not used as part of industrial policy as in many rival countries, and partly because of the suspicion that BT's needs might not be the same as those of other potential buyers."[55]

Trojan Horse

By the end of 1985, GEC, whose telecom operations in Coventry alone employed more than 10,000 people, had announced redundancies and was blaming BT for lack of support.[56] BT's response was that the UK manufacturers were not delivering the new equipment quickly enough and overseas producers such as Ericsson, which had lined up a Trojan horse joint venture with Thorn, were ready to supply.

Among the contracts placed by BT with non-traditional sources were big orders for the System Y exchange offered by Thorn Ericsson. The bulk of this equipment was imported, and the difficult implications for the British telecom producers were spelt out in a review by the newly formed regulatory body, Oftel.

The government washed its hands of responsibility for BT procurement. A prominent government backbencher in the House of Lords expressed concern, explaining that the British telecommunications industry needed time to adjust before having its firm home base eroded by overseas suppliers.[57]

Meanwhile, Mercury Communications, the fledgling network operated by recently privatised Cable & Wireless, placed a key order for a digital exchange with Canada's Northern Telecom. This dashed the hopes of STC, which had been shortlisted and saw it as the last opportunity to keep a presence in the British public exchange business.[58]

At the same time System X exports were struggling. It had not been launched on the international market until 1979, and critics claimed that it was good but overengineered to suit UK specifications.[59] Since its progenitor was John Whyte, BT's chief engineer, this was hardly surprising.

System X was competing in a sector already dominated by established players such as Alcatel, AT&T, LM Ericsson, Siemens and the Japanese, most of whom could depend on domestic markets far less open than the UK's. Ericsson was also strong in Australia, Latin America and Scandinavia, Siemens had penetrated Asia and Africa, and India had been pocketed by Alcatel in a shady backdoor deal between the French and Indian governments in 1982.[60]

GEC Plessey Telecommunications

In 1987, in a move that should have occurred a decade earlier, the British manufacturers merged their interests to form GEC Plessey Telecommunications (GPT). STC had pulled out of the consortium in 1982, but in return was given the monopoly to supply TXE4A exchanges to BT. A slower pace of BT ordering, coupled with the arrival of Ericsson in the UK market, dimmed the prospects for STC[61] and in the mid-1980s there were hefty cutbacks at its plants in Ulster.[62]

Having effectively been out of the British market since 1948[63] Ericsson had sidled back into the UK. As the *Financial Times* put it, "[w]hen Thorn Ericsson won its bid to become a supplier of digital exchanges to British Telecom, the name of Thorn was an important component in gaining the upper hand over other foreign competitors". By 1988, when orders were coming through from BT,[64] the joint venture with Thorn was no longer needed and it was dumped when Ericsson bought out its partner's share.[65]

Within a few years the dire results of government policies in the UK – and also in the US, where the magnificent Bell system had been broken up in obedience to the prevailing dogma[66] – were all too apparent. A study by the Logica consultancy noted that "Britain and the US – the first nations to liberalise telecommunications without analysing the broader consequences – are the main victims of the tilt in the hi-tech balance of power to Japan".[67] Within a few years the *Financial Times* was reporting a dismal situation "in which all or part of the UK's largest domestic equipment suppliers have been sold to overseas companies".[68]

Privatisation Privations

Did the privatisation of BT at least bring advantages to consumers? A mid-1987 survey found that, far from improving, relations between the telecom giant and its customers had significantly worsened since privatisation.[69] And a survey later the same year indicated that productivity levels were among the lowest in the industrialised world.[70] UK investment in telecommunications was among the most meagre in the 13 countries studied.[71]

Nor did the picture improve. A 2012 study found that download speeds via the BT network were among the slowest in Europe.[72] In the words of a former BT engineer, "[i]n terms of broadband, the UK is at the back of the pack. We're beaten by almost every other European country and Asia leaves us for dust." BT was also failing in more mundane areas, such as the simple provision of landlines.[73]

The telecoms privatisations featured shabby instances of revolving doors between government and industry. Norman Tebbit, who had been secretary of state for industry from 1983 to 1985, did not let this stop him taking a BT directorship in 1987. And David Young, a prominent member of the government which sold off the old workhorse of imperial communications, Cable & Wireless (C&W), eventually took over as chairman. As with many privatisations the record of Cable & Wireless under private ownership was dismal. After five years and as many CEOs, Young left the company.[74]

Digitalisation Delays

BT investment spending remained meagre and the digitalisation of its whole system was not achieved until 1998. In the meantime the telecoms manufacturers had faced still greater pressures. In its traditional cable areas STC could still display major strengths. It remained the world's largest supplier of submarine cable in the early 1980s, claiming 60 per cent of the market. And in 1983 the company won an important contract for the world's first optic fibre transatlantic submarine cable.[75]

But at home its position was eroding. One of the last significant moves by STC under the management of the distinguished industrialist Kenneth Corfield[76] was its acquisition of ICL. With profitability still fragile, however, the company was vulnerable to takeover.

STC was one of the few remaining British-owned high-tech companies, and the possibility that it might be sold to an overseas buyer naturally aroused concern. This was in no way allayed when its chairman, Arthur Walsh, breezily dismissed the need to preserve British ownership as a "macho" consideration which should not enter into business decisions.[77]

The buyer that emerged in 1990 was Canada's Northern Telecom (Nortel), which already held 27 per cent of STC. Under new ownership STC became a much-reduced player in UK telecommunications. Its demise was mourned by many who recalled the company's important innovations in the communications field.[78, 79]

The last significant British presence was GEC. In 1998, when GEC was being reshaped by the new regime that had succeeded Arnold Weinstock, the company tried to turn itself into a force in telecoms by acquiring Siemens' 40 per cent stake in GPT. This was followed by the extraordinary sequence of events in which GEC attempted to buy its way back into the front line of telecoms only to dice with bankruptcy.

Worse, when the time came for BT to award the £10bn contracts for its 21st Century Network project in 2005, not a penny of the business was awarded to Marconi, GEC's successor. The result of this disaster was that most of what was left of Marconi went to Ericsson.

This meant the end of a British telecoms manufacturing industry. From doctrinaire and feckless privatisation of the biggest customer in the land to belated modernisation of its complacent successor, it took only a decade or two to destroy what had taken a century to build.

Racy Racal

Racal Electronics was a much more recent entrant to British telecoms than the venerable organisations serving the telephone network. Racal's dramatic rise was followed, as with so many British companies, by swift dismemberment.

The company started life as an instrumentation supplier to the radio communications industry in the early 1950s.[80] Through a mixture of astute acquisition, high-risk initiative and shrewd management it grew to be the third largest British electronics company. At peak it had a dozen factories and a labour force of 30,000.

The base for Racal's early expansion was the development of tactical radios for the military. The first big breakthrough came with Ministry of Defence orders for the celebrated RA17 receiver in 1955. This was followed by variants such as Larkspur and Clansman in the 1970s.

The man who was to drive the company for much of its life had meanwhile taken the reins. One of Racal's first employees, Ernie Harrison, was CEO from 1966 to 1992 and chairman for even longer.[81] A popular manager, he ran his arm's length operations with style and ruthlessness. Between 1976 and 1985 *Management Today* magazine named Racal "best managed company" every year.[82]

An early coup was a link with US-based Milgo Electronics Corporation. In 1979 Harrison took over Decca Radar. But Harrison's biggest feat was winning one of the first two mobile phone franchises in 1982. His gamble quickly paid off. Within three years Vodafone had been launched, by the end of the decade it had been partially floated on the Stock Exchange as Racal Telecoms and in 1991 the balance was floated as Vodafone.

The flotation had, however, left the erstwhile parent prey to takeover, with City opportunists focusing on what they charmingly called Rump Racal. A bid from acquisitive Williams Holdings was swatted away without much difficulty, but break-up was in the wind.

In 1994 Decca Radar was sold to Litton Industries of the US, and within a decade the once-famous name had disappeared. In 1999 Racal Telecoms was sold to another US company, Global Crossing, for £1bn.

A few months later came the most dramatic sale of all. In its quest to build a credible position in marine electronics, France's state-controlled Thomson-CSF made a £1.8bn bid for Racal. An Anglo-French deal in the opposite direction would be impossible to imagine. But this one evinced little more than a shrug from the (Labour) government of the day. The bid was too good to turn down. An insouciant Harrison received the City's gratitude for another lucrative fix, and retired to the golf course.

For Thomson, now portentously renamed Thales after the Greek father of Western philosophy, it was a brilliant deal. It brought access to the lucrative defence market of the UK, still running the largest military budget in Europe and building two giant aircraft carriers. So strong was the Thales position that in 2003 it won the design competition for the new vessels and became a member of the construction consortium. Racal's new owner was now earning half its revenues from its international business, of which the UK subsidiary was the biggest single source.

Quite why a British company could not be enjoying those revenues while serving queen and country remains hard to understand.

Consumer Electronics

Like computers, British consumer electronics took off in the 1950s. Many of the manufacturers had their origins between the wars, an era marked by depression but also by the birth of promising new industries within a nurturing framework of protection. Like other light industries, consumer electronics was concentrated in the south of England, often in the London area.

Radio ownership raced up and firms such as Bush, Cossor, Dynatron, Ecko, Ferguson, Hacker, Mullard, Murphy, Philips, Pye, Rank, Roberts and Ultra became household names. Some were also heavily involved in TV set production when the television market boomed in the late 1950s. By 1960 there were more than 11m TV sets in use, far more than anywhere except the USA.[83]

For a while, wirelesses, record players, tape recorders and TV sets were supplied almost entirely by domestic producers, including Mullard and other British subsidiaries of Philips of the Netherlands. Yet, in recent times almost all the traditional makes have disappeared, and most of the best known are no more than a memory.

Even in 1970 three-quarters of TV sales came from the four major British-based companies and another 20 per cent from smaller brands such as EMI, Pye and Ultra. However, the early 1970s brought the arrival of foreign TV manufacturers. The Japanese producers gained a significant toehold during the Barber boom of the early 1970s and then continued to gain market share.

An increasingly concerned British government fostered an agreement limiting Japanese imports to 10 per cent of the market while encouraging the Japanese to establish joint ventures with British companies. These initiatives allowed them to consolidate their hold in the UK and achieve duty-free entry to the EEC.

For a while the strategy worked. It helped to promote greater efficiency, better product quality and higher exports. But in the long run the incursion of overseas producers spelt the death of a significant indigenous TV receiver industry.

EMI Triumph to Tragedy

Few stories in electronics are more poignant than that of EMI. Inventive and internationally renowned, the company's history ended in ignominious litigation, dismemberment and interment.

Its origins were in the 1920s, when the Columbia Gramophone Company and the Gramophone Company combined to form Electrical and Musical Industries. Much of the impetus for EMI's expansion in electronics came from the work of Isaac Shoenberg.

The consumer market did not at first dominate EMI's activities. During the Second World War the group pursued military goals and developed the first defensive radar system. With the return of peace EMI redirected itself to civilian activities while still supplying military avionics.

Shoenberg's achievements had not ended with his triumph in television, since he moved on to the development of video recording. Thanks to a major manufacturing and research centre at the company's headquarters in Hayes, west London,[84] EMI became an iconic name in the world of broadcasting and sound reproduction.

A jewel in the dowry of the Gramophone Company was His Master's Voice (HMV), the leading brand for what was now the world's biggest gramophone record manufacturer. EMI also deepened its involvement in television equipment and developed Britain's first transistorised computer, the EMIDEC 1100, in the 1950s.

The profits from the music side financed impressive developments at Hayes. One of the most spectacular was the body scanner, unveiled in 1971. EMI's new product pioneered chromatic axial tomography (CAT or CT) and was hailed as the most significant advance in radiography since the X-ray. It earned research manager Godfrey Hounsfield a Nobel Prize for Physiology or Medicine – an extraordinary distinction for an industrial engineer with only a brief involvement in medical sciences.

US rival General Electric (GE) threw huge resources into competing, however, and within a few years it had caught up. Litigation for patent infringement proved inconclusive and EMI gave up.[85] Eight years after launching its superb invention it sold the scanner business to GE, and at the end of the 1970s merged with Thorn to form Thorn EMI.

The hope was that EMI research would benefit Thorn Consumer Electronics. Unfortunately, the financial climate had changed profoundly. By the mid-1980s new management was proving susceptible to the City mantra of short-term shareholder value and embarked on a decade of divestment. This brought the group little benefit, and in 1996 EMI was floated off again as the EMI Group.

With the closure of its record pressing operations in 2000 the company was entirely dependent on music recording and publishing – the largest such business in the world – and retailing. The next few years were marked by shrinking markets and a failed bid for Warner Music, on which EMI spent an "incredible" £43m.[86] Such setbacks did not prevent Eric Nicoli from collecting over £3m when he stepped down as chief executive after the company was taken over in 2007.[87]

The new owner was Terra Firma Capital Partners, an opportunistic private equity outfit headed by executives devoid of music industry experience. Typically, the deal had been financed with vast borrowings and the group staggered from crisis to crisis, shedding thousands of employees along the way.

Things only got worse when Terra Firma called in Blackstone Group financial associate John Studzinski.[88] In 2011 the company's main financier, Citigroup, wrote off £2.2bn and took ownership of the company.[89] What was left of the world's most famous music group was then progressively dismembered between Universal Music Group, Sony and other aspirants to the challenging world of recorded music. An illustrious history came to an ignominious end.[90]

Thorn Electrical

Jules Thorn, an energetic Austrian émigré, founded his eponymous company in Edmonton in the late 1920s and built it into a leading producer of lamps and lighting products. The company became Thorn Electrical Industries in 1936.[91]

It was not until after the war that there was a significant move into consumer electronics. The boom in TV demand prompted takeovers of Ferguson Radio in the late 1950s and Ultra Radio and Television a few years later. In the 1970s Thorn became the most efficient and productive of the UK TV makers, and best placed to withstand the Japanese.

There was a spate of acquisitions in consumer durables, followed by the merger with EMI in 1979 and the purchase of a privatised Inmos in 1984. Thorn EMI was now a substantial conglomerate, with interests ranging from household appliances and consumer goods to recorded music and industrial and military electronics.

This made it an obvious target. At this point a new team took over, with Colin Southgate, ominously popular with analysts and financial journalists, at the helm. Urged on by City fantasies about the profit potential from demerger, he spent the next decade doing the fashionable thing – diluting and selling off the group's manufacturing operations.[92]

By the early 1990s Thorn EMI had dumped more than 60 companies and sold its core lighting business to General Electric. Other major disposals included the sale of Ferguson to France's market-hungry Thomson, the sale of Missile Electronics to another arm of Thomson and the sale of Thorn Sensors – again to the French.

The group now comprised two branches, the prosaic business of TV rentals and the more exotic world of music. All to no avail. The sad reality was that "the old overgrown version produced better returns for shareholders than the lovingly pruned and reshaped group".[93] But the City at last got its destructive demerger. In 1996 EMI was floated off as the EMI Group. This was saddled with a millstone of debt, carved up and picked to pieces by private equity and investment banking interests.

Most of what was left of Thorn was acquired in 1998 by an arm of Japanese banking group Nomura. This was run by Guy Hands, later of Terra Firma Capital Partners, the outfit which subsequently took over EMI. The balance of Thorn went to a private buyer in 2007.

A Reckoning

How does the balance sheet for British electronics look? What is the legacy of that extraordinarily rich scene still evident in the 1970s? The question was asked in a *Financial Times* survey in the late 1980s. James Blyth, retired managing director of Plessey, noted a striking paradox. On the one hand, British companies had an enviable profit record when compared with their international peers. On the other hand, they had not managed to expand in step with those peers.[94]

Blyth put it bluntly. If these great British electronics companies were to be world players, they had to "take a margin diminution". In other words, be less greedy and short-termist, and lower their profit requirements. It was already getting late. The trade deficit, negligible in the 1970s, had surged since 1980, the relative size of electronics in the economy was stagnating, and there was growing concentration in the hands of foreign companies.

Three decades on, these problems have only become more pronounced. The trade deficit has continued to balloon. Electronics output has stagnated. And the concentration of the industry in the hands of foreign companies has become overwhelming. With the sale of Arm Electronics to a Japanese company there is barely a single significant British contender right across the sector.

For the *FT* writer in the late 1980s, "these ills can be traced to the... policies of the present government".[95] That the criticism can be extended to the administrations of the 1990s and the 2000s does not mitigate the original charge. The successors to the Thatcher years were trapped by the fundamental changes ushered in by that baneful era.

The impact varies, of course. In computers the ultimate supremacy of the Americans and their Asian disciples would have been impossible to prevent. Britain could never realistically have hoped for more than a niche role in manufacture and a more significant role in design and software. In semiconductors the outcome is more debatable, and the insouciance with which Inmos and other promising initiatives were abandoned the more culpable.

In telecoms, the crass way in which BT and other public assets were privatised simply crippled the domestic equipment suppliers. Across the

Channel, a responsible and determined reshaping of industry guided the genesis of a French telecom manufacturing giant.

In consumer electronics the strategy of encouraging non-EEC companies to use the UK as a stepping stone to the Continent, with no regard for the incumbents, proved a failure. For a while it looked benign as the UK enjoyed a boom in TV sets and hi-fi equipment, but when the newcomers went away they left an industrial wasteland. And in industrial and military electronics the official indifference to changes of ownership allowed the flagships to be dismembered and snapped up by foreign interests, to an extent unthinkable in any other country.

Trading Chips

Above all, a climate in which companies became financial counters rather than generators of wealth promoted short-term priorities at the expense of traditional approaches to ownership and investment. This allowed scores of companies to be carved up or traded on the narrowest financial criteria.

The experience elsewhere is revealing. True, other European countries, the US and even Japan have followed some of the same paths as Britain. Philips, the giant of European consumer electronics, has ended all TV production on the Continent.[96] And the mass market for music centres, CD players, DVD players and their successors has largely been ceded to Asian producers.

On the other hand, while companies like Siemens and Bosch have retreated from consumer electronics they have built very successful stakes in household appliances and, of course, go from strength to strength in the industrial field.

The Japanese giants have drawn lessons from their experience.[97] Sony, Panasonic and Sharp have lost billions of dollars on their consumer goods.[98] They built their empires on complex electromechanical devices. But the digital revolution changed both the way they function and the way they are made. They involve far more investment in design and software, and far less in hardware. The Japanese were left behind by the Koreans and now the Chinese.

Hitachi's response has been to return to its core businesses: heavy engineering, gas turbines, steam turbines, nuclear power, high-speed trains

– the infrastructure of modern civilisation.

Britain once had a company which could do these things. It was called GEC. Criminally, it was downsized, streamlined, refocused and, in the end, picked to bits and looted by short-term financial operators. And what was left of a cohort of fine companies which could do the other useful things – Decca, EMI, Mullard, Plessey, Racal, STC, Thorn – was sold off and their ownership scattered across the European mainland.

The disappearance of most British names in electronics does not always mean the demolition of their operations. Some have survived their sale to other owners, often foreign. But many have not, and those that still exist are ghosts of what they once were.

Industry comment remains improbably optimistic. A government-sponsored ESCO (Electronic Systems Challenges and Opportunities) report in 2013 put the output of the industry at £78bn, equivalent to 5.4 per cent of GDP.[99] But the total includes a large development and services sector, suggesting a much smaller share for manufacturing and far below the 6.5 per cent seen as inadequate for a modern economy in the 1980s.

The UK may, in the grand claims of another recent survey, be a "leader in independent electronics system design…as well as microprocessor design, video, graphics, audio and many other areas". But the notion that Britain might rectify the omissions of "successive governments who have missed opportunities to build on electronic engineering successes and build an industry that rivals South Korea" is surely fanciful.

CHAPTER 13

Textiles Unravel

> *All the people were going clattering down the street in their clog-irons on the pavement. Yes, it was a happy feeling: everybody was going to work and you were part of a huge family.*
>
> *Millworker, All Our Working Lives Revisited, BBC[1]*

The Oldest Industry

Textiles vies with shipbuilding as Britain's oldest manufacturing industry. In time it became the largest. At its zenith British textiles were a wonderfully rich tapestry of mills, factories, finishers, warehouses, workshops, exchanges, merchants, dealers and traders – the greatest on earth.

Prior to the eighteenth century, textiles in the British Isles meant mainly wool and woollen products. Linen could be combined with wool to make the linsey-woolsey and fustian cloths worn by all but the wealthiest.[2] And for them there was also lustrous silk, introduced to England by refugee Huguenot weavers in the seventeenth century.

For much of their history cotton, wool and other materials followed distinct development paths. Producers tended to specialise in one fibre or the other and they were often based in locations specific to their particular trade. It was not until quite recent times that there was significant integration between one branch of the industry and another.

There is one exception to this. With the arrival of man-made fibres in the twentieth century, major substitutes became available to most textile manufacturers. Nevertheless, the latter still tended to be associated with their traditional raw materials and the activities which had defined them. Only in a few materials, such as rayon and nylon, did new variants of textile manufacturing arise.

Though wool had an ancient tradition in England and other parts of the British Isles, cotton eventually overtook it and for long remained king. It became the largest sector of employment, made the biggest contribution to the economy, generated the biggest export earnings, and received the most attention from government.

By the eighteenth century, Britain's trading reach had improved the availability of cotton from the East, and this inexpensive and versatile material quickly came to rival more traditional fabrics. However, England's cotton textile industry, so often seen as a centrepiece of the Industrial Revolution, in part owes its existence not to free trade but to protection.[3] Governments intervened in favour of English wool interests against cotton, then advanced wool and cotton against linen, and finally favoured all indigenous textiles over foreign producers.

Historically, the main source of cotton textiles was India, whose handloom weavers produced high-quality cloth for export. This threatened British wool textile makers and traders. Pressure from vested interests in the eighteenth century secured a succession of tariffs and import controls on Indian goods, and ultimately these were barred from the British market.[4] The effect was the opposite to what was intended, since it encouraged the growth of indigenous cotton textiles.[5] The stage was set for a huge new industry in Britain.

Two more ingredients were necessary. One was a series of inventions which allowed cotton to be machine-processed into textiles on a factory basis. Among the more renowned advances were the spinning jenny, developed by Thomas Highs and James Hargreaves in the 1760s, Richard Arkwright's spinning frame, patented in 1769, and Samuel Crompton's mule, widely adopted by the end of the eighteenth century.[6]

Slavery

The other ingredient for a new industry was a dependable source of inexpensive raw material. This began to flow from the southern states of the newly independent USA in the 1780s.[7] Over the next century the market for cotton became more differentiated as higher qualities were cultivated. One of the first premium grades was Sea Island cotton from the coastal plantations of the Carolinas and Georgia. Later came Egyptian and Sudanese cottons, celebrated for their long staple and the lustrous finishes they bestowed on the textiles for which they were used.

The slave plantations of the American south quickly became the main source of raw material to the rapidly growing textile industry in the former colonial power. Britain's mill owners were now able to benefit from exploited labour on both sides of the Atlantic. Many of the new English mills employed women on low wages and children on none. Juveniles from workhouses and orphanages were indentured to work as unpaid apprentices in conditions of slavery.[8] It was only in 1833 that child labour began to be regulated through the first Factory Act. And a 70-hour adult working week was the norm in the mills of Lancashire until the Ten Hour Act was passed in 1847.

The combination of cheap labour, mechanised production, ample raw material and import protection proved a potent mix, and by the end of the eighteenth century Britain was the world's leading producer of cotton textiles. Rapid expansion in the nineteenth century generated two distinctive features to the industry. One was a high degree of geographical concentration. The other was a low level of vertical integration, with most firms specialising in a single stage of processing.

The cotton industry became concentrated in the north-west of England, mainly in Lancashire.[9] There was a classic growth pole effect. As the industry grew, the cotton mills benefitted from a widening local pool of skilled labour, a concentrated network of related activities, and access to seaports such as Liverpool.

The output of finished goods rose 30-fold during the nineteenth century, and by its close Britain had over half the world's cotton spindles. In exports the main outlets of earlier years, Europe and North America, had been largely replaced by vast semi-captive markets in India and China.

Protection and After

Whole towns became identified with a particular country or product. Blackburn wove for India, Burnley for China.[10] Nottingham was famous for cotton hosiery and lace,[11] Londonderry/Derry for shirts.[12]

Textiles assumed huge importance in Britain's export trade. Having overtaken wool as Britain's main export in the early 1800s,[13] cotton reinforced its ascendancy. By the early twentieth century textiles – the great bulk of which were cotton – comprised a quarter of all exports.

This was its zenith. The boom came to a sudden end in the years after the First World War. Indeed, the interwar period was the watershed when British textiles ceased to be predominantly an export industry.[14] Its main competitor was Japan, whose exports overtook those of the UK in the 1930s.

Britain's traditional overseas outlets were racing down the road to self-sufficiency, closing the open markets so long taken for granted by British mills. India imposed import tariffs and set about rebuilding its own domestic production,[15] cutting imports from the UK by 70 per cent. Protection was also hitting British exports elsewhere. So, while global textiles production was rising, British output was falling and its share of the international market was slipping even faster.

Domestic demand for textiles proved relatively resilient during the Depression but it was not immune. A big surplus of capacity emerged in spinning, weaving and finishing. But restructuring proved as elusive in the famously fragmented textile business as it did in machine tools, steel or shipbuilding.

Among the main supports for the industry were tariffs and import restrictions. The McKenna Duties imposed since 1915 applied to luxury products, and there were restraints on lower value items. However, there were major concessions to empire and Commonwealth countries. Since these were developing great textile industries of their own, this was to prove very damaging to British interests.

Even during the Second World War the issues facing the industry were not forgotten. In 1944 a study mission confirmed that US productivity was far higher than it was in the UK. The main factors were the use of modern machinery and standardised bulk production. These themes became an obsession with at least one of Britain's key players in years to come.

The post-war Labour government took an active role in fostering textiles. Development councils for wool and clothing were established in 1947, and a Cotton Industry Board soon after. Concentration and investment were encouraged in the Cotton Industry (Re-equipment Subsidy) Act of 1948. However, the response from the textiles sector, particularly cotton, was disappointing. The industry was enjoying a post-war revival in the absence of Japan and other players whose trade had been crippled by the war.

Commonwealth imports now became the main challenge.[16] Producers in India, Pakistan and Hong Kong were often using more modern machinery than their UK counterparts. So rapid was their advance that by the end of the 1950s Britain had become a net importer of cotton cloth. By 1960 per capita UK imports of Asian textiles were the highest in the world.

Though less interventionist than its predecessor, the Conservative government that assumed office in 1951 imposed import quotas on India, Hong Kong and Pakistan. It also passed the 1959 Cotton Industry Act, with incentives for replacing obsolete machinery. The Act triggered a succession of events that were to have a profound effect on the textiles and clothing industry. In a business where restructuring had been rare, alliances, mergers and takeovers quickly became the norm. Many were led by a handful of remarkable figures who came to dominate the industry.

Courtaulds, Viyella

Few companies made more of a mark on textiles than Courtaulds.[17] After specialising in silk and mourning crape in the nineteenth century,[18] Courtaulds was reborn in the twentieth as a producer of man-made fibres. Following acquisition of the rights to a process developed by British scientists in the 1890s, its specialism was viscose. Courtaulds remained a dominant player in viscose, rayon and acetate (closely related materials) throughout the interwar period.

In 1947 the chairmanship of the board went to John Hanbury-Williams, who presided over substantial investment in fibres. This included nylon through the huge British Nylon Spinners joint venture with ICI. After Hanbury-Williams retired in 1962 the chairmanship passed to Frank Kearton.

Frank Kearton, a director since 1952, had come to the fore in fighting off a bid for Courtaulds from ICI. A manager of outstanding ability,[19] he got on well with the politicians of the day[20] and became a towering figure in the industrial landscape of the 1960s and 1970s.[21] He was a technical optimist and a patriot who, in a striking contrast to the defeatism that was to characterise much of political and business opinion in the 1970s and 1980s, believed that even in a downbeat sector like textiles British industry could – and should – be revived.

At the time he took over Courtaulds was a giant – the world's biggest producer of cellulosics and the third largest in man-made fibres. Yet despite its successful battle with ICI it was seen as staid and slow-moving. It was heavily involved in artificial fibres, but in the slowest-growing sector. Where should it go next?

Kearton's answer was downstream into textiles and clothing. Almost a third of the company's output of viscose staple went to textile mills. Man-made fibres were becoming the dominant raw material in textiles. Kearton wanted to be on the front line of this revolution. And he believed that, with hefty investment, product standardisation and longer production runs, British textiles "have every prospect … of becoming a growth industry once more".

Quite how the industry was going to beat back the inroads of Commonwealth producers was never really clear. But Kearton hoped the interventionist Labour government that came to power in 1964 would accept an infant industry argument and impose meaningful protection.

He pursued his goal with extraordinary determination. There was investment in new facilities and in takeovers. Early acquisitions included major concerns such as Lancashire Cotton and Fine Spinners & Doublers and over the course of the 1960s Courtaulds bought more than 50 textile and clothing companies.

The expansion chimed with the economic policies of the new Labour government. Kearton was close to an administration which believed bigger industrial units were vital to Britain's competitiveness. He was, indeed, the first chairman of the Industrial Reorganisation Corporation, set up in 1966 to promote restructuring.

The 1959 Act prompted a cascade of restructuring across the industry and the reverberations have echoed down to the present day. The detail is inevitably quite dense and complex but the story involves some of the most redolent names in British manufacturing and tracks the downward evolution of one of the country's oldest industries. One whose decline owes less to the three villains – macroeconomic mismanagment, privatisations and City meddling – so often identified elsewhere and perhaps more to the evolutionary pattern beloved of economic determinists.

In 1960 J&P Coats merged with Patons and Baldwins to form the world's largest manufacturer of woollen yarn and cotton thread. Four years later the group bought Pasolds, maker of Ladybird childrenswear, and in 1967 it acquired Jaeger. Among other classic names changing hands in those years were Tootal, bought by English Sewing Cotton in 1963,[22] and Rael-Brook, taken over by Calico Printers in 1965.

Another dramatic growth story was that of Viyella. Following its abortive bid for Courtaulds in 1962 ICI bought out Courtaulds' stake in British Nylon Spinners but remained uncomfortable with the growing presence of its rival in the textiles field. Instead of outright acquisition, however, ICI opted for minority stakes in companies like Carrington & Dewhurst and Viyella as counters to Courtaulds.

A key ally was Joe Hyman.[23] Descended from émigré Russian merchants, Hyman was another moderniser who became a business superstar of the 1960s. With the help of ICI he built Viyella into one of the largest textile groups in the country, with dozens of mills and many thousand employees. Among Hyman's bolder acquisitions was Combined Egyptian Mills, once the world's second biggest spinning company.

Despite his spectacular reign at Viyella, however, the board eventually evicted Hyman, probably at the prompting of ICI, in 1969.[24] Hyman tried to relive his successes with Viyella in the wool textiles industry, but failed to make the same impact.

Courtaulds and English Calico

Meanwhile, Courtaulds was still busy. In 1969 it made one of its largest forays yet with a bid for English Calico. The takeover target had been formed the previous year by the merger of English Sewing Cotton and Calico Printers' Association (CPA). CPA's main claim to fame had been the pioneering work that led to terylene, one of the most successful of all the artificial fibres.[25]

The authorities were now harbouring second thoughts about the pace of concentration in textiles, and put a ban on further mergers involving what were now the big five – Courtaulds, English Calico, Viyella, Carrington & Dewhurst and Coats Paton.

It was not the end of restructuring. Under a new government in 1970 ICI took control of Viyella and Carrington & Dewhurst to form Carrington Viyella. And there were many more textiles restructurings in years to come. But for Courtaulds the great acquisitions drive was at an end.

Kearton may have been disappointed in his hope for greater protection for his dream of a reborn industry. Nevertheless, 1964 had seen the imposition of a blanket 15 per cent import surcharge, and the 1967 sterling devaluation had been equally – if temporarily – helpful. The far-sighted Industrial Training Act of 1964 encouraged apprenticeships in knitting, lace, carpet, wool, cotton and clothing. And there was public funding for export promotion in woollens, hosiery and clothing.

Yet the industry remained under pressure. It was not until 1972 that tariffs replaced the very loose quotas set in 1959 for imports from India, Pakistan and Hong Kong. Worse, the first Multi Fibre Agreement that came into place the following year still exempted Commonwealth producers. The same was true of the second Multi Fibre Agreement, in 1978.

An almost slavish adherence to free trade principles on the part of the government ensured that life would remain very tough for British textiles.

The Fall of Courtaulds

Kearton retired from Courtaulds in 1975 and went off to fresh battlegrounds. Back at Courtaulds his formidable creation began to unravel. Though the closure of a large mill at Skelmersdale in 1976 cost 1,000 jobs, cutbacks were generally cautious. This changed soon after Christopher ("Cash Comes First") Hogg arrived as chief executive in 1979. The skies over Courtaulds were darkening with the changing political and commercial climate in the country at large.

One of the first results was a recession that in just 12 months closed over 200 textile mills. Yet, although 1980/81 was described as the "worst year in the company's history", Courtaulds still managed a small profit. Indeed, in striking contrast to its European counterparts, some of whom needed hefty state assistance, it never made a loss throughout the bleak years of the 1980s.

This did not stem the retrenchment. With companies now freer to kill off operations seen as a drag on short-term financial performance, Courtaulds waded in with indecent eagerness. Job losses rocketed from 8,000 in 1979 to 15,000 in 1980 and over 40,000 in total by 1985. Textiles bore the brunt,[26] with two dozen Courtaulds-owned plants terminated.[27]

Though Hanson had bought a small "warning" stake, this was for the moment enough to keep the carpet-baggers at bay. Nevertheless 1985 saw institutional pressure force Courtaulds into the fatal step of carving itself into two divisions, one for textiles and one for other interests. The final stage in the dismemberment of the group came in 1990, when the two divisions were floated off as separate companies.

Courtaulds Textiles was now run by an able former journalist, Martin Taylor, and there was an echo of Kearton's ambitions in his quest for big brand acquisitions. Courtaulds plc went to Sipko Huismans, once a protégé of Kearton.[28] Huismans greeted the crippling recession of the early 1990s, born of the Lawson boom and the Major/Lamont ERM fiasco, as a "stimulating experience, more like a cold shower" and "not made in Downing Street".[29]

It seems unlikely that the shop-floor employees laid off in yet another round of factory closures would have shared his callous enthusiasm.

After Martin Taylor stepped down from Courtaulds Textiles in 1994 the succession passed to Noel Jervis and then Colin Dyer. More retrenchment followed. There were also acquisitions, but these had the unfortunate effect of making the company even more dependent on Marks & Spencer, which now took nearly half the output of Courtaulds Textiles. The dangers were underlined when Marks & Spencer abruptly dumped its time-honoured tradition of buying British and began sourcing overseas.

The following year there was a bid for Courtaulds Textiles by Sara Lee, a US mini-conglomerate. In opposing the bid, Dyer offered the sorry defence that in the previous five years the Courtaulds Textiles board had ended 40 per cent of its UK manufacturing and doubled its offshore sourcing of clothes.

The bid was successful,[30] but Sara Lee struggled and investor pressure prompted another break-up. In 2005 what was left of Courtaulds Textiles and Clothing was divided between a US private equity outfit and a Chinese entrepreneur.[31] Before long the former Courtaulds factories in the UK were down to just one and today, while some of the businesses still exist, little of what they sell is made in Britain.

The other arm of the old empire, Courtaulds plc, had been also sold to another foreign buyer, Akzo Nobel of the Netherlands.[32] Like many Continental companies, Akzo Nobel had articles of association which made it almost impregnable to takeover yet allowed it to take its pick of more open counterparts. One day it was to take over what was left of Courtaulds' great rival, ICI.

There was foolish press comment that the deal could launch the rebirth of Courtaulds as one of the great names of UK industry. But Akzo had absolutely no intention of loosening the reins on the company that had founded the man-made fibres business. The reality was the familiar pattern of divestment, cutbacks and absorption that so often follows the takeover of British companies by foreign competitors.

Courtaulds was no more. Britain's industrial heritage, and its productive capacity, had been severely weakened. Perhaps the most poignant comment came from one of its erstwhile directors, a good and thoughtful man. Asked in after-years to explain what on earth had happened to the great company, he pondered the question for a while before simply saying that he couldn't.[33]

Cyril Harrison

In 1948 one of the more notable figures in textiles, Cyril Harrison, became managing director of English Sewing Cotton, one of the top three textile groups listed on the Stock Exchange.[34] English Sewing Cotton was a household name as Britain's second biggest supplier of thread through its popular Sylko brand.

No stranger to restructuring, in 1963 Harrison organised the takeover of Tootal, a sizeable maker of clothing and well-known for its shirts. Oddly, both ICI and Courtaulds took minority stakes in the new group.

The following year English Sewing Cotton took over Barlow and Jones, noted for Osman Towels and other luxury household products. And 1968 brought an agreed merger with Calico Printers' Association to form English Calico.

Founded at the end of the nineteenth century, Calico Printers had become the main producer of printed cloth in Britain and was the fourth largest textile company on the Stock Exchange.[35] In 1941 its research department had synthesised polyethylene terephthalate, the building block from which ICI was to develop terylene.

Another large textile group fostered by both ICI and Courtaulds was Carrington & Dewhurst. The company had become a large user of rayon between the wars and remained a big consumer of synthetic fibres after the Second World War. In 1963 Courtaulds took a minority stake and ICI also acquired an interest.

Courtaulds relinquished its stake in 1968 and ICI was left to steer the company into a merger with Viyella the following year. At about the same time the man who had made a spectacular success of Viyella over the previous decade, Joe Hyman, was forced out of his post as chief executive.[36]

David Alliance

The 1980s brought a spate of fresh restructurings. This time it was the turn of David Alliance to make his mark.[37] Yet another resourceful immigrant to have left a lasting impression on British industry, Alliance came to the UK from Iran as a young man and soon took the first steps to building a business empire. By the time he had left textiles he had made at least as great an impact as Frank Kearton.

In contrast to Kearton, however, Alliance's purchases were guided by opportunism rather than strategy. Textiles afforded lots of scope for low-cost acquisitions. By the late 1960s Alliance's interests were centred on corsetry maker Spirella, from which he launched a £5m bid ("shrewdly judged rather than generous") for a leading maker of household textiles, Vantona, in 1975.[38]

Meanwhile, Alliance was building good relations with Marks & Spencer. Under the benign guidance of Marcus Sieff M&S was then in its glory years. Many years later Alliance was to observe in his autobiography that Sieff would have been "shocked by the short-term culture that drives the City – and the company – today".[39]

In 1982 Alliance made his boldest move yet with an offer for Carrington Viyella, now eight times the size of Vantona. His target controlled classic brands like Dorma, Van Heusen and Viyella itself, but it was also regarded as a struggling giant. ICI and the minority shareholders were easily bought out. The new group was named Vantona Viyella.

Alliance's standing was reinforced by an alliance with Nottingham Manufacturing, a leading manufacturer of hosiery and knitwear owned by Harry Djanogly, in 1985. The merger brought stronger links with Marks & Spencer, to which Nottingham Manufacturing was an important supplier, and greater financial stability to Alliance's operations.

Coats Patons

An even more ambitious move came the following year with a bid for Coats Patons. Coats Patons was one of the most venerable names in textiles. Its enduring speciality, the manufacture of cotton thread, had been developed in the 1820s and for most of the nineteenth century J&P Coats was the world leader. A merger with the rival Clark Thread Company in 1952 reinforced its position, and a union with Patons & Baldwins in 1960 brought the group dominance in woollen yarns.

To win Coats Patons Alliance outbid a rival approach from knitwear group Dawson International with a huge offer of £715m. The group was renamed Coats Viyella.[40] Alliance continued his quest to fashion a textile company of international stature[41] with a strong UK production base,[42] but more jobs were lost.[43] Other deals followed over the next few years, with some, such as the 1987 purchase of Youghal Carpets, taking Alliance deeper into wool textiles.

The last of Alliance's significant textiles acquisitions was Tootal in 1990/91.[44] This brought domination of the international thread market. Alliance now headed the largest textile group in the UK. In building it he had clearly overreached. Like most older industries, textiles had contracted much faster in the 1980s than in the preceding decade. The year 1988 saw well over 1,000 job losses in Alliance's operations and the 1990s were a sorry story of repeated cutbacks. Between 1995 and 2000 Coats Viyella shed more than 5,000 jobs as the company ended its 70-year tie with Marks & Spencer.

By the end of 2000 the company had shut four Midlands factories and was planning to shed all its remaining UK clothing activities.[45] In future it would concentrate on its thread interests, mostly overseas. The sombre news was, naturally, welcomed in the City.

Meanwhile, David Alliance stepped down as chairman and handed over to Harry Djanogly. For all the travails of textiles, both men had done extraordinarily well out of Britain's oldest industry. And Alliance acknowledged it, graciously. A friendly reviewer described his autobiography as "a hymn to the openness and generosity of British society that gives the frailest of saplings from faraway lands a chance to root and grow".[46]

Yes, his adopted land had been generous. The *Sunday Times* Rich List 2015 put Alliance's personal fortune at £650m. That of Harry Djanogly has been estimated at £300m.

Shopping Abroad

The problems of British textiles at the close of the twentieth century only partly reflected broader influences such as adverse exchange rates, commitments to the Commonwealth and free trade with the European Union. They were also due to developments much closer to home, in particular the readiness of retailers to switch their supplies of clothing and household textiles from domestic sources to overseas.

This was made easier by the way British clothing manufacturers traditionally sold their output under the names of the companies which retailed their products and did not invest in their own brands, styles and images. Among their Continental rivals, independent brands for manufacturers of clothing and household textiles have been much more common. Strong images meant they could build premiums into their pricing, offsetting the cost disadvantages of a European manufacturing base.

In recent years the UK has seen a shift towards the Continental pattern. A number of brands have gained market share by reinterpreting traditional British style and selling their output through their own concessions. This has not done much, however, to reverse the offshoring of production. Here the damage has been done.

Notable among British companies which deserted their home base in favour of overseas suppliers was Marks & Spencer. After becoming the world's most profitable single brand retailer, M&S faced tougher conditions in the late 1990s. The company remained profitable but for the

City, with its unblinking gaze on the short term, the profitability setback was unacceptable. In 1999 the forceful Richard Greenbury was replaced as chief executive by Peter Salsbury, who confirmed a huge swing to overseas sourcing by a company which had always made a virtue of buying British.[47]

M&S Switch

M&S was still the outlet for up to a quarter of all UK clothing production,[48] so the new policy left few suppliers unscathed.[49] Two major clothing makers were devastated. William Baird had to retrench in Scotland,[50] the North East and the Midlands,[51] and squandered huge sums on closures and redundancies.[52] Dewhirst Group,[53] dependent on M&S for 90 per cent of its sales, closed factories in Cheshire,[54] Stoke-on-Trent, Teesside[55] and Wales.[56]

In that sad reaction of self-blame often encouraged in victims of economic adversity, one of its employees in the principality said: "When I heard that Dewhirst was closing in Lampeter, I blamed myself and many other workers did the same."[57] Needless to say, they were blameless. As nearly always in textiles and clothing, labour relations in Dewhirst had been excellent.

Today most retailers in Britain cheerfully import their lower-price garments from the East. Their trade is rarely interrupted by reports of conditions in suppliers' factories that echo the dark satanic mills of the Industrial Revolution.

Despite the debacle, Dewhirst survived but by 2010 its operations were nearly all overseas. In a total labour force of 20,000 just 4 per cent were in the UK.[58]

Meanwhile, Coats Viyella was closer to oblivion. A proposal to demerge into two main groupings, the dependable threads business and the more problematic textiles and clothing, was now reactivated.[59] What little was left of Viyella was sold, as were venerable brands such as Jaeger. Within a few years Viyella filed for bankruptcy.[60]

The main survivor was Coats. It was bought in 2003[61] by Guinness Peat Group,[62] which adopted the illustrious name of its main asset[63] and allowed it to resume what it been for the two centuries before it was bought by David Alliance – the world's leading manufacturer of industrial threads.

The difference this time was that its operations were now all overseas rather than in the UK.

Wool: the Oldest Textile

The second of the great strands in England's textile industry is wool, which long predates the Industrial Revolution.[64] Exports of English sheepskins, wool and broadcloth were well established before the arrival of the Normans[65] and sustained for centuries after.

Wool textiles became factory-based much later than in the case of cotton, and some activities remained the preserve of handloom weavers until late in the nineteenth century.[66] Nevertheless the mechanised spinning of finer grades of material, such as worsteds, was well established by mid-century.

The transition to a factory industry was accompanied by concentration into well-defined areas. Worsteds became centred on the West Riding of Yorkshire,[67] in Bradford, Halifax, Huddersfield[68] and Keighley.[69] Bradford also became the commercial centre of wool textiles. At peak 70,000 people were at work in 300–400 mills, factories and warehouses in and around the great city.[70] Though working conditions could be appalling,[71] the Bradford millionaire became a byword.[72] Premises ranged widely in size and were not all devoted to wool. The largest included the magnificent complexes of Salts Mill at Saltaire, on the edge of Bradford, and Manningham Mills.

Woollens were located predominantly in the West Riding, in Batley, Dewsbury and Leeds. Heckmondwike and Ossett were the centre of the Heavy Woollen District, noted for the manufacture of heavyweight cloth, blankets, cheaper clothing and industrial products.

There were significant centres elsewhere, notably the West Country and the Scottish Borders. Towns such as Elgin are still the location for the production of fine quality woollens to this day. The traditional weaving of Harris tweeds has survived in the Hebrides into modern times. The East Midlands saw the emergence of a major hosiery and knitwear industry centred on Leicester[73] and Loughborough. And the manufacture of wool carpets was established in the West Midlands, West Yorkshire and Glasgow.[74]

Business was considerably less volatile in wool than in cotton. Wool was less dependent on exports than cotton, and was spared the worst of the interwar collapse. Domestic demand was strong and protection ensured that imports fell and output rose markedly.[75]

Conditions remained favourable in the post-war years, when wool faced none of the problems of low-cost Commonwealth imports. In the mid-1950s, when imports of cotton textiles were making rapid inroads, imports of woollen fabrics supplied just 5 per cent of UK demand.[76]

The number of insured workers in cotton fell by over a third between the mid-1920s and the end of the 1930s, whereas those in woollens and worsteds fell less than a fifth. During the 1950s the numbers employed fell 30 per cent in cotton but only 10 per cent in wool.

The manufacturers of woollens and worsteds enjoyed considerable prosperity through the 1950s and well into the 1960s. More volatile economic conditions posed unfamiliar challenges in the 1970s and there was some retrenchment, but it was not until the 1980s and 1990s that there were major cutbacks, closures and redundancies.

Illingworth Morris

For much of the post-war period the wool textiles industry remained fragmented. Apart from Coats Patons and Crossley, giants in yarn-spinning and carpet making, the biggest name in wool textiles was Illingworth Morris.[77] The firm achieved a kind of fame in the 1970s when its main shareholder, Pamela Mason, wife of the actor, vowed to revitalise its business.[78] The company had been hit by sales setbacks – first in Iran after the Islamic revolution, and then in the US after the imposition of a 50 per cent tariff on wool fabrics.[79]

Illingworth Morris had acquired some notable assets in its 125 years. Among these was the Salts Mill,[80] taken over in 1958 and surviving until the 1980s.[81] With it, Salts brought Crombie, maker of fine outerwear since the Napoleonic Wars. In a nice piece of product placement, James Mason is seen in the 1970 film *Spring and Port Wine* reverently unwrapping the beautiful overcoat his character Rafe Crompton has ordered for himself. The coat would likely have been made in Huddersfield, Mason's birthplace.

In 1982 Illingworth Morris came under the control of another of the distinctive figures[82] who have made their names in textiles. Alan Lewis[83] is credited with the revival of the group, which still employed 6,000 people in the early 1980s. Unfortunately, the recipe for revival included the eventual end of all UK manufacturing by the company. More recently Alan Lewis has been a government adviser on industrial strategy, vowing, apparently without irony, that he was "determined to restore the importance of manufacturing to the UK economy".[84]

Corah

One of the biggest sectors in wool textiles was knitwear. For many years the largest presence in an industry of small family-run firms was N. Corah, which originated with a Leicester hosiery dealer in the 1820s. In mid-century Corah moved into one of the biggest factories in the city, where its operations were the first to be powered by a steam-driven beam engine. The company was a progressive employer and still evokes affectionate memories in Leicester.[85]

Corah formed a close association with Marks & Spencer and was eventually supplying over half its output to the retail chain. For a considerable time Corah's operations grew on the back of M&S's high street popularity. There was some retrenchment in the consumer recession of the mid-1970s but it was not until the 1980s that radical change finally arrived.

In 1987 the company reported a modest loss. The following year it appointed a new chief executive. With a background in Hanson Trust, John Foulkes[86] was no stranger to ruthless cost-cutting and downsizing. Within months he had conducted a "critical review"[87] – a euphemism for closure of the knitwear division and nearly 800 job cuts.[88]

Unfortunately, Corah was now locked into a downward slide.[89] More redundancies[90] were followed by outright sale of its socks division to Courtaulds,[91] and after the departure of the last member of the founding family what remained was picked up by an investment group in 1989. Few were surprised when, not long after, the Leicester factory closed for good.

Dawson International

Dawson International concentrated on the top end of the market, making high-value knitwear from cashmere wool. The group's origins were at Otley, in the West Riding, where Joseph Dawson pioneered the processing of cashmere at a mill opened in 1871.

From the late 1960s the company began to acquire downstream producers of knitwear. Its targets were not in the West Riding but mainly in the Scottish Borders, long noted for makers of high-grade knitwear.[92] Among the illustrious names taken over by Dawson were Pringle, Ballantyne, Barrie, Braemar and Todd & Duncan. Courtaulds bought Lyle & Scott at about this time, and it was not long before most of the independent mills in the Borders had been snapped up by larger groups.

Meanwhile, Dawson International had built a presence in Western Europe and the US, where its brands had a particular cachet. At peak it had 12,000 employees. Unfortunately, conditions became much tougher. Chinese mills benefitted from the lifting of trade barriers ushered in by the World Trade Organization at the end of 2004. They could now flood the international market with bargain-basement cashmere products, and where they left off multinationals like Iqlo took over.

Dawson International had to sell off most of its assets. Pringle went to Hong Kong's SC Fang[93] in 2000, and other changes of ownership followed.[94] Most of the group's production was transferred to Italy and the Far East. Dawson struggled on at a reduced scale at the Barrie mill in Hawick,[95] only to sink under the weight of its pension commitments.[96] One of the last remnants of the group, Barrie, was sold to Chanel in 2012.[97]

Scotland's high-quality knitwear industry is now a shadow of what it was.[98] Lyle & Scott found that there was life after Courtaulds and other long-established Hawick names are still in business. The greatest survivor in Scottish knitwear is Johnstons of Elgin. Johnstons has pursued verticalisation and claims to be the only textile firm in Britain that takes its raw material – merino wool and cashmere – through all the stages to finished garment.[99] Selling both to retailers and to the leading international brands the company hopes to restore its fortunes[100] on the back of the "reshoring" trend of recent years.[101]

Unfortunately, Borders knitwear continues to face difficult conditions. The year 2015 saw losses at Lyle & Scott[102] and cutbacks at Peter Scott; 2016 opened with Hawick Knitwear, the largest producer of knitwear left in the UK, going into administration.

How long before yet another fine traditional industry faces complete oblivion?

Carpets

The manufacture of high-quality woven carpets in Britain goes back 300 years. The main operations were in the West Midlands, the west of Scotland, the West Country and the West Riding of Yorkshire.

The biggest was Dean Clough Mills in Halifax, built for Crossley's Carpets in the mid-nineteenth century.[103] A colossal complex, Dean Clough once employed many thousands. After business collapsed in the 1980s, however, the whole operation closed.[104]

Conditions have been difficult for all carpet-makers. Imports have swept in. From almost nothing in 1970, imports rose to two-thirds of the market by 2003. Among the domestic casualties have been Carpets International, Britain's biggest manufacturer, which went into receivership in 2003,[105] and Kilmarnock-based Stoddard Carpets,[106] which closed two years later. More recently, two venerable names, Axminster Carpets[107] and Brintons,[108] have had to be rescued and only survive on a much-reduced scale.

The effect on employment has been sombre. Numbers working in the sector fell from 45,000 in the early 1970s to just 7,500 three decades later. The impact on Kidderminster, host to Brintons, Crossley and other famous names, has been dramatic. At peak, between the 1950s and the 1970s, the town was "wall to wall carpets", boasting 25 factories with 15,000 employees.[109] Now there is just a handful of operations, employing a few hundred people.[110]

Jute, Linen and Silk

In the nineteenth century other textile sectors, such as silk, lace, linen and jute, were well represented in Britain. Even before the First World War, however, a US study noted that although the UK maintained a "great lead over all competitors" in flax processing it was now "greatly distanced" by India in jute manufacturing. In silk, where the UK had formerly been successful, the industry had greatly declined.[111] A century later, these industries have virtually disappeared.

In Victorian times the manufacture of jute products, such as bags, sacks and carpet backing, employed 50,000 workers on Tayside in Scotland. Almost half the workforce of Dundee was employed in jute. The city had a whaling industry, whose oil output was needed for softening the unprocessed fibre when it arrived from India.

By end of the nineteenth century the "jute barons" were setting up mills in the subcontinent, and the industry in Dundee declined.[112] However, Tay Spinners, the city's last jute mill, survived until 1998.[113] Of the three Js that were once Dundee's economic bedrock – jute, jam and journalism – only the latter remained.

Linen has been used for many centuries for clothing, sailcloth and furnishing fabrics. Its production employs fibres obtained from flax, probably introduced to Britain by the Romans.[114] During the seventeenth century the growing of flax in England was restricted to help the woollen industry, and linen production became concentrated in Ireland.

Ireland remained the focus of the industry and linen, where milling was based mainly in Belfast,[115] became its principal export. By the end of the nineteenth century the industry was dominated by the York Street Flax Spinning Company, which had 63,000 spindles and 1,000 looms.

The threat from cotton receded once Ireland's cotton industry fell victim to the competitive strength of Lancashire. It was not until the twentieth century that man-made fibres and cheap imports finally forced the linen industry in the British Isles into serious retreat. From time to time there have been reports of a renaissance,[116] but this has proved elusive.

Silk had been processed in England on a small scale for centuries, but it was given tremendous impetus by the arrival of Huguenot refugees from France in the seventeenth century. It became an industrial activity after the invention of the Jacquard loom in France at the beginning of the nineteenth century.[117]

The new device reached England, and silk-weaving became associated with Cheshire towns such as Macclesfield,[118] Congleton, Bollington and Stockport. However, by the end of the nineteenth century silk-weaving was already in decline. Today there is only a modest UK output of fabrics and finished articles.

Neglect, Delusion and Aspiration

Like all industries in long-term decline, textiles have received extensive study and analysis. A 2003 government comparison of the UK industry with its more successful Italian counterpart found that state aid to manufacturing industry, including textiles, had generally been far higher in Italy, and indeed in the EU15 as a whole, than was the case in the UK.[119] Moreover, the Italian textile and apparel industry is dominated by private firms, often family-owned, in contrast to the predominance of public companies in the UK, and this has fostered independence, flexibility and long-term commitment.

More recently the industry has itself made appreciable efforts to promote its role. A study sponsored by David Alliance in 2013 pointed to enduring capabilities in yarn-spinning, knitting and weaving alongside growth in technical textiles, materials and composites.[120] It also cited commitments from leading retailers and industry associations[121] to reshore their sourcing.[122] The report hoped that the textile and clothing industry could add 15,000 jobs to its workforce by 2020.

History suggests that textiles are one of the few UK industries where neglectful, clumsy or dogma-driven government policies do not bear a heavy burden of responsibility for their decline. Textiles and clothing were not subject to the privatisations that crippled special steels, shipbuilding, railway rolling stock, power engineering, commercial vehicles and other sectors. True, they were unquestionably damaged by the stumbling incompetence with which macroeconomic affairs were handled in the 1980s and 1990s. But this affected all of Britain's manufacturing.

Nevertheless, government was extremely complacent in the face of the import threat from the Commonwealth textile producers in the 1950s and 60s and 70s. This placed heavy pressures, not faced by their Continental counterparts, on British textiles and clothing. The voice of British industry in the face of these policies was remarkably feeble, not least because in a nation of shoppers retailers have always been so powerful.

The optimistic outlook postulated in the Alliance Report probably depends far more on the individual players in the sector than on anything the government can do. Addressing a conference around the Alliance themes in 2012, industry minister Vince Cable voiced his enthusiastic support.[123] But he had to remind his audience that there would be little government money to help a scheme trying to coax hundreds of millions of pounds in new investment into textiles and clothing.

Ambiguous Attitudes

Industry figures[124] proclaim their support for bringing clothing and textile manufacture back to Britain.[125] Yet they remain heavily compromised. Stuart Rose, former Marks & Spencer chief executive, said the ideas were not "pie in the sky…but…we will need to see a big change in the mindset of retailers, which currently devote little thought to UK-based sourcing".

This was the Stuart Rose who, in swatting away a nuisance bid from Philip Green of British Home Stores only a few years earlier, had initiated yet another "review of the group's supplier relationships" – a specious name for still more cutbacks in the domestic sourcing of M&S. The result was factory closures in Northern Ireland, including Desmonds' 165-year-old operation in Derry, the Courtaulds mill at Limavady and an Invista facility at Maydown.[126]

Reshoring faces new challenges from multi-stage processing. The "British" suit chosen for the England football team at Euro 2016 was made from cloth woven in Leeds. But before arriving in the UK the wool had been topped in China, dyed in Italy and spun into yarn in Romania. The worsted cloth was then shipped out from Leeds, this time to Cambodia, where it was cut into finished product before being sent back to Marks & Spencer.[127]

Many seem scarcely even aware of the issues. With the closure of its Rhondda factory in 2006,[128] Burberry was reduced to just two small manufacturing operations in Britain. Yet in 2012 its highly paid American chief executive proclaimed: "We are selling Britishness all around the world …all the music [sic] we use is British, all the models [sic] are British, the design team is 80 per cent from British design schools like St Martins." Since the UK is home to a third of the world's top art and design colleges, the surprise is that all the company's designers are not from British schools. And, after winning Veuve Clicquot Businesswoman of the Year in 2012, Anya Hindmarch proudly described her company as "very British", but had to concede that the proportion of her fine handbags actually made here was perhaps 5 per cent.[129]

Even with a will there may not be a way. The biggest challenge in bringing manufacturing back to the UK is the restoration of productive capacity. The director of commercial operations at John Lewis pointed out in 2013 that it was "difficult to manufacture fashion products in large numbers [in the UK] because there are not enough big factories to source the numbers it needs". And the founder of Hackett's stylish British clothing was even more blunt, claiming that it was impossible to make clothes in the UK as the skills had simply disappeared.[130]

If the hopes of the Alliance Report are to be realised, there is a very long way to go. The industry's revival clearly cannot be left to the private sector alone. As in Italy and other countries, it will require a significant well-judged input from government.

CHAPTER 14

Chemical Waste

> *There is a public duty to go on making the essential, basic chemicals even though the sales may appear to be less progressive and less profitable. ICI could not, for example, withdraw from the production of industrial explosives without giving the government and the public many years' notice of its intentions.*

Paul Chambers, ICI Chairman, 1961[1]

Imperial Industry

As a distillation of corporate philosophy, the quotation from Paul Chambers would prompt a guffaw in today's switched-on investor. Where is the aggression, the jargon, the hype that any self-respecting commercial organisation feels it needs these days? Where is the focus on aims, ambitions, aspirations? Where is the focus on – focus?

Yet, for much of the twentieth century any reference to British chemicals prompted the image of three letters – ICI. There were, of course, other significant players, notably oil companies with interests in petrochemicals. But none cast such a giant shadow as Imperial Chemical Industries.

For glib commentators, ICI was run on lines more suited to the Foreign Office than a modern commercial concern.[2] But then it wasn't exactly an import warehouse, a hedge fund or a casino. When it was formed in 1926 Imperial Chemical Industries had 33,000 employees. By the 1960s its workforce had grown fourfold and was spread across hundreds of locations in dozens of countries, making it Britain's biggest company.

True to its name, the focus was the UK and Commonwealth, but there was a growing presence in Continental Europe and the Americas. And, as the dominant force in a disparate industry, ICI's output was vast, ranging from acids, alkalis, ammonia, artificial fibres, explosives, fertilisers, non-ferrous metals and plastics to dyestuffs, medicines, paints, pesticides and many other intermediate and finished products. The lifeblood of modern industrial civilisation.

ICI was created by the 1926 merger of Brunner, Mond & Co,[3] Nobel Industries, British Dyestuffs and United Alkali Company, and brought together most of Britain's heavy chemicals industry.[4] The alliance was prompted partly by government concern at the weaknesses of the sector, particularly in relation to that of Germany. The chemical industry there had built a strong technical lead in the closing decades of the nineteenth century and, worried about losing this in the aftermath of the First World War, established a giant cartel, IG Farbenindustrie (IG Farben) in the 1920s. Cartels and other market-sharing agreements also dominated the US industry.

The architects of Britain's new flagship were Harry McGowan of Nobel Industries and Alfred Mond of Brunner, Mond. The latter had its origins in an ammonia works founded at Northwich, in Cheshire, in 1874. The partners in this enterprise were John Brunner, son of a Swiss schoolmaster, and Ludwig Mond, a German chemist who had moved to England in the 1860s. Though he became wealthy, Brunner was strongly associated with radical causes,[5] and both these remarkable men followed a progressive approach in running their business.

Among other policies they pioneered were reduced working hours (the norm for chemical workers in the 1880s being 84 hours a week), paid holidays and long service awards. Brunner and Mond brought a modern German business ethos to their activities, fostering employee consultation through the establishment of works committees. These were succeeded by the works councils that made an important contribution to the industrial cooperation characteristic of ICI throughout its existence.[6] As one commentator has put it, ICI had, "without flattery, most of the qualities of a first class German company".[7]

The emergence of ICI ensured that Britain had a strong contender in a world of managed markets, its designated territory being the Commonwealth and Southern Europe. Like many British companies ICI went from strength to strength in the era of protectionism. Despite the break-up of regional monopolies and the erosion of tariff and trade agreements after the Second World War, it remained for many years a dominant presence at home, where it had nearly half the market for industrial chemicals, and overseas.

Rich Hinterland

This prominence was not built on protectionism and tradition alone. From early on there was a strong emphasis on research and development, and by the Second World War the company had hundreds of high-quality engineers and scientists on its staff. The stark shortcomings in British technical education and training vis-à-vis Germany in Victorian and Edwardian times were redressed in the interwar period and particularly during the post-war years. And the company developed strong links with the universities. With its base in Britain it could draw on a rich intellectual hinterland. Since the first Nobel Prize for Chemistry was awarded in 1901, the UK has produced nearly as many laureates as Germany and if Commonwealth countries are included the score exceeds that of Germany.

A steady stream of important discoveries and pioneering initiatives emerged from ICI and in total it registered more than 33,000 scientific patents during its lifetime.[8] The company claimed, with justifiable exaggeration, that, in 1927, it was first to coin the word "plastics".[9] And among its notable subsequent developments were the first modern coatings – Dulux paints, developed with DuPont of the US – polythene, acrylics, high-grade thermoplastics and synthetic fibres such as Terylene and Crimplene.

ICI also proved very inventive in the field of biosciences. One of its first major discoveries was Paludrine, for many years the standard malaria prophylactic, and this was followed by halothane anaesthetics, Inderal and Tenormin beta-blockers, Tamoxifen cancer treatment, and other path-breaking drugs. In the crop protection field important developments included Gamoxone, a major pesticide, and the synthetic pyrethroids.

ICI's creativity was supported by high levels of investment. The company was active in pioneering the shift from coal feedstock to oil in the 1940s and opened a massive petrochemical complex at Wilton on Teesside, a few miles from the older works at Billingham, in the early 1950s. Not quite the first UK petrochemical complex, Wilton was nevertheless among the biggest, and required, of course, a huge capital commitment. But it fitted well with ICI's tradition of running integrated operations, supplying big tonnages of intermediate products to other divisions as well as outside customers.

A readiness to sanction the investment budget of each division on a rollover basis did not prevent the active pursuit of major areas of promise, such as the new science of pharmaceuticals. Here in contrast to its US rival DuPont ICI was ultimately very successful, thereby playing an important role as the progenitor of Britain's leading high-tech industry.

The base for the Pharmaceuticals Division, established in 1957, was a major new laboratory complex at Alderley Park in Cheshire. It was here that James Black, a Nobel Prize winner, worked on the development of heart drugs, and it subsequently became a centre of excellence in cancer research. In its overall approach to the development of its pharmaceuticals interests, ICI was an exemplar of the long-term approach, soldiering on for 20 years before the business returned its first profit.

ICI had the knack of choosing the right man at the right time to head the company, and was fortunate in the early decades to have had a main board dominated by scientists and engineers rather than money men and salesmen. The 1940s and 1950s were marked by the burial of the old pre-war market carve-ups and the re-emergence of the three giants of German chemicals, BASF, Bayer and Hoechst, now untangled from IG Farben and distancing themselves from that demonic union. Meanwhile, there were the stirrings of freer international trade and a loosening of the old ties that bound ICI to the Commonwealth and empire.

Yet business conditions remained very buoyant for ICI, and the company continued to be headed by technical men of a high calibre. Glaswegian Harry McGowan, the first president of ICI and for many years chairman of the board, was succeeded in 1950 by fellow Scots John Rogers and then Alexander Fleck, who saw their task as that of keeping the great ship steady on its course.

The 1960s brought new challenges to ICI in the wake of keener international competition. It also brought Paul Chambers, a tax expert who had been the company's finance director, to the chairmanship. Despite the ponderous quotation at the start of this chapter Chambers was an able reformer. Following a study by the McKinsey consultancy, he set about a sensible reorganisation of the company structure. Among other changes, he put the non-ferrous metals interests into a separate company, which would one day be the first significant subsidiary hived off from the parent.

He also pursued higher productivity through schemes modelled on the renowned Fawley Agreement implemented by Esso at its refinery near Southampton. He encouraged a programme of major capital projects in a corporate dash for growth, and ensured that ICI would participate in North Sea oil and gas exploration. This far-sighted initiative secured long-term supplies of natural gas at extremely favourable prices, allowing its fertiliser operations to generate exceptional profits for many years.

New Worlds

One of Chambers' few mistakes was a failed bid for Courtaulds, at a time when hostile takeovers were almost unknown. Trends in the use of artificial fibres by UK textile manufacturers, to which Courtaulds was a major supplier, looked promising and ICI wanted more of the business. However, Courtaulds put up a spirited defence and the approach failed.

In contrast to many British executives, Chambers took an interest in developments across the Channel and encouraged the first decisive moves into mainland Europe. In 1961 the company bought a large site in Rotterdam and earmarked it for a major new plant to supply the fast-growing Common Market. A European Council was established, and the Continental operations became ICI Europa.

Meanwhile, there were the first steps to build a US presence through acquisition and investment in greenfield capacity. The high point of the company's standing was the late 1960s, its zenith coinciding with the chairmanship of the highly regarded Peter Allen between 1968 and 1971. The year 1969 saw ICI restored to second place in the *Chemical Age* ranking of world chemical companies, closing the gap with the world number one, DuPont, and far ahead of its European rivals.[10]

One of the first heads of ICI Europa was Jack Callard, who presciently moved its headquarters from London to Brussels soon after his appointment in 1965. Calm, clever and fair-minded, Callard was a classic ICI figure, earning a steady advancement entirely on his merits.[11] Finally beating his rival, Michael Clapham,[12] to the top job in 1971, he proved a distinguished chairman during a tenure that ended with his retirement in 1975.

Jack Callard worked with the consensual grain of the organisation, rationalising where sensible, shunning a confrontational approach to issues and sustaining a rapid expansion on the Continent. It was on his watch that ICI became the nation's biggest exporter.

He also proved a redoubtable champion of the company's cause with government. This was testing for Callard, an avowed Conservative, when a Labour administration with radical aspirations took office in 1974. But Labour instinctively and rightly favoured industry, and relations remained constructive. Callard was able to report a doubling of profits between 1972 and 1974, to avoid losses in the 1975 recession and to sanction capital investment of over £400m (£4bn in today's money) in that same year.

The short reign of Rowland Wright, chairman from 1975 to 1978, saw little radical restructuring, though the non-ferrous metals activities were floated off as Imperial Metal Industries (IMI), in 1977.

The heavy investment of the 1960s and 1970s gave ICI the resilience to ride out a more challenging commercial environment in the second half of the decade, and profits held up well. On the whole, ICI enjoyed remarkably good labour relations. A tradition had been built by outstanding personnel managers like Geoffrey Gilbertson, whose charm and humour enabled him to work closely with union leaders such as Jack Jones and Hugh Scanlon to keep the group largely free from industrial strife.[13]

Among Gilbertson's achievements was the conclusion in 1969 of a far-reaching productivity agreement covering ICI's 60,000 UK blue-collar workers. Much of the work was done by union leaders travelling the country to explain the proposals.[14] The framework was the system of German-style works councils set up when Brunner and Mond founded the company.

Lurch into Loss

This benign story came to a shattering close in the 1980s. True, there were challenges in the late 1970s, when trends in fibres and plastics remained sluggish and expanding oil company capacity was eroding margins in petrochemicals. But what happened next cannot be explained by such longer-term trends. Structural fissures may eat away at margins and eventually cause a great company to stall. But a sudden lurch from hefty profit into unprecedented loss can only be explained by special events.

From a respectable profit in 1979 ICI plunged to a loss in the third quarter of 1980 and the dividend was halved. True, the loss, £10m, was not large. But it was the first in the company's 54-year history – as was the dividend cut. Britain's biggest blue-chip company, bulwark of countless pension funds, was not supposed to do that. The problem, of course, was a domestic recession on a scale not experienced since the 1930s.

By 1981 a third of ICI's UK customers had gone out of business and few of the company's activities were escaping the fallout. The recession was caused by appalling economic mismanagement and inflamed by cuts in public spending and soaring interest rates. Together with a petrocurrency effect as Britain became a major oil exporter, this prompted a gross overvaluation of the pound. Since ICI's bulk chemicals exports were priced in Deutsche Marks in Continental Europe and dollars in other markets, this put a cruel squeeze on margins in much of its traditional business.

The response was to accelerate the ultimately fatal process already set in train by Maurice Hodgson, a scion of Paul Chambers and unassuming but formidable chairman of the board since 1978. For a corporate captain who wants to jettison cargo and crew, there is no time like recession. Cheered on by City bystanders, Hodgson pressed ahead with cutbacks, closures and sell-offs in petrochemicals, plastics and fibres, and by the end of his term in 1982 the company had shed a quarter of its UK labour force.

Maurice Hodgson's succession might have gone to the popular Bob Haslam, now one of three deputy chairmen after more than 30 years with the company. But he was "late in throwing his hat in the ring",[15] and the most prestigious job in British industry went to another zealous proponent of the reform school of ICI management, John Harvey-Jones.[16]

It was a measure of the crisis atmosphere surrounding British industry at the time that Harvey-Jones was given chief executive powers. An able but unconventional figure with a navy rather than science or engineering background, he sold off the Millbank headquarters, slashed head office staff and drove through sweeping restructuring. He swapped assets with other big players in the industry and approved significant acquisitions in the US. The broad theme was still the shift from heavily cyclical bulk commodities to higher-value products. It meant dramatic withdrawal from some traditional areas of business, and it meant more redundancies.

For a while – after a fashion – it all seemed to work. The classic mix of job cuts, investment curbs and ambitious pricing did the trick. In 1985 ICI became the first British company to report profits of over £1bn. Although he undoubtedly drew in the short term from the work of his predecessor, Harvey-Jones became a business legend.

Courageous Critic

He was also that rare phenomenon among captains of industry: a courageous critic of the Conservative government. Asked by a foreign journalist why he thought the recession was far deeper in Britain than in other European countries, he replied: "That's simple. It's because we've got Margaret Thatcher running the country."[17] He accused her of decimating Britain's manufacturing base and reckoned that 30 per cent of ICI's UK customers had disappeared since the Conservatives had come into office in 1979.[18] She reciprocated by calling him "her least favourite businessman"[19] – a select field in which Harvey-Jones was being joined by some of the ablest industrialists of the age.

The reaction of the prime minister's closer colleagues was unforgiving. Senior minister Cecil Parkinson remarked that the quickest way to cause silence at an ICI lunch was to say something nice about Harvey-Jones.[20] Inevitably, Harvey-Jones had to wait longer for his knighthood than any previous head of ICI.

Nor was Harvey-Jones sparing of fellow businessmen. At the height of the savage onslaught on its unions by News International, he denounced Rupert Murdoch's vindictive sacking of 5,000 print workers as "monstrous. …I would be deeply ashamed if I had to operate my plant from behind a barbed wire fence in order to keep going."[21]

Harvey-Jones was also a forthright critic of the City, commenting: "We were all brainwashed years ago into thinking that the City of London exists to allocate money in a cleverer way, to make sure that the country's businesses would succeed in the longer term. …But the City is in no position to judge good businessmen, nor is the stock market. Everything is far too short term these days."[22]

Inevitably, the City came out on top. Years into retirement Harvey-Jones confided that after meetings with investment bankers he would sometimes make discreet enquiries and find that he, the head of the nation's biggest industrial company and its greatest wealth creator, was invariably the lowest-paid person in the room.

By driving through the initiatives of his predecessor Harvey-Jones probably made as much impact on ICI as any of the company's chairmen. Paradoxically, though heavily compromised by his own actions he gave a powerful voice to those questioning the new economic orthodoxy. And he restored confidence to a company reeling under the impact of that orthodoxy. More interestingly, he tried to foster a radical role for middle and senior management, reminding them that a key part of their job was not to avoid risk but to manage it.[23]

And yet, somehow, somewhere in those turbulent and terrible years something precious was lost. A new theme had taken virulent hold on the company's philosophy. From now on management would be preoccupied as much with shedding activities as with building new ones. This was the case with Denys Henderson, who took over as chairman in 1987. Although bulk chemicals was now back in decent profit and eminently saleable, Henderson's relations with the City were double-edged and he was personally uncomfortable with divestment.

As Henderson rightly pointed out, "[y]ou look at most successful chemical companies, of which we are one, [and] you don't see the Americans, the Japanese or the Swiss unbundling".[24] Nevertheless, he was bullied by the City into seeking further asset disposals. Fertilisers, one of the building blocks of ICI, was sold off – despite doctrinaire objections from trade secretary Peter Lilley that the buyer was a state corporation, Kemira of Finland.

Turning its back on the discovery successes of the past, ICI also sold its oil interests. This was standard stuff from the new business school textbook. The oil market had become global; ICI was not an oil company, so it should get out. While a few of the chemical giants have followed this dim rubric, others have not. Once very much a runner-up to ICI, Germany's BASF has remained highly diversified, with interests in bulk chemicals and even its own oil exploration arm. This has proved no bar to its becoming the world's largest and most successful chemical company, with 30,000 employees at its Ludwigshafen home alone.[25]

Like his predecessor, Denys Henderson was forthright on issues of government policy.[26] And like Harvey-Jones he was not impressed by the economic record of the 1980s. Speaking to *The Times* in 1990, Henderson said that growth in the future had to be based on "solid industrial substance – not the shadow or 'fluff' of the second half of the Eighties, which so swiftly evaporated in the current harsher economic climate".[27]

Carpet-Baggers

Despite ICI's divestment efforts, the cold eye of City scribblers was still on the company. "Unbundling" had entered their unlovely lexicon in connection with ICI, mainly because of its success in pharmaceuticals. Rumour was succeeded by reality in 1991 when a 2.8 per cent stake in the company was acquired by a pair of corporate stalkers. This, for the *Daily Telegraph*, was the beginning of ICI's fall – the first step on its long road to oblivion.[28]

The raiders were James Hanson and Gordon White. Major contributors to Conservative Party funds, the predatory pair had thrived on – indeed been rewarded by – a looser business environment in the 1980s, allowing them to build exactly what ICI was being told not to be, a conglomerate. It was a measure of the demented climate at the time that Hanson, a company whose return on capital had been lower than that of its prey in three of the previous four years and had a research budget just a twentieth the size of ICI's, could for a single second be regarded as a serious contender to take over Britain's industrial flagship.[29]

The menace from Hanson was nevertheless backed by a propaganda campaign in the tame press. At the prompting of Downing Street *The Times* called for the replacement of Denys Henderson.[30] With all the confidence of those who have never been near a factory floor, *The Economist* offered a specious defence of asset-stripping ("finding the assets new and better homes") and asserted, without any supporting evidence, that "ICI should be shaken up".[31]

To the surprise of many in the City, Henderson marshalled a sterling defence, mustering up a small platoon of that rare breed – the independent-minded Tory backbencher – in support.[32] His advisers revealed that Hanson had planned to raid the pension fund when his Hanson Trust acquired Imperial Group a few years earlier, and that he had subsequently filched the Courage family portraits from the brewer's boardroom.[33] As for his accomplice, Gordon White was not even on Hanson's board when he had squandered millions of pounds of company money on horse race betting. Few were surprised to learn that he was also a self-proclaimed admirer of Adolf Hitler.

Their credibility in tatters, the dodgy duo slunk away and sold their shares in 1992.

But the deadly damage was done. The bleat of shareholder value became a mantra, unbundling evolved into demerger, and two activities in which ICI had been brilliantly successful, pharmaceuticals and crop sciences, were carved off into a new company. This was floated on the stock market as Zeneca in 1993. A key figure in pillaging ICI for the Zeneca sell-off was John Mayo, who was recruited from merchant bankers SG Warburg in 1992 to orchestrate the demerger and become Zeneca's first finance director.[34] Mayo was to float up again a few years later in the fiasco which torpedoed Britain's other industrial flagship, GEC.

The new company's first chief executive was Tom McKillop, a chemist who had been technical director of ICI since 1989. His inelegant comment was: "For us it was like a great stone had been lifted off our backs."[35] The exact nature of that stone was not specified, but presumably it was not ICI's "fantastic set of values":[36] the priority that the great company had traditionally given to the application of science through long-term research, non-opportunistic investment and sheer hard work. And integrity. All those dull old virtues that went out of fashion in the get-rich-quick 1980s.

McKillop went on to chair the Royal Bank of Scotland in 2006. A couple of years later his ruined bank was at the front of the queue for countless billions in taxpayer handouts to the financial sector.

Syngenta

By the end of the decade Zeneca had merged with a Swedish group to form AstraZeneca and not long after that its celebrated "agro-business" was swallowed by a secretive Swiss-based biosciences entity called Syngenta.[37]

Startling as it seemed at the time, the demerger would set a pattern endlessly repeated by other companies.[38] Many of Britain's industrial giants were reduced to weaklings which became prey to repeated takeovers, asset reshuffling, obscurity and potential oblivion.

What remained of ICI went on being gnawed away. Ronnie Hampel, who took over as chairman in 1995, and Charles Miller-Smith, the company's first "chief executive", plodded on down the road of dumping bulk chemicals and chasing fine chemicals. In a deal described as "disastrous" by the Chemical Industries Association,[39] they paid an astonishing £4.9bn for Unilever's specialty chemicals[40] but failed to realise sufficient funds from the sale of unwanted assets. The process involved 50 separate disposals, including the knock-down resale of former Unilever interests. In the end the "strategy" left a burden of debt hanging over the company and a future as uncertain as ever.

Brendan O'Neill took over the baton in a short innings as chief executive between 1999 and 2003. Incredibly, an unpopular rights issue in 2002[41] left a company which only a decade earlier had been the bellwether of British industry with junk status hanging over it.[42] O'Neill stepped down and was replaced by John McAdam.[43] McAdam had spent much of his career as a mid-level executive with, of course, Unilever. Among his first comments in the new role, McAdam asserted: "This is a great company, with strong market positions and considerable potential."

Sinking the Flagship

That didn't, of course, deter him from grabbing at an £8bn bid for ICI by the Dutch conglomerate Akzo in 2007. And, in the final folly that sank what had been Britain's greatest company, ICI went down for the last time.[44] The new owners wasted little time dumping the ICI brand in the dustbin of history.[45] The *Daily Telegraph* reported that McAdam stood to collect £20m from this sickening debacle.[46]

The story was not denied. McAdam went on to chair the board at Rentokil. This "royal rat-catcher" had been turned into a kind of ragbag conglomerate in the 1980s by Clive Thompson, favourite of Margaret Thatcher and City stockbrokers.[47] Rentokil became notorious for the remuneration taken by a chief executive, Bart Becht, who awarded himself £91m in 2009.[48]

Conservative yet progressive, austere yet generous with ideas and investment, scholarly yet practical, ICI represented the best of British industry. In his survey of Britain's industrial economy *From Empire to Europe*, former *Financial Times* editor Geoffrey Owen concludes a summary of the company's history with the observation: "ICI held its position as one of the world leaders in its field from the 1950s to the 1990s."[49]

So how did things go so disastrously wrong? The answer is the power of the financial markets. After the Thatcher government took over in 1979 the stock market played a vastly greater role in ICI's affairs, the status of institutional investors was greatly enhanced and corporate predators were unleashed on the real economy. Companies came under intense pressure to maximise their shareholder value – without ever being clear exactly how this should be defined or measured, or why the chancers, carpet-baggers and corporate looters whose reign culminated in the fiasco of the 2008 financial crisis should, for a single second, have been the arbiters.

Nevertheless, these developments are claimed in *From Empire to Europe* to have been good for British industry and, by inference, to have stimulated desirable changes in strategy and organisation in ICI. The assertion would be a shade less preposterous if, at the end of their long ordeal, exemplary companies like ICI had not simply ceased to exist.

Epitaph

Others have had a very different take. Ronnie Hampel's "biggest regret [was] that the demand of the market for short-term results has destroyed the ability of companies to run the large research establishments which were the basis of ICI's growth and success in the 1950s, 1960s and 1970s".[50]

In a thoughtful if understated *Financial Times* epitaph, John Kay recalled "a national institution which nurtured some of Britain's best managerial talent and developed the skills and knowledge behind the country's most successful post-war industry [pharmaceuticals]. But in Britain…companies are no longer institutions, but creatures of the capital market. This is a policy choice we may one day regret."[51]

And a moving comment from a former ICI executive spoke for many: "All that will now be left is the legacy of its inventions, and [the memory of] the high standards with which it operated."[52] Another said: "There is little doubt that ICI's demise means the long term future of the UK as a centre of excellence in chemistry, and with it the country's ability to generate wealth, have been damaged."[53]

It would, of course, be wrong to infer that the villainous destruction of ICI implied the annihilation of the entire British chemicals industry. Indeed, vestiges of ICI's legacy live on in at least four of the five regional hubs identified by an AIChE (American Institute of Chemical Engineers) round-up of UK chemicals a few years ago.[54]

The Runcorn and Widnes district was the centre of ICI's inorganic chemicals activities from the company's earliest days, and is still among the bigger chemical clusters in Britain. At least as important is the Teesside grouping, based around the Wilton complex opened by ICI in the 1950s.[55] And not far to the north of Teesside lies the older Billingham works, founded before the First World War.

Even at Grangemouth, Europe's first major petrochemicals plant when it was opened in 1951 by British Petroleum Chemicals (a joint venture by Distillers Company and the forerunner of BP Chemicals), ICI was involved in adjacent downstream operations.

At all these sites some of the former ICI plants may still be in operation. But often they are under foreign ownership. And most are shadows of what they once were.

The BOC – Losing Air

The history of British chemicals is dominated by the story of ICI. And for a while it looked as though the oil companies would be major long-term players through petrochemicals. Those hopes have long been dashed. But there has been a handful of other outstanding companies in the chemicals sector, particularly in the more traditional areas of business. What has been their fate?

British Oxygen was for decades a giant of industrial gases, one of a small group of multinationals that dominate this rarefied business. It was founded as Brin's Oxygen Company by two French brothers, Arthur and

Leon Brin, in the 1880s, and the production of oxygen has remained an enduring theme ever since.

Business was initially on a small scale but it expanded greatly with oxyacetylene welding in the early years of the twentieth century. At around this time Brin's Oxygen adopted a new cryogenic air separation process developed by a German associate, Carl von Linde. The Linde connection was to be re-established in a much more final way nearly a century later.

The British Oxygen Company, as it became in 1906, gradually extended its geographical reach throughout the empire and Commonwealth. A loss of direction after the Second World War ended with the arrival of Leslie Smith, first as managing director and then as chairman from 1972 on. Highly regarded, Smith modernised the group and secured better relations with government, notably the Labour administration of the 1970s.[56] His biggest success was the takeover of Airco, a major US competitor.

The BOC itself nearly acquired new owners in 1999, when the management agreed an $11bn carve-up between France's Air Liquide and Air Products of the US. The deal was blocked on competition grounds, but the board's indecent appetite for the proposed surrender made it clear that the BOC would remain an all-too-ready target for takeover.

The BOC was indeed an attractive proposition. It had invested heavily in the right areas and the right products at the right time, and was earning a third of its income in the fast-growing markets of the Far East. In global market share it was second only to Air Liquide and ahead of US-based Praxair and Air Products. It also surpassed Germany's Linde. It was, in the words of one observer, "one of Britain's best companies – well managed and with an attractive spread of assets".[57]

When the decisive bid came in early 2006 it was from Linde, despite its smaller size.[58] The BOC board rejected an offer of £15 a share, with one commentator noting: "BOC had said a number of times that it saw no point in a merger or acquisition between ourselves and Linde."[59] However, the lofty disdain vanished when the offer was raised by just a pound. The BOC board promptly rolled over, with chief executive Tony Isaacs reportedly lifting more than £24m from the deal. The hugely strengthened Linde became number one in global gases, and a delighted company president, Wolfgang Reitzle, commented: "We will combine German engineering with Anglo-Saxon shareholder management."[60] Since the deal had been financed by Linde's banks, very much in traditional Rhineland style, the comment carried a touch of sarcasm.

A Labour government pathetically in thrall to the City received in silence the spectacle of another great British company capitulating to foreign ownership. This was just the latest in a flurry of takeovers of major UK concerns, recent victims including Pilkington, P&O, Exel, BPB and British Airports. It was left to CBI director general Digby Jones to voice in an uncharacteristically oblique way a more general unease, calling on Europe to operate a level playing field for takeover bids and citing the example of Spain: "I just wish that Blair and Brown would make a far greater noise about the fact that Spain actually gives a tax break to companies which make an overseas acquisition."[61]

It is a measure of the quality of Linde's acquisition that the takeover didn't bring the familiar aftermath of rationalisation – cutbacks, closures and redundancies. Yet, already the legend of British Oxygen has been erased in some of the lands where it was once a household name.[62]

Albright & Wilson

No other companies in the UK chemicals industry have come near to rivalling ICI for industrial stature or intellectual distinction. Albright and Wilson, founded in the nineteenth century to supply potassium and phosphorus for the match industry, subsequently struggled in its diversification quest. Eventually it passed into the hands of US conglomerate Tenneco and was then broken up and sold off to France's Rhodia. Its rival Marchon Products was absorbed by Albright and eventually disappeared.[63]

Though some of the bigger multinationals, such as Unilever, are still represented, much of today's chemicals industry comprises medium-size businesses. Observers quote a figure of over 3,000 for the number of companies with a presence in the UK. Typically these firms concentrate on higher-value specialty products rather than commodity chemicals.

Croda International is one example. After the Second World War Croda diversified into more specialised areas, and by the 1970s it was making hundreds of intermediate chemicals used in industrial and consumer goods. Like everyone else in the chemical industry, Croda endured a searing experience during the recession which hit the economy in 1980, and by mid-decade its customer base had shrunk alarmingly.

Like his counterpart at ICI, chairman Frederick Wood was an outspoken critic of the government, claiming that it was perverting the business climate and making no effort to understand industry's troubles.[64] His finance director, Richard Heseltine, put it cogently: "Who has been profitable in the last two or three years? It has been the high street retailer. The UK has been a consumers' paradise, not an exporters' paradise. North Sea oil has found its way into consumers' pockets."[65]

Laporte was another company which ventured into the specialty chemicals field, though with less success. By the 1980s Laporte's business was declining and the company's manufacturing operations were closed, and in 2000 what was left of Laporte was bought by Degussa, the German precious metals refiner.

Pharma Stalls

The only sector where unambiguously British-based companies still figure in the big league is pharmaceuticals. Two of the world's larger pharmaceutical companies have their operational headquarters in England and most of the other leading players have manufacturing or R&D activities in the UK. Britain was in the recent past host to the largest research and development budgets in Europe and responsible around for 10 per cent of world spending in this area.

As in chemistry, the UK can draw on deep intellectual wellsprings to nurture its successes in pharmaceuticals. Britain is second only to the US in Nobel Prizes for Physiology or Medicine and can claim more than the next two countries (Germany and France) combined. At least a fifth of the world's major drugs used to originate in research laboratories in Britain, and many of them will have been made in the UK and exported.

One of the oldest British manufacturers was Allen & Hanbury, founded in London in the early eighteenth century. The company became well-known for dietary supplements and patent medicines, and was eventually taken over by Glaxo Laboratories in 1958 – one of the first steps on the long road by which Glaxo would emerge as one of the giants of the industry.

Another familiar name was May & Baker, which originated in London in the 1850s. In the 1930s the company developed a pharmaceuticals division, becoming famous for its "M&B" sulpha drugs, which offered the first effective treatments for bacterial diseases before modern antibiotics. After many years of ownership by France's Rhone-Poulenc, May & Baker was sold off in 1999, most of its assets going to German's Hoechst and Bayer. Shortly afterwards its research and development facilities were closed and its manufacturing operations run down.

AstraZeneca

Today's British-owned pharmaceuticals industry is dominated by two companies, GlaxoSmithKline (GSK) and AstraZeneca. The latter is actually only half British, its other progenitor being Swedish. When under City pressure Zeneca was carved off from ICI in 1993, it was bequeathed two exceptional businesses in pharmaceuticals and agrochemicals. Shortly after Zeneca merged with Sweden's Astra in 1999, agrochemicals was sold off, leaving pharmaceuticals to form the backbone of the new company.

The record since then has been far from untroubled. Efforts to cut costs have prompted a series of spectacular job losses across the group, with 12,600 jobs going in 2007–09 and another 9,000 in 2010–11.[66] But this was not the end of the retrenchment. In 2012 the company's chief executive, David Brennan, was ousted by shareholders restless over falling sales and a threadbare drugs pipeline.[67] Brennan's disappointing performance was typically well-rewarded, with the *Daily Telegraph* reporting a pay-off of £4.5m and a pension fund of £14m. This followed a total remuneration package of over £9m the previous year.[68] After so many people had been made redundant this package was, for at least one investor, "obscene".[69]

The company then initiated more restructuring. It meant, of course, further retreat. The Alderley Park complex, centre of so much distinguished research after it was opened in 1957, was shut down and the company's London headquarters closed. Nearly 4,000 jobs were lost, taking the total cutbacks between 2011 and 2013 into five figures.[70] Many of the employees affected were research staff.

The company was increasingly following an industry trend whereby the pharmaceutical giants were buying in their development stage products through high-tech acquisitions, such as the Cambridge-based KuDOS Pharmaceuticals in 2005.[71] Not all shareholders were convinced, with one commenting: "What future is there for British industry if this is happening? This company will not survive if it does not do its in-house research."[72]

AstraZeneca pledged to spend $500m on a new research and development facility in Cambridge and move its head office to the city, reflecting its status as a centre for high-tech industries. Ominously, its research and development headquarters remained in Sweden.

A year later a poorly handled takeover approach from US-based Pfizer, the world's second largest pharmaceutical company, was being unenthusiastically contested by AstraZeneca. There was public and political disquiet in Britain, particularly in the scientific community. Business secretary Vince Cable proposed that a public interest test of such takeovers should be expanded to protect Britain's "strategic" science base. Conservative Party chairman Grant Shapps misjudged the public mood with a clumsy dismissal of the Cable proposal as "anti-business, anti-jobs and anti-jobs security".[73]

The AstraZeneca board eventually turned down the final offer. Claims that a merger would enhance industrial logic by expanding Pfizer's product pipeline were tarnished by suspicion that the real motive was tax avoidance by the US giant. This would be achieved simply by moving Pfizer's domicile (though not its headquarters) from the US to the UK, where corporation tax was lower. Since Pfizer has been the most profitable pharmaceutical company in the world, such considerations were unlikely to be far from the surface.

Pfizer Puzzle

AstraZeneca retained its independence, though dismayingly it emerged that its directors had actually been in secret talks with Pfizer for some time. The *Pharmaceutical Journal* asserted that corporate takeovers do not threaten the UK pharmaceutical industry.[74] But it then spoilt its own case by reminding readers of the fate of AstraZeneca's Fisons laboratories in Leicestershire, closed in 2010, and of Pfizer's facility at Sandwich, its largest R&D centre in Europe. Sandwich closed with the loss of 2,400 jobs in 2011.[75]

Sandwich had invented Viagra, and one of the team responsible expressed the feelings of many: "It is difficult to understand the closure of Sandwich, which was the most productive research site in the world. The position of the UK as a centre of excellence for pharmaceutical research has been significantly compromised."[76] It is worth recalling that Pfizer had closed its manufacturing operations at Sandwich in 2007. As one seasoned commentator noted, "[w]hen production moves overseas, R&D eventually follows".[77]

The unpopularity of Pfizer's bid for AstraZeneca prompted some long-overdue reflection in the financial community. The *Financial Times* warned: "The ideology of shareholder primacy has overemphasised the importance of near-term share price performance", turning managers into "what Professor John Kay has termed 'meta fund managers', who perceive their job to be about buying and selling assets", when their "real role…is to run a business that adds value primarily by means of the goods and services it provides".[78]

There was predictable City grousing at AstraZeneca's decision. Sue Noffke of Schroders Prime UK Equity futilely demanded that AstraZeneca directors "recommence their engagement with Pfizer". But others at last seemed to be learning something from the years of damaging free-for-all in company takeovers.[79] The *FT*'s comments were endorsed by leading fund manager Simon Robertson: "In considering value, directors should be prepared…to take a long-term view, ie seven to ten years, of the prospects for the business…to give their honest view of what they believe is best for the company both financially and socially."[80]

GlaxoSmithKline

GlaxoSmithKline (GSK) remains the flagship of the British pharmaceuticals industry, with one of the top corporate listings on the London Stock Exchange.

The group has been built up through a long succession of mergers. One of the earlier milestones was the establishment of the Glaxo Laboratories research department at Greenford in west London in 1935. Other important events were Glaxo's takeover of Allen & Hanbury in 1958 and the merger of the Beecham Group with US-based SmithKline Beckman in 1989. In 1995 Glaxo linked with the Wellcome interests of Burroughs Wellcome, and in 2000 Glaxo Wellcome combined with SmithKline Beecham to join the world's top five pharmaceutical companies.

Many of the critical stages in the evolution of GSK occurred under the exemplary guidance of Austin Bide, who became chairman of Glaxo in 1973.[81] Bide reorganised and strengthened the company, which up to then had been a disparate group of concerns each with its own tradition and way of doing things. Above all, he recognised the importance of investing in research and development. One of the fruits of this approach was Zantac, the anti-ulcer drug that transformed the company into a significant international presence.[82]

Presiding over the giant formed in 2000 was a combative new chief executive, Jean-Pierre Garnier. JP, as he is known, drew vocal criticism over the size of his pay package. Chairman Christopher Hogg, never the most adroit at handling such controversies, somehow thought he could defuse the row by pointing out that Garnier's remuneration – a proposed £11.4m for 2002 – was not exceptional by the grotesque norms of many multinationals.[83]

JP might have evoked more empathy but for an abrasive public manner and a refusal to reside in the country one of whose leading institutions he had the privilege to serve. His attitude doubtless reflected the observation, reported in the *Financial Times*, that "he hates everything British – the people and the country",[84] an ugly reminder of the often bizarre choices of the appointments boards and remuneration committees charged with the safekeeping of British industry.

When he retired in 2008, Garnier claimed that he left GSK in a better state than at the start of the decade, with a coherent structure, a longer and healthier drugs pipeline and streamlined research and development operations.[85] And he was unusual among chief executives in reshaping a major British company without triggering mass redundancies or leaving a business that may have improved its short-term appeal to investors but in its long-term potential was actually weaker.

Garnier's successor, Andrew Witty, brought a refreshing change of tone to one of the Britain's very few remaining industrial flagships. At a time when it was becoming increasingly fashionable for companies to prioritise the minimisation of their contributions to the Exchequer, he delivered a stinging attack on organisations that shift their headquarters abroad in search of lower taxes.[86] And GSK has managed to steer a relatively steady course at the pinnacle of British pharmaceuticals, opening its first new factory in 40 years[87] and holding its own in an increasingly competitive international field.

Pharma Headaches

Though there are areas of unquestioned strength in UK pharmaceuticals, such as the biosciences, there have been disquieting trends. Of the leading pharmaceutical companies operating in the UK in 2013, only two British-based groups – GSK and AstraZeneca – were among the top ten in terms of market share.[88] And that same year saw another fall in research and development spending, the lifeblood of drug development.[89] According to the Federation of European Pharmaceutical Industries and Associations (EFPIA), in 2011 the UK had the highest research and development expenditure in Europe.[90] But the following year the British total fell 15 per cent and in 2013 it fell another 3 per cent.

Moreover, output also fell significantly, dropping by nearly a third between the 2009 peak and a low point in 2013.[91] This produced the alarming result that for the first time in memory the UK became a net importer of drugs and medicines. If there has since been a return to surplus, the balance remains wafer thin.

The government of the day included one competent minister who was alert to these developments. In his response, business secretary Vince Cable pointed to the £3.5bn in new investment announced since his strategy for the industry was launched in 2011. But if Britain is to restore its place as Vince Cable's "world leader in life sciences" it will have to sustain a much stronger revival in pharmaceuticals.

Relegation

Where have the upheavals of the recent past left UK chemicals? In a 2015 publication to celebrate its fiftieth anniversary, the Chemical Industries Association (CIA) pointed out that the industry is our country's largest manufacturing exporter, with overseas sales of nearly £50bn a year.[92] "The chemical and pharmaceutical industry is a positive force for good in this country and beyond", the CIA declares, highlighting successes in fine chemicals and pharmaceuticals.

The claim is more or less factual, but it is impossible to argue that Britain has kept pace with a fast-moving world. Back in the 1950s the Central Office of Information (COI) was able to point to a tripling of production from pre-war levels, a labour force of 400,000 and the largest petrochemicals sector in Europe.[93] By 1973 Britain remained a major global presence in fertilisers, pesticides, plastics, paints and above all the new world of pharmaceuticals, and had 458,000 people working in chemicals.[94] For all the turbulence of the 1970s, the broad picture remained remarkably resilient, and in 1979 the COI noted that although employment had slipped to 429,000 Britain was still the second largest chemicals producer in Europe (Germany having regained its pre-war pre-eminence) and fourth in the Western world.[95]

The 1980s brought a marked erosion of Britain's position. By 1991 the COI round-up was giving the UK only third position in Europe and fifth rank in the Western world.[96] A decade on and the official picture was relying more heavily on pharmaceuticals for reassurance, pointing out that the UK industry was the world's second largest exporter and could claim credit for 13 of the world's top 50 bestselling medicines.

More recently, the international picture has changed rather radically – but not in Britain's favour. In 2014 the European Chemical Industry Council (Cefic) put the UK no higher than fifteenth in chemicals output, only just ahead of Mexico and below Belgium.[97] Indeed, there were no fewer than six other European countries above the UK and newcomers such as Korea, India and China were far ahead. If pharmaceuticals are included, even Switzerland ranks higher.

Nor does the UK have a significant corporate presence. In a 2013 report the University of York listed the world's top 20 chemical companies, but not one was headquartered in the UK.[98] China, of course, got into the rankings, as did Korea, and the US had three groups in the list. But Europe was also still doing well, with two for France, three for the Netherlands (including Shell) and no less than four for Germany. Sadly, the Old World is getting by rather well without Britain.

This should be no great surprise. As *The Manufacturer* has pointed out, Britain's historic chemicals industry is no longer even British. It is now 70 per cent foreign-owned.[99]

CHAPTER 15

Sea of Dreams

My formula for success: rise early, work late, strike oil.

John Paul Getty, Founder, Getty Oil Corporation

There won't be a major field in the North Sea.

Sir Eric Drake, BP Chairman, April 1970

Oil Gusher

It took just a decade – from the mid-1970s to the mid-80s – for Britain to come from nowhere to the front rank of oil producers, a pace of development unmatched in history. Accomplished in the hostile waters of the northern North Sea, the technical achievement was staggering. And it brought opportunity unprecedented in the history of these islands. There was the promise of extending big modern industries such as petrochemicals. There was the chance to establish major offshore supply services. Above all, there was the potential to put aside some of this extraordinary windfall for the benefit of future generations. How well were these hopes realised?

The last is easily answered. In the early days there was broad consensus on the need to handle the North Sea bounty responsibly. For the 1974 Conservative Party manifesto: "The British people must retain control of, and enjoy, the maximum benefits from our off-shore oil…we will establish an Oil Conservation Authority to act as a watchdog…its job will be to regulate exploration for oil, investment, production and sales…a Scottish Development Fund will lay the foundation for Scotland's long-term economic prosperity."[1] Although slightly more interventionist in tone, Labour's themes were not dissimilar.[2]

However, meaningful intervention was strangled at birth. The notion was no more than aired under the Heath government in the early 1970s. When Labour was in office later in the decade it was foolishly opposed by the more conservative members of the government, such as Harold Lever.[3] And by the 1980s, when free market dogma was triumphing over common sense, it was too late. There was no attempt to take a lead from other countries and tap off profits into a fund for the future. The example of Norway, Britain's North Sea twin, was not followed. Indeed, *The Economist*, ever the cheerleader for the new laissez faire, scoffed at the approach of Britain's oil twin as "[a]n object lesson in how not to run an oil industry".[4]

But Norway got it exactly right.[5] After switching on its oil at around the same time as Britain, it has produced similar amounts (3.8–4.0bn tonnes by 2018), in similar conditions. There the parallels end. Because it adopted a policy of slower depletion and more gradual development, Norway achieved better prices for its oil and used its share of taxes and profits to build a treasure chest of titanic size. The world's biggest, Norway's sovereign wealth fund is worth a trillion dollars.[6] That's one thousand billion dollars – nearly half the entire national income of Britain.

Norway has managed to raise significantly more in tax revenues than the UK, without deterring investment in its sector of the North Sea.[7] It has fostered a thriving supply services industry and a modern oil refining and petrochemicals sector. It has retained democratic control through majority public ownership of its oil industry. And the country that in living memory was one of Europe's poorest[8] is now its wealthiest.

For the UK, which has retained only an emaciated supply services industry, has lost most of its downstream activities and has saved nothing into a sovereign wealth fund,[9] the comparison is humbling. For Scotland, geographic owner of 95 per cent of Britain's oil,[10] it is appalling.[11]

Adulation and Atrocity

Conditions may have been testing, but the oil companies were offered an exceptional deal in the British North Sea. Keith Taylor, head of exploration and production at Esso UK, enthused: "The UK sector of the North Sea is one of the most attractive places in the world for the oil industry to be."[12] A major appeal was that the oil companies did not face the more stringent tax system and interventionist climate governing the Norwegian sector.

Within a year of the Conservatives taking office in 1979, the industry was back in the free-wheeling atmosphere it had enjoyed a decade earlier. The companies loved it. In his memoir *Fear*, the distinguished explorer Ranulph Fiennes recalls an all-too-telling moment when the principal guest spoke at an industry dinner in the mid-1980s:

"As she [Margaret Thatcher] left the ballroom, the entire room, over a thousand oil bosses, stood up, cheering and stamping their feet, and they continued to do so for several minutes after she had disappeared."[13]

The laxity of government policy applied to production, where any idea of meaningful depletion policy was postponed in the 1970s and killed off in the 1980s. At one moment of lunatic profligacy Britain was pumping more oil than Saudi Arabia.[14] Ironically, the refusal to join Opec and Norway in tailoring output to a weaker market merely ensured that the oil was sold at prices even lower than they would otherwise have been.[15]

The laxity extended to operating procedures. Working conditions, in an industry where the response to employee complaints could include intimidation and blacklisting[16] and unions were excluded,[17] ranged from gruelling to abusive.

And the laxity applied, even more shockingly, to safety.[18] By the late 1980s the years of free-for-all had fostered a climate of abysmal complacency. To oversee the safety of over 200 offshore installations, the UK Continental Shelf (UKCS) had just five inspectors. They were drawn, moreover, not from the Health and Safety Executive but from the Department of Energy, whose mission was to promote the maximisation of output. The heedless rush for production culminated in catastrophe.

The worst disaster in the entire history of oil occurred not in some far-flung anarchic corner of the globe but in our very own once well-run British Isles. The story has been carefully reconstructed in Stephen McGinty's book *Fire in the Night*.[19] On 6 July 1988 a lucrative rust-bucket called Piper Alpha, a North Sea rig operated by Occidental Petroleum (Oxy) which should have stopped pumping oil and gas while it was being upgraded, suffered a series of explosions. The resulting inferno raged 300 feet above the platform and was visible for 80 miles. It killed nearly 170 employees, many of whom had sought pitiful refuge in the mess hall. The blaze took three weeks to douse.

It was reported[20] that Prime Minister Thatcher took tea next day in Downing Street with the founder of Oxy, Armand Hammer. Hammer was a rum mix of visionary and huckster, approvingly recalled by Tony Benn,[21] yet one of Thatcher's favourite businessmen ("a marvellous person").[22] The Prime Minister briskly rejected a call for statutory no-fault compensation to provide immediate financial support for the victims of the disaster.[23] From his personal fortune of perhaps £800 million Hammer offered all of £1 million. Indeed most of the compensation paid by Oxy to victims' families came not from its own coffers but from Lloyd's of London. And the company was never prosecuted, fined or sanctioned in any way for the Piper Alpha atrocity.[24]

On this abominable episode, Thatcher's memoir,[25] her official biography[26] and even David Cannadine's exemplary profile[27] are strangely silent.

Lost Opportunity

Less lethal, but longer lasting, was the failure to foster an enduring offshore supply industry of international standing. At the outset the potential had been promising. The UK was home to no fewer than three major oil companies, Shell, BP and Burmah. Two were leading members of the mighty "Seven Sisters" which dominated world oil and were active in offshore fields such as the Niger Delta and Abu Dhabi Marine Areas. The UK had two big state corporations, British Gas (BG) and the National Coal Board (NCB), both with offshore experience. And in 1975 these were joined by the new state-owned British National Oil Corporation (BNOC), headed by Frank Kearton, one of the ablest industrialists of the age.

At the same time Britain was a leading industrial power with a broad manufacturing base and marine engineering companies which should have been well placed – given time – to offer most of the equipment and services required by an indigenous oil industry.

Yet for his authoritative history of the offshore supply industry, Norman J. Smith chooses the haunting title *The Sea of Lost Opportunity*. He concludes, with memorable understatement: "British industry's failure to use the North Sea opportunity to establish a prominent position among the leaders in the global offshore service and supply market, or even to have a significant share of many important sectors of its domestic market, was clearly a disappointment."[28]

The roots of the failure go back to the early days of the North Sea adventure. The mid-1960s saw the confirmation of big natural gas occurrences in the southern basin of the North Sea. Subsea national boundaries were quickly agreed among most of the littoral states, though the settlements included one which might have been more problematic.

This was with Norway, where Britain could have made a legitimate case that its continental shelf extended to the western edge of a deep (800-metre) trench close to the Norwegian coast. In the event the UK conceded a median line settlement. The Foreign and Commonwealth Office (FCO) had probably been anxious, for political/military reasons, to avoid contention with Norway, the only European member of NATO with a (modest) land border with the USSR.

Not for the first time, Whitehall's absurd geopolitical pretensions were to cost Britain dear, since much of Norway's vast oil and gas deposits were subsequently found in what might conceivably have been British waters. The eagerness to please Norway was to be a recurring theme over many years of North Sea activity. Whereas Norway followed a heavily protectionist approach to its own North Sea activities, its companies were allowed a remarkably free hand in pursuing business on the UKCS.

Speed was also a crucial source of weakness. Britain's hydrocarbon deposits were developed remarkably rapidly, and by 1967 the first gas was being piped ashore.[29] Accompanied by the conversion from town gas of every domestic and commercial appliance in the country, the advent of natural gas was driven through with great tenacity and skill by the Gas Council, later British Gas, under the formidable leadership of Denis Rooke.[30]

Hostile to Whitehall interference, Rooke was nevertheless treated with "beautiful manners" by Tony Benn in the Labour government of the 1970s. But he had bruising encounters with the more intransigent members of the Thatcher administration, notably Nigel Lawson, in the 1980s.[31] Rooke favoured a conservative depletion policy and opposed the plunder of his highly successful British Gas for privatisation. Among the most objectionable proposals was the disposal of its thriving North Sea oil interests, peddled off as Enterprise Oil in 1984.

Rooke's most important legacy to the North Sea hydrocarbon industry was, however, a negative one. It arose from his disdain for British companies in the supply of equipment and services. It was no accident that all 24 gas production platforms in the southern North Sea were designed in the US and fabricated in the Netherlands. And development drilling, submarine pipe and offshore installations of all kinds were sourced mainly from abroad. This set a precedent that was to prove all too enduring.

The Birth of Giants

The critical moment in Britain's oil story came at the dawn of the 1970s. Between late 1969 and early 1971, three huge fields were confirmed in British and Norwegian waters. The unthinkable was really happening. Britain was about to join the ranks of the energy giants. Not only did it have the biggest coal reserves in Western Europe and its greatest renewables potential; it was now clear that it was blessed with oil and gas resources on a vast scale.

Among the new discoveries was Forties, announced by BP in October 1970. The rush to develop was now on. The UKCS quickly became the world's largest single theatre of offshore operations, with over 30 per cent of the total seaboard market for goods and services.[32] British industry had a huge opportunity on its doorstep. The government was slow to realise the potential of this new market, but at the end of 1971 Conservative prime minister Heath urged that the UK content of equipment and services to the Forties development be maximised.

However, it was not until 1973 that the International Management and Engineering Group of Britain (IMEG) published an urgent report and an Offshore Supplies Office (OSO) was at last established to implement some of its recommendations. IMEG was interventionist rather than protectionist, and a minimalist interpretation of that philosophy was to shape official attitudes towards the North Sea for many years to come.

The impact of official policy was not radically different when a new government took office. The Labour administration elected in 1974 was strangely diffident in its approach to the new industry on its doorstep. True, some ministers insisted that the development of the North Sea be actively guided in the long-term interests of the British people, rather than allow short-term market forces to reign supreme. But they were handicapped by three issues.

One was the so-called Varley Assurances, under which the new administration's first secretary of state for energy had saddled it with a fateful undertaking to the participants in the North Sea. Eric Varley promised the oil companies, of which he was excessively in awe, that no investment or production constraints would be imposed on any field discovered before 1975 until 1982 or later.[33] Since the biggest fields had mostly been identified by the mid-1970s, this made any overall depletion policy, and a moderation of development, impossible to pursue.

Linked to this were capacity constraints that had emerged in the UK supply sector. Even radical Labour ministers like Tony Benn were resigned to disappointment. He acknowledged that the British industrial equipment industry had been so "stressed and strained" by the investment boom following the free-for-all of the early 1970s that it was "simply unable to meet the demand".[34]

And finally, one of the intended instruments of intervention, the British National Oil Corporation (BNOC), met relentless hostility from a powerful established industry in its attempts to develop a meaningful role in the North Sea.[35] Bizarrely, one of its foremost antagonists was a company that was actually majority-owned by the taxpayer – British Petroleum (BP). BNOC could have provided OSO with substantial support in developing a UK supply sector. But by the time it was privatised in 1982 its life had been too short to achieve the kind of radical results that its counterpart in Norway, Statoil, was so successful in securing.

The Labour government of 1974–79 did at least establish a proper statutory framework for the industry and issued more restrictive licences with each licensing round. It also introduced a petroleum revenue tax, though Chancellor Denis Healey grumbled that the investment allowances were so generous that even as late as 1978 the North Sea was still yielding little for the Treasury.[36] The revenues that began to flow soon after were instead scooped up and squandered by the Conservative governments of 1979–97. The administrations that followed did little better.

Even with more considered licensing policies development continued in a rush. That rush forced the oil companies – by no means all averse to doing business with British companies – to rely heavily on foreign contractors and suppliers, or their UK-based subsidiaries. The dream of a major domestic supply industry, fully competitive with the world, was already in jeopardy.

OSO SOS

Promoting the cause of British suppliers fell almost entirely on the OSO. To implement the full and fair opportunity criterion which might keep the market open for British suppliers, the OSO kept detailed information on all contracts, from rigs to pipelines to supply vessels. Energy ministers could take these into account when awarding or renewing oilfield licences. Policy would, however, be applied cautiously and officials would work through consultation rather than diktat.

At the time the OSO was launched in 1973, the broad target was to raise the role of UK suppliers to Britain's new oilfields from less than a third to over two-thirds, and there were some successes in the second half of the 1970s. However, there were claims that, far from sustaining the high level (over 70 per cent) hailed by ministers, UK content in the 1980s actually averaged 40 per cent or less.[37]

Within the framework set by government policy – no depletion regime, short-term maximisation of production and no effective controls on the sale and processing of oil – the OSO did what it could. John D'Ancona, its forceful head in the 1980s, pointed out that his organisation was never remotely able to enforce a Buy British policy.[38]

The contrast with Norwegian activities was stark. By the mid-1980s Norway was taking a 30 per cent share in the provision of supply boats to the UKCS, while conceding just 3 per cent of its own market to outsiders.[39]

In dealing with pressures from foreign governments, the Office had little support from the FCO. Worse, it had to contend with the Treasury, where a blinkered attachment to rapid project development in the interest of short-term revenue maximisation reigned supreme. Ultimately, the eye of the Treasury, and of the Chancellor at its head, was on the long-dreamed goal of tax cuts for the wealthy.

OSO pinpointed the weaknesses of the UK supply industry, where the UK was strongest when location was important and output labour-intensive.

This meant the provision of shore bases, platform yards and supply vessels. Cynics dubbed the British the coolies of the North Sea as the fabrication industry became OSO's flagship for UK content.[40] But of course this activity did not travel well. Every time its domestic market subsided, it was unable to compensate with overseas business.

The supply industry was weakest where heavy capital expenditure and complex technology were required. This included offshore installation, pipelay, mobile drilling, drilling fluids, underwater equipment and technical services. And the oil companies were far from pliable in cooperating with the OSO. Shell, whose Expro subsidiary controlled a third of all North Sea expenditure, was "implacably opposed" to using British-built MSVs (multiple function field support vessels).[41] While BP and British Gas had research and development facilities in this country, Shell's main centre was in the Netherlands, and US and French companies tended to base their activities at home.

Astonishingly, in a country so boastful of its sophisticated financial markets, the OSO highlighted an acute shortage of large-scale equity and a persistent lack of venture capital in North Sea-related projects.[42] When it came to the crunch, all those buccaneering financiers were remarkably timid about risk in areas where they lacked experience.

Depletion Dumped

As the Varley Assurances approached the end of their term, the issue of depletion policy was diffidently aired by the Thatcher government's first energy minister, David Howell.[43] But his weak submissions were briskly stamped on by his successor, Nigel Lawson, ever the standard-bearer for dogmatic adherence to the cruder interpretations of free market ideology. And within a few years other measures, such as dropping any reference to benefits to the UK economy and industry from licensing criteria, brought to an end two decades of support – lukewarm but bipartisan – for the offshore supplies sector.[44]

Domestic procurement again began to suffer. The year 1984 saw one of the first major platform orders go abroad when Sun Oil of the US signed up for a £111m rig from Götaverken of Sweden rather than British Shipbuilders. This dealt a lethal blow to the Cammell Laird shipyard. The decision was heavily criticised by an unusually energetic energy minister, Alick Buchanan-Smith, MP for Aberdeen, who warned that he would "scrutinize carefully" future attempts by the company to win British offshore licences.[45]

As so often, any conscientious attitudes among junior ministers were not encouraged higher up the Thatcher administration. And an atmosphere of complacency anyway prevailed. By the late 1980s the *Glasgow Herald* was making the dubious claim that the UK offshore supplies industry was the second largest in the world, with US-based companies supplemented by multinationals from other countries and indigenous firms such as the Weir Group, the John Wood Group and the Balmoral Group.[46]

Clipping the Wings

By the end of the decade even the most notional intercession was abandoned, with the OSO "having its wings severely clipped as the single European market comes into force".[47] The constraints of the single market were much exaggerated, since its implementation was phased in only from 1993 on. Nevertheless, it provided a convenient excuse for neglect of the offshore sector by John Major's government.

The oil companies wasted no time in going abroad. Somehow Britain's very own oil flagship, BP, often seemed to be in the vanguard, this time placing major orders for its Bruce gas field with French and Spanish yards.[48] In the view of the *Financial Times* the orders could just as easily have been placed at home, in a sector where there was still adequate capacity.[49]

With a decent revival in North Sea oil activity under way, there were reports a year later of another tide of orders flowing overseas, with BP resorting to Korea for a rig for its Forties field. Part of the problem was a renewed attrition of capacity at home, where the *Daily Telegraph* reported that the number of Scottish platform builders had now fallen from eight to three.[50]

While there was some revival later in the 1990s, UK offshore supply never really recovered even the limited momentum it had built in the 1970s. This was particularly true of the yards where exploration and production rigs were constructed. Where there were once 40 UK yards producing platforms and jackets, by 2015 there was only a tiny handful still in business.

One of the more recent disappointments was the decision by Chevron in 2015 to exclude the Tyneside-based OGN from the shortlist for one of the last major North Sea contracts.[51] In a typically feeble response to complaints that North Sea oil companies win breaks from the British taxpayer without any requirement to use local suppliers the industry's regulator, the Oil and Gas Authority merely said its job was to ensure a level playing field rather than tilt contracts towards the UK.

Little had changed since even tentative intervention went out of fashion in the 1980s.

Refining Rise and Fall

The downstream involvement of the oil companies has been even more disappointing than their role upstream. Yet, the primary oil industry that sprang into life in the 1970s inherited a rich hinterland of downstream activities, not only in petrochemicals but also in refining. The Institute of Petroleum could justifiably boast: "One of the most important UK industrial investment programmes undertaken during the post-war years has been that associated with this country's oil refining capacity…increasing capacity progressively from some 2.5 million tonnes immediately post-war to a peak of 149 million tonnes. …Such a development programme must be regarded as outstanding even by contemporary industrial standards."[52]

The investment in domestic refining had taken Britain from a high degree of import dependency in petroleum products to self-sufficiency. However, the mid-1970s proved to be the high-watermark of the UK refining industry. Within a few years it all began to unravel, though there was a pause before the retreat began in earnest.

True, there was a modest reduction in national refining capacity in the second half of the 1970s, when the aftershocks of the 1973/74 oil crisis were working through the refinery sector. But the only British plant of any consequence to shut was Heysham, one of Shell's five UK facilities. Spread across the country were another 20 oil refineries, including 15 big installations.[53] Most were in excellent seaboard locations, well placed to scoop up the crude now starting to gush from indigenous sources.

Incredibly, the UK refining industry saw no benefit from the North Sea bonanza. Unlike every other important oil producer, including the US,[54]

Britain had no policy for regulating the destination of its oil. When output soared to over 100 million tonnes in 1982, an astonishing 60 per cent was shipped abroad for refining.[55] And as production raced towards 130 million tonnes, the amount processed at home remained less than 50 million tonnes, far short of total UK refining requirements. There was a technical requirement to import some heavier grades of oil for blending with the lighter crudes from the North Sea, but this was a scandalous neglect of domestic potential.

The results were as mad as they were predictable. The first half of the 1980s saw the destruction of no less than six refineries, including huge facilities at Milford Haven and the Isle of Grain, at the very moment the North Sea was in full flow. In just a few years the UK was to close more refining capacity than any of its Continental counterparts, none of whom were significant oil producers.

By the end of the 1980s the British refining industry had shrunk to a dozen plants. And there was more destruction to come. The 1990s brought two big closures, and recent years have seen another spate, with three important plants shut since 2012. By 2015 the UK had closed more capacity since the 1970s than all European countries bar one, and had just six refineries still in operation.

Petrochemicals Retreat

For oil companies with integrated refining capacity, downstream means petrochemicals and their derivatives. Here the retreat has been even more extraordinary. Decades of cheap oil (prior to Opec) and advances in extractive and transformative technology meant that by the 1970s petrochemicals accounted for about a third of the output of the UK chemicals industry. The production of plastics, derived from petrochemicals, had enjoyed spectacular growth in the 1950s and the 1960s, and there were further advances in the 1970s.

Up to this point the progress had been built on imported oil. But the arrival of the North Sea prompted well-founded hopes that with an indigenous source of feed the industry would be launched on a new era of growth. Industry figures repeatedly urged the government to ensure that the North Sea output was used for the benefit of UK petrochemicals.

However, 1983 saw the Chemicals Economic Development Committee (EDC) flag up a dramatic slump in the British share of European ethylene production, a ballooning trade deficit in plastics and UK plant closures "considerably in advance" of its competitors. The EDC made a desperate appeal to the government to develop a North Sea oil and gas policy which "gives incentive to the use of gaseous and liquid feedstocks in the UK as petrochemicals raw materials and to the maximum addition of added value by further processing within the UK".[56]

Such pleas were ignored and a once-in-a-lifetime opportunity went to waste. True, there were some downstream projects linked in to the North Sea, but they were limited in scale and outweighed by retreat elsewhere.

ExxonMobil

The charge that the oil majors have walked away from downstream involvement is perhaps least applicable to ExxonMobil. The world's biggest oil company continues to refine and manufacture petrochemicals on a sizeable scale at Fawley, on Southampton Water. Established in 1921, the refinery was rebuilt in 1951 and subsequently enlarged and upgraded. At peak in the 1970s its annual throughput of nearly 20 million tonnes of crude made it one of Europe's biggest refineries, accounting for a fifth of UK consumption. It remains the UK's largest plant of its kind and the most complex – complexity being a measure of the flexibility of the installation with regard to feed and products.[57]

Having pioneered flexible working in the 1960s, Fawley has long been an exemplar in labour relations and remains a technical showpiece. Since 1966 it has been the base for a substantial petrochemicals operation, producing up to 750,000 tonnes of chemical products a year.[58]

Where ExxonMobil has made a major retreat is in refining. In 1960 the company opened a large facility at Milford Haven, which offered deep-water anchorage ideal for the larger tankers coming on stream. Esso, as it then was, was only the first of four oil companies to establish itself on the Pembrokeshire coast. After enlargement its operation became the second biggest refinery in the UK, with a capacity of 15 million tonnes a year. However, it was one of the victims of the collapse in oil refining in the 1980s and was closed and sold on to Ajman in 1983.[59] Ajman, unlike fellow Emirates, produces not a single drop of oil.[60]

Exxon has committed itself to one of the very few downstream initiatives born of the North Sea. This was Mossmorran, undertaken as a joint venture by Exxon and Shell in the early 1980s. Completed on time and within budget in 1984, this impressive project was designed to utilise the natural gas liquids (NGLs) recovered from a dozen wells in the northern UK sector.

The gases were collected by the FLAGS (Far North Liquids and Associated Gas System) pipeline and pumped to a gas-gathering plant at St Fergus, north of Aberdeen. This separated the dry gases for British Gas and then sent the NGLs down to Mossmorran in Fife. There they were separated and the main product, ethane, piped to an adjacent facility for making ethylene, the basic building block for plastics.

Ethane's attraction was that it was a cheaper feedstock for petrochemicals than the traditional raw material, naphtha, which derives from oil. With Mossmorran on stream, BP switched its Grangemouth operations from naphtha to ethane. However, both of these initiatives, Mossmorran and the Grangemouth conversion, only came about after the oil companies had levered secret tax concessions out of the government.[61]

The story of previous proposals for gas-gathering from the UKCS had been a sorry one. An ambitious scheme backed by energy secretary David Howell in 1980 had been rejected by the prime minister and her Chancellor Geoffrey Howe for narrow doctrinaire reasons. Their objection? That state-owned British Gas would provide some of the finance.

This ran counter to the Treasury's obsession of the day, the public sector borrowing requirement (PSBR). So, while Norway was installing an eastward running pipeline to collect its own rather smaller natural gas output, Britain would continue to let a major resource go to waste. For one editorial, it was "the economics of the madhouse".[62] Worse, the government stood by while the oil companies (notably BP) turned down a smaller project a couple of years later.[63]

Mossmorran Milestones

In Mossmorran and FLAGS, however, Whitehall at last supported a scheme with compelling logic. The oil industry was belatedly following in the footsteps of Saudi Arabia, which was building an entire export-oriented petrochemicals industry on the back of flare-gas conversion.[64]

Mossmorran caused waves in a volatile energy market. The tax concessions which catalysed the new operation prompted litigation by ICI, which was now facing a serious competitive disadvantage on its feedstock costs. In 1973 it had struck a long-term deal under which BG supplied methane at a fixed price to ICI's operations at Billingham. ICI then built the biggest gas conversion complex in Europe and enjoyed huge profits after the 1973/74 oil shock hiked energy costs for its competitors.[65]

The termination of the ten-year Billingham contract faced ICI with a jump in its raw material costs. Because it was being fattened for privatisation, BG was under government pressure to hike the price of its methane. Meanwhile, ICI's other big petrochemical operation, Wilton, used naphtha, which put it at a severe disadvantage to its ethane-based rivals. ICI finally won its case in 1988.[66] Ironically, oil-derived naphtha was by then at less of a disadvantage to ethane simply because oil prices had fallen while gas prices had risen.[67]

A technical and environmental success, Mossmorran has been a disappointment in terms of further development downstream.[68] It did not, after all, form the nucleus of a chemical cluster and there was no associated investment in the manufacture of plastics and other derivatives. Half the output of what ExxonMobil calls the Fife Ethylene Plant[69] goes to customers in the UK – once mainly Shell operations – while the balance is shipped to Belgium for use in Exxon's polyethylene operations near Antwerp.[70]

At commissioning the complex was a 50/50 joint venture, with the gas separation plant operated by Shell Expro (Shell Exploration and Production) and the ethylene facility run by Esso Chemicals. Since then Shell has walked away from Mossmorran, leaving it in the hands of ExxonMobil.[71]

The last big shoreside investment by the oil industry is the Shetland Gas Plant, opened by Total in 2016.[72] The £3.5bn facility processes natural gas from the Laggan and Tormore fields. Strictly, these are not part of the North Sea basin but lie under deep water west of the Shetlands. Throughput from this ambitious project is rated at 500m cu ft of gas a day, equivalent to 8 per cent of UK consumption.

Shell Shortfall

The deplorable record of Shell UK confounds the promise of its early days. The company was the first to establish a modern refinery in the UK when it opened Shell Haven in the Thames estuary in 1916, nine years after the merger of Royal Dutch Petroleum and Shell Transport & Trading. New facilities were opened at Stanlow in Cheshire and Ardrossan in Scotland in the 1920s, and enthusiastic support for the Nazis proved no impediment to Shell's further growth in Britain in the 1930s.[73] The post-war period saw two new refineries commissioned – at Heysham and Teesport – and by the late 1970s Shell had the largest refining capacity (nearly 35 million tonnes) of any oil company in the UK.

In the meantime Shell established Europe's first production of petroleum-based organic chemicals at Stanlow, in 1941. The company went on to commission chemical plants at Carrington, in Manchester, and at Shell Haven in the 1950s. Its last important initiatives were the St Fergus and Mossmorran projects developed with ExxonMobil in the 1980s.

By then a long retreat was well under way. The closure of Heysham in 1976 was more than offset by additional capacity elsewhere. But the 1980s brought successive closures at Teesport[74] and Ardrossan, and cutbacks at Stanlow[75] and Shell Haven. The latter closed for good in 1999, leaving only Stanlow still in operation. Even then, Shell's withdrawal was not finished. In 2011 it sold its sole remaining refinery to India's Essar group. Essar then belatedly found that the operation needed major updating.[76]

Meanwhile, the petrochemicals side was shrinking. Carrington saw swingeing cutbacks in the mid-1980s.[77] And despite upbeat rhetoric[78] by the mid-2000s its operations had been sold off or closed.[79] Petrochemical operations established at Shell Haven in the 1950s largely disappeared with the refinery in 1999. After being cut back in the 1980s, only the petrochemicals operation at Stanlow still belongs to Shell Chemicals, and even this is operated by Essar.

The outcome in Britain contrasts shockingly with the buoyant picture just across the Channel. It cannot be coincidence that Shell, notionally a binational company incorporated in the UK but in practice run from The Hague, retains huge refining and petrochemical operations in the Netherlands.[80] The Pernis[81] refinery in Rotterdam is Europe's biggest and the integrated petrochemicals complexes there and at Moerdijk[82] are among its largest. Operations such as these have been benefitting from large tonnages of crude from the UKCS since its early days.

BP Retreat

Despite its undiluted British parentage, the story of BP's downstream involvement with UK oil parallels the dismal record of Shell. The forerunner of BP established a processing facility in Scotland in the late nineteenth century and more modern refineries at Llandarcy in Wales and Grangemouth in Scotland in the 1920s. A big refinery was built at the Isle of Grain in the 1950s and a smaller one at Belfast in the 1960s. By the end of the 1970s BP was the country's third largest refiner, with over 25 million tonnes of annual capacity.

Within five years, three of its four plants had closed. By the mid-1980s the workforce of BP Oil, the refining and marketing arm, had fallen 50 per cent since 1976.[83] Llandarcy was a particularly sorry story. Though the unions had proposed radical measures – including substantial job losses – to save the refinery, and could show that the plant was profitable, its closure still went ahead. By the end of 1985 BP had cut refining capacity in Europe's biggest oil producer by nearly 70 per cent.[84] Britain's flagship oil company was down to just one refinery in the whole of the British Isles – Grangemouth.

The latter was a big complex, with substantial downstream activities. In the 1960s an expansionist BP set its sights on building up its chemicals interests and formed BP Chemicals as the vehicle.[85] And in 1968 there was further development at Grangemouth, eventually Britain's sole refining and petrochemicals operation directly tied into the North Sea.

Among other new BP ventures in that buoyant decade was a petrochemicals plant at Baglan Bay in South Wales, opened early in the 1960s to draw feedstock from nearby Llandarcy. By the late 1960s Baglan Bay was one of the biggest petrochemical complexes in Europe. At this point BP had a very substantial presence in South Wales, since in addition to Llandarcy and Baglan Bay it also operated a PVC plant at Barry, south of Cardiff.

BP Chemicals also acquired the Chevron Chemicals operation at Salt End, on the north bank of the Humber, and emphasised its commitment to Grangemouth by buying out the minority interests there.

Hatchetman Hubris

This phase came to a halt in the first half of the 1980s, when BP backpedalled on its involvement in petrochemicals. Directing this retrenchment was Robert Horton, who seized the helm at BP Chemicals in 1980. The recession and the new commercial climate – in which it became as acceptable simply to kill off operations as to manage them through their challenges – earned Horton the nickname Hatchetman. By the time he left the division at the end of 1983 he had closed 20 plants and axed two-thirds of the staff.[86]

Horton was apparently rather well qualified. "Because I am blessed by my good brain, I tend to get to the right answer rather quicker and more often than most people," he boasted to *Forbes* magazine.[87] His answers proved less than brilliant when yet another recession struck in the early 1990s. Horton, by now group chairman, was himself ousted in 1992.[88] He went on to exercise his enviable decision-making skills at Railtrack, about to leave the station ahead of the fiasco that became rail privatisation.[89]

Among the victims of the Horton hatchet was Barry. The early 1980s saw activities heavily curtailed, with the workforce falling from nearly 2,000 in 1981 to only 300 three years later.[90] Indeed, Barry's petrochemicals industry, which included plants operated by Dow Corning, Dow Chemical and ICI in addition to BP, suffered particularly severely at this time, with employment falling more than 80 per cent in less than ten years.[91]

Baglan Bay was also slimmed down. The site suffered another hefty cutback in 1993–94 when it lost its ethylene plant,[92] and in a few more years it had closed entirely.[93] And with the sale of the refinery at Grangemouth in 2005 went the adjacent petrochemicals interests. Since the turn of the decade the only remaining BP interest in UK chemicals has been the Salt End aromatics and acetyls plant.[94]

Moreover, BP has continued to jettison its downstream involvement in the North Sea, withdrawing from a new gas sweetening plant at Sullom Voe.[95] And more recently the company has announced plans to sell part of its stake in the facility itself. The buyer, Enquest, is a kind of corporate scavenger "known for managing end-of-life assets".[96]

Ineos Impact

Events at Grangemouth have dramatically highlighted some of the issues facing UK petrochemicals. Despite cost-cutting and hefty investment at the start of the century,[97] BP decided in 2004 that its olefins and derivatives activities, which included Grangemouth, were not making an adequate return. The operations were grouped into a single division called Innovene and in 2005 this was sold for £5.1bn.

Grangemouth's new proprietor was a privately owned enterprise whose rise to riches is one of the more startling business stories of modern times.[98] Ineos had its origins in a small operation acquired from BP in 1992 and went on to build one of the world's largest chemical concerns, much of it from the rubble of Britain's once-mighty chemical industry.

After a refusal by government (soon after it had thrown hundreds of billions into rescuing the City) to alleviate a financial squeeze in 2010, the company moved to Switzerland.[99] Ineos also laid off some of its exposure on Grangemouth by selling a half share in the refinery to PetroChina.[100]

Ineos majority owner Jim Ratcliffe has used a debt-funded private equity model to sweep up "orphaned assets in blue chip majors" – unwanted operations from the international chemicals industry.[101] The strategy – and the historic giants of UK chemicals – has rewarded Ratcliffe by making him one of the wealthiest British industrialists of the age.[102]

His management style has prompted inevitable friction, and in 2008 there was a 48-hour walkout at Grangemouth – the first UK refinery strike in 73 years – over changes to retirement provisions. Though the management retreated, it came back with fresh demands in 2013, claiming Grangemouth was losing £10m a month. There was another strike and the company threatened to walk away. For a couple of days there was the nightmare prospect of Scotland losing its sole refinery and biggest industrial complex.

In the event the workforce capitulated and conceded all the management demands.[103] Linked to the cost-cutting was a project to buy cheap shale gas from the US. The new investment in Grangemouth was partly financed with a loan guarantee of £230m from Westminster and a £9m grant from the cash-strapped Scottish government.[104] Ineos hopes eventually to be allowed to access domestic shale gas, but in the meantime the US deal offers 15 years of secure energy at low prices.[105] And Ineos has also acquired North Sea gas fields from a forced sale by their Russian owner.[106]

For all its controversies, Grangemouth is defying the obituaries of observers eager to write off yet another British basic industry.[107] If giant petrochemical plants can survive in Germany (BASF Ludwigshaven), Belgium (Total Antwerp)[108] and the Netherlands (Shell Moerdijk),[109] there is no obvious reason why they should not do so in the UK.

Events at Grangemouth were bruising.[110] Yet Ratcliffe is unusual in voicing a belief in the importance of British manufacturing: "If you look at chemicals in the UK all you see is plant closure following plant closure; there have been no new ones [but] a successful economy must have a strong manufacturing base."[111]

His personal commitment to his homeland is, however, less impressive. Ratcliffe promised in 2015 to repatriate his corporate headquarters to London from Switzerland. Yet, he himself remained a resident of that enigmatic Alpine tax haven – before moving to Monaco[112] – to reduce his fiscal dues to the country that has been so generous to him.[113]

The Second Division

It is a curious fact that in the 1980s the closures disfiguring the UK refining industry were largely confined to the big three – Exxon, Shell and BP. The only other shutdown was Burmah Oil's small facility at Ellesmere Port, not far from Shell's Stanlow, which closed in 1981. After almost a century of independence Burmah was itself swallowed up by BP in 2000.

The next significant closure was the Gulf Oil refinery at Milford Haven. Opened in 1968, the plant had a capacity of five million tonnes a year and an integrated petrochemicals operation. The chemicals plant was a victim of the market collapse in the 1980s and shut down in 1981. Eventually the refinery also closed.

It was not until well into the new century that the next phase of refinery attrition occurred. First to go was the refining and petrochemicals complex near Teesport in County Durham, which had a throughput capacity of five million tonnes a year. This had been established in the 1960s by Phillips Petroleum and ICI to supply the feedstock needs of the great works at Billingham and Wilton.

With the rundown and fragmentation of ICI's operations the outlets for Teesside were shrinking, the petrochemicals side was cut back and in

2000 the refinery was sold to Petroplus. Swiss-based Petroplus was building a position as Europe's largest independent oil refiner, but the company eventually ran into financial difficulties and in 2009 Teesside was closed.

Petroplus Minus

In the meantime Petroplus had also bought the Coryton refinery, originally established by Mobil Oil in 1953. Coryton was sited on the Thames estuary, a favoured location for oil storage and refining, and with a throughput capacity of 11 million tonnes of oil a year was one of the country's larger refineries. The sale to Petroplus was not the first time the plant had changed hands. In 1996 it was put into a joint venture with BP, which became the operator and then sole owner after the Exxon takeover of Mobil. In 2007 BP sold it on to Petroplus.

By this stage it was a substantial facility, having expanded from its initial capacity of 3.2 million tonnes to a final rating of 11 million tonnes. Within a few years Petroplus had filed for bankruptcy. The search for a buyer was unsuccessful and Coryton closed in 2012.[114] The site has been turned into a fuel import terminal. Products will no doubt be shipped in from the big facilities still active – even thriving – in the Netherlands, Belgium and Germany.

With the end of refining at Coryton the remaining refinery capacity of the UK was becoming so out of balance with the market that there was an immediate impact on the supply of kerosene/jet fuel, and imports promptly rose 25 per cent. There was also renewed pressure on diesel supplies, and imports have also jumped.[115]

However, the retreat from refining was still not finished.[116] There was yet another closure on the Pembroke coast when one of the Milford Haven refineries shut down at the end of 2014. Opened by Amoco in 1973, the plant was part owned by Murco from 1983 and then by Elf, which bought out Amoco in 1990. Elf was taken over by Total and finally Murco bought out the Total interest to become sole owner in 2007. In November 2014 it announced the end of refining at Milford Haven.[117] The site became another storage and distribution terminal.

The conversion of refineries such as Coryton and Murco Milford Haven into mere storage and distribution depots was taking the EU's only major oil producer still further down the dismal road away from downstream processing, and still faster towards import dependence in petroleum products.

Six Survivors

By 2015 there were just six refineries left in the United Kingdom – four in England and one each in Scotland and Wales. The latter still has the Pembroke Refinery, the last of the four built in the 1960s. The Pembroke plant was opened in 1964 by Texaco. Noted for close links with both the Franco insurgency in Spain and the Nazi regime, Texaco had long enjoyed good business in the UK and needed Pembroke to supply its Regent petrol brand. The plant was eventually expanded from an initial 5.9 million tonnes capacity to its current nine million tonnes. It changed hands when Texaco was taken over by Chevron in 2000 and again in 2011, when the operation was sold to Valero Energy Corporation.

Apart from Fawley and Stanlow, the only remaining refineries in England are at Lindsey and Humber. Opened as the Killingholme joint venture by Total and Fina in 1969, Lindsey is now wholly owned by Total. Having commissioned its new £3.5bn gas collection plant in Shetland in the teeth of a severe downturn, Total has undoubtedly earned its place among the long-term stayers in UK hydrocarbons. However, in 2015 even Lindsey saw its capacity halved.

Lindsey's smaller neighbour to the south, the Humber Refinery (6.5 million tonnes), was established by Continental Oil in 1969, but is now run by Phillips 66, a spin-off from the parent company.

The collapse in UK refining capacity has opened the way to much greater import dependency in oil products. In lines such as diesel and aircraft fuel, half the national requirement is now imported.[118] Without firm interventionist policies on the part of government, the possibility of reversing this egregious situation looks remote.

That great industry-building exercise of which the Institute of Petroleum was once so justly proud has fallen a long, long way back from its 1970s zenith.

Song of Norway

Could it all have been different? A glance at the Continent gives the answer. By the 1970s an entrepreneurial state had developed effective offshore industries in Norway, France, the Netherlands and even Italy – though only one of these had significant indigenous oil resources.

Measures included unstinting promotion and support for oil companies that were all, apart from Royal Dutch Shell, creatures of the state. There was generous public funding for research and development, finance for training and effective protection. These were necessary in an industry dominated by US (and to a modest extent British) companies. The US offshore industry benefitted greatly from protection through the Jones Act, which excluded foreign companies from offering shipping services in US waters.

The record for Norway is particularly impressive. From the outset it adopted a highly integrated strategy to exploit its new-found North Sea riches. The issue of exploration licences was tightly controlled by the government, with the early concessions going mostly to Norsk Hydro, Norway's leading natural resources company. And in 1972 Statoil was established with the specific mission of retaining Norwegian sovereignty over its hydrocarbon industry.

Statoil was required to work closely with the appropriate ministry and report regularly to the Norwegian parliament. Despite the subsequent dilution of the government stake through the sale of a third of its shares, the company has remained the main official vehicle in guiding oil and gas development throughout the Norwegian North Sea.

With a 60 per cent share of total production Statoil remains the dominant operator on the Norwegian continental shelf. This has not prevented it from building a major international presence. Since taking over the hydrocarbon interests of Hydro in 2006, Statoil has joined the top ten of the global oil industry, and is now the undisputed leader in offshore oil and gas. It is an extraordinary achievement.

A crucial feature of Statoil's role in the North Sea has been to make haste slowly. It has followed a depletion policy which husbanded the oil and gas reserves and avoided the development rush that yielded such disappointing long-term results on the UKCS. This allowed it to open new fields at a sensible pace. While production from the British sector raced from a standing start to 100 million tonnes in just eight years, Norway's output took almost two decades to reach a comparable level.

This strategy enabled it to secure Norway's secondary goals for its oil. Statoil's role included the encouragement of significant industries in refining and petrochemicals and fostering a specialist supply sector. A typical comment from a Danish trade organisation was: "The Norwegian offshore sector is almost entirely sealed off from foreign competition even where foreign supplies are offered at decisively lower prices."[119]

Norway's success has been hugely helped by the application of common sense rather than ideology. The dogmas that infected the British political arena in the 1980s and have blighted so much of its economy since have been blessedly absent from the Norwegian scene. The role of the state in the industry has been uncontroversial. Active interventionism has been pursued by Conservative, Christian Democrat and Labour administrations alike. Yet, Norway's policies have also survived the country's membership of EFTA (European Free Trade Area) and the EEA (European Economic Area), both of which are closely aligned with the European Union and pay similar lip-service to free market principles.

Yes, there is an alternative to wasting the manna of North Sea oil. Shamefully, in Britain it was never even tried.

CHAPTER 16

Paper Trail

> *To look at the paper is to raise a seashell to one's ear and be overwhelmed by the roar of humanity.*
>
> *Alain de Botton*

Late Arrival

Paper and printing are usually bracketed together in the statistics. Yet they make odd bedfellows. One is a commodity industry producing big tonnages of standard-grade materials such as newsprint and bulk packaging, with some higher-value lines. The other is a complex business producing tailor-made products to diverse specifications, and requiring considerable craft skills. Moreover, grouping the two sectors together has disguised very different fortunes. Where trends in printing have remained buoyant, in papermaking they have been little short of calamitous.

Papermaking came relatively late to England. Brought to Europe from the Islamic world in the twelfth century, it was not recorded in the British Isles for another 300 years.[1] By Elizabethan times, however, textile-based paper production appears to have become quite well established. But more centuries were to pass before the first attempts at mechanised papermaking.

Early in the nineteenth century a French process for the machine production of paper was taken up in England by the Fourdrinier brothers.[2]

The Fourdriniers were stationers and engaged an engineer, Bryan Donkin, to develop the new technique for commercial use. Eventually a successful machine was installed at the Frogmore mill, in Hertfordshire, and the process was soon acknowledged as the leading technique for papermaking.

Other inventors, such as John Dickinson and Robert Crompton, were attracted into the business. By the middle of the nineteenth century Britain had a thriving paper industry,[3] with important centres in the south-east of England and lowland Scotland. From the mid-nineteenth century on the industry rapidly shifted over to using woodpulp and other cellulose-based materials.[4]

The main demands for paper focused on stationery, book-printing and packaging requirements, but by the end of the nineteenth century a big new outlet was emerging with the world's first popular press. To feed this voracious market, large mills were built by entrepreneurs such as Edward Lloyd and Albert Reed. The new plants were typically sited within range of cities like London and Manchester, where the newspapers had their printing works.

This set the geographical pattern of the paper industry for many years, with the towns of the Thames estuary, north Kent and the north-western seaboard of England sustaining major paper mills right up until modern times. Other papermaking, particularly for higher-value products, tended to be centred on smaller mills.

The interwar period proved relatively benign for the paper industry. Its business was less badly hit by the Depression than some of the more traditional sectors, and there was a measure of protection for most of the 1920s and 1930s. Production more than doubled, and omens for the post-war world were good.

Following the Second World War, the environment for the UK paper industry – still almost entirely British- or Commonwealth-controlled – remained favourable for well over a decade. Demand was sustained by post-war recovery, and the industry was buttressed by import tariffs and quotas, and by price-fixing agreements. Substantial investment in additional capacity was made by companies such as Bowater, Reed, St Anne's Board Mills, Tullis Russell and Wiggins Teape.

Production was not particularly expansionary, however, and it was not until the 1960s that output really took off, drawing on the investment that had taken place in the 1950s. The growth was slightly surprising in that the advent of the European Free Trade Area (EFTA) in 1960 opened the British market to imports from the highly competitive Nordic paper producers. Nevertheless, UK production rose from around three and a half million tonnes in 1960 to almost five million tonnes at the end of the decade, making the British paper and board industry the second largest in Europe after Germany.

This was the peak of the upswing, however, and a combination of economic slowdown, stagnant demand and rising imports pulled output down to under four million tonnes a year in the first half of the 1970s. Concerned at this decline in a hitherto thriving industry, an interventionist Labour government introduced the Paper and Board Industry Scheme to promote the use of waste paper and domestic woodpulp.

The initiative fostered a revival, and by 1979 output had recovered to 4.2 million tonnes. This proved to be a peak, however, and the subsequent downturn was exacerbated by the onset of severe recession. An overvalued pound hampered the competitiveness of the industry, and in 1981 imports exceeded domestic production for the first time.

Once the economy began to recover, paper became one of the few traditional sectors in the 1980s to see a decent upturn. For once restructuring had meant more than job loss, silent factories and a hollowed-out industry. Assets changed hands, sleepy conglomerates floated off subsidiaries and there was significant new investment by US and Continental papermakers. However, the advance of foreign firms was accompanied by a general retreat on the part of UK interests as British owners sold up and left the business.

For a while the broader trends looked encouraging. Helped by a rise in the availability of domestic woodpulp and higher recycling rates, UK output of paper and board grew to five million tonnes in 1990 and went on rising, reaching 6.6 million tonnes in 2000. So had the upheavals of the 1980s and 1990s given birth to a new-found strength in British papermaking?

Unfortunately not. The year 2000 proved to be an all-time peak, and since then the industry has been on a relentless downward slide. Output was badly hit by the recession which began in 2008 and has not seen a sustained recovery since. In recent years production has fallen to barely four million tonnes, the lowest level in 30 years and little higher than it was half a century ago.

Bowater

Few of the companies which were once household names in British papermaking survived the upheavals of the 1980s and 1990s or the collapse of recent years. For many decades one of the most prominent was Bowater.[5] Originally a wholesaler in newsprint and waste paper, Bowater built a large business with the popular press and opened a paper mill at Northfleet in Kent in the mid-1920s.

Within a few years this was doubled in size and a new plant, the Mersey mill, was built at Ellesmere Port, near Manchester. And in the mid-1930s the company purchased yet more capacity, in the form of the Sittingbourne[6] and Kemsley[7] mills originally built by Edward Lloyd, an early pioneer in bulk papermaking. With over half the domestic market Bowater was now the dominant force in British newsprint.

The post-war period was marked by another burst of growth, this time overseas. By the mid-1950s Bowater was the world's biggest manufacturer of newsprint,[8] with other interests in woodpulp and shipping. The expansionary momentum ended with the death of Eric Bowater in 1962 and from that point the empire started to crumble. There was a series of divestments and in 1972 the entrepreneur Jim Slater – notorious for asset stripping – contrived a controversial merger with a commodity trader called Ralli.

The 1980s brought further restructurings, culminating in the sale of most of Bowater's paper capacity to a management buyout (MBO) which called itself UK Paper. Before long the MBO had off-loaded the bulk of its assets. Sittingbourne ended up in the hands of Finland's Matsäliitto Group (M-Real), which eventually closed the mill in 2007. Northfleet has closed and, after becoming a subsidiary of AbitibiBowater through its Bridgewater Paper offshoot, the Mersey mill went into administration and closed in 2010. The only former Bowater mill still operating is Kemsley, taken over by a relative newcomer to the paper industry, DS Smith, in 1988.

Reed

For much of its existence Bowater's closest rival was the Reed group. Reed's origins go back to 1894, when Albert Reed bought a paper mill at Maidstone in Kent.[9] After expanding the factory and opening half a dozen small operations the company eventually centralised its activities on a big new mill at Aylesford, also in Kent, opened in 1922. By 1939 Aylesford was the largest plant of its kind in Europe.

Reed used the post-war boom to extend its paper interests at home and invest in pulp mills overseas. The end of pricing agreements and the loss of protection from the integrated Nordic producers brought this phase to an end, and Reed was seen as increasingly vulnerable. In a succession of corporate manoeuvres by the megalomaniac newspaper publisher Cecil King in the 1960s, Reed came under the formal control of its largest shareholder, the International Publishing Corporation (IPC).

The relationship was reversed in 1970 when Reed itself took over IPC to form Reed International. With the energetic Don Ryder as managing director, the group was now a conglomerate spanning paper, publishing, wallpaper, paints and building products, and employing 85,000 people. Though Ryder rationalised some operations, he continued to invest in the more promising ones. By the end of the decade profitability was stagnating, however, and his successors made extensive disposals overseas. But it was not until the 1980s that drastic cutbacks, closures and asset sales were implemented at home. In 1988 the last of the group's big industrial interests, paper and packaging, were handed to a management buyout, Reedpack, in collaboration with Cinven private equity.

As so often, the MBO proved to be a stalking horse for a rival manufacturer, and within months the UK paper operations were sold on to Svenska Cellulosa Aktiebolaget (SCA). SCA brought in South Africa-based Mondi as a partner in the Aylesford operations.

Meanwhile, having finally shed all its commodity manufacturing, Reed merged itself with Dutch publisher Elsevier to become Reed Elsevier, which then dropped its evocative name to call itself RELX Group.[10]

Initially SCA and Mondi worked hard to sustain their acquisition, investing £250m in 1994–95 to build the most modern newsprint recycling plant in Europe. The mill could turn half a million tonnes of waste into 400,000 tonnes of saleable product and benefitted from good industrial relations and a highly skilled workforce. Yet in 2012 the owners decided to sell up.[11]

SCA had indicated that it wanted to concentrate on the tissue sector, while Mondi stressed the losses being incurred by the plant.[12] Ownership of the mill went, for a nominal consideration, to the Martland Holdings,[13] a US-based "investment holding company".[14] The new owner declared itself a long-term investor committed to building lifetime relationships with customers,[15] but little more than two years later the operation was put into receivership,[16] the mill was closed for good and its equipment was sold off overseas.[17] It was yet another case of asset stripping.

Wiggins Teape

The third of the big three that dominated the paper industry[18] in the mid-twentieth century was Wiggins Teape.[19] With origins in Kent dating back to the 1760s, the company was involved from an early stage in the manufacture of fine papers and remained a specialist producer throughout its life. The range of products was gradually extended during the nineteenth century, with production coming mainly from relatively small mills. The interwar period brought another phase of expansion, based on the acquisition of a sizeable mill at Dartford in 1931, and on the eve of the Second World War Wiggins Teape had 17 mills in different parts of the country.

By the end of the 1950s it had over 30 plants and more than 10,000 employees. The biggest development in the 1960s was a new mill at Fort William in the Scottish Highlands,[20] backed by a £10m Board of Trade loan. It emulated the ventures typical of the Nordic countries as a fully integrated pulp and paper operation. The only one of its kind in the British Isles, the mill would draw on softwood supplies from Scottish forests within a radius of 100 miles.

The plant opened in 1969 and operated for over a decade, but technical problems with the Stora process were never fully resolved. The 1980s brought a combination of severe recession, government hostility to the promotion of industry and a climate in which companies could more easily wash their hands of challenging industrial endeavours. Fort William closed.

In the meantime, British American Tobacco (BAT) had completed a gradual takeover of Wiggins Teape by 1970,[21] and had the resources for successful development of specialist paper products in the 1970s and 1980s. Unfortunately, BAT itself came under pressure from opportunistic speculators during the 1980s, and in 1989 it demerged and floated off its UK and US paper interests as Wiggins Teape Appleton.

Within a couple of years the company had merged with a French counterpart to form Arjo Wiggins Appleton. Another ten years and it had become a subsidiary of the financial group Worms & Cie and was sinking fast. The mid-2000s saw the closure of Scottish paper capacity and in 2009 the former heartland of Wiggins Teape, the mill at Dartford in Kent, was closed.[22]

BAT's purchase of Wiggins Teape may have been prompted by the example of its rival Imperial Tobacco, which had long had its own paper and packaging subsidiary. This was the St Anne's Board Mills, a major feature of Bristol's industry since it was opened before the First World War to provide carton for cigarette packets. In time the St Anne's mill became one of the country's top three board makers. It remained a successful producer of packaging material until the 1970s, when competitive pressures grew more intense. Heavy cutbacks in the late 1970s presaged the end.[23] The plant was closed in 1980 and demolished four years later.[24]

Thames Board Mills

Another big producer of packaging was Thames Board Mills. Thames Board was established in 1902 to supply manufacturers of food and household commodities such as Unilever, which eventually took a 50 per cent stake. The first facility was opened at Purfleet on the Thames estuary and another mill was built at Workington in Cumbria. Purfleet was eventually sold to British Plasterboard (BPB), which used large tonnages of linerboard for its plasterboard products and ran its paper interests under the Davidson Radcliffe name.

Among other operations, BPB bought the long-established mill in the Manchester suburb of Radcliffe in 1961. Together with nearby Ramsbottom, Radcliffe had become a centre for papermaking following the decline of the cotton industry. Indeed, the other main producer in Radcliffe, East Lancashire Paper, had originally been a textile mill but switched to paper earlier in the century. After trading as a quoted company for many years, East Lancashire was sold to a group of investors in the late 1980s and then to a management buyout in 1990.

Having employed as many as 2,000 people in the mid-1990s, however, papermaking in Radcliffe went into an "abrupt and brutal" collapse at the end of the decade.[25] The Radcliffe mill closed in 1998 and East Lancashire went bankrupt[26] and shut soon after.[27] The demise of Radcliffe was followed by that of Purfleet in 2004 and the Muggiemoss mill in Aberdeen the following year. BPB had abandoned its UK papermaking ambition and signed up to buy large quantities of paperboard from DS Smith and from a German producer.[28]

Meanwhile, Unilever's mill at Workington had been substantially upgraded with government financial assistance in the late 1970s. The intention at Workington was to meet rapidly rising demand for Duplex packaging board. Originally it was to utilise home-grown raw material, though the emphasis later switched to waste paper processing.

One reason why the government supported the scheme was Unilever's commitment to purchase its equipment as far as possible in Britain, a policy where it had a good record.[29] Though it proved a sustained success, the mill was sold to Iggesund of Sweden in 1987. In 2012 Iggesund announced a £108m investment in Workington,[30] making the mill one of the few survivors of recent years.

John Dickinson

Some of the oldest papermakers in England were involved from an early stage in high-grade and other specialist products. John Dickinson[31] founded his operations on stationery and in the course of an inventive life patented many innovative approaches to papermaking.

Established in the early years of the nineteenth century, his company opened several mills in Hertfordshire and went on to develop a range of famous stationery brands, including Lion, Basildon Bond, Croxley and Queen's Velvet. These were added to in 1966, when Dickinson took over Bristol-based ES & A Robinson to create one of the world's largest stationery and packaging companies, Dickinson Robinson Group (DRG).

Further acquisitions were made in the UK and in France, but 1989 brought a controversial leveraged (junk bond) buyout by Bermuda-registered Pembridge Investments.[32] Among many alarmed at the threatened asset stripping, Conservative MP Nicholas Winterton revealed a hitherto well-concealed radical streak when he questioned whether "[i]t is correct for people based overseas, who can remit profits overseas, to take over and break up British companies which are of great value to the economy merely to make money for a few people and not for the general public".[33]

Secretary of State John Redwood showed his customary touching faith in financiers with the inelegant comment: "Junkiness is in the eye of the beholder. The Government believe that these decisions are best made by shareholders and bankers, who have to make important decisions on behalf of the companies in which they are investing."[34]

As predicted, Pembridge Investments set about dismembering DRG. Packaging was sold to Bowater and other interests went to a succession of owners. Among these was John Dickinson Stationery, though this at least ended up in the hands of a company from a country which, like Britain, has a long tradition of fine stationery – France. The Dickinson paper mills were handed to SAPPI of South Africa and after centuries of successful operation they eventually closed.

Peter Dixon

Peter Dixon & Son established itself as a significant papermaker by buying a mill at Oughtibridge, on the outskirts of Sheffield, in 1871.[35] The company was integrated with a substantial forestry and pulp operation in Finland, and became the leading privately owned newsprint producer in the UK. Shortly after the turn of the century a second mill was opened at West March, Grimsby, and this took over newsprint production to leave Oughtibridge free to concentrate on other types of paper.[36]

Following a fire and difficult trading conditions, Grimsby closed in 1973. But Oughtibridge continued in operation despite passing through a bewildering succession of new proprietors after the Dixon family sold up. The final owner was Sweden's SCA, which bought the mill in 2014. The paper mill had actually closed in 2007 after severe flooding, but the site continued to be used for converting raw paper[37] into a range of finished products.[38]

This ended in 2015 when Capita, "the UK's leading provider of business process management and integrated professional support service solutions" – whatever that means – was asked to "bring the site to market". What that meant, in plain English, was to turn Oughtibridge into another dull housing estate.[39]

Scottish Mills

Scotland once had a large and thriving paper industry, with many mills active in the 1950s and a workforce of over 17,000. Among the biggest producers was Inveresk, which was founded in Musselburgh in 1922 and eventually had a dozen plants north of the border and several in England. The company came under pressure with British membership of EFTA and the EEC, and several mills were closed in the 1970s. However, overall capacity remained pretty much the same until more recent times.

The downhill slide really became evident around the turn of the century, when a Swedish corporate investor, reportedly with a stake in a competitor, took an interest in Inveresk and began a sequence of downsizing. Mills such as Inverkeithing were decommissioned and their sites put to other uses. Inveresk evolved into a real estate developer rather than a papermaker.

The process was nearly complete with the closure of Inveresk's last Scottish mill in 2005, when the company's Carrongrove plant at Denny in Stirlingshire was shut after two centuries of papermaking.[40] Carrongrove had received financial support from the Scottish government, and its closure prompted angry accusations of asset stripping. Inveresk's retreat culminated in the suspension of the St Cuthbert[41] mill in Somerset when the company went into receivership in 2010.[42]

More poignant still was the demise of another great name in Scottish papermaking, Tullis Russell. Founded in 1809, the company was based for much of its existence at Markinch in Fife, and produced high-quality board for use in cards, covers and premium packaging.[43] In 1994 the owners stepped down and the firm was turned into an employee-owned cooperative.

However, after the recession triggered by the financial crisis, Tullis Russell found recovery elusive. The final blow came in 2015, when the firm was hit by the insolvency of a major client and forced into administration.[44] Within weeks two centuries of papermaking at Markinch had ended.[45]

David Erdal, who had led the transfer from his family to employee ownership (as distinct from management buyout), paid handsome tribute to the workforce at Markinch: "Employee ownership is not the cause of this closure. All the evidence points to extra productivity, innovation and longevity being characteristic of employee-owned companies."[46] The blame lay with "international pressures [which] have closed pretty well the whole of the UK printing paper industry".[47]

The shutdown at Markinch left just two mills active in the whole of Scotland. These were the specialist Stoneywood facility in Aberdeen and the big Caledonian mill operated by United Paper Mills-Kymmene (UPM) at Irvine. UPM had come on to the UK paper scene during the great retreat by British owners that began in the 1980s. Among other operations the Finnish group opened a newsprint mill at Shotton, on Deeside. In 2015 this was cut back by closing one of its two big machines.

The decision was presented as part of a scheme to reduce UPM's European capacity for publication paper by 800,000 tonnes a year.[48] At the same time the company reduced its commitment to the UK still further by centralising supply chain planning and order fulfilment at its main facility in Germany.

Another overseas company to make its entry to the UK was US-based International Paper, which bought the mill making fine papers at Inverurie. The plant had been acquired by Federal Paper of the US in the late 1980s, and was then sold on to International Paper in the mid-1990s. Inverurie has subsequently gone the way of most other Scottish mills and closed in 2009.

Survivors

Jefferson Smurfit, with origins in a box-maker founded in Ireland in the 1930s, had only a small presence in the UK until the 1970s. There was then a drive to turn the company into a significant international player. In 2002 the group was the subject of a management buyout, financed by a trio of private equity concerns – notably Cinven, a veteran of such episodes. In 2005 there was a merger with Kappa Packaging, and in 2007 Smurfit Kappa was floated as a public company under the name Smurfit Kappa.

Smurfit Kappa's main UK papermaking interests have been mills at Townsend Hook and Snodland, in Kent, and a plant in Birmingham. Townsend Hook was a medium-sized newsprint manufacturer owned by the *News of the World*, which switched to packaging and printing paper in the 1970s and was bought by Smurfit as part of its expansion initiative. In 2015 Townsend Hook was the focus of substantial investment to replace two existing containerboard machines with a single lightweight modern machine.[49]

The sole British-owned group to sustain a prominent position in paper since the upheavals of the 1980s and 1990s is DS Smith. Based on a business founded by David Smith, a Polish immigrant,[50] in the early twentieth century, the company was only listed on the Stock Exchange in the 1950s. And the group did not begin its big expansion until the 1980s. The critical steps were the purchase of the St Regis Paper Company in 1986 and Bowater's Kemsley mill some years later.[51]

Kemsley was modernised at a cost of £110m in 1993–96[52] and its capacity supplemented by the purchase of the adjacent New Thames Mill from M-Real (Finland's Metsäliitto Group) in 2008.[53] New Thames had been a maker of high-quality office paper,[54] but the mill was converted by its new owner[55] to the production of lightweight recycled corrugated case material (CCM).[56] This drew hostile comment on the grounds that New Thames was Britain's sole remaining facility for recycling and manufacturing high-quality paper. Its reshaping would mean the transfer of operations to France, leaving only the de-inking process still in operation at New Thames.[57]

This was not the only rationalisation of British papermaking by DS Smith. In 2001 its subsidiary St Regis had disposed of the East Lancashire paper mill site, after buying it as a failed concern from the administrators. A relatively small operation based in a former cotton mill at Radcliffe, in Bury, East Lancashire had been involved in a management buyout some time before but the venture had gone bankrupt.

The first significant downsizing by DS Smith occurred in 2011, when the Hollins paper mill at Darwen, in Lancashire, shut down, and the company's Higher Kings Mill operation was sold the same year.[58] More salutary was the closure of the Wansbrough Paper Mill at Watchet, in Somerset. The mill,[59] the largest manufacturer of coreboard in the UK,[60] had been in existence for over two centuries and was one of the main commercial employers in the area.[61]

Germans and Spanish to the Rescue

Dismal though trends have been in British papermaking, the picture has not been entirely bleak. As a partial offset to the swathes of capacity lost in recent years there have been two significant developments. Both are the result of large-scale investment by EU-based family-owned private groups specialising in paper.

The first is a recycling facility set up by Papier Fabrik Palm of Germany, which opened a large mill at Kings Lynn in Norfolk in 2009. Reportedly using the world's largest recycled newsprint machine,[62] the Palm mill is highly efficient and supplies approximately 450,000 tonnes a year of uniform-grade newsprint to regional and national publications.[63] It also produces papers for a variety of printing processes. The downside to the arrival of Palm was the 2015 closure of the former Reed mill at Aylesford.

The other positive development is a new facility opened at Partington, in Manchester. This is an initiative by the Spanish group SAICA, which has been building an impressive international business in papermaking.[64] In 2008 SAICA bought some of the conventional corrugated packaging interests of SCA for around £100m.[65] The purchase appears to have included a discreet understanding that SCA would close its containerboard mill at New Hythe in Kent. Soon after the deal was reported, SAICA announced a project for a big lightweight board mill in Partington, Manchester.[66] The new plant[67] was commissioned in 2012[68] and has an output capacity of 400,000 tonnes a year.[69]

Though a couple of producers have helped to stem the tide, British papermaking has long been on a remorseless downward trend. At less than four million tonnes in recent years, output has been heading for its lowest since the dire days of the 1980s.[70] True, consumption has fallen back from its 13mt peak at the end of the millennium. But the demand is still there.

Despite all the familiar reasons for using less paper – the advance of electronic communication, the decline of print journalism, growing environmental awareness – at well over nine million tonnes a year UK consumption remains far above domestic production. Indeed, in packaging, construction and specialist lines it looks set for growth a long way into the future.

Ironically, there is no shortage of raw material. But it's in the form of waste paper. Thanks entirely to EU directives UK waste paper collection has risen from less than three million tonnes a year at the end of the 1980s to over eight million tonnes in recent years.[71] However, the collapse of capacity has meant that less and less of this is being processed at home.

In 2014 the UK recycled less than half the waste paper it recovered. Exports of unprocessed waste paper have shot up from under a million tonnes a year at the start of the century to four to five million tonnes a year more recently. In effect, the trend in paper has been following the same disastrous pattern as in ferrous metals, non-ferrous metals, plastics, textile fibres and other raw materials.

World's Largest Importer

The lack of domestic processing capacity has drawn angry comment from municipal authorities and their agents. Obliged by Brussels to raise their waste collection targets they have had to ship much of their material 11,000 miles to China for recycling.[72] China is already putting a brake on the amount of waste materials it can absorb, and if this outlet is entirely blocked the industry may have to go back to the wasteful and environmentally degrading practice of dumping scrap paper in landfill.

Concern has also been voiced at the poor quality of much of the paper still being reclaimed in the UK. This growing problem reflects serious weakness in the regulation of scrap sorting, segregation and wholesaling, which has been largely abandoned to crude market forces. The poor quality of its raw material was a factor in the closure of the Aylesford mill in 2015.[73]

In contrast to high-profile activities like steelmaking, the collapse of British papermaking has gone strangely unremarked. However, with an extraordinary tally of 50 mills lost between 2000 and 2010[74] and more since, the industry's representatives at last sounded the alarm. In September 2015 the Confederation of Paper Industries (CPI) pointed out that, after a pause in the decline of the sector, four more mills and 13 machines were expected to close by the year end, cutting 20 per cent of UK output and putting the UK in the dismal position of being the world's largest importer of finished paper.[75]

The CPI might have added that other industrial countries without big domestic lumber resources, such as Japan, Germany, Korea and France, still manage to make several times as much paper as the UK – and achieve higher levels of recycling.

For the CPI the villain is energy costs. While UK industrial gas prices are roughly in line with European neighbours (though twice the level of shale gas-rich North America), direct and indirect industrial electricity costs are higher than virtually anywhere else in the world. Two taxes have been particularly burdensome – the Carbon Price Floor and the Carbon Price Commitment.[76]

Both of these reflect official recognition of the need to decrease fossil fuel consumption. But, if consumption of the end product is not cut and the only result of reductions in UK carbon release is to divert the productive activity from British shores to other countries, the policy neither makes moral sense nor, in the long run, is it economically sustainable. Paper is a sector crying out for firm and constructive government intervention.

CHAPTER 17

Meltdown

The divine drink, which builds up resistance and fights fatigue; a cup of this precious drink [cocoa] permits a man to walk for a whole day without food.

Montezuma, Aztec emperor

Food and drink is Britain's largest industry, accounting for 15 per cent of total industrial output. Though the industry has vibrant sectors, overall trends are far from vigorous, with self-sufficiency in foodstuffs falling, import dependency rising and a growing trade deficit.[1] In corporate terms the UK has also been faring badly. Of the top 500 global brands in recent years just two were British.[2] One was Unilever, which is actually Anglo-Dutch and tried recently to decamp to Rotterdam. The other was Cadbury, which has since ceased to be British.

The fate of Cadbury epitomises the weakness even in what was historically one of the most flourishing areas, chocolate and sugar confectionery. The way this once-thriving British industry has been allowed to slip away is an appalling story.

Joseph Fry

Britain has long had one of the highest levels of confectionery consumption in the world, well ahead of other industrialised countries. Many of the confectionery brands developed in the UK have international recognition, though British products have been associated more with the popular segments of the market rather than the premium end.

Historically, chocolate was consumed as a drink or in roughly cut pieces sold by weight and individually wrapped by the retailer. As it was rather expensive, it tended to be less accessible to the poorer members of the population. All this changed with the development of the moulded chocolate bar by JS Fry & Sons in 1847.[3]

The firm had been established by Joseph Fry in Bristol in the 1750s. Fry was a Quaker and maintained high ethical standards and good employment practices, themes which came to characterise much of the confectionery industry. By the 1820s Fry was the biggest maker of chocolate merchandise in the country.

Following success with the chocolate bar, a range of other products was developed and by the end of the century Fry was still a leading supplier to the British market, and one of the largest employers in Bristol. Just after the First World War the company merged with its main rival, Cadbury, to form the British Cocoa and Chocolate Company.

Four years later production was moved to a new factory at Somerdale, near Bristol, and the operation retained its identity as the Fry's division of British Cocoa and Chocolate for many years. Some of the quintessential Fry's products, such as Turkish Delight and Peppermint Creams, are still being distributed under the traditional banner. Unfortunately, they are now made in Poland.

John Mackintosh

Mackintosh's started life as a small confectioner in Halifax in the 1890s.[4] Ambition and enterprise took the company into wider markets at home and abroad, and by the First World War John Mackintosh Ltd had 1,000 employees. Acquisitions between the wars included Caley's of Norwich, which strengthened the position of Mackintosh in the chocolate field.

Famous brands developed in the 1930s included Quality Street and Rolo, and there was further expansion post-war. The year 1969 saw the company merge with Rowntree to form Rowntree Mackintosh, which continued to market the best selling Mackintosh products under their familiar names.

Quality Street, the world's best selling boxed chocolate, gained a moment of dubious publicity in 1991 when the Iraqi dictator Saddam Hussein greeted a respectful visitor, George Galloway MP, with his favourite confectionery.

Terry's of York

Terry's was another chocolate maker with origins dating back to the eighteenth century, when Robert Berry opened a confectionery business in York.[5] After Joseph Terry joined the business in the 1820s it was renamed Terry's of York. The rest of the century brought recurrent expansion, particularly in chocolate making.

In the 1920s the next generation of Terrys brought a fresh lease of life, and 1926 saw the opening of a new factory near the centre of York.[6] Like Cadbury's Bournville headquarters, the new initiative reflected the paternalistic philosophy of its owners, with spacious facilities for the welfare of employees.[7] Built in art deco style and designated Terry's Confectionery Works, the new operation developed such distinctive products as Terry's Chocolate Orange and Terry's All Gold.

By the 1960s the Terry family had lost control of the business. For a while it was owned by Trust House Forte before being sold on to Colgate Palmolive. Colgate in turn sold it to United Biscuits (UB), but before long UB was shedding activities. The year 1993 saw Terry's sold to Philip Morris, owner of Kraft General Foods. Kraft promptly merged it with its new acquisition, the Swiss chocolate maker Jacobs Suchard, to form Terry's Suchard.

This proved fatal. In 2000 Terry's of York became plain Terry's and over the next few years it was downsized into oblivion.[8] In 2004 production of the remaining product lines was switched to Kraft factories abroad. These included sites in Poland and Slovakia, but also locations not noted for low costs, such as Belgium and Sweden.[9] And in 2005 the famous factory[10] finally closed.[11] The Grade II listed building has become a museum named, apparently without irony, the Chocolate Factory. The rest of the site has a familiar if banal future as a commercial and residential development.

Rowntree's

Not quite as old as Terry's, Rowntree's also had its origins in York but had a history that was even more distinctive, developing a philosophy imbued, like other confectioners, with a Quaker ethos. Originally founded by the Tuke family, the business was taken on by Henry Isaac Rowntree and his brother Joseph in the 1860s. By the 1880s the company had moved into chocolate production and in the 1890s it expanded by opening a purpose-built factory on the outskirts of York.

Business in the early years of the twentieth century was relatively pedestrian and by the 1920s the company was struggling financially. In the 1930s, however, new management brought more dynamism and iconic brands such as Black Magic, Aero, Kit Kat and Smarties were developed. By the 1960s Rowntree was manufacturing in Continental Europe and becoming an acquisition target for the bigger multinationals. In 1969 it turned down a bid from General Foods, itself eventually taken over by Kraft, and instead merged with Mackintosh to form Rowntree Mackintosh.

The 1980s brought heavy investment, both in manufacturing facilities and in corporate acquisitions, mainly in US food and confectionery, and in 1987 the business was floated on the London Stock Exchange. At this point Rowntree Mackintosh held over a third of the UK market and was rated the fourth largest chocolate manufacturer in the world after Mars, Hershey and Cadbury. Despite some rationalisation,[12] the group was a major employer. It had over 30,000 employees, about half located in the UK. It was also a highly rated multinational, with 60 per cent of its business overseas.

This was a time before the leading confectionery makers in Continental Europe had yet to make a big impact outside their home countries. Turning Rowntree Mackintosh into a public quoted company may have made it easier to raise funds for investment, but it also turned it into a tempting acquisition target for others keen to expand their presence in branded confectionery. And in the looser climate ushered in by the Conservative government in the 1980s Rowntree became much more vulnerable to predators.

The first to take a bite, in a dawn raid, was Jacobs Suchard, which swooped on Rowntree Mackintosh in April 1988. Suchard snapped up 15 per cent of the company's shares and then built up a 30 per cent stake. At this point rival Nestlé offered to act as a "white knight" with a takeover offer that would be less unattractive to a reluctant Rowntree board.

The Nestlé bid was, of course, controversial. Overseas takeovers of British companies were still infrequent and there was public unease at the prospect of a cherished household name falling into foreign hands. And after nearly a decade of industrial collapse and mass unemployment there was concern for the future of what had seemed one of the few secure sectors of industry.

But the official reaction was complacent to the point of indifference. Interviewed for radio, industry minister Kenneth Clarke breezily remarked that most of his constituents called the putative new owner Nestles and thought it was British anyway, so he wasn't bothered. Only John MacGregor, at the Ministry of Agriculture, Fisheries and Food, asked David Young, secretary of state for trade and industry, to refer the bid to the Monopolies and Mergers Commission. His case was based on principle. As there was no reciprocity in the positions of the bidding company and the target company – "an unfriendly takeover of a Swiss company…is, for all intents and purposes, impossible" – the free operation of market forces to which the Thatcher government was supposedly committed was being thwarted.[13]

The government dismissed the case for a Monopolies Commission investigation, citing a narrow interpretation of the competitive picture rather than the wider issues traditionally considered.[14] Indeed, the takeover of Rowntree appears not even to have been discussed in Cabinet.[15] The secretary of state for trade and industry, in a government so committed to market forces, let the largest ever foreign takeover of a British firm – by a protected company – go through without a murmur.[16]

"A Lot of Pinkos"

Not quite without a murmur. Years later it emerged that "one source close to Downing Street described the company [Rowntree] as just a lot of pinkos".[17] The observation was revealing. It shed light on both the prejudices of leading members of the government and their ignorance. The charitable trusts established long ago by the Rowntree family, renowned for sponsoring social research, had no influence whatever on the commercial activities of the companies which had been the source of their funding.

Ironically, the most trenchant criticism came from Conservative MP Rodney Atkinson, known for the driest of Thatcherite economic views. Writing in *Crossbow*, the publication of the Conservative Bow Group, he said that the prime minister's statements welcoming the Swiss bids as "inward direct investment" displayed "appalling ignorance of business economics" and added that, contrary to what David Young had said, takeovers of large regional groups like Rowntree usually result in the loss of jobs.[18]

How right he was.

Nestlé secured acceptance for its £2.55bn bid with three commitments.[19] The York headquarters would remain the centre of the company's UK activities. It would serve as a strategic headquarters for Nestlé's international confectionery business. And chairman Kenneth Dixon would remain on the group's management committee. In other words, Nestlé was pledging business as usual.

These undertakings were not worth the paper they were written on. In six months Kenneth Dixon had gone. And within a few years the York operation had lost its autonomy and the Rowntree corporate name had been dropped.[20] True, the path taken by Nestlé has been less dire than that followed by Kraft with Terry's, and Nestlé has invested in a grandly named Product Technology Centre in the UK.

Yet much has been lost, not least jobs. On the eve of takeover Rowntree had 16,000 UK employees. In 2018 Nestlé reported a total UK labour force – including coffee, food and other products – of barely 8,000. From over 5,000 in the 1980s the workforce in York has fallen by two-thirds.[21]

Other Rowntree operations have disappeared. These include factories in Glasgow[22] and Norwich, which closed in 1993–94 when production was moved to France. Worse, in 2006 production of some of the most popular brands was moved abroad – not necessarily to low-wage economies. Black Magic went to the Czech Republic, but Smarties migrated to Hamburg and Dairy Box to Spain.[23] Four years later the Castleford factory closed and After Eight moved to Hamburg.[24] In 2017 Blue Riband biscuits went to Poland.[25]

It would be difficult to argue that becoming a minor branch of the world's largest food company has really enhanced the standing of the once-great firm of Rowntree.[26]

Cadbury Ascendancy

The fate of Terry's and Rowntree was much in the minds of observers at the 2010 takeover of Britain's only remaining major in the confectionery industry, Cadbury. Britain's biggest confectionery company had its origins in Birmingham in the 1820s, when John Cadbury began retailing tea, coffee and chocolate. His motive was partly to encourage alternatives to alcohol. Like the Frys and the Rowntrees the Cadburys were a Quaker family and imbued their work with their ethical principles.

Within a few years they had built a small factory, but it was not for another couple of decades that chocolate took precedence. Later in the century the company moved to Bournville, outside Birmingham, and developed a model estate for the benefit of its employees.[27]

The 1900s brought successful new products such as the Dairy Milk bar, and by the First World War Cadbury had overtaken Fry to become the biggest producer of chocolate products in the country. In 1919 Cadbury merged with Fry, and a few years later built the Somerdale factory for its subsidiary.

The interwar period saw the launch of more successful brands, including Flake, Crème Eggs, Fruit and Nut, and Dairy Milk Whole Nut. There were also moves into overseas markets, particularly in the Commonwealth, a trend continued after the Second World War. There were increasingly large mergers and acquisitions, the biggest being a tie-up with Schweppes in the late 1960s. The 1970s and 1980s saw considerable diversification, mainly through acquisition, and at one point the group was one of the world's largest soft drinks manufacturers and a significant producer of processed foods.

The diversification tide then ebbed. A forerunner was the sale of Burton's Foods, based in Moreton, in the Wirral. After more than 30 years as a Cadbury's subsidiary, Burton's was hived off to a management buyout in 1986. As so often, this was the prelude to repeated changes of ownership. A private equity intervention predictably left the firm saddled with debt, and it ended up in the hands of Canadian Imperial Bank of Commerce and Apollo Global Management. After a final year, in which its directors' pay had doubled, the factory closed in 2011.[28]

Meanwhile, Cadbury had continued to divest away from foods and back towards the company's historic strengths in chocolate. The process ended in 2008 with the untying of its involvement in soft drinks. The demerger which launched Dr Pepper Snapple proved astonishingly expensive, with a bill of £130m from investment bankers, lawyers and the tax authorities.[29]

Cadbury was now closer to its roots.[30] It was the world's second largest confectionery group, with an excellent name and pedigree. It had 40,000 employees around the globe, including 6,000 in the UK, sales of £5.4bn and profits of £400m. And it was strong in fast-growing markets such as India, Brazil, Mexico and Turkey.

All of which made it an appetising proposition. For dowdy Kraft Foods, still looking to reduce its dependence on slow-moving domestic groceries, Cadbury was particularly attractive. When Kraft launched a debt-financed £10bn offer for the company in September 2009 the move at first prompted only a subdued response. For Geoffrey Owen, senior fellow at the LSE Institute of Management, this demonstrated a change in attitudes since the controversial Nestlé takeover of Rowntree: "We take these acquisitions in our stride now."

It was soon apparent that we don't. A groundswell of hostility quickly built up, not just from unions and employees quick to cite the Terry's takeover and fearful of job losses[31] but from a general public weary of seeing an endless procession of household names go abroad. The ghost of Terry's and the shade of Rowntree were invoked.[32]

The Cadbury board at first mimed stalwart resistance. For chairman Roger Carr there was an "unappealing prospect of being subsumed by Kraft's low growth, conglomerate business model" and the offer was "derisory".[33] Chief executive Todd Stitzer warned that a tie-up with an "unappealing" conglomerate such as Kraft would stifle growth at the British confectioner. The approach "fundamentally undervalued" the business.[34] There were invocations of the "ethical values" of the Cadbury brand.[35] And there were rumours of a rescue mission by Hershey, the world's third largest confectionery group,[36] Ferrero, the secretive Italian family-owned chocolate giant,[37] or even Nestlé.

None of these saviours materialised. Nor did the Labour government raise meaningful objections. A warning from business secretary Peter Mandelson that Kraft would face government opposition if it tried to make a "fast buck" by slashing Cadbury's operations sounded hollow when he claimed that he could not block a bid.[38] And the opposition party was even more complacent. Once again Kenneth Clarke bobbed up, this time as shadow business secretary. He ducked out of the debate with a shrug: "Ultimately this is a matter for Cadbury's shareholders."[39]

Cadbury Cave-In

Urged on by a pack of those shareholders – hedge funds who had gone long of Cadbury shares on the whisper of a deal – Kraft steered a canny course through the City and made a modest increase in its offer. The move was well judged. Abruptly swallowing its apparent misgivings,[40] the Cadbury board rolled over.[41] Describing the decision to accept the deal as a "bittersweet moment",[42] chairman Roger Carr declared the revised offer to be "good value" and said he was "pleased with the commitment that Kraft Foods has made to our heritage, values and people throughout the world".

Press comment was unenthusiastic. *The Mirror* quoted an angry descendant of the founding father of Cadbury.[43] Jeremy Warner reminded *Daily Telegraph* readers that takeover deals almost always fail to deliver on their promises to "create value" and Chris Hope argued that the French would never have allowed such an important company to be taken over by foreigners.[44] The point was broadened by Larry Elliott of *The Guardian* to include the Germans, the Japanese and the Americans,[45] while for Nils Pratley that "derisory" offer simply meant "give us another 10 per cent and our defences will crumble".[46]

The *Wall Street Journal* pointed out that Continental European countries frequently block foreign takeovers and whole sectors of industry in the US and emerging markets such as China and India are protected. But since Margaret Thatcher had begun in the 1980s to remove barriers to foreign ownership of UK companies and state-owned assets "almost everything in Britain has been fair game".[47] Even *The Economist* could only find feeble generalisations to support the Cadbury sale.[48]

That commitment and those values that Roger Carr had found so reassuring were soon looking less impressive. Within a week Kraft reneged on its undertaking to keep open the Somerdale plant that had – prior to the bid – been scheduled for closure, and 400 shop-floor job losses were confirmed. And within two years another 200 jobs had gone at Bournville and elsewhere. The House of Commons Business Select Committee was not impressed when Kraft's executive vice-president said soon after the takeover that he was "sorry to the people who we disappointed".[49]

Others did rather better out of the takeover. Fees of at least $400m went to investment bankers, lawyers and accountants.[50] Goldman Sachs was incentivised with higher fees if the company was successfully sold. The incentive came not from Kraft but, shamefully, from Cadbury, for whom Goldman was acting as adviser. Irene Rosenfeld, head of Kraft, saw her pay rise 40 per cent to $26.3m. And Cadbury's management did not go hungry. On his departure chief executive Todd Stitzer took £40m in salary and allowances, cashed-in shares and pension contributions.[51] An executive called Bob Stack pocketed £3.8m and a £700,000 a year pension merely for having been personnel manager.[52]

What Roger Carr, veteran of foreign sell-offs – Chubb to a Swedish company, Thames Water to a German group – and of the debt fiasco at Mitchell & Butlers, took home is not known. By the end of the year he had collected a knighthood for services to business and was bleating about how open British companies were to foreign takeovers. He laid much of the blame for the Cadbury debacle at the door not of himself and his directors but of the hedge funds, which had apparently made the bid a "self-fulfilling prophecy".[53]

Cadbury Law?

Liberal Democrat Treasury spokesman Vince Cable called for the reintroduction of a public interest test for future takeovers. He pointed out that the Labour government had blundered in 2002 when it formalised a new regime under which mergers and acquisitions were assessed purely on competition grounds. With the prospect of a general election imminent the government proposed a "Cadbury Law". This would require a two-thirds majority of shareholders for a takeover to succeed and might exclude from the vote any opportunistic newcomers to the shareholders register.[54]

Before the year end it was revealed that Kraft was hiving Cadbury and other confectionery interests off into a new holding company called Mondelez, to be based in Switzerland.[55] According to the *Daily Mail* the move would deprive Britain of more than £60m in tax every year.[56] The prediction has proved all too true. Mondelez has since paid not a penny in UK corporation tax. Public indignation was not assuaged when the *Financial Times* revealed that Cadbury, so boastful of its ethical values, had itself indulged for many years in what a former director called some "pretty aggressive" tax reduction schemes.[57]

A year after the event, Kraft's chief executive Irene Rosenfeld was still dodging attendance at a House of Commons committee studying the deal. The US legislature, of course, has little problem in arraigning foreign businesspeople – for example Tony Hayward of BP and Akio Toyoda of Toyota – for cross-examination when it is vexed about the activities of foreign companies in its domain.[58]

A revealing comment did come from the last family member of the Cadbury board. Delivering a Cass Business School lecture in 2013, Dominic Cadbury praised the new owner of the business so diligently nurtured by his Quaker forebears, but rather dampened his enthusiasm by dwelling on the downside. He reminded his audience that there was now a problem with public trust in business and that the country had lost another UK headquarters (Kraft having briskly closed Cadbury's head office). The deal went through so easily partly because "the UK is the most open market when it comes to takeovers… the City likes takeovers because the fees are so high…and the takeover rules favour the short term investor".[59]

Of course, it explains it all.

Life on Mars

One company which had not been considered as a possible white knight for Cadbury was Mars. Even in the laissez faire climate that has tainted the British takeover scene since the 1980s, its market share was large enough to trigger potential monopoly objections. As a private company Mars has a reputation for secrecy but is also regarded as a well-run concern that has made efforts to address ethical criticisms in recent years.

The UK has been an important market for Mars since the 1930s, when it opened two factories in Slough. Popular brands such as Mars Bars, Twix and Snickers were developed there and production remained at a high level for many years. In 2005, however, Mars restructured its European operations, with the main brunt falling in Britain. The production of Starburst was transferred to the Czech Republic and Twix went to Veghel in the Netherlands. One of the Slough factories closed and there were 700 job cuts there and elsewhere in Britain.[60]

Thorntons Goes Italian

Outside the small group of big suppliers to the UK market – Mars, Kraft/ Cadbury and Nestlé – Thorntons has until recently been the only remaining domestic manufacturer of significance. The company had its origins in a confectionery shop opened by Joseph William Thornton in Sheffield in 1911. After the First World War it began manufacturing on a small scale, and for most of its existence it has had a high level of integration from factory to retailing.

Additional manufacturing capacity was developed at Belper, in Derbyshire, in the 1950s, and the company fostered the good industrial relations which have characterised all the great British chocolate and confectionery makers. In the 1980s another factory was opened in Derbyshire, and within a few years there was a public share issue. By the turn of the decade Thorntons had several hundred shops and was developing sales to supermarkets and other outlets.

Conditions have subsequently been more challenging. The recession that began in 2008 hit luxury products like presentation boxes of chocolates. In early 2011 the company issued a profits warning and announced store closures,[61] and by the year end it was looking to shut a third of its outlets.[62] Since then business appears to have stabilised. Nevertheless, the company has retreated on domestic manufacture, with a swing to imports from Belgium. This process may be taken further following the 2015 takeover of Thorntons by Ferrero. Secretive and recently exposed as a major tax-evader, the privately owned Italian giant is now the world's third largest manufacturer of chocolate confectionery.

Small Players

For the rest of the traditional chocolate confectionery industry the picture has been as downbeat as it has for the bigger names. Elizabeth Shaw had its origins in a Bristol confectionery maker in the 1880s, and was established as a chocolate brand when the firm built a factory in the locality in 1901. After passing through various hands, the firm eventually ended up in the grasp of a financial group and in 2006 the Bristol factory was closed.

Bendicks was founded by Oscar Benson and Bertie Dickson as a purveyor of specialty chocolates in the 1930s. After a change of ownership, the company moved from Kensington to a purpose-built factory in Winchester. In 1988 it was taken over by Germany's August Storck and in 2009 production was to the parent's works in Germany. Two years later the Winchester factory closed, with the loss of 140 jobs.[63]

Set against the absorption, subjugation or annihilation of Britain's big confectioners has been a succession of newcomers, though all have been small. They include Green & Black's, set up in 1991 and invoking environmental awareness and Fairtrade in its identity. Production comes from factories not in the UK but in Canada, Italy and Poland. In 2005 the operation was sold to Cadbury for £20m. Founder and erstwhile "hippy" Craig Sams claimed to be uneasy at the subsequent Kraft/Mondelez fiasco.[64]

Hotel Chocolat at least makes the effort to manufacture in the UK, operating at a Cambridgeshire factory after initially importing from the Continent. Founded in the 1990s, the company claims to be the only chocolate maker in the world with its own cocoa plantation.[65]

Divine Chocolate is a serious attempt to involve cocoa producers in the production and distribution of chocolate. A leading purveyor of Fairtrade chocolate, it is owned jointly by Ghanaian cocoa farmers, an "alternative trading organization" and a Dutch microfinance institution, but manufactures in Germany.

A number of other "artisan" chocolate makers typically import raw material from the giant industrial operations of Callebaut in Belgium and Valrhona in France, and hand make their products on a small scale in the UK.[66]

The decimation of Britain's once-celebrated confectionery industry clearly cannot be laid at the door of privatisations, since there haven't been any. Nor, on the whole, can macroeconomic mismanagement be blamed, since in common with most food and drink confectionery demand is largely immune to the vicissitudes of the economy.

The real villain, notably in the cases of Terry's, Rowntree Mackintosh and Cadbury, has been predatory capitalism, accompanied by extraordinary government complacency. Cadbury also had the misfortune of a board of directors who were clearly swayed by personal avarice and an indifference to the longer-term fate of their charge.

CHAPTER 18

Brassed Off

> *I liked the way the British built things to last. I liked the way they used solid brass fittings in their ships and railway trains. Great slabs of pure metal, with plenty to spare for sheer bulldog strength. This was a thing I noticed everywhere; lamp brackets, toilet appliances, motor-cars, ash-trays – it was part of a sense of solidarity that permeated the whole of British life.*
>
> Negley Farson, *The Way of the Transgressor*[1]

Europe's Largest

"The non-ferrous metals industry is the largest in Europe, and as a consumer of aluminium, copper and lead Britain is second only to the United States among Western countries." This was the proud claim of the annual guide to the UK published by the Central Office of Information.[2]

But it was the 1970s. Britain had a full complement of metal processing plants serving a wide hinterland of customers at home and overseas. There were four aluminium smelters, several copper refineries, one of Europe's largest lead refiners, and significant smelters for zinc and tin.

The output of these plants typically went to rolling mills, tube mills, wire mills, foundries and other metal-forming operations in the UK. The semi-manufacturing industries were large enough to sustain their own research centre, the British Non-Ferrous Metals Research Association (BNF), with 600 members at home and abroad.

In addition to the base metal processors there were also precious metals refiners of international standing and important producers of the more specialised elements used in nuclear, aircraft, electronics and other advanced applications.

Today's non-ferrous industry is so different as to be almost unrecognisable. Semi-manufacturing and end-use industries have dwindled or disappeared. The BNF has long closed. And in smelting and refining the non-ferrous industry is a ghost of what it was. Copper refining, zinc smelting and tin refining have vanished. Aluminium smelting is confined to a single operation that is little more than a pilot plant. Gold and silver refining have almost disappeared and there have been major retreats across the range of specialty metals. In the base metals only lead refining still survives.

Aluminium Ambitions

One of the sorriest stories is that of aluminium. Prior to the 1970s the UK had only one primary aluminium smelter, the Lochaber plant near Fort William in Scotland. Developed with financial assistance from the government, Lochaber was opened by British Aluminium in 1929.[3]

The operation was a useful domestic source of aluminium ingot, particularly during the Second World War. But with an output capacity of less than 50,000 tonnes a year Lochaber has been little more than a curiosity in an industry of giants. Nevertheless, the plant has seen some upgrading in recent years. In 2016 the operation was sold by its owner, Rio Tinto, to Sanjeev Gupta's Liberty group.[4] The price for what had always been a fairly marginal operation was a remarkable £330m.

The rapid post-war growth in demand for aluminium, "the metal of tomorrow", meant that by the 1960s the UK was importing most of its requirements. Eager to address weaknesses in the country's industrial structure, the Labour government that took office in 1964 saw the development of a significant aluminium industry as a worthwhile aim.

The view was that two major obstacles could be addressed. The cost of electricity, an important factor in aluminium smelting, would be lowered with the development of nuclear power and natural gas. And the capital cost of new projects could be cut by calling on regional investment and construction grants available under the Industrial Development Act 1966. The interest in aluminium was not some British peculiarity. A drive for greater self-sufficiency, supported by import duties, was encouraging the expansion of the industry in Germany and elsewhere in Continental Europe.

After intensive negotiations three projects were announced in 1968. Two involved active official encouragement. Under the Industrial Expansion Act 1968 they received interest-bearing loans of £29 million and £33 million, respectively, to help finance long-term power supply contracts.

The first scheme was a smelter to be opened by British Aluminium at Invergordon in north-east Scotland, taking electricity from the new nuclear plant at Hunterston. The second was a joint venture smelter at Holyhead in Anglesey. This was to draw its power from the nuclear power plant sited on the coast at Wylfa, not far away. Initially the investors in Anglesey Aluminium were to be RTZ (now Rio Tinto) and British Insulated Callender's Cables (BICC). The third new plant, to be constructed by Alcan at Lynemouth in Northumberland, would build its own power station based on locally mined coal.

There were strong protests from a fellow member of the European Free Trade Area (EFTA). Norway, which had built a large aluminium industry on cheap hydroelectric power, was accustomed to shipping a quarter of its output duty-free to Britain. Its objections were met by generous concessions on the part of the UK government. The start-up capacities of Invergordon and Anglesey would be trimmed and Norway's share of the UK market would be assured.

Invergordon

After commissioning in 1971, Invergordon lasted for just a decade.[5] Efficient and well-located, its main challenge was that familiar noxious cocktail posed by nuclear energy – completion delays, cost overruns and high generating expenses. There were wrangles with the power suppliers and the government had to step in to cover the deficits incurred by the generators.

The change of government in 1979 brought recessionary economic conditions, soaring interest rates and a reluctance to provide any official debt write-offs or power cost subsidy. British Aluminium suspended operations in December 1981. Half-hearted attempts to find a new owner failed and government intervention was predictably inadequate.[6] In 1982 the plant closed, with the loss of 900 jobs.

Anglesey

Anglesey Aluminium proved more durable. By the time the plant was commissioned in 1971, ownership was split between RTZ, Kaiser Aluminium of the US and BICC. Kaiser supplied the smelting technology and BICC, as Britain's leading cable maker, an outlet for the product.

The partners were required to take aluminium in proportion to their shareholdings. Before long, however, BICC had reduced its interest from 27 per cent to 19 per cent, and then finally to zero when it left the consortium in 1975.[7] Thereafter RTZ and Kaiser remained sole partners with stakes of 51 per cent and 49 per cent, respectively.

Despite power supply headaches due to delays in completing Wylfa, operations were mostly profitable and product quality was high. The plant was expanded from 100,000 tonnes of output a year at start-up to nearly 150,000 tonnes a year.[8] This made Anglesey Aluminium the biggest single commercial consumer of electricity in Britain.

As with all aluminium smelters, the cost of power was a critical issue for its long-term viability. Although the company had a favourable power supply contract in a domestic context, many of its international competitors were benefitting from better terms. And when it was revealed that Wylfa would close in 2010 Anglesey Aluminium faced a major challenge in finding new sources of electricity at acceptable prices.

Under a scheme called Project 2010 the smelter's management made heroic efforts to raise revenues by £10m and cut costs by £10m. But the attempt to replace the Wylfa deal with an acceptable contract with the privatised electricity generators proved fruitless. A government that could usually be relied on to cite European Union rules as an excuse for not intervening nevertheless offered a £48m support package.

The shareholders rejected this as inadequate in the context of the long-term power supply issue. It was not entirely coincidental that for the first time in many years Rio Tinto was short of cash, having recently squandered

$38.1bn on the purchase of Aluminium Company of Canada (Alcan), the world's second biggest aluminium company.[9]

Rio Tinto's advisers and consultants would have been more deserving of their vast fees if they had simply pointed out that overpaying for a company at the top of the cycle in a business that has been volatile since the dawn of history might not be the most sensible use of shareholder funds.[10]

Within five years of the Alcan takeover Rio Tinto had to write down its aluminium assets by up to £20bn. CEO Tom Albanese was rewarded for some of Rio's more disastrous initiatives with almost £22m in cash and share options while head of the company.[11]

Against this background of self-inflicted injury by Rio it was perhaps not surprising that Anglesey Aluminium was cut back in 2009[12] and closed for good in 2013.[13]

Lynemouth

The third smelter in the new trio, Lynemouth, was the last to come on line when it was commissioned in 1973. As the second largest player in the global aluminium business, Alcan was an obvious spearhead for major expansion of the UK industry – particularly as it already had sizeable downstream operations. But the company reportedly felt sidelined in the early consultations, which had focused on Invergordon and Anglesey. So Alcan directly approached the National Coal Board and secured a favourable long-term supply contract for its project.[14] The coal would be mined nearby.

Alcan's operational management was competent, Lynemouth proved successful and the smelter was consistently profitable. Expansion from an initial 100,000 tonnes a year to almost 180,000 tonnes made it the largest of the four plants in the UK. However, the purchase of Alcan by Rio Tinto in 2007 imposed new commercial straitjackets on Lynemouth. Rio's profit target was much higher and the dire financial situation into which it had been dragged by the acquisition of Alcan only aggravated the position.

Meanwhile, energy and environmental protection costs were mounting. The EU's Large Combustions Plant Directive (LCPD) was a challenge.[15] And the UK carbon price floor was perhaps pushing the operating expenses of energy-intensive British industries above those of their Continental rivals.

Though it was one of the most efficient smelters in the industry, this posed a threat to the future even of Lynemouth, despite its having reduced its emissions by a remarkable 65 per cent since 1990 – far ahead of the UK goal of a 34 per cent reduction by 2020.

The issue of energy costs was cited in Rio's announcement in 2011 that it would close Lynemouth. Yet the plant was still profitable. The problem was actually the very high financial hurdle it had been set by Rio Tinto. Corporate affairs director John McCabe put it, candidly if inelegantly: "Rio Tinto is streamlining its global aluminium business in order to focus on its top assets globally; unfortunately Lynemouth isn't considered to be one of them as it does not return 40 per cent rate of return for the business." In the words of the local MP, "[m]ost people would be happy with £40m, but they want 40 per cent profits on the investments they make". Efforts to sell the power station continued, but this undermined the viability of the smelter and it closed in May 2012.[16]

With its supply of aluminium once again largely dependent on imports, the UK has thus travelled full dismal circle. Ironically, more than half its supplies come from the rest of the European Union, whose smelters are subject to climate change and environmental considerations not very different to those facing UK industry.

Downstream Devastation

As with other base metals, a sizeable proportion of aluminium supply is obtained from recycled scrap. The secondary smelters involved naturally faced a difficult time when demand for their products collapsed in the 1980s. One of the biggest casualties was the International Alloys operation at Aylesbury, established by Alcoa, the world's biggest aluminium producer, in the 1940s. Most of the output from Aylesbury went to make engine blocks and cylinder heads for the motor industry, and when car production crashed the operation was plunged into financial crisis. With prices undermined by the recession there was little prospect of imminent recovery. The plant closed, with the loss of 244 jobs, at the end of 1981.[17]

The problems of the aluminium smelters were echoed downstream, and the 1980s saw sweeping cutbacks at rolling mills, extrusion plants and foundries. Following a merger of Alcan Aluminium (UK) and British

Aluminium in 1982, British Alcan Aluminium became much the largest producer of semis in the UK. It then spent months cutting capacity and shedding a quarter of its workforce. In early 1983 the company announced the loss of 1,200 jobs across three of its sites.

The main casualty was the big facility at Falkirk, where two-thirds of the workforce was laid off when rolling operations ended. Other activities affected were extrusion at Rogerstone, in South Wales, and foil production at Kitts Green, near Birmingham.[18] Little more than a decade later the whole of the great Falkirk works was closed and the site cleared by a firm from one of the few industrial sectors to have flourished in the 1980s, demolition contractor David Morton & Co.[19]

Alcan's long retreat from the UK was nearly complete with the closure in 2002 of the company's research and development centre at Banbury.[20] The company had been in the town for more than 70 years, and, in the words of the laboratory director, "[t]he high level of talent, expertise and experience of our team at Banbury is widely recognised by Alcan". So was this widely respected R&D unit moving to some low-cost base, perhaps in Eastern Europe? Far from it: the department was going to Canada and Switzerland.

Copper Refining

The mining, smelting, refining and working of copper were important features of Britain's Industrial Revolution. Firms such as Thomas Bolton, based in Staffordshire, led the world in the production of copper wire, tube and sheet.

Copper mining has long ceased, as has the smelting of primary ores. But refining continued right up until modern times, and the manufacture of wrought products continues today, though on a vastly reduced scale by comparison with the past.

Prior to the 1980s there was just one significant exit, that of the Brimsdown copper refinery in north London, which was closed by Delta Metal some years after it bought Enfield Rolling Mills in the 1960s. But even in the late 1970s there still were half a dozen refiners of copper in Britain – even though only three were of any standing. The other refiners included small by-product and recycling operations.

By 2003 the whole of this industry had vanished. First to go was a recycling unit operated by McKechnie Brothers at Widnes in Lancashire.

This was a small operation based on fire refining, a process for purifying copper since ancient times. McKechnies used scrap and residues for feed, and output was a few thousand tonnes a year. The plant closed in 1978.

More significant was the closure of Elkington Copper Refiners' plant at Walsall in the West Midlands. With an annual output of around 25,000 tonnes, this had been in existence for many years and had built up expertise in the recycling of scrap, on which it was entirely based. In 1984 ownership passed from metals trader Brandeis Goldschmidt to Imperial Metal Industries (IMI), the former base metals arm of ICI. IMI already ran a copper refinery in the same town as Elkington, and few were surprised when Elkington closed soon after.

The Capper Pass smelter at Melton on Humberside processed complex tin-bearing ores and ran circuits for the recovery of by-products such as copper, of which it recovered around 2,000 tonnes a year. For environmental reasons the works was closed in 1991.

British Copper Refiners

The same year saw the demise of a much more significant name, British Copper Refiners (BCR). BCR was an integral part of the BICC complex at Prescot on Merseyside. Britain's leading manufacturer of cables and conductors, and indeed a world leader, BICC sold more than half its output overseas in the mid–late 1970s.[21] The company operated from ten different sites and had a substantial research and engineering facility in west London. Its main cable-making operations were on Merseyside, where at one time it employed 10,000 people.

BICC was, however, a curious mix of ancient and modern. The manufacture of electric cables was a mature business, with production techniques little changed in generations. This was reflected in some of the equipment at Prescot. A well-known example was the Krupp looping mill, used to make trolley wire since the nineteenth century. On the other hand, BICC was one of the first cable makers to invest in the new technology for producing copper wire-rod – continuous casting – in the mid-1970s, and was a leader in optic fibre cables in the 1980s.

Between 1984 and 1992 BICC was led by Sir William Barlow, who throughout a distinguished career was a consistent and far-sighted champion of British manufacturing.[22] When he arrived at BICC, however, the company was already facing severe challenges. There had been several years of grim industrial recession, and investment in wire and cable products had slumped. The Merseyside workforce was down to less than 2,000, and by the time Barlow left office it had shrunk still further.

The company had long been involved in copper refining, based since the 1960s on an electrolytic refinery. In addition to domestically sourced scrap, the refinery imported "blister" copper. Much of the latter was obtained through British Kynoch Metals (BKM), an imaginative joint initiative by BICC, Delta Metal and IMI to facilitate long-term offtake contracts with overseas copper producers.[23]

These contracts could be offset against equipment and services supplied by UK manufacturers such as GEC (electrical plant), BTR (conveyors), Hunslet (locomotives) and others. Major copper mines were developed at Toquepala and Cuajone in Peru with the help of long-term deals with customers in the UK and Germany.

By the late 1980s, raw material for the Prescot refinery had become more difficult to find on acceptable terms. Much worse, there had been a calamitous decline in UK consumption of copper-using products. In 1991 BICC announced the closure of its plant, with the loss of 230 jobs.[24]

By the end of the decade BICC's century-old presence in cables was being dismembered. Its promising fibre optics business was handed to US-based Corning, while its traditional wire and cable interests went to a succession of owners. First in line was General Cable. Next came the cable-making arm of Pirelli, and finally an irrelevant oddity called Prysmian, whose commercial heart lay in metal trading rather than manufacturing. None of these owners invested in the long-term viability of Prescot. Indeed, each inflicted severe cutbacks. The successive rundown culminated in the closure of the wire-rod mill by Prysmian in 2006.[25]

James Bridge

The largest of the UK copper refineries was the James Bridge plant at Walsall in the West Midlands.[26] It was operated by IMI, whose origins lay in one of the founding businesses of ICI.[27]

ICI's metals interests were grouped into the Imperial Metal Industries division, and indeed in the early 1960s it was the biggest single contributor to ICI profits. IMI was listed on the Stock Exchange in 1966 and became fully independent in 1977. Headquartered in Witton, Birmingham, the company combined activities in the non-ferrous field with pioneering the commercial production of titanium, zirconium and beryllium. Among its main activities were the production of copper and brass semi-manufactures, including copper tube, copper and brass sheet, and a range of fittings for plumbing and other products.

The James Bridge plant[28] became a significant operation in the 1960s, when its output capacity was raised to 50,000 tonnes a year. IMI became the sole owner in 1968[29] and expanded the refinery to 60,000 tonnes a year.

The main role of the plant was to produce raw material for associates such as Yorkshire Copper Tube, formerly Yorkshire Imperial Metals (YIM).[30] YIM was originally located in Leeds, but in response to government incentives it moved to Kirkby on Merseyside. Raw material for the James Bridge works comprised scrap and primary blister copper, partly sourced on similar arrangements to those for BCR.

The 1980s saw some investment in more efficient refining and casting techniques.[31] Though market conditions were grim, the company was greatly helped by the disappearance of other domestic producers of copper-based semis. Nevertheless, its ultimate end-market was shrivelling, and by the end of the 1990s its economics were looking unsustainable. After a "fruitless" year-long search for a buyer[32] the company announced in September 1999 that the refinery would be closed by the year end.[33]

The story has a familiar ending. After rationalising its copper tube activities and investing in the Kirkby mill in the 1990s, IMI then sold off most of its copper interests. In 1992 Yorkshire Copper Tube went to the German group KME (Kabelmetal Europa) and became KME Yorkshire.[34] KME claims to be the world's largest maker of copper and copper alloy semi-manufactures, but little of its impressive output is made in the UK.

After the closure of James Bridge the only other copper refinery still operating in the UK was a small by-product circuit at Britannia Zinc, at Avonmouth. This closed, along with the parent operation, in March 2003.

Avonmouth Zinc

Lead and zinc smelting had long been established at Avonmouth. Large-scale zinc production in Europe was established in the Bristol area in the eighteenth century. More modern operations were set up during the First World War to process zinc concentrates that had previously gone to Germany for smelting.[35] The new plant was run by the National Smelting Company and then by the newly formed Imperial Smelting Corporation (ISC).[36]

ISC was controlled by Zinc Corporation of Australia and became part of Rio Tinto Zinc Corporation (RTZ). The plant came close to closure in the gruelling economic conditions of the early 1980s, but survived after hefty cutbacks in 1983.[37] It was eventually taken over by Australia's Pasminco and, in 1993, by Mount Isa Mines (MIM).[38] The operating company became Britannia Zinc.

By this stage the smelter was operating the largest and most efficient zinc blast furnace in the world,[39] using the imperial smelting process developed in the 1950s. Its feed was complex polymetallic materials.

The rationale for MIM's $100m purchase of Avonmouth was to allow the company's mines in Australia to be fully integrated with downstream processing. Barely a decade had passed, however, when new management at the parent company announced its intention to dispose of Avonmouth, along with its other European smelter at Duisburg, on the grounds that they were suddenly not regarded as core businesses.[40] Avonmouth was said to be losing £2m a month.[41]

Quite how an integrated and efficient operation could lose money separately from its feed source was not clear. The likelihood is that in a tight market for zinc concentrates the parent could get attractive terms from other smelters. Duisburg was duly sold in December 2002.[42] But the sale of Avonmouth to US trader Marco fell through, and in February 2003 the operation closed with the loss of 400 jobs.[43]

The undoing of Britain's industrial heritage has spawned an entire sector – a kind of debased industry – of companies engaged in the prompt and terminal removal of its physical presence. It took David Morton[44] just nine months to have the 212-acre Avonmouth site cleared and ready for the St Modwen property company to turn into an "employment park".[45]

Capper Pass

In modern times Britain's sole tin smelter was Capper Pass at Melton on Humberside. Having moved from Bristol to Yorkshire in the 1930s, the company was eventually bought by RTZ in 1967.

From the outset the Melton plant was a specialised venture, treating low-grade and complex materials. Its activities prompted concerns over its environmental impact, however, and in 1971 a 600ft chimney was built to aid emissions dispersal.

By 1980 the plant was the largest smelter of tin from secondary sources and contributed 10 per cent of world tin processing capacity. Five years later, however, business conditions deteriorated abruptly with the collapse of the International Tin Buffer Stock, prompting a dramatic fall in the tin price and cutbacks in the mining industry. The availability of tin-bearing feedstocks became much tighter and processing margins narrowed. By the end of the decade RTZ announced that the plant was no longer viable, and in 1991 the smelter was closed.

A contributory factor in the closure may have been the controversy over the plant's impact on the health of the local population. In subsequent years the debate intensified, and after two decades of denying responsibility RTZ grudgingly offered recompense to a limited number of claimants who cited Capper Pass in the incidence of cancers and pulmonary disorders. After the smelter closed the Melton site was designated for warehousing and other commercial uses.

Britannia Lead

The sole remaining base metals smelting and refining unit in the UK is the Britannia Refined Metals (BRM) plant at Northfleet in Kent.[46] BRM was developed by MIM to process lead concentrates from its Australian mines in the 1930s. Between 1931 and 1968 the annual output capacity of Northfleet was 70,000 tonnes of lead, together with significant amounts of silver by-product. Subsequently there were substantial programmes of modernisation and expansion, eventually making the plant the largest of its kind in Europe and capable of producing over 180,000 tonnes of refined lead and 400 tonnes of silver a year.

In marked contrast to other operations in the British non-ferrous metals industry, BRM has changed hands only once in its history. This was when MIM was taken over by Xstrata for £1.95bn in 2003. Since then the plant has in general been successfully run at or close to full capacity and, unlike the rest of the UK non-ferrous industry, it survived the recession of 2008/9 and appears to have a future.

Precious Metals

In the precious metals sector the UK had a long history of refining gold, silver and platinum group metals. These operations were based partly on the processing of output from overseas mines and partly on the recycling of scrap and other materials. As more of the countries where gold and silver are mined installed their own refining capacity, the amount of raw material available for processing in Europe became scarcer. And there was strong competition from Swiss refiners able to provide the kind of services not possible – or legitimate – for UK companies to offer.

Nevertheless companies such as Johnson Matthey, with a gold refinery at Royston in Hertfordshire, Engelhard, with a gold refinery at Chessington on the southern edge of London, and Sheffield Smelting, with a silver refinery in Sheffield, were able to sustain their refining operations into the 1980s.

Thereafter conditions became more difficult. One of the first operations to go was the solvex refinery for platinum group metals at Royston. This closed in 1986 when the operation moved to South Africa.[47]

Meanwhile, ugly developments were sealing the fate of Sheffield Smelting, a large scrap refining operation dating back more than two centuries and centrepiece of Sheffield's long-established silver industry.[48] In the early 1980s, Engelhard, the owner of Sheffield Smelting, embarked on an aggressive programme of destocking and reported the resulting inventory profits as operating income. Coupled with a failure to make prompt disclosure of major plant shutdowns at the company's US and UK refining facilities, this did wonders for company profits, the share price and the chief executive's bonus.

When that chief executive abruptly left Engelhard one step ahead of the investigators, he took at least $7m in severance pay and share options, while a thousand refinery employees on both sides of the Atlantic lost their jobs.[49] Today the shade of Sheffield Smelting lingers on as Thessco, reclaiming scrap and making silver alloys on a modest scale.

In more recent years both Johnson Matthey and Engelhard have closed their mainstream gold refining operations. The former concentrates on specialty alloys, platinum group metals and autocatalysts, while the latter sold its UK interests to a French company with roots in the precious metals business, Comptoir Lyon Alemand (CLAL).

The potential for spontaneous revival of Britain's once-flourishing base metals industries looks remote in the extreme. The whole complex of activities on which they depended has disappeared. The process, which really got under way in the 1980s, was confirmed in the 1990s and 2000s.

Non-ferrous metals is one of the few sectors where the influences so baneful to other industries, such as privatisation or City meddling, cannot be fully arraigned as leading culprits in their destruction.

Directly relevant, however, is the economic mismanagement, particularly in the 1980s and 1990s, which hollowed out the industrial base and wrecked the domestic demand for the metals producers. The downstream industries and end-users which could once support smelting and refining industries of the kind which survive in Germany, France, Italy and elsewhere on the Continent have been decimated. And except in rare niches any possibility of technical leadership has vanished. Dependence on imports has ratcheted up to extremely high levels, and this will prove very difficult to roll back.

CHAPTER 19

Stalling Speed

> *British aviation of the 1930s was overwhelmingly military, was strong, was strengthened by the demands of empire, and was central to the peculiarly modern war-fighting strategy of the British state.*
>
> David Edgerton, *England and the Aeroplane*[1]

Empire of the Skies

The world's first operational jet fighter, the first jet bomber, the first jet airliner, the first turbo-prop airliner, records for speed, altitude, and performance of every kind. And often involving test pilots, inventors and industrialists with charisma, flair and valiant war records. For anyone growing up in the decade after 1945 the achievements of the British aircraft industry were often thrilling and sometimes astounding. And they were part of the popular culture – through comics, newspapers, books and radio – in a way impossible to imagine today.

The atmosphere is vividly evoked in James Hamilton-Paterson's *Empire of the Clouds*.[2] After an exhilarating flight through the racier realms of British aircraft, however, Hamilton-Paterson touches down on a gloomy note. His claim is that the UK is no longer capable of producing a new aircraft without help from abroad, contrasting the British picture with that in countries as diverse as Brazil, China, India, Israel, Japan and Sweden. Normally classed as second-division players, all have developed lively aircraft industries. The UK, meanwhile, has doomed itself to a kind of vassal status in the aircraft business, a mere subcontractor to others.

Is Hamilton-Paterson's sombre conclusion justified?

As David Edgerton conclusively shows in his brilliant accounts of Britain's warfare state, English aviation and its aircraft industry were strong for most of the twentieth century – before the Great War, through the interwar years and during and after the Second World War. This strength derived from "the vital place of technology, industry and economic thinking within the grand designs of English strategy…and from English enthusiasm for the aeroplane".[3]

Far from being sleepy, backward or blinkered, relative to the size of its armed forces Britain had the strongest air service on the eve of the First World War, and its industry saw huge growth over the course of the conflict. In the 1920s its aircraft industry was the largest in the world, and, although other countries – notably France, Germany and Italy – became important players, sustained government support ensured that Britain remained in the front rank. For most of the early history of the aeroplane its development was driven by military rather than civil needs, and in the latter field Britain's achievements during the interwar period were less impressive.

Rearmament built on an already vigorous culture in military aircraft and the outbreak of hostilities triggered a surge in output. By 1940 Britain was the world's largest producer, making considerably more airframes and engines than Germany.[4] This, and a reluctance to commit its full strength before the fall of France, ensured that Britain was by no means a prostrate target when the Luftwaffe attacked in the summer of 1940.

Following the Battle of Britain aircraft production was given even greater priority and the industry which supported it became still more gigantic. By 1943–44 it accounted for 8 per cent of the employed population and a third of all manufacturing labour. By the end of the war Britain had produced over 130,000 aircraft.

For reasons only half acknowledged by many historians, the bomber assumed a central (though subsequently deeply controversial) role in British military strategy,[5] and the output of the Lancaster, Halifax, Wellington and other powerful machines assumed prodigious proportions. Because of the large share of bombers in overall production, the total airframe weight manufactured in Britain was second only to that of the US and exceeded the output of the Axis powers put together.

This achievement, orchestrated by Stafford Cripps, Air Marshal Freeman,[6] and other public servants, reflected the huge resources poured into the sector. Involving little help from external sources, it remains an enduring tribute to the breadth and depth of Britain's industrial power and its technological expertise and vigour.

Fragmented Leadership

In 1945 the manufacture of aircraft was, on most counts, Britain's biggest industry. Though peace brought the closure of subsidiaries, shadow factories and satellite plants, and a rapid shrinking of a workforce that had peaked at nearly two million, the capacity of the sector remained huge. However, the scramble to maximise British production left a very fragmented industry. There were nine independent aero engine manufacturers, led by Bristol Aircraft, Rolls-Royce and Armstrong Siddeley. And there were 22 airframe builders, including such illustrious names as de Havilland, Handley Page, Hawker, Supermarine and Vickers.[7]

Post-war tensions reinforced government interest in military aircraft, and large resources continued to pour into the industry. The Second World War had ended with the Gloster Meteor established as the world's first jet plane in series production, and new speed records were claimed for it in 1945 and again in 1946. With little competition Britain achieved startling successes overseas, sending nearly 1,000 Meteors to export customers.

Jet engine technology advanced rapidly, and airframe design raced to keep up. The de Havilland Vampire was launched at the end of the war, and notched up 1,500 direct and indirect exports. Other new jets included Hawker's Sea Fury, Sea Hawk and Hunter, the English Electric Canberra, and the Gloster Javelin. All sold in substantial numbers at home and abroad.

Among the most successful of the post-war generation was the Hunter, of which Hawker Aircraft Company made almost 2,000. This elegant little plane gave a good account of itself against MiGs and Sabres in two of India's wars and against Mirages and MiGs in Middle East conflicts. Perhaps the lowest point was its role in the savage attack on Chilean democracy by the head of its armed forces, General Augusto Pinochet, in September 1973.

Though long overtaken by more advanced aircraft, the Hunter was still on active service – in Lebanon and elsewhere – till recently.

Another major success was the Canberra, the world's first jet bomber, which launched in 1949 and was one of only three major British aircraft to sell in significant numbers to the US. Including overseas assembly, a total of 1,350 Canberras were produced, and it remained in service with the RAF until the 1990s.

When the de Havilland Comet, the first jet airliner, took to the skies in the late 1940s, the *New York Times* acclaimed Britain's "leadership in jet planes". Ironically, Britain's supremacy had already begun to wane. In the military field the US and Russia had had major successes with the Sabre and the MiG, and the rebirth of French aviation was under way. Development activity nevertheless remained at a high level in the UK. In the mid-1950s Fairey Aviation's beautiful little delta-winged FD2 raced to a new record of over 1,130 miles an hour and by the close of the decade the English Electric Lightning was routinely flying at 1,300 miles per hour.

Thanks to remarkable levels of government spending on defence, at least a dozen new fighters and bombers were brought to production during the 1950s. None sold in the numbers enjoyed by their predecessors, however, and by the 1960s the industry had been radically restructured and the pace of development slowed.

Civil Initiatives

Meanwhile, the civil airframe builders were busy. A 1942 agreement allowing the US primacy in civil aircraft did not stop British manufacturers coming up with a succession of new contenders. Of the earlier ventures the most successful was the de Havilland Dove short-haul carrier, of which over 540 were built.

However, the headlines were soon going to remarkable advances in airliners. The Comet was far and away the pioneer. Sadly, it was to pay the price. An exceptionally elegant aircraft, Comet had structural flaws in its cabin design. After three fatal crashes all flights were suspended for a couple of years. By the time a redesigned Comet 4 was launched the competition had caught up.

The setbacks to the confidence of the aircraft industry were soon assuaged by the Vickers Viscount, the first turbo-prop airliner. This superb aircraft immediately made its piston-engined counterparts redundant and sold nearly 450 at home and abroad.

The industry never again matched this achievement. Despite a debacle over the Vickers V-1000 (described by a waspish French industrialist as a "stupid project" but actually a promising contender for the transatlantic airliner market), the 1960s brought a flurry of initiatives. They were led by the Hawker Siddeley Trident and the Vickers VC10 in 1962, and the BAC-111 in 1965.

The latter had appreciable export success but all struggled to compete with the new US jet airliners. By the middle of the decade the sheer extravagance of launching three major civil aircraft within three years was all too apparent. The industry began to think in terms of cooperation with overseas companies. The first fruits of such initiatives were Concorde, commissioned in 1969, and Airbus, launched in 1972.

Riddle of the Sandys

The industry was undergoing radical restructure. The government was increasingly uneasy over funding a business that lived off cost-plus pricing. This had led to repeated duplication of effort, wasted resources and damaging delays in project completion.

The profligate approach to aircraft procurement was exemplified by the V-Bomber force developed for the RAF in the 1950s. The Air Ministry had invited proposals for a jet bomber that would equal anything conceived by the US or the USSR. The new British aircraft would be able to deliver free-fall bombs or, later, ballistic missiles.

Where the US approach was to build one design per category, however, the RAF insisted on multiple choices in case one proved abortive. The result was three aircraft, the Vickers Valiant, Avro Vulcan and Handley Page Victor,[8] all of which were in active service by the late 1950s. Magnificent aircraft they proved to be, but they epitomised a fantastically extravagant philosophy.

The catalyst for change was the 1957 Defence White Paper. Defence minister Duncan Sandys proposed a sweeping restructuring of the aircraft sector. The focus was on the role of the fighter. Here Sandys held the bizarre view that the future lay entirely with missiles, so the RAF would not require any new fighter aircraft.

All development that was not too far advanced had to be stopped. The implication was a drastic concentration of the industry. The year 1959 saw two of the big engine builders merge into Bristol Siddeley, itself eventually swallowed up by Rolls-Royce. And in 1960 most of the airframe makers were gathered into either the British Aircraft Corporation (BAC) or Hawker Siddeley Aviation. Hawker had been one of the powerhouses behind British aircraft development and was served by brilliant leaders such as Arnold Hall, managing director from 1963 to 1977.[9] Accusations of profiteering on government contracts did little to tarnish Hawker's reputation for technical excellence and commercial vigour.

The restructuring did not bring a halt to new aircraft development. By the mid-1960s the TSR-2 advanced fighter-bomber was well on the way to completion. But its role in domestic defence was not clear and export prospects were dealt a severe blow when the Australian airforce opted for a US rival. One of the painful decisions of the Labour government of 1964–70 was the cancellation of this ambitious aircraft.[10]

Much more successful were the Harrier Jump Jet and the Hawk jet trainer. Originally conceived by Hawker in the 1960s both were further developed by successor companies, including the BAC, British Aerospace (BAe) and BAE Systems (BAES). More than 1,000 Hawks have been built and it has been adopted by many air forces as a trainer. It has undoubtedly been used, in Indonesia and elsewhere, for domestic repression.

The Harrier was bought by half a dozen governments. It retired from UK service in 2011 when, controversially, the Royal Navy's fleet of 74 aircraft was handed to a grateful US Marine Corps. They were casualties of the coalition government's 2010 defence review,[11] which had beached the Royal Navy's last aircraft carrier and retired its incomparable aircraft.

Since the Hawk and the Harrier, the British aircraft industry has never again produced a fighter plane conceived, designed and built at home.

Nationalisation and Privatisation

Another major restructuring of aviation came with nationalisation by the Labour government in 1977, when Hawker Siddeley Aviation and Scottish Aviation were merged with the BAC to form British Aerospace (BAe).

Arnold Hall had left the industry when the aircraft interests of his company were taken over.[12] Although initially hostile to state ownership he had voiced reservations about the Conservative commitment to "total denationalisation" [since] "there are ways in which we can introduce private capital, private enterprise disciplines, maximum autonomy from government, which will be effective for all our main purposes".[13] The story of aviation's development in other European countries – notably France, Germany and Italy – proved these observations all too percipient.

BAe had been under public ownership for only four years when the Conservative government that assumed office in 1979 sold half the state's holding. At this point the total compensation paid to the previous owners since nationalisation, plus interest on the related government debt, amounted to £215m, and the corporation had received £140m in investment funding.[14]

As with so many state sell-offs, the motivation for privatising BAe was "primarily political not economic".[15] Inevitably, the arrangements were controversial. The sale was at an unfavourable time and the proceeds were just £148.6m before costs of £5.6m. Of the net revenue, £100m went back to the company to window-dress its balance sheet, and the Treasury received just £43m. Even this was wiped out by cancellation of dividends on public dividend capital. The government's net loss of £12m was severely criticised by the Public Accounts Committee.[16]

A more serious issue was the long-term direction that private ownership would bring. Opposition MP Jon Silkin accused the government of permitting the rundown of the aerospace industry so that "we would become mere sub-contractors to the Americans".[17] The path by which the industry would go to meet its subcontractor fate – through Europe as much as America – was more complex. But Silkin's prediction is one of the more far-sighted observations in the post-war history of British aviation.

As a sop to the concerns of government backbenchers, the privatisation set a 15 per cent limit on foreign ownership and retained government ownership of 48 per cent plus 25 per cent of the voting rights for the "foreseeable future". These conditions were watered down when the balance of the state's shares was sold in 1985. This time the sale was more successful, with the government realising £363m for its 48 per cent. The only remaining restrictions on the now fully privatised company were the 15 per cent limit on foreign holdings and the retention of a government "golden share".

Twelve years later BAe was restyled BAE Systems (BAES) to reflect the broadening of the company into a conglomerate with wide-ranging interests in naval shipbuilding, armoured vehicles and other military products.

Rolls-Royce Reborn

The other major player in today's British-owned aerospace industry is Rolls-Royce. Founded by Henry Royce, an engineer for whom there was "no such thing as an insoluble problem", this unique company has surmounted great challenges in more than a century of existence.[18] Perhaps its finest hour was when its engines powered the aircraft – Hurricane, Spitfire, Mosquito, Lancaster and Mustang – that ensured Britain would not come out on the losing side in the Second World War. This is fitting. Before the war Rolls had been almost entirely a supplier of engines for military aircraft.

Like many of the world's best manufacturers, Rolls-Royce has, for most of its life, been run by engineers. "A basic engineering training is a good training for management and for top engineering decisions" was the view of James Denning Pearson, who played a leading role in building the company's standing in civil aircraft in the 1950s and 1960s.[19] Naturally, Denning Pearson's own credentials – a first-class degree won in his spare time – were exemplary.

Another striking feature of the company was extraordinary employee loyalty. Before Rolls merged with Bristol Siddeley in 1966, only one of its eight directors had been with the company less than 25 years. Even in the mid-1960s over a third of the employees at the great Derby works had been there since before the Second World War.[20]

The 1960s were a time of strong growth for Rolls-Royce, not least because of the 1966 merger with Bristol Siddeley. The tremendous commitment to aero engines can be measured in the size of the company's labour force. This rose to 87,000, of whom 50,000 were working on aero engines and a further 18,000 were in research, design and development.[21]

Rolls's crisis came in 1971 when it overreached in developing a new engine, the RB-211, for Lockheed's contender in the wide-body airliner market. Having been allowed to go bankrupt in order to break its ruinous contract with Lockheed, the company was nationalised by the Conservative government. For all its early talk of a more ruthless approach ("Selsdon

Man"), Ted Heath's Tory regime was essentially a pragmatic and patriotic administration concerned to limit unemployment, foster Britain's technical prowess and preserve its industrial base.

Rolls-Royce remained in public ownership until privatised in the late 1980s by the Thatcher government. When the company had faced new challenges earlier in the decade, more than 20,000 employees paid the price through redundancy. But sustained engineering excellence and a recovery in the airliner market took Rolls back into profit and by 1987 it was being tailored for stock market flotation.[22]

Despite bizarre proposals for cutbacks in aero engines and diversification into unrelated activities,[23] privatisation involved keeping the existing business intact. The flotation generated a larger revenue than projected, raising £1.08bn for the Treasury after an injection of £283m to clear the balance sheet of debt.[24] As so often in the privatisations of the 1980s and 1990s, the shares were absurdly underpriced and in the first day's trading they rose 80 per cent.

Roller Coaster

Rolls-Royce was to face another test in the late 1980s, when it was developing and marketing a new generation of engines. A critical feature of such an initiative would normally be launch orders from the national flag-carrier, especially one as important as British Airways (BA), which called itself the world's largest airline.

But flying the flag did not stop BA, newly privatised on excessively generous terms from the taxpayer,[25] from giving every impression that along with public ownership it had shed any such old-fashioned patriotic loyalties. Under the leadership of Lord King, its executives repeatedly went off to the US to specify rival products from General Electric and Pratt & Whitney to power its new airliners.

Moreover, those airliners themselves were often made in the US rather than closer to home. In 1988 there were protests at a BA decision to buy McDonnell Douglas MD-11 jets instead of the excellent A340 made by Airbus, the European consortium in which British Aerospace had a 20 per cent stake.[26] The chairman of the European Parliament Economic Committee, Dr Barry Seal, described the decision as "short sighted and absolutely ridiculous".[27]

Predictably, opting for the MD-11 was a foolish choice. The aircraft was a commercial disappointment and within a decade its production had ended with the takeover of McDonnell Douglas by Boeing.

Worse was to follow. In August 1991 BA announced $5bn worth of orders for Boeing's new 777 design, coupled with engines from General Electric. Since BA was supposedly the lead customer, other airlines followed. Air India and All Nippon Airways switched from Rolls-Royce to rival engine builders.[28] Meanwhile, BA strengthened General Electric's grip on the European market by selling the US company its giant maintenance base in South Wales for £272m. This left Rolls-Royce to embark on an increasingly urgent search for an airline to launch its newly developed Trent engine on the Boeing 777.[29]

Such events sapped the strength of Britain's aerospace industry. Its rivals in France, Germany, Japan and the US were buoyed by protected domestic markets, lavish government assistance with research and development, and a sympathetic investment community. But thanks to the supposed benefits of a free market British firms were expected to fight their corner alone.[30]

Lord King's captaincy of British Airways was meanwhile becoming increasingly megalomaniac. A dirty tricks campaign orchestrated by King against Richard Branson's Virgin Airlines[31] culminated in litigation which cost BA millions and King his position as chairman.[32]

Rolls-Royce staged a remarkable fightback from BA's treachery. Though his reputation was later tarnished by revelations of corruption in the securing of overseas contracts, the company enjoyed outstanding leadership in the 1990s under Ralph Robins. Robins had been with the company since 1955 and commanded "enormous respect" among colleagues and customers.[33] Nevertheless, by the early 2000s he was under investor pressure to step down in favour of chief executive John Rose, who had an investment banking background.

The complaint against Robins was the familiar bleat of the short-termist: "From the City's perspective he is just not focused on shareholder value."[34] In reply, he simply pointed to his huge achievement: "Transforming the Rolls-Royce of 1984 from a third tier player with seven per cent of the world's civil jet engine market into a market leader with more than 30 per cent."[35]

The company continued to build the range and capacity of its products throughout the 1990s and 2000s. Unwise initiatives, such as the acquisition of Northern Engineering Industries, were rectified, and the traditional businesses were sustained and extended. This was achieved through organic growth and judicious acquisition, until Rolls emerged as undisputed giant of the European aero engine business and number two to General Electric worldwide. Among planes now flying with Rolls-Royce engines are the Airbus A350 and A380 and the Boeing 787 Dreamliner.

Corruption and Activists

Critics of Britain's engineering flagship have not been without ammunition. One problem has been corrupt practice in contracts for Brazil, China, India, Indonesia and Russia.[36] For some the culprit was the company's bonus culture.[37] As the *Financial Times* put it, a Serious Fraud Office fine on Rolls-Royce was a humbling moment for the most blue-chip of British companies.[38]

A major misjudgement for which the company has also been criticised is opting out of engines for the narrow-bodied smaller airliners which have been the main growth area in recent years. For these and other reasons there have been job losses at both the company's main plants, Derby and Bristol.[39]

And there has been a series of profit setbacks. These culminated in a startling loss of £4.6bn in 2016, due to the impact of the EU referendum vote on sterling and the cost of settling corruption charges. The company had to reassure a domestic workforce – now down to just 22,000 from the near 90,000 in its 1960s heyday – with a £150m investment in engine testing facilities, its biggest single commitment to the UK in over 10 years.[40]

Nevertheless, the string of bad news was enough to prompt "activist shareholders" to break cover.[41] Among their demands were board representation and break-up of the group. Given the dismal fate of British companies dismembered in the pursuit of shareholder value (ICI, GEC, Courtaulds, Thorn EMI and many others) it is difficult to see why anyone other than an opportunist short-term investor would regard this as desirable. Outright takeover by foreign interests is, however, unlikely as long as the government retains a "golden share" in the company.

Nevertheless, Rolls-Royce faces major challenges. Despite a competent 14 years at the helm, these remained daunting when John Rose stepped down as chief executive in 2010.[42] Perhaps the greatest accolade to Britain's leading engineer was the comment of one insider: "There remains a sense that Rolls is less appreciated in the City than it ought to be. When Sir Ralph Robins bowed out as chairman in 2003, he launched a blistering attack on the City's short term thinking. Rose's quieter sermons have been better received."[43]

Of course they have. Having returned to investment banking, Rose had to pull his punches.

The challenges faced by Britain's leading wealth creator have been recognised even by the *Daily Mail*.[44] Rolls-Royce's challenges are, of course, made all the more daunting by the cause so shrilly espoused by that same organ – the exit of the UK from the European Union.

Foreign Hands

Apart from suppliers of structures and components such as Dowty, Melrose/ GKN, Meggitt, and Smiths, and subcontractors working for Boeing, the other significant players in the UK aero industry are foreign-owned. The biggest employer, Airbus UK, operates the sites formerly owned by BAES before it sold its stake in the consortium to EADS.

Among other companies involved in UK aerospace is Boeing, which employs around 2,000 in the manufacture of components for its aircraft products. The chief executive of the company's commercial aeroplanes division has issued clear warnings that the UK is under-investing in technology and failing to map out a cogent industrial vision.[45]

Westland Helicopters

Westland emerged from the Sandys restructuring of the aircraft industry as Britain's sole manufacturer of helicopters, an area where the UK had generated many innovative developments before and after the Second World War. At the start of the 1960s Westland took over the helicopter interests of its two main rivals, Bristol and Fairey, and also acquired the hovercraft division of Saunders-Roe.

The restructuring of the sector left Westland a strong contender in the European helicopter industry, with substantial plants in the West Country – at Yeovil and Weston-super-Mare – and smaller operations at Cowes and Milton

Keynes. Products included the Sea King and Sioux, made under licence, and Westland's own well-regarded Lynx, Scout, Wasp, Merlin and Wildcat.

Surprisingly often, however, Westland has looked less like a national flag-carrier than an orphan. It ran into difficulties in the 1980s, when domestic recession and defence spending cuts hit sales, and by mid-decade there were large job losses and growing financial strains. Characteristically, the government insisted that the company's problems had to be solved in the private sector and no Treasury assistance would be forthcoming.[46]

By 1986 there were urgent efforts on the part of defence secretary Michael Heseltine to find a rescuer among European peers. These included Agusta, a subsidiary of Italy's state-owned Finmeccanica, France's Aerospatiale – partly state-owned – and Germany's MBB. Meanwhile, Westland was sounding out alternative links with the US giant Sikorsky. The dilemma triggered a bizarre political row, since a private-sector American solution was strongly favoured by a Europhobe prime minister.

Two of Thatcher's assistants, Bernard Ingham and Charles Powell, undermined Heseltine with a shabby subterfuge in which the prime minister's own hands were "not entirely clean".[47] That is, she "lied to the House of Commons".[48] And rational consideration of the future of Britain's sole contender in helicopters evaporated in a row in which Heseltine stormed out of the Cabinet.

In the event, the government's solution, involving a £75m cash injection from Sikorsky, proved a typically short-term palliative. UK orders for Sikorsky's Black Hawk did not materialise and within a year Westland announced 2,000 redundancies. These were followed by further cutbacks and plant closures in the recession of the early 1990s.

Ironically, a European option did in the end prevail when GKN took a stake in Westland in 1988. Six years later the engineering group sold its interest on to its partner, Finmeccanica, for £1bn.[49] From then on it was downhill again. GKN retained a facility at Yeovil making fuselages on contract for what was now known as Leonardo, while the main site worked on joint venture projects with the Italian parent. Essentially, what had been Westland was now increasingly diluted as it became more dependent on overseas associates for design, assembly and production. It was sliding more and more into a subcontracting role.

Meanwhile, the company has been hit by the affliction that has beset so much of Britain's defence industry in recent years, corruption in export contracts. Allegations that AgustaWestland, as it then was, had used bribes prompted India to terminate a £466m order in 2013, and fears were expressed for the future of the remaining jobs at Yeovil.[50]

There have been other problems following the award of a $2bn MoD contract for 50 Apache helicopters direct to Boeing and the loss of GKN's contract with Leonardo, which had transferred the work to its operational base in Italy. In early 2017 the UK head of Leonardo had to issue sweeping assurances about the plant's long-term future.[51] Vacuous statements from the local MP and a junior minister did little to allay the fears for an operation whose workforce had dwindled over the years from 10,000 to a couple of thousand, and was still shrinking.[52]

Short Shrift

Short Brothers, the world's first manufacturer of production aircraft, has changed hands many times in over a century of existence. During the Second World War the state commandeered all the company's shares. And as one of the biggest manufacturing operations in Belfast Shorts became an instrument of official efforts to sustain employment during the Troubles. By the mid-1980s, however, the Thatcher government had it on its list for privatisation.

Eventually Shorts was sold to Canada's Bombardier, the world's third largest civil aircraft maker. The purchase price to Bombardier was £30m, but the net revenue for government was heavily negative. This was because the deal involved a taxpayer write-off of £390m in accumulated losses and injection of another £390m to restore Shorts' balance sheet.[53] Bombardier then invested heavily, putting in more than £1bn over the following decade.[54]

Output has comprised components for Bombardier's business and short-haul jets, and parts for other plane and engine makers. Much of the focus is now on Bombardier's C Series regional jets, with Shorts manufacturing the wing and part of the fuselage. Conditions in the short-haul sector have become intensely competitive, however, with the industry leaders, Airbus and Boeing, pursued by Brazil's Embraer, China's Comac and others.

The challenges were intensified by the Trump regime's imposition in 2017 of a huge anti-dumping duty on planes for US customers. This problem seems to have been obviated by Airbus USA taking a majority stake in the project.[55] The next few years could, however, prove even more testing for Shorts than the recent past and there were substantial job losses in late 2018. The year 2019 saw Bombardier announce the sale of Shorts to US-based Spirit Aerosystems, a spin-off from Boeing.[56]

Collaborative Road

According to the European Commission, the UK aircraft industry has "an outstanding track-record for international collaboration".[57] Bluntly, Britain has long ceased to develop new military aircraft or airliners of its own.

The first significant international cooperation was the Sepecat Jaguar ground attack aircraft, launched by BAC and Breguet of France in 1968. The Jaguar was petulantly dismissed by Marcel Dassault, founder of the company which bears his name, as a "camel...designed by a committee",[58] and after Dassault took over Breguet in 1971 it advanced its own products, such as Mistrale and Super Etendard, rather than the Jaguar. Nevertheless, nearly 550 Jaguar were built and it is still on active service in India.

The biggest technical challenge tackled by international cooperation was Concorde, jointly developed by BAC and Sud-Aviation/Aerospatiale and funded by the British and French governments. The cost of the world's first supersonic airliner (over £1bn) seemed daunting at the time it first flew in 1969, but in comparison with the staggering financial bailouts of recent years it now looks almost modest.

Concorde's design drew on experience with delta-wing planes like the Vulcan in the 1950s, and used a variant of the Olympus engines developed by Bristol/Rolls-Royce. Though popular with passengers Concorde failed to gain enough routes for commercial viability, and its production was eventually suspended with just 20 built.

Missing the Bus

The Airbus story reflects the most remarkable collaborative effort in aviation history. Here, unfortunately, Britain has become a much less central player.

The original concept goes back to the late 1950s, when Hawker Siddeley advertised a low-cost "Airbus" variant of an existing product. Early initiatives were funded by the governments of France, Germany and the UK, but the latter's vision failed and the Labour government withdrew from the project in 1969.

However, Hawker Siddeley showed characteristic entrepreneurial spirit, and when the Airbus Industrie consortium was established the following year Hawker took a 20 per cent stake. This bestowed the invaluable status of "privileged subcontractor" to Airbus, giving Hawker security of tenure in the work for the consortium. The involvement in the Airbus project was inherited by BAC and its successors BAe and BAES.

The funding of successive Airbus models naturally required recurrent injections of finance. Each time there was grumbling on the part of the British institutional shareholders, with their unsleeping eye for short-run gain rather than long-term investment. In September 2006 BAES caved in and sold its 20 per cent to EADS, the Franco-German company into which the other partners had vested their stakes.

BAES dressed up its decision as part of a strategy of concentrating on defence. But it can be no coincidence that as a result the UK share of airframe work for Airbus has been dropping, slipping from the historic 20 per cent to below 15 per cent. Apart from the wings made at Broughton and the landing gear supplied by Smiths the main contribution to the Airbus is now the Rolls-Royce engines which power its airliners. The larger ones, that is. For reasons that are still unclear, Rolls-Royce has remained out of the smaller narrow-bodied airliner business, a sector that has boomed in recent years.

BAES's last major involvement in civil airliners was the BAe 146, a reasonably successful initiative in the regional airliner market. Production ended in 2001 after abortive attempts to involve a Taiwanese company in the manufacture of the aircraft.

Other civil aviation programmes which came to an end were the Jetstream and ATP turboprops and the RJ series of short-haul aircraft. For the *Financial Times*, "[a] tumultuous half-century for Britain's civil aerospace industry is coming to an inglorious end with BAE Systems' decision to abandon the production of regional jets".[59] The successful initiatives in short-haul aircraft by other manufacturers, such as Embraer and Bombardier, make the BAES strategy look increasingly foolish.

Business Jets

British Aerospace had made another ill-judged move in 1993, when it sold its corporate jets division to US-based Raytheon. Raytheon had offered BAe an apparently irresistible £250m. The division's main product was the BAe 125, originally offered by Hawker as a first-generation executive jet in 1963. By the 1990s the 125 had long been a well-proven product, with sales of over 800 since launch. Following their acquisition the new owners sold it as the Hawker 800 in direct competition with market leaders Cessna, Gulfstream and Dassault.

Less than a year after buying the business, however, Raytheon announced the transfer to the US of the assembly work on the aircraft.[60] This meant the closure of Hatfield, Hertfordshire, one of the cradles of British aviation. Some of the airframes for the 125 and its successors continued to be made at the former BAe plant at Broughton, now owned by EADS.

However, production of the 125 and its derivatives came to an end in 2013, when Hawker Beechcraft went bankrupt. Ironically, the 125 series had proved to be one of the most successful British-inspired commercial aircraft ever devised, selling more than 1,600 for civil and military uses around the world. Moreover corporate jet demand has gone from strength to strength, with more aircraft delivered to the UK in recent years than any other country in Europe.[61]

Development Grounded

"British Aerospace has been so busy dismembering the country's industrial base that it's hard to perceive it as a company that actually makes money."[62] Prompted by the closure of Hatfield, this sombre newspaper comment reminded readers that BAe's profit prospects were actually improving. The relentless retreat from aircraft production had simply left BAe looking increasingly like a property developer rather than a manufacturer.

Valuable sites at Brooklands, Kingston, Weybridge, Preston and other former aviation centres were being supplemented by BAe acquisitions such as Rover and Royal Ordnance (RO). Notable among these were Enfield and Waltham Abbey, valued by an investment bank at £450m rather than the few million pounds received by the taxpayer when RO was privatised. There were soon calls for the Public Accounts Committee to investigate claims that BAe was set to make a £1bn "killing" from RO and Rover.[63]

With no less than 35,000 acres of land accumulated by 1989, BAe bought developer Arlington Securities for £267m and within a year it was indeed making substantial profits from property.[64] There is little evidence that these profits were ploughed back into research and development, or new aerospace products, rather than handouts to a restless investor following.

Tornado and Typhoon

British collaboration in the military field has become almost routine. Following Jaguar the next major venture was the Tornado combat aircraft, launched in 1974 by the Panavia consortium, owned 42.5 per cent each by the UK and Germany and 15 per cent by Italy. Series production ran from 1979 to 1998, and amounted to almost 1,000 of these excellent planes. The large production run allowed economies of scale and proved a sensible approach to the production of a military aircraft for use by fellow members of the NATO alliance.

Tornado sales included a large consignment for Saudi Arabia, a major customer for British military aircraft since the English Electric Lightning in the 1960s. The Tornado was bought under the Al Yamamah ("Dove") contracts, much the largest set of export deals in British history. In its early stages Al Yamamah tided BAe/BAES over a critical period when the group was coping with slacker business and distractions such as Rover. The company was guided through this difficult phase by its energetic chief executive Richard Evans.

Al Yamamah involved huge secret commissions, a widespread feature of international arms deals.[65] An official enquiry was, however, eventually dropped and there were no criminal prosecutions.

Rival Fighters

The Tornado was followed by the Typhoon, a high-performance multi-role fighter. This has been built by the Eurofighter consortium, a joint venture between BAES (33 per cent) and German, Italian and Spanish groups. France's Dassault dropped out at an early stage to develop its own Rafale jet fighter.

Eurofighter production has been allocated according to procurement, with BAES getting the largest share, and 650 aircraft had been completed by the end of 2018. The main buyers are the UK, Germany, Italy, Spain and Austria,[66] while export customers include Saudi Arabia, Kuwait, Oman, Qatar and Peru.

Hopes of further export sales were frustrated when a major potential deal with India went to Eurofighter's rival Dassault, which won "preferred bidder" status for the Rafale jet fighter.[67] One of the more respectable explanations for the exclusion of Eurofighter was that the Rafale demonstrated greater flexibility during operations in Libya.[68] Dassault is very secretive and, like other French firms, scores poorly on Transparency International's measures of political and corporate corruption.[69]

The uncertainties that lie ahead for BAES were highlighted again in October 2017, when the company announced the loss of almost 2,000 jobs at its UK operations.[70] Under the euphemisms about a "sharper" competitive edge for the company lay the reality of a slowdown in the production rate for the Typhoon. The two other Eurofighter lines, in Germany and Spain, were due to close by the end of 2018,[71] and BAES will face difficult dilemmas when UK production is wound down in the next few years.

Meanwhile, the French and German governments have announced a collaborative fifth-generation combat aircraft. The programme excludes the UK. This confirms a clear warning from the head of Airbus's military aircraft arm that a "Continental" approach to new developments was likely following Brexit.[72] There has since been a worrying "chill towards Britain [within Airbus], mainly through a drip feed of small changes collectively representing…an insidious threat to UK relevance".[73]

For its last big project, BAES has signed up for the F-35 Joint Strike Fighter (JSF) programme, a vastly expensive collaborative project led by Lockheed Martin. Including subcontractors, the UK share is barely 20 per cent.

An increasingly important branch of aviation technology are unmanned aerial vehicles (UAVs) and unmanned combat air vehicles (UCAVs), and many countries now include them in their arsenals. The deployment of drones was confirmed in the UK Defence Industrial Strategy of 2005 and they have played a significant role in long-range conflicts in the Middle East.

The main British contender is BAES, which is working with other contractors, including Dassault, on such products as Taranis and Mantis. UAVs have demonstrated flexibility and effectiveness and are replacing assault aircraft in some of their combat roles.

Losing the Edge

Is James Hamilton-Paterson's claim that Britain is no longer capable of producing an entire aircraft on its own – in the way that France's Dassault has developed the superb Rafale – valid? The fact that significant British initiatives have for many years been mostly on a collaborative basis points to the answer.

Does it matter? Collaboration has kept order books filled and production lines reasonably busy. But a notable feature of each successive venture is that the UK share has fallen. The danger is a cumulative loss of the engineering expertise that Britain could once take for granted.

Britain's standing in aerospace nearly took another big step back in September 2012 when it was proposed that BAES become a minority partner in EADS.[74] The scheme foundered on antagonism from UK investors, opposition by German politicians and EADS insistence that group headquarters should be in Munich. The debacle left a sour taste in Germany, where a senior official cautioned that the future of EADS (and Airbus) would lie in Franco-German cooperation.[75]

Without a British shareholder in Airbus the UK has lost any control over the greatest aircraft venture of all time. That UK involvement would be seriously at risk from Brexit has been clearly spelt out by Airbus executives on more than one occasion. Spokesperson Katherine Bennett pointed out that wing design was still the "crown jewel" of airframe building but that the location of the work in the UK was vulnerable to any new customs obstacles.[76] And chief executive Tom Enders followed this up with a much blunter warning in January 2019 – well-meant advice which prompted a typically crass response from at least one prominent Leave-fixated politician.[77]

France Flies

UK aerospace is often presented as a national champion, one of the few sectors where Britain's industrial prowess is undisputed. This is a half-truth. For those nostalgic for the high-flying days of the 1940s, 1950s and 1960s, today's industry is clearly a shadow of what it once was. Employment has been declining for many years. It dropped from a quarter of a million in 1980 to less than 200,000 a decade later and well below 100,000 more recently.[78]

The fall partly reflects rising productivity. But it also signals slower trends in output. True, recent years have seen more buoyancy, with turnover rising from £25bn in 2012 to £30.6bn in 2016, and value added lifting from £6.1bn to £8.7bn.[79] There was, however, a lot of catching up to do. A European Commission study noted that between 2001 and 2008 the value of UK production declined at an average rate of 1.6 per cent a year, pushing Britain into second place in Europe.[80]

Thanks to its grip on Airbus, now a global titan with annual sales cruising past €70bn, France has continued to soar ahead. On most estimates the UK is now barely level with Germany in terms of output and exports of aerospace products. And it is not that far ahead of Italy. Moreover, where France has a huge trade surplus in aerospace products and Germany is also in credit,[81] the UK has shown deficits in most years since 1996.[82]

Civil Business Neglect

So it is difficult to avoid a negative verdict on Britain's aerospace record. The industry's badly handled privatisation brought investment constraints, a pronounced narrowing of focus and a rush to dependence on military business. Many milestone advances were left behind. The sale of civil aviation sites following privatisation marked a huge change of course and the BAES opt-out, under City pressure, from its Airbus shareholding looks even more foolish in retrospect. The retreat from civil aviation at all levels has opened the door to newcomers to the industry who were unknown a generation ago.

This may have made limited sense for BAES during the long period of expansion in military spending. But it made the group vulnerable to the defence cutbacks which swept the Western world after the 2008 financial crisis. And it has left its aircraft activities dependent – to an extent that is both morally reprehensible and commercially perilous – on an execrable and unstable client base in the Middle East. Moreover, the industry will face a void if a replacement is not found for the Eurofighter Typhoon programme set to close in the near future.

In aero engines the powerful momentum built by Denning Pearson and Ralph Robins in the 1980s and 1990s has somehow been lost, with Rolls-Royce ceding big tranches of the market to rival manufacturers. And in helicopters what was once a world-class presence is now a shadow of what it once was, with Britain's main player reduced to subcontracting for its Italian owner.

One area where the UK has a strong position is maintenance, repair and overhaul, where nearly half the industry's workforce has been employed in recent years. However, this mainly reflects the historic market position of Rolls-Royce rather than the airframe makers. And it is clearly vulnerable to the migration of aircraft servicing to overseas locations.

The policies governing state support for the aircraft industry have in the past ranged from indecisive to capricious. Reversals of policy over the choice of jets for the Royal Navy, prompted by severe budgetary constraints, have been not untypical. The 2009 European Community report refers to a "less supportive framework of conditions for research and development in the UK than in France and Germany". Yet the scale of public funding has continued to fall in real terms. If it were to decline much further the implications for any significant remaining British aircraft industry could be sombre indeed.

CHAPTER 20

Farewell to Arms

> *The supreme excellence is not to win a hundred victories in a hundred battles. The supreme excellence is to subdue the armies of your enemies without even having to fight them.*
>
> *Sun Tzu*

Warfare State

Among my childhood keepsakes is a Centurion tank, a scale model made in Liverpool when Meccano was the world's biggest toy company. In 1950, with Second World War triumphs still vivid, the celebration of Britain's prowess in the production of armaments, even through children's toys, seemed normal. And for me, age, reason and pacific tendencies have never entirely exorcised the fascination of these ugly and awesome machines.

The UK has long been a major producer of the weapons of war. Since for much of the past century Britain was at least as much a warfare as a welfare state,[1] this is not so remarkable. Unlike its Continental peers, however, Britain has traditionally maintained only a small standing army. Despite their limited scale, Britain's land forces have long sustained substantial armouries and weapon stocks, typically produced at home. Britain has also been a big exporter, selling large amounts of arms overseas.

However, the industry that has historically underpinned these has been in steep decline. Contrary to popular belief, most of the export trade has now gone. What is left has two distinctive features. It is heavily concentrated in terms of products, and it is narrowly based geographically.

UK arms exports are now dominated by aircraft, and these go mostly to the Middle East, notably Saudi Arabia. The aircraft are of high value, of course, and this is mainly what keeps Britain in the top rank of arms exporters. Apart from upgrades of existing models and subcontracts to foreign designs, tanks, armoured cars, troop transport, self-propelled guns, artillery, landmines and many types of land-based ancillary equipment have been largely abandoned by UK companies. Small arms manufacture is confined to specialist items, and where other products are required by British armed forces they are mostly imported.

The decline of arms exports is surely welcome, but the shrinking of the industry raises questions over self-sufficiency for legitimate self-defence and should prompt concern at the dramatic slide into import dependence.

Light Arms

For much of the period of imperial expansion the small arms weaponry of the army was based on variants of the Brown Bess muzzle-loaded musket. By the mid-1800s, however, the breech-loading rifle had been adopted and Ferguson, Baker and Brunswick rifles were widely used. Most were made by specialist gunsmiths or assembled at the Royal Small Arms Factory (RSAF) at Enfield in north London.

The disappointing performance of British small arms in the Crimean War prompted urgent further development. By 1871 the army was using the new Martini-Henry rifle, named after a Swiss designer who modified an existing pattern and a Scotsman who devised the rifling.

Within 30 years a much more modern weapon had been adopted. This was the bolt-action Lee-Enfield 303, named after its designer James Paris Lee and the RSAF where he worked. Two World Wars and numerous smaller conflicts generated huge demand for the 303 and many millions were produced in the UK and overseas. Though it has been superseded in the British Army by German and Belgian weapons it is still in use in the developing world.

Another RSAF product which achieved considerable success was the Sten gun. This was a light portable submachine gun rushed into production after the huge equipment losses at Dunkirk. The Sten gun was simple, cheap and easy to operate, but unreliable. Nevertheless, it saw widespread use in many theatres during and after the Second World War, and by the time it was superseded in the 1960s several million had been produced.

The Sten was partially replaced by the Sterling submachine gun, developed in 1944 by the Sterling Armaments Company of Dagenham. Reliable and accurate, the Sterling was in service with the British Army for half a century. It also sold in substantial numbers in export markets, with total output over the years approaching half a million.

Among heavier machine guns, the most successful of earlier designs was the Maxim, invented by Hiram Maxim in 1884. More efficient and wieldy than predecessors such as the Gatling and the Gardner, the Maxim developed a fearsome reputation as a weapon of colonial aggression. It enabled small groups of British soldiers to butcher much larger opposing forces in Southern Africa, Sudan, Tibet and elsewhere. A notorious engagement was Omdurman in 1898, when the Maxims slaughtered 10,000 tribesmen for the loss of 48 British troops.[2]

The Maxim was superseded by the Vickers machine gun, developed after Vickers bought Maxim's company in the 1890s. The Vickers gun became a byword for durability, reliability and versatility during the First World War. It was shipped to many customers overseas, and was still in service with the British Army as recently as the 1960s.

Other notable British machine guns were based at least partly on developments elsewhere. The Lewis gun, used by the army until the 1950s, was an American design modified by Birmingham Small Arms Company (BSA). The Bren gun took its name from its birthplace, Brno in Czechoslovakia, and its adopted home, RSAF Enfield. Thanks to extensive service in the Second World War and subsequent operations in the twilight of empire, the Bren became almost a household name.

Artillery

Notable advances in cannons, mortars, howitzers and other artillery passed Britain by until the mid-nineteenth century, when a revolutionary new piece was developed by the industrialist William Armstrong at his Elswick works in Newcastle on Tyne. The design marked the birth of modern artillery. It was a breech-loader, requiring robust firing components made to a fine tolerance. The barrel was rifled, and formed of high-quality wear-resistant steel to withstand far greater pressures than previous patterns.

Among the larger pieces subsequently produced in Britain were the 17–18-inch guns for the capital ships of the Royal Navy early in the twentieth century. These were generally made at the Elswick factory, by now owned by Vickers-Armstrong.

Arms for Iraq

Britain's only brush with the world of superguns was through Project Babylon, commissioned by Iraq's President Saddam Hussein in 1988. Designed to launch a projectile hundreds of miles from a fixed site, the Iraqi supergun incorporated specialised components from various Western sources.

Among leading firms involved in the programme was Sheffield Forgemasters. One of very few companies that could tailor-make the giant steel tubes for the barrel, Forgemasters claimed it was making specialised pipes for the petrochemical industry.

The project reached the trial stage but was halted in 1990 when Gerald Bull, the Canadian scientist who had masterminded the venture, was assassinated by Israeli agents. Components were belatedly seized by customs on their way from Europe to Iraq. The *New York Times* was puzzled by the refusal of Downing Street to acknowledge the Supergun project: "One of the enduring mysteries of the Bull story is the behaviour of the British authorities."[3]

There was no mystery. Envious of France's covert sale of $5bn worth of arms to Saddam Hussein during the Iran–Iraq War,[4] the British government had for years turned a blind eye to sanctions-busting.[5] This became obvious when UK executives involved in the business faced prosecution. Their firms included Walter Somers, a West Midlands steel fabricator, Matrix Churchill, a machine tool maker, and munitions manufacturer Ordtec.

The cases collapsed when it became clear that ministers had long been encouraging British suppliers to ignore the arms embargo. Kenneth Clarke, Michael Heseltine, Douglas Hurd, Norman Lamont, Peter Lilley, Nicholas Ridley, Malcolm Rifkind and others had acquiesced in the suppression of evidence that would have helped the defence of the accused.[6] In a rare moment of conscience leading Conservative Alan Clark blew the whistle on the whole sordid affair.

Ironclads, Landships and Tanks

One area where Britain has a strong history of innovation is armoured vehicles. Before the First World War trials of ironclads, landships and other devices had come to nothing, but a Royal Engineers officer, Ernest Swinton, persuaded the War Office to take up some of the more promising ideas, and the first British tank – designed by Sir William Tritton and his firm William Foster of Lincoln – was born. Britain led the way in putting the tank on to the battlefield. Several dozen were deployed at the Somme in 1916 and Ypres in July 1917, and at Cambrai in November the same year.

More lasting gains were secured at Amiens on 8 August 1918 when, with the aid of 600 tanks Britain's Fourth Army at last spearheaded a crucial victory.[7] Described by General Erich Ludendorff as the "Black Day of the German Army", the battle launched the Hundred Days of Allied advance which culminated in the November Armistice.

Despite its wartime successes, there was still debate about the appropriate role for tanks in modern warfare, and the UK let its momentum falter. By the late 1930s British interest was reviving, however, and after the disasters of May 1940 production was given a high priority. The results were impressive in scale but mixed in quality.

In all 28,000 tanks and self-propelled guns – slightly more than in Germany – were manufactured in British factories over the course of the war. Vickers generally sustained a good standard of quality, as did Royal

Ordnance at Leeds, but firms such as Leyland, Nuffield and Vauxhall made an uncertain start. Their products tended to be underpowered and outgunned when they came up against the Wehrmacht machines.

Matilda I, a low-cost light tank built by Vickers-Armstrong, was in service for only a couple of years at the start of the war, but Matilda II, a heavier vehicle, was deployed throughout. The Covenanter, a so-called Cruiser tank, was taken out of service in 1943 after only three years of production. In the meantime, another model, the Crusader, had gone into service and its greater speed brought some success in North Africa and elsewhere.

The most successful British tank in the early years of the war was the Valentine. Designed by Vickers-Armstrong in 1938 and produced from mid-1940 on, over 8,000 were manufactured in the UK and Canada – more than any other British tank.

Another model produced in large numbers – well over 7,000 – was the Churchill, one of the heaviest tanks of the war. The Churchill's performance was at first flawed when it was rushed into production in 1940. But after urgent improvements it performed better in North Africa and Normandy, becoming a favourite with the troops for its toughness, terrain handling and the protection afforded to crews – a striking contrast to the gruesome "Tommy Cooker" reputation of the American Sherman tank. Churchills were among the 2,000 British tanks shipped to Russia and made their contribution on the battlefields of Kursk.

Towards the end of the war other products were coming out of British tank factories. Among the most successful were the Cromwell, of which over 4,000 were built, the Centaur and the Comet. These were Cruiser tanks of medium weight, good manoeuvrability and high top speed.

Centurion Conquest

The closing weeks of the war saw the birth of a tank whose design was based on the Comet but which was, at last, to outshine both its predecessors and its contemporaries. This was the Centurion, conceived in 1943 and delivered to the front just as the titanic struggle with the Third Reich was ending. Technically a medium tank, at 52 tonnes it outweighed all its British forebears.[8]

Having missed the Second World War, the Centurion promptly became a main battle tank (MBT) for the Cold War. Though not noted for speed or range, it was formidably protected with six-inch armour, better armed than its predecessors and dependably powered by the Rolls-Royce Meteor engine. It proved the finest tank of its era. Nearly four and a half thousand were produced and the Centurion sold widely in Europe, the Commonwealth and the Middle East.

Battle experience included legendary encounters in Korea, the Indo-Pakistan war of 1965 and the liberation of Bangladesh in 1971. The most testing engagement was on the Golan Heights during the Yom Kippur War. By the time the Syrians had capitulated to 100 Israeli Centurions they had left 1,000 advanced Russian-built tanks wrecked on the battlefield.

The Centurion remained in service with the British Army into the twenty-first century.

Vickers MBT

Much of the effort in tank development during the 1960s was funded by the government. An exception was the Vickers Main Battle Tank, developed primarily for export. The Vickers Mark I was a low-cost vehicle, borrowing significant components from its contemporaries. Eventually it also included the engine, transmission, steering and fire control system proposed for the Army's next MBT, the Chieftain.

The catalyst was a 1961 agreement for Vickers to provide an MBT design for the Indian Army. India received a prototype of its new tank, to be called Vijayanta (Victorious), and 90 production models assembled at Elswick. Subsequent Vijayanta output came from a factory built by Vickers in India.

The share of Indian-made components was escalated until virtually all were sourced in India.[9] For better or worse, the deal was a successful example of technology transfer from developed to developing country. India went on to build nearly 2,000 of the new tanks. They served the country well in 1971, when the incomparable Sam Manekshaw[10] led India to victory over Pakistan.

Production of the Vickers MBT continued at Elswick from 1963 to 1994. In addition to India export markets included Kenya, Kuwait, Malaysia, Nigeria and Tanzania. It was not taken up by the British Army.

Mighty Chieftain

This was because the army's MBT replacement for the Centurion was the Chieftain. A descendant of the Centurion, the Chieftain was assembled at ROF Leeds and Vickers-Armstrong on Tyneside. Billed as the most advanced tank of the era when it was unveiled in the mid-1960s, around 900 units were delivered to the British Army and subsequently modified with Stillbrew armour developed at the Military Vehicles and Engineering Establishment (MVEE).

An important potential customer was Israel, which had cooperated in the Chieftain's development and envisaged local manufacture. After strong opposition from Israel's Arab neighbours and signs that the Middle East could become a major market, the British government backpedalled on its commitment. Israel went on to develop its own formidable contender, the Merkava.[11]

One hundred and seventy Chieftains were earmarked for King Idris of Libya, 175 MBTs went to Kuwait and 27 to Oman. The most remarkable sales were those to the Shah of Iran, who was "besotted" with the Chieftain.[12] Thanks to agent Shapoor Reporter, who had haunted the back alleys of Middle East arms deals for decades,[13] the Shah signed up for 1,350 MBTs in the next few years.

A further 250 Chieftain armoured recovery vehicles (ARVs) were bought in 1976 and, to the delight of the Labour government of the day, there were indications that another 2,000 MBTs could follow.[14] The Iranian deals would have constituted the biggest peacetime MBT sales in European history. The two Chieftain variants – Shir 1 and Shir 2 – were to be assembled initially in Britain and then in a new defence industries complex in Iran.[15]

With only part of the contract completed, however, it lapsed after the 1979 revolution in Iran. Whitehall hastily searched for alternative outlets. A total of 279 MBTs went to Jordan in 1981 in a version of Shir 1 called Khalid ("Sword").[16] And under a secret embargo-busting deal the Thatcher government shipped 29 ARVs to Saddam Hussein.

The Iran deal story has an epilogue, indeed a testimony to the dour single-mindedness of the Islamic regime. The Shah had paid for the whole package in advance. His successors demanded repayment for the tanks not delivered, but the British government did not feel bound to reimburse its customer once the deal lapsed. However, the Iranians pursued the case with impressive tenacity and in 2014 they gained a favourable arbitration (though not their frozen assets) from the International Chamber of Commerce in The Hague.

The Shir I tanks inherited by Iran's Islamic regime were deployed at the Battle of Dezful in the Iran–Iraq War in January 1981. Jordan was later gifted a fleet of the Iranian tanks captured by Baghdad during the war. Kuwait fielded its Chieftains in the 1990 Gulf War, but also lost large numbers of these to Iraq.

Challengers

Some of the vehicles left over from the abortive deal with the Shah were modified to meet NATO requirements and reborn as Challenger 1. This was seen as an interim contender for MBT with the British Army after many years of service by the Chieftain. The tank was built at ROF Leeds, which had been sold to Vickers Defence Systems in 1986.

In all 420 Challenger 1 tanks were supplied to the army. Their active deployment was mainly in two theatres – peacekeeping in the former Yugoslavia and Operation Desert Storm in the first Gulf War.

When the replacement for Challenger 1 was being phased in during the 1990s, efforts were made to sell the tanks on to overseas customers. A substantial number were taken by Jordan to replace its Tariq MBT, an upgraded variant of the Centurion.[17] In total the Royal Jordanian Army – long one of the best run and best equipped in the Middle East – has taken around 400 Challenger 1 tanks.

The successor to Challenger 1 was Challenger 2, the finest of all MBTs to serve the British Army and affectionately known to squaddies as the Chally. Vickers was awarded a substantial development contract by the British government in 1989. The Challenger 2 that emerged had features in common with Challenger 1,[18] but was extensively redesigned and rebuilt.[19] In all nearly 400 were bought for the British Army.

Production began in 1994 at Leeds and Elswick – both eventually owned by BAES, which was to take over Vickers defence operations in 2004. The main deployment for Challenger 2 was in the 2003 invasion of Iraq. The two Challengers are thus distinguished from most of their contemporaries by having proven battlefield experience. Overseas sales of Challenger 2 were nevertheless limited to 38 tanks for Oman in 1994.

After taking over Vickers in 2004 BAES eventually terminated all Challenger production.[20] In 2014 the factory at Elswick, chosen by William Armstrong as the site of his Tyneside engineering works in 1847 and a maker of tanks since the First World War, fell silent.[21]

BAES has joined two other European MBT makers in closing production lines. France's Nexter has mothballed production of its Leclerc MBT. The line for the Ariete, Italy's MBT, has also shut down. The only manufacturer still active is Krauss-Maffei Wegmann, whose Leopard series has sold widely. Even so, the company is now "sharing the road ahead" with Nexter.[22]

This is unlikely to change. There is a widespread belief that there will never be another Kursk or Alamein.[23] And anyway the main NATO partners all have modern tank fleets good for another generation.

When in 2015 the British Ministry of Defence was offered several hundred second-hand Leopard 2 tanks they were turned down in favour of a £700m upgrade of the Challenger 2 fleet. "Worry about negative press headlines" was cited.[24]

The MoD may have regretted the rejection of the German offer. Yet for once the popular press may have got it right. If defence of the realm is not a motive for sustaining a domestic manufacturing capacity, it is quite difficult to see what is.

Armoured Cars

The history of other armoured vehicles goes back even further than that of tanks. Again, Britain was active in the early days. FR Simms designed an armoured quadricycle in the 1890s, and followed it with a Motor War Car. By the First World War armoured cars were in use as reconnaissance vehicles, troop carriers, machine gun carriers, anti-aircraft carriers and ambulances.

The interwar years saw experimentation with light armoured vehicles. One of the most successful was the Carden-Lloyd Tankette, which became part of the Vickers stable.[25] Vickers went on to develop the Universal

Carrier, which was adopted by the British Army in the 1930s. Armed with a machine gun, typically the Bren, they were deployed in all the main theatres of the Second World War and for many years afterwards. Production of the Universal Carrier in the UK, USA, Canada and Australia amounted to well over 100,000, the largest output of any armoured vehicle in history.

The Second World War prompted demand for more substantial armoured vehicles to carry machine guns, small artillery pieces or anti-aircraft guns. Many of the car and lorry makers answered the need, with AEC, Daimler, Guy, Humber, Lanchester and others turning out armoured cars, scout cars and field ambulances.

Over the next half century British manufacturers of armoured vehicles enjoyed remarkable success in export markets, selling thousands of vehicles to a wide range of countries. Prominent among those involved were Alvis, Daimler and GKN.

Daimler Ferret

Daimler was a manufacturer of passenger cars which had turned its hand to military vehicles during the Second World War. With the end of hostilities the company resumed civilian activities but continued to make armoured cars. A notable product was the Ferret, thousands of which were supplied to the British Army and to overseas customers in the 1950s and 1960s.

Ideal for challenging urban environments, the Ferret inevitably ended up serving in ugly colonial settings such the French war in Algeria, UDI Rhodesia and apartheid South Africa. On the other hand, it was also used to protect Irish peacekeepers in the 1962 UN Congo mission and in legitimate operations elsewhere. It epitomised the familiar ethical dilemmas facing those who make and sell armaments for a living.

Immediately after the Second World War the British Army needed new tracked armoured personnel carriers, and GKN was contracted to supply the FV430 series to the Army. This grew to ten variants capable of a dozen roles. Production ran for a decade from the early 1960s and around 3,000 vehicles were delivered to the MoD. The series, notably the FV432 armoured personnel carrier, has proved extremely durable and successive improvements have enabled this old warhorse to remain in service into the twenty-first century.

All the Ss

Many of the armoured cars which served the British Army between the 1960s and the 2000s were made by Alvis. One of the most distinctive products was the Saladin, which spearheaded the FV600 series of armoured vehicles. A larger vehicle than the Ferret, the Saladin shared components with the Saracen, the Stalwart amphibious truck ("Stolly") and the Salamander fire tender.

Saracen became a familiar sight during the Troubles in Northern Ireland, and like the Saladin enjoyed strong sales overseas, sometimes to severely repressive regimes. Alvis also developed the Fox armoured car as a replacement for the Ferret. One of the last wheeled vehicles from Alvis was the Saxon armoured personnel carrier, a mine-resistant lorry introduced in the 1980s.

Devised partly as replacements for the FV600 suite was the Combat Vehicle Reconnaissance (Tracked) – CVR(T) – series. This was an impressive family of small, mobile, air-transportable vehicles conceived in the 1960s and produced from the 1970s on. All shared common features and components.

Many hundreds were delivered to the British Army, and many more were sold overseas. Among the most successful were the Scorpion, bought by more than 20 foreign governments, the Spartan and the Scimitar. Though the series was conceived in the 1960s, some variants are still in active deployment at home and abroad.

Warrior

A bigger contender in armoured vehicles is the Warrior, which in style and size – 25 tonnes – is more akin to a light tank. Warrior was GKN's contribution to a new family of larger armoured vehicles for the British Army in the 1980s.

Manufacture was initially by the Sankey division of GKN, then by Alvis, which bought the operation from GKN, and finally by BAES after its purchase of Alvis. Over 1,000 vehicles were manufactured, with nearly 800 going to the British Army and the balance to Kuwait. Having seen testing conditions in the Balkans, the Gulf and Afghanistan, the Warrior has been undergoing extensive upgrading.

The decade following the fall of the Berlin Wall saw a growing impression that the army needed more versatile equipment. The MoD response was the Future Rapid Effect Systems (FRES) programme, under which several thousand advanced vehicles would be purchased for the army.

The two targets were a utility vehicle (UV) to replace such units as the Saxon, the FV432 (eg Bulldog) and some of the CVR(T) series, and a specialist vehicle (SV). Though the FRES has subsequently been modified, its philosophy has dominated defence vehicle design.

An attempt to develop a new vehicle in cooperation with Germany in 2004 opened the door to a much less domestically oriented sourcing policy on the part of the army. Within a couple of years it was evaluating three contenders for the UV, one made in Germany, one made in France and one an imported design with only final assembly in Britain. Subsequent decisions have taken the UK still further down the road to dependence on foreign suppliers of sophisticated equipment.

Acronyms and Argot

Britain's MoD may have had to slow its spending but one thing it is clearly not short of is abbreviations, acronyms and argot. This does not ease the difficulties of the layman in following MoD development and procurement. Nor does it help any politician striving to bring this juggernaut under control.

One thing is clear, however. Despite budgetary constraints, armoured vehicle funding has remained lavish. Some years ago it was set at £10bn for the decade from 2013. The main projects include Challenger 2 Life Extension Programme (LEP), Warrior Capability Sustainment Programme (CSP), Scout Specialist Vehicle (SV), Utility Vehicle (UV) and Armoured Platform Support Vehicle (APSV).[26]

The budget has also included vehicles acquired under the Urgent Operational Requirements (UOR) mandate for Iraq and Afghanistan. Many were hastily procured from overseas suppliers, typically in the US, in response to the horrific British casualties of those missions.

In 2014 an enormously costly SV procurement programme went not to the traditional British contender, BAES, but to the UK subsidiary of a US company. In its biggest single order for land vehicles in 30 years the MoD signed a £3.5bn deal with General Dynamics for nearly 600 Scout armoured vehicles for use by the Armoured Cavalry. With a weight of over 40 tonnes the Scout has more in common with a tank than with the armoured cars it is replacing. Deliveries were to run from 2017 to 2020.[27]

The announcement was, of course, window-dressed with claims that the order would secure nearly 1,300 direct jobs in the UK, but the reality was just 200–300 jobs at General Dynamics' operation in South Wales, plus 1,000 indirect jobs across the UK supply chain. The sophisticated technology embodied in the equipment would be the preserve of the supplier.

The continuous erosion of the UK's heritage in defence technology has been further reinforced by the choice of weaponry for the Scout and the upgraded Warrior. True, BAES is involved in the supply of the main gun. But it is being built by a joint venture with France's Nexter Systems. Naturally, the factory is in France.[28] Grudgingly, the joint venture has conceded that the component supply chain "will include" UK companies.

Transport Reverse

Ever since the Second World War the British Army has had an extensive and effective transport fleet. The British Expeditionary Force went into France in 1940 enviably well-equipped and fully motorised, and contrary to popular belief the War Office was able to call on Britain's industrial resources to replenish its Dunkirk losses quite quickly. Once the conflict had ended the Cold War sustained military requirements at a high level.

The Army's transport has typically included large numbers of four-by-fours and support trucks. There are still many thousands of Land Rovers in use, and this brand is unlikely to be displaced by imports. But further up the scale the situation has changed radically. Here there has been a far-reaching erosion of domestic sourcing.

The critical event was the award of a huge Ministry of Defence contract in 2004. Worth over £1bn, the biggest in 25 years, the plan was to replace thousands of long-serving cargo trucks such as Bedfords. The Bedford factory had been killed off by the recession of the 1980s, but there was a strong contender in an LDV-led consortium which would have made the vehicles in Birmingham.[29]

To the shock of many, the contract went to Germany's MAN, which reneged on understandings to manufacture in Cheshire by sourcing from Austria.[30] The relevant minister, Labour's Lord Bach, offered the lame excuse that the contract would provide "value for money for the taxpayer".

The claim was unfortunate, since the trucks were found to be hopelessly inadequate for their tasks and needed extensive and expensive modification for hot-climate service in Iraq and Afghanistan.[31]

Royal Ordnance

Historically, the manufacture of weapons, ammunition and explosives was controlled by the monarch through the Royal Ordnance factories (ROFs). Important ROFs included the Royal Gunpowder Factory at Waltham Abbey, founded in 1560,[32] and the Royal Arsenal at Woolwich.

During the First World War the Royal Arsenal became a gigantic complex of factories, stores and research facilities with up to 80,000 employees. With the help of large numbers of women workers, other plants opened as the war dragged on. Leeds started up in 1915 and by the end of the conflict it had become Britain's biggest producer of artillery shells, turning out half a million tonnes of heavy ammunition.

So colossal was the demand for munitions, however, that from quite early on the Allies had to turn to the US for additional supplies. In addition to paying for its own imports, the British government took the momentous decision to finance those of Russia and Italy from 1915 and France from 1916. From an initial estimate of $50m in total, by 1917 expenditure had soared to an incredible $80m a week.[33] By the end of the war Britain had squandered its gold reserves, liquidated overseas assets and incurred vast debts to the US. This appalling legacy was to haunt the economy for much of the century.

The ROFs retrenched between the wars but the outbreak of the Second World War prompted the opening of more than 40 plants, employing over 300,000 people. In the post-war years there was a gradual winding down of

ROF activities and by the 1980s the MoD ordnance sites had dropped to around 20.

Royal Ordnance Sell-Off

Privatisation had now become one of the obsessions of the Conservative government and the ROFs were seen as eminently saleable. They had broadened their activities, developed joint ventures with the private sector and won three Queen's Awards for Export Achievement. Above all they were remunerative, reporting an after-tax profit of £26m in 1985.

Yet even before privatisation had begun severe cutbacks were initiated. Among the first were at Bishopston (Glasgow), Birtley (near Gateshead), and Chorley and Blackburn in Lancashire, all announced in November 1984.[34] The following March saw more job losses, this time at Bridgwater, in Somerset, and in January 1986 Birtley and Chorley were again cut back.

Particularly galling at this time was the revelation that the MoD had switched orders for tank shells from the UK to Belgium.[35] By the middle of 1986 other operations, such as the RO tank factory at Leeds, were being targeted for increasingly controversial cutbacks.

Meanwhile, in January 1985 Royal Ordnance was vested as a state-owned company, with a turnover of £500m and a workforce of 18,000 at 16 manufacturing sites. However, privatisation was delayed by wrangles with private-sector arms suppliers such as Vickers. Ominously for the future of manufacturing in the UK, the government confirmed that Royal Ordnance would lose its status of preferred supplier to the MoD.[36]

As so often, privatisation proved unrewarding to the taxpayer. In addition to rationalisation the government had to pad the balance sheet and the pension fund. The privatisation bill in Parliament grudgingly acknowledged that, far from benefitting the public purse, the sell-off could cost a net £100m.[37]

Royal Ordnance was sold to British Aerospace (BAe) in early 1987 for £188.5m. The National Audit Office pointed out that the sale value of the company was "significantly less than the net asset value".[38] This was an understatement. The acquisition brought matchless property development potential on the edge of London. City analysts reckoned that BAe could make £1.1bn from the land that came with Royal Ordnance and Rover. The deal was made all the shabbier by suspicion that government ministers had been secretly plotting the 7,000 job losses linked with privatisation for five years in advance.[39]

In the meantime, Leeds ROF, builder of the Centurion, Chieftain and Challenger tanks and one of RO's most important facilities,[40] had been sold separately to Vickers. The price was just £11.2m, plus a deferred payment towards its net asset value.[41]

Before long retrenchment resumed. Despite assurances about job security, two sites, Patricroft and Bishopston, near Glasgow, were targeted. When Bishopston closed, an all-party House of Commons committee demanded to know why a £100m Ministry of Defence propellants contract had gone to an overseas supplier, and why Royal Ordnance had no access to the expertise of the Defence Evaluation and Research Agency (DERA) when its overseas competitors routinely received government research funding.[42]

Meanwhile, other Royal Ordnance facilities were closing. Notable was the Royal Small Arms Factory (RSAF) at Enfield Lock, which shut in 1988. The site where the Lee-Enfield rifle had been conceived became a humdrum business park and housing estate. As so often with the industrial graveyards of the 1980s and 1990s, the developer was Trafalgar House.

One ROF suffered a particularly cruel fate. The Whitehall official responsible for MoD munitions procurement in the 1980s, Gordon Foxley, was convicted of taking bribes to divert purchases from ROF Blackburn, the traditional supplier, to Germany, Italy and Norway.[43] Foxley served time but, incredibly, neither this crook nor his family returned the £1.5m forfeited as a condition of his light sentence.[44] Deprived of millions in revenue, ROF Blackburn closed, with the loss of hundreds of jobs.

Vickers

Vickers, the company which bought the Leeds ROF, was the oldest and best known of the British arms manufacturers. The company's origins were in Sheffield steel, and it was not until late in the nineteenth century that it became a producer of artillery.[45] The involvement with armaments accelerated rapidly after 1897, when along with the Barrow Shipbuilding Company Vickers acquired the Maxim machine gun company and the services of Basil Zaharoff.

Among his talents Zaharoff was an extraordinary salesman. During the First World War the company produced vast quantities of armaments, ranging from submarines to battleships, and from cannons to aeroplanes. Zaharoff bought the patronage of Lloyd George, a string of honours and a personal fortune. He was the inspiration for the arms dealer Andrew Undershaft in Shaw's play *Major Barbara*. Like many wealthy people with controversial reputations, he nurtured a philanthropic image.

A merger with Armstrong Whitworth in 1928 brought Vickers the Elswick works and a naval shipyard on Tyneside.[46] A significant initiative was taken in the interwar years with the development of the 6-Ton tank, and Vickers remained an important manufacturer of tanks, such as the Valentine, during the Second World War.

The company's armaments activities only retreated a little with the post-war peace. In the 1960s its successful aircraft business was absorbed into the newlyformed British Aircraft Corporation. Meanwhile, tank production continued on Tyneside, where one of Vickers' biggest commitments was the MBT for the Indian army.

Both Vickers' shipbuilding and aircraft interests were nationalised in the 1970s. This was reversed in the following decade, when privatisations and economic crisis brought the bewildering and destructive patterns of sale, resale and rationalisation of assets that was to become as familiar in the arms sector as in the wider economy. Vickers' former warship yard was sold to GEC and aircraft assembly was returned to the private sector with the privatisation of British Aerospace.

During the privatisation of Royal Ordnance the sale of the Leeds factory brought the production of MBTs, in the shape of Challenger 1 and then Challenger 2, back into the Vickers fold. Rolls-Royce plc (the aero engine maker) bought what was left of Vickers in 1999 but sold the company on to Alvis in 2002. The ghost of Vickers lingered on as Alvis Vickers until 2004, when the combined group was bought by BAES and the venerable name was finally interred.

Alvis

Alvis started life as a Coventry-based manufacturer of high-quality cars just after the First World War.[47] The company diversified into armoured vehicles in the 1930s and in collaboration with a Hungarian inventor, Nicholas Straussler, developed the first true armoured car. After concentrating on aero engines during the Second World War the company returned to armoured vehicles, and in 1950 launched the first of the FV600 family of six-wheeled products which included the Saladin, Salamander, Saracen and Stalwart.

Alvis also produced the Fox armoured reconnaissance vehicle as a replacement for the Saladin and for Daimler's Ferret armoured car. But its greatest success was with the CVR(T) range of tracked vehicles such as the Scorpion, Striker and Scimitar.

Alvis was taken over by Rover Ltd in 1965 and was part of British Leyland (BL) when the group became state-owned ten years later. However, the Alvis operations kept their company name and a distinct identity in military vehicles. When privatisation came along in the 1980s Alvis's successful record made it a contender for an early sale.

In 1981 United Scientific Holdings was delighted to pick it up for a modest £27m, adopting the name of its main asset and becoming Alvis plc. The group bought Sweden's Hägglunds in 1997, the armoured vehicles business of GKN the following year and Vickers' defence operations in 2002.[48]

Alvis could now claim to supply 90 per cent of the British Army's armoured vehicles.[49] Within a decade this proud position was lost. But in the short term Alvis was a ripe target for takeover by one of the giants of the arms business. In 2003 the minority stake held by GKN was bought by BAES,[50] and the following year BAES acquired full control. The renowned name of Alvis was finally interred.

GKN Sankey

In contrast to Alvis, military products were far from being a core activity for GKN.[51] It was not until the 1980s, when the group was forced into heavy rationalisation by ferocious recession, that GKN made a concerted move back into the military field. Its initial bid was the Warrior, made by GKN Sankey and sold in substantial numbers to the British Army and to Kuwait. Other vehicles produced by GKN included the Saxon mine-proof lorry, the Simba "battlefield taxi", the Piranha, the Tactica and the Aquatrack.[52]

In 1994 GKN bought Westland Aircraft, the sole British helicopter builder, which had significant involvement in the military field. By the end of the decade, GKN was feeling less confident about its new subsidiary, however, and put it into a joint venture with Italy's Finmeccanica to form Augusta Westland. Four years later it sold out entirely to Finmeccanica, and yet another historic British company went into foreign hands.

In the meantime, in return for a minority stake GKN had sold its armoured vehicle business to Alvis. The latter closed its historic factory in Coventry in 1998 and concentrated its military vehicle operations on the GKN site at Telford.[53]

BAE Systems

The company which in 2004 became the final repository for so much of Britain's defence industry was a very different creature to Britain's traditional manufacturers of armoured vehicles and ordnance such as Alvis, GKN, Royal Ordnance and Vickers. BAE Systems was already one of the UK's biggest companies, having been formed from the £7.7bn merger of Marconi Electronic Systems, GEC's defence electronics and naval shipbuilding division, and British Aerospace (BAe) in 1999.

Within a couple of years the new group was diluting its dependence on UK military spending by buying major defence manufacturers in the US. At the same time BAES was on its guard against further encroachment by US groups in its own back yard. It bought GKN's minority stake in Alvis in 2003, and when General Dynamics of the US offered £309m for Alvis the following year BAES trumped it with an offer of £355m.

Long before Basil Zaharoff the arms business was notorious for corrupt practices. Inevitably a player as big as BAES has been accused of illicit payments to win contracts, particularly in the Middle East. While a series of investigations have been inconclusive, the company has stated that it "regrets and accepts full responsibility for past shortcomings" and has made out-of-court settlements.

Naturally it has worked on its image, devoting great tracts of annual reports to long-winded accounts of governance, compliance and regulatory matters. However, in contrast to European counterparts such as Dassault, BAES has greatly improved its standing in the Transparency International accountability ratings. And it has commissioned research to confirm its wider role in the UK, though an adulatory report from Oxford Economics managed to endorse the importance of the company to the British economy while disclosing almost nothing about the products and services it sells.[54]

It is unlikely that questions over the probity of BAES will have significantly affected its business. Which makes it harder to explain a major setback at the hands of the British government in 2010, when the MoD handed the first phase of its huge contract for new armoured cars to General Dynamics rather than to the British contender. One explanation may be a history of wrangling over cost overruns at projects managed by BAES, such as the Nimrod surveillance aircraft and the Astute-class submarine.

Whatever prompted the MoD decision, the event was particularly ironic. BAES had taken over Alvis, traditional supplier of armoured vehicles to the MoD, for strategic rather than commercial reasons. The MoD action had an inevitable consequence. After concluding that once the last of its Terrier specialist vehicles had been completed in 2014 there was no prospect of new vehicle contracts from the MoD, BAES closed the Newcastle plant. This left the UK division of BAES with just two areas of traditional military business surviving from all the land-based activities it had inherited. One is the support of legacy platforms such as Challenger 2. The other is the supply of munitions to the UK armed forces.

General Dynamics

The armoured vehicle contract confirmed General Dynamics as a significant player in the UK.[55] Yet its activities are a shadow of its British forerunners. Its main product, the Scout SV, is a variant of the ASCOD (Austrian Spanish Cooperation Development) armoured vehicle. It has a Spanish hull, a German engine and transmission, and sights from French-owned Thales UK. The turret is supplied by the local subsidiary of US-based Lockheed Martin. Not only does Lockheed Martin have a significant slice of the Scout project; it also has an important part of the Warrior upgrade.[56]

General Dynamics established its first real foothold in the UK with a major contract from the MoD some years earlier. In 2001 its Canadian subsidiary CDC was awarded a £1.8bn deal to supply the Bowman battlefield radio system for the armed forces. This was a bitter blow for

Thales UK, which had positioned itself as the only domestic contender after buying Racal Electronics for £1.3bn the previous year, and would have undertaken all the work in the UK.

QinetiQ Questions

A significant new presence in the UK military sector in recent years is QinetiQ. Actually, it is an old presence, since at its birth in 2001 the company simply took over the intellectual cream of the MoD's Defence Evaluation and Research Agency (DERA), the largest research organisation in the entire country.

QinetiQ's clumsy sell-off vividly demonstrated the pitfalls of privatisation. Having been allowed to tailor the organisation for sale to the private sector, the managers of QinetiQ reserved for themselves a lavish slice of equity and handed a big stake to Carlyle Group, a private equity outfit whose directors have included John Major,[57] ex-president G.H.W. Bush and former CIA chief George Tenet.[58]

When the Labour government floated QinetiQ on the stock market in 2006 ten managers made an immediate paper profit of over £100m on their paltry stake (under £540,000) and Carlyle Group pocketed a ninefold tax-free gain on its £42m. In return for a modest personal investment executive chairman John Chisholm and chief executive Graham Love each had shares worth over £20m.[59] Within a few months Love, a former public relations hack, had sold some of his stake for almost £6m, and Carlyle Group had cashed in 67.7m shares for £140m.[60]

The National Audit Office verdict was blistering. Because QinetiQ was undervalued and its sale badly timed, taxpayers could have gained "tens of millions more". And accusing the management of "profiteering at the expense of the taxpayer" and the senior management of "behaving dishonourably", the chairman of the Public Accounts Committee observed that the MoD "conducted the deal like an innocent at a table of cardsharps".[61] Unfortunately, the stakes had been the public assets of every citizen in the land, while the winnings went to a tiny bunch of insiders.

There have been no reports of subsequent efforts to reclaim this money for the taxpayer.

Equipment Retreat

At least there was something to show for the QinetiQ give-away, with the MoD still committed to buy important services from a domestic supplier. This is more than can be said for much of the equipment now used by the British Army. From small arms to battlefield radios,[62] and from guided weapons to armoured vehicles, the army's requirements draw heavily on overseas sources. Small arms and equipment come from Heckler & Koch, Herstal and Glock, protected patrol and reconnaissance vehicles (apart from Land Rover) are at best UK-modified US designs, logistics vehicles come from MAN and Oshkosh, and aircraft are sourced mainly from the Continent (Airbus and Aerospatiale) and the US.

Peacetime sourcing from overseas is nothing new, but the pace has speeded up. The Chief Executive of BAES has claimed that it is operating in "the only truly open defence market", competing for British defence projects with US and European companies which are themselves protected in their home markets. The Helsinki European Council meeting of 1999 steered members towards European defence integration and to sourcing in Europe rather than the US. Nevertheless, France supports a thriving defence sector by shopping mainly at home, as does Germany.

The UK has become much more import-dependent in arms but this has not been offset by broader export sales. The Department for Trade (DIT) claimed in July 2019 that the UK had risen to second biggest global arms supplier, with exports of £14bn in 2018.[63] This is simply deceptive. The figures are based on export orders, which can bunch several years together. Moreover, they are heavily weighted toward aircraft, which represent 90 per cent of the total; exports of land-based (and for that matter naval) weaponry are now modest compared with the past.

For reasons best known to itself the DIT is exaggerating. Sources such as the Stockholm International Peace Research Institute (SIPRI) put the UK in sixth place, behind the US, Russia, France, Germany and China, and a little ahead of Spain and Israel, in the league table for international arms supplies. Other sources put the UK still lower.[64]

Arms Trade Iniquity?

Not surprisingly, none of this reassures critics of the arms trade. Organisations such as Campaign Against the Arms Trade (CAAT) rightly claim that exports have put weapons in the wrong hands – such as brutal tyrants in the Middle East. Critics include those who believe that the subsidy of arms exports promotes economic inefficiency and is a strategic and ethical failure.

The ethical case was well put many years ago by Conservative MP Alan Howarth[65] and is difficult to refute, and the plea that if Britain does not do it someone else will – usually the old rival France – does not advance the moral argument.

The practical (inefficiency) case put by commentators like the *FT*'s Samuel Brittan is also difficult to answer. And to point out that other industries, such as agriculture and the financial sector, also receive big subsidies from the taxpayer merely spreads the context of the debate.

Both sets of critics show a touching faith in the power of market forces to reallocate capital and labour into other productive activities in the event of a drastic curtailment of arms exports. What few of the critics propose, however, is that the entire industry should be closed down. It has already shrunk dramatically in recent decades, and on present trends it is set to decline for the foreseeable future.

We should temper a heartfelt welcome for this trend by flagging up the drastic fall in the domestic sourcing of British Army arms purchases. From either economic or strategic perspectives this cannot be sensible. The restoration of Britain's arms industry to anything like its former scale is both very undesirable and very unlikely. But simply ensuring that more of the requirements of the military are met from domestic sources is surely a reasonable aim for any responsible government.

CHAPTER 21

Look Back in Anger

The Thatcher years were the time when it seemed much easier to make money out of money rather than by making things.

Julian Critchley, Some of Us – People Who Did Well under Thatcher[1]

Enduring Legacy

Julian Critchley was an engaging backbench Conservative MP who couldn't resist telling uncomfortable truths to his party from time to time. He outlived the Thatcher years, but only by a decade. If he had survived he could have applied his strictures almost as readily to the administrations that succeeded Thatcher. Her baneful legacy has proved all too enduring, making it difficult for manufacturing to survive and thrive, let alone rediscover long-term growth.

Technical accounts of deindustrialisation simply do not explain the scale and speed of the cataclysm that hit the British economy. People may spend more on services than on goods as they become better off, but this tells us nothing about why the goods they still buy are no longer made here. Measuring the output of the economy in constant rather than current prices merely makes the decline of manufacturing slightly less startling.

This leaves an awful lot of room for other factors. The histories of the companies and industries visited in this book point to some of them. True, many firms, for example in consumer electronics, have been the victims of the evolutionary process familiar to conventional theory – the cycle of growth and decay so beloved of determinists of right and left. But often enough much more has been at work. Many commentators on Britain's deindustrialisation have been quick to attribute blame in areas where it does not belong. And they have been all too ready to absolve individuals, organisations and governments where it does.

This chapter looks briefly at some of the wider developments cited by historians pondering the loss of Britain's industrial heritage. And it focuses on the malign influences that are so often overlooked.

They should prompt concern, dismay – and anger.

Labour Pains

Debate about the challenges that have faced the British economy has often invoked labour relations and attitudes to work. Few commentators adopt the shrill tone of a book published as recently as 2012: "Once they enter the workplace, the British are among the worst idlers in the world."[2] But some still lay the difficulties of the past at the door of employees and the trade unions that have represented them.

Hostility to the unions rose to a crescendo in the early 1980s. The year 1982 saw the director general of the Institute of Directors, Walter Goldsmith, declare: "I am attacking, without apology, the trade union leadership which disgracefully misrepresents its members."[3] He took a lead from Treasury Secretary Leon Brittan: "Misuse of excessive industrial power by the unions is the main…cause of high and rising unemployment."[4]

Such intemperate views paved the way for sweeping changes in the legal position of unions and employees. But even reflective academic research has claimed that the industrial relations reforms of the 1980s raised productivity growth and that the sedate advance of manufacturing in the 1950s, 1960s and 1970s owed something to poor working relations.[5]

The case has always looked distinctly flimsy. During the 1960s Britain actually had quite a respectable industrial relations record. *The Times* reported: "Of the largest industrial nations only Sweden and West Germany had better strike records than the UK during the period 1959-68."[6] And although the incidence of strikes rose sharply in the 1970s Britain was still not far from the average, since industrial unrest was a broad-based international phenomenon.[7]

Foreign companies with British subsidiaries actually had few complaints. A 1977 survey of Scandinavian firms found labour relations in their British subsidiaries to be "excellent", with strikes virtually unknown and an industrial relations climate "as good or better" than at home. Moreover, absenteeism in their UK operations was lower than at home.[8]

That same year a *Der Spiegel* survey of German companies cited the chemicals producer Hoechst, which had 8,000 employees in Britain and only two days' strike loss in 20 years. And Mercedes-Benz: "Our British motor mechanics work as well as those in Germany".[9] The report bluntly attributed underperformance at British companies to stinginess in investing in the newest technology, poor quality management and the bad treatment of staff, claiming that "most British top managers treat their workmen like dirt".[10] Many of the problems that would lead to strikes under British managements were peacefully settled by the works councils that were the norm in German companies.

Remarkably, this favourable take on British industrial relations was sustained right through the 1970s. Towards the end of a supposedly strife-wracked decade the German Chamber of Commerce & Industry was reporting that its 152 members had enjoyed good labour relations, two years of "excellent" productivity and a good return on their operations in Britain.[11]

A few years later the reaction of visitors to the UK was still pretty much the same. "There is no such thing as the British disease. It's complete nonsense, absolute rubbish." This was the robust view of US-based engineering entrepreneur Tim Kelleher, who went on to say: "Our workforce here [UK] is better than any I have come across anywhere in the world."[12]

Easy Copy

Of course, the experience of foreign companies was not necessarily a guide to the whole of industry. Yet by the end of the 1980s a succession of studies was showing that the simplistic assumptions so current earlier in the decade were largely baseless. A paper published in 1988 questioned the supposed link between unionisation and lower productivity.[13] Indeed research showed that strikes have a marginal impact on productivity and unions have actually aided productivity growth.[14]

The truth is that Britain did have assertive unions, but major strikes were concentrated in the public sector, transport services and a relatively narrow spectrum of industry. Car factories, shipyards and parts of mechanical engineering suffered recurrent conflict, but in other industries – textiles, chemicals, electronics, arms and aircraft, food processing, non-ferrous metals, paper, printing (aside from newspapers), oil refining, and countless other trades – stoppages were rare. Even the steel workers put up with years of savage attrition before walking out in 1980 – their first national stoppage in half a century.

While cars and steel suffered, there is no tangible evidence that total GDP was directly cut by labour stoppages. But for a popular press looking for easy sensation the strife in town halls and car factories made better copy than the peace more customary in great tracts of British industry.

It has often taken a foreign eye to offer a detached perspective. Though the focus of his 1996 study was the steel industry, Japanese economist Harukiyo Hasegawa's account of changes in industrial relations applied much more widely.[15] He described industrial relations in British Steel as traditionally "'co-operative' on the basis of industrial democracy, namely the co-existence of capital and labour". But by the 1990s this had been replaced by "powerful managerial authority".

The ultimate drivers identified by Hasegawa were, of course, negative – the legislative attack on the unions, their weaker financial position and changes in the attitudes of members, reflecting the pressure of high unemployment created by the "long-running economic decline".[16]

For the historians who attribute shortfalls in UK economic performance to labour difficulties a big question lingers. If these were indeed a major drag on industry in 1945–79, why has the economy not performed vastly better and manufacturing not taken off since union power was subjugated in the 1980s?

Tax Tantrums

Another preoccupation for some historians trying to explain economic underperformance was high taxation. This was said to discourage enterprise and "crowd out" the wealth-creating private sector.

According to the Institute for Fiscal Studies, government revenue increased quite sharply in the 1960s, rising from about a third of GDP in 1964 to 42 per cent in 1970. Over the following 15 years, however, the tax share fluctuated "without any obvious trend up or down".[17] There were sharp spikes in the mid-1970s, after the first oil shock, and there were big jumps during the Thatcher recessions of the 1980s. But by the end of the century the trend had long been relatively flat. Meanwhile, the tax take in other EU countries had risen, leaving the UK a relatively low-tax country.

This still leaves the issue of tax rates on higher earners, said to include the country's "wealth creators". At the end of the 1970s the top rates of tax were what appeared to be a startlingly high 80–90 per cent. But these were marginal rates, set in 1939, applying only to a small proportion of income and levied on a tiny minority of taxpayers. Since there were plenty of ways in which income, profits and rent could be retained by entrepreneurs, there is no tangible evidence that they acted as a drag on the economy.

Objectors to high marginal rates of income tax claimed they would prompt an exodus of top talent from British industry. Yet a study by the Institute for Fiscal Studies in the 1970s was able to find only a single case.[18]

More recently, a rather candid director of Shell put the executive rewards issue nicely in perspective. After criticism for the size of his remuneration retiring chief executive Jeroen van der Veer conceded: "You have to realise, if I had been paid 50 per cent more, I would not have done it [the job] better. If I had been paid 50 per cent less, *I would not have done it worse.*"[19] [my italics]

Thanks to obsessive coverage in the *Sunday Times*, the crowding out thesis enjoyed a brief vogue in the late 1970s. The problem was that it treated the economy like a cake of fixed size, where growth in one sector can only be at the expense of another. This is not how the world, or the economy, actually works.

Crowding out did not survive the realities of the 1980s, when the emergence of vast underutilised resources in the form of unemployed labour and silent factories (before they were demolished) did not prompt a surge in manufacturing. Indeed, just the opposite.

State Intervention

There has been state involvement in the economy for centuries. The 1960s saw cautious intervention to prompt further restructuring. Such policies are often described as the promotion of "national champions" or "picking winners", though it is difficult to find any such term in the official pronouncements of the time. The industries included electrical engineering, aluminium smelting, bearing manufacture, papermaking, computers and cars.

Some of these initiatives – notably the formation of the enlarged GEC – were successful. Yet the total commitment of state funds via the Industrial Reorganisation Corporation – around £100m – was limited, and often recouped through subsequent asset sales.[20]

The 1970s brought more intervention, though this time the beneficiaries included some distress cases. Most were eventually gathered together in the National Enterprise Board. Excluding British Leyland, which had cost the state £846m, Rolls-Royce (£234m) and Alfred Herbert (£44m), the total book value of about 60 small and medium businesses was just £67m.[21]

True, considerably larger funds went to support the car industry, steel, shipbuilding, aircraft manufacture and computers. But even before privatisation proceeds the interventions of the 1970s and 1980s probably cost no more than £10bn – a modest total compared with the hundreds of billions for bailing out the financial system a generation later.

In all this, Britain was far from alone. Except in the early 1950s its industrial subsidies were not even the largest among comparable countries.[22] For much of the 1960s and 1970s subventions as a proportion of GDP in the UK were around 2–2.5 per cent – similar to the levels in France and Italy. Perhaps surprisingly, the figure was not that much more than in Germany, where industrial subsidies were supplemented by tax concessions averaging 1.8 per cent of GDP in 1975–85.[23]

Of course, the fact that Britain was not exceptional in its use of industrial subsidies does not deny that their removal may have speeded up deindustrialisation. But it does mean their disappearance is not much help in explaining why the decline of industry has been so much more severe in the UK than elsewhere.

It would be wrong to leave the issue of state intervention without at least a brief reference to protection. This has typically taken the form of import tariffs, import quotas and voluntary export restraints (VERs).

For much of the twentieth century Britain levied tariffs on a range of imports. The most sweeping were the McKenna Duties introduced during the First World War and other tariffs and levies came in under imperial preference in the 1930s. Some were still in place at the start of the 1970s. Following Britain's accession to the EEC in 1973, however, the tariffs on goods from the European Community were steadily reduced to zero.

Clearly this would have added to the competitive pressure on UK manufacturers. Tariffs had been declining for many years, however, and by the 1970s there were generally at a fairly low level. Again, their gradual removal does not explain the scale and speed of the deindustrialisation that occurred in the 1980s and 1990s.

Investment Anaemia, Training Tribulations

Investment activity in Britain in the first couple of decades after the Second World War was quite respectable. In the 1960s and the early 1970s the rate of addition to the capital stock averaged almost 4 per cent a year, well below Germany (over 6 per cent) and France (8 per cent) but close to the US at 4.4 per cent. Even in the second half of the 1970s the UK record at 2.1 per cent was surprisingly close to Germany's 2.5 per cent.[24]

This changed abruptly. The 1980s saw virtually no overall growth in manufacturing investment, and by 1991 the capital equipment available to each worker in UK manufacturing was two-thirds of the German equivalent, less than half that in France and 20 per cent of the Dutch figure.[25] Over the 1989–2007 period annual investment growth in UK industry was just 0.8 per cent. Something had changed, profoundly.

Industrial training was another area of major setback. In 1964 a sensible non-partisan approach[26] replaced the traditional informal arrangements. The new system involved industrial training boards (ITBs), financed by levies on the companies in each sector. The ITBs were eventually undermined by three developments. First was the arrival of laissez faire individualism in the 1980s. Second was the huge contraction of the workforce under the impact of the two recessions that started in that decade. And third was the desperate corporate need to cut costs during those recessions. Before long the results were obvious. By 1991 the *Financial Times* was reporting a huge gulf between Britain, which had 65,000 manufacturing apprentices, and Germany, with ten times as many.[27]

Investment in training had gone the way of investment in plant and equipment; both contributed to the abrupt collapse of industry from the 1980s on.

Serenity and Mayhem

It is claimed that economic management has had only a limited impact on the long run status and standing of industry.[28] This may be true of the first three decades after the war but can it be argued for the period since?

Between 1945 and 1973 the UK enjoyed growth in every single year. This was accompanied by moderate inflation, a decent balance in international trade and very low levels of unemployment. Because expansion was sedate, the record was derided on the political left. And because it embodied a consensus Keynesian approach it has been scorned on the right.

Yet in many respects the record was remarkably good. Outside the older sectors such as textiles and shipbuilding, the broad structure of industry remained intact. Major casualties such as Rolls-Royce were rescued by government. Rather startlingly, a future Thatcherite extolled Britain as "a model of [economic and social] perfection".[29]

The Labour government of 1974–79 pursued traditional principles of economic governance, rescuing lame ducks and fostering cautious industrial restructuring. This was despite constraints attaching to a largely unnecessary[30] IMF loan in 1976. An exaggerated response by both right and left continues to overstate the scale of the Fund's assistance. It was just £2.3bn,[31] of which only half was ever drawn down.[32]

Out in the real world 1976 was, on some measures, Britain's best, an "all-time peak for national well-being",[33] and a record high in its "genuine progress indicator".[34] Things can't have been so terrible for business either. Legendary entrepreneur James Goldsmith extolled Britain as "the last bastion of good old-fashioned buccaneering private enterprise".[35]

All this changed in the 1980s. Under the banner of monetarism – briefly in vogue in the US and the UK but nowhere else – the Thatcher government abrogated the broader responsibilities that had hitherto gone with the job. A fixation with money supply, coupled with soaring interest rates and deflationary budgeting, plunged the economy into a recession of exceptional severity. The result was the demise of hundreds of companies, thousands of factories and millions of jobs. About a third of UK industrial capacity disappeared.[36]

Even in industries not hit quite so hard by recession the climate ushered in during the 1980s opened the way to pressures on individual companies that proved incredibly damaging. Despite their evident destructiveness, government economic policies made few concessions to the crises in industry. The crude mantra was: "there is no alternative" (TINA).

Triumphalism and Myth

Refighting old wars is best left to hobbyists. But the 1980s was such a critical point in the industrial history of Britain that a return to the battlefield cannot really be avoided. In negotiating the minefields it is surprisingly easy to avoid party invective, simply because the most cogent critiques often came not from the Opposition but from within the Conservative Party itself and from its erstwhile friends in business.

The Thatcherite approach was contested early on: 364 professional economists of varying persuasions publicly censured Chancellor Geoffrey Howe's savagely deflationary 1981 budget, and warned of dire consequences.[37] They were, of course, right. Unemployment raced on up, industry continued to collapse and it took nearly a decade for manufacturing output to struggle back to its 1978–79 levels.

With triumphalism reigning in Tory ranks, it took courage to defy Julian Critchley's "garagistes"[38] – the direct successors to Stanley Baldwin's 1918 contingent of "hard faced men who looked as if they had done well out of the war".[39]

In his elegant demolition of Thatcherism, *Dancing with Dogma*, Tory MP Ian Gilmour puzzled over "the Thatcherites' persistent belittling of the importance of manufacturing industry".[40] He was perhaps thinking of Jock Bruce-Gardyne MP, who dismissed manufacturing as "the tie-clip making sector".[41] Gilmour blamed "very few Thatcherites knowing anything about industry".[42] Jim Prior, a rare industrialist in Thatcher's first Cabinet, took a withering view of his Treasury colleagues: "None of them had any experience of running a whelk stall, let alone a decent-sized company. Their attitude to manufacturing industry bordered on the contemptuous."[43]

Even more pointed comment came from Conservative backbenchers. By the mid-1980s Hugh Dykes MP publicly despaired of a "quite chilling picture of economic decline".[44] Sir Peter Tapsell angrily denounced "mass unemployment, industrial output lower than it was six years ago, the first deficit on Britain's manufactured trade, the lowest sterling exchange rates and almost uniquely high real interest rates". He blamed "a small group of theorists who have hijacked economic policy. Having produced disaster, they proclaim success".[45] Ted Heath condemned the "ghastly economic legacy" Thatcher would bequeath to her successor.[46]

As for the casualties of this legacy, the government worked up a fine line in victim blaming. For Norman Tebbit, chairman of the Conservative Party, the economic wounds of the north of England were "self-inflicted".[47]

In the sheltered south of the country, the noisiest bastion of support for Thatcherism was the City, where a new breed of overpaid economists was vying for the headlines. The City enjoyed exceptional favours during the Thatcher years, and with a couple of honourable exceptions its "teenage scribblers" – Nigel Lawson's contemptuous term for the analysts[48] – fawned on the hand that fed them.

They might not have shared his eventual enthusiasm for the European Monetary System (EMS), but Jim O'Neill of Swiss Bank spoke for many when he described himself as "a Lawson freak".[49] And his predecessor at Goldman Sachs, Gavyn Davies, was later to make the lame confession: "Many of us believed a miracle had happened."[50] He had perhaps taken a lead from Kevin Boakes at Greenwell Montagu, who fantasised about "Britain's productivity miracle".[51] Nor was hyperbole restricted to City hothouses. Over at the supposedly independent Institute for Fiscal Studies, director Bill Robinson was daydreaming about the "continuing British supply side miracle".[52]

What Robinson and so many City commentators were getting excited about was an apparent upturn in manufacturing productivity. Unfortunately, this turned out to be no more than a batting average effect: if you drop the slower members of your team, the average score goes up.

For a short time it was superficially impressive – provided you did not worry about the total score – but how this tawdry "miracle" was going to be sustained was never clear. It turned out that 95 per cent of the belated investment revival between 1985 and 1991 went not into manufacturing but into services, nearly half into the City. Yet as a share of GDP the export of those very services that were to replace manufacturing as Britain's bread and butter actually *fell*.[53]

It was left to Neil MacKinnon at Yamaichi Securities to restore a shred of professional integrity to his calling: "Talk of a supply-side miracle was a load of flannel. The government started to believe its own rhetoric."[54] As it all went hopelessly wrong and the Lawson boom blew up, Geoffrey Dicks of the London Business School put it bluntly: "A lot of forecasters were trying to monitor what was going on; very few thought that things would turn out as badly as they did."[55]

Fairy Tales and Courage

Yet, the fairy-tale miracle lived on long after it should have been discreetly buried. City commentator Tim Congdon dusted it off for an article in *The Times* ("A Christmas Miracle") in the mid-1990s.[56] And the moth-eaten relic was disinterred as recently as February 2018 when Bernard Jenkin MP was fantasising about Brexit.[57]

Some of the most trenchant protests at the wrecking of industry came, appropriately, from industrialists. But not, at first, from the Institute of Directors, unkindly known as the club for laundrette owners and garage proprietors. In 1981 Director General Walter Goldsmith hailed the unemployment and industrial collapse sweeping the country as signs of a "productivity miracle".[58] A decade later, however, his successor, Peter Morgan, was reduced to blaming the "pernicious influence of senior civil servants" for what he had to call "the calamitous errors" of the Conservative government.[59]

More telling was the position of the CBI. At its 1980 conference Director General Terry Beckett – a brilliant former head of Ford UK – won a standing ovation for his "bare knuckle fight" over government policy.[60] The 1984 conference heard spirited calls to re-establish manufacturing industry as a vital component of the economy,[61] a view reiterated the following year by the Association of British Chambers of Commerce.[62]

Individual industrialists felt even less constrained, an embittered businessman speaking for many in the early 1980s: "The trouble with this lot is they think that if you cut industry's balls off they'll grow again."[63] Arnold Weinstock of GEC joined ICI's John Harvey-Jones in dismissing as "absolute rubbish" the government claim that the growth and development of service industries would compensate for the loss of production and jobs through the collapse of manufacturing.[64]

And every so often the press was enlivened by denunciations of "the massive and damaging interference by Thatcherite interventions in the economy" from intrepid entrepreneurs like Bill Abbotts, a manufacturer of computer-controlled industrial machinery.[65]

Barely had the recession of the first half of the 1980s eased than industry was struggling with renewed crisis. Believing his own ludicrous pretensions to be an economic wonder-worker[66] the Chancellor had stoked a credit-fuelled mini-boom and then had to hike interest rates. For Gilmour, in *Dancing with Dogma*, he had achieved the grotesque combination of booming consumption, weak investment and surging trade deficits.[67]

Interest rates rocketed, and stayed high to sustain the foolhardy and politically driven decision in 1990 to join the Exchange Rate Mechanism (ERM) of the European Monetary System (EMS). The resulting downturn brought more factory closures, surging unemployment and further destruction of the country's industrial base.

The onset of yet another recession prompted fresh anger. For the *Financial Times*, "given the severity of the recession and the clear culpability of the government" this was not surprising.[68] Much of the resentment focused on trade and industry secretary Peter Lilley, "a man of unbelievable arrogance and extraordinarily rigid views [with] a very low opinion of British manufacturers".[69] Those struggling manufacturers were not assuaged by Lilley's half-apology: "A foolish impression was created that we were not interested in manufacturing industry. That was wrong."[70]

In 1991 CBI head Brian Corby voiced fierce criticism of the government's economic policies,[71] and pleas for the survival of manufacturing were often repeated over the following months and years.

The government's apologists were unsleeping. Never having been near a factory floor was no deterrent to Charterhouse Tilney's Richard Jeffrey, who breezily opined: "It's so simple when you're in the CBI, but that's not how the economy works."[72] Such sniping from the cosseted world of money management rarely silenced the protests of those on the front line of wealth creation. Infuriated by the remarks of former trade and industry secretary David Young that Britain could subsist as an ice cream economy, Neil Johnson at the battered Engineering Employers Federation exploded: "Many companies are in total despair at the apparent ignorance of government towards industry."[73]

Rhineland Rumours

Meanwhile, some commentators had gone back to fantasy-building. As chief secretary to the Treasury, John Major had set the ball rolling in 1988 with the claim that Britain was undergoing "an economic miracle similar to that enjoyed by West Germany in the 1960s".[74] The following year saw business economist Douglas MacWilliams predict that UK living standards could overtake those of Germany by the end of the century.[75] For Thatcher adviser Douglas Hague, Germany, along with the other heavily industrialised "Germanics" – Austria and Switzerland – was the "odd man out" in a Europe moving away from manufacturing.[76]

A new theme was emerging. The fantasists were contrasting an outdated "Rhineland" model – dominated by manufacturing and doomed to slow growth – with a spritely deindustrialised Anglo-Saxon alternative. Economic guru Brian Reading pronounced Germany the "sick man of Europe".[77] Douglas MacWilliams assured his faithful that Mercedes-Benz and Porsche were "losing out".[78] Centre for Policy Studies apparatchik Sheila Lawlor deplored a "sclerotic" Germany, whose carmakers were moving abroad in pursuit of lower wages.[79]

Frowning across the Rhine at Ludwigshafen, Bill Robinson, now adviser to Norman Lamont, tut-tutted at BASF's magnificent chemicals complex as outmoded and irrelevant to the future of the European economies.[80] Tory MP Teresa Gorman wrote off the German economy as "geared to the past, dominated by old-fashioned heavy industry selling to sluggish European markets".[81] Imprimatur was bestowed by unrepentant monetarist Patrick Minford, who attacked the "myth of German industrial invincibility" and predicted the wasting away of its industry and jobs.[82]

German policymakers took not the slightest notice of such nonsense. They were busy taking aboard an entire impoverished country called East Germany. The new Germany turned out to be the old Germany. To the chagrin of Charles Powell,[83] erstwhile foreign policy adviser to Margaret

Thatcher, it remained a benign industrial and economic giant, the world's biggest exporter and a triumphant leader across vast swathes of industry, ancient and modern. Its manufacturers confirmed the insight of French thinker Jean-Pierre Chevènement: "There are no condemned industrial sectors, only outdated technologies."[84]

Contrary to the beliefs of a management consultant as seasoned as Charles Handy, most industries nowadays require considerable intellectual input. Handy had commented approvingly that in dumping manufacturing in favour of services in the 1980s the UK moved into activities "where brains count more than brawn".[85]

Somehow, BASF has gone on to be the world's largest and strongest chemical company. Mercedes-Benz is in the front rank of global vehicle manufacture. And Porsche – now owned by Volkswagen, the world's largest car company – is still the world's most profitable carmaker.

As for those other "Germanics" who were misguidedly fostering their manufacturing, Austria's average income is now a third higher than Britain's. And Switzerland's is double that of the UK, thanks to a manufacturing output per head *three times* that of Britain.[86]

Sleepy Recovery

Once the British economy was in the sleepier hands of Ken Clarke as Chancellor, it could begin its recovery from the Lawson/Major/Lamont debacles. Though it was spared the macroeconomic mess of the Thatcher era, however, manufacturing was still vulnerable to the pressures unleashed by financial deregulation, the erosion of sound corporate governance and the corruption of traditional commercial mores.

This went hand in hand with the philosophy of non-intervention enshrined during the Thatcher years. The Major government remained fatalistic in the face of developments that were obviously detrimental to the country's manufacturing future. Much of the ruinous damage to rolling stock manufacture and electrical engineering from privatisation of rail and power generation was played out in the dying days of the Major administration.

There were fewer major casualties under the 1997–2010 Labour government, partly because so much had already gone. Nevertheless, early in its tenure there were two big losses in semiconductors. These were the Siemens microchip plant on north Tyneside in 1998 and a similar Fujitsu operation at Newton Aycliff soon after. These disasters came to epitomise Labour's industrial policies – or lack of them.

The immediate culprits were high interest rates and an overvalued pound, but the underlying cause was the hollowing-out of electronics over the previous two decades. The episode aroused concern that because it had accepted so much of the Thatcherite ethos the government was much too complacent about such erosions of industrial capacity. The suspicion was inflamed by comments from the City's Gavyn Davies, now a government confidant, that job losses of up to 500,000 were "a fact of life in the battle to keep the lid on inflation".[87]

Hot Air

There were other industrial setbacks and by the 2000s even moderate ministers were admitting to errors in the Labour approach. After a year in which manufacturing had lost 150,000 jobs, industry secretary Patricia Hewitt confessed: "In our first term we quite inadvertently gave the impression that British manufacturing did not matter...we gave the impression that manufacturing was not a priority." And she criticised the fashionable texts of the dot-com economy, *Living on Thin Air*[88] – "so much hot air" – and *The Weightless World*,[89] which had informed a vacuous government White Paper on the knowledge economy.[90]

Yet the conventional wisdom on manufacturing remained negative. After a visit in 2006 to the industrial wastelands of York (once a great railway engineering and confectionery centre), writer Andrew Martin recounted the insouciance of Martin Weale, director of the National Institute of Economic and Social Research: "Most people would say it was a good thing that we switched to services early, that we didn't make the mistake of hanging on to our manufacturing at all costs like Germany and Japan."[91]

There is no evidence whatever that Germany or Japan have in some sense stubbornly clung on to their industry. What they have done is continue to afford it sensible support and encourage it to flourish. Weale's attitude was looking distinctly out of touch when the global financial crisis struck only 18 months later.

By Labour's closing years it was clear that if it wanted to conserve manufacturing it had little to be proud of. True, up until the financial crisis there had been no recurrence of the devastation of the Thatcher/ Major years. Nevertheless, there had been some appalling episodes. These included the extinction of what was left of GEC and ICI and big factory closures by Massey Ferguson, Peugeot Citroen and Ford. Not surprisingly, manufacturing output stagnated and its share of GDP fell as fast as ever.

As a country which had allowed deindustrialisation to run rampant and had become so dependent on the financial sector, Britain was naturally among the hardest hit by the 2008 credit crunch. Despite a breezy dismissal by former *Economist* editor Bill Emmott,[92] the economic crisis was all too real. Nor was it, as Labour peer Lord Desai improbably claimed, merely "a middle-class recession in the south".[93] When manufacturing output and employment slumped, the worst affected regions were once again the West Midlands, the North East and the North West.

Recession Restricted

Paradoxically, Labour dealt much better with the crisis in the City than it did with the decay of manufacturing. Thanks to Prime Minister Gordon Brown and Chancellor Alistair Darling the situation received a prompt, imaginative and radical response. Measures included a subsidised scrap-and-buy scheme to support the car industry. They worked, and the lasting damage to industry was much less grievous than in the Thatcher/Major recessions.

The dangerous instability of the finance sector nevertheless rekindled a forlorn search for alternatives. "I am unashamedly talking about the reindustrialisation of the British economy", leading government minister Peter Mandelson suddenly declared at the end of 2009. But he added: "Not by going back to the old smokestack manufacturing past; we know we can't turn the clock back."[94] At a time when steel, shipbuilding, and electrical and mechanical engineering were still going strong on the Continent (where nobody scoffed at "metal-bashing" or "smokestack" industries) his qualification signalled an administration still in thrall to the dot-com idiocies that had floored GEC.

Worse, it signalled the malign influence of the government adviser who had recently told industrialists and union leaders: "Manufacturing and engineering have no real value…only financial services and the City have any real value [and] must be supported at all costs. The rest of the country can be turned over to tourism."[95]

When the coalition government took over in 2010 at least the rhetoric improved, with Chancellor George Osborne invoking a March of the Makers in his 2011 budget. Unfortunately, rhetoric was all there was. Despite the strong case for industrial promotion made by business secretary Vince Cable, funding was reduced, and even for deserving cases such as Sheffield Forgemasters financial assistance was cut. Only when the Conservative government that took office in 2015 was faced with the real possibility of a terminal collapse of the steel industry did the Treasury make a panicky intervention. And the longer-term results of that episode remain distinctly uncertain.

Privatisation Perils

An oddly neglected aspect of the privatisation programmes of the 1980s and 1990s is the profound damage they did to Britain's industries. The effects worked through in several ways.

First, even before they had been sold off, ministers in the Thatcher and Major governments encouraged the breaking of long-standing links between state-owned industries – railways, power supply, road freight, road passenger transport, aviation and defence organisations – and their traditional UK suppliers. Their policies were quite different to typical practice in Britain's Continental counterparts, such as Belgium, France, Germany, Italy, Sweden and Switzerland, where railways and power generation routinely look to local sources for their plants, equipment and services.

Once the public industries had been sold – often to become sleepy quasi-monopolies – there were no restraints on ditching the cause of buying British. Particularly egregious examples were British Airways over its airliner orders in the late 1980s, British Telecom's major upgrade at the turn of the century and railway rolling stock investment.

Second, the very prospect of privatisation could stop the buyers dead in their tracks. Either there was a Whitehall decree to halt new investment or potential owners in the management did not want to move the price of their prospective purchase against them. The worst case was the railways, where rolling stock orders dried up for years on end. There was a similar impact in electricity generation, where a chaotic approach to power station renewal killed off a large slice of UK manufacturing capacity. Lorry and bus manufacturing were also hit by a buyers' strike ahead of privatisation.

Third, the way industries were privatised often had damaging implications for domestic suppliers. Management buyouts were a convenient way for the state to dump its assets, but often they were just cosy insider deals which acted as stalking horses for overseas manufacturers looking to buy UK market share. A particularly egregious example involved Leyland Bus.

Damning Indictment

"Overall, the City has been one of the main drivers of the decline in UK engineering." This is Tom Brown's damning indictment in *Tragedy & Challenge*, his perceptive account of the fate of British engineering.[96] What has been true for engineering in particular has been true for manufacturing as a whole, and Tom Brown's book is an invaluable corrective to much of the comment from gullible journalists over the years.[97]

The City's malign influence goes back at least as far as the return to the gold standard in 1925 "to make the pound look the dollar in the face".[98] An exchange rate wrenched from its post-war rate of $3.40 to its 1914 parity of nearly $5 to the pound devastated Britain's export industries.

The charge that high finance has caused grave damage to individual companies is more recent. Until the 1980s the City was a mix of reasonably useful activities. They included trade finance, commercial insurance, commodity broking, bullion dealing, ship broking, gilts trading, bond dealing and securities, and currency dealing. It played a minor role in raising finance for industry. And it provided an occasional forum for company flotations, mergers or takeovers.

The 1980s brought profound change to the operating environment for businesses, corporate governance and, above all, the latitude within which financial players could operate. This was not just a matter of regulation or legislation. It was also a question of business climate – what constituted legitimate activity as much as what was licit.

Many practices that would once have been regarded as unethical, and discouraged through moral suasion, became acceptable. Management fads with little empirical basis became accepted wisdom. Otherwise sober journalists were absurdly impressed by the status of the City and suspended judgement.[99]

The pivotal moment was the deregulation and liberalisation that accompanied the Big Bang in 1986. Traditional activities continued but were joined by newer variants. Abysmal investment records and exorbitant fees did not stop fund managers becoming vastly influential. As did the brokers who scrambled for their custom and the grandstanding analysts who strayed so eagerly into political partisanship.

Merchant banks were taken over by investment banks and became much more aggressive in their pursuit of business. This was emulated by, of all things, the retail banks. Swept up in the frenzy after Big Bang, the high street banks ditched their traditional role as quietly supportive providers of liquidity to worthy industrial enterprises in a kind of mimicry of investment banks. Their traditional approach to business – cautious and constructive – was replaced by a grotesquely aggressive pursuit of new business. Among the results was the bullying of small commercial borrowers by the Royal Bank of Scotland,[100] and an approach by others that strayed into the criminal.

Venture capitalists, hedge funds, private equity partnerships and other players have all made their pitch in an increasingly busy field, usually with detrimental effects on manufacturing businesses. Often they have simply put a smoother face on what used to be called crude asset stripping.

Among the most destructive newcomers are activist investors. Their dismal role has been neatly summarised by Terry Smith, an unusually successful fund manager.[101] First, take a stake in a company using short-term derivatives (ie someone else's money). Next, noisily pressure the target into unwanted, unnecessary and expensive actions that will drive up the short-term share price but cripple the firm's long-term prospects. Finally, take profit on your initial stake and walk away from the wreckage.

One of the main results of City pressure has been the short-term focus on profit that has blighted the sensible development of so many major businesses. The intellectual underpinning has been one of the great illusions of the age, shareholder value.

Shareholder value was a fad that took flight in the parallel universe of business schools in the 1980s. It has been repeatedly brought back to earth[102] by John Kay[103] and had a silver stake plunged through its heart by none other than Jack Welch, management icon of the age. Repenting his former pursuit of something suspiciously like shareholder value at General Electric, Welch described it as "the dumbest idea in the world…a result, not a strategy [because] your main constituencies are your employees, customers and products".[104]

M&A Mayhem

A pernicious myth of recent decades is the notion that the surge in merger and acquisition (M&A) activity since the Big Bang has been a constructive development, helping with the efficient distribution of capital. For Professor Karel Williams of Manchester University, "[h]ostile takeovers do not defend industries in decline or bring benefits to shareholders in the long term".[105] The stories of many of the firms described in this book show that buyouts, mergers, takeovers and forced restructurings have often been profoundly destructive.

Among the first to sound the alarm was Hector Laing of United Biscuits, who warned the 1988 CBI conference that UK companies were uniquely vulnerable to takeovers. The openness of the Stock Exchange meant it had become both stock and company market, with a double price list for shares – the trading price and the takeover price. He predicted, accurately, that Britain was in danger of following the US route of highly leveraged buyouts, making it very difficult to finance productive investment in the businesses involved.[106]

A couple of years later corporate affairs minister John Redwood – a fervent Thatcherite – made a surprising observation: "Takeovers are good news for shareholders in the target companies and for advisers [but] evidence is rising that, except in the very short term, takeovers can all too often damage the wealth of shareholders of the bidding company rather than improve it."[107] And a major survey by accountancy firm KPMG (which shabbily withheld publication of the report because of its own ambitions in M&A) found that 30 per cent of cross-border deals failed to add value to their participants and 53 per cent actually destroyed it.[108]

A close relative of M&A is the management buyout (MBO). This came into vogue in the 1980s, not least as an expedient whereby the government dumped publicly owned assets into the private sector. In theory MBOs will unleash the entrepreneurial spirit of managers. In practice they have often been examples of financial engineering, putting a lot of money in the pockets of a few insiders.[109] Some of the most egregious instances involved the rail, bus, shipbuilding and defence industries. The ink has barely been dry on some MBOs before the new owners have sold the business on, often to overseas interests looking to buy UK market share. The result is usually the same – a painful reduction in UK industrial capacity.

Does It All Matter?

Does the decimation of industry matter? Are we – as a former Labour politician put it – just mourning for the dinosaurs?[110]

The answers are, respectively, yes and no. The demise of many of Britain's manufacturers, and with them the industries they served, matters intensely. The distress to those directly involved matters. The damage to local and regional economies matters. And the damage to the long-term economic viability of the UK matters.

It is a commonplace that the shattering of the economic base in areas whose identity was closely bound up with industry has lasting consequences. The contemporary effects may have been worst in the 1980s and 1990s but the legacy endures in high unemployment – camouflaged through statistical window dressing[111] – disability, ill health and poverty.

One of the striking features of the legacy of industrial collapse is its sheer persistence. The areas with the highest levels of workless households still tend to be former industrial powerhouses lying north of a line drawn from the Severn estuary to the Wash.[112] They include Glasgow, Liverpool, Hull, Birmingham and Wolverhampton.[113]

Districts which have experienced both the collapse of coal mining and its associated activities, such as South Wales and the North East, have continued to generate terrible stories of demoralisation and despair.[114] In the haunting words of artist Grayson Perry, after a visit to Sunderland, "[t]hough heavy industry has gone, the emotional scaffolding is still there".[115]

Perhaps the most enduring memorial is the death of aspiration and civic cohesion. The decay of civil society was eloquently evoked by historian Neil Ferguson in his 2012 Reith Lectures.[116] But for him the causes were state education and welfare dependency. For many of his listeners this completely missed the crucial link with the wellspring of that dependency – the collapse of traditional forms of employment and their associated ways of life in former industrial areas. The consequences of deindustrialisation run far beyond the loss of well-paid jobs and economic security. The deeper wounds lie in the collapse of what Ferguson aptly termed "working class associational life" and "working class civil society".

In a typically thoughtful piece for *The Guardian* in 2009 Jonathan Glancey neatly invoked the consequences of the Labour government's superficial approach to rebalancing the economy towards manufacturing: "How we will become a high-tech neomanufacturing nation, given the decline of industrial culture, is a mystery. Manufacturing is not simply about brute or emergency economics. It's also about a *sense of involvement and achievement engendered by shaping and crafting useful, interesting, well-designed things.*"[117] [my italics]

The Kindness of Strangers

This is not the place to analyse the merits of the services that have so inadequately supplanted manufacturing. But the decline of manufacturing certainly requires a brief look at the more obvious financial consequences.

One is the persistence of vast deficits on overseas trade. The collapse of industrial capacity in the 1980s pushed UK trade into its first shortfall on manufactures since the Industrial Revolution. Chancellor Nigel Lawson brushed this aside with the complacent assertion that the export of services would make up for the deficit in manufactures. He might also have conceded that oil exports were providing a hugely convenient mask for the adverse trend.

Neither services nor oil did the trick. Lawson's legacy has ballooned. Income from overseas investments helped for a while, but in recent years even this seems to have turned negative. Since 2013 the UK has been running a current account deficit of 5 per cent of GDP, much the largest for any industrialised country.[118]

Moreover, the quality of the income stream from services is problematic. About half the export revenue comprises the overseas earnings of the City, which the financial crisis has shown to be a dangerously volatile and unreliable focus of economic activity. In no sense is it a reassuring alternative to the export of manufactures by which Britain has, for centuries, earned its bread.

Because of the sluggish trend since the 1980s, the UK has one of the lowest levels of exports per capita in Europe. Underlying this are still more sobering statistics. In manufacturing per head, the UK is only twenty-sixth in the world, and for manufacturing as a share of GDP it has slumped to 118th.[119]

The payments deficit has been covered partly by the sale of UK businesses to overseas companies. More than half of UK quoted companies are now controlled by overseas interests.[120] Clearly there is a finite limit to this sell-off.

Does Britain now depend on "the kindness of strangers" who lend to the UK on a short-term basis?[121] This view is not refuted by the observation that much of the deficit has been financed not by borrowing but by the sale of overseas assets by British investors,[122] since this is simply the other side of the same coin.

History tells us that domestic residents are no more likely than strangers to show kindness to Britain. There is no evidence that they would be any slower to withdraw their kindness – by keeping their assets overseas or transferring their liquid assets abroad – in the event of a crisis of confidence or political developments they disapprove of. It happened in 1976, it happened in 1992 (the Black Wednesday fiasco) and it could easily happen again.

Make Peace with the Past?

Much of the worst damage to Britain's industrial base could have been avoided. True, there may have been technical influences which explain a part of the process and manufacturing would likely have lost some of its relative importance. But the stories of many companies and their industries make it clear that the speed and extent of the disaster can be laid at very different doors.

These were the dreadful mishandling of the economy in the 1980s, dogmatic privatisations in the 1980s and 1990s, and the malign role of the City. Because it has been less doctrinaire, short-term economic management has since improved. Because the response was bold but deft, the 2008 financial crisis caused far less damage than it might have. Privatisations have dried up because there is little left to sell off. But the destructive influence of the City continues unabated.

For the near future the biggest uncertainty obviously relates to Britain's relations with our biggest trading partner, the European Union. The short-term problems that Brexit could pose for manufacturing operations heavily dependent on trade with the EU have been frequently aired. Tariffs on imports of components and exports of finished products will put immense pressure on manufacturing operations that are already marginal.

Brexit could, however, be an opportunity to make belated amends for the follies of Thatcherism and the neo-liberal blight it passed to its successors. In particular, it could open the door to a return of interventionism of an appropriate kind. Future governments should feel much less fenced in by the supposed constraints of EU rules – though they have often been overstated – and could set about serious programmes to foster manufacturing industry.

There are a number of obvious areas, many of which have been visited in this book. Domestically oriented public-sector purchasing needs to be urgently reinstated, if only to bring it up to the levels of our Continental neighbours. Beneficiaries would include motor vehicles, shipbuilding, railway rolling stock, aircraft assembly, armaments and pharmaceuticals.

The restoration of basic industries is a perfectly reasonable aim. There is an urgent ethical and economic need for greater self-sufficiency in the processing of raw materials, particularly scrap and waste – for example in paper, plastics, and non-ferrous and ferrous metals, where dependence on overseas processors is vast and growing.

In engineering, the motor industry cries out for attention. The big carmakers, who import finished products from the Continent and the Far East on a huge scale, should be prevailed upon to assemble in Britain. Such a policy was implemented even under Thatcher. This time there will have to be much more demanding local content requirements, which would call a halt to the wasting away of the components sector. It would provide a long-term framework for the regeneration of this industry and of other linked activities that have been allowed to wither.

If something positive can be gained from Brexit, we may look forward to a time when we no longer have to look back in anger. We may even be able to make peace with the past.

There is, however, a shadow over what lies ahead. In so far as Brexit has any ideological coherence, much of the running has been made by a small coterie of economists, mostly with City provenance. Eerily, the group includes names that go all the way back to Thatcherism at its most virulent. Economists for Free Trade, which includes Patrick Minford, Roger Bootle and Tim Congdon, and others such as Ruth Lea, have cheerfully countenanced the complete disappearance of British manufacturing industry as a real possibility in the kind of post-Brexit world they look for.[123]

How telling – and how appallingly fitting – if the final act in the deindustrialisation of Britain were played out in the wake of one of the greatest acts of self-harm that this country could have inflicted on itself.

APPENDIX

Immigrants in British Industry

Immigrants have long played an important role in the development of British industry. From the Huguenots who brought their skills in silversmithing and silk-weaving to London in the eighteenth century to the labourers who migrated from the Indian subcontinent to toil in the foundries and textile mills of the Midlands and North in the 1950s and 1960s, industrious folk from around the world have made a huge contribution to manufacturing in the UK.

Easiest to identify individually, however, are those who played a key part in the establishment, development and management of many of our great companies. Some, indeed, were to found what became the centrepieces of entire industries. The list below includes a selection of the better known or more celebrated. Most, but not all, were first-generation immigrants.

Many of the more prominent came from Germany, a tribute to the strong historic links Britain has had with that extraordinary country. It is possible to trace two streams of migration from Germany. One was associated with the later Hanoverian monarchs, whose benign reigns coincided with the emergence of industry in the British Isles and who looked favourably on the arrival on these shores of their fellow countrymen. The second coincided with the enlightened influence of the prince consort during the nineteenth century.

The late nineteenth and early twentieth century brought a new influx of engineers, entrepreneurs and industrialists into the UK. Often these were people who were attracted to Britain by its advanced technical development, its supplies of investment capital and its high standard of living – implying a ready market for their talents, ideas and potential products.

Sometimes they came as refugees from racial or religious persecution. The interwar years saw another spate of such arrivals, often from Germany and central Europe, where conditions were becoming increasingly perilous for people of independent attitude or minority heritage. This pattern continued into the post-war period. It has remained a phenomenon of incalculable benefit to the British economy.

More recently there have been a number of instances where entrepreneurs from overseas have established or revitalised individual companies and industries in Britain. These have included food manufacture, textiles, engineering and steel. Many of these interventions have been by entrepreneurs from the Indian subcontinent. Though they have often retained an allegiance and residential status in the lands of their birth as much as in the UK, such individuals have made important contributions to the resilience, sometimes the very survival, of significant British manufacturing operations. A small sample is listed below.

Immigrant	Family Origins	Industry/Company
Frederick Accum	Germany	London's first gas works
David Alliance	Iran	Textiles and clothing
Paul Angois	France	Raleigh bicycles
Siegfried Bettman	Germany	Velocette motorcycles
Gustav Binswanger	Germany	Electrical engineering (GEC)
Max Binswanger	Germany	Electrical engineering (GEC)
Arthur Brin	France	British Oxygen Company
Leon Brin	France	British Oxygen Company

John Brunner	Switzerland	Brunner, Mond (ICI)
Charles Francis Brush	USA	Brush electrical engineering
Alfred Deutsch	Austria	Consumer electronics
Hugo Frye	Germany	Machine tools
David Gestetner	Hungary	Duplicators
Johannes Gütgemann	Germany	Velocette motorcycles
Hugo Hirst (Hirsch)	Germany	Electrical engineering (GEC)
Ernst Hoffmann	Switzerland/USA	Ball bearings
Joe Hyman	Russia	Textiles, clothing
Emmanuel Kaye	Russia	Lansing Bagnall lift trucks
Bernard Laporte	Germany	Chemicals
Henry Lobnitz	Denmark	Shipbuilding
Guglielmo Marconi	Italy	Radio development
Ludwig Mond	Germany	Brunner, Mond (ICI)
Hidalgo Moya	Spain/US	Typewriters
Swraj Paul	India	Structural steel
Harry Railing	Germany	Electrical engineering (GEC)
Max Railing	Germany	Electrical engineering (GEC)
Hans Renold	Switzerland	Industrial chains
Alphonse Reyrolle	France	Switchgear
Moritz Schulte	Germany	Triumph motorcycles
Isaac Shoenberg	Russia	Television
August Siebe	Germany	Diving gear

Wilhelm Siemens	Germany	Siemens Brothers
David Smith	Poland	Papermaking
Nicholas Straussler	Hungary	Armoured cars
Jules Thorn	Austria	Consumer electronics
George Westinghouse	USA	Electrical engineering
Frederick Winzer	Germany	London's first gas works
Gustav Wolff	Germany	Shipbuilding
Alfred Yarrow	Spain	Shipbuilding

Endnotes

Foreword

1   eg Liberal England, Tory England, Europe, English cricket.

Chapter 1   Introduction

1   Yanis Varoufakis, Question Time, BBC1, 28 March 2019.
2   Jim Tomlinson, De-industrialisation rather than globalisation is the key part of the Brexit story, Economic History Society Annual Conference, 2017.
3   Martin J. Wiener, English Culture and the Decline of the Industrial Spirit, Cambridge University Press, Cambridge, 1981.
4   Victoria Bateman, Cambridge University, Money Box Live: What Britain Sells, BBC Radio 4, 21 February 2018.
5   Robert Rowthorn and Ramana Ramaswamy, Deindustrialization – Its Causes and Implications, IMF, Washington, September 1997.
6   Stephen Broadberry and Tim Leunig, The Impact of Government Policies on UK Manufacturing since 1945, London School of Economics, October 2013.
7   Ibid.
8   Michael Kitson and Jonathan Michie, The Deindustrial Revolution: The Rise and Fall of UK Manufacturing, 1870–2010, Centre for Business Research, University of Cambridge, Working Paper No 459, June 2014.

9   Ibid.

10   Taxpayer support for UK banks, National Audit Office.

11   Michael W. Flinn, Roy Church, Barry Supple, John Hatcher, William Ashworth, The History of the British Coal Industry, Volumes 1–5, Oxford University Press, 1984.

12   Francis Beckett and David Hencke, Marching to the Fault Line, Constable, London, 2009.

13   Seumas Milne, The Enemy Within, Verso, 1994.

Chapter 2   Steel Rusts

1   Fred Dibnah and David Hall, Memories of Industrial Britain, BBC Books, 2010.

2   G.C. Allen, British Industries and Their Organization, Longmans, London, 1959.

3   Maev Kennedy, World's first iron bridge given €1m gift from Germans to maintain links, The Guardian, 13 November 2017.

4   G.C. Allen, British Industries and Their Organization, Longmans, London, 1959.

5   Ibid.

6   Ibid.

7   Ibid.

8   Ibid.

9   Brian Groom, The long, slow decline of the British steel industry, Financial Times, 1 April 2016.

10   Harukiyo Hasegawa, The Steel Industry in Japan, A Comparison with Britain, Routledge, London, 1996.

11   Ibid.

12   A. Cockerill and A. Silberston, The Steel Industry, Comparisons of Industrial Structure and Performance, Cambridge University Press, London, 1974.

13   A. Cockerill, Steel, The Structure of British Industry, Ed P.S. Johnson, Granada Publishing, London, 1980.

14   Martin Upham, Can Britain's steel industry survive a third assault? The Guardian, 23 April 1980.

15   A. Cockerill and A. Silberston, The Steel Industry, Comparisons of Industrial Structure and Performance, Cambridge University Press, London, 1974.

16   Introduction to continuous casting, ccc.illinois.edu.

17   British Steel, Grace's Guide to British Industrial History.

18   A. Cockerill, Steel, The Structure of British Industry, Ed P.S. Johnson, Granada Publishing, London, 1980.

19   Lord Brookes, obituary, Daily Telegraph, 6 August 2002.

20   History of British Steel, Tata Steel.

21   Harukiyo Hasegawa, The Steel Industry in Japan, A comparison with Britain, Routledge, London, 1996.

22   Jonathan Aylen, Prospects for Steel, Lloyds Bank Review, April 1984.

23   Harukiyo Hasegawa, The Steel Industry in Japan, A comparison with Britain, Routledge, London, 1996.

24   Clyde Iron Works, Grace's Guide to British Industrial History.

25   Stoke-on-Trent History: Shelton Iron & Steel Works, potteye.co, 21 November 2013.

26   Rupert Neate, Online bets record lifts gambling boss's pay to £199,305,000, The Guardian, 13 November 2017.

27   Harukiyo Hasegawa, The Steel Industry in Japan, A comparison with Britain, Routledge, London, 1996.

28   Richard Littlejohn, Mr Pastry and the myth of public spending cuts, Daily Mail, 17 February 2012.

29   Ian Rodger, Steel users favour cuts in capacity, Financial Times, 23 November 1982.

30   Majority pared by Ravenscraig, Financial Times, 21 June 1988.

31   Alasdair M. Blair, The British Iron and Steel Industry Since 1945, The Journal of European Economic History, Rome, Volume 26, 1997.

32   US company helps British Steel sell equipment, Wire Technology, Spring 1982.

33   Keith Harper, Llanelli furnace sold to Pretoria, The Guardian, 7 June 1983.

34   Anthony Hyman, Pakistanis flock to buy Britain's used bargains, The Guardian, 23 August 1983.

35   BSC may sell plant to China, Financial Times, 27 September 1983.

36   James McLoughlin, EEC strategist advises closure of Ravenscraig, The Guardian, 29 September 1983.

37   Keith Harper, Llanelli furnace sold to Pretoria, The Guardian, 7 June 1983.

38   North-East steel town that felt the icy blast of change, The Northern Echo, 9 April 2013; A.J. Ayles, Diary of a Closure, March 1981; Gavin Havery, Memories of a steel town, Darlington & Stockton Times, 5 September 2011.

39   Nigel Fisher and Selina Maycock, Scunthorpe steelworkers "still reeling from Thatcher's term in office", Scunthorpe Telegraph, 11 April 2013; House of Commons Debate on the Steel Industry, 16 December 1980.

40   Anthony Moreton and Stewart Dalby, Shattered towns that prove there can be life after steel, Financial Times, 9 January 1992.

41   Jonathan Aylen, Prospects for Steel, Lloyds Bank Review, April 1984.

42   Geoffrey Goodman, Lord Haslam of Bolton, obituary, The Guardian, 4 November 2002.

43 Nick Garnett, Measuring up to great expectations, Financial Times, 9 November 1988.

44 Selling steel to biased buyers, Financial Times, 29 February 1988.

45 Ibid.

46 Geoffrey Owen, From Empire to Europe, HarperCollins, London, 1999.

47 David Parker, The Official History of Privatisation, Volume II, Routledge, Abingdon, 2012.

48 Ibid.

49 The Davignon plan for Europe's steel, Executive Intelligence Review, 3–9 April 1979.

50 F. Gillett, Putting UK steel in perspective vis-à-vis other EEC countries, Letter to the Financial Times, 21 December 1982.

51 Ian Rodger, Why ministers are poised to push the clock back, Financial Times, 22 March 1985.

52 German Steel Federation, cited by Geoffrey Owen, From Empire to Europe, HarperCollins, London, 1999.

53 John Glover, Ilva plant turns to Japanese for reversal of ailing fortunes, The Guardian, 30 January 1993.

54 Charles Leadbeater, Passing of an industrial symbol, Financial Times, 9 January 1992.

55 James Buxton, BSC chief warns on Scots plant, Financial Times, 22 September 1987.

56 Jeremy Bray, obituary, Daily Telegraph, 5 June 2002; House of Commons Debate on Ravenscraig Steelworks, 20 July 1988.

57 Editorial, Financial Times, 9 January 1992.

58 Ivor Owen, Scholey's line on Ravenscraig seen as insulting, Financial Times, 5 July 1990.

59 Sir Robert Scholey, obituary, Daily Telegraph, 16 January 2014.

60 Mark Meredith, British Steel invests in Life after the Gartcosh closure, Financial Times, 5 February 1986.

61 Charles Leadbeater, Passing of an industrial symbol, Financial Times, 9 January 1992.

62 Sir Robert Scholey, obituary, Daily Telegraph, 16 January 2014.

63 James Buxton and Chris Tighe, Workers show refusal to look back in anger, Financial Times, 9 January 1992.

64 David Gow, Nicholas Bannister, Patrick Wintour and Michael White, Steel: more jobs may go, The Guardian, 2 February 2001.

65 David Gow and Nick Bannister, Man of steel who loathes politicians, The Guardian, 2 February 2001.

66 Michael Harrison, Anger at 103% pay rise for Corus boss who sacked 6,000 workers, The Independent, 5 April 2002.

67   Roland Gribben, Chairman would not be bullied by Blair, Daily Telegraph, 2 February 2001.

68   Shutting down steel, The Guardian, 2 February 2001.

69   Roland Gribben and George Jones, Corus steel unions fight a losing battle, Daily Telegraph, 2 February 2001.

70   Peter Marsh, Tata looks to close the gap in Europe, Financial Times, 7 May 2011.

71   Ibid.

72   170 years of steelmaking ends in fury as the last blast furnace on Teesside is closed down, Daily Mirror, 20 February 2010.

73   Mark Milner, Corus deal secures Teesside's 1,700 jobs, The Guardian, 17 December 2004.

74   Chris Tyghe and Andrew Bounds, UK steel furnaces roar back into life, Financial Times, 13 May 2012.

75   About SSI UK, ssi-steel.co.

76   Tata Steel, Goodwill hunting, The Economist, 18 May 2013.

77   Robert Lea, Steel "at risk of being taxed out of UK", The Times, 3 May 2011.

78   Alan Tovey, British Steel hails "turnaround" of loss-making Scunthorpe plant it purchased from Tata, Daily Telegraph, 1 June 2017.

79   Ibid.

80   Sean Farrell, Steel industry reels as Caparo announces 450 more job losses, The Guardian, 31 October 2015.

81   Katrine Bussey, Liberty House formally takes over Tata's Scottish steel mills, The Scotsman, 8 April 2016.

82   Alan Tovey, Liberty snaps up more steel mills from Tata as buying spree continues, Daily Telegraph, 11 July 2017.

83   Alan Tovey, Tata steel returns to profit in UK and Europe, Daily Telegraph, 7 February 2017.

84   Peter Hain welcomes Spanish interest in Allied Steel and Wire, Wales Office, 11 November 2002.

85   Tanya Powley, High energy costs hit UK steelmaker Celsa, Financial Times, 19 February 2014.

86   Geoffrey Owen, From Empire to Europe, HarperCollins, London, 1999.

87   David Parker and Hsueh Liang Wu, Privatisation and Performance: A Study of the British Steel Industry under Public and Private Ownership, Economic Issues, Vol 3, Part 2, September 1998.

88   World Steel in Figures, World Steel Association, 2017.

89   John Burnside, The Iron Lady's lethal legacy, New Statesman, 1 March 2010.

90   Toni Jones, No love for Scunthorpe: Industrial town is voted the least romantic place in the UK, Daily Mail, 6 February 2013; Joanna Moorhead, The real life Shameless, Daily Mail, 31 May 2013.

91   Just why is millionaire Paul Sykes determined to take us out of the EU?, Yorkshire Post, 25 November 2013.

92   Understanding the economic contribution of the Foundation Industries, PwC for Tata Steel, January 2014.

93   Mathew Lawrence and Alfie Stirling, Strong Foundation Industries, IPPR, March 2016.

94   Nick Cole, Scunthorpe steel to be used for Royal Navy fleet – but Sweden gets the lion's share of contract, Scunthorpe Telegraph, 13 July 2017.

Chapter 3   Mechanical Engineering – Spanner in the Works

1   Negley Farson, The Way of a Transgressor, Victor Gollancz, 1935.

2   G.C. Allen, British Industries and Their Organization, Longmans, fourth edition, 1959.

3   Lee Child, Made in Birmingham, The Guardian, 8 September 2018.

4   Britain – An Official Handbook, Central Office of Information, 1959.

5   G. C. Allen, British Industries and Their Organization, Longmans, fourth edition, 1959.

6   Ibid.

7   Negley Farson, The Way of a Transgressor, Victor Gollancz, 1935.

8   G.C. Allen, British Industries and Their Organization, Longmans, fourth edition, 1959.

9   Ibid.

10   Ibid.

11   Dava Sobel, Longitude – The True Story of a Lone Genius Who Solved the Greatest Scientific Problem of His Time, Walker, 1995.

12   Britain – An Official Handbook, Central Office of Information, 1959.

13   Ibid.

14   Britain – An Official Handbook, Central Office of Information, 1973.

15   Britain – An Official Handbook, Central Office of Information, 1980.

16   Patience Wheatcroft, Surviving on fruit juice and fireworks, Sunday Times, 25 July 1982.

17   Christopher Lorenz, editor, Survival, we now see, is not enough, Financial Times, 28 December 1983.

18   Terry Dodsworth and Nick Garnett, A wealth of contradictions, Financial Times, 23 November 1987.

19   Nick Garnett, Home territories must be defended now, Financial Times, 6 December 1989.

20   Nick Garnett, Quieter year may be ahead, Financial Times, 4 January 1988.

21   Peter Marsh, UK engineering 11th out of 14 in the EU, Financial Times, 14

December 1998.

22 Peter Marsh, Step into the engine room of the world, Financial Times, 16 September 1999.

23 Peter Marsh, Knowledge plays big role in spurring productivity growth, Financial Times, 14 December 1998.

24 Steaming on: The engineer, Mr Harry Hacking, keeps a close watch on a 1922 steam engine at Syke cotton mill, Haslingden, Lancashire, The Guardian Weekly, 19 January 1974.

25 James Simpson & Co, Grace's Guide to British Industrial History.

26 Hathorn, Davey & Co, Grace's Guide to British Industrial History.

27 George Kent, Grace's Guide to British Industrial History.

28 Dewrance & Co, Grace's Guide to British Industrial History.

29 Schäffer & Budenberg, Grace's Guide to British Industrial History.

30 Kew Bridge Engines Trust, London Museum of Water and Steam, Brentford.

31 Textile Machinery Industry – A Review, teonline.com.

32 About the BTMA, British Textile Machinery Association.

33 Nick Garnett, European Textile Machinery, Financial Times Survey, 12 October 1987.

34 Made in East Manchester, Museum of Science & Industry, Manchester, 2006.

35 A Brief History of the Globe Works, Hyndburn Borough Council, 2015.

36 Grace's Guide to British Industrial History.

37 Platt – Makers of Quality Textile Machinery & Parts, platt.co.uk/history.

38 Grace's Guide to British Industial History.

39 Hansard, House of Commons Debate, 8 April 1982.

40 Mackie – Built to Last, BBC1 Northern Ireland, 19 November 2012.

41 The Industrial Heritage of West Belfast, culturenorthernireland.org.

42 Premiere for Mackie's "glory days" documentary, Motherwell Times.

43 David Parker, The Official History of Privatisation, Volume 2, Routledge, London, 2012.

44 Maurice Neill, Meltdown at Mackie's, Belfast Telegraph, 2 September 1999.

45 Jürg Repp, Germany: The Premier League in Textile Machinery Production, textileworld.com.

46 Fritz P Mayer, Ibid.

47 G.C. Allen, British Industries and Their Organization, Longmans, fourth edition, 1959.

48 Ian Rodger and Peter Bruce, The uphill struggle to survive, Financial Times, 15 February 1983.

49 Ibid.

50 Andrew Fisher, Machine tools orders surge, Financial Times, 1 April 1985.

51 Andrew Fisher, A fight-back at the eleventh hour, Financial Times, 3 April 1985.

52 Simon J. Brown, Beaver dammed, Letter to the Guardian, 23 July 1992.

53 Peter Bruce, Machine Tools, Steady climb in new orders, Financial Times, 4 July 1984.

54 Nick Garnett, Yamazaki plans machine tool exports to Japan, Financial Times, 16 June 1987.

55 Nick Garnett, Halifax tooling up to face an optimistic but uncertain future, Financial Times, 2 September 1987.

56 Peter Marsh, UK slips down European league in production of machine tools, Financial Times, 30 June 2001.

57 Roger Lloyd-Jones and Merv Lewis, Alfred Herbert Ltd and the British Machine Tool Industry, 1887–1983, Ashgate, 2006.

58 Grace's Guide to British Industrial History.

59 The Alfred Herbert News, Herbert Art Gallery and Museum, 2015.

60 Michael Shattock, Sir Richard Young: Industrialist with an incisive and analytical mind, and a passion for technological innovation, The Independent, 16 June 2008.

61 About Us, Alfred Herbert (India) Ltd, 2011.

62 Grace's Guide to British Industrial History.

63 Ibid.

64 Company profile, Wadkin.com.

65 Nick Garnett, Wood working machinery surge, Financial Times, 24 July 1987.

66 Ibid.

67 Ibid.

68 David Connett, Matrix Churchill case was "ludicrous": Former minister could not see justification for trial, The Independent, 15 December 1993.

69 The Core of Engineering Based Manufacturing – Basic Facts 2014, The Manufacturing Technologies Association, 2014.

70 The Mazak Way, About Mazak Europe, Yamazaki Mazak, 2015.

71 George Orwell, The Road to Wigan Pier, Victor Gollancz, 1937.

72 Huw Beynon, Andrew Cox and Ray Hudson, The Decline of King Coal, The Coalfields Research Programme: Discussion Paper No 1, Cardiff University, ESRC, University of Durham, 1999.

73 Lord Ezra, NCB chairman – obituary, Daily Telegraph, 22 December 2015.

74 John Lloyd, obituary: Derek Ezra, coal executive, 1919–2015, Financial Times, 22 December 2015.

75 Victor Keegan, Lord Ezra – Former chairman of the National Coal Board who spent his working life in the industry, obituary, The Guardian, 24 December 2015.

76   Peter Bruce, Mining Equipment, Best prospects for growth lie overseas, UK Engineering, Financial Times, 4 July 1984.

77   John Hooper, Stand by "cheap" coal appeal, The Guardian, 18 November 1987.

78   Peter Luff MP, House of Commons Debate, Hansard, 2 December 1992.

79   Dobson Park Industries, Grace's Guide to British Industrial History.

80   Harnischfeger in talks to buy Dobson Park of London, New York Times, 2 September 1995.

81   Broom & Wade, Grace's Guide to British Industrial History.

82   Anderson Strathclyde, Grace's Guide to British Industrial History.

83   Anderson Boyes, Grace's Guide to British Industrial History.

84   Mavor and Coulson, Grace's Guide to British Industrial History.

85   Anderson Boyes closes its doors for a final time, Daily Record, 30 December 2010.

86   Charter Consolidated, Grace's Guide to British Industrial History.

87   Anderson Strathclyde, House of Commons Debate, Hansard, 22 March 1983; Anderson Strathclyde (Prevention of Take-over), House of Commons Debate, Hansard, 30 March 1983.

88   House of Commons PQs, 21 December 1982, margaretthatcher.org.

89   John Scouller, Mergers and Acquisitions.

90   House of Commons Debate, 22 March 1983.

91   Ian Bruce, Fears of further job losses at mine company, Glasgow Herald, 16 May 1989.

92   PR Newswire, 9 July 2001.

93   Ben Laurence, City Focus: Charter buyer's mysterious past, MailOnline, 10 November 2011.

94   About ABMEC, Association of British Mining Equipment Companies, 2014.

95   Britain – An Official Handbook, Central Office of Information, 1959.

96   Britain – An Official Handbook, Central Office of Information, 1973.

97   Diesel Engines, Financial Times Survey, 8 January 1979.

98   Nick Garnett, Perkins offshoot to shed 90, Financial Times, 27 April 1987.

99   RA Lister and Co, Grace's Guide to British Industrial History.

100   Petters, Grace's Guide to British Industrial History.

101   Ian Rodger, A diesel struggles back on to the tracks, Financial Times, 15 June 1984.

102   Martyn Halsall, Darlington to take jobs appeal to the US, The Guardian, 29 December 1986.

103   700 Scots jobs go south – Shotts closure as Cummins switches work, The Herald on Sunday, 21 February 1996.

104   Chris Price, Cummins to close manufacturing operations in Manston and move it to Daventry, China and India, kentonline, 16 February 2016.

105   Mike Humble, Cummins in the UK – Darlington celebrates 50 years, AROnline.co, 25 February 2015.

106   Herbert Morris, Grace's Guide to British Industrial History.

107   Report on Proposed Merger of Babcock & Wilcox and Herbert Morris, Monopolies and Mergers Commission, February 1977.

108   Ibid.

109   Management buyout of Morris UK operations, Cranes Today, 12 April 2001.

110   Ian Griffin, Poor handling of Morris closure, Leicester Mercury, 21 October 2009.

111   Grace's Guide to British Industrial History.

112   Nick Garnett, The long haul back to recovery, Financial Times, 12 October 1983.

113   Nick Garnett, How Steet Crane has become a thorn in its competitors' sides, Financial Times, 21 November 1984.

114   Ibid.

115   Sarah Stoner, Reunion will give ex-Sunderland crane workers a lift, Sunderland Echo, 18 November 2015.

116   Britain – An Official Handbook, Central Office of Information, 1959.

117   Britain – An Official Handbook, Central Office of Information, 1979.

118   Duncan Campbell-Smith, An industry that is fighting back, Financial Times, 28 March 1985.

119   Nick Garnett, Eye of a whirlwind, Financial Times, 25 October 1985.

120   Tom Brown, Tragedy and Challenge, Matador, Kibworth Beauchamp, 2017.

121   William Weir, The Weir Group, The history of a Scottish engineering legend, 1872–2008, Profile Books, 2008.

122   Ibid.

123   Rhys David, Why it's all hands to the pump, Financial Times, 17 December 1984.

124   Nick Garnett, Pump-priming "ruinous" management systems, Financial Times, 7 October 1988.

125   William Weir, The Weir Group, The history of a Scottish engineering legend, 1872–2008, Profile Books, 2008.

126   Scott McCulloch, Weir Group to cut jobs and close factories in £35m annual savings drive, Daily Record, 4 November 2014.

127   Jon Yeomans, Weir Group sheds 400 jobs as falling oil and commodity prices take toll, Daily Telegraph, 3 November 2015.

128   Weir Group hit by oil slump, BBC News, 30 July 2015.

129   James Howden & Co, Grace's Guide to British Industrial History.

130   Patrick Harverson, No great escape from tunnelling factory closure, Financial Times, 4 October 1990.

131   History of Howden, howden.co.

132   William Weir, The Weir Group, The history of a Scottish engineering legend, 1872–2008, Profile Books, 2008.

133   Gordon Thomson, Jobs fears as Howden axes plant, Evening Times, 2 May 2014.

134   Gordon Thomson, Glasgow jobs at risk as engineering firm switches manufacturing to Europe, Evening Times, 2 May 2014.

Chapter 4   Mechanical Engineering – The Wheels Come Off

1   Robert M. Pirsig, Zen and the Art of Motorcycle Maintenance, William Morrow & Co, New York, 1974.

2   Abe Aamidor, Shooting Star: The Rise and Fall of the British Motorcycle Industry, ECW Press, 2009.

3   Decline of British motorcycle industry, wheels.ca.

4   The baffling case of motorcycles in the UK, themotorcycleobsession.com.

5   Jonathan Boorstein, What Did Happen to the British Motorcycle Industry? theridersdigest.co.uk.

6   Steve Koerner, The Strange Death of the British Motorcycle Industry, Crucible Books, 2012.

7   Bert Hopwood, quoted in The British Motorcycle Industry: Rise and Fall, freecapitalists.org.

8   Joe Heaton, An Examination of the Post-Second World War Relative Decline of UK Manufacturing 1945–1975, Viewed through the Lens of the Birmingham Small Arms Company Ltd, PhD Thesis submitted to the University of Birmingham, July 2007.

9   Tom Waterer, This Is What Happened to the British Motorcycle Industry, Motorcycle Industry Association.

10   Japanese Motorcycle, classic-british-motorcycle.com.

11   See Lynden Briscoe, The Textile and Clothing Industries of the United Kingdom, Manchester University Press, 1971.

12   Triumph Motorcycles, Grace's Guide to British Industrial History.

13   Triumph Motorcycles: The Rise, Fall and Revival of an Icon, knowledge. wharton.upenn.edu, 15 May 2014.

14   Roland Gribben, The Great British motorcycle comeback, The Daily Telegraph, 20 July 2014.

15   The Motorcycle Industry in a Nutshell, Statistical Pocket Guide, Motor Cycle Industry Association, January 2015.

16   Emily Davies, Triumph Motorcycles accelerates back into profit after crashing to an £8m loss, This is Money, 22 December 2015.

17   Rover Safety Bicycle, 1885, Making the Modern World.

18   The History of Starley Bikes, starleybikes.com.

19   BSA: Bicycles, Grace's Guide to British Industrial History.

20   Tracing the roots of Nottingham cycle brand Raleigh, BBC News, 1 May 2012.

21   Raleigh: history of the bicycle maker, Daily Telegraph, 3 April 2012.

22   Company History, Raleigh.co.

23   History: The Heron Evolves: Raleigh from 1975 to 2002, Bicycle Business, 13 February 2002.

24   "I worked at Raleigh" website chronicles life at iconic Nottingham bike factory, road.cc.

25   Tube Investments, Grace's Guide to British Industrial History.

26   Armstrong Cycles, Grace's Guide to British Industrial History.

27   Norman, Grace's Guide to British Industrial History.

28   Sun Cycle and Fittings Co, Grace's Guide to British Industrial History.

29   Raleigh Bicycles – Manufacturer Profile, ebicycles.co.

30   Raleigh Chopper history, BBC Home, November 2002.

31   Pedalling Dreams: the Raleigh Story, BBC4, 5 August 2019.

32   Martin Wainwright, On yer bike, as Raleigh shuts frame plant, The Guardian, 11 December 1999.

33   Alan Sillitoe, Saturday Night and Sunday Morning, WH Allen, 1958.

34   Matt Seaton, Here comes the chopper, The Guardian, 10 May 2002.

35   On your bike – Raleigh move to the Far East costs 280 jobs, The Guardian, 29 November 2002.

36   A century of bicycle production ends, BBC News, 27 November 2002.

37   Peter Walker, Leading British bike brand Raleigh could go Dutch, The Guardian, 3 April 2012.

38   Peter Walker, Dutch cycle firm gears up to buy Raleigh, The Guardian, 4 April 2012.

39   Raleigh Cycle bought by Dutch rival Accell for $100m, BBC News, 26 April 2012.

40   Tina Nielsen, Wheels on Fire, Director Magazine, November 2010.

41   Ben Laurance, Cycling hits the wild side as Britain gets back in the saddle, Sunday Times, 29 May 2011.

42   Industry and Market Profile, European Bicycle Market, COLIPED Association of the European Two Wheeler Parts and Accessories Industry, 2013.

43   Jonathan Guthrie, Cyclical business rides high, Financial Times, 20 April 2009.

44   Heritage, The Moulton Bicycle Company, 2014.

45   Jonathon Harker, British Manufacturing Special: Bicycles, bikbiz.com, 2 June 2014.

46   Laurence Dodds, Holdsworth bikes targets return to Britain, Daily Telegraph, 7 July 2014.

47   John Murray Brown, UK bicycle component producers ride sales boom, Financial Times, 8 April 2014.

48   G.C. Allen, British Industries and Their Organization, Longmans, fourth edition, 1959.

49   Peter Small, Gaining traction: Britain's other post-war boom, The Courier, 12 February 2014.

50   Britain – An Official Handbook, Central Office of Information, 1980.

51   Fordson History, Friends of Fordson, 2014.

52   Ford Dagenham, Wikia, 2015.

53   New Holland celebrates 50 years of tractor production at Basildon, Farmers Guardian, 6 February 2014.

54   Joe Finnerty, Britain: Home of the tractor, Auto Express, 10 August 2014.

55   Tractor Manufacturing – Dominating the field, The Economist, 31 May 2014.

56   David Brown Tractors, University of Reading.

57   Andrew Gowers, Call for investment in Case tractor plant, Financial Times, 5 July 1986.

58   David Brown – History, The David Brown Tractor Club, 2005–8.

59   Grace's Guide to British Industrial History.

60   Records of International Harvester Company of Great Britain Ltd.

61   International Harvester Company of Great Britain Limited, University of Reading.

62   Harvester to Shut Plant in England, New York Times, 27 July 1982.

63   Hansard, House of Commons Debate, 29 July 1982.

64   Peter Marsh, Shopfloor flexibility leaves rivals in the cart, Financial Times, 26 July 1996.

65   Grace's Guide to British Industrial History.

66   Mervyn Bailey, A tearful farewell to tractor production in Doncaster, Farmers Guardian, 20 December 2015.

67   Peter Hill, McCormick's Doncaster tractor factory shuts its doors, Farmers Weekly, 14 December 2007.

68   Mervyn Bailey, McCormick tractors to close Doncaster plant after 60 years, Farmers Guardian, 22 December 2006.

69   Grace's Guide to British Industrial History.

70   The Massey Ferguson Years, Coventry Telegraph.

71   Our Heritage, Massey Ferguson.

72   Employment (Kilmarnock), House of Commons Debate, Hansard, 12 December 1978.

73   A Life with Massey Ferguson, Tractor Magazine, 9 March 2010.

74   Helen Hague, Jobs blow reflects world tractor slump, The Independent, 17 April 1987.

75   David Brindle, Massey-Ferguson turns the corner, Financial Times, 30 November 1987.

76   Who We Are, Agco Corporation.

77   Kevin Maguire, US owner may close tractor factory hit by strong pound, The Guardian, 18 May 2000.

78   End of an era for Massey Ferguson, BBC News, 25 June 2002.

79   Redundancies "a disgrace" says MP, BBC News, 25 June 2002.

80   "Euro" fears raised over factory closure, BBC News, 25 June 2002.

81   What Massey Ferguson workers did after factory closure, BBC News, 13 February 2013.

82   Andy Walker, Is this the world's favourite second-hand tractor?, BBC News, 13 June 2016.

83   Grace's Guide to British Industrial History.

84   Short history of tractors in West Lothian, Workers' Educational Association.

85   Marshall, Sons & Co, Grace's Guide to British Industrial History.

86   Ibid.

87   Nick Garnett, Lean times for farm machinery, The Financial Times, 6 November 1987.

88   Grace's Guide to British Industrial History.

89   Britain – An Official Handbook, Central Office of Information, 1959.

90   Britain – An Official Handbook, Central Office of Information, 1973.

91   Lynton McLain and Ian Rodger, A litany of gloom, Financial Times, 25 October 1983.

92   Komatsu plant completes first excavators, Financial Times, 22 December 1986.

93   Lynton McLain, Caterpillar to close plant with loss of 960 jobs, Financial Times, 1 September 1983.

94   Nick Garnett, Caterpillar cocoons itself against cool business climate, Financial Times, 16 January 1987.

95   Jean Stead, Tractor firm for talks with Rifkind on closure, The Guardian, 17 January 1987.

96   25 Years on: Workers look back on Caterpillar factory sit in, aggregateresearch.com, 8 March 2012.

97   Caterpillar in the United Kingdom, Caterpillar, 2012.

98   Aveling-Barford, Grace's Guide to British Industrial History.

99   Michael Pointer, The Rise and Fall of Aveling-Barford, 1933–1988, BG Publications, 1997.

100   Ibid.

101   Maamba Collieries, visited by the author in 1971.

102   Ibid.

103   Memory Lane: Last truck rolls out of Grantham's Aveling-Barford, Grantham Journal, 17 October 2015.

104   Joseph Bamford, Daily Telegraph, 2 March 2001.

105   Sean Farrell, JCB to cut 290 jobs after big fall in demand for machines, The Guardian, 5 November 2015.

106   Aditya Chakrabortty, What JCB's yellow digger tells us about our manufacturing malaise, The Guardian, 8 February 2011.

107   Kaye, Sir Emmanuel, Jewish Virtual Library, 2008.

108   Robert Brown, The growth of fork-lift firm, Basingstoke Gazette, 8 July 2007.

109   Bob Bischof, Invensys sale: UK manufacturing on the fast track to oblivion?, Daily Mail, 7 August 2013.

110   Why Lansing Bagnall had to cut back, Financial Times, 12 May 1982.

111   Charles Leadbeater and Patrick Harverson, Forklift truck industry sheds jobs, Financial Times, 15 October 1990.

112   Lucy Clark, End of an era: 350 jobs set to go at major town firm, Basingstoke Gazette, 18 June 2009.

113   Linde closes Basingstoke plant with hundreds of job losses, Material Handling Wholesaler, 18 June 2009.

114   Linde: Jobs threat in Merthyr forklift factory closure talks, BBC News, 31 January 2013.

115   Self-preservation instinct wins day, Andrew Baxter, Financial Times, 8 October 1992.

116   Sir Neville Bowman-Shaw, forklift truck magnate – obituary, Daily Telegraph, 11 August 2015.

117   Ibid.

118   Will Hutton, The deadly cocktail that has seen off quality engineering, The Guardian, 6 May 1994.

119   David Bowen, Lancer Boss "forced under", The Independent, 11 June 1994.

120   Obituary: Sir Neville was the Boss of the forklift industry, Leighton Buzzard Observer, 30 July 2015.

121   Nick Garnett, Swedish facelift revitalises Coventry Climax, Financial Times, 2 March 1988.

122   Ibid.

Chapter 5   Mechanical Engineering – Bearings to Chains

1   Census of World Casting Production, Modern Casting, December 2016.

2   Ian Rodger, Castings and Forgings, Financial Times Survey, 12 May 1983.

3   The effects of semi-finished steel imports on the US iron and steel scrap industry, US International Trade Commission, May 1985.

4   Ian Rodger, Castings and Forgings, Financial Times Survey, 12 May 1983.

5   Maggie Brown, Foundries are foundering, The Guardian, 13 March 1984.

6   Ian Rodger, Cuts planned at Ley's Foundries, Financial Times, 13 March 1984.

7   Ibid.

8   Michael Smith and Maggie Brown, Another 1,000 jobless in cut-backs, The Guardian, 24 November 1984.

9   Ian Rodger, Birmid offshoot to close foundry and cut 700 jobs, Financial Times, 23 January 1986.

10 Mark Meredith, New broom sweeps into dusty world of steel castings, Financial Times, 31 May 1985.

11 Ibid.

12 Ian Rodger, Castings and Forgings, Financial Times Survey, 12 May 1983.

13 Ford's Dagenham car plant: 80 years of a British giant, mirror.co.uk, 1 March 2009.

14 Ian Rodger, Castings and Forgings, Financial Times Survey, 12 May 1983.

15 50 years in the melting pot, Yorkshire Evening Post, 26 November 2004.

16 Census of World Casting Production, Modern Casting, December 2016.

17 Forging Facts, www.forging.org.

18 Christopher Carr, Britain's Competitiveness, The Management of the Vehicle Components Industry, Routledge, London, 1990.

19 Ian Rodger, Castings and Forgings, Financial Times Survey, 12 May 1983.

20 205 Production per specialities, Euroforge, 2016.

21 Britain – An Official Handbook, Central Office of Information, 1973.

22 Britain – An Official Handbook, Central Office of Information, 1979.

23 Obituary, Sir John Buckley, Daily Telegraph, 11 December 2000.

24 Head Wrightson & Co, Grace's Guide to British Industrial History.

25 Head Wrightson, Grace's Guide to British Industrial History.

26 Maggie Brown, Hard times fear for process plant sector, The Guardian, 17 April 1984.

27 Report on Proposed Merger of Babcock & Wilcox and Herbert Morris, Monopolies and Mergers Commission, February 1977.

28 Ibid.

29 FK Electricals, Grace's Guide to British Industrial History.

30 Simon Beavis, FKI Babcock to shed 4,000 jobs, The Guardian, 27 November 1987.

31 James Buxton and Nick Garnett, Babcock Power to cut 475 jobs at Renfrew plant, Financial Times, 27 October 1987.

32 David Fishlock, Babcock seeks powerful partner, Financial Times, 11 April 1988.

33   Clay Harris, FKI Babcock to shed 4,000 jobs worldwide, Financial Times, 27 November 1987.

34   Lord King of Wartnaby, obituary, Daily Telegraph, 13 July 2005.

35   Bridging the gap: great British bridges through history, Country Life, 31 August 2015.

36   Grace's Guide to British Industrial History.

37   Sir William Arrol, Engineering Achievements, Scottish Engineering Hall of Fame.

38   Grace's Guide to British Industrial History.

39   Duncan Leatherdale, Dorman Long: The Teesside firm that bridged the world, BBC News, 3 October 2015.

40   Tomas Farrell, Building Bridges: Dorman Long, Let's Look Again, 15 January 2016.

41   Grace's Guide to British Industrial History.

42   Ibid.

43   Erik Ipsen, Kvaerner is close to bidding for troubled group: Lifeline bid for Trafalgar House?, The New York Times, 28 February 1996.

44   Magnus Grimond, Trafalgar House clears decks, The Independent, 18 April 1996.

45   About Cleveland Bridge, clevelandbridge.com.

46   Alan Pike, Dunlop faces protest strike, Financial Times, 20 February 1979.

47   James Erlichman, Dunlop awaits Japan's avenging fire, The Guardian, 20 September 1983.

48   James Erlichman, Dunlop's £142m kiss of life, The Guardian, 16 January 1985.

49   Martin Dickson, A culture shock that won ardent converts, Financial Times, 13 January 1987.

50   Lorne Barling and Kenneth Gooding, Michelin to cut 2,600 tyre jobs, Financial Times, 9 June 1985.

51   Charles Leadbeater, A painstaking route to job security, Financial Times, 9 February 1987.

52   St Modwen set to start demolition at ex-Pirelli site, Burton upon Trent, St Modwen, 31 May 2013.

53   BTR Industries, Grace's Guide to British Industrial History.

54   Tony Jackson, "Magic dust" loses glitter, Financial Times, 15/16 September 1990.

55   Siebe Gorman, Grace's Guide to British Industrial History.

56   Peter Marsh and John Kipphoff, From a change of control to a change of identity at Invensys, Financial Times, 16 February 2002.

57   Malcolm Withers, Invensys plans split and a £1.5bn sell-off, Evening Standard, 19 February 2002.

58 Peter Marsh, One step backwards in pursuit of the future, Financial Times, 20 February 2002.

59 Ibid.

60 Re-invensys, The Guardian, 8 January 2002.

61 Robert Bischof, Invensys Sale: UK Manufacturing on the Fast Track to Oblivion?, The Daily Mail, 7 August 2013.

62 Nicholas Comfort, The Slow Death of British Industry, Biteback Publishing, 2012.

63 Joseph Lucas Ltd, Grace's Guide to British Industrial History.

64 Adrian Smith, The Lucas Plan: what can it tell us about democratising technology today, Comments, The Guardian, 22 January 2014.

65 Stefan Wagstyl, Electrical side faces testing time, Financial Times, 28 January 1985.

66 Ibid.

67 Richard Tomkins, The word "re-rating" is suddenly in the air, Financial Times, 21 October 1988.

68 GKN, Grace's Guide to British Industrial History.

69 Andrew Lorenz, GKN, The Making of a Business, John Wiley & Sons, Chichester, 2009.

70 Tom Brown, Tragedy and Challenge, Matador, Kibworth Beauchamp, 2017.

71 Nick Garnett, GKN steels itself for further changes, Financial Times, 19 March 1987.

72 Sir Trevor Holdsworth, obituary, Daily Telegraph, 13 October 2010.

73 Ray Maughan, GKN lifts pre-tax profits to £88m, 15 March 1984.

74 Extract from the 1984 annual report, Financial Times, 16 April 1985.

75 Hazel Duffy, Standard bearer for manufacturing, Financial Times, 11 May 1988.

76 Ibid.

77 John Griffiths and Maggie Urry, GKN makes £215m but 1,000 more jobs to go, Financial Times, 7 March 1991.

78 Michael Kavanagh, GKN reaps rewards of change in direction, Financial Times, 13 March 2011.

79 James Shotter, Manufacturers in striking comeback, Financial Times, 2 April 2012.

80 Kevin Brown, Revolutionary cells at work in dark satanic mill, Financial Times, 9 November 1999.

81 Head of Vauxhall Motors, The Guardian.

82 Tom Brown, Tragedy and Challenge, Matador, Kibworth Beauchamp, 2017.

83 Ransome & Marles Bearing Co, Grace's Guide to British Industrial History.

84   Hoffmann Manufacturing Co, Grace's Guide to British Industrial History.

85   History of the Stonehouse factory, SKF website.

86   Hoffmann Bearings History, hoffmannbearings.co.

87   Ransome Hoffman Pollard Co, Grace's Guide to British Industrial History.

88   Bearings that made the world go round, Essex Chronicle, 29 October 2012.

89   SKF UK History, SKF Website.

90   NSK in Europe – Facts and Figures, nskeurope.com.

91   Renold, Grace's Guide to British Industrial History.

92   Company History of Renold, renold.com.

93   Nick Garnett, Restructuring Renold, The long struggle to regain profitability, Financial Times, 30 March 1984.

94   Andrew Cornelius and Simon Beavis, Manufacturing job cuts support CBI pessimism, The Guardian, 8 November 1986.

95   Shelina Begum, Jobs axed as Renold confirms closure of chains factory, Manchester Evening News, 22 October 2013.

96   Karl West, Pilkington's glass is half empty, This is Money, 2 July 2010.

97   Company History, pilkington.com.

98   John Holusha, Alastair Pilkington, 75, Inventor of a Process to Make Flat Glass, The New York Times, 24 May 1995.

99   Ibid.

100   Greg Morris, Ardagh Glass confirms UK production line closure, Glass International, 3 February 2016.

101   Pilkington plc, encyclopedia.com.

102   Tony McDonough and Mike Chapple, Pilkington Takeover: End of an era for glass giant, thefreelibrary.com.

103   Emily Davies, Christian Grysin and Jason Groves, Japan takeover of UK tech giant ARM could net directors £35 million, Daily Mail, 20 July 2016.

104   Lina Saigol, Kaori Suzuki and David Turner, NSG and Pilkington in £2.2bn deal, Financial Times, 27 February 2006.

105   Tony McDonough and Mike Chapple, Pilkington Takeover: End of an era for glass giant, thefreelibrary.com.

106   Keith Jackson and Shigeru Matsumoto, The acquisition of Pilkington by Nippon Sheet Glass as a failure of cross-border synergy, Paper Proposal, SOAS & Doshisha University, 2016.

107   Ibid.

108   Pilkington glass factory in St Helens cuts 140 jobs, BBC, 7 November 2013.

109   Julie Froud, Adam Leaver, Gindo Tampubolon and Karel Williams, Everything for Sale: How Non-executive Directors Make a Difference, CRESC, The University of Manchester, January 2008.

110   Ibid.

111   Grace's Guide to British Industrial History.

112   Caradon plc, referenceforbusiness.com.

113   Ibid.

114   Maggie Brown, 1,139 jobs axed at Metal Box, The Guardian, 22 June 1985.

115   Ian Rodger, Metal Box to cut over 1,000 jobs, Financial Times, 22 June 1985.

116   Tony Jackson, A believer in focusing on a few key issues, Financial Times, 23 May 1986.

117   Cracking entente, The Guardian, 16 February 1993.

Chapter 6   Cars – Changing Gear

1   René Cutforth, Order to View, Faber and Faber, London, 1969.

2   Geoff McGarry, When Acton powered the UK, Ealing Gazette, 19 August 2011.

3   Jonathan Wood, The British Motor Industry, Shire Publications, Oxford, 2011.

4   Roy Church, The rise and decline of the British motor industry, Cambridge University Press, Cambridge, 1995.

5   Jonathan Wood, The British Motor Industry, Shire Publications, Oxford, 2011.

6   Ibid.

7   Stephen Bayley, The Morris Minor: A British Miracle, Daily Telegraph, 2 January 2011.

8   In praise of Stirling Moss, The Guardian, 14 June 2011.

9   Maurice Gatsonides, obituary, Daily Telegraph, 2 December 1998.

10   Ulrike Gutzmann, Cars and Democracy, Talk at National Archives, Kew, 11 July 2013.

11   Jonathan Wood, The British Motor Industry, Shire Publications, Oxford, 2011.

12   In praise of the Mini, The Guardian, 14 September 2006.

13   James Ensor, Jaguar increasing output, Financial Times, 16 September 1969.

14   James Ensor, Car manufacturers: the squeeze becomes a strait-jacket, Financial Times, 10 July 1969.

15   The car lord who laughed his way to a Swiss bank, Evening Standard, 23 July 2008.

16   Roy Church, The rise and decline of the British motor industry, Cambridge University Press, Cambridge, 1995.

17   Roger Cowe, Lord Ryder, obituary, The Guardian, 16 May 2003.

18   Andrew Lorenz, How the Warrior rescued GKN from 1980s slump, Daily Telegraph, 20 September 2009.

19   Clifford Webb, The MG factory at Abingdon closes today, classics. honestjohn.co.uk.

20 Michael Smith and John Palmer, BAe snaps up Rover for £150m, The Guardian, 30 March 1988.

21 Andrew Cornelius, Down, Rover: an old friend is laid to rest, The Guardian, 23 September 1988.

22 Shady dealing by UK plc, Financial Times, 22 February 1991.

23 Michael Smith and John Palmer, BAe snaps up Rover for £150m, The Guardian, 30 March 1988.

24 Kevin Done, Honda's backroom role in fly-drive synergy, Financial Times, 2 February 1990.

25 Call to investigate prospect of BAe £1bn property "killing", Michael Smith, The Guardian, 29 November 1988.

26 Michael Harrison, Rover on the road into Europe in a second-hand sale by BAe, The Independent, 9 August 1992.

27 Chris Brady and Andrew Lorenz, End of the Road, The true story of the downfall of Rover, Pearson Education Limited, Harlow, 2001.

28 John Griffiths, Carmaker claims it has confounded sceptics who predicted early collapse, Financial Times, 9 May 2001.

29 Rover wins Car of the Year, BBC News, 23 February 1999.

30 Stuart Marshall, Rover's make-or-break marque, Financial Times, 1 April 1999.

31 John Griffiths, UK's biggest car plant now 400 acres of pure paradox, Financial Times, 20 December 1999.

32 Anthony Hilton, The only road to salvation for Longbridge, Evening Standard, 22 March 1999.

33 A tale of greed and gullibility, Financial Times, 9 April 2005.

34 Simon Goodley, Deloitte told it failed to manage MG Rover conflict of interest, The Guardian, 30 July 2013.

35 Larry Elliott, Rare as an Aston Martin, for the price of a Lada, with instant obsolescence, The Guardian, 15 November 2004.

36 About MG, MG Motor UK Ltd.

37 MG to end UK car production at Longbridge with switch to China, BBC News, 23 September 2016.

38 Chris Brady and Andrew Lorenz, End of the Road, The True Story of the Downfall of Rover, Pearson Education Limited, Harlow, 2005.

39 Louis Schweitzer, Biography, Reference for Business.

40 Vincent Frigant and Yannick Lung, Are the French Car Companies PSA and Renault the European Automobile Industry's Champions of Shareholder Value?, INSEAD, Fontainebleu, France, April 2001.

41 Paul Betts, A French renaissance, Financial Times, 20 October 1988.

42 Alix Christie, The state stays in the driving seat at Renault, The Guardian, 17 September 1994.

43   Ibid.

44   Vincent Frigant and Yannick Lung, Are the French Car Companies PSA and Renault the European Automobile Industry's Champions of Shareholder Value?, INSEAD, Fontainebleu, France, April 2001.

45   Paul Betts, A critical period for the car sector, FT Survey of France, 20 September 1983.

46   Renault assistance, The New York Times, 31 March 1988.

47   David Owen and Tim Burt, Renault keeps a French accent, Financial Times, 8 December 1999.

48   Nick Matthews, French lessons in manufacturing, Tribune, 28 April 2006.

49   Paul Betts, Peugeot aims high, Financial Times, 20 October 1988.

50   Ben Hall and Peggy Hollinger, France opts for €6bn car bail-out, Financial Times, 10 February 2009.

51   Mark Binelli, How Detroit was laid low, The Guardian, 22 July 2013.

Chapter 7   Cars – Back on the Road?

1   Chris Arnot, When the wheels came off the dream, The Guardian, 25 February 2009.

2   Jonathan Glancey, End of the line, The Guardian, 19 February 2002.

3   Lord Varley, obituary, The Guardian, 31 July 2008.

4   David Gow, Peugeot seeks aid for Ryton plant, The Guardian, 23 October 2002.

5   Analysis – why Ryton is closing, Autocar, 20 April 2006.

6   James Mackintosh and Martin Arnold, Peugeot admits Ryton plant could build new car profitably, Financial Times, 19 May 2006.

7   Jonathan Wood, The British Motor Industry, Shire Publications, Oxford, 2011.

8   Sam Toy, obituary, The Guardian, 1 May 2008.

9   Sir Terence Beckett, obituary, Daily Telegraph, 10 May 2013.

10   Sir Terence Beckett, obituary, The Guardian, 13 May 2013.

11   The Ford Factor, aronline.co.

12   Ford's Dagenham Dream, BBC4, 5 June 2010.

13   Robin Reeves, Ford plans to cut up to 1,800 jobs this year, Financial Times, 21 March 1986.

14   Abby Bolter, There are "major concerns" over the future of Ford's engine plant in Bridgend, www.walesonline, 1 February 2017.

15   Jon Menon, End of line for Dagenham carmaking, The Business, 10 February 2002.

16   Geoffrey Owen, Don't shed too many tears when the last Ford rolls out of

Dagenham, The Independent, 18 February 2002.

17   Ian Jack, Fear and loathing in Dagenham, The Guardian, 21 November 2009.

18   John Griffiths, Vauxhall's vanquished workers decide that they will go out on a high note, Financial Times, 19 February 2002.

19   David Gow, General Motors to shut British engine factory, The Guardian, 10 April 2004.

20   Tom Mcghie, Vauxhall will save Ellesmere Port car plant, creating hundreds of jobs and boosting production, This is Money, 12 May 2012.

21   Vauxhall's Ellesmere Port boost for Welsh workers, BBC News, 17 May 2012.

22   British manufacturing, Reality bites, The Guardian, 25 April 2011.

23   Jon Yeomans, Peugeot buys Vauxhall and Opel from General Motors for £1.9bn: But what happens next?, Daily Telegraph, 6 March 2017.

24   Dearball Jordan, Why is Vauxhall being sold to Peugeot's owner?, BBC Business, 6 March 2017.

25   Nick Gibbs, Vauxhall could thrive as "unique survivor" post-Brexit, Automotive News, 28 February 2019.

26   Richard Williams, Goodbye happiness, The Guardian, 1 March 2014.

27   David Parker, The Official History of Privatisation, Volume I, Routledge, Abingdon, 2009.

28   Steven Prokesch, Ford to Buy Jaguar for $2.38 billion, The New York Times, 3 November 1989.

29   Kevin Done, Ambitious plans for Jaguar, Financial Times, 6 June 1990.

30   Michael Cassell, Subsidy for Ford tests political will, Financial Times, 18 January 1995.

31   Karl West, In the driving seat: pioneering Jaguar Land Rover leaves dark days of recession behind, The Guardian, 29 July 2014.

32   Kevin Done, Jaguar unveils £200m XJ range, Financial Times, 28 September 1994.

33   Tim Burt, Jaguar rolls out its project X, Financial Times, 10 February 2001.

34   Jorn Madslien, Who gains most as Tata buys UK legends?, BBC News, 27 March 2008.

35   Ibid.

36   Tata buys Jaguar in £1.15bn deal, BBC News, 26 March 2008.

37   Lionel Barber, Seven days in South Asia, Financial Times Weekend Magazine, 20/21 November 2010.

38   Ben Oliver, Made in Britain, Saved in India, Craved in China, MailOnline, 25 August 2012.

39   Nils Pratley, Jaguar can still jump, The Guardian, 27 May 2011.

40   Terry Macalister, China sales boost behind 45% rise in Jaguar Land Rover profits, 10 August 2012.

41   Queen unveils Jaguar Land Rover engine plant, Auto Express, 30 October 2014.

42   Motor Industry Facts and Figures 2017, Society of Motor Manufacturers and Traders, London.

43   Peter Pugh, The Magic of a Name, The Rolls-Royce Story, Part Three, Icon Books, Cambridge, 2002.

44   Kevin Done, Time runs out on the road to survival, Financial Times, 25 February 1992.

45   Michiyo Nakamoto, Vickers in talks on sale of Rolls-Royce, Financial Times, 9 December 1991.

46   John Griffiths, Rolls-Royce keeps hold of the steering wheel, Financial Times, 20 December 1994.

47   Lucy Kellaway, Arms and the manure expert, Financial Times, 12 July 1998.

48   Peter Pugh, The Magic of a Name, The Rolls-Royce Story, Part Three, Icon Books, Cambridge, 2002.

49   Ibid.

50   Ibid.

51   Chris Barri, Germans to be the power behind Rolls, The Guardian, 20 December 1994.

52   Peter Wilkinson, "Affordable" Rolls-Royce powers record sales figures, CNN, 1 January 2012.

53   Octav Botnar dies fighting, Motor Trader, 20 July 1998.

54   Why Nissan prefers to forget Octav Botnar, inpmedia.com, 16 September 2011.

55   Nissan UK chief guilty of tax fraud, The Herald, 28 June 1993.

56   Shadowy figure who ended his years as a fugitive from justice, Octav Botnar Obituary, Financial Times, 14 July 1998.

57   Michael White, McAlpine stands by Tory donor who fled fraud case, The Guardian, 28 June 1993.

58   Reduction in Japanese car imports proposed, Financial Times, 13 September 1982.

59   John Griffiths, Daewoo tops car productivity league, Financial Times, 22 October 1999.

60   Rhys Jones, Nissan seeks to extend Sunderland car plant, Britain's biggest, Reuters, 20 August 2013.

61   Graham Ruddick, Nissan warns that increased French stake in partner firm Renault threatens UK jobs, The Guardian, 3 December 2015.

62   Ibid.

63   Chris Tighe, After a resounding Brexit vote, Sunderland fears for Nissan plant, The Guardian, 28 June 2016.

64   Why Toyota located here, Toyota Manufacturing (UK) Ltd, 2013.

65   James Mackintosh, Toyota moves into black in UK, Financial Times, 31 August 2006.

66   David Gow and Jon Henley, Toyota apologises for slur on UK workers, The Guardian, 4 March 2003.

67   Toyota to invest £240m in UK plant at Burnaston, BBC Business, 16 March 2017.

68   Graham Ruddick, Toyota to invest £240m in UK factory as government throws in £21m, The Guardian, 17 March 2017.

69   Tim Burt and John Griffiths, Mass car assembly has "no future in Britain", Financial Times, 24 May 2001.

70   Suzannah Hills, Britain now producing more cars than Germany, Daily Mail, 28 September 2012.

71   Federico Mor and Jennifer Brown, The motor industry: statistics and policy, House of Commons Briefing Paper, 11 April 2017.

72   Ibid.

73   Julia Kollewe, "Terrible blow" to Wales as car parts factory is shut with loss of 900 jobs, The Guardian, 16 January 2010.

74   David Bailey, The UK's auto industry. At a crossroads?, Birmingham Post – Business Blog, 25 April 2011.

75   Dan Milmo, Ellesmere Port news is good in parts, The Guardian, 15 May 2012.

76   Professor Karel Williams, Radio 4 Today Programme, 26 July 2013.

77   Duncan Weldon, Foreign-owned UK car industry offers economic lesson, BBC Business, 15 May 2014.

78   Motor Industry Facts and Figures 2017, Society of Motor Manufacturers and Traders, London, 2017.

79   Abby Bolter, Jaguar Land Rover lands blow to Ford Bridgend as it ends engine deal, Wales Online, 28 September 2017.

80   Peter Campbell and Jim Pickard, Ford plans to cut more than 1,100 jobs at UK's Bridgend plant, Financial Times, 1 March 2017.

81   Roy Church, The rise and decline of the British motor industry, Cambridge University Press, Cambridge, 1995.

82   James T. Walker, Voluntary Export Restraints between Britain and Japan: The Case of the UK Car Market (1971–2001), Henley Business School, 22 May 2015.

83   David Curry, France asks Japan to curb car sales, Financial Times, 28 July 1977.

84   Motor Industry Facts, Society of Motor Manufacturers and Traders, London, 2017.

85   The failure of Triumph in Speke, BBC Local, 8 December 2009.

86   The Motor Industry, Taking the High Road, The Economist, 17 November 2012.

87   Motor Industry Facts, Society of Motor Manufacturers and Traders, London, 2017.

88   Franziska Scheven, The United Kingdom is a big export market for German car companies and experts fear a Brexit could dampen sales, Handelsblatt Global, 23 June 2016.

89   Obituary: Sir George Turnbull, The Independent, 24 December 1992.

90   Unite launches plan to build growth and support for the UK automotive industry, Unite the Union press release, 21 May 2012.

91   James Fairrie, Letter to the Financial Times, 20 April 2009.

92   John Hooper, Automotive therapy, The Guardian, 29 October 2011.

93   Mary McMurray, Letter to The Guardian, 6 October 2009.

Chapter 8   Truck Stop

1   Survey Through the Years, Cars and Commercial Vehicles, Society of Motor Manufacturers and Traders, London.

2   Decade of change in the 1970s, Commercial Motor, 7 March 2013.

3   Ibid.

4   Steven Rattner, British companies in buy-out trend, The New York Times, 15 October 1982.

5   Sandy McLachlan, The National Freight Buy-Out, Macmillan Press, London, 1983.

6   Bedford, Grace's Guide to British Industrial History.

7   British truck industry is stuck in low gear, Chicago Tribune, 23 July 1985.

8   Kenneth Gooding, Bedford to phase out production of medium and heavy trucks, Financial Times, 10 September 1986.

9   Ibid.

10   John Griffiths, Receivers take control of AWD, Financial Times, 5 June 1992.

11   John Nevill, Ford Dagenham's 80 year history, BBC News, 6 October 2009.

12   Chris Godsmark, Iveco to close Langley factory, The Independent, 1 March 1997.

13   Rootes Group, Grace's Guide to British Industrial History.

14   Leyland Motors, Grace's Guide to British Industrial History.

15   Kenneth Gooding, Leyland and Daf to steer joint course, Financial Times, 20 February 1987.

16   Ibid.

17   A Brief History of Leyland Motors, its predecessors and successors, leylandtrucksltd.co.

18   Laura Run, Marriage of true minds behind Anglo-Dutch success, Financial Times, 5 July 1988.

19   Kevin Done and Laura Raun, DAF set to raise £250m from flotation, Financial Times, 9 December 1988.

20   Michael Smith, Leyland deal "may cost up to 5,000 jobs", The Guardian, 21 February 1987.

21   Michael Smith and John Carvel, 2,200 jobs go as Leyland is sold to Dutch, The Guardian, 20 February 1987.

22   Peter Hetherington, Leyland workers lobby in fight for 2,200 jobs, The Guardian, 3 March 1987.

23   Michael Harrison, DAF skids off the highway, The Independent, 7 February 1993.

24   Celia Weston, Mark Milner, Alan Travis and Martyn Halsall, Major refuses to join DAF rescue effort, The Guardian, 5 February 1993.

25   David Bowen, Hard road back from despair, The Independent, 2 January 1994.

26   Ibid.

27   Wim Oude Weernink, Paccar acquires Leyland Trucks, Automotive News Europe, 11 May 1998.

28   DAF Worldwide, daf.com.

29   George Archer, Andrea Thompson – Team captain, The Manufacturer, 5 January 2012.

30   Cable lays foundations for manufacturing growth in Lancashire, Lancashire Business, 14 January 2013.

31   John Griffiths, Truck group's move kills off Leyland name, Financial Times, 15 December 1999.

32   Austin and Morris Trucks, AROnline, aronline.co.

33   Morris, Grace's Guide to British Industrial History.

34   Associated Equipment Company, Grace's Guide to British Industrial History.

35   Albion Motor Company, Notable Commercial Vehicle Manufacturers in Britain, igg.org.

36   Guy Motors, Grace's Guide to British Industrial History.

37   The History of Scammell Lorries Limited, scammellregister.co.

38   Arthur Smith, Closure marks the end of a family affair, Financial Times, 27 February 1987.

39   Stephen Pullen, British Leyland, The history, the engineering, the people, Heritage Commercials, Mortons Media Group.

40   Scammell Commander, Tank transporter, military-today.com.

41   Universal Power Drives, History, tractors.wikia.com.

42   Arthur Smith, Closure marks the end of a family affair, Financial Times, 27 February 1987.

43   Kenneth Gooding, Scammell managers in plan to save jobs, Financial Times, 24 February 1987.
44   Tim Parry, Oshkosh signs UK deal, Fleet Owner, 17 December 2001.
45   Stephen Pullen, British Leyland, From steam wagons to seventies strife, Heritage Commercials, Mortons Media Group, Horncastle.
46   History, ERF Historic Vehicles Limited, erfhistoricvehicles.co.
47   Dai's inside story about ERF, thisisstaffordshire.co, 22 December 2009.
48   Ibid.
49   A Brief History of Dennis Brothers of Guildford – 1895–2011, dennissociety. org.
50   Dennis Brothers, Grace's Guide to British Industrial History.
51   John Griffiths, Hope in coaches as vehicles for success, Financial Times, 19 March 1985.
52   Dennis Eagle celebrates the best of British manufacturing with Top Gear, Dennis Eagle Ros Roca press release, 2 September 2013.
53   Foden, Grace's Guide to British Industrial History.
54   Tim Burt, Paccar transfers assembly of Fodens to Leyland, Financial Times, 13 September 1999.
55   Seddon, Grace's Guide to British Industrial History.
56   Atkinson, Grace's Guide to British Industrial History.
57   History of Seddon Atkinson.
58   End of the line for Seddon Atkinson, Commercial Motor, 4 January 2010.
59   Survey Through the Years, Cars and Commercial Vehicles, Society of Motor Manufacturers and Traders, London.
60   Ford Commercial Vehicles, Grace's Guide to British Industrial History.
61   Keith Naughton and Alex Webb, Ford to cut 5,700 jobs with three European plant closings, Bloomberg, 25 October 2012.
62   Len McCluskey, The Guardian, 27 October 2012.
63   Ibid.
64   Angela Monaghan, Ford considers Southampton factory closure, Daily Telegraph, 24 October 2012.
65   Mary Fagan, Buyout bid for Leyland DAF vans to go ahead, The Independent, 1 March 1993.
66   David Bowen, Leyland DAF in £8.6m rebound: Management buyout brings a change in fortunes – and name, The Independent, 23 April 1994.
67   End of the road for Mandy's white van, Evening Standard, 19 March 2009.
68   Jonathan Guthrie, Jobs axe hangs over 3,500 as hopes fade, Financial Times, 30 April 2009.
69   Jonathan Guthrie, Landscape of industrial decay emerges, Financial Times, 5 May 2009.

70   History of Leyland Motors, Leyland, Lancashire, Made in Preston, the engineer's story, madeinpreston.co.

71   Survey Through the Years, Cars and Commercial Vehicles, Society of Motor Manufacturers and Traders, London.

72   Peter Gould, The Leyland Story, Part Two: 1946–1991, petergould.co.

73   History of Leyland Motors, Leyland, Lancashire, Made in Preston, madeinpreston.co.

74   Christian Wolmar, John Hibbs, obituary, The Guardian, 29 January 2015.

75   David Hencke, Bus station buyers "made millions", The Guardian, 3 May 1991, summarising the Ninth Report of the Public Accounts Committee, Sale of the National Bus Company.

76   Robert Rice, Andrew Adonis, Chris Tighe, MMC condemns Stagecoach over "predatory" action, Financial Times, 4 August 1995.

77   Geoff Andrews, Retired bus chief rebukes Ridley over his "inexplicable" privatisation plans, The Guardian, 4 January 1984.

78   Geoff Andrews, Ridley is jeered by bus industry leaders, The Guardian, 27 September 1984.

79   Nick Garnett, Not yet the best but already transformed, Financial Times, Financial Times, 27 February 1985.

80   Sam Phipps, Colin Curtis, obituary, The Guardian, 29 September 2012.

81   Peter Stonham, Letter to the Financial Times, 11 April 1995.

82   Mike Humble, The Bus Section: Leyland Bus – 20 years since closure, AROnline, 10 July 2013.

83   John Griffiths, Leyland Bus to close HQ with loss of 757 jobs, Financial Times, 23 August 1986.

84   John Griffiths, Leyland Bus sold by buyout team to Volvo group, Financial Times, 31 March 1988.

85   Ibid.

86   Marcus W. Brauchli, Volvo agrees to buy Leyland Bus of Britain, Wall Street Journal, 31 March 1988.

87   Michael Smith, Volvo to get Leyland Bus "for £23m", 31 March 1988.

88   John Griffiths and Kevin Done, Swedish shoppers pick privatised bus bargain, Financial Times, 31 March 1988.

89   Paul Thompson and Terry Wallace, Volvo truck and bus in the UK: The clash of the Titans, Ending Production: Perspectives on Volvo's Uddevalla Plant, University of Stockholm, 1995.

90   Ibid.

91   Volvo to close Workington, Commercial Motor, 12 December 1991.

92   John Griffiths, Volvo factory closure signals end for Leyland Bus, Financial Times, 7 December 1991.

93   Robert Spano, Letter to the Financial Times, 16 December 1991.

94   Volvo closes Scottish truck factory, BBC News, 28 January 1999.

95   Paul Thompson and Terry Wallace, Volvo Truck and Bus in the UK: The Clash of the Titans, Ending Production: Perspectives on Volvo's Uddevalla Plant, University of Stockholm, 1995.

96   Ibid.

97   Ibid.

98   Hélène Mulholland, Boris Johnson unveils redesigned Routemaster bus for London, The Guardian, 16 December 2011.

99   Orders secured for 1,000 buses as ADL steps up the technology race, Alexander Dennis, 6 November 2012.

100   Peter Campbell, Alexander Dennis backs away from Optare bid, leaving road clear for rival Ashok Leyland, This is Money, 29 December 2011.

Chapter 9   Train Wreck

1   Maeve Kennedy, The Guardian, 1 May 2002.

2   British Railways 1920–1970, Locomotive Works of Independent Builders, britishrailways.info.

3   Portrait of an Engineer, A Merton Park Production in association with The Film Producers Guild, 1954.

4   Newton-le-willows.net.

5   Ibid.

6   English Electric, Grace's Guide to British Industrial History.

7   The North British Locomotive Company, Serving the Railways of the World, cat-flap.demon.co.

8   W.G. Bagnall, Grace's Guide to British Industrial History.

9   Ruston & Hornsby, Grace's Guide to British Industrial History.

10   Keith Farr, The Deltic Dynasty, Railway Magazine, September 2001.

11   GEC, Grace's Guide to British Industrial History.

12   A Brief History of the Metropolitan Carriage and Wagon Company Ltd, 1845–1945, metcam.co.

13   London Transport Locomotives and Rolling Stock, Ian Allan, London, 1969.

14   David Black, Indebted Alstom calls halt to shares trading, The Guardian, 5 August 2003.

15   Brush Traction, Grace's Guide to British Industrial History.

16   Brush in the Hawker Siddeley Group 1957–1991, www.brushtraction.com.

17   Peter Semmens and Yves Machefert-Tassin, Channel Tunnel Trains, Channel Tunnel Rolling Stock and the Eurotunnel System, The Channel Tunnel Group, Folkestone, 1994.

18   Ibid.
19   Wabtech strengthens its services with acquisition of LH Group, wabtecrail.co.
20   Ian Jack, When it comes to railways, the government is on the wrong track, The Guardian, 14 June 2008.
21   British Rail Workshops, railwaybritain.co.
22   Ibid.
23   Christian Wolmar, Broken Rails, How Privatisation Wrecked Britain's Railways, Aurum Press, London, 2001.
24   Ian Jack, The Crash That Stopped Britain, Granta Books, London, 2001.
25   Andrew Martin, There's a patriotic case for renationalising our railways, Daily Telegraph, 12 October 2013.
26   Ed Crooks, Radical soul chose to rock status quo, Financial Times, 1 May 2001.
27   Ibid.
28   Hamish McRae, Everyone thought Glengeagles was sold cheap – well they were right, The Guardian, 5 January 1984.
29   Peter Hetherington, Job-starved railway town gets £1.6m cash package, The Guardian, 22 August 1984.
30   Peter Hetherington, No rich pickings for redundant 900 as their line runs out of time, The Guardian, 23 June 1984.
31   Ibid.
32   Ivor Owen, BR "will not be forced to buy British", Financial Times, 11 June 1985.
33   Robert Wright, Chinese rail unit looks at building plant, Financial Times, 9 February 2009.
34   Woodrow Wyatt, Patriotism that would work, The Times, 23 March 1985.
35   Sir Robert Reid, obituary, Financial Times, 18 December 1993.
36   Hazel Duffy, Tough hall on a tighter track, Financial Times, 10 October 1984.
37   British Rail is accused of connivance with Tories in running down network, 8 January 1987.
38   Martin Linton, Tory MP criticises ministers for "shameful" rail cash cuts, The Guardian, 24 March 1990.
39   Ridley faces fury over job losses, Financial Times, 21 May 1986.
40   Richard Tomkins, A new locomotive for British Rail, Financial Times, 1 October 1990.
41   The Iron Lady: Margaret Thatcher: From Grocer's Daughter to Iron Lady, Vintage, London, 2012.
42   Jeremy Seabrook, Engineering a retreat into the museum society, The Guardian, 21 December 1985.

43   Doncaster Works to close, The Railway Magazine, January 2002.

44   Closure at Plant Works means the end of the line for 150 years of history, Doncaster Free Press, 20 December 2007.

45   Redundancy blow for 83 Horwich engineering workers, Lancashire Telegraph, 7 October 2004.

46   British Rail Workshops, railwaybritain.co.

47   Nicholas Bannister, Brel blames government for risk to jobs, The Guardian, 5 April 1993.

48   Andrew Baxter, Nervous end to roller-coaster ride, Financial Times, 8 February 1993.

49   Andrew Cook, Putting our business interests first, Letter to The Times, 16 April 1993.

50   Jonathan Foster, Death knell imminent for York train works as the railway industry prepares for privatisation, historians and innovators reflect on the past and argue the way of the future, The Independent, 12 January 1995.

51   Andrew Baxter, York train works to close with the loss of 750 jobs, Financial Times, 12 May 1995.

52   Charles Batchelor, Freight wagon maker to open plant, Financial Times, 3 March 1997.

53   Jonathan Glancey, The beauty of Crewe, The Guardian, 6 November 2005.

54   Crewe Locomotive Works Training School, Chief Mechanical and Electrical Engineer's Office, London Midland Region, Derby, September 1955.

55   John Harris and Les Summers, members of the design team, Letters to The Guardian, 14 September 2013.

56   Andrew Mist, The Australian XPT, The Railway Magazine, June 2000.

57   Gerry Bates, Letter to the Guardian, 13 July 2001.

58   Rebecca Smithers, Job losses blamed on BR privatisation, The Guardian, 8 June 1993.

59   Richard Marsh, Off the Rails, Weidenfeld and Nicholson, London, 1978.

60   Julia Langdon, Lord Marsh, obituary, The Guardian, 3 August 2011.

61   Sir Peter Parker, obituary, The Railway Magazine, July 2002.

62   David Walker, Sir David Serpell, obituary, The Guardian, 11 August 2008.

63   Sir Peter Parker, obituary, Daily Telegraph, 30 April 2002.

64   Andrew Clark, Network "too big to run profitably", The Guardian, 13 May 2002.

65   Gwyn Topham, Should railways be turned into bus lanes?, The Guardian, 4 February 2015.

66   John Wells, University of Cambridge, Letter to the Financial Times, 16 December 1988.

67   Andrew Cornelius, Government attacked on British Rail cash cuts, The Guardian, 15 July 1987.

68   Privatisation and After: Key Dates and Documents, Factsheet No 13, The Railway Forum, December 2000.

69   Christian Wolmar, Rail supply firms face "annihilation", The Independent, 3 December 1992.

70   Christian Wolmar, Rolling stock faces last siding: The Rail Privatisation Bill will bring little hope to Britain's train makers, The Independent, 20 January 1993.

71   That was a year that was…and from one extreme to the other, The Railway Magazine, April 1999.

72   Privatisation of the Rolling Stock Leasing Companies, National Audit Office, 3 March 1998.

73   Sean McCartney and John Stittle, "Engines of extravagance": The privatised British railway roling stock industry, Critical Perspectives on Accounting, Volume 23(2).

74   Professor Bill Bradshaw, Low priced rolling stock, Letter to the Financial Times, 4 April 1995.

75   Privatisation of the Rolling Stock Leasing Companies, National Audit Office, 3 March 1998.

76   Michael Harrison, Inquiry into how public lost £300m on gravy train, The Independent, 6 January 1997.

77   David Parker, The Official History of Privatisation, Volume II, Routledge, Abingdon, 2012.

78   Andrew Cave, Rail deals lost taxpayers £700m, Daily Telegraph, 5 March 1998.

79   Ibid.

80   David Wighton, Sale of BR depots "quite appalling", Financial Times, 17 December 1996.

81   Simon Beavis, Rail sell-off advice fees "cost £450m", The Guardian, 5 August 1996.

82   Rebecca Smithers, Rail sell-off fees to be kept secret, The Guardian, 17 February 1995.

83   Simon Beavis and Daniel John, BR sale "another poll tax", The Guardian, 2 June 1992.

84   Andrew Clark, Train fleet owners face scrutiny over profits, The Guardian, 16 July 2004.

85   Mary Fagan, I was right to sell the railway, Daily Telegraph, 3 December 2000.

86   Rachel Sylvester and Paul Marston, Tories: we were wrong on rail, Daily Telegraph, 13 December 2003.

87   Andrew Martin, Going up the line, The Guardian, 6 October 2012.

88   Rebecca Smithers and Martin Wainwright, ABB "sacrificed for the election", The Guardian, 9 December 1994.

89   Rebecca Smithers, £750m Tube contract compounds "misery" for British train builders, The Guardian, 9 December 1994.

90   Building a Better Railway: £1 Billion Rolling Stock Deal Means More Seats for South West Trains' Passengers, Strategic Rail Authority, 24 April 2001.

91   Colin Blackstock, £7m line to UK rail misery, The Guardian, 25 April 2002.

92   House of Commons Debate, 12 February 2009, cited in Louise Butcher, Railways: rolling stock, House of Commons Library, 2 August 2012.

93   Ray Massey, Hitachi moving headquarters of lucrative rail business to Britain in pre-emptive bid to build trains for HS2 line, MailOnline, 20 March 2014.

94   Press Association, Hitachi moves its rail business to Britain, The Guardian, 21 March 2014.

95   UK Rolling Stock Procurement, Written evidence to Parliament from Unite, the majority union at the Bombardier Transportation plant in Derby, 9 September 2011.

96   Jack Blanchard, Stabbed in the back again, Daily Mirror, 23 January 2016.

97   Sean Farrell, Derby Bombardier train factory wins £1bn deal to build carriages for Abellio network, The Guardian, 11 August 2016.

98   Bombardier wins £1bn Crossrail order, BBC News, 6 February 2014.

99   Ian Traynor, Angelique Chrisafis and John Hooper, How a British industry came off the rails, The Guardian, 7 July 2011.

100   Chris Bovis, Professor of European business law at the University of Hull, quoted in The Slow Death of British Rail Manufacturing, christianwolmar. co, 6 July 2011.

101   Ibid.

Chapter 10 Shipbuilding Founders

1   Michael Mason, Basil Greenhill and Robin Craig, The British Seafarer, Hutchinson/BBC in Association with the National Maritime Museum, London, 1980. The radio series was outstanding even by BBC standards – a long, painstaking and vivid tribute to Britain's huge maritime history.

2   Anthony Slaven, British Shipbuilding 1500–2010, Crucible Books, Lancaster, 2013.

3   All Our Working Lives Revisited – Shipbuilding, Peter Pagnamenta, BBC, 1984.

4   The History of Clyde Shipbuilding 4: Workshop of the British Empire.

5   Ibid.

6   A.J. Arnold, Iron Shipbuilding on the Thames, 1832–1915, eh.net/book, 2002.

7   Alan W. Cafruny, Ruling the Waves, The Political Economy of International Shipping, University of California Press, London, 1987.

8   End of an era for Germany's most famous shipyard, motorship.com.

9   Anthony Slaven, British Shipbuilding 1500–2010, Crucible Books, Lancaster, 2013.

10   Duncan Philip Connors, The Decline of British Shipbuilding: Negotiations between the British Government and the Scott Lithgow Company 1960–1987, Essays in Economic and Business History, Vol XXV, 2007.

11   Ian Hargreaves, Why time is running out for Tyneside shipbuilders, Financial Times, 16 May 1978.

12   Anthony Slaven, British Shipbuilding 1500–2010, Crucible Books, Lancaster, 2013.

13   Duncan Philip Connors, The Decline of British Shipbuilding: Negotiations between the British Government and the Scott Lithgow Company 1960–1987, Essays in Economic and Business History, Vol XXV, 2007.

14   Anthony Burton, The Rise and Fall of British Shipbuilding, The History Press, Stroud, 2013.

15   Closure Dates of Clyde Yards, inverclydeshipbuilding.co.

16   Frank Broadway, Upper Clyde Shipbuilders, A Study of Government Intervention, Centre for Policy Studies, London, 1976.

17   Anthony Burton, The Rise and Fall of British Shipbuilding, The History Press, Stroud, 2013.

18   Ibid.

19   Alan W. Cafruny, Ruling the Waves, The Political Economy of International Shipping, University of California Press, London, 1987.

20   David Bowen, Britain misses the boat, The Independent, 4 September 1994.

21   Ian Hargreaves, Why time is running out for Tyneside shipbuilders, Financial Times, 16 May 1978.

22   Britain holds place on slipway, Financial Times, 25 February 1970.

23   David Bowen, Britain misses the boat, The Independent, 4 September 1994.

24   Marshall Meek, obituary: Admiral Sir Anthony Griffin, The Independent, 22 October 1996.

25   Sir Robert Atkinson, businessman – obituary, Daily Telegraph, 2 February 2015.

26   Anthony Slaven, British Shipbuilding 1500–2010, Crucible Books, Lancaster, 2013.

27   Ibid.

28   Peter Hetherington, Battle is on as Tyneside yards run out of work, The Guardian, 6 November 1984.

29   Stephen Ward, Shipyard grants "sacrificed", The Independent, 1 September 1993.

30   John Newman, Numast, Letter to The Guardian, 2 September 1986.

31   Martyn Halsall, Lamont had an obsession to kill off shipyards, The Guardian, 1 September 1993.

32   Adam Sweeting, How a shipyard got that sinking feeling, The Guardian, 21 May 1991.

33   Kevin Brown, Aid to halt shipping fleet urged, Financial Times, 15 December 1986.

34   Shipping call for a lifeboat, Financial Times, 17 September 1990.

35   Lisa Wood, Heseltine "excluded" Treasury from DTI reviews, Financial Times, 3 August 1994.

36   Engineers' chief to quit IoD in protest, Financial Times, 15 August 1994.

37   Peter Hetherington, Worse to come as shipyards fight 9,000 lost jobs, The Guardian, 3 May 1983.

38   Anthony Slaven, British Shipbuilding 1500–2010, Crucible Books, Lancaster, 2013.

39   Seumas Milne, Storm over closure of Cammell Laird yard, The Guardian, 3 December 1992.

40   Anthony Slaven, British Shipbuilding 1500–2010, Crucible Books, Lancaster, 2013.

41   Ian Jack, Industrial miracle of a Scottish wasteland given up for dead, The Guardian, 16 August 2008.

42   Sarah Bridge, Full Speed Ahead: …how building boats has become a £3bn industry, This is Money, 10 July 2011.

43   Britain's richest woman splashes out £100m on 96-metre yacht – the biggest ever built in the UK, Daily Mail, 14 September 2011.

44   Michael Trebilcock, Marsha Chandler and Robert Howse, Trade and Transitions, A Comparative Analysis of Adjustment Policies, Routledge, London, 1990.

45   Options for the Scottish yards, The Referendum on Separation for Scotland, Scottish Affairs Select Committee, House of Commons, 20 January 2013.

46   BAE Systems in £133m deal to provide Brazilian Navy with 3 ocean patrol ships, This is Money, 3 January 2012.

47   Some words of history, stxeurope.com.

48   Raphael Minder, French shipyard puts to sea on its own, Financial Times, 13 August 2001.

49   David Woodruff, Aging French shipbuilder thrives as it kicks the subsidy habit, Wall Street Journal, 2 February 2000.

50   Raphael Minder, French shipyard puts to sea on its own, Financial Times, 13 August 2001.

51 Ben Hall, Paris to acquire shipbuilder stake, Financial Times, 8 November 2008.

52 Larrie D. Ferreiro, Shipbuilders to the world, International Journal of Naval History, December 2010.

53 Patrick Knox, Whatever happened to British shipbuilding?, Daily Echo, 10 November 2013.

54 David Watt, Royal Australian Navy to purchase UK ship, FlagPost, Parliament of Australia, 8 April 2011.

55 German Shipbuilding Industry, GlobalSecurity.org.

56 Cruising ahead, Italian Shipbuilding, The Economist, 21 September 1996.

57 Clay Harris, Clan Line's feuding heirs fight for Caledonia, Financial Times, 13 September 2003.

58 David Wighton, Plan to introduce tax breaks for shipowners, Financial Times, 12 August 1999.

59 Alan W. Cafruny, Ruling the Waves, The Political Economy of International Shipping, University of California Press, London, 1987.

60 Sir Lindsay Alexander, obituary, Daily Telegraph, 24 May 2000.

61 Japan gets ship order, Financial Times, 4 May 1985.

62 Charles Batchelor, P&O orders the world's biggest ferries, Financial Times, 26 January 1999.

63 Charles Batchelor, P&O places $2bn order for five new cruise ships, Financial Times, 23 June 1999.

64 P&O's new global Aurora, Financial Times, 21 August 1999.

65 Maggie Urry, Lord Sterling rings the changes, Financial Times, 13 May 2005.

66 Godfrey Holmes, Zeebrugge ferry disaster, 30 years on, The Independent, 3 March 2017.

67 Steve Bird, Work begins on £538m queen of the seas, The Times, 5 July 2002.

68 Richard Wray, Cunard contract goes to Italian yard, The Guardian, 15 December 2001.

69 Dan Milmo, The decline of the UK shipbuilding industry was not inevitable, The Guardian, 6 November 2013.

70 South Korea wins Royal Navy tanker deal, BBC News, 22 February 2012.

71 Ian Drury, MoD rejected defence company's offer to build the navy's tankers in Britain, MailOnline, 24 February 2012.

72 Dan Milmo and Severin Carrell, Defence contracts that keep British shipbuilding sector afloat, The Guardian, 16 August 2011.

73 Adam Nicholson, The call of the sea, The Guardian, 26 May 2007.

Chapter 11 Electric Shock

1   John Dummelow, Metropolitan-Vickers Electrical Co Ltd, 1899–1949, published by Metropolitan-Vickers Electrical Company, 1949, and digitised by Jim Lawton as a "labour of love".

2   Martin Doppelbauer, The invention of the electric motor 1800–1854, Elektrotechnisches Institut.

3   Ibid.

4   Maev Kennedy, First Edison light bulbs may fetch £300,000, The Guardian, 9 December 2006.

5   Robert Jones and Oliver Marriott, Anatomy of a Merger, Jonathan Cape, London, 1970.

6   Martin J. Wiener, English Culture and the Decline of the Industrial Spirit, 1850–1980, Cambridge University Press, Cambridge, 1981.

7   History of Metropolitan Vickers Ltd, www.britishtelephones.com.

8   Josef Reindl, Collusion and Competition: The Electrical Engineering Industry in the United Kingdom and West Germany between 1945 and the late 1970s, Business and Economic History, Vol 26, no 2, Winter 1997.

9   Metropolitan Vickers, Grace's Guide to British Industrial History.

10   Jo Carley, Fifty years on, the spare parts run out, Financial Times, 12 July 1991.

11   John Dummelow, Metropolitan-Vickers Electrical Co Ltd, 1899–1949, digitised by Jim Lawton as a "labour of love".

12   Associated Electrical Industries Ltd (AEI), www.britishtelephones.com.

13   History of Metropolitan Vickers Ltd, www.britishtelephones.com.

14   Judith Court, Source of power and pride; from Willans & Robinson to GEC and Alstom – the life and turbulent times of a "family" that was the dynamo for industry, Coventry Evening Telegraph, 31 October 2003.

15   Ibid.

16   Josef Reindl, Collusion and Competition: The Electrical Engineering Industry in the United Kingdom and West Germany between 1945 and the Late 1970s, Business and Economic History, Vol 26, no 2, Winter 1997.

17   Briefing: Power Generating Industry, International Socialism, October 1977.

18   Associated Electrical Industries Ltd (AEI), www.britishtelephones.com.

19   Robert Jones and Oliver Marriott, Anatomy of a Merger, Jonathan Cape, London, 1970.

20   English Electric Co, Grace's Guide to British Industrial History.

21   Robert Jones and Oliver Marriott, Anatomy of a Merger, A History of GEC, AEI and English Electric, Jonathan Cape, London, 1970.

22   History of GEC, britishtelephones.com.

23   Ibid.

24   Ibid.

25   Stephen Aris, The accountant who was Lord Weinstock's alter ego at GEC, Financial Times, 15 June 2006.

26   Michael Grylls MP and John Redwood MP, National Enterprise Board, A Case for Euthanasia, Centre for Policy Studies, 1980.

27   Nick Garnett, GEC Turbines axes 650 jobs at three plants, Financial Times, 16 November 1983.

28   Nick Garnett, New orders will go to the survivors, Financial Times, 16 February 1987.

29   Ian Rodger, RR and GEC in turbine venture, 15 June 1984.

30   Lord Weinstock, obituary, Daily Telegraph, 24 July 2002.

31   A failing giant, editorial, New Statesman, 13 January 1989.

32   Jean Shaoul, Lord Weinstock and the near terminal decline of British industry, wsws.org, 27 July 2002.

33   Lord Weinstock, obituary, Daily Telegraph, 24 July 2002.

34   Dan Sabbagh and Sean O'Neill, Marconi: from boom to bust in a year, Daily Telegraph, 7 September 2001.

35   Simon Caulkin, GEC Alsthom – A marriage a la Jack Sprat, Management Today, 1 July 1993.

36   Andrew Baxter and Ronald van de Krol, GEC Alsthom sets 1990s agenda, Financial Times, 10 January 1991.

37   Crossed wires for electricity, Lex Column, Financial Times, 30 July 1990.

38   David Thomas, Labour sees costs in power sell-off exceeding £100m, Financial Times, 27 March 1990.

39   Maurice Samuelson, Electricity industry switches on the lawyers, Financial Times, 28 March 1990.

40   David Thomas and Maurice Samuelson, Hanson ghost at PowerGen's feast of figures, Financial Times, 1 August 1990.

41   Maurice Samuelson, Tory peer attacks power sell-off, Financial Times, 21 May 1988.

42   Patrick Wintour, Electricity sell-off attacked by Tories, The Guardian, 15 July 1988.

43   Andrew Baxter, GEC Alsthom plant in N Ireland to shut, Financial Times, 26 April 1991.

44   Simon Caulkin, GEC Alsthom – A marriage a la Jack Sprat, Management Today, 1 July 1993.

45   Andy Blamey, Copper holds the key to electrical energy efficiency, Reuters, 19 February 2001.

46   Mary Brasier, French criticise UK power industry, Daily Telegraph, 25 February 1993.

47   Mark Milner, PowerGen's £300m order helps boost Siemens profit to £270m, The Guardian, 25 April 1990.

48   Nick Garnett, Equipment suppliers fear a power vacuum, Financial Times, 22 November 1989.

49   Nick Garnett, Power struggle, Financial Times, 20 April 1990.

50   Andrew Clark, Wakeham brushed aside Enron crisis warnings, board papers show, The Guardian, 15 April 2006.

51   Rob Evans and David Hencke, Ambassador promoted cause of Enron boss, The Guardian, 22 December 2003.

52   Crash of the cult, Enron tolls the bell for deregulation, The Guardian, 30 November 2001.

53   Tom Leonard and George Jones, Wakeham quits in Enron scandal, Daily Telegraph, 1 February 2002.

54   Irwin Stelzer, Why Enron deserves our gratitude, The Guardian, 29 January 2002.

55   Larry E. Hoffman, Chris J. Harrison, James J. Shields, Combustion Turbine Triple Fuel System for Teesside, England, Project. American Society of Mechanical Engineers, 1994.

56   Sandra Laville, Anger over £10m fattest cat of all, Evening Standard, 28 August 1996.

57   Dan Sabbagh and Sean O'Neill, Marconi: from boom to bust in a year, Daily Telegraph, 7 September 2001.

58   Nick Gilbert, Profile: Sir Roger Hurn – an Unsung Hero, The Independent, 7 September 1997.

59   Jane Martinson, GEC's Darth Vader makes a biotech transformation, The Guardian, 18 August 2006.

60   Last great industrialist – livid to the end, The Guardian, 24 July 2002.

61   Michael Harrison, Corporate Profile: The man spending GEC's £6bn, The Independent, 5 May 1999.

62   GEC Alsthom to be floated, Railway Gazette, 1 January 1998.

63   Simon Bowers, Alstom blames UK for job losses, The Guardian, 11 August 2003.

64   Ibid.

65   Julian Birkinshaw, The destruction of Marconi, Business Strategy Review, Spring 2004.

66   Reinventing Marconi, The Economist, 30 November 2000.

67   Edmond Warner, Stop bleating about the Marconi bust, The Guardian, 31 August 2002.

68   The £11bn wreckers, This is Money, 17 July 2001.

69   Dan Sabbagh, Nightmare on Bruton Street, Daily Telegraph, 16 February 2002.

70   Mark Milner, Four years after the Marconi fiasco, John Mayo is back, The Guardian, 25 June 2005.

71   Marconi shares collapse, BBC News, 5 September 2001.

72   Dominic White, Parton in line for £17m if he revives Marconi, Daily Telegraph, 19 March 2003.

73   Philip Aldrick, Marconi chief to quit after pocketing £8.5m, Daily Telegraph, 2 November 2004.

74   Neil Collins, Marconi payoff that sticks in the craw, Daily Telegraph, 2 November 2004.

75   Maija Pesola, Sundeep Tucker and Mark Odell, Marconi value slashed after failure to win role in £10bn BT network rebuild, Financial Times, 29 April 2005.

76   BT blamed for Marconi job losses, The Guardian, 14 July 2005.

77   Richard Wray, Marconi dealt fatal blow as BT shuts it out of 21st century, The Guardian, 29 April 2005.

78   Richard Wray, Marconi cuts 800 jobs and pulls out of Liverpool, The Guardian, 7 May 2005.

79   Maija Pesola and Jean Eaglesham, DTI will urge Marconi to retain R&D activity in UK, Financial Times, 21 May 2005.

80   Malini Guha and Carlos Grande, Marconi seeks talks with unions, Financial Times, 4 May 2005.

81   Terry Macalister, Marconi up for sale with 2,000 jobs at risk, The Guardian, 4 May 2005.

82   Richard Wray, Marconi faces backlash over Huawei talks, The Guardian, 9 August 2003.

83   Mark Milner and Charlotte Moore, Ericsson deal closes Marconi's final chapter, 26 October 2005.

84   Richard Wray, Former Marconi boss to quit rump firm Telent, The Guardian, 12 August 2006.

85   Alstom ex-boss refunds pay-off, BBC News, 18 August 2003.

86   Mary Bellis, Steam Turbines – Charles Parsons, inventors.about.com.

87   F.R. Harris, The Parsons Centenary – a Hundred Years of Steam Turbines, Proceedings of the Institution of Mechanical Engineers, Part A; Journal of Power and Energy, August 1984.

88   CA Parsons & Co, Grace's Guide to British Industrial History.

89   CA Parsons: The Tyneside factory that powered nation, chroniclelive.co, 25 March 2013.

90   A Reyrolle and Co, Grace's Guide to British Industial History.

91   Reyrolle, abb.co.

92   Clarke Chapman, A Brief History, www.pharoah.co.

93   John Lloyd, A growing power beside the Tyne?, Financial Times, 6 November 1979.

94   Nick Garnett, New order will go to the survivors, Financial Times, 16 February 1987.

95   John Hooper, Power progress at a snail's pace, The Guardian, 2 April 1984.

96   Nick Garnett, A slimmer, fitter NEI moves nearer a clean bill of health, Financial Times, 6 November 1994.

97   Richard Tomkins, NEI plans reorganisation with loss of 7,500 jobs, Financial Times, 1 October 1986.

98   Rolls' steam bath, Lex column, Financial Times, 20 July 1996.

99   Stefan Wagstyl, Rolls-Royce to sell steam turbine generator business, Financial Times, 20 July 1996.

100   Stefan Wagstyl and Chris Tyghe, Siemens agrees to buy most of Parsons, Financial Times, 10 April 1997.

101   Stefan Wagstyl, Siemens believes its time has yet to come, Financial Times, 11 April 1997.

102   Stefan Wagstyl, Re-engineering a grand old name, Financial Times, 10 April 1997.

103   Siemens Brothers and Co, Grace's Guide to British Industrial History.

104   History of Siemens Brothers, britishtelephones.com.

105   About US, Crompton Lighting, Crompton.com.

106   Crompton Parkinson, Grace's Guide to British Industrial History.

107   South Wales Switchgear, Grace's Guide to British Industrial History.

108   Aberdare Cables, Grace's Guide to British Industrial History.

109   Hawker Siddeley Switchgear, hss-ltd.com.

110   75 jobs to go at Blackwood's Hawker Siddeley Switchgear, BBC News, 6 December 2011.

111   History – Loughborough, www.brush.eu.

112   Ibid.

113   Andrew Baxter, A clean sweep at the old Brush, Financial Times, 9 October 1991.

114   Britain, An Official Handbook, Central Office of Information, 1959.

115   Britain, An Official Handbook, Central Office of Information, 1973.

Chapter 12 Electronic Short Circuit

1   R.W. Burns, British Television, The Formative Years, IEE History of Technology Series 7, Peter Peregrinus, 1986.

2   Jane Gatrell (née Shoenberg), Shoenberg's role in development of TV, Letter to The Guardian, 2 July 2015.

3   Ibid.

4   EMI – a long, slow, painful death, Kevin Tennant, The Business History Blog, 1 February 2011.

5   Rex Malik, What's Wrong with British Industry?, Penguin Books, 1964.

6   The Structure of British Industry, Edited by P.S. Johnson, Granada Publishing, 1980.

7   Simon Lavington, A brief history of British computers: the first 25 years (1948–1973), computinghistory.org.

8   Jack Schofield, Sir Maurice Wilkes, scientist who built the first practical computer, Obituaries, The Guardian, 1 December 2010.

9   Hilary J. Kahn, Tom Kilburn, brilliant scientist at the heart of the computer revolution, Obituaries, The Guardian, 23 January 2001.

10   Georgina Ferry, A Computer Called LEO, Fourth Estate, 2003.

11   Paul Fisher, Down the tube, The Guardian, 5 May 1994.

12   The Structure of British Industry, Edited by P.S. Johnson, Granada Publishing, 1980.

13   Michael Grylls MP and John Redwood MP, National Enterprise Board, A Case for Euthanasia, Centre for Policy Studies, London 1980.

14   Deborah Wise, ICL stays in profit while trying to remain British and in Europe, The Guardian, 17 April 1991.

15   Guy de Jonquieres, ICL to make 650 redundant, Financial Times, 18 January 1985.

16   Fading away, editorial, The Guardian, 20 July 1990.

17   Ibid.

18   Alan Cane, ICL slips into a kimono…but keeps its identity, Financial Times, 30 November 1990.

19   Michael Skapinker, ICL ousted from research programme, Financial Times, 27 March 1991.

20   Geoff Gibbs, ICL name joins computer history, The Guardian, 22 June 2001.

21   Paul Fisher, Down the tube, The Guardian, 5 May 1994.

22   Bull computers chronological history, feb-patrimoine.

23   Atos to buy Bull in all-French IT services deal, Reuters, 26 May 2014.

24   Jason Crisp, They're walking off the shelves, Financial Times, 12 December 1983.

25   Terry Dodsworth, Electronics industry faces harsh home truths, Financial Times, 27 June 1988.

26   David Manners, 50 Years of the UK semiconductor industry, Electronics Weekly, 17 September 2010.

27   Inmos, Domesday Reloaded, BBC.

28   BTG chief Dame Louise Makin in line for £20m windfall after firm's sale, This is Money, 25 November 2018.

29   Deborah Wise, End of the road for UK hi-tech pace-setter, The Guardian, 14 March 1992.

30   Alun Williams, ST to close its former Inmos design centre Bristol site, Electronics Weekly, 5 July 2013.

31   The idea that died, The Guardian, 26 June 1990.

32   Michael Skapinker, Great divide of the Plessey spoils, Financial Times, 4 April 1990.

33   Hugo Dixon, Asset stripping threat to chip operation, Financial Times, 13 January 1989.

34   Michael Skapinker, Chipping away at the market, Financial Times, 16 October 1990.

35   Steven Hugill, Calls to save north-east microchip factory from closure, The Northern Echo, 22 March 2013.

36   Shock at Siemens jobs loss, BBC News, 31 July 1998.

37   Siemens Brothers and Co, Grace's Guide to British Industrial History.

38   Standard Telephones and Cables, Grace's Guide to British Industrial History.

39   Automatic Telephone and Electric Company, Grace's Guide to British Industrial History.

40   Abridged History of the British Ericsson Company, britishtelephones.com.

41   Tony Benn, Out of the Wilderness, Diaries 1963–67, Hutchinson, 1987.

42   UK's first electronic phone exchange to be completed next year, Electronics Weekly, 1 February 1961.

43   Brian Groom, Manufacturing chief William Barlow dies, obituary, Financial Times, 2 June 2012.

44   Sir William Barlow, obituary, Daily Telegraph, 23 May 2012.

45   Alan Tuffin, Press button BT and listen to the sound of plunder, The Guardian, 19 November 1984.

46   David Simpson, City to get £127m from BT sale, The Guardian, 28 November 1984.

47   Stockbrokers simply cannot believe their luck at the Telecoms flotation, The Guardian, 22 November 1984.

48   Alex Henney, The consumer is left out in the cold, Financial Times, 7 March 1984.

49   BT wrings its suppliers, Lex Column, Financial Times, 13 May 1985.

50   Peter Riddell, Lord Weinstock's public protest, Financial Times, 28 March 1984.

51   Guy de Jonquieres, The BT sale: why the stakes are so very high, Financial Times, 3 May 1984.

52   Peter Large, BT's foreign phone deal hits STC shares, The Guardian, 9 October 1984.

53   Peter Large, British Telecom spurns ICL for IBM, The Guardian, 4 May 1985.

54   Jason Crisp, BT aims for the world stage, Financial Times, 11 May 1985.

55   Telecom still part of Great Britain Ltd, The Times, 24 July 1985.

56   Seumas Milne, Telecom plan UK firms, The Guardian, 17 November 1984.

57   GEC, Financial Times, 15 June 1985.

58   Jason Crisp, Mercury order for Northern Telecom, Financial Times, 10 May 1985.

59   Guy de Jonquieres, A crucial test for System X, Financial Times, 11 April 1983.

60   Ibid.

61   David Simpson, STC to cut Belfast workforce by 240, The Guardian, 30 November 1984.

62   STC to cut 300 jobs in Ulster, Financial Times, 18 May 1985.

63   Abridged History of the British Ericsson Company, britishtelephones.com, 6 March 2010.

64   David Thomas, Thorn Ericsson wins BT order, Financial Times, 28 January 1988.

65   Terry Dodsworth, Telecoms partners grow apart, Financial Times, 10 June 1988.

66   Christopher Reed, Charles Brown, the man who killed Ma Bell, obituary, The Guardian, 25 November 2003.

67   Peter Large, Logica says UK is victim of new telecom moves, The Guardian, 15 June 1988.

68   Andrew Adonis, Nice benefits, what about the borders, Financial Times, 24 February 1994.

69   Victor Keegan, Sell your house in London, move to the North and you may never have to work again, The Guardian, 6 July 1987.

70   Terry Dodsworth, BT investment levels "lagging behind rivals", Financial Times, 19 October 1987.

71   Ibid.

72   Juliette Garside: Britain's broadband is stuck in the slow lane, The Guardian, 8 May 2012.

73   Miles Brignell, Owners of new-build homes waiting six months for landline; one of Thatcher's privatisations is still failing to deliver, The Guardian, 20 April 2013.

74   Paul Vallely, Five years of crossed lines at Cable & Wireless, The Independent, 17 November 1995.

75   Jason Crisp, Optical fibre cable for Atlantic, Financial Times, 17 November 1983.

76   Gordon Cramb, Kenneth Corfield: Engineer with an agile eye for the trajectory of technology, obituary, Financial Times, 6/7 February 2016.

77   Michael Skapinker, STC in talks with likely buyers, Financial Times, 16 October 1990.

78   Peter Young, More than just another takeover, Letter to the Financial Times, 18 November 1990.

79   Eye of storm, Alistair Gooch, director, Fibreoptic Transmission Technology, Letter to The Guardian, 10 July 1991.

80   Racal, Grace's Guide to British Industrial History.

81   Sir Ernest Harrison, obituary, Daily Telegraph, 22 February 2009.

82   Racal Electronics plc History, fundinguniverse.com.

83   Zichun Gao and Clem Tisdell, Television Production, The Product Cycle and China, University of Queensland, January 2004.

84   The Old Vinyl Factory, Hayes, Cathedral Group PLC.

85   EMI – Advantage Lost, venturenavigator.co.uk, August 2007.

86   EMI scratches £43m, Financial Times, November 25/26 2000.

87   Joshua Chaffin, Andrew Edgecliffe-Johnson, Maggie Urry, EMI chief to leave with £3m, Financial Times, 30 August 2007.

88   Tom Fairless, EMI: a history of a deal gone wrong, Financial News, 4 November 2010.

89   Matthew Sparkes, From the Gramophone Company to Citigroup, Daily Telegraph, 11 November 2011.

90   EMI: the sad demise of a very British company, Music Blog, The Guardian, 11 November 2011.

91   Thorn Electrical Industries, Grace's Guide to British Industrial History.

92   Dominic Midgley, UK: Thorn EMI's Fissile Future, Management Today, 1 August 1994.

93   Patrick Hosking, Profile: Reformer badly in need of a good result: Sir Colin Southgate: The man who pruned Thorn EMI down to two core businesses has yet to see the fruits of the changes, The Independent, 28 November 1993.

94   Terry Dodsworth, Electronics sector shows plenty of profit but not enough growth, Financial Times, 24 November 1987.

95   Ibid.

96   Philip Smet, Philips switches off TV production, Radio Netherlands Worldwide, 20 April 2011.

97   What happened to Japan's electronic giants?, BBC News, 2 April 2013.

98   Jonathan Soble, Japanese TV manufacturers admit defeat, Financial Times, 2 November 2011.

99   Christopher Williams, Electronics sector in UK "could expand by 55 per cent", Daily Telegraph, 24 June 2013.

Chapter 13 Textiles Unravel

1   All Our Working Lives Revisited – Cotton and Textiles, BBC4, 27 September 2010.

2   Claire Hopley, British textiles clothe the world, British Heritage, 29 July 2006.

3   Pat Hudson, The Industrial Revolution: A New History, newleftproject.org.

4   The Early British Industrial Revolution and Infant Industry Protectionism: The Case of Cotton Textiles, Social Democracy for the 21st Century: A Post Keynesian Perspective, 22 June 2010.

5   Lynden Briscoe, The textile and clothing industries of the United Kingdom, Manchester University Press, 1971.

6   The Early British Industrial Revolution and Infant Industry Protectionism: The Case of Cotton Textiles, Social Democracy for the 21st Century: A Post Keynesian Perspective, 22 June 2010.

7   Ibid.

8   Ibid.

9   G.C. Allen, British Industries and Their Organization, Longmans, fourth edition, 1959.

10   The British textile industry – after decades of decline, down but not out, Workers, May 2005.

11   A Brief History of Hosiery Manufacture and Lacemaking in Nottingham, based on The Lace Market, Nottingham, by Geoffrey Oldfield, Nottingham Civic Society, 2001.

12   The textile industry in Derry, the shirt industry, Culture Northern Ireland.

13   G.C. Allen, British Industries and Their Organization, Longmans, fourth edition, 1959.

14   Ibid.

15   Ibid.

16   Ibid.

17   Geoffrey Owen, The Life and Fall of Great Companies: Courtaulds and the Reshaping of the Man-Made Fibres Industry, Pasold Research Fund, Oxford University Press, 2010.

18   Courtaulds, Grace's Guide to British Industrial History.

19   Chris Mullin, Tony Benn: he was a life-enhancer and fizzed with ideas, The Guardian, 14 March 2014.

20   Tony Benn, Out of the Wilderness, Diaries 1963–67, Hutchinson, 1987.

21   Norman Wooding, obituary, Lord Kearton, The Independent, 29 July 1992.

22   Grace's Guide to British Industrial History.

23   Nicholas Faith, obituary: Joe Hyman, The Independent, 12 July 1999.

24   Alan Cowell, Joe Hyman, 77, established British textile empire in 60s, The New York Times, 17 July 1999.

25   Russia: Textile Institute Member Wants Terylene Inventors to be Honoured, just-style.com, 24 November 2000.

26   Courtaulds "inconsiderate" record attacked, Financial Times, 2 July 1985.

27 Courtaulds closing four Lancashire textile mills, Financial Times, 15 September 1988.

28 Chris Blackhurst, Profile – Sipko Huismans of Courtaulds, Management Today, 1 November 1992.

29 Interview, BBC Radio 4, 22 January 1992.

30 Courtaulds bows to £150m takeover, BBC News, 24 March 2000.

31 Harry Wallop, Hong Kong firm buys Courtaulds, Daily Telegraph, 10 May 2006.

32 Courtaulds goes Dutch in £1.8bn Akzo takeover, BBC News, 20 April 1998.

33 John Parker, in conversation with the author, late 1990s.

34 Lynden Briscoe, The Textile and Clothing Industries of the United Kingdom, Manchester University Press, 1971.

35 Ibid.

36 Robert Heller, Joe Hyman – Financial genius who built and lost an empire, The Guardian, 12 July 1999.

37 Antonia Feuchtwanger, Maestro of mail-order: Sir David Alliance, The Independent, 16 October 1994.

38 Grace's Guide to British Industrial History.

39 David Alliance, My time as a supplier to Marks & Spencer, Retail Week, 12 February 2015.

40 Grace's Guide to British Industrial History.

41 Debra Isaac, Strong steps at Viyella, Financial Times, 20 September 1988.

42 Alice Rawsthorn, Knitwear factory closes, Financial Times, 5 October 1988.

43 Alice Rawsthorn, Coats closure costs 800 jobs, Financial Times, 8 October 1988.

44 Grace's Guide to British Industrial History.

45 Anna Minton, Coats Viyella to close UK production, Financial Times, 9 March 2000.

46 Amir Taheri, Home Lifestyle & Culture Book Reviews, 3 June 2015.

47 Textiles in decline, BBC News, 6 December 1999.

48 Rob Griffin, 1,900 jobs go as Coats cuts out Marks, Financial Times, 7 September 2000.

49 Textiles unravelling, The Economist, 31 December 1998.

50 Baird jobs to go as M&S severs 30-year contract, The Independent, 23 October 1999.

51 Axe hangs over William Baird jobs, BBC News, October 1999.

52 William Baird plunges into loss, BBC News, 29 February 2000.

53 Tom Stevenson, Dewhirst profits from Marks & Spencer, The Independent, 10 April 1996.

54 David Blackwell and Susanna Voyle, 1,000 jobs to go as Dewhirst factories close, Financial Times, 14 January 2000.

55   Dewhirst closure "cannot be halted", BBC News, 19 July 2002.

56   Dewhirst shuts last clothes factory, BBC News, 28 August 2002.

57   Dewhirst jobs have been taken to hotter climes, Cambrian News, 17 October 2002.

58   Richard Tyler, Strategic planning is the key to Dewhirst's overseas drive, Daily Telegraph, 24 May 2010.

59   Coats Viyella postpones plans to split, BBC News, 9 September 1998.

60   Zoe Wood and Julia Kollewe, After 225 years, Viyella joins casualty list putting 450 jobs at risk, The Guardian, 8 January 2009.

61   Sir William Coats Obituary, The Herald, 23 May 2009.

62   Guinness Peat told to boost Coats pension fund, BBC News, 22 December 2014.

63   Geoff Foster, End of an era as Guinness Peat Group dons its new coat, This is Money, 26 February 2015.

64   G.C. Allen, British Industries and Their Organization, Longmans, 1959.

65   A brief history of the wool trade in the Witney area. www.witneyblanketstory.org.uk

66   G.C. Allen, British Industries and Their Organization, Longmans, fourth edition, 1959.

67   Linda Whitwam, Focus on Huddersfield's proud textile heritage, Huddersfield Examiner, 9 April 2011.

68   History of weaving in Huddersfield, C&J Antich, 2012.

69   Ibid.

70   Tony Phillips, The rise and fall of Wool City, Yorkshire Post, 22 November 2007.

71   Terrible Times for Children During Bradford's Textile Revolution, Bradford Industrial Museum.

72   David Goodhart, A tale of three cities, Prospect Magazine, July 2011.

73   The City of Leicester – Hosiery Manufacture, British History Online.

74   Lynden Briscoe, The textile and clothing industries of the United Kingdom, Manchester University Press, 1971.

75   G.C. Allen, British Industries and Their Organization, Longmans, fourth edition, 1959.

76   Ibid.

77   Lynden Briscoe, The textile and clothing industries of the United Kingdom, Manchester University Press, 1971.

78   Jerene Jones, Her claws as sharp as ever, Pamela Mason tells her old family firm to "stuff its stuffiness", People Magazine, 22 October 1979.

79   Sandra Salmans, How Pamela Mason is rattling British wool, The New York Times, 27 June 1981.

80   Nigel Grizzard, Run of the mill they're not, The Guardian, 17 June 2008.

81 Jim Greenhall, Mill doors close, but not for long…, Bradford Telegraph and Argus, 14 February 2011.

82 Gail Counsell, Profile: The recession player: Alan Lewis believes in God, making money, and the disciplines of karate, The Independent, 6 September 1992.

83 Profile: Alan Lewis, Yorkshire Post, 17 July 2012.

84 This university means business, University of Huddersfield, 8 November 2012.

85 No encore for Corah, Leicester Chronicler.

86 Alice Rawsthorn, Troubled knitwear maker sheds 780 jobs to cut costs, Financial Times, 28 May 1988.

87 M&S supplier axes 800 clothing jobs, The Guardian, 28 May 1988.

88 Alice Rawsthorn, Knitwear makers fight for survival, Financial Times, 28 May 1988.

89 Debra Isaac, Corah to close Troon plant in new management shakeout, The Guardian, 30 July 1988.

90 Alice Rawsthorn, Corah cuts 380 jobs in move to save costs, Financial Times, 31 July 1988.

91 David Green, Corah sells off socks sector to Courtaulds, Daily Telegraph, 31 August 1988.

92 Alistair Moffat, The Borders: A History of the Borders from Earliest Times.

93 William Hall, Joseph Dawson returns to its Yorkshire roots, Financial Times, 4 September 2004.

94 Crisis time for cashmere giants, Yorkshire Evening Post, 15 December 2007.

95 Hawick cashmere firm Dawson's share price plunges, BBC Scotland Business, 20 July 2012.

96 Jack Mathieson, Fears for 200 jobs at Scots textile firm after shares suspended, Daily Record, 9 August 2012.

97 Hawick jobs saved as Chanel buys Barrie Knitwear after Dawson collapse, The Southern Reporter, 16 October 2012.

98 Alan Cowell, Cashmere moves on, and Scotland feels a chill, The New York Times, 27 March 2004.

99 Peter Marsh, Special breed with knitwear products to dye for, FT Series Made in Britain, Financial Times, 2 October 2010.

100 Erikka Askeland, "Time is now" to back Scots textile firms, The Scotsman, 22 September 2013.

101 Lucy Siegle, Should I worry about cheap cashmere?, The Guardian, 7 December 2014.

102 Scott Wright, Profits fall as Lyle & Scott battles headwinds in the UK and Europe, HeraldScotland, 2 January 2015.

103 Run of the mill they're not, The Guardian, 17 June 2008.

104 150 years on Hugh threads the story of the Crossley dynasty, Halifax

Courier, 17 September 2012.

105 Angelique Chrisafis, Pile of trouble for carpet makers, The Guardian, 25 August 2003.

106 Carpet firm closes after 168 years, The Guardian, 26 February 2005.

107 John Murray Brown, Axminster Carpets bounces back, Financial Times, 7 April 2014.

108 Axminster Carpets: Consortium saves Devon firm and 100 jobs, BBC News, 6 April 2013.

109 Industrialising carpet making – a report of a visit to the Kidderminster Museum of Carpet, Wyre Forest and District University of the Third Age, 24 November 2014.

110 Julia Leonard, Kidderminster carpet traders dispute the decline of the industry, BBC News, 1 September 2012.

111 W.A. Graham Clark, Linen, Jute and Hemp Industries in the United Kingdom, US Department of Commerce, 1913.

112 Jim Tomlinson, The Decline of Jute and the De-globalization of Dundee.

113 Stephen Goodwin, Just journalism left as jute joins jam, The Independent, 20 October 1998.

114 About Linen – History of Irish Linen, Thomas Ferguson Irish Linen, 2015.

115 Emily Boyle, Linenopolis: the rise of the textile industry, Irelandseye.com.

116 Peter Lennox-Kerr, Linen makes a comeback in Ulster, Financial Times, 18 July 1985.

117 Invention of the Jacquard Loom, ideafinder.com.

118 How a northern town became a silk powerhouse, BBC News, 23 October 2015.

119 Nicholas Owen and Alan Cannon Jones, A Comparative Study of the British and Italian Textile and Clothing Industries, DTI Economics Paper No 2, April 2003.

120 The Alliance Project Team, Repatriation of UK Textiles Manufacture, January 2015.

121 Shelina Begum, Brands look to rebuild British textile manufacturing, Manchester Evening News, 6 January 2012.

122 Steve Hawks, John Lewis to "repatriate" textile manufacturing in made in Britain push, Daily Telegraph, 21 July 2013.

123 Peter Marsh, Cable backs plan to boost textile industry, Financial Times, 1 November 2012.

124 Lucy Siegle, Britain's rag trade revival, The Guardian, 15 February 2014.

125 Natalie Graham, Making it in Britain, Financial Times, 26 August 2011.

126 Heather Stewart and Angelique Chrisafis, Nearly 300 jobs lost after Marks cancels contract, The Guardian, 4 June 2004.

127 Can an English suit be made in Cambodia?, BBC News, 10 February 2016.

128   Stephen Moss, "They've got no reason to take it away from us", The Guardian, 12 December 2006.

129   Interview on Radio 4 Today programme, 20 April 2012.

130   Tanya Powley, "Made in Britain" demand prompts rise in textile manufacturing, Financial Times, 5 December 2013.

Chapter 14   Chemical Waste

1   Richard Wachman, How competition ate away Britain's chemical giant, The Observer, 24 June 2007.

2   Matthew Gwyther and Andrew Saunders, The MT interview: Sir John Harvey-Jones, Management Today, 1 September 2006.

3   Brunner, Mond & Co, Grace's Guide to British Industrial History.

4   Grace's Guide to British Industrial History.

5   Stephen E. Koss, Sir John Brunner, Radical Plutocrat 1842–1919, Cambridge University Press, London, 2008.

6   Alkali News, November 1948.

7   Edward Pearce, Hanson is as Hanson does, The Guardian, 22 May 1991.

8   Imperial Chemical Industries plc History, fundinguniverse.com.

9   Julia Kollewe and Graeme Wearden, ICI: from Perspex to paints, The Guardian, 18 June 2007.

10   Harold Bolter, ICI second in world chemical sales, Financial Times, 1969.

11   Sir Jack Callard, obituary, Daily Telegraph, 30 September 1998.

12   Sir Michael Clapham, obituary, Daily Telegraph, 14 November 2002.

13   Sir Geoffrey Gilbertson, obituary, The Times, 15 February 1991.

14   The end of the beginning, Men and Matters, Financial Times, 18 July 1969.

15   Geoffrey Goodman, Lord Haslam of Bolton, obituary, The Guardian, 4 November 2002.

16   Sir John Harvey-Jones: Ebullient business leader who chaired ICI and found fame as the BBC's "Troubleshooter", obituary, The Independent, 14 January 2008.

17   James Erlichman, Sir John Harvey-Jones, obituary, The Guardian, 11 January 2008.

18   James Erlichman, ICI slips despite record, The Guardian, 26 April 1985.

19   Matthew Gwyther and Andrew Saunders, The MT interview: Sir John Harvey-Jones, Management Today, 1 September 2006.

20   Lucy Kellaway, Self-styled hero in a kipper tie, Financial Times, 21 April 1993.

21   Financial Times, 7 March 1986.

22   Matthew Gwyther and Andrew Saunders, The MT interview: Sir John Harvey-Jones, Management Today, 1 September 2006.

23   Paul Hodges, Farewell to tragic ICI, ICIS Chemical Business, 12–18 November 2007.

24   Ben Laurance, ICI: Learning to live with hard times, The Guardian, 6 February 1991.

25   Stanley Read and Melissa Eddy, BASF, an industrial pillar in Germany, leans abroad, The New York Times, 24 October 2014.

26   Christopher Huhne, ICI chief warns on Lawson policy, The Guardian, 4 January 1989.

27   Philip Bassett, ICI chairman doubts recession will be over within two years, The Times, 28 November 1990.

28   Philip Aldrick, ICI finally consigned to history, Daily Telegraph, 2 January 2008.

29   Ben Laurance, ICI: too important to be left to the numbers game, The Guardian, 18 May 1991.

30   Martin Adeney, Sir Denys Henderson, obituary, The Guardian, 31 May 2016.

31   ICI digs in, The Economist, 25 May 1991.

32   Ralph Atkins, A party divided in a testing time for free marketers, Financial Times, 30 May 1991.

33   Penny-wise Hanson, The Times, 1 January 1988.

34   Richard Wachman, How competition ate away Britain's chemical giants, The Observer, 24 June 2007.

35   Ratcliffe, the alchemist, ICI faces the Akzo, Daily Telegraph, 12 August 2007.

36   Ibid.

37   Company History, syngenta.com.

38   Martin Adeney, Sir Denys Henderson, obituary, The Guardian, 31 May 2016.

39   Claudia Flavell-While, Changes: The Evolution of the Chemicals Industry in the UK, AIChE, 28 December 2012.

40   Jenny Luesby, ICI pays £4.9bn for Unilever arm, Financial Times, 8 May 1997.

41   Paul Murphy, ICI rescue plan unravels, The Guardian, 4 February 2002.

42   Terry Macalister, Junk rating threat hangs over ICI, The Guardian, 1 February 2002.

43   BBC News, ICI chief quits, 9 April 2003.

44   Angela Jameson, Business big shots: John McAdam, The Times, 21 March 2008.

45   Sarah Spikes, ICI brand may be consigned to history, Financial Times, 22 November 2007.

46   Katherine Griffiths, ICI chief McAdam may collect £20m payoff in Akzo's £8bn purchase, Daily Telegraph, 14 August 2007.

47   Terry Macalister, Rentokil rids itself of bosses and calls in ICI crew, The Guardian, 21 March 2008.

48   Ibid.

49   Geoffrey Owen, From Empire to Europe, The Decline and Revival of British Industry Since the Second World War, HarperCollins, London, 1999.

50   Ratcliffe, the alchemist, ICI faces the Akzo, Daily Telegraph, 12 August 2007.

51   John Kay, Chain reaction that burned out ICI, Financial Times, 3 September 2007.

52   Paul Hodges, Farewell to tragic ICI, ICIS Chemical Business, 12–18 November 2007.

53   Will Beacham, RIP ICI, ICIS, 4 February 2008.

54   Claudia Flavell-While, Changes: The Evolution of the Chemicals Industry in the UK, AIChE, 28 December 2012.

55   Karen McLaughlan, Once just ICI, Wilton is now home to eight global giants, Evening Gazette, 14 May 2013.

56   Sir Leslie Smith, obituary, Daily Telegraph, 20 July 2006.

57   Saeed Shah, BOC rejects £7bn-plus offer from German rival Linde, The Independent, 25 January 2006.

58   Richard Milne and Lisa Urquart, BOC rejects £7.6bn Linde offer, Financial Times, 25 January 2006.

59   BOC Turns Down Linde Offer, Sky News, 24 January 2006.

60   Richard Milne and Lina Saigol, Linde and BOC confirm £8bn deal, Financial Times, 6 March 2006.

61   Nick Goodway, BOC falls to Linde of Germany for £8.2bn, MailOnline, 6 March 2006.

62   Farhan Zaheer, Five years after merger, BOC gives way to Linde brand, The Express Tribune, 20 September 2011.

63   Ibid.

64   Carla Rapoport, Diet and diversity for slimline revival, Financial Times, 10 January 1985.

65   Ibid.

66   Nils Pratley, AstraZeneca may discover that it has overdosed on the bitter pill of job losses, The Guardian, 3 February 2012.

67   Julia Kollewe, £4.6m payoff for former chief of AstraZeneca, The Guardian, 17 July 2012.

68   AstraZeneca chief David Brennan leaves with up to £19m, Daily Telegraph, 16 July 2012.

69   Julia Kollewe, AstraZeneca boss David Brennan quits under pressure from investors, The Guardian, 26 April 2012.

70   Louise Armitstead, Cambridge: home of Britain's biotech boom offers relief to UK economic ills, Daily Telegraph, 2 April 2013.

71   Caroline Muspratt, AstraZeneca buys biotech company for £120m, Daily Telegraph, 23 December 2005.

72   Julia Kollewe, AstraZeneca boss David Brennan quits under pressure from investors, The Guardian, 26 April 2012.

73   Nicholas Watt and Katie Allen, Coalition rift over £63bn offer for UK drugs group, The Guardian, 5 May 2014.

74   Stephen Goundrey-Smith, Corporate takeovers do not threaten UK pharmaceutical industry, Pharmaceutical Journal, 5 July 2014.

75   Amelia Gentleman, Science is our future? That sounds hollow here, The Guardian, 24 March 2011.

76   Viagra plant closure may compromise UK research, The Guardian, 7 February 2011.

77   Larry Elliott, Pfizer exposes Britain's big fantasies, The Guardian, 2 February 2011.

78   The real choice that AstraZeneca faces, Financial Times, 11 May 2014.

79   Rupert Neate, AstraZeneca boss tells disgruntled shareholders that takeover is dead, The Guardian, 21 May 2014.

80   Sir Simon Robertson, Letter to the Financial Times, 12 May 2014.

81   Edgar Jones, Chemist made Glaxo a worldwide great, obituary, Sir Austin Bide, Financial Times, 17 May 2008.

82   Ibid.

83   Patrick Jenkins, A Frenchman who would rather be in Philadelphia, Financial Times, 23 November 2002.

84   Ibid.

85   Nick Huber, JP Garnier leaves a bitter-sweet pill for Glaxo to swallow, The Guardian, 20 May 2008.

86   Andrew Clark, GlaxoSmithKline boss: firms shouldn't quit Britain for tax reasons, The Observer, 20 March 2011.

87   Ben Griffiths, GlaxoSmithKline hopes to create 1,000 jobs with its first new UK factory in 30 years, This is Money, 30 October 2011.

88   Leading pharmaceutical corporations' UK market share, 2013, Association of the British Pharmaceutical Industry.

89   Peggy Hollinger and Andrew Ward, UK drug manufacture drops by a quarter, Financial Times, 1 March 2015.

90   The Pharmaceutical Industry in Figures, Key Data 2013, European Federation of Pharmaceutical Industries and Associations.

91   Peggy Hollinger and Andrew Ward, UK drug manufacture drops by a quarter, Financial Times, 1 March 2015.

92   UK Chemical and Pharmaceutical Industry Facts and Figures, Chemical Industries Association, 2015.

93   Britain – An Official Handbook, Central Office of Information, 1959.

94   Britain – An Official Handbook, Central Office of Information, 1973.

95   Britain – An Official Handbook, Central Office of Information, 1979.

96   Britain – An Official Handbook, Central Office of Information, 1991.

97   The European Chemical Industry, Facts and Figures 2014, European Chemical Industry Council (Cefic), 2014.

98   The Essential Chemical Industry online, University of York, 21 July 2013.

99   Ruari McCallion, Chemicals industry: UK manufacturing's unique element, themanufacturer.com, 11 May 2015.

Chapter 15 Sea of Dreams

1   Putting Britain First – A National Policy from the Conservatives, Conservative Party, October 1974.

2   United Kingdon Offshore Oil and Gas Policy, HMSO, 11 July 1974.

3   Tony Benn, Conflicts of Interest, Diaries 1977–80, Hutchinson, London, 1990.

4   Norwegian crone, The Economist, 18 February 1989.

5   Keith Myers and David Manley, Did the UK Miss Out on £400 Billion Worth of Oil Revenue?, NRGI – Crystol Energy, 28 October 2015.

6   Aditya Chakraborty, Dude, where's my North Sea oil money?, The Guardian, 13 January 2014.

7   Gordon MacIntyre-Kemp, Research Briefing: The Resource Governance and Taxation Track Record of the UK Government in UK's Oil and Gas Sector, Business for Scotland.

8   David Lennon, OECD says Norway oil tax revenues could be halved, Financial Times, 11 February 1986.

9   Guy Lodge, Thatcher and North Sea Oil – a failure to invest in Britain's future, New Statesman, 15 April 2013.

10   Steven Brocklehurst, Who has a right to claim Scotland's oil?, BBC Scotland News, 16 April 2013.

11   Gordon MacIntyre-Kemp, Research Briefing: The Resource Governance and Taxation Track Record of the UK Government in UK's oil and gas sector, Business Scotland, 23 April 2017.

12   Lucy Kellaway, Life goes on past Forties, Financial Times, 7 September 1987.

13   Ranulph Fiennes, Fear, Hodder & Stoughton, London, 2016.

14   Dominic Lawson, N Sea tops Saudis in oil output, Financial Times, 9 May 1985.

15   Ian Hargreaves, Cold comfort for struggling Opec, Financial Times, 10 January 1985.

16   Celia Weston, North Sea: why more oil is being spilled on troubled waters, The Guardian, 7 September 1990.

17   Robert Taylor, Oil unions held over a barrel, Financial Times, 2 June 1993.

18   Peter Hetherington, Piper's lament on deaf ears, The Guardian, 15 July 1988.

19   Stephen McGinty, Fire in the Night, the Piper Alpha Disaster, Macmillan, London, 2008.

20   Charlie Gall, Piper Alpha disaster 25 years on: Survivor recalls how he fled to Australia in bid to escape haunting horrors of tragedy, Daily Record, 8 July 2013.

21   Tony Benn, Conflicts of Interest, Diaries 1977–80, Hutchinson, London, 1990.

22   Remarks visiting Aberdeen (Piper Alpha oil rig disaster), Margaret Thatcher Foundation.

23   Gas build-up theory in worst oil disaster, The Times, 8 July 1988.

24   Terry Macalister, Piper Alpha disaster: how 167 oil workers died, The Guardian, 4 July 2013.

25   Margaret Thatcher – The Downing Street Years, HarperCollins Publishers, London, 1993.

26   Charles Moore, Margaret Thatcher – The Authorized Biography: Volumes One and Two, Allen Lane, 2013 and 2015.

27   Margaret Thatcher, A Life and Legacy, David Cannadine, Oxford University Press, 2017.

28   Norman J. Smith, The Sea of Lost Opportunity, Elsevier, Oxford, 2011.

29   The National Gas Archive, National Grid, 2005.

30   Sir Denis Rooke, obituary, Daily Telegraph, 5 September 2008.

31   Ibid.

32   Norman J. Smith, The Sea of Lost Opportunity, Elsevier, Oxford, 2011.

33   Ibid.

34   Tony Benn, Conflicts of Interest, Diaries 1977–80, Hutchinson, London, 1990.

35   Ibid.

36   Denis Healey, The Time of My Life, Michael Joseph, London, 1989.

37   Norman J. Smith, The Sea of Lost Opportunity, Elsevier, Oxford, 2011.

38   Steven Butler and Lucy Kellaway, Government to relax scrutiny of oil industry, Financial Times, 2 May 1990.

39   Norman J. Smith, The Sea of Lost Opportunity, Elsevier, Oxford, 2011.

40   Ibid.

41   Ibid.

42   Ibid.

43   Depletion Policy, Development of the Oil and Gas Resources of the United Kingdom, 1981.

44   Ibid.

45   David Young, N Sea warning to Sun Oil after order goes abroad, The Times, 22 March 1984.

46   Vital role of the offshore supplies, Glasgow Herald, 22 June 1989.

47   Steven Butler and Lucy Kellaway, Government to relax scrutiny of oil industry, Financial Times, 2 May 1990.

48   Steven Butler, Platform orders go to Continental companies, Financial Times, 23 June 1990.

49   Steven Butler, The revival of the fittest, Financial Times, 5 July 1990.

50   North Sea boom, Daily Telegraph, 23 May 1991.

51   Terry Macalister, Jobs fear as UK firm loses out on North Sea deal, The Guardian, 31 August 2015.

52   Know more about oil, The United Kingdom Refining Industry, Institute of Petroleum Information Services, 1989.

53   Ibid.

54   Professor Peter Odell, UK oil exporting and refining policies, Letter to the Financial Times, 13 October 1983.

55   Ibid.

56   The Chemicals Industry, Report to NEDC by Chemicals EDC, June 1983.

57   Fawley Refinery, ExxonMobil in the UK, exonmobil.co.

58   Fawley chemical manufacturing plant, ExxonMobil in the UK, exxonmobil.co.

59   Andrew Taylor, Ex-Esso refinery for Emirates, Financial Times, 18 June 1984.

60   Richard Johns, Esso refinery to be shipped abroad soon, Financial Times, 13 August 1985.

61   John Hooper, Oil giants hit as ICI wins court tax battle, The Guardian, 25 February 1986.

62   Gas pipes and tunnel vision, The Guardian, 12 September 1981.

63   Dominic Lawson, Oil industry rejects plan for gas-gathering pipeline, Financial Times, 10 January 1984.

64   The impact of Saudi chemicals, Financial Times editorial, 19 November 1984.

65   James Erlichman, A hungry giant looks east for fuel, The Guardian, 17 January 1984.

66   James Erlichman, Outright victory for ICI over tax, The Guardian, 2 May 1988.

67   Ibid.

68   Mark Meredith, Mossmorran, A £353m feat of co-operation, Financial Times, 16 November 1984.

69   Fife Ethylene Plant, ExxonMobil in the UK, exxonmobil.co.

70   Peter Marsh, Exxon and Shell in £130m chemicals plant expansion, Financial Times, 8 June 1989.

71   ExxonMobil Chemical, Mossmorran, UK, shell.com.

72   Laura Chesters, French giant Total opens £3.5bn gas plant off the Shetland Islands delivering a much-needed boost to North Sea jobs, This Is Money/ Daily Mail, 15 May 2016.

73   Royal Dutch Shell and the Nazis, John Donovan, quoting from A History of Royal Dutch Shell, University of Utrecht, March 2011.

74   Michael Smith, Shell closing Teesside plant, The Guardian, 27 September 1984.

75   Alan Dunn and Mary Brasier, Oil firm blames competition as 1,000 jobs go, The Guardian, 7 March 1985.

76   James Crabtree, Essar to sell UK's second biggest refinery, Financial Times, 12 June 2014.

77   Brian Groom and Nick Garnett, Shell Chemicals to cut 700 jobs at Carrington, Financial Times, 21 June 1985.

78   Revolution at the Chemicals Factory, Shell Chemicals advertisement in the Financial Times, 19 June 1987.

79   Shell Carrington Development Strategy, tcproperty.

80   Evolution of the port of Rotterdam, 1400–2030, The Geography of Transport Systems, people.hofstra.edu.

81   Shell Nederland Chemie BV – Pernis, Rotterdam, The Netherlands, shell.com.

82   Shell Moerdijk clocks 40 years of petrochemical production, Shell Global News and Media Releases, 28 February 2014.

83   Dominic Lawson, BP Oil reports first profit for four years, Financial Times, 28 March 1984.

84   Dominic Lawson, BP to close oil refinery with loss of 750 jobs, Financial Times, 11 August 1985.

85   BP Chemicals, Grace's Guide to British Industrial History.

86   BP chairman ousted as directors seek solution to dismal first-quarter figures, The Guardian, 26 June 1992.

87   Cal McCrystal, Profile: Tough of the Track: Robert Horton, The Independent, 18 June 1994.

88   BP chairman ousted as directors seek solution to dismal first-quarter figures, The Guardian, 26 June 1992.

89   Richard Tomkins, Hatchet honed to a softer point, Financial Times, 31 July 1993.

90   Philip Bassett, TGWU warns BP Chemicals on staff deal, Financial Times, 6 December 1984.

91   Robin Reeves, Barry – a case for self-help in Wales, Financial Times, 4 December 1984.

92   Patrick Donovan, The chemical equation that adds up to crisis, Evening Standard, 13 January 1994.

93   BP Chemicals Announces Baglan Bay Closure, contractorsunlimited.co.uk, 17 February 2004.

94   Hull – Saltend Chemicals Park, bp.com.

95   BP scraps Sullom Voe gas processing plant plans, BBC Scotland Business, 10 June 2016.

96   Chris Foote, BP to sell stake in Sullom Voe oil terminal in £68m deal, STV News, 24 January 2017.

97   BP to shed jobs at Grangemouth, Financial Times, 13 November 2001.

98   Ineos, Britain's biggest private companies: Chemical elements of success, Daily Telegraph, 22 August 2008.

99   Douglas Fraser, The tycoon behind the Grangemouth dispute, BBC News Scotland Business, 19 October 2013.

100 Grangemouth Petrochemical Plant Expansion, United Kingdom, chemicals-technology.com.

101 Sylvia Pfeifer, Jim Ratcliffe, Financial Times, 20 November 2014.

102 Rich List 2018: Jim Ratcliffe is UK's richest man, BBC News, 13 May 2018.

103 Ian Jack, I first saw Grangemouth's flames as a boy. It's a relief they will burn a little longer, The Guardian, 26 October 2013.

104 Europe's largest ethane storage tank allows shale ethane imports, kci-world.com, January–February 2015.

105 Sean Farrell, Ineos calms fears over Grangemouth future, The Guardian, 17 February 2015.

106 Ineos buys North Sea gas fields from Russian group, The Guardian, 12 October 2015.

107 Andrew Critchlow, UK petrochemicals industry is a lame duck, Daily Telegraph, 23 October 2013.

108 Jacky Naegelen, Total plans €1.2bn investment in Antwerp refinery, Reuters Business News, 24 September 2012.

109 Shell Moerdijk clocks 40 years of petrochemical production, Shell Global News and Media Releases, 28 February 2014.

110 Richard Seymour, How Ineos humiliated Unite in Grangemouth, The Guardian, 9 November 2013.

111 Alex Bell, Meet billionaire Ineos boss Jim Ratcliffe, one of Manchester's most successful entrepreneurs of all time, Greater Manchester Business Week, 14 September 2015.

112 Adam Forrest, Sir Jim Ratcliffe: UK's richest man and ardent Brexiteer is moving to Monaco, The Independent, 9 August 2018.

113 Oliver Shah and Caroline Wheeler, Richest man quits UK to save billions, Sunday Times, 17 February 2019.

114 Dan Milmo, 850 jobs at risk in Coryton closure, The Guardian, 27 June 2012.

115 Economic Contribution and Refinery Economics, UK PIA Statistical Review 2015.

116 John McKenna, Refined Capacity: the future of UK refineries, Process Engineering, 7 January 2015.

117 Andrew Trotman, The UK is losing one of its seven oil refineries – Milford Haven, Daily Telegraph, 4 November 2014.

118 John Kemp, Lindsey oil refinery falls victim to UK policy and shale, Reuters, 12 February 2015.

119 Hilary Barnes, Sweden tops Danish export barrier list, Financial Times, 11 June 1985.

Chapter 16 Paper Trail

1 British Association of Paper Historians.

2 Confederation of Paper Industries Fact Sheet, March 2013.

3 Geoffrey Owen, From Empire to Europe, HarperCollins, 1999; this provides an excellent summary account of the structure and development of the British paper industry.

4 Geoffrey Owen, From Empire to Europe, HarperCollins, 1999.

5 Bowater-Scott, Grace's Guide to British Industrial History.

6 Sittingbourne Mill – History, www.sittingbournemill.com.

7 DS Smith History, www.dssmith.com.

8 Bowater-Scott, Grace's Guide, British Industrial History.

9 Reed International plc, Encyclopedia.com.

10 Financial Times, 26 February 2015.

11 SCA press release, 2 October 2012.

12 Aylesford Newsprint sold to US equity firm, letsrecycle.com, October 2012.

13 Aylesford Newsprint: the real story behind the paper mill's closure, The Kent Messenger, 30 March 2015.

14 The Martland Holdings Company – News, 2014.

15 New Aylesford owner in long-term pledge, letsrecycle.com.

16 Aylesford Newsprint set to appoint administrator, Print Week, 24 February 2015.

17 Aylesford Newsprint in administration, Mortons Print, 24 February 2015.

18 Wiggins Teape, Grace's Guide to British Industrial History.

19 Arjo Wiggins Appleton plc History, Funding Universe Company Profile.

20 Hansard, 10 April 1963.

21 A Little History, Wiggins Teape Pensioners.

22 Paper mill could close causing more Dartford job losses, News Shopper, 20 November 2008.

23   This week's pride of Bristol looks at the demise of the once mighty St Anne's Board Mills, Bristol Evening Post.

24   Board Mills employed hundreds of workers in production of packaging, Exeter Express and Echo.

25   Reinventing Radcliffe – Next Steps, Bury Council.

26   PRN million fails to help avoid closure of East Lancs paper mill.

27   East Lancs closure hits 180 mill staff, Print Week, 1 March 2001.

28   BPB to close paper mill, This is Money, 3 March 2005.

29   Hansard, 29 November 1977.

30   Iggesund invests in green future at UK board mill, Packaging Today, 31 July 2012.

31   John Dickinson, Grace's Guide to British Industrial History.

32   Richard Roberts and David Kynaston, City State, Profile Books, 2001.

33   Hansard, 1 November 1989.

34   Hansard, 1 November 1989.

35   P. Dixon and Son Limited, National Archives.

36   Grimsby's Paper Makers, Grimsby Telegraph.

37   History coming to an end with plan to close Sheffield paper mill, The Star, 22 May 2013.

38   Jobs blow as historic Sheffield paper mill to close, The Star, 23 May 2013.

39   Capita brings former SCA paper mill to market, Capital News, 3 March 2015.

40   Inveresk closes last Scottish paper mill, The Herald on Sunday, 10 June 2005.

41   Inveresk in receivership, Print Week, 14 October 2010.

42   Jobs at risk as mill firm goes bust, Western Daily Press, 14 October 2010.

43   Fife paper maker Tullis Russell in administration, BBC News, Scotland, Business, 27 April 2015.

44   Tullis Russell: Another paper tiger turns to ashes, The Scotsman, 2 May 2015.

45   Tullis Russell collapsed with "over £50m debts", The Scotsman, 12 July 2015.

46   Employee-owned mill closes, with almost 475 jobs lost, Co-operative News.

47   Losses ballooned at Tullis Russell paper making business in final year, The Herald on Sunday, 22 January 2016.

48   UPM cuts capacity, Shotton's PM1 among closures, Print Week, 13 November 2014.

49   Smurfit Kappa advances closure of paper machines, letsrecycle.com.

50   DS Smith company history.

51   DS Smith company history.

52   DS Smith announces £104m investment for Kemsley mill, letsrecycle.com.

53   M-Real sells its New Thames paper mill in the UK, Metsä Board Corporation press release, 1 February 2008.

54   M-Real pulls out of UK paper production with sale of New Thames mill, Print Week, 1 February 2008.

55   DS Smith plc acquires New Thames Paper Mill and 50% of Grovehurst Energy from M-real for £60m, Allen & Overy press release, 4 February 2008.

56   £104m deal secures papermaking jobs, Kent Messenger, 7 February 2008.

57   Paper mill closure is bad news for the environment, Kent News, 12 February 2008.

58   DS Smith plc – Disposal of Higher Kings Mill Paper Mill, Company press release, 19 September 2011.

59   Jobs at risk as DS Smith mill faces closure, Print Monthly, 27 August 2015.

60   Watchet paper mill set to close with "tragic" loss of 170 jobs, BBC News, 28 August 2015.

61   DS Smith Considers Closure of Wansbrough Paper Mill in UK, Paper Age, 31 August 2015.

62   A paper mill actually opens in the UK, Justinsamazingworldatfennerpaper, 7 September 2009.

63   Open day at Palm Paper, Palm Paper press release, 19 September 2010.

64   Profile: SAICA sets sights on long-term success in UK, Packaging News, 1 September 2010.

65   SAICA plans £250m recycled paper mill in Manchester, Print Week, 26 June 2008.

66   Mill to complete SAICA's UK jigsaw: Profile special, Packaging News, 9 December 2011.

67   SAICA starts production at new paper mill, Place North West, 25 January 2012.

68   Most Advanced Paper Machine in Europe Officially Opened by Minister of State for Business and Energy, SAICA press release.

69   SAICA thanked by Cameron for new paper mill, letsrecycle.com.

70   Annual Reviews, Confederation of Paper Industries.

71   Annual Reviews, Confederation of Paper Industries.

72   Farce of 11,000 mile journeys to China to recycle Hampshire's paper, Hampshire Chronicle, 13 August 2015.

73   The mythical "march of the makers", TUC.

74   Mill closures mask shift in UK paper manufacturing, Print Business, 4 May 2015.

75   UK Papermakers Alert MPs to the Effects of High Energy Costs, Confederation of Paper Industries, 30 September 2015.

76   Devastating effect of uncompetitive pricing on UK paper industry, ACM Environmental Press Release.

Chapter 17 Meltdown

1   Harry Wallop, Britain is least self-sufficient in food since 1968, Daily Telegraph, 25 September 2010.
2   Value of Food and Drink Manufacturing to the UK, IfM Centre for Industry and Government, University of Cambridge, July 2010.
3   Grace's Guide to British Industrial History.
4   Ibid.
5   Ibid.
6   Terry's of York: The history of the chocolate maker, BBC News, 2 February 2010.
7   Charlotte Harriman, Terry's factory workers reminisce, BBC News, 22 December 2009.
8   Nick McCarthy, What happened when Kraft took over Terry's of York, The Birmingham Post.
9   Victoria Gibson, Still sweet and rosy?, Bqmagazine, 11 July 2012.
10   Terry's calls time on York chocolate factory, The Guardian, 1 October 2005.
11   Andrew Martin, Financial Times Magazine, June 3 2006.
12   Lisa Wood, Rowntree products cut, Financial Times, 12 January 1988.
13   John MacGregor's "dynamite" letter disclosed for the first time, York Press, 23 December 2013.
14   Ben Laurance, Young casts doubt on British policy, The Guardian, 5 October 1988.
15   Nestle-Rowntree takeover never debated in Cabinet, York Press, 23 December 2013.
16   The trade and industry secretary was David (Lord) Young; later economic adviser to Prime Minister David Cameron, he resigned in 2010 after referring to the "so-called recession".
17   Dismay over "pinkos" comment, York Press, 23 December 2013.
18   Daniel John, Rowntree: PMs "appalling ignorance", The Guardian, 5 August 1988.
19   Rowntree accepts bid by Nestle, The New York Times, 24 June 1988.
20   Jenny Wiggins, Jonathan Guthrie and Andrew Bounds, The hard truth about soft centres, Financial Times, 16 September 2009.
21   Andrew Martin, Financial Times Magazine, 3 June 2006.
22   Ben Laurance, 550 jobs may go at Nestlé plant, The Guardian, 5 February 1993.
23   Hans Kundnani and Martin Wainwright, 645 jobs lost as Nestlé ships Smarties abroad, The Guardian, 21 September 2006.
24   Jill Treanor, 40 years and billions of mints later, After Eight factory closes, The Guardian, 11 December 2010.
25   Blue Riband biscuit production to be moved to Poland, BBC News, 25 April 2017.

26   Peter Wilsher, Nestle Rowntree – A bittersweet tale, Management Today, 1 March 1993.

27   Deborah Cadbury, Chocolate Wars: From Cadbury to Kraft – 200 Years of Sweet Success and Bitter Rivalry, HarperPress, London, 2011.

28   John Harris, How the home of Mini Rolls and Smash was gobbled up, The Guardian, 23 March 2011.

29   Simon Bowers, Cadbury demerger will cost £130m for advisers and tax, The Guardian, 12 March 2008.

30   Jenny Wiggins, Cadbury's solo status offers sweet rewards, Financial Times, 26 February 2009.

31   Richard Wachman, Kraft takeover could be bitter experience for Cadbury, The Observer, 20 September 2009.

32   Michael Skapinker, Ethics will not keep Cadbury independent, Financial Times, 8 December 2009.

33   Simon Duke, Cadbury chief exec to warn Kraft takeover would stifle growth, MailOnline, 25 August 1009.

34   Adam Arnold, Cadbury Rejects Kraft's "Derisory" Takeover Bid, Sky News, 9 November 2009.

35   Jenny Wiggins, American at home in Cadbury, Financial Times, 28 November 2009.

36   Jenny Wiggins, Cadbury warms to Hershey tie-up, Financial Times, 28 October 2009.

37   Andrew Hill, More questions than answers in the Cadbury saga, Financial Times, 28 November 2009.

38   Kraft/Cadbury, The Lex column, Financial Times, 5 December 2009.

39   Heather Stewart, Nick Mathiason, Tasty deal in the City – but bitter and hard to digest in Bournville, The Guardian, 20 January 2010.

40   Dan Roberts, Swallowed up for £12bn: Kraft wins Cadbury takeover battle, The Guardian, 19 January 2010.

41   Zoe Wood, How Cadbury rhetoric of value, Quaker ethics and tradition foundered on a rock of hard cash, The Guardian, 19 January 2010.

42   Takeover will mean job cuts, says the boss of Cadbury, The Independent, 20 January 2010.

43   Clinton Manning, Kraft's Cadbury takeover marks the end of a British institution, Daily Mirror, 20 January 2010.

44   Graham Ruddick, Kraft buys Cadbury for £11.9bn: a Q&A, Daily Telegraph, 19 January 2010.

45   Larry Elliott, The sad lesson of Cadbury: the City still holds the whip, The Guardian, 20 January 2010.

46   Nils Pratley, Cadbury board rolls over too cheaply, The Guardian, 19 January 2010.

47 Alistair Macdonald, Foreign takeovers take a toll in the UK, Wall Street Journal, 26 January 2010.

48 Small island for sale. The takeover of Cadbury by Kraft seems to symbolise a hollowing-out of corporate Britain. The truth is rather more complicated, The Economist, 25 March 2010.

49 Kraft sorry for "dashing hopes" over Cadbury factory, Evening Standard, 16 March 2010.

50 Jill Treanor, Banks share $390m in fees as criticism mounts over deal, The Guardian, 20 January 1010.

51 Tim Webb and Zoe Wood, Stitzer departs with £40m after selling off Cadbury to Kraft, The Guardian, 17 April 2010.

52 Jonathan Freedland, Our anger over runaway top pay is more about merit than money, The Guardian, 23 November 2011.

53 Graeme Wearden, UK firms "need more protection from foreign takeovers", The Guardian, 10 February 2010.

54 Nils Pratley, Save only two cheers for Labour's Cadbury Law, The Guardian, 13 April 2010.

55 Simon Goodley, Julia Finch and Paul Lewis, Cadbury's secret Swiss move will save millions in tax, The Guardian, 4 December 1010.

56 Dan Atkinson and Jonathan Petre, Cadbury goes Swiss to avoid British tax: move by US bosses will cost Treasury £60 million a year, MailOnline, 5 December 2010.

57 Simon Bowers and Jennifer Rankin, We played by the rules, says Cadbury insider, The Guardian, 22 June 2013.

58 Julia Finch, Silence is not an option for Kraft chief, The Guardian, 16 March 2011.

59 Rupert Steiner, Sweet on Kraft: Ex-Cadbury's boss hails chocolate firm's new owners, This is Money, 31 October 2013.

60 Henry Tricks, Mars to close Slough factory and cut 700 jobs, Financial Times, 11 March 2005.

61 Thorntons announces plan to shut some stores, The Guardian, 17 February 2011.

62 Julia Kollewe, Shop closures and falling profits leave bitter taste for Thorntons, The Guardian, 22 December 2011.

63 Tim Webb, Bendicks to be made in Germany, The Guardian, 5 March 2011.

64 Cahal Milmo, Cadbury deal turns sour for Green & Black's, The Independent, 18 January 2011.

65 Our Story – Find Out About Hotel Chocolat, hotelchocolat.com.

66 Xanthe Clay, Why doesn't Britain make its own chocolate from scratch? Daily Telegraph, 14 October 2013.

Chapter 18 Brassed Off

1   Negley Farson, The Way of a Transgressor, Victor Gollancz, London, 1935.

2   Britain – An Official Handbook, Central Office of Information, 1973.

3   Aluminium in the Highlands, aluminiumville.co.

4   Alan Tovey, Rio Tinto to sell Scottish aluminium smelter to Liberty for £330m.

5   Aluminium in the Highlands, aluminiumville.co.

6   Aluminium smelter (Invergordon), House of Commons Debate, Hansard, 28 July 1982.

7   Monopolies and Mergers Commission Report, 1977.

8   The Power to Succeed, Venture Magazine, 31 October 2006.

9   John W. Miller, Ales MacDonald and Robb M. Stewart, Miner Rio Tinto Ousts CEO as Bad Bets Cost Billions, Wall Street Journal, 17 January 2013.

10   Giles Turner, Should bankers share the blame for Rio Tinto?, Financial News, 24 January 2013.

11   Simon Goodley, Ousted Rio Tinto boss pocketed £22m in cash and shares, The Guardian, 17 January 2013.

12   Anglesey smelter gearing to shut, American Metal Market, 14 August 2009.

13   Robin Latchem, Remelt operation ending on Anglesey, Materials Recycling Week, 22 February 2013.

14   Roland Gribben, Chancellor too late to save Britain's aluminium smelters, Daily Telegraph, 11 December 2011.

15   UK aluminium industry in crisis, Process Engineering, 17 September 2009.

16   David Merlin-Jones, The closure of the Lynemouth aluminium smelter: an analysis, Civitas, April 2012.

17   Roy Hodson, When the growing had to stop, Financial Times, 28 October 1981.

18   Peter Hetherington, Scotland hit hard as 1,200 Alcan jobs go, The Guardian, 9 February 1983.

19   Novelis (Ex Alcan) David's Loan, Falkirk, davidmortonltd.co.

20   Jonathan Goode, End of an era and 110 jobs as Alcan leaves, Banbury Guardian, 26 September 2002.

21   Monopolies and Mergers Commission Report, 1977.

22   Sir William Barlow, obituary, Daily Telegraph, 23 May 2012.

23   British Kynoch Metals Ltd, Company brochure.

24   BICC to close Prescot copper refinery, Metal Bulletin, 17 January 1991.

25   UK's last copper wire rod mill to close at year end, crumonitor.com, 22 June 2006.

26   James Bridge Copper Works, Grace's Guide to British Industrial History.

27   ICI Metals Division, Grace's Guide to British Industrial History.

28 Walsall – Economic History, british-history.ac.

29 Wolverhampton Metal Company, Grace's Guide to British Industrial History.

30 Yorkshire Imperial Metals, Grace's Guide to British Industrial History.

31 IMI automates anode production, Metal Bulletin Monthly, March 1986.

32 Peter Thal Larsen, IMI plans to cease copper smelting, Financial Times, 7 September 1999.

33 IMI to Close Its 60,000 tpa Secondary Copper Plant, Daily Metals Report, Prudential-Bache International Limited, 7 September 1999.

34 The KME Yorkshire History, kme.com.

35 Downstream innovation – chemical and zinc production at Avonmouth, humanities.uwe.ac.

36 Imperial Smelting Corporation, Grace's Guide to British Industrial History.

37 Michael Smith, Avon smelter jobs vanish, The Guardian, 9 July 1983.

38 Bruce Hextall, MIM Buys Pasminco's UK Zinc Smelter for $100m, Sydney Morning Herald, 2 July 1993.

39 Downstream innovation – chemical and zinc production at Avonmouth, humanities.uwe.ac.

40 Arthur Hagopian, MIM plans to exit Europe zinc smelting, American Metal Market, 27 August 2001.

41 400 jobs to go at zinc works, BBC News, 18 February 2003.

42 Barry Fitzgerald, MIM walks from Duisburg zinc mine for $53m, The Age, 29 August 2002.

43 No more zinc, The Engineer, 20 February 2003.

44 Britannia Zinc, davidmortonltd.co.

45 St Modwen acquires former smelter site at Avonmouth to create a £150m Employment Park, 27 May 2003, stmodwen.co.

46 Description and Brief History, Britannia Refined Metals, xstrata.com.

47 Royston refinery shut, Metal Bulletin, 17 June 1986.

48 Sheffield Smelting Company, Grace's Guide to British Industrial History.

49 Jeff Blyskal, All is not gold, Forbes, 30 July 1984.

Chapter 19 Stalling Speed

1 David Edgerton, England and the Aeroplane – Militarism, Modernity and Machines, Revised Edition, Penguin Books, London, 2013.

2 James Hamilton-Paterson, Empire of the Clouds – When Britain's Aircraft Ruled the World, Faber and Faber, London, 2010.

3 David Edgerton, England and the Aeroplane – Militarism, Modernity and Machines, Revised Edition, Penguin Books, London, 2013.

4   David Edgerton, Britain's War Machine, Allen Lane, London, 2011.

5   David Edgerton, Warfare State – Britain, 1920–1970, Cambridge University Press, Cambridge, 2006.

6   Paul Kennedy, Engineers of Victory: The Problem Solvers Who Turned the Tide in the Second World War, Allen Lane, London, 2013.

7   James Hamilton-Paterson, Empire of the Clouds – When Britain's Aircraft Ruled the World, Faber and Faber, London, 2010.

8   Donald C. Clayton, Handley Page, An Aircraft Album, Ian Allan, London, 1970.

9   Kevin Done, obituary: Sir Arnold Hall, brilliant academic and aviation engineer, Financial Times, 12 January 2000.

10   Ben Dryer, Concorde's daddy, Metro, 1 October 2003.

11   Lewis Page, Britain's Harrier jump-jets reprieved to fly and fight again, The Register, 15 November 2011.

12   Anthony Tucker, Sir Arnold Hall, obituary, The Guardian, 11 January 2000.

13   Quoted in a letter from Keith Joseph to Michael Heseltine, 10 September 1976.

14   David Parker, The Official History of Privatisation, Volume I, Routledge, Abingdon, 2009.

15   Ibid.

16   Ibid.

17   Ibid.

18   Peter Pugh, The Magic of a Name, The Rolls-Royce Story, Parts One to Three, Icon Books, Cambridge, 2001–2.

19   David Huddie, Sir Denning Pearson, Obituary, The Independent, 14 August 1992.

20   Robert Gray, Rolls on the Rocks, Panther Books, London, 1971.

21   Ibid.

22   Terry Dodsworth, Flying, but maybe not high enough, Financial Times, 8 April 1987.

23   Michael Smith, Rolls "may close factory and move into banking", The Guardian, 19 March 1987.

24   David Parker, The Official History of Privatisation, Volume I, Routledge, Abingdon, 2009.

25   Michael Smith, British Airways may well be under-valued, says NAO, The Guardian, 22 July 1987.

26   Larry Elliott, Boeing order "kick in the teeth for Europe" says union, The Guardian, 22 October 1988.

27   Outcry over BA move on US jets, The Guardian, 9 January 1988.

28   David Housego, R-R may sue Air India over loss of £87m order, Financial Times, 14 October 1991.

29   Charles Leadbeater, BA order is setback for Rolls-Royce, 22 August 1991.

30   Patrick Donovan, Aerospace loses ground, The Guardian, 26 September 1991.

31   Patrick Donovan and Daniel John, BA under fire for Virgin "campaign", The Guardian, 4 December 1991.

32   Lord King of Wartnaby, obituary, Daily Telegraph, 13 July 2005.

33   Peter Pugh, The Magic of a Name, The Rolls-Royce Story, Part Three: A Family of Engines, Icon Books, Cambridge, 2002.

34   Julia Finch, Investors seek Rolls chairman's scalp, The Guardian, 15 February 2002.

35   Dominic White, Robins pulls away from Rolls-Royce, Daily Telegraph, 8 March 2002.

36   Ruth Sutherland, Dark Shadow looms over Britain's standard-bearer Rolls-Royce, This is Money, 6 December 2012.

37   Rupert Neate, Rolls scandals blamed on "bonus culture", The Guardian, 7 March 2014.

38   Peggy Hollinger and Catherine Belton, Rolls-Royce humbled by long list of corruption offences, Financial Times, 18 January 2017.

39   Graham Ruddick, Julia Kollewe, Sean Farrell, Rolls and BAE deliver double blow to march of the makers, The Guardian, 13 November 2015.

40   Rob Davies, Rolls-Royce cash injection safeguards 7,000 jobs, The Guardian, 30 June 2017.

41   Graham Ruddick, Hedge fund's Rolls-Royce stake raises breakup fears, The Guardian, 1 August 2015.

42   Jonathan Russell, Sir John Rose: profile of Rolls-Royce chief executive, Daily Telegraph, 23 November 2010.

43   Nils Pratley, Thorny issues, The Guardian, 1 October 2010.

44   Ruth Sutherland, Can Rolls-Royce make the nation proud again?, This is Money, 17 February 2016.

45   Dan Milmo, Boeing boss: UK lacks industrial vision and technology investment, The Guardian, 1 June 2012.

46   Michael Smith, 2,000 face Westland's axe, The Guardian, 6 April 1987.

47   Charles Moore, Margaret Thatcher – The Authorized Biography, Volume Two, Penguin, London, October 2015.

48   Richard Jinman, Margaret Thatcher "lied to the House of Commons" over the Westland affair, The Independent, 17 October 2015.

49   Terry Macalister, Westland goes to Italians for £1bn, The Guardian, 27 May 2004.

50   Simon Goodley, Fears for 3,300 jobs after helicopter bribe scandal, The Guardian, 3 January 2014.

51   Alan Tovey, Britain's helicopter industry is safe "for decades", says new Leonardo boss, Daily Telegraph, 30 January 2017.

52   UK Helicopter Industry, Bankbench Business, 24 January 2017.

53   David Parker, The Official History of Privatisation, Volume I, Routledge, Abingdon, 2009.

54   Kevin Done, Bombardier plan welcomed as a vote of confidence, Financial Times, 1 June 2000.

55   Hannah Boland and Alan Tovey, Airbus takes majority stake in Bombardier's C Series programme, 17 October 2017.

56   Jasper Jolly, Bombardier's Belfast factory sold to Spirit in £850m deal, The Guardian, 31 October 2019.

57   Competitiveness of the EU Aerospace Industry, ECORYS for the European Commission, December 2009.

58   Peter Spiegel, End of an era at BAE: how Sir Richard Evans changed the UK defence industry, Financial Times, 17 July 2004.

59   Kevin Done and Alexander Nicoll, A national champion takes flight, Financial Times, 28 November 2001.

60   Paul Betts, Raytheon's UK jet plants set to close, Financial Times, 16 September 1994.

61   Simon Goodley, Britain flying high in Europe for private jets, The Guardian, 15 October 2014.

62   BAe's lean, mean and hungry for greater profit, The Guardian, 16 September 1994.

63   Michael Smith, Call to investigate prospect of BAe £1bn property "killing", The Guardian, 29 November 1988.

64   John Willcock, Profit bonanza likely from redeveloping disused sites, The Guardian, 1 December 1990.

65   Richard Norton-Taylor, Study points to corruption risk in arms trade, The Guardian, 29 January 2013.

66   Ralph Atkins, Austria to phase out Eurofighter jets, Financial Times, 7 July 2017.

67   Richard Wachman and Patrick Wintour, Fears for British jobs after BAE loses out on £7bn Indian fighter contract, The Guardian, 2 February 2012.

68   Carola Hoyos, Sales: Battle-readiness clinched biggest deal, Financial Times, 7 July 2012.

69   Richard Norton-Taylor, BAE/EADS merger "will create company beyond law", The Guardian, 4 October 2012.

70   Holly Christodoulou and Brittany Vonow, 2,000 UK jobs will be axed at Eurofighter Typhoon jet plant, The Sun, 10 October 2017.

71   Thomas Seal and Benjamin D. Katz, It's a battle for Britain to sell the Eurofighter, Bloomberg, 2 August 2017.

72   Ibid.

73   Tim Hepher, UK sidelined as Europe looks beyond Brexit in aerospace, Reuters, 21 July 2017.

74   Dan Milmo, BAE and EADS announce plans for £29.8bn merger, The Guardian, 13 September 2012.

75   Dan Milmo, Ministers reaffirm loyalty to aerospace industry in wake of failed BAE merger, The Guardian, 14 January 2013.

76   Dan Roberts, Aerospace UK could lose "crown jewels" due to Brexit, Airbus says, The Guardian, 22 November 2017.

77   Brexiter Tory MP Mark Francois accuses Airbus boss of "German bullying", BBC News, 25 January 2019.

78   Philip Brien and Chris Rhodes, The aerospace industry: statistics and policy, House of Commons Briefing Paper Number 00928, 8 November 2017.

79   Ibid.

80   Competitiveness of the EU Aerospace Industry, ECORYS for the European Commission, December 2009.

81   Daniel Workman, Aerospace Exports by Country, worldstopexports.com, 4 July 2017.

82   Philip Brien and Chris Rhodes, The aerospace industry: statistics and policy, House of Commons Briefing Paper Number 00928, 8 November 2017.

Chapter 20 Farewell to Arms

1   David Edgerton, Warfare State – Britain, 1920–1970, Cambridge University Press, Cambridge, 2006.

2   Luke Johnson, Merchants of death display mixed virtues, Financial Times, 23 July 2008.

3   Kevin Toolis, The man behind Iraq's supergun, The New York Times, 26 August 1990.

4   David Pallister, A war machine built by willing foreign hands, The Guardian, 3 August 1990.

5   Richard Norton-Taylor, Howe "urged silence on Iraq arms", The Guardian, 28 July 1993.

6   Richard Norton-Taylor, Victims of a Whitehall conspiracy, The Guardian, 8 November 1995.

7   Despite his involvement in the disaster on the Somme in 1916, Britain's citizen Fourth Army was headed by General Sir Henry Rawlinson. On appointment to his extraordinary new command, Rawlinson's laconic comment was: "It is not the lot of many to command an army of over half a million men".

8   Marcia Malory, A41 Centurion Mark 13 Main Battle Tank, tanks.net, 25 February 2011.

9   Marcia Malory, Vijayanta Main Battle Tank, tanks.net, 5 May 2011.

10   Field Marshal Sam Maneckshaw, obituary, Daily Telegraph, 3 July 2008.

11   Files reveal British-Israel tank secrets, BBC News, 2 January 2003.

12   Cahal Milmo and Nick Dowson, The MoD, the arms deal and a 30-year-old bill for £400m, The Independent, 24 April 2010.

13   Peter Wright, Spy Catcher, William Heinemann Australia, Richmond, Victoria, 1987.

14   David Leigh and Rob Evans, The Iranian deals, theguardian.com.

15   Cahal Milmo and Nick Dowson, The MoD, the arms deal and a 30-year-old bill for £400m, The Independent, 24 April 2010.

16   Khalid Main battle tank, army-guide.com.

17   Challenger 1 Main battle tank, army-guide.com.

18   Challenger 2 Main battle tank, army.mod.

19   Marcia Malory, FV4034 Challenger 2 Main Battle Tank, tanks.net, 11 May 2011.

20   Peter Almond and Christopher Leake, Tanks for the memories…Britain ends tank production after 93 years, MailOnline, 2 May 2009.

21   Carola Hoyos, The end of the British tank, Financial Times, 31 May 2012.

22   Krauss-Maffei Wegmann and Nexter Systems plan alliance, Company press release, 1 July 2014.

23   Tom de Castella, Kursk legacy: Will there ever be another massive tank battle?, BBC News, 6 July 2013.

24   Lucy Pasha-Robinson, Ministry of Defence "turns down German tank deal for fear of negative press", The Independent, 5 January 2017.

25   Bren/Universal carriers, angelfire.com.

26   Berenice Baker, future armoured vehicle fleet, Army Technology, 23 July 2013.

27   Alan Tovey, Army places £3.5bn order for new tanks with General Dynamics, Daily Telegraph, 3 September 2014.

28   Alan Tovey, BAE Systems to build main gun for British Army's new tanks, Daily Telegraph, 2 July 2015.

29   LDV and Stewart & Stevenson to bid for UK MoD contract, Automotive World, 28 June 2002.

30   Michael Harrison, Anger as MoD hands £1bn Army truck contract to German supplier, The Independent, 13 October 2004.

31   Christopher Booker, How UK defence firms suffer for MoD Euro-mania, Daily Telegraph, 28 February 2009.

32   Royal Ordnance, Grace's Guide to British Industrial History.

33   Clive Ponting, 1940: Myth and Reality, Hamish Hamilton, London, 1990.

34   Lynton McLain, Government confirms Ordnance job losses, Financial Times, 3 November 1984.

35   Lynton McLain, Ordnance to shed 831 at ammunition factories, Financial Times, 31 January 1986.

36   David Simpson, Royal Ordnance jobs threat, The Guardian, 9 April 1985.

37   Michael Smith and Richard Norton-Taylor, Ordnance factories sell-off will cost government £100m, The Guardian, 20 December 1983.

38   Lynton McLain, Royal Ordnance sold for "under net asset value", Financial Times, 27 November 1987.

39   Simon Beavis, Royal Ordnance job loss plan "known to ministers", The Guardian, 24 October 1988.

40   Royal Ordnance Factory Barnbow, Leeds Engine Builders, 27 June 2014.

41   David Parker, The Official History of Privatisation, Volume I, Routledge, London, 2009.

42   Alexander Nicoll, Battle to prevent munitions factory closure, Financial Times, 11 March 1999.

43   Chris Blackhurst, The millionaire civil servant, The Independent, 12 December 1993.

44   Clare Dyer and Owen Bowcott, Corrupt MoD official can keep £1.5m, The Guardian, 18 January 2008.

45   Vickers, Grace's Guide to British Industrial History.

46   Vickers Armstrong, Grace's Guide to British Industrial History.

47   Alvis, Grace's Guide to British Industrial History.

48   Alvis Plc History, fundinguniverse.com.

49   Alvis PLC, Army Guide.

50   David Black, BAE buys strategic Alvis stake, The Guardian, 23 August 2003.

51   GKN, Grace's Guide to British Industrial History.

52   Alvis and GKN to create enlarged armoured vehicle business in transaction announced today, Coventry and Warwickshire News, 15 September 1998.

53   Review of Operations, GKN Annual Report for 1998.

54   The economic contribution of BAE Systems to the United Kingdom in 2012, Oxford Economics, December 2013.

55   About GDUK, General Dynamics United Kingdom Limited, generaldynamics.uk.

56   Warrior Infantry Fighting Vehicle upgrade gets initial design approval, lockheedmartin.co, 28 January 2014.

57   George Monbiot, A good model for a mugging, The Guardian, 14 February 2006.

58   Dominic Rushe, Carlyle Group's three founders share $400m windfall, The Guardian, 12 January 2012.

59   Lewis Page, Top Qinetiq raider to retire with vast treasure chest, The Register, 9 February 2009.

60   QinetiQ chief sells £6m shares, Evening Standard, 15 February 2007.

61   Jonathan Sibun, Qinetiq chairman Sir John Chisholm set to retire, Daily Telegraph, 7 February 2009.

62   Kevin Done, N American group wins £1.8bn army radio deal, Financial Times, 20 July 2001.

63   Dan Sabbagh, UK reclaims place as world's second largest arms exporter, The Guardian, 30 July 2019.

64   Arms exports by country: Ranking the top ten in 2018, Army Technology, 8 May 2019.

65   Alan Howarth, Weapons that make us weaker, The Guardian, 17 November 1994.

Chapter 21 Look Back in Anger

1   Julian Critchley, Some of Us, People Who Did Well under Thatcher, John Murray, London, 1992.

2   Kwasi Kwarteng MP, Priti Patel MP, Dominic Raab MP, Chris Skidmore MP, Elizabeth Truss MP, Britannia Unchained, Palgrave Macmillan, Basingstoke, 2012.

3   Financial Times, 7 October 1981, quoted in Huw Beynon, False Hopes and Real Dilemmas, The Politics of the Collapse in British Manufacturing, SSRC Working Paper, 1983.

4   Ibid.

5   Nicholas Crafts, Deindustrialisation and economic growth, The Economic Journal, 1996.

6   Rodney Cowton, UK placed third in strike league, The Times, 27 November 1969.

7   Industrial stoppages, 1972–81, Employment Gazette, March 1983.

8   David Freud, Scandinavian companies favour UK as sphere for investment, Financial Times, 3 November 1977.

9   Der Spiegel, 31 July 1977, Managers blamed for British "sickness", The Times, 1 August 1977.

10   Ibid.

11   Rod Chapman, Germans who like the look of Britain, The Guardian, 4 September 1979.

12   David Goodhart, Backing British engineering, Financial Times, 25 October 1986.

13   Peter Nolan and Paul Marginson, Skating on Thin Ice?, University of Warwick, 1988.

14   Charles Leadbeater, Dispelling some myths about the impact of unions on workplaces, Financial Times, 29 August 1989.

15   Harukiyo Hasegawa, The Steel Industry in Japan, A Comparison with Britain, Routledge, London, 1996.

16   Ibid.

17   Tom Clark and Andrew Dilnot, Long-Term Trends in British Taxation and Spending, Institute for Fiscal Studies Briefing Note No 25.

18   Dick Taverne, Letter to the Financial Times, 10 September 2011.

19   Carola Hoyos and Michael Steen, Shell chief calls for pay reforms, Financial Times, 8 June 2009.

20   Industrial Reconstruction Corporation, Grace's Guide to British Industrial History

21   Michael Grylls MP and John Redwood, National Enterprise Board, A Case for Euthanasia, Centre for Policy Studies, London, 1980.

22   Michael J. Trebilcock, Marsh A. Chandler and Robert Howse, Trade and Transitions, Routledge, London, 1990.

23   Ibid.

24   Michael Kitson and Jonathan Michie, The Deindustrial Revolution: The Rise and Fall of UK Manufacturing, 1870–2010.

25   Alex Brummer, Labour's problem, The Guardian, 13 November 1991.

26   Hugh Pemberton, The 1964 Industrial Training Act: A Failed Revolution, paper to the conference of the Economic History Society, Bristol, 30 March 2001.

27   David Marsh, A hard act for Britain to follow, Financial Times, 15 April 1991.

28   Stephen Broadberry and Tim Leunig, The impact of government policies on UK manufacturing since 1945, Government Office for Science, October 2013.

29   William Davis, Gnome truths in a summer of violent unrest, The Guardian, 4 August 1973.

30   Denis Healey, The Time of My Life, Michael Joseph, London, 1989.

31   Benedict Brogan, The debt crisis of 1976 offers a vision of the blood, sweat and tears facing David Cameron, Daily Telegraph, 22 October 2009.

32   Denis Healey, The Time of My Life, Michael Joseph, London, 1989.

33   Sarah Womack, Remember 1976? Britain's best ever year, Daily Telegraph, 17 March 2004.

34   Viv Groskop, Lazy, hazy, crazy days of summer, The Guardian Weekend, 30 July 2016.

35   Michael Cockerill, The Lost World of the Seventies, BBC2, 13 May 2012.

36   Ian Gilmour, Dancing with Dogma, Simon & Schuster, London, 1992.

37   Stephanie Flanders, Were 364 economists all wrong?, Newsnight, BBC 2, 13 March 2006.

38   Andrew Grice, Irreverent rebel Tory MP Julian Critchley dies at 69, The Independent, 10 September 2000.

39   J.M. Keynes, The Economic Consequences of the Peace, Harcourt Brace, New York, 1920.

40   Ian Gilmour, Dancing with Dogma, Simon & Schuster, London, 1992.

41   Bringer of division and bitterness, letter from Edward Pearce to The Guardian, 27 December 2011.

42   Ian Gilmour, Dancing with Dogma, Simon & Schuster, London, 1992.

43   Jim Prior, Member of the Awkward Squad, The Observer, 12 September 1986.

44   Hugh Dykes MP, The figures that underline our chilling economic decline, The Guardian, 13 December 1985.

45   Martin Linton, New assault by Tory "wet" on Thatcher policies, The Guardian, 28 February 1985.

46   Patrick Wintour, Heath outburst over Thatcher "lies", The Guardian, 19 June 1991.

47   James Lewis and David Mckie, North's economic decline is a self-inflicted wound, says Tebbitt, The Guardian, 9 November 1986.

48   Christopher Huhne, Lawson berates City "scribblers", The Guardian, 1 July 1988.

49   The Financial Week, BBC Radio 4, 26 October 1990.

50   Peter Marsh, Economists open inquest on Lawson era, Financial Times, 4 October 1990.

51   Ralph Atkins, UK productivity "to go on rising", Financial Times, 23 May 1988.

52   Christopher Huhne, Lawson "to give £1.5bn in tax cuts", The Guardian, 2 February 1989.

53   Bill Robinson, Painful adjustments, Financial Times, 17 August 1993.

54   Peter Marsh, Economists open inquest on Lawson era, Financial Times, 4 October 1990.

55   Ibid.

56   Tim Congdon, A Christmas miracle, The Times, 20 December 1995.

57   The Ministry of Leave, BBC Radio 4, 19 February 2018.

58   Huw Beynon, False Hopes and Real Dilemmas, The Politics of the Collapse in British Manufacturing, SSRC Working Paper, 1983.

59   Michael Cassell, Direct hit by boss of bosses, Financial Times, 1 May 1993.

60   Sir Terence Beckett, obituary, Daily Telegraph, 10 May 2013.

61   Plea for more investment in industry, The Guardian, 6 November 1984.

62   New demand for boost to industry, Financial Times, 29 April 1985.

63   Michael White and David Hencke, What did John Major really say at the time?, The Guardian, 5 May 1993.

64   New demand for boost to industry, Financial Times, 29 April 1985.

65   Bill Abbotts, "Essentials" for a survivor's Budget, Financial Times, 19 March 1991.

66   Alan Travis, Lawson's economic miracle came into view "after dinner", The Guardian, 30 October 1992.

67 Peter Marsh, Economists open inquest on Lawson era, Financial Times, 4 October 1990.

68 Dream time for industry, Financial Times, 12 October 1991.

69 Michael Cassell, Time for minister to show his mettle, Financial Times, 7 October 1991.

70 Ibid.

71 CBI chief attacks economic policies, Financial Times, 27 February 1991.

72 The Financial World This Week, BBC Radio 4, 18 June 1993.

73 Keith Harper, Heading towards an ice-cream economy, The Guardian, 28 October 1992.

74 Peter Riddell, UK undergoing "economic miracle", Financial Times, 19 March 1988.

75 Peter Norman, Britain "may be growth leader", Financial Times, 23 February 1989.

76 Sir Douglas Hague, Germany is not the model: it's the odd man out, Financial Times, 5 June 1991.

77 Brian Reading, The Financial Week, BBC Radio 4, 6 November 1992.

78 Professor Douglas MacWilliams, The Financial Week, BBC Radio 4, 13 December 1991.

79 The Moral Maze, BBC Radio 4, 15 April 1993.

80 Bill Robinson, The Guardian, 1992.

81 Teresa Gorman, The wrong example to follow, Letter to the Financial Times, 16 May 1995.

82 Patrick Minford, Industrially invincible no more, Letter to the Financial Times, 22 May 1995.

83 Charles Powell, Germany through rose-tinted glasses, Financial Times, 27 April 1995.

84 David Marsh, Elegant intellectual shapes techno-strategy, Financial Times, 16 November 1982.

85 The British at Work: To Have and to Have Not, BBC2, 24 March 2011.

86 Chris Rhodes, Manufacturing: international comparisons, Briefing Paper, House of Commons Library, 5 January 2018.

87 Peter Hetherington, £500m blow in Blair's back yard, The Guardian, 4 September 1998.

88 Charles Leadbeater, Living on Thin Air, Viking, Penguin Books, London, 1999.

89 Diane Coyle, The Weightless World, Capstone Publishing, Oxford, 1997.

90 Hewitt admits Labour's industry errors, The Guardian, 16 May 2002.

91 Andrew Martin, Financial Times Magazine, 3 June 2006.

92 Bill Emmott, Crisis, what crisis? Enough kerfuffle, it's just a slowdown, The Guardian, 12 August 2008.

93 John Harris, An all too familiar plot, The Guardian, 9 April 2009.

94   Jonathan Glancey, The art of industry, The Guardian, 22 December 2009.

95   Comment, Tribune, 6 March 2009.

96   Tom Brown, Tragedy & Challenge, Matador, Kibworth Beauchamp, 2017.

97   John Torode, Evening Standard, 2005.

98   Tony Warwick-Ching, The International Gold Trade, Woodhead Publishing, Abington, Cambridge, 1993.

99   John Torode, Evening Standard, 2005.

100   Martin Arnold, Failings of RBS small business unit laid bare, Financial Times, 13 February 2018.

101   Terry Smith, Eighth annual letter to owners of the Fundsmith Equity Fund, January 2018.

102   John Kay, Profits without honour, Financial Times, 29 June 2002.

103   John Kay, The City serves only itself. This is how it could serve us all, Daily Telegraph, 9 September 2015.

104   Simon Caulkin, It's time to explode the myth of the shareholder, The Observer, 29 March 2009.

105   Thinking Aloud, BBC Radio 4, 7 July 2010.

106   Hazel Duffy, Laing warns on foreign bidders, Financial Times, 8 November 1988.

107   Ben Laurance, Minister admits bids can be damaging, The Guardian, 8 December 1990.

108   Norma Cohen, KPMG withdraws merger study, Financial Times, 29 November 1999.

109   Vanessa Houlder, The spoils of enterprise, Financial Times, 31 January 1990.

110   Ed Balls, chief economic advisor to the Treasury, quoted by Tom Brown, Tragedy and Challenge, Matador, Kibworth Beauchamp, 2017.

111   Larry Elliott, Full employment? Why Blackpool begs to differ, The Guardian, 30 October 2017; Richard Partington, Unemployment figures should be 3m higher, says research, The Guardian, 17 October 2019.

112   Larry Elliott, Economically speaking, London is a different country, The Guardian, 23 September 2013.

113   Simon Johnson, Glasgow has the UK's most workless households, Daily Telegraph, 4 September 2013.

114   Adrian Clarke, The end of the tracks?, The Guardian Weekend, 1 September 2007.

115   All in the Best Possible Taste, Channel 4, 5 June 2012.

116   Professor Neil Ferguson, The Rule of Law and its Enemies, Reith Lectures, BBC Radio 4, 14 July 2012.

117   Jonathan Glancey, The art of industry, The Guardian, 22 December 2009.

118   Economic and financial indicators, The Economist, 3 March 2018.

119   Chris Rhodes, Manufacturing: international comparisons, Briefing Paper, House of Commons Library, 5 January 2018.

120   Alex Brummer, Britain for Sale, Random House Business Books, London, 2012.
121   Mark Carney, A Fine Balance, The Mansion House, London, 20 June 2017.
122   Stephen Burgess and Rachana Shanbhogue, A prince not a pauper: the truth behind the UK's current account deficit, Bank Underground, 7 December 2017.
123   Professor Patrick Minford, Brexit will cut the cost of BMWs and even brie, The Sun, 15 March 2016.

Bibliography

Alexander, William, and Arthur Street, Metals in the Service of Man, Penguin, 1944.

Allan, Ian, London Transport Locomotives and Rolling Stock, Ian Allan, 1969.

Allen, G.C., British Industries and Their Organization, Fourth Edition, Longmans, 1959.

Benn, Tony, Conflicts of Interest, Diaries 1977–1980, Hutchinson, 1990.

Brady, Chris, and Andrew Lorenz, End of the Road, Pearson Education, 2001.

Briscoe, Lynden, The Textile and Clothing Industries of the United Kingdom, Manchester University Press, 1971.

Britton, A.J.C., Macroeconomic Policy in Britain 1974–87, Cambridge University Press, 1991.

Brown, Tom, Tragedy and Challenge, Matador, 2017.

Brummer, Alex, and Roger Cowe, Hanson, a Biography, Fourth Estate, 1994.

Brummer, Alex, Britain for Sale, Random House, 2013.

Burns, R.W., British Television, The Formative Years, Peter Peregrinus.

Burton, Anthony, The Rise and Fall of British Shipbuilding, The History Press, 2013.

Cafruny, Alan W., Ruling the Waves, University of California Press, 1987.

Carr, Christopher, Britain's Competitiveness, The Management of the Vehicle Components Industry, Routledge, 1990.

Central Office of Information, Britain – An Official Handbook, HMSO, 1959.

Central Office of Information, Britain – An Official Handbook, HMSO, 1973.

Central Office of Information, Britain – An Official Handbook, HMSO, 1979.

Central Office of Information, Britain – An Official Handbook, HMSO, 1980.

Central Office of Information, Britain – An Official Handbook, HMSO, 1985.

Central Office of Information, Britain – An Official Handbook, HMSO, 1991.

Central Office of Information, Britain – An Official Handbook, HMSO, 2000.

Chang, Ha-Joon, 23 Things They Don't Tell You About Capitalism, Penguin, 2011.

Chapman, Colin, Selling the Family Silver, Hutchinson Business Books, 1990.

Church, Roy, The Rise and Decline of the British Motor Industry, Cambridge University Press, 1995.

Cockerill, A. and A. Silbertson, The Steel Industry, Cambridge University Press, 1974.

Comfort, Nicholas, Surrender, Biteback Publishing, 2012.

Cooper, Richard, and Peter Lyth (Ed), Business in Britain in the Twentieth Century, Oxford University Press, 2009.

Coyle, Diane, The Weightless World, MIT Press, 1998.

Davis, Evan, Made in Britain, Little, Brown, 2011.

De-industrialisation, Frank Blackaby (Ed), National Institute of Economic and Social Research, 1979.

Delbridge, Rick, and James Lowe, Manufacturing in Transition, Routledge, 1998.

Dibnah, Fred, and David Hall, Memories of Industrial Britain, BBC Books, 1999.

Dickson, Tony, and David Judge, The Politics of Industrial Closure, Macmillan, 1987.

Edgerton, David, Warfare State, Britain 1920–1970, Cambridge University Press, 2006.

Edgerton, David, Britain's War Machine, Allen Lane, 2011.

Edgerton, David, England and the Aeroplane, Revised Edition, Penguin, 2013.

Elliott, Larry, and Dan Atkinson, Going South, Palgrave Macmillan, 2012.

Farson, Negley, The Way of a Transgressor, Victor Gollancz, 1935.

Ferry, Georgina, A Computer Called Leo, Harper Perennial, 2004.

Gilmour, Ian, Dancing with Dogma, Simon & Schuster, 1992.

Gray, Robert, Rolls on the Rocks, Panther Books, 1971.

Hamilton-Paterson, James, Empire of the Clouds, Faber and Faber, 2010.

Hamilton-Paterson, James, What We Have Lost, Head of Zeus, London, 2018.

Hasegawa, Harukiyo, The Steel Industry in Japan, A Comparison with Britain, Routledge, 1996.

Hothi, Nicola R., Globalisation and Manufacturing Decline, Arena Books, 2005.

Hutton, Will, The State We're in, Jonathan Cape, 1995.

Jack, Ian, The Crash That Stopped Britain, Granta Books, 2001.

Johnson P.S. (Ed), The Structure of British Industry, Granada Publishing, 1980.

Jones, G.P., and A.G. Pool, A Hundred Years of Economic Development in Great Britain, Duckworth, 1940.

Jones, Robert, and Oliver Marriott, Anatomy of a Merger, Jonathan Cape, 1970.

Keeling, B.S. and A.E.G. Wright, The Development of the Modern British Steel Industry, Longman, 1964.

Landes, David S., The Unbound Prometheus, Cambridge University Press, 1969.

Landström, Björn, Das Schiff vom Einbaum zum Atomboot, Bertelsmann, 1973.

Leadbeater, Charles, Living on Thin Air, Viking, 1999.

Lorenz, Andrew, GKN, The Making of a Business 1759–2009, Wiley, 2009.

Luffman, George A., and Richard Reed, The Strategy and Performance of British Industry 1970–80, Macmillan, 1984.

Malik, Rex, What's Wrong with British Industry?, Penguin, 1984.

Mason, Michael, Basil Greenhill and Robin Craig, The British Seafarer, Hutchinson, 1980.

Mathias, Peter, The First Industrial Nation, Methuen, 1969.

Mazzucato, Mariana, The Entrepreneurial State, Public Affairs, 2013.

McCart, Neil, Canberra The Great White Whale, Patrick Stephens, 1982.

McLachlan, Sandy, The National Freight Buy-Out, Macmillan, 1983.

Moore, Charles, Margaret Thatcher, The Authorized Biography, Volume One, Allen Lane, 2013.

Moore, Charles, Margaret Thatcher, The Authorized Biography, Volume Two, Allen Lane, 2015.

Murphy, Brian, A History of the British Economy 1740–1970, Longman, 1973.

O'Brien, Patrick (Ed), and Roland Quinault, The Industrial Revolution and British Society, Cambridge University Press, 1993.

Owen, Geoffrey, From Empire to Europe, HarperCollins, 1999.

Owen, Geoffrey, The Rise and Fall of Great Companies, Oxford University Press, 2010.

Parker, David, The Official History of Privatisation, Volume I, Routledge, 2009.

Parker, David, The Official History of Privatisation, Volume II, Routledge, 2012.

Pollard, Sidney, The Development of the British Economy 1914–1967, Edward Arnold, 1969.

Ponting, Clive, 1940: Myth and Reality, Hamish Hamilton, 1990.

Prest, A.R. (Ed), and D.J. Coppock, The UK Economy, Ninth Edition, Weidenfeld & Nicholson, 1982.

Pugh, Peter, The Magic of a Name, The Rolls-Royce Story, The First 40 Years, Icon Books, 2000.

Pugh, Peter, The Magic of a Name, Part Two, Icon Books, 2001.

Pugh, Peter, The Magic of a Name, Part Three, Icon Books, 2002.

Reece, Reviving British Manufacturing, Civitas, 2011.

Roberts, Richard, and David Kynaston, City State, Profile Books, 2001.

Robinson, Colin, and Jon Morgan, North Sea Oil in the Future, Macmillan, 1978.

Rubinstein, W.D., Capitalism, Culture and Decline in Britain 1750–1990, Routledge, 1993.

Slaven, Anthony, British Shipbuilding 1500–2010, Crucible, 2013.

Smith, David, The Rise and Fall of Monetarism, Penguin, 1987.

Stainless Steel Special, Metal Bulletin, London, 1972.

Thatcher, Margaret, The Downing Street Years, HarperCollins, 1993.

Trebilcock, Michael J., Marsh A. Chandler and Robert Howse, Trade and Transitions, Routledge, 1990.

Walker, Fred M., Shipbuilding in Britain, Shire Publications, 2013.

Wells, S.J., British Export Performance, Cambridge University Press, 1964.

Wiener, Martin J., English Culture and the Decline of the Industrial Spirit, Cambridge University Press, 1981.

Wild, Trevor (Ed), and Philip Jones (Ed), De-industrialisation and New Industrialisation in Britain and Germany, Anglo-German Foundation, 1991.

Wolmar, Christian, Stagecoach, Orion, 1999.

Wolmar, Christian, Broken Rails, Aurum, 2001.

Wood, Jonathan, The British Motor Industry, Shire Publications, 2010.

Worswick, G.D.N., and P.H. Ady, The British Economy in the 1950s, Clarendon Press, 1962.

Wrigley, Chris, British Trade Unions since 1933, Cambridge University Press, 2002.

Index

Dennis 160
Depletion and refining policy neglect 330-331
Derby works - survival 189
Derby works - technical achievements 188-189
Deritend 86
Devaney, John 238
Dewhirst Group 287
Dewrance & Co 37
Dibnah, Fred x, 8
Dick, Kerr 227
Dickinson Robinson Group (DRG) 351
Dicks, Geoffrey 443
Diesel engines - strength of UK industry 47
Diesel engines - rivalry with Germany 47
Divine Chocolate 371
Djanogly, Harry 285
Dobson Park 43
Doncaster works closure 184
Dorman 47, 48
Dosco Mining 43
Dowty Engineering 43
Doxford 47
DS Smith 347
Du Cann, Edward MP 211
Dunlop - BTR takeover 95
Dunlop - Dunlop-Pirelli Union 94-95
Dunlop - sale to Sumitomo 95
Dunlop 2, 94-95
Duport 18
Dykes, Hugh MP 442
East Hecla 28
East Lancashire Paper 350
East Moors 16
Ebbw Vale steelworks 11
Economic 'miracle' 442
Economists for Free Trade 457
Edgerton, David - *England and the Aeroplane* 387
Edgerton, David - *Warfare State* 388
Edwardes, Michael - criticism of government 120
Edwardes, Michael 119
Electrical engineering 223-248
    1930s catch-up 226
    UK shrinks 247-248
    Privatisation fiascos 233, 234
Electronic engineering 249-273
Elizabeth Shaw 370
Elkington Copper Refiners 380
Ellesmere Port 132
Elliott Automation 228
EMI - Emitron to oblivion 268-269
EMI 2
EMI body scanner 269
EMI Emitron 250

Emmott, Bill 448
Enfield Rolling Mills 379
Engelhard 385, 386
Engineering Employers Federation 212
English Calico 281
English Electric 227-228
    Electrical engineering 227-228
    English Electric Canberra 389
    English Electric Lightning 390
    Rail interests 177-178
English Sewing Cotton 280
Enron supporters 235-236
ERF 160
Ericsson 240
Ericsson Telephone (ETL) 259
Ernest Scragg 38
Ernesto Che Guevara - La Poderosa 58
EU Referendum 4
European Free Trade Area (Efta) 346, 375
European Monetary System 442
Ever Ready - Hanson run-down 98-99
Ever Ready 98-99
Eversholt Leasing 191
ExxonMobil 332-333
Fairey Aviation 390
Fairfield Experiment 206
Fairfields 200
Farson, Negley x, 30, 32, 373
Fenner Gullick 43
Ferguson shipyard 213
Ferguson, Harry 67, 69
Ferranti - Mark I computer 252
Fiat 116
Fina 341
Fine Spinners & Doublers 279
First World War - shipping losses 202
Firth Brown 86
Foden 160
Ford Motor Company 113, 114, 129-131
    Bridgend 131
    Dagenham car production ends 131
    Foundry closures 84, 86
    Halewood 131
    Sourcing from Continent 130
    Anglia 130
    Escort 130
    Ford New Holland 67
    Ford Transit 163
    Ford trucks - Dagenham, Southampton, Langley 153
    Ford's Dagenham Dream 130
    Fordson tractors 66-67
Forging industry 86-87
Forgings - market collapse early 1980s
Fork lift trucks 79-82